2013
Business Reference Guide

The Essential Guide to Pricing Businesses and Franchises

23rd Edition

business
brokerage
press

Written and Compiled by Thomas L. West
800.239.5085 | bbpinc.com

Important Note to the Reader
"This publication is designed to provide accurate and authoritative information with regard to the subject matter covered. It is sold with the understanding that the authors, editors and publisher are not engaged in rendering legal, accounting or other professional advice. If legal advice or other expert assistance is required, the services of a competent professional should be sought."

Notes to the 2013 Business Reference Guide and the Business Reference Guide Online

Just a few explanations concerning the information in this year's Guide.

In the Statistics sections of the Benchmark Data, the figures from IBISWorld are based on their 2013 projections.

Also in the Statistics, the number of businesses refers to individual establishments. Some may be owned by a single enterprise.

Some sentences may be grammatical incorrect or some words are not capitalized that usually are. In some cases we may have made changes to make the sentence more readable .

Due to space requirements, General Information, Advantages and Disadvantages are not included in the hard copy Guide, but are available in the Online Edition.

Pricing Methods

Pricing methods such as multiples of SDE, EBIT and EBITDA all have two things in common; one must calculate SDE, EBIT and EBITDA and then calculate a multiple based on many factors relating to the business. Multiplying the two should then produce the rule of thumb for that business. These methods are based on two figures that are calculated by the person doing it.

The other method used in the Guide is a rule of thumb that calls for a multiple of sales. One advantage to this method is that it doesn't call for calculating any figures as the methods above require. One simply takes the total annual sales (less sales taxes) and multiplies it by a percentage that experts are comfortable with based on their knowledge and experience. The annual sales of a business are a provable figure. An argument could be made, especially in very small businesses that the owner could be "taking money off the top," thus reducing sales. However, unless the owner is really "stealing" from the business, small amounts shouldn't influence the price dramatically.

The purpose of the above information is to show that although multipliers may stay about the same, the final result is based on figures that do reflect the impact of the economy. Sales are down and costs go up especially in relation to sales. Therefore, we are comfortable with the final pricing results. As we keep saying, rules of thumb are just that. The purpose in supplying Benchmark and other data is so the user can adjust the rule of thumb up or down based on this information.

The pricing of businesses is based on the sales and earnings for the most part. However, other factors enter the process. The price of a business is not "cut and dry." It is not just based on earnings as a valuation may be. The price of a business is ultimately what someone will pay for it – it is market driven.

Pricing and the Economy

The number of businesses still in business has been reduced considerably since the economy went downhill. This is especially true in those states that have been impacted the most such as California, Florida, and Nevada. In doing the franchise section of this year's book, we have also noticed that in almost all cases the number of franchised units was also down from the previous year, which was also down from the previous one. This would indicate that the franchise community also paid a price for the economic maladies. They may have added new units in 2011, but not enough to cover the losses.

In our opinion, many business owners have put off a decision to sell until the economy picks up. Buyers too have put off purchasing a business. However, we continue to believe that the unemployed will think that owning their business is a good way to go. You can't lose your job if you own it. Sellers will realize that the price they would have received a few years ago is not coming back.

How does all of this impact the rules of thumb for pricing businesses? The information in this book presents a "ballpark" for putting a price on a business. The marketplace determines the ultimate price. However, marketplace is just a word for supply and demand. We feel that buyers will want to own their piece of the American Dream – owning their own business. The "boomers," as they say, will soon be ready to "pack it in" and move on. A perfect supply – and demand -- situation.

We think that the rules of thumb can come just about as close to what a business is worth as most other pricing methods, whether you call it a price, a value, an opinion of value, or whatever.

Using the Rules of Thumb

Despite all of the caveats about using rules of thumb in pricing businesses, they are commonly used to do just that. The answer is quite simple—the rules are very easy to use and almost seem too simplistic. But how accurate are they? A lot more accurate than many people think. They may supply a quick fix, but if used properly, rules of thumb can come pretty close to what the business will ultimately sell for.

Rules of thumb in the Guide usually come in two formats. The most commonly used rule of thumb is simply a percentage of the annual sales, or better yet, the last 12 months of sales/revenues. For example, if the total sales were $100,000 for last year, and the multiple for the particular business is 40 percent of annual sales, then the price based on the rule of thumb would be $40,000.

Quite a few experts have said that revenue multiples are likely to be more reliable than earnings multiples. The reason is that most multiples of earnings are based on add-backs to the earnings, which can be a judgment call, as can the multiple. Sales or revenues, they're the same, are essentially a fixed figure. One might want to subtract sales taxes, if they have not been deducted, but the sales are the sales. The only judgment then is the percentage. When it is supplied by an expert, the percentage multiplier becomes much less of a judgment call.

The second rule of thumb used in the Guide is a multiple of earnings. In small businesses, the multiple is used against what is termed Seller's Discretionary Earnings (SDE). It is usually based on a multiple (generally between 0 and 4), and this number is then used as a multiple against the earnings of the business. Many of the entries also contain a multiple of EBIT and/or EBITDA.

The terms used to express earnings are as follows, along with a definition of SDE:

EBDIT (EBITDA) Earnings before depreciation (and other noncash charges), interest, and taxes.

EBDT Earnings before depreciation (and other noncash charges), and taxes.

EBIT Earnings before interest and taxes.

Source: Pratt et al., *Valuing a Business*

SDE Seller's Discretionary Earnings

Seller's Discretionary Earnings: "The earnings of a business enterprise prior to the following items:
- income taxes
- nonrecurring income and expenses
- nonoperating income and expenses
- depreciation and amortization
- interest expense or income
- owner's total compensation for one owner/operator, after adjusting the total compensation of all owners to market value."

Source: The International Business Brokers Association (IBBA)

The above definition of Seller's Discretionary Earnings, although completely accurate, is a bit confusing. If you change the words "prior to the" and substitute the word "plus" it may be easier to understand. We would also suggest that the highest salary be used in the calculation of SDE. The reason is that we must assume that the buyer will replace the highest compensated employee or owner – at least for the SDE calculation. We should also add that this is our definition and not necessarily that of the IBBA.

Keep in mind that the multiples for the different earnings acronyms mentioned above will be different than the multiple of SDE, which, as mentioned, generally is a number between 0 and 4. The rules contained in the Guide are specific about what is being used. It will say 2 times SDE or 4 times EBIT, etc.

The Basics

The businesses are arranged alphabetically. In some cases, the business may go by two name descriptions, for example, gas stations and service stations. We use the one that we feel is the most common, and we try to cross-reference them. If you can't find what you are looking for, see if it is listed under another name. If there is a particular franchise you are working on and it's not in the rules, check the type of business for more information. For example, if the franchise is an ice cream store, check the name of the franchise; and if it's not there, go to ice cream stores and other ice cream franchises. If the business is not listed, find a similar business and start there.

Name/Type of Business

The information just below the type of business is the approximate number of businesses of that type in the U.S. Where there was an IBISWorld report, we used that number. In the top section where the type of business is located, in most cases we have rounded the number of businesses for ease of use.

IBISWorld provides wonderful reports on many, many different businesses -- www.ibisworld.com. Most of these reports are well over 20 pages and are not only extensive, but most informative. They are well worth the price.

We have also provided the Standard Industrial (SIC) Classification code and the North American Industry Classification System (NAICS).

The Rules of Thumb

The price, based on the rule of thumb, does not include inventory (unless it specifically states that it does include inventory), real estate, and other balance-sheet items such as cash and accounts receivable. Interestingly, we have noticed an increase in Industry Experts telling us that inventory is included in the multiples. The price derived from the rule of thumb is for the operating assets of the business plus goodwill. It also assumes that the business will be delivered free and clear of any short -- and long-term debt. If any debt is to be assumed by a purchaser, it is subtracted from the price based on the rule of thumb method.

In other words, the rules, unless mentioned otherwise, create a price that includes goodwill, FF&E (furniture, fixtures & equipment), and leasehold improvements, less outstanding debt including, accounts payable, loans on FF&E, bank loans, etc. The business, unless otherwise mentioned, is assumed delivered to a purchaser free and clear of any debt or encumbrances. Accounts receivable are not included as they are generally handled outside of any transaction and usually belong to the seller. Work in progress, prepaid memberships, etc. also normally belong to the seller. Items such as these may be divided between buyer and seller. For example, in a dry cleaning business, the seller may have taken in a customer's clothing for dry cleaning, but the buyer may take over the business before the work has been completed and delivered back to the customer. This is generally handled outside the transaction and does not usually figure in a pricing or valuation.

Benchmark Data

This is a valuable section. We feel it is very important, in analyzing and pricing a business that you compare it to similar businesses, or benchmarks that are unique to this type of business. One common benchmark unique to each business is the expenses. We have included as many of these as we could find. Many have been contributed by Industry Experts. If no source is mentioned, then you can assume that an Industry Expert(s) has supplied them. In many cases we have used a breakdown of expenses from IBISWorld.

The figures in the "Expenses as a Percentage of Annual Sales" may not always add up to 100 percent. We provide only the major categories, and there may be other expense items not included which would make up any difference. Also, in many cases, we have to meld the figures from several different industry experts or sources. This may also cause some totals to slightly exceed 100 percent.

Critics of rules of thumb claim that a rule is simply an average and doesn't allow for the variables of each individual business. Comparing the business under review with industry standards—benchmarks—can allow one to raise or lower the percentage accordingly.

The Benchmark section can help you look at the vital signs of the business and compare them to similar businesses. Looking at the expenses as a percentage of annual sales can be a good start. For example, the business under review has an occupancy percentage of 12 percent against an average eight percent benchmark, perhaps the price then should be reduced to compensate for the higher rent. The rent is pretty much a fixed expense; but the higher the rent, the lower the profit. Certainly a new owner could lower some of the expenses, but a trained labor force, for example, is hard to replace. Obviously, reducing the percentage multiple is a judgment call; but let's face it, even business valuation is not a science, but an art—and judgment plays a large part in it.

Some Final Notes

We know that some of the information may be contradictory, but since we get it from those whom we believe to be experts, we still include it. The more information you have to sort through, the better your final conclusion. We think the information and data are reliable, but occasionally we find an error after the book has been printed. Also, keep in mind that rules of thumb can vary by area and even by location. For example:

Keep in mind that the rules of thumb can vary by region. For example, businesses in the western states tend to have the highest average prices in the country, followed by the eastern states, and then the central states.

Thanks to our Industry Experts

We want to thank all of those that contributed rules of thumb, industry data, and information to the Guide. It is a tribute to them that they are willing to contribute not only a rule of thumb, but also their knowledge on pricing.

We are focusing on the Industry Experts and are offering to put them on our Web site, provide BBP Industry logos and anything else we can do to set them apart, in gratitude for their contribution to the Guide and the profession. And, we give them a free one-year subscription to the BRG Online – our online edition of the Guide itself. If you're interested and feel that you are qualified, go to www.bbpinc.com and click on Industry Experts. Or, just pick up the phone and call me, Tom West, at 978-692-0323 or email me at tom@bbpinc.com.

And When All Else Fails

Keep in mind that if it's not in the Guide, we really don't have a rule of thumb for that business. We get calls from people asking for a rule of thumb for some oddball type of business like Elephant Training Schools (not really). Honestly, if we knew of one, it would be in the Guide. We're always happy to help if we can, but unless there is sufficient sales data, there generally isn't a rule of thumb available. Here are some suggestions if you can't find what you need in the Guide:

- Call a similar business in your area and see if they are aware of one.

- Check with a vendor, distributor, or equipment manufacturer and see if someone there can help.

- Call a trade association for that particular industry and see if they can direct you to someone who can help. Don't do it by email or fax, but call and speak to someone. Trade associations really don't want to get involved, but an individual might get you to the next step.

If none of the above helps, then we're afraid you just have to accept the fact that there isn't one for the business you are checking on.

Businesses in the 2013 Guide

Introduction

Introduction

Introduction

Introduction

Introduction

Introduction

Introduction

Franchise

A&W Restaurants (A&W Root Beer)

Approx. Total Investment		$1,039,000 to $1,623,500
Estimated Annual Sales/Unit		$565,000
SIC 5812-06	NAICS 722211	Number of Businesses/Units 625

Rules of Thumb

➢ 45 to 55 percent of annual sales plus inventory

Resources

Websites

- www.awrestaurants.com

Franchise

AAMCO Transmission (See also Auto Transmissions Centers)

Approx. Total Investment		$225,000 to $299,000
Estimated Annual Sales/Unit		$800,000
SIC 7537-01	NAICS 811113	Number of Businesses/Units 900

Rules of Thumb

➢ 40 to 42 percent of annual sales plus inventory

➢ 2 to 3 times EBITDA

➢ An industry rule of thumb for AAMCO is 20 times average weekly sales for the past 16–26 weeks for a shop that has average weekly sales of less than $20,000 per week, and up to 27 times average weekly sales for shops above $20,000 per week.

Pricing Tips

- "One observation is that franchised shops who are following the model with a good manager are successful. The typical shop has three technicians, a rebuilder and two mechanics, and a manager. Most of the franchised shops have an owner who oversees but might be considered absentee.
  "The better way to analyze a business is from a well-defined proforma as opposed to tax returns and financial statements. Looking at the top line on the tax return, I sell from a proforma using market values for parts, cost and labor."

- "An old rule of thumb for valuation is 2 x SDE for this industry, whereby one adds back the manager's comp (which is typically 10% of the sales) for valuation, does not fit unless the new buyer is experienced. More often than not this leads to failure and is one reason there are so many resales— overstated earnings that go away. Most of the buyer's I deal with are first-time buyers from corporate entities. The rule that works for me is 3 times earnings (EBITDA) with the manager left in the expenses."

- "Detailed weekly reports provided to the franchisor are more important documents for analyzing historical performance than financial statements and tax returns, as these reports will reveal the prices charged ratio of major/minor repairs and warranty repairs."

- "Nothing has really changed regarding pricing on franchised transmission shops. I sold one a couple weeks ago for 3 times SDE. The challenge is getting one available that is profitable and that an owner will finance."

- "Established shops with a manager in the expenses:

Small Shops—Less than $20,000 per weekSixteen to twenty (16–20) times weekly sales for the last 26 weeks—and/or one and one half (1.5) to three (3) times adjusted earnings (EBITDA). If the seller is the manager or builder—assets plus one year's SDE.

"Minimum sale price for an established, poorly performing, franchised transmission shop that is in a proven location which historically has been profitable but has recent sales which at least are 'breakeven' ($8,000 to $10,000 per week) is no less than the total cost it would take to put in a new franchise and reach breakeven—typically $195,000 to $225,000."

"Large Shops—$20,000 per week and higher Twenty to Thirty (20–30) times average weekly sales for the last 26 weeks—and/or two (2) to three (3) times adjusted earnings (EBITDA).

High parts cost implies theft and/or high warranty repairs.

Usually the buyer assumes responsibility for warranty repairs for previous work. If they are unusually high, a provision in contract price might be a consideration.

If the owner is the manager, be careful in adding back manager's salary and replacing with first-time buyer unless the shop is a national franchise with a training program."

Expert Comments

"Typically a buyer assumes responsibility for warranty repairs. In my analysis I look at this very carefully and at the compensation to the rebuilder to see if it is too low.

"The Internet has changed the marketing and advertising model—lowering cost but making it more difficult for the small independent to compete with the franchises in the major market areas."

Benchmark Data

Expenses as a percentage of annual sales

Production labor costs	20%
Sales/Labor	08% to 10%
Occupancy	06% to 10%
Profit (estimated pretax)	10% to 20%

- "A shop should generate $3,500 to $4,000 per technical employee per week."
- "It seems that the parts suppliers have consolidated and parts cost are higher—typically were 18–20% now in the 25–30%."
- "If parts costs are less than 15 percent, suspect that used parts are sold, which will go up if a new owner uses new parts."
- "A typical shop has four employees—1 manager, 2 mechanics (Remove & Replace), and a builder; the manager and the builder are key employees. Typical breakeven is $8,000 to $10,000/week, with the manager included in the expenses."

Percentage of Gross Sales: (where they should be)

Sales 100%

Cost of Sales:
Parts & Fluids 22%
Production Labor (All Technical Employees) 20%
Towing 1%
Misc. Production Supplies 3%
Total Cost of Sales 46%

Sales & Administration Expenses:
Salaries (Center Mgr. & Office) 10%
Rent 08%
Insurance 03%
Utilities 01%
Advertising-Yellow Pages 08%
Telephone 01%
Legal/Accounting 01%
Bank Fees/Bad Debt 01%
Training 01%
Total Sales & Administration Expenses 34%
Net Profit 20%

Seller Financing
- "50 percent down—five (5) years"

Resources

Websites
- www.aamcofranchises.com

Accounting Firms/CPAs (See also Accounting Firms)

SIC 8721-01	NAICS 541211	Number of Businesses/Units 89,188

Rules of Thumb

➢ 100 to 125 percent of annual revenues plus inventory

➢ 2 to 3 times SDE plus inventory

➢ 2 times EBIT

➢ 2.2 times EBITDA

Pricing Tips
- "No individual client or industry type over 20% of Gross Revenue. Gross Revenue earned from Audit, Accounting, or Tax Returns"
- "Even distribution of revenue from tax return preparation and accounting fees is better."
- "CPAs commonly use 1 times gross although we have frequently exceeded that amount."
- "Product mix and any special areas of practice can affect selling price to the right buyer. There is always the possibility to split up a practice among two or more buyers if specialty work is involved."

- "Pricing levels have increased slightly over past several years. In general, pricing ranges from a low of 75% of sales for firms under $50K in revenue to 130% for larger firms in excess of $1M in sales."
- "SDE should be 40% to 60% of gross revenue. The higher the percent of SDE, the more valuable the practice. Other important factors: no client over 20% of revenue, and type of work mix (audit, tax, consulting, bookkeeping)"
- "Many buyers want an earnout but there is demand for practices, and buyers will pay more than 1 times gross."
- "Revenue composition is important; retail tax, write-up, monthly accounting, review work, audit, consulting, types of revenue streams—all have an effect on sale's price."
- "Generally sold based on an annual multiple of gross revenue."
- "Biggest factor is the terms and whether seller will guarantee part or all of the income."
- "SDE should be between 40% and 60% of revenue."
- "Many accountants automatically expect all practices to be worth one times gross. We find that is not true. Most practices will sell for higher than that amount."
- "Selling price is usually based on percent of gross sales. Small practices, under $100K, will usually sell for less than 100%. Large firms, over $500K, may sell for $120% or higher."
- "CPA buyers always want to pay 1 times gross . . . sellers tend to want more . . . terms drive price."
- "Generally will sell for a multiple of annual GROSS revenues (billings)."
- "1 to 1.25 times revenue, with SDE of 30% to 60% of gross revenue."
- "Employees on non-compete will increase; composition of services, accounts receivable, pricing of client work, recovery percentages. These last few will swing price in both directions."
- "Accounting, tax, bookkeeping, EA and/or CPA firms typically sell for 100% to 135% of annual gross revenue. They tend to sell for 2–4 times SDE."
- "Sale price should yield an SDE range of 40% to 60%."
- "Location is paramount. Same practice will sell for 1.3 times gross revenue in one location and 1 times gross revenue in another."
- "The composition of billings is important. The split between recurring/one time. The split among taxes/accounting/audit/consulting/other is important in determining staff composition. Labor costs are extremely important in bottom line. Accounts receivable levels may indicate problems with billings and/or clients."
- "The commonly accepted rule of thumb is one times annual gross sales. The biggest cause for variation from this (50% more or less) is location. Prices in big metro areas are seldom that low. Prices in rural areas are often not that high. Also, it is VERY important to consider the wide variation in definition of 'one times annual gross.' One definition is a total 'work out' situation paying seller 20% of collection each year for five years. On the other end of the scale is a check for all cash at closing with no seller risk regarding retention of clients. These differences in definition of 'price' can mean that actual present value can vary by as much as 100% depending on definition used. Owners (sellers) and buyers are often very confused and misled regarding these issues."

- "EBIT and EBITDA are difficult to use in this industry. This depends a great deal on the staffing requirements, which in turn are dependent on the services provided. It is important to understand the composition of the billings—audits, annual bookkeeping, monthly write up, composition of tax returns (corporate, partnerships & individuals) and the average fees for each of the client lists. Non-recurring consulting billings must also be examined. If regular and for existing clients more valuable than for non-clients (one time consultations). Existing staff represents the greatest danger to the buyer, non-compete agreements are important. State laws vary widely on who can perform what services and what they can call themselves."
- "Sales price will be the lesser of 1.3 times gross revenues or 3 times SDE—and will include FF&E."
- "Accounting firms generally sell based on a multiple of annual gross revenues. That multiple is generally 1 times billings. Premium factors may add to this multiple, such as fee structure, location, services provided, length of time the firm has been established, etc."
- "Type of professional service for clients, client industry mix, no client over 10% of practice revenue, professional staff with firm, time & billing records or charge by service, length of time as a client with the firm, economic outlook for geographic area of service."
- "CPA firms typically sell for 100 to 130% of Annual Gross Sales. Larger firms typically demand a higher percentage. Small single CPA offices may only warrant 100%. The size, training, and qualifications of the firm's staff have an impact on pricing."
- "Earnouts are used for most do-it-yourselfers."

Expert Comments

"Most smaller CPA firms either specialize in a type of industry audit or avoid all audits. The special industry audit firm may be more difficult to sell due to small demand."

"Great buyer demand…difficult industry to grow organically."

"Competition is aging and the regulating agencies are making an impact on various areas of practice, in particular taxation. Accountants are usually not very good at generating new business so acquisitions are a key growth strategy."

"The profit trend and industry trend is upward due to increased tax and government regulations on businesses and individuals. Location and facilities are located in office or upscale retail locations. A profitable, well-balanced CPA practice is highly marketable to those entering the profession from corporate and established firms to expand their client base. Replication or opening a practice is not difficult. Establishing a client base is the challenge for a new CPA practice. "

"Easy to start but takes a lot of time to build good client base."

"In general CPA firms are low risk and high profit. Profit can easily reach 30% of revenues. Existing firms are easily marketed with well-qualified buyers."

"Industry outlook is increasing due to a complex tax code and need for business financial reports and services."

"Business owners continue to age, and the sole proprietorship is at risk if he or she does not plan an exit, something they are poor at."

"Marketability is high because practice purchase is a quick and low-cost method of increasing revenue and long-term SDE."

"CPA firms are easily marketed. The pool of buyers usually has significant financial resources to close a deal."

"Although a very stable industry, current government regulations and the changes of such have put increasing demand on service. There is also a decline in numbers of people entering and staying in public accounting."

"Risk of client loss is the biggest factor in a purchase."

"CPAs benefit from changes in tax law. Due to upcoming change of President, expect many tax changes to be enacted that will drive tax work to CPAs."

"Demand for client service is increasing. Purchasing a client base may be less expensive and quicker than new client marketing."

"The marketability of accounting firms is much greater in major metro areas but still fairly marketable even in rural areas."

"People don't leave their CPA often—so there's competition but it doesn't affect established firms much. Very low risk—very few CPAs go out of business. Profits are up although firms can be adversely affected by local trends—i.e., Silicon Valley fallout where CPAs have a concentration in a particular industry. Facilities are often Class A buildings. There's definitely a market for CPA firms but finding the right buyer is difficult. The industry is increasing while fewer people enter the profession. Replicating an existing practice is often very difficult and the reason we sell 400+ practices a year."

"Competition is of minor consideration in the industry. Location is key. Good firms are in hot, growing areas and 'good customer services' and high prices run hand in hand with quality office spaces."

"The accounting/tax industry as it pertains to small privately owned locations has been steady for some years. Profitability has always been high and replication difficult, especially in the CPA field. As for risk, CPAs are the second best rated business loans to make—their default rate is very low."

"The industry is aging and recent decisions by the professional groups have made it difficult to enter. The ability to perform even basic marketing is limited, resulting in acquisition being a key growth criteria. Specialization in terms of market and product continues and while entry is easier, breaking into profitable niches is difficult."

"CPA firms usually have high client and revenue retention when properly transitioned to a new owner."

"It's easy to create a CPA firm but costly and time consuming to get the clients."

Benchmark Data

Statistics (Accounting Services)

Number of Establishments	89,188
Average Profit Margin	15.6%
Revenue per Employee	$154,500
Average Number of Employees	5
Average Wages per Employee	$65,930

Source: IBISWorld, March 2012

Products and Services Segmentation

Auditing	44.7%
Corporate tax services	21.8%
Consulting	17.4%
General accounting	16.1%

Source: IBISWorld, March 2012

Industry Costs

Profit	15.6%
Wages	42.5%
Purchases	3.0%
Depreciation	3.0%
Marketing	4.3%
Rent & Utilities	7.0%
Other	24.6%

Source: IBISWorld, March 2012

Market Share

PricewaterhouseCoopers	10.2%
Deloitte Touche Tohmatsu	10.1%
Ernst & Young	10.1%
KPMG International	5.3%

Source: IBISWorld, March 2012

Distribution of Employer Enterprises by Employment Size

Number of Employees	Number of Enterprises	Percentage of Total
0 to 4	35,787	68.5
5 to 9	9,874	18.9
10 to 19	4,210	8.1

Source: IBISWorld, March 2012

- "SDE should be 45% to 60% of Gross Revenue for the three- to five-person firm."
- "Staff wages no more than 33% of revenue. Professional staff should annually bill 3 to 5 times their salary."
- "SDE as a percentage of sales should be, as a minimum, 35%."
- "Gross is the key."
- "Most net approximately 40% to 50% annually."
- "Employee should bill three times salary cost."
- "Diversification of revenue source by industry and from individual clients. No single client over 10% of total revenue."
- "Labor costs less than 1/3."
- "Payroll should be less than 30% of gross receipts. Net earnings to the owner, including salary, can easily range from 30% to 50% of gross revenue."

- "Adjusted net income of SDE can have a big impact. Industry average tends to be 33% of sales but can be much higher in a very good office."
- "$100,000 billings per employee."
- "Solid accounting firms with gross revenues of $100K to $2 million tend to have SDE of 35% to 50% and even more in some cases."
- "Hard to benchmark due to high fluctuations of billable rates. CPAs in the same community may bill from $75 per hour to $250 per hour or more depending upon size of firm and expertise. Professional staff should be able to bill 3 times their base salary."
- "There should be gross revenue of $100,000 to $150,000 per employee if you expect to be profitable. Most practices have 35% to 50% of gross revenues dropping to the bottom line as SDE."
- "Labor should be no more than 1/3 of gross receipts."
- "We consider gross receipts of $100,000 per year per person in the office is a benchmark indicating profitability. For a typical small firm from $250,000 to $450,000 of annual receipts, the cash flow to owner should be at or above 50% of gross in order to be a top firm. Cash flow percentages vary greatly and decline as annual gross increases."
- "Should be $100,000+ in revenue per full-time staff person, including the owner— more in given markets. SDE should be 40% to 50% of gross to sell for premium price. Anything under 40% and we start looking for problems."
- "A successful CPA practice will value employees as well as clients. Finding and keeping good employees for work in public accounting is a distinguishing feature of a successful firm. Flex hours, on-premises nursery, and production bonuses are a few of the successful firm employee benefits."
- "Annual growth rate in excess of 7 percent owner profit, SDE in excess of 40% of sales, stable revenues from recurring billings—approx. 80% of total billings."
- "Many firms generate gross revenues of $100,000 to $150,000 per staff person. Labor costs generally run around 32% of gross revenues."
- "A successful CPA firm should bill $100,000 to $200,000 per professional staff member per year. Gross wages should be in the 30% to 35% range."
- "Employee cost below 30% is excellent"
- "Billing at 3 times employee cost"

Expenses as a Percentage of Annual Sales

Cost of goods:	0% to 05%
Payroll/labor Costs:	25% to 35%
Occupancy:	10% to 20%
Profit (estimated pretax):	35% to 45%

Industry Trend

- "Increased government regulations that will require more need by the small business for accounting and tax advice."
- "Many baby boomers are getting ready to retire."
- "Industry trend is upward due to increased tax and government regulations on businesses and individuals."
- "Still a seller's market"
- "Industry regulation makes entry difficult yet demand for services continually increase."

- "An increase in the number of small single-owner firms billing $100K or less as laid- off industry CPAs open their own firms."
- "Shortage of staff accountants for public accounting "
- "Many baby boomers will begin to retire."
- "Changes in govt. regulation continue to increase. Strong likelihood of licensing for tax preparation will reduce competition, and aging practitioner base will reduce competition."
- "More consolidations. More minority and foreign ownership."
- "Steady to upward trend continues."
- "Increased demand for tax advice"
- "Number of sellers may increase."
- "Specialty shops can be in the wrong sector and therefore be hit heavily by current downturn in economy. Market for new business and small business continues to be strong."
- "Continued upward trend"
- "CPAs may see increased revenues in years to come with tax changes. Costs not impacted by oil crisis, so rate increases go more to bottom line."
- "An increase in the number of small firms changing hands due to the average age of firm owners approaching retirement age"
- "More outsourcing and more retiring practice owners"
- "Increasing exit from the profession. I see prices decreasing as supply of firms increases vs. a relatively decreasing number of persons entering the profession. This exit is because the profession is in decline and margins are shrinking."
- "Although the marketplace of accountants is aging, there are excellent opportunities for the future entrants into the industry. Future government legislation will result in fewer competitors in taxation. The audit market has slowed with legal difficulties, but other sectors have expanded with government legislation."
- "As baby boomer owners start to retire, more firms will come to market possibly lower prices."
- "Consolidation of the marketplace continues, Specialization in terms of product and customer. More regulation imminent, especially in tax preparation."
- "Consolidation as smaller firms (1 to 4 professionals) are purchased and merged into mid-size firms of 5 to 10 professionals."

Seller Financing

- "Four years earnout method with 25% to 50% down"
- "Seller financing is usually only a last resort."
- "3 to 5 years"

Questions

- "What period of time will they guarantee the billings."
- "Any client concentrations, risks of client losses."
- "Why are you selling? Is any individual client fee over 10% of the Gross Revenue? Is any single industry over 10% of Gross Revenue? How much of Revenue is earned from tax return preparation and how much from accounting or auditing? What percent are corporate returns or individual returns? What type of client audits? What type of work does your staff do? What tax and

accounting software do you use? What is the billing rate per hour? Do you bill by hour or project? How long have your clients been with this firm? How long have the employees been with this firm?"

- "(1) Why are you selling? (2) Do you have any open complaints with the state CPA board? (3) Do you have any clients that represent more than 5% of revenue? (4) Do you require your staff to sign non-compete agreements? "What are the strengths of your firm? What areas can be improved? Have you attempted to sell on your own?"
- "Client mix, services mix, average billings for services, accounts receivable and status of employees"
- "How close is the seller to the end customer?"
- "Why are you selling? Will you work part time? Will your staff stay?"
- "Info relating to clientele, fee structure, employee information, pending litigation, office lease, type of services performed, need for licenses/ certifications"
- "Do you do any audit work? Are your licenses current? How many hours do you personally bill per year?"
- "Why are you selling? Is any one client or industry over 10% of gross revenue? What percent of revenue is from tax, audit, bookkeeping? Client length of time with the firm? Staff knowledge and client contact?"
- "Gross revenue for the last three years (trend). Percent of revenue from tax, audit, bookkeeping, or other. Number of tax returns by type, Audits by industry, bookkeeping clients monthly or quarterly. Client mix—by industry, profession, etc. and revenue per type. Client location by zip code. Any client over 10% of total revenue. Length of time as a client. Are there time and billing records? Staff-number, location, length, duties, competency, salary. Office lease time period. Tax software in use."
- "The quality of the fees should be investigated both by looking at the cash flow percentages and investigating the billing rates of the personnel and the owner. Post- sale competition is a major risk factor so this possibility should be investigated carefully."
- "Nature of clients and services, market definition, geography of practice, employees have a non-compete, accounts receivable status"
- "Are there any concentration issues—any 3–5 clients that represent 10% or more of gross revenue? Take a look at A/R aging—could be a sign of deadbeat clients. Is there the potential for staff members to leave and take clients with them? Age of clients—if 80% over 65 years old, could be a problem. And the list goes on."
- "Why you are selling, growth rates, stability of clients, composition of services offered and average fees"
- "Revenue level? Growth rate for each of past 5 years? How many employees? What are rates charged to clients? Are there time and billing records? Why are you selling? How long have you been in business? What are the demographics of the client base? Age, location, size of businesses. What software products are used? Do clients come to your office or do you go to them?"

Resources

Associations

- American Institute of CPAs: www.aicpa.org

Accounting Firms/Practices

(See also Accounting Firms/CPAs/Tax Practices)

SIC 8721-01	NAICS 541219	Number of Businesses/Units 140,000

Rules of Thumb

➤ There are three rules of thumb generally cited: #1—.75 to 1.25 annual revenues, depending on characteristics of practice; #2—9 to 15 times monthly net sales, depending on characteristics of practice; and #3—2 to 5 times the seller's SDE. Rules of thumb normally include FF&E, Lease and Intangibles. Current assets, real estate, and all related liabilities must be considered separately.

➤ 2.5 to 3.5 times SDE plus inventory (if any)

➤ One to 1.25 times annual revenues (non-CPA) plus inventory

➤ Generally sold for a multiple of 1 to 1.5 times gross revenues depending upon net earnings. Rarely sell below one times gross.

➤ One times gross for low-level billings, up to 1.5 times gross for high-level billings

➤ 100 percent to 115 percent of one-year's revenue + FF&E with one-year guarantee of gross

➤ 90 to 110 percent of anticipated annual revenues under new ownership, subject to seller guarantee and earnout provisions

➤ 100 to 115 percent of annual revenues, plus fixtures & equipment; seller keeps accounts payable & accounts receivable

➤ Sales price generally 100 to 125 percent of annual revenue; higher in some metropolitan areas such as New York City, Dallas, Atlanta, etc.

➤ 45 percent times EBIT

Pricing Tips

- "Terms are a huge factor in determining value."
- "Fee structure, client complexity, location and overall staffing requirements affect practice desirability."
- "Typically, accounting firms are sold on a percentage of collections and based on a client retention clause. This number can range from 1.0 times to 1.50 times revenues depending on location, average rates, etc."
- "Priced based on a multiple of annual gross revenue."
- "Good ones should sell for more than 1 times gross."
- "Accounting and tax practices' purchase price is typically based on a multiple of the gross billings anywhere from 1.0 to 1.5 times. There is also usually a discount for an all-cash deal or no-retention clause (fixed price) deal."
- "Accounting firms generally sell for 100 to 125 percent of annual revenue. Equipment, furniture, etc. is sometimes included in this pricing structure and sometimes is asked for on top of the revenue multiplier. It is common for these types of practice sales to have some type of an earnout feature. Location of the practice, profitability, average billing rates and client demographics all play an important role in the marketability of the firm."

- "Client mix and buyer personality are key to a successful transition."
- "The rule of thumb is from .75 to 1.5 times annual gross revenues; the higher number is usually for CPA firms or firms that have an excellent profit margin."
- "In the larger deals ($350K and up), usually the furniture, fixtures and equipment are included; in the smaller deals they are sold at fair market value."
- "Name recognition and reputation in the area. Fee structure, length of service of firm's clientele."
- "Higher percentage of write-up work, higher multiple (versus tax work). Higher hourly rate charged to customers, higher multiple. Higher average monthly fee (write-up) or tax return, higher multiple. Prolonged cooperation, involvement of seller post-closing, higher multiple. Flexible lease terms, higher multiple."
- "One-third down payment and one-year guarantee of gross."
- "Location, fees, length of time in business, length of relationships with clients, quality of client base, quality of staff & profitability."
- "...steady, historical growth in number of accounts and revenues. High 'averages' per monthly accounts and tax returns (corporate & individual). Reasonable, documentable relationships between dollars charged and total work completed. At least 50 percent of revenues generated from monthly write-ups to balance hectic tax season. Lengthy, committed transition phase to maximize retention. Existing trained staff willing to remain at new owner's discretion. Dollar-for-dollar seller guarantee (difficult/impossible to sell without). Either short-term or month-to-month lease allowing new owner to eventually move clients to his/her existing location. Lack of substantial 'one-time only' work such as IRS representation or specialized consulting services. Substantially all revenues collected as earned; i.e., no material advance billings (unearned revenue). Absence of 'audit work,' which carries great liability (insurance is often cost-prohibitive)."
- "Sales of accounting practices range from .5 to 1.6 times gross revenues, with a very high concentration at 1.0 times annual gross revenue. However, in the majority of cases, the price was contingent on retaining the clients for some period of time, most typically one year, with the final price reduced by the amounts for any clients not retained. The median ratio of price/SDE was 1.64."
- "Metro areas on the high side (New York City maybe 200 percent of annual billings). High fee structure adds to price unless highly specialized. Compliance work (recurring type) increases price. All tax work reduces price."
- "One times gross annual billings retained during first year of new ownership plus the FMV (fair market value) of equipment."
- "Perhaps the most unique feature of accounting/tax practice sales is the presence of a dollar-for-dollar seller guarantee; i.e., the purchaser will ultimately pay only for the business (revenues) retained during an agreed-upon time period (typically the first year after closing). Secondly, cash flow... is not extremely important (as opposed to revenues). Obviously, without a seller guarantee, the price would be substantially less. Also of importance (all other things being equal) is the mix of monthly write-up work versus seasonal tax work. Generally, the greater the write-up percent, the more valuable. Also, any highly specialized consulting is less valuable. Finally, the higher the 'averages' the better (e.g... average monthly write-up, and average personal and corporate tax returns). The amount and length of cooperation from the seller during the transition phase also impacts value and the ease with which

the practice is sold. The seller will often introduce the buyer as a new partner to allow clients to become familiar with the new practitioner (this maximizes retention). Additionally, the presence of a long-term lease actually detracts from value (most acquisitions are made by established practitioners with an existing office)."

Expert Comments

"There seem to be plenty of buyers for a good accounting practice."

"With technology today, accountants can process the client's work from anywhere. Office location is not as important unless it is an all-1040 tax practice."

"Regarding ease of replication—if you are looking to buy an accounting practice, you must be in the industry and have an educational background to purchase. This will decrease the buyer pool significantly."

"A new owner will assume risk by trying to retain the previous owner's clients."

"Generally works the same as CPA firms. Fee structure may be somewhat lower in some cases."

"Accounting firms located in major cities tend to be very marketable. A pool of prospective buyers includes most any firm located near the selling firm and also includes many talented accountants who currently do not own their own firm."

Benchmark Data

- "Labor at less than 33% is best."
- "Each employee should generate around $100k–$150k in annual billings. Owners/Partners—$200k–$250k."
- "Net income should be at least 40%. Owners expected to bring in around $200k in annual billings."
- "Generally revenue based on employee costs."
- "Not moving the office will help retain the client base."
- "Number of repeat clients on the book; it usually takes at least 250–350 to break even and above that to be profitable."
- "Accounting firms will typically have an SDE of at least 33%."
- "More than half of gross income is earned, on average, from the preparation of tax returns. The typical firm charges an average of $208 to prepare an itemized Form 1040 and $102 for a non-itemized Form 1040. Fees average $92 an hour to prepare financial statements and $112 an hour for estate and financial planning services. Fees vary sharply by state and region."

Source: National Society of Accountants

Expenses as a Percentage of Annual Sales

Cost of goods	n/a
Payroll/labor Costs	30% to 35%
Occupancy	08% to 12%
Profit (estimated pretax)	30% to 40%

Industry Trend

- "More people preparing own returns with 'off-the-shelf' software."
- "Any new tax laws that would take effect that could decrease people's needs for accountants (i.e., Fair Tax)."
- "Steady to upward"
- "More and more small businesses are using accounting software, which is reducing the amount of monthly write-up work accounting firms used to perform."
- "Generally an upward trend"
- "Strong growth trend with more outsourcing in the industry to keep labor costs down. Substantial amount of this work is repetitious and clerical driven."
- "Consolidation and firms sending work offshore"
- "Technology is changing the way accounting practices operate. The firms owned by older practitioners who do not keep up with IT updating will either die off, or will provide younger and more savvy CPAs great opportunities (at lower P/R multiples). More CPA firms are finding that it is necessary to use 'off-site' employees who have computers at home. Firms without adequate non-compete and employment contracts in place may pose greater risks to potential buyers. I think we will see many smaller firms being put on the market, because they cannot attract the talent to keep them going in this 'standards-overloaded' environment. Mid-size firms will develop more innovative ways to bring professionals into the profits of the firm, and eventually into equity positions. Group practices will grow, as there is strength in numbers and it is easier to spread fixed overhead costs over a greater number of professionals."

Seller Financing

- "5 years"
- "Earnouts are very typically between one and two years."
- "30 percent down payment, 70 percent seller carry back, five years, 8 to 10 percent"
- "20 to 40 percent down, financing three to five years for small practices; seven to 10 years for larger ones"
- "Three years average"
- "Three to five years"
- "30 to 35 percent down, balance financed over three to five years with one-year client retention guaranteed by the seller to the buyer"
- "Usually seller financed—25 percent to 40 percent down. From three to 10 years, depending on size of the practice"

Questions

- "Demographic of the client base. Number of years average client has been with the firm."
- "What is the firm's net income? How long has the practice been established? What price is the owner looking to get? Does the staff know the owner is looking to sell the business?"
- "Gross revenue, revenue type, number of clients, fees generated from each client, employee compensation and experience, lease on facilities, type of software used, net income."

- "Why are you selling? Will you stay? Will you sign a non-compete? Will the staff stay?"
- "Will clients likely stay with new owner?"
- "Break down the composition of fees on an annual basis (percent from tax, bookkeeping, payroll, accounting, auditing, technology, consulting, etc.). Also ask if fee structure is based on hourly or fixed-fee arrangements. What is the effective percent of production hours (total firm hours billed/total firm hours spent)? What are the rate realizations (total fees billed/standard rates x hours billed)? Clients making up over 10% of annual fees? Any major clients coming to end of service agreements, and details? Answers indicating poor production and rate realizations have a negative impact on pricing, while positive statistics have positive impacts on pricing."

Resources

Websites
- www.cpasales.com

Associations
- National Society of Accountants: www.nsacct.org
- American Institute of Certified Public Accountants (AICPA): www.aicpa.org

Accounting/Tax Practices

(See also Accounting Firms/Practices/CPAs)

SIC 7291-01	NAICS 541213	Number of Businesses/Units 120,119

Rules of Thumb

➤ 1 to 1.35 times annual revenues plus inventory

➤ 2.5 to 3 times SDE plus inventory

➤ 5 to 7 times EBIT

➤ 4 to 6 times EBITDA

Pricing Tips

- "Most practices are sold on a multiple of the gross billings. This is typically anywhere from 1.0 to 1.30."
- "Even distribution of revenue from tax return preparation and accounting fees is better."
- "Buyers generally want earnouts, sellers want cash."
- "Repeat clients, accounting vs. tax preparation work."
- "Tax related revenues are priced at 1 to 1.25 times annual revenues. Monthly write-up revenues are priced at 1.25 to 1.5 times annual revenues. Other revenues priced at one times annual revenue."
- "Be careful of competition from current employees starting their own firm. Get non-competes from current employees."
- "National franchises can hurt sale price due to franchise, royalty, and advertising fees charged."
- "Higher average price per return results in higher asking price."

- "Priced based on annual gross revenue."
- "Accounting, tax & bookkeeping practices are valued typically at 1 to 1.3 times gross revenue + hard assets."
- "Higher end practices will net 40%"
- "Generally sell for a multiple of annual gross revenues."
- "Dependent on type of clients; 1040 clients result in lower pricing; monthly and retainer clients result in higher pricing. Audit only preferred by a minority of firms."
- "Generally sold based on a multiple of one times annual gross revenues"
- "Typically practices sell for multiples of revenue from 1x to 1.75x based on location and demand in area and type of practice."

Expert Comments

"Accounting work growing due to outsourcing"

"The profit trend and industry trend is upward due to increased tax and government regulations on businesses and individuals. There is a greater need of business bookkeeping and records for proof of compliance with government regulations. Location and Facilities are located in office or retail locations. A profitable, well balanced practice is highly marketable to those entering the profession from corporate and established firms to expand their client base. Replication or opening a practice is not difficult. Establishing a client base is the challenge for a new accounting practice."

"Historically profitable practices will sell for a higher price."

"Lots of competition. Marketing for new clients is difficult, so building a large client base takes time."

"The major concern for any buyer should be retaining the clients they are purchasing. An owner willing to stay on after the sale to help with transition should help the buyer feel more comfortable. Practices where owners do not stay on should be sold at a discount and less than market price."

"With a good computer program and little training, anyone can prepare a basic tax return."

"Tax preparation has become a commodity. Anyone with $5,000, a PC, and software can easily open a tax prep office. A number of recent national franchises have over-saturated the market. "

"Fair amount of competition in the industry. Very profitable businesses when compared to many others. Accounting practices in major metro areas are highly marketable."

"Industry is in need of personnel and has no lack of new regulations which necessitate new audit or forensic work."

"Not a location-dependent business...service usually at the client's business address. Tough business to grow organically but many with financial wherewithall to purchase firms or accounts."

"High risk, as it is easy to duplicate this type of business. Customer loyalty is not as strong in this business as in a CPA practice."

"Easily transferable. High visibility of offices necessary to attract large number of walk-in clients. Majority of clients are seen only once a year for tax preparation and filing of tax returns. Office location is critical."

Benchmark Data

Statistics (Tax Preparation Services)

Number of Establishments	120,119
Average Profit Margin	18%
Revenue per Employee	$31,000
Average Number of Employees	3
Average Wages per Employee	$12,660

Source: IBISWorld, March 2012

Products and Services Segmentation

Standard tax preparation services	57%
Basic tax preparation services	23%
Full-service tax preparation services	14%
Tax-related financial products	06%

Source: IBISWorld, March 2012

Industry Costs

Profit	18.0%
Rent	2.0%
Utilities	1.5%
Depreciation	2.3%
Other	33.2%
Wages	41.0%
Purchases	2.0%

Source: IBISWorld, March 2012

Enterprises by Employment Size

# of Employees	# of Enterprises	% of total
1 to 4	10,797	67.6
5 to 9	2,492	15.6
10 to 19	1,505	9.4

Source: IBISWorld, March 2012

Market Share

H&R Block Inc.	32.0%
Jackson Hewitt Inc.	2.1%

Source: IBISWorld, March 2012

- "SDE should be 45% to 60% of Revenue"
- "Write-up work and monthly payroll preparation should provide approximately 75% of total revenues. Taxes should provide the remaining 25%."
- "Taxpayers may also benefit by obtaining tax preparation estimates from more than one preparer from different size companies. For example, the survey found that tax preparation fees for an itemized Form 1040 with Schedule A and a state tax return averaged only $217 at one-person firms, and rose to an average of $245 for firms with three or more staff.
- "Employees should bill out around $100,000 per year. Net income should be around 40%. Typically, audit and review practices are less desirable and may be more difficult to find a buyer for."
- "Most net approx. 45+ percent."
- "Employee cost should be under 25%. Occupancy cost may be high for newer offices as they move into newer strip centers with higher rents."

- "SDE on most firms ranges from 30%–50%."
- "Per employee sales/billings of approx. $100,000."
- "Labor costs below 30%"
- "Generates approx. $100,000 in fees per employee. Franchise operations compensate tax preparers based on a percentage of fees billed to client— 30%."

Expenses as a Percentage of Annual Sales

Cost of goods	02%
Payroll/labor Costs	25% to 30%
Occupancy	05% to 10%
Profit (estimated pretax)	30% to 40%

Industry Trend

- "With so many small businesses closing due to the poor economy, independent accounting firms are experiencing a decline in both new clients and total clients. "
- "Industry trend is upward due to increased tax and government regulations on businesses and individuals."
- "Short term declining, longer term growing."
- "Computers are making it easier and easier for businesses and individuals to prepare their own taxes, but people will always need professionals to help with audits, the tax code, etc."
- "Upward trend with more electronic filing"
- "More industry regulation from IRS."
- "Any new tax laws would greatly affect the accounting and tax industry."
- "I see the trend to remain about the same as it has been the past 10 years."
- "Continued upward trend"
- "Growth...consistent growth due to regulations."
- "Continued demand for acquisitions and continued exiting by aging population of CPAs."
- "IRS free e-file along with PC software continues to pull customers away from paid preparers. More tax preparation franchises opening will take business away from established firms."

Questions:

- "Repeat clients, accounting vs. tax preparation work"
- "Why are you selling? Is any individual client fee over 10% of the Gross Revenue? Is any single industry over 10% of Gross Revenue? How much of Revenue is earned from tax return preparation and how much from accounting or bookkeeping? What type of work does you staff do? What tax and accounting software do you use? What is the billing rate per hour? Do you bill by hour or project? How long have your clients been with this firm? How long have the employees been with this firm?"
- "How long will you stay around and help with transition? How long have the clients been clients?"
- "Strengths and weaknesses of the firm. Information about the area."
- "What is the breakdown between tax, write-up, consulting and audit revenues?

Also, who else in the firm can do the tax and write-up work? Who reviews the work?"

- "How long has the firm been in business? List of clients that have left within the past 3 years. List of new clients within the last 3 years. Does the owner plan on being available after the sale? Review sample returns and work papers to get a feel for the amount of work that is done for each client."
- "Why are you selling? Are the clients because of location or other reason? What type of software is used now? If the clients are not walk-in, how long have they been tax clients? What industry are most of the clients? What % of clients are personal returns or business returns? Are bookkeeping services included with any client?"
- "What are the seller's goals in the sale of the practice? They are not the same for all sellers."
- "Fee structure, number of clients, services performed, employee costs, franchise fees paid, licenses required."
- "Any clients not in the local service area?"
- "Years in practice? Type of practice? Number of clients? Dispersion of client revenues?"
- "Do employees have a non-compete agreement? Are you aware of any new tax offices opening in the area in the last year?"

Ace Cash Express (See also Check Cashing Services)		
SIC 6099-03	NAICS 522390	Number of Businesses/Units 1,750

Rules of Thumb

➢ 1.25 times annual sales plus inventory

Resources

Websites

- www.acecashexpress.com: This company is publicly held. Their annual report is available online and is an excellent resource.

Ace Hardware (See also Hardware Stores)		Franchise
Approx. Total Investment		$400,000 to $1,100,000
Estimated Annual Sales/Unit		Not Available
SIC 5251-04	NAICS 444130	Number of Businesses/Units 4,100

Rules of Thumb

➢ 45 percent of annual sales plus inventory

Pricing Tips

- Sales seem to indicate that smaller sales bring a higher multiple (50%+) than stores with sales over $1 million, which seem to bring lower multiples. Price is plus inventory, and that may be the reason for lower multiples for larger stores. Note: There is some excellent information on Ace Hardware in the Hardware Store entry.

Questions

- "For Ace Hardware stores: Are you Vision 21-compliant? Do you have the Eagle 4 Windows level Activant computer? If answer is no to either question, there will be substantial costs to upgrade the store that Ace will require of the new owner. Vision 21 requires store to have proper signage, decor, inventory layout, enroll in various marketing programs, have Activant Computer, attend Ace hardware shows etc. If a store isn't Vision 21-compliant AND doesn't have Activant, costs to upgrade may be in the $150,000 range!!"

Resources

Websites
- www.myace.com

Adam & Eve Stores	Franchise
Approx. Total Investment	$151,550 to $345,700
Estimated Annual Sales/Unit	Not Available

	NAICS 451120	Number of Businesses/Units 40

Rules of Thumb

➤ 35 percent of annual sales plus inventory

Resources

Websites
- www.adamevestores.com

Adult Clubs/Nightclubs (See bars)	
	NAICS1 722410	

Advertising Agencies		
SIC 7311-01	NAICS 541810	Number of Businesses/Units 13,000

Rules of Thumb

➤ 50 percent of annual revenues (billings) plus inventory. May require an earnout.

Benchmark Data

Statistics (Advertising Agencies)

Number of Establishments	13,563
Average Profit Margin	8.0%
Revenue per Employee	$197,000
Average Number of Employees	12
Average Wages per Employee	$89,584

Source: IBISWorld, April 2012

Products and Services Segmentation

Advertising services 69.5%
Other 9.9%
Creative services 9.0%
Media planning and buying 6.4%
Media representation services 2.6%
Public relations services 2.6%

Source: IBISWorld, April 2012

Major Market Segmentation

Automotive sector 17.5%
Other industries 17.3%
Telecommunications sector 12.7%
Food and candy sector 12.5%
Local services and amusements sector 11.1%
Financial services sector 11.2%
Miscellaneous retail sector 9.4%
Direct response 8.3%

Source: IBISWorld, April 2012

Industry Costs

Profit 8.0%
Wages 46.0%
Purchases 10.5%
Depreciation 2.5%
Marketing 1.0%
Rent & Utilities 6.7%
Other 25.3%

Source: IBISWorld, April 2012

Market Share

Omnicom Group Inc. 10.4%
The Interpublic Group of Companies Inc. 7.3%
WPP PLC 6.7%
Publicis Groupe SA 4.3%

Source: IBISWorld, April 2012

Enterprises by Employment Size

Number of Employees	Number of Enterprises	Share %
0 to 4	8,367	66.1
5 to 9	1,913	15.1
10 to 19	1,191	9.4

Source: IBISWorld, April 2012

Agency Revenue by Category

Advertising 33%
Direct marketing and Customer Relation Management 17%
Digital 14%
Public Relations 11%
Promotion 9%
Media 7%
Other Billings 9%

Source: www.statisticbrain.com and the Gale Group, Inc.

Industry Trend

- "eMarketer predicts 3 ad formats will dominate 2012

  "The majority of U.S. online ad spending will go on three formats over the next few years, according to a new forecast from eMarketer.

  "Video, banner and search advertising will account for upwards of 80% of all spending through 2016, predicts eMarketer.

  "Video will be the fastest-growing of all formats, growing 54.7% over 2010 to account for 7.9% of all online ad buying this year. eMarketer predicts video's share to rise to 15% by 2014.

  "However, video remains in third place to search and banner advertising. Search is forecast to maintain its lead, comprising 49.4% of total online spending this year, but its share of overall online advertising budgets will slowly decrease from 2012 to 2016.

  "The continued dominance of search as the leading digital advertising format comes as little surprise, with its near-universal adoption rates among consumers and popularity on both the desktop and mobile web," says eMarketer.

  "Banners will comprise 23.4% of the total online ad spend this year falling to 20.5% by 2016."

  Source: "eMarketer predicts 3 ad formats will dominate 2012" by Helen Leggatt, www.bizreport.com/2012

Resources
Websites

- www.aaaa.org

Advertising Material Distribution Services		
(See also Money Mailer, Supercoups, Valpak, etc.)		
SIC 7319	NAICS 541870	

Rules of Thumb

➢ 40 to 45 percent of annual sales plus inventory

➢ "If a cooperative direct mail business, such as Money Mailer or Supercoups is making $100,000, it could be sold for $150,000 to $225,000, and $250,000 if it was a perfect situation. Now, on the other hand if it is a Valpak, I believe you could get up to 3 times what it is making because Valpak is the undisputed leader."

Benchmark Data
- See Direct Mail Advertising for Benchmark information

Aero Colours, Inc		Franchise
Approx. Total Investment		$49,400 to $65,000
Estimated Annual Sales/Unit		Not Available
SIC 7532-02	NAICS 811121	Number of Businesses/Units 32

Rules of Thumb

➢ 70 percent of annual sales

Resources

Websites

- www.aerocolours.com

Air Conditioning Contractors (See HVAC)		
		Number of Business/Units 59,500

Aircraft Cleaning (See also Airport Operations)		
SIC 4581-04	NAICS 561720	

Rules of Thumb

➢ 100 percent of annual sales plus inventory
➢ 3 times SDE plus inventory

Pricing Tips

- "Minimum 3 yrs. in business, 2.5 x net if owner operated, as much as 4x net if work is performed by a crew or crews."

Expert Comments

"Strong barrier to entry; quality equipment is a must; high profit; labor intense; and a current downturn in general aviation"

"Aviation is a very difficult industry as a startup business."

Benchmark Data

- "Labor should run approximately 25% of sales"
- "Corporate aircraft cleaning is a very specialized service; if it survived the first 18 months, chances are it will do well."
- "All services are mobile."

Expenses as a Percentage of Annual Sales

Cost of goods:	05% to 10%
Payroll/labor Costs:	25% to 35%
Occupancy:	10%
Profit (estimated pretax):	55% to 60%

Industry Trend

- "The industry will bounce back, as always"
- "Increase in demand"
- "Private aviation is a rapidly growing industry."

Questions

- "Number of accounts, how long servicing those accounts, percentage of sales from which accounts"

- "How many aircraft do you service per week, per month? Number of employees? The buyer is going to need to keep the employees."
- "Transition period is very important"

Resources

Associations
- National Business Aviation Association : www.nbaa.org

Aircraft Manufacturing—Parts, Supplies, Engines, etc.		
(Kit-built & Ultralight aircraft industry)		
SIC 3724	NAICS 336412	

Rules of Thumb

➢ 40 to 70 percent of annual sales includes value of equipment

➢ 4 times EBIT

Pricing Tips
- "Add for any FAA approvals and for high-value equipment."
- "FAA approvals and/or contracts with major OEM's very important."
- " Each business varies so greatly from the next. It takes someone who knows the industry to know the exact business being described before a price can be established."
- "When very specialized equipment is needed, add some if a good business. Add value of real estate."

Expert Comments

"Sales and profits declining due to technological factors such as increased time between overhauls"

"Low competition based on high barriers to entry."

Benchmark Data

- "Revenue per employee should be at least $100,000 per annum."

Expenses as a Percentage of Annual Sales
Cost of goods:	35%
Payroll/labor Costs:	35%
Occupancy:	20%
Profit (estimated pretax):	10%

Industry Trend

- "Highly cyclical with the economy and military spending"
- "Highly cyclical. Down in short term due to current recession. Growth in longer term due to continued worldwide growth in air travel."

Seller Financing

- "3 years max, 1 year least"
- "We've never sold a 'seller-financed' ultralight aircraft business. It is always a cash deal."

Questions

- "Approvals and contracts"
- "What is the reputation of the aircraft or related product being sold? What is the reputation of the company? Is business up or down? What about accidents—any deaths? A company with a great reputation may be worth little because of their product—or, vice versa."
- "Where are sales today in comparison to one, two . . . years ago? Why are they up or down?" [We don't know if the pun was intended or not.] Have there been any structural failures or successful liability suits against them? Is it movable or must buyer move?"

Airport Operations		
SIC 4581-06	NAICS 488119	Number of Businesses/Units 1,700

Rules of Thumb

➢ 100 percent of annual sales includes inventory

➢ 3 to 4 times SDE includes inventory

➢ 4 to 5 times EBIT

➢ 3 to 4 times EBITDA

Pricing Tips

- "While the Trajen FBOs (Fixed - base operators) sold to Macquarie for about 16x EBITDA, that was not the norm, despite Macquarie subsequently having its IPO with over 18x P/E ratio. The FBO business is really a real-estate play. Take a careful look at the city leasehold agreements and the fuel farm, as EPA regulations can be costly to implement. Most fuel farms now must be built above ground. For air charter companies, take a close look at the age/condition of the aircraft used and existing contracts. When Sentient reformed Jet Direct, it imploded because of excessive growth issues, i.e. too much overhead. "First, if a fixed base operator, perform due diligence on EPA regulation adherence (e.g. fuel farm) and hangar leases with city or county"
- "Need to consider time remaining on municipality leases and at what rate these could be renewed. First-tier airports will demand higher premium, maybe 6 times EBITDA. With cash flow financing at a maximum now of 4 to 6 times cash flow, selling at a higher multiple than a target of 5 times is not reasonable. Municipalities have also reduced the time of the leases from 30 years to 20 years. It typically takes 15 to 17 years to break even on new hangar construction. In theory, buying a fixed base operator is really a real-estate play, as revenues are either from hangar/office rents or fuel purchases."

Expert Comments

The private jet industry has taken an economic hit the past few years, as a luxury brand. Industry growth rate is under 2%. The political climate has not helped, despite the fact that the President has used Oprah's private jet. The high growth areas now are in southeast Asia and in Brazil.

Benchmark Data

Statistics (Airport Operations)

Number of Establishments	1,719
Average Profit Margin	3.8%
Revenue per Employee	$116,400
Average Number of Employees	36
Average Wages per Employee	$30,959

Source: IBISWorld, February 2012

Products and Services Segmentation

Fixed base operations	59.3%
Ground handling services	30.4%
Other airport services	5.1%
Administration and operational services	3.3%
Airport traffic control operations	1.9%

Source: IBISWorld, February 2012

Major Market Segmentation

Airlines	62%
Retail outlets	17%
Car parks	12%
Other	9%

Source: IBISWorld, February 2012

Industry Costs

Profit	3.8%
Wages	27.3%
Purchases	14.0%
Depreciation	12.9%
Rent & Utilities	16.0%
Other	26.0%

Source: IBISWorld, February 2012

- "Variable cost for pumping fuel is about 40 cents per gallon. Thinking of the eventual exit strategy, the FBO should be pumping 80,000 gallons a month to attract a global buyer. Such an FBO would have about 30 employees and generate from $8 million to $15 million in annual sales, depending on location."
- "Strictly on EBITDA; a fixed base operator must sell 80,000 gallons of fuel each month to be profitable; a company of this minimum level would have at least 30 employees."
- "Standard & Poor's Benchmark Data are a good starting place. Premiums placed on location, e.g., Van Nuys, CA or major cities."
- "High private-jet-traffic airports. Jet fuel sales a plus. General aviation service only and/or airports with less than 5,000-foot runways sell at a discount."

Expenses as a Percentage of Annual Sales

Cost of goods	35% to 45%
Payroll/labor Costs	25% to 35%
Occupancy	10% to 20%
Profit (estimated pretax)	05 to 15%

Industry Trend

- "Major research firms are showing a delivery of over 10,000 private jets in the next 10 years, implying a need for more airport service providers, including FBOs. City governments are now taking ownership of some FBOs, which is a threat to entrepreneurship. The inability of FBO owners to get more than a 25-year lease from a city is also a threat to profitability."
- "Private jet aviation is the main driver of many of these airport businesses; how the business jet industry goes is how these services will go."
- "More consolidation, particularly among first-tier airports; FBOs typically 'bundled' and sold as a package exceeding $20 million, which generates more interest from private equity groups."

Seller Financing

- 3 to 5 years

Questions

- "Why sell now? Any trouble with city/local governments? Status of existing leases/agreements? Trouble with EPA? Labor issues?"
- "City leasing contracts; tenant contracts; EPA investigations; fuel farm inspection status; labor agreements."
- "Is the site EPA-compliant? How is the relationship with the airport manager? The local community? Is there any moratorium against expanding the fuel farm?"
- "What percentage of revenue from jet fuel, hangar rental? Do you own your own fuel farm? How long is left on your lease?"

Alarm Companies (See also Security Services/Systems & Guard Services)

SIC 7382-02	NAICS 561621	Number of Businesses/Units 10,000

Rules of Thumb

➢ See Pricing Tips

Pricing Tips

- "It's all about the recurring monthly revenue, the RMR. You know that alarm companies sell subscriber contracts for a multiple of the RMR. But why is some company getting 12 times RMR, and others are even commanding 45 times RMR or more? And why are some companies surprised that no one is interested in buying the subscriber accounts?

  "You should take some comfort knowing that you are in a business that deals with subscriber contracts as negotiable instruments. The contracts have intrinsic value, are assignable, tradable, and have real value. That $30 a month subscriber account can be worth $360 to $1,500. If you have 1,000 or 5,000 or more of those subscriber contracts you have a valuable business to protect."
- "A new Barnes Associates study shows that alarm companies that specialize in vertical markets within residential security are likely to have a greater return on investment when it comes time to sell. 'We analyzed more than 120 transactions over the past 10 years (those involving $100,000 to $10 million of RMR) and looked for correlations across a number of variables [including size, metrics and operational focus],' Michael Barnes told Security Systems News.

"Barnes defined focus as companies with a concentration in vertical markets, geography, and product/service offerings. Noting the term 'vertical markets' is generally reserved for commercial concerns, Barnes said he 'included segments of the residential market as vertical markets—for example if a company focused only on entry-level residential using low/no-cost systems, we considered that a vertical market, as we did someone that did only ultra-high-end residential to the very wealthy.'"

Source: "The Legal Side: Valuing your alarm business" by Ken Kirschenbaum, ESQ., SecurityInfoWatch.com, Updated March 3, 2010

Benchmark Data

Statistics (Security Alarm Services)

Number of Establishments	10,188
Revenue per Employee	$140,500
Average Number of Employees	30.8
Average Wages per Employee	$43,241

Source: IBISWorld, February 2012

Products and Services Segmentation

Security alarms and monitoring services	58.4%
Fire-alarm systems	28.3%
Locksmith services	13.3%

Source: IBISWorld, February 2012

Industry Costs

Profit	5.0%
Wages	30.9%
Purchases	39.0%
Depreciation	3.0%
Rent & Utilities	5.5%
Other	16.6%

Source: IBISWorld, February 2012

Market Share

Tyco International Ltd. 25.7%

Source: IBISWorld, February 2012

Enterprises by Employment Size

Number of Employees	Enterprises	Share
0 to 4	5,538	61.6%
5 to 9	1,694	18.9%
10 to 19	975	10.9%

Source: IBISWorld, February 2012

	Franchise
All Tune and Lube (See also Auto Lube, Grease Monkey, Jiffy Lube)	
Approx. Total Investment	$150,000
Estimated Annual Sales/Unit	Not Available
SIC 7549-03 NAICS 81191	Number of Businesses/Units 358

Rules of Thumb

➢ 20 to 25 percent of annual sales

Resources

Websites

- www.alltuneandlube.com

Allegra Printing (See also Printing)	Franchise	
Approx. Total Investment		$172,348 to $520,814
Estimated Annual Sales/Unit		Not Available
	NAICS 323114	Number of Businesses/Units 300

Rules of Thumb

> 60% to 65% of annual sales plus inventory

Resources

Websites

- www.allegranetwork.com

AlphaGraphics	Franchise	
Approx. Total Investment		$242,000 to $412,000
Estimated Annual Sales/Unit		$1,125,700SIC 7336-02 NAICS 541430
		Number of Businesses/Units 272

Rules of Thumb

> 60 to 65 percent of annual sales plus inventory

Aluminum Smelting Machinery		
	NAICS 331316	

Rules of Thumb

> 70 percent of annual sales plus inventory

> 5 times EBITDA

Pricing Tips

- "If balance sheet is sound, business is worth an average between twice net assets and 5 times EBITDA."

Expert Comments

"Highly specialized market. Vendor must establish himself on short list of major EPCMs through references. Spare parts market captive and profitable."

Benchmark Data

- "$250,000 per employee"

Expenses as a Percentage of Annual Sales

Cost of goods	70%
Payroll/labor Costs	25%
Occupancy	05%
Profit (estimated pretax)	10%

Industry Trend

- "The aluminum market is growing fast. New smelters are being built. Older are being extended or revamped. Market for machinery will be excellent for next 5 years at least."

Questions

- "Indebtedness? Officers' loan or debt? Backlog and list of references."

Ambulance Services

SIC 4119-02	NAICS 62191	Number of Businesses/Units 4,935

Rules of Thumb

➤ 40 percent of annual revenues plus inventory

➤ 2 to 4.0 times SDE includes inventory

➤ 2 to 5 EBITDA

Pricing Tips

- "Approximately 12 different factors affect the Multiple & Pricing/Selling range, from one company to another; unless broker understands the industry and how these factors affect value, it is very challenging to properly price and sell these companies."
- "Large pricing range due to a larger number of key variables that affect valuation. Transition period with seller is critical (should be at least 6 months to a year, even on smaller businesses)."
- "Payer mix & breakdowns very important; breakdowns on advanced life support (ALS) vs. basic life support (BLS) transports; reimbursements; rural vs. urban mix; wheelchair transports diminish profitability."

Expert Comments

"CHALLENGES are understanding ambulance billing, cash flow, collections, logistics management; Medicare comprises high percent of sales"

"Degree of risk depends on buyer's familiarity of Medicare & other insurance payers & billing. Medicare makes up over 50% of sales; Medicaid brokerage impacts valuation & marketability, etc.

"Growing number of transports, but tougher for the smaller provider (all under $5–$7 million in sales) to compete effectively against the mid-sized players; trend is to sell, merge or acquire; knowledge of ambulance billing is very important."

"Every market is different; some companies truly dominate 70%–90% of their markets; profit margins are affected by many factors: income can vary significantly; high risk for buyers unfamiliar with healthcare billing."

Benchmark Data

Statistics (Ambulance Services)

Number of Establishments	4,935
Revenue per Employee	$90,900
Average Number of Employees	32
Average Wages per Employee	$38,249

Source: IBISWorld, March 2012

Products and Services Segmentation

Emergency ground transportation	41.5%
Non-emergency ground transportation	28.4%
Emergency air transportation	19.3%
Other services	7.7%
Non-emergency air transportation	3.1%

Source: IBISWorld, March 2012

Major Market Segmentation

Private insurance providers	40%
Medicare	35%
Fees or subsidies	10%
Medicaid	10%
Out-of-pocket payments	5%

Source: IBISWorld, March 2012

Industry Costs

Profit	8.1%
Wages	42.5%
Purchases	20.4%
Depreciation	4.3%
Marketing	0.9%
Rent & Utilities	3.6%
Other	20.2%

Source: IBISWorld, March 2012

Market Share

Emergency Medical Services Corporation	11.3%
Air Methods	5.2%

Source: IBISWorld, March 2012

Establishments by Employment Size

No. of Employees	No. of Establishments	Share of total
1 to 4	731	15.3%
5 to 9	366	7.7%
10 to 19	718	15.1%
20 to 99	1,349	28.3%
100 to 499	565	11.9%
More than 500	1,037	21.7%

Source: IBISWorld, March 2012

- "UHU rating .35 or higher"
- "Payroll costs should be under 58%, fully loaded."
- "Can be very lucrative, with EBITDA in the 22%–27% range if properly run & managed."
- "4–6 transports per day, per ambulance; logistics are critical and impact profitability, as does scheduling."

Expenses as a Percentage of Annual Sales

Cost of goods	08%
Payroll/labor Costs	58%
Occupancy	01%
Profit (estimated pretax)	05% to 22%

Industry Trend

- "Higher CAPEX cost due to need to implement technology for both logistics management and patient record management"
- "More challenging to maintain profits & margins"
- "Brokerage of Medicaid increasing"
- "Solid upward growth in transports, however more pressure on smaller operators to become larger or they will be forced out of business."
- "Ambulance providers face unique financial challenges due to inadequate Medicare payments and barriers to receiving federal homeland security funds."

Source: American Ambulance Association

- "Positive; aging population"
- "Growth in transports, increased operating costs and equipment costs"

Questions:

- "LOTS; There are a lot of fraudulent practices and brokers need to understand the industry and billing guidelines OR they should avoid taking a listing/representing the owner; need to know the quantity of dialysis patients; businesses with a high percentage of dialysis runs get discounted in valuation/pricing"
- "Who does billing: in-house or sub out to 3rd party? What software is used? What systems do you have in place & utilize for billing and for logistics? Do you prescreen your transports/patients?"
- "Medicare & Medicaid audits & status of these? Billing processes & procedures; qualifying transports."

Resources

Associations

- American Ambulance Association—primarily for members : www.the-aaa.org

	Franchise
American Poolplayers Association (APA) (See also Billiards)	
Approx. Total Investment	$17,080 to $20,150
Estimated Annual Sales/Unit	Not Available
SIC 7999-12 NAICS 713990	Number of Businesses/Units 300

Rules of Thumb

➢ 1.4 times annual sales

➢ $1,000 to $1,800 per team in sales: selling price—$2,000 to $2,500 per team

Pricing Tips

- "These franchises are purchased by areas. Pricing is normally based on the number of teams in the area. The general rule of thumb is $2000 per team in a well-managed area."

Benchmark Data

Expenses as a Percentage of Annual Sales

Cost of goods	n/a
Payroll/labor Costs	n/a
Occupancy	n/a
Profit (estimated pretax)	35%

Industry Trend

- "Increase in popularity and participation in recreational billiards"

Resources

Websites

- www.poolplayers.com

Amusement Routes (See Routes & Vending Routes)	
NAICS 713990	

	Franchise
Andy OnCall	
Approx. Total Investment	$56,150 to $79,050
Estimated Annual Sales/Unit: Not Available	
NAICS 236118	Number of Businesses/Units 50

Rules of Thumb

➢ 25 percent of annual sales

➢ Andy OnCall connects unemployed craftsmen with homeowners who need home repairs.

Benchmark Data

Statistics (Handyman Service Franchises)

Number of Establishments	2,051
Average Profit Margin	10.1%
Revenue per Employee	$132,400
Average Number of Employees	9.3
Average Wages per Employee	$25,155

Source: IBISWorld, August 2012

Products and Services Segmentation

Maintenance services	63.1%
Plumbing	12.4%
Other	11.7%
Painting	8.5%
Flooring	63.1%

Source: IBISWorld, August 2012

Major Market Segmentation

Households	69%
Property owners and managers	18%
Commercial clients	10%
Other	3%

Source: IBISWorld, August 2012

Industry Costs

Profit	10.1%
Wages	18.4%
Purchases	50.2%
Depreciation	4.8%
Marketing	3.2%
Rent & Utilities	2.0%
Other	11.3%

Source: IBISWorld, August 2012

Resources

Websites

- www.andyoncall.com/andy-on-call-franchises.html

Antique Malls

		Number of Business/Units 10,000

Rules of Thumb

➢ 2 to 4 times EBITDA with a minimum of $100,000 EBITDA not including real estate

Resources

Associations

- National Association of Antique Malls (NAAM): www.antiqueandcollectible.com

Antique Shops/Dealers

SIC 5932-02	NAICS 453310	Number of Businesses/Units 32,000

Rules of Thumb

➢ 20 percent of annual sales plus inventory

Resources

Websites

- www.artantiquedealersleague.com

Apartment Locators

SIC 6531-11	NAICS 531110	Number of Businesses/Units 441,976

Rules of Thumb

➢ 80 percent of annual revenues

Pricing Tips

- "This is generally a secondary revenue source to real estate sales."
- Note: A real estate license is required for the operation of this business.

Benchmark Data

Statistics (Apartment Rental)

Number of Establishments	441,976
Average Profit Margin	33.3%
Revenue per Employee	$195,300
Average Number of Employees	1.5
Average Wages per Employee	$15,322

Source: IBISWorld, September 2012

Products and Services Segmentation

Rental of one-unit structures	31.3%
Rental of two- to four-unit structures	21.0%
Rental of five- to nine-unit structures	13.4%
Rental of 10- to 19-unit structures	12.0%
Rental of 20- to 49-unit structures	9.0%
Rental of 50- or more unit structures	9.0%

Source: IBISWorld, September 2012

Major Market Segmentation

One-person households	37.5%
Two-person households	27.1%
Three-person households	15.3%
Four-person households	11.3%
Five-person households	5.3%
More than five-person households	3.5%

Source: IBISWorld, September 2012

Industry Costs

Profit	33.3%
Wages	7.9%
Purchases	8.0%
Depreciation	11.0%
Marketing	1.0%
Rent & Utilities	2.8%
Other	36.0%

Source: IBISWorld, September 2012

Market Share

Equity Residential	1.9%
Apartment Investment and Management Companies	0.9%

Source: IBISWorld, September 2012

- "Fees are most often paid by the apartment owner, usually about 10% to 15% or one month's rent."

Questions

- "How long have they been in business? How do they locate apartments? Do they have an online database? How many apartment communities do they work with?"

Source: www.austinapartmentfinder.com,

Appliance Repair

SIC 7629	NAICS 811412	Number of Businesses/Units 47,500

Rules of Thumb

➢ 30 to 35 percent of annual sales plus inventory

➢ 1 to 1.5 times SDE, plus fixtures, equipment and inventory

Benchmark Data

Statistics (Appliance Repair)

Number of Establishments	52,705
Average Profit Margin	6.3%
Revenue per Employee	$50,700
Average Number of Employees	1
Average Wages per Employee	$17,425

Source: IBISWorld, December 2011

Products and Services Segmentation

Appliance repair services	61%
Home and garden equipment repair services	21%
Other personal household goods repair services	11%
Electronic and precision equipment repair services	06%
Sale of spare parts	01%

Source: IBISWorld, December 2011

Industry Costs

Profit	6.3%
Rent	5.5%
Utilities	2.5%
Depreciation	3.8%
Other	15.8%
Wages	33.5%
Purchases	32.6%

Source: IBISWorld, December 2011

Market Share

Sears Holdings Corporation	35.2%
Best Buy Co., Inc.	22.6%

Source: IBISWorld, December 2011

Appliance Stores (See also Furniture/Appliance Stores)

SIC 5064	NAICS 443111	Number of Businesses/Units 17,000

Rules of Thumb

➢ 2 times monthly sales plus inventory

Benchmark Data

- "Markup is about 27 percent with some discounters working on a 25 percent markup."

Resources

Trade Publications
- Appliance Service News: www.asnews.com

Associations
- National Appliance Parts Suppliers Association: www.napsaweb.org
- North American Retail Dealers Association: www.narda.com
- Association of Home Appliance Manufacturers: www.aham.org

Appraisal/Valuation Services	
SIC 7389	NAICS 541990, 531320

Pricing Tips

- "For a firm with less than 10 professionals—1.25 to 1.5 times EBITDA. This would include all FF&E and related software and exclude Accounts Receivable and Accounts Payable. Most of the deals are where there is a merger of firms or a buyout by a CPA firm wanting to get into the appraisal business. They usually want the seller to manage the operation for several years."

Benchmark Data

Statistics (Real Estate Appraisal)

Number of Establishments	67,593
Average Profit Margin	12.9%
Revenue per Employee	$75,700
Average Number of Employees	1.3
Average Wages per Employee	$27,833

Source: IBISWorld, August 2012

Products and Services Segmentation

Commercial real estate appraisal	50.2%
Residential real estate appraisal	26.5%
Real estate consulting	10.9%
Appraisal management	6.6%
Real estate brokerage and other services	5.8%

Source: IBISWorld, August 2012

Major Market Segmentation

Financial institutions and brokers	58%
Law offices	15%
Private owners	13%
Government and other	8%
Accountants	6%

Source: IBISWorld, August 2012

Industry Costs

Profit	12.9%
Wages	37.9%
Purchases	18.1%
Depreciation	2.3%
Utilities	2.1%
Rent	5.8%
Other	20.9%

Source: IBISWorld, August 2012

Market Share

CB Richard Ellis Group Inc. 6.2%
Source: IBISWorld, August 2012

Statistics (Business Valuation Firms)

Number of Establishments... 13,419
Average Profit Margin 14%
Revenue per Employee $82,690
Average Number of Employees... 2.52
Average Wages per Employee $42,233
Source: IBISWorld, December 2011

Products and Services Segmentation

Comprehensive appraisals 55.2%
Preliminary value studies.. 23.4%
Limited partnership appraisals.. 17%
Other.. 4.4%
Source: IBISWorld, December 2011

Major Market Segmentation

Service sector 30.1%
Retail trade 25.7%
Manufacturing 19.8%
Other industries 12.7%
Finance, insurance and real estate... 6.1%
Wholesale trade... 5.6%
Source: IBISWorld, December 2011

Industry Costs

Profit 14.0%
Rent 2.0%
Utilities 1.5%
Depreciation... 2.0%
Other... 21.3%
Wages... 53.7%
Purchases... 5.5%
Source: IBISWorld, December 2011

Resources

Associations

- American Society of Appraisers: www.appraisers.org
- Institute of Business Appraisers (IBA): instbusapp.org
- National Association of Certified Valuation Analysts (NACVA): www.nacva.com

Arcade, Food & Entertainment Complexes		
SIC 71312	NAICS 713120	

Rules of Thumb

➢ 25 percent of annual sales includes inventory

➢ 3 times SDE includes inventory

➢ 3 to 3.5 EBITDA

Pricing Tips

- "Make sure the equipment is either owned and is in current, 'fashionable' condition, or make sure there is an attractive lease arrangement that enables simple trade-in for more current gaming. These games are only as valuable as the current trend. There are 'stability' games such as air hockey, certain pinball games and redemption games where you can win toy prizes straight from the machine. The store must have a mix of current trend equipment and the stability games. Stability games are the work horses but the trendy games are very expensive to stay on top of."

- "This industry is not for everyone! Although, if you are an experienced retailer and have a stomach for high rent-to-gross sales percentages, this could be a great opportunity for you to enter into a fun and rewarding industry! It is a simple business model and can be improved SIGNIFICANTLY by introducing customer promotions combining game tokens with redemption prize incentives and local food retailers."

Expert Comments

"Games must also be attractive/specific to area demographics. Interestingly, my clients that owned a chain of stores in and around New York City found that the Asian neighborhoods demand more high-tech, challenging games and they will correspondingly pay a higher price per use. This is not a business that a client should jump into ill-informed or insufficiently researched. Only buy tried and true locations. Don't build new locations unless on a massive scale like Dave & Busters. They are a one-stop entertainment supercenter including food, bowling and usually booze. The smaller locations in malls and plazas are way too risky given the fact that kids don't need to leave the home anymore to get the most current and challenging gaming. So, if there is a location that has withstood the transition to home-based gaming through the 80s, 90s and up to now, it is likely a winner. These arcade formats only now work in certain neighborhoods, need high volume given the price of commercial real estate, etc. Get a long lease."

"Location is KEY. This is a capital-intensive industry but a proven location is a very valuable semi-absentee opportunity. If you are buying existing units, you can use the assets in the purchase to back part of the financing."

Benchmark Data

Statistics (Arcade, Food & Entertainment Complexes)

Number of Establishments	2,674
Average Profit Margin	9.6%
Revenue per Employee	$47,500
Average Number of Employees	12
Average Wages per Employee	$11,915

Source: IBISWorld, November 2011

Products and Services Segmentation

Coin-operated games and rides	53.2%
Other rides, games and attractions	24.9%
Food and beverages	13.0%
Corporate and party event services	5.0%
Resale of merchandise	2.2%
Rental or lease of goods and equipment	1.7%

Source: IBISWorld, November 2011

Industry Costs

Profit	9.6%
Rent	8.0%
Utilities	3.0%
Depreciation	3.9%
Other	16.6%
Wages	26.9%
Purchases	32.0%

Source: IBISWorld, November 2011

Market Share

CEC Entertainment Inc.	52.2%
Dave & Buster's Holdings Inc.	35.0%

Source: IBISWorld, November 2011

- "Game costs range from $2,500 to $15,000 per new machine. You DO NOT have to buy new machinery! Sell older technology online and buy new circuitry for new games and put them in your existing game machines. It will save tremendous operating capital and the customer will not know the difference."

Expenses as a Percentage of Annual Sales

Cost of goods	05% to 10%
Payroll/labor Costs	15%
Occupancy	40% to 50%
Profit (estimated pretax)	15% to 20%

Industry Trend

- "This industry has seen a significant decline since the advent of in-home video gaming. HOWEVER, it is my estimation that the business has seen its bottom and consistent sales should continue indefinitely, given good gaming technology for your clients."

Questions

- "Asset values?"

Resources

Websites

- http://www.coastergrotto.com/theme-park-attendance.jsp

Architectural Practices

SIC 8712-02	NAICS 541310	Number of Businesses/Units 101,000

Rules of Thumb

➢ 40 percent of annual sales plus inventory

Pricing Tips

- "Goodwill is at a minimum due to the non-repetitiveness of the clients. It is also a personal service business. The stature, reputation and contacts of the principal(s) are generally not transferable, especially in a smaller firm."

Benchmark Data

Statistics (Architects)

Number of Establishments	103,304
Revenue per Employee	$148,900
Average Number of Employees	3
Average Wages per Employee	$82,161

Source: IBISWorld, April 2012

Products and Services Segmentation

Basic design services	61.5%
Construction phase services	14.5%
Expanded design services	11.5%
Operation, maintenance and other services	7.0%
Drafting services	5.5%

Source: IBISWorld, April 2012

Major Market Segmentation

Institutional organizations	35%
Commercial and industrial developers	25%
Residential developers and individuals	20%
Other	20%

Source: IBISWorld, April 2012

Enterprises by Employment Size

Number of Employees	Number of Enterprises	Share
0 to 4	17,930	64.7%
5 to 9	5,157	18.6%
10 to 19	2,662	9.6%

Source: IBISWorld, April 2012

	Franchise

Arctic Circle

Approx. Total Investment	$95,000 to $160,000
Estimated Annual Sales/Unit	$650,000
NAICS 722211	Number of Businesses/Units 73

Rules of Thumb

➢ 40 percent of annual sales plus inventory

Resources

Websites
- www.acburger.com

Art Galleries and Dealers	
SIC 5999-69	NAICS 453920	Number of Businesses/Units 22,500

Rules of Thumb

➢ 30 percent of annual revenues plus inventory

Pricing Tips

- In some galleries, much of the art work may be on consignment.
- "A surprising number of people search for answers to these and similar questions in attempts to quantify the art market. The art market, however, is not quantifiable, and the answers to these questions don't exist. To begin with, art is not a commodity that can be regulated. Anyone can call him or herself an artist, anyone can call anything that they create 'art,' and anyone can be an art dealer. Anyone can sell art wherever, whenever and under whatever circumstances they please, and price or sell whatever they call 'art' for whatever amounts of money they feel like selling it for, as long as that art is offered without fraud or misrepresentation."

Source: www.artbusiness.com

Benchmark Data

Statistics (Art Dealers)

Number of Establishments	23,015
Average Profit Margin	5.2%
Revenue per Employee	$236,700
Average Number of Employees	1.6
Average Wages per Employee	$29,391

Source: IBISWorld, June 2012

Products and Services Segmentation

Paintings	73.7%
Drawings	12.5%
Sculptures	7.8%
Prints	2.7%
Photography	2.3%
Other media	1%

Source: IBISWorld, June 2012

Industry Costs

Profit	5.2%
Wages	12.1%
Purchases	62.2%
Depreciation	1.6%
Marketing	4.0%
Rent & Utilities	5.1%
Other	9.8%

Source: IBISWorld, June 2012

Market Share

Sotheby's Holdings Inc.	3.85
Christie's International	1.6%

Source: IBISWorld, June 2012

Resources

Associations
- Art Dealers Association of America: www.artdealers.org

Art Supplies (See also Arts & Crafts and Hobby Stores)		
SIC 5999-65	NAICS 453998	Number of Businesses/Units 7,000

Rules of Thumb

➤ 30 percent of annual sales plus inventory

Pricing Tips
- Many hobby stores and related businesses may carry a line of art supplies. A store specializing in just art supplies requires an owner with the appropriate knowledge.

Benchmark Data
- For Benchmark Information see Retail Stores—Small Specialty

---

Arts & Crafts/Retail Stores (See also Hobby Shops)		
SIC 5085	NAICS 45113	

Rules of Thumb

➤ 35 percent of annual sales plus inventory

➤ 2 times SDE plus inventory

Pricing Tips
- "Inventory should be priced separately and should include any costs associated with shipping the inventory to the place of business. Also, any needed labor required to re-package product should be part of COGS and not part of labor. As with most other business valuations, look hard at attractors and detractors to the 36% rule of thumb."
- "You should be able to tell if a 'crafter' is operating the business as opposed to a 'business person,' by their financials."
- Note: The people who actually create the finished arts and crafts (craftspeople) are unique and their business might be difficult to sell because of the very nature of what they produce. Their skill is usually not transferable.

Expert Comments

"Relatively easy to get into the craft businesses but difficult to obtain and maintain profitability. Smaller independently owned stores tend to be operated by owners with a passion for the craft rather than a passion for business. As a result, turnover is common."

Benchmark Data

Statistics (Fabric, Craft & Sewing Supplies Stores)

Number of Establishments	18,566
Average Profit Margin	1.9%
Revenue per Employee	$72,900
Average Number of Employees	3.3
Average Wages per Employee	$9,831

Source: IBISWorld, June 2012

Products and Services Segmentation

Fabrics	40.0%
Sewing and craft supplies	33.0%
Other	12.0%
Seasonal decorations	8.0%
Fabric home décor	7.0%

Source: IBISWorld, June 2012

Industry Costs

Profit	1.9%
Rent & Utilities	3.0%
Depreciation	2.2%
Other	12.8%
Wages	13.8%
Purchases	64.3%

Source: IBISWorld, June 2012

Market Share

Jo-Ann Stores Inc.	26.0%
Michaels Stores Inc.	13.7%
Hobby Lobby Stores Inc.	9.6%
Hancock Fabrics Inc.	6.8%

Source: IBISWorld, June 2012

- "Rent at 10% of GAS (Gross Annual Sales). Sales per square foot at $150–$175. Sales per employee at $75,000–$125,000. Advertising at 3%–4% of GAS."

Expenses as a Percentage of Annual Sales

Cost of goods	50%
Payroll/labor Costs	15%
Occupancy	15%
Profit (estimated pretax)	20%

Questions

- 1. "Their background in business
  2. The profitability of the target business
  3. Historical GAS of the target business
  4. Local and historical competition
  5. Excitement! How are they creating it?"

Resources

Websites
- www.craftandhobby.org

Trade Publications
- The Crafts Report—excellent publication: www.craftsreport.com

Assisted Living Facilities (See also Nursing Homes)		
SIC 8361-05	NAICS 623311	Number of Businesses/Units 39,000

Rules of Thumb

➤ 75 percent of annual sales

➤ $30,000–$60,000 per bed. Pricing above this range typically raises a red flag for individual buyers.

➤ This business is based on net operating income divided by a capitalization rate of 10 to 14 percent.

Pricing Tips

- "Real-estate-intensive business. SBA pays extra attention to this industry to ensure that the buyers are not acting as 'passive real-estate investors,' but rather as small-business owners."

- "Capitalization of income for going concern value including real estate"

- "Occupancy in market area. Going cap rates at that specific time. Whether Medicaid or private pay?"

Benchmark Data

Statistics (Retirement Communities)

Number of Establishments	21,109
Revenue per Employee	$60,200
Average Number of Employees	42
Average Wages per Employee	$23,950

Source: IBISWorld, May 2012

Products and Services Segmentation

Assisted living facilities	41%
Independent living facilities	37%
Continuing care retirement communities	22%

Source: IBISWorld, May 2012

Major Market Segmentation

Females with incomes greater than $20,000	55%
Females with incomes less than $20,000	20%
Males with incomes greater than $20,000	18%
Males with incomes less than $20,000	7%

Source: IBISWorld, May 2012

Industry Costs

Profit	9.8%
Wages	39.3%
Purchases	15.0%
Depreciation	9.0%
Marketing	5.0%
Rent & Utilities	13.5%
Other	8.4%

Source: IBISWorld, May 2012

- "The national average monthly base rate in an assisted living community rose 5.6% from $3,293 in 2010 to $3,477 or $41,724 annually in 2011."
  Source: www.metlife.com/mmi/research/2011
- "Assisted living communities provide housing for those who need help in day-to-day living, but who do not need the round-the-clock level of skilled nursing care found in nursing homes. Many communities, however, have nurses on staff and provide health care monitoring."
  Source: www.metlife.com/mmi/research/2011

Long-Term Care Spending by Payer

Medicaid	42%
Medicare	25%
Out of Pocket	22%
Private Insurance and Other Sources	11%

Source: www.leadingage.org/facts

- "The average assisted living center resident is an 85-year-old female who pays close to $3,000 a month—though many needing greater care pay closer to $4,000 or $5,000. While the assisted living industry is currently strong, experts said a major shift in demographics and the looming threat of federal regulation could transform the industry over the next two decades."
  Source: "Assisted Living Centers Are Costing the Elderly a Pretty Penny" www.foxbusiness.com
- "Total expenses excluding debt service should average 68 percent."
- "Operating expense ratio—65 to 70 percent"

Industry Trend

- "By 2026, the population of Americans ages 65 and older will double to 7.5 million."

  "Between 2007 and 2015, the number of Americans ages 85 and older is expected to increase by 40 percent.

- "By 2020, 12 million older Americans will need long-term health care."
  Source: HIAA, "A Guide to Long-Term Care Insurance,"

Seller Financing:

- "5 to 10 years"

Resources

Websites
- www.ncal.org

Trade Publications

- The Directory of Retirement Facilities, published by HCIA Inc., (800) 568-9429 : www.hcia.com

Associations

- Assisted Living Federation of America : www.alfa.org
- Leading Age : www.leadingage.org

	Franchise
Atlanta Bread Company	
Approx. Total Investment	$650,000–$1,000,000
Estimated Annual Sales/Unit	$1.1 million
SIC 5812-08	NAICS 722211	Number of Businesses/Units 170

Rules of Thumb

➤ 25 to 30 percent of annual sales plus inventory

Audio and Film Companies		
	NAICS 512120	

Rules of Thumb

➤ 4 to 6 times EBITDA

Pricing Tips

- "Ownership of the intellectual property is key to value. Companies that provide work-for-hire services are not as valuable as those that own the final production. Since this medium ages quickly, the economic life span of the films/ videos is critical."

Seller Financing

- "3 to 7 years"

Audio/Video Conferencing		
SIC 4822-06	NAICS 518210	

Rules of Thumb

➤ 3 to 4 times EBITDA

Expert Comments

"Cost of setting up public centers is substantial. Industry is upgrading services and equipment."

Industry Trend

- "New technology is outdating old. Tele-presence is the new upgrade name."

Questions

- "How long are the contracts? What services are being provided?"

Auto Body Repair

SIC 7532-01	NAICS 811121	Number of Businesses/Units 119,399

Rules of Thumb

➤ 2 to 4 times EBITDA

➤ 28 to 35 percent of annual sales plus inventory

➤ 1.7 to 2.3 times SDE plus inventory

Pricing Tips

- "Because of the difficulty of obtaining licensing in many urban areas including the real estate is highly desirable. A knowledgeable buyer would probably not buy a shop unless it is large—$1,500,000 plus and includes real estate."
- "The price can be 2 to 3 times EBITDA based on the age of the equipment and how long the owner has been in the business."
- "Poor books & records less than $1 million sales—2X EBITDA. Good books $3–4 million with Direct Insurance Referrals—3X–4 X EBITDA with earnout"
- "Shops doing less than $1.5 million tend to have no more than $125,000 profit. Bigger shops make more money."
- "Body shops doing less than $500,000 in sales are only worth asset value."
- "Number of DRPs and length of time active a critical item."
- "Pricing usually 2.5 x owner benefit [SDE] plus fair market value of FF&E."
- "Shops doing less than $100,000 monthly sales are worth $125,000 or less, regardless of any other rule of thumb. Shops doing less than $40,000 in monthly sales are worth $75,000 or less."
- "Market value of FF&E is critical to accurate price development. Also—number of years in business, diversity of supplier base; with auto body shops the number & quality of DRP contracts, stability of labor pool, ease of replacing skilled employees & diversity/ stability of supplier base."

Expert Comments

"Insurance referrals can go away very easily with ownership changes."

"It is difficult for people in the industry to succeed, which means that new people have twice as difficult a time."

"The insurance companies control who gets the customers and what price the vendor can charge."

"Volume continues for a good quality shop even in a flat to declining economy."

"Body shops should only be purchased by experienced buyers in this industry. Shops doing less than $100,000 a month in sales all make around the same profit, which is $60,000 to $100,000 for a working owner. Working owner means one who physically works on cars some of the time. Only shops with a multiple of insurance contracts are easy to market. Shops without insurance contracts are very difficult to sell."

Benchmark Data

Statistics (Car Body Shops)

Number of Establishments	119,399
Average Profit Margin	4.5%
Revenue per Employee	$112,000
Average Number of Employees	3
Average Wages per Employee	$40,680

Source: IBISWorld, May 2012

Products and Services Segmentation

Bodywork	51%
Paintwork	25%
Glass replacement and repair	14%
Upholstery and interior repair	03%
Van conversions	03%
Merchandise sales	02%
Other services	02%

Source: IBISWorld, May 2012

Major Market Segmentation

Private households	45%
Commercial and business clients	25%
Insurance companies	18%
Car dealers	09%
Other	03%

Source: IBISWorld, May 2012

Industry Costs

Profit	4.5%
Wages	35.4%
Purchases	50.0%
Depreciation	1.6%
Marketing	1.5%
Rent & Utilities	5.1%
Other	1.9%

Source: IBISWorld, May 2012

Number of operational bays at a facility

5 or under	7.7%
5–10	22.1%
11–16	27.8%
17–22	18.3%
23–29	12.5%
30 or more	11.5%

- "Ownership Status: 86% Independent
  14% Franchise/Network/Consolidator, Dealership
- "Overall average repair order in 2011—$2,165
- "Percentage of Ticket: Paint and Materials 12%, Labor 47%,
  Parts 41%
- Estimated Gross Annual Sales for 2011 (Single facility)
  $1M–$2M—according to 34% of respondents: 22% reported $2M–$4M; and
  15% reported $750K–$1M."

  Source: "How's Your Business? 2011, Collision," www.AutoInc.org December 2011

- "The successful shop generates $150K per bay."

- "Rent can't be over 10% of gross income."
- "Shops doing over $100,000 per month in sales have a wide variation in profit, depending on the quality of the general manager and his ability to keep costs under control."
- "Annual gross volume of approximately $150,000 per year per employee, including hands-on owner."

Expenses as a Percentage of Annual Sales

Cost of goods	35% to 40%%
Payroll/labor Costs	20%
Occupancy	05% to 10%
Profit (estimated pretax)	15% to 20%

Industry Trend
- "More and more small shops will close and a greater percentage of the business will go to the insurance shops."
- "Upward for established, quality-oriented operations with DRP relationships with clients, mainly insurance companies."

Seller Financing
- "Sellers carry for three to five years with SBA requiring the seller not to receive payments for the first two years."

Questions
- "Age and condition of equipment. A downdraft spray booth is desirable and, with maintenance, can last 15 or 20 years. DRP relationships? Does the owner work in the shop? Any relationships that are important to the revenues?"
- "How many insurance contracts do they have and what percentage of the gross income are they."
- "Do you supply loan cars? If so, do you get rebates from rental companies for the loaners? When will a job be booked as a sale? Do you have steady referrals from dealerships? When are initial assessments made? Is any charge made for them? After the initial estimate is made, how are contacts made with the insurance company?"
- "What is your real sales volume? How many DRP contracts do you have? Which insurance companies are your DRP contracts with? What is the labor rate paid by the insurance companies? How many employees do you have? Are your employees paid a salary or a percentage of the production they produce? How many frame machines do you have? is your spray booth heated?"
- "Show me your profit & loss statements, tax returns, environmental compliance & OSHA documents."
- "If real estate is part of the deal, are the painting/baking facilities included as part of the real estate or part of the FF&E?"

Resources

Trade Publications
- Body Shop Business is an excellent publication and Web site; it also offers back issues. www.bodyshopbusiness.com

- Collision Repair Industry Insight is also an excellent publication and Web site. It's interesting that body shops with two good publications also have informative Web sites. : www.collision-insight.com
- AutoInc.org — great, great site : autoinc.org

Associations

- Automotive Service Association, (ASA) - Great site with lots of information : www.asashop.org

---

Auto Brake Services (See also Auto Repair)

SIC 7539-14	NAICS 811118	Number of Businesses/Units 31,500

Rules of Thumb

> 30 percent of annual sales plus inventory4 times monthly sales plus inventory

---

Auto Dealers—New Cars

SIC 5511-02	NAICS 441110	Number of Businesses/Units 17,000

Rules of Thumb

> 0 to 10 percent of annual sales plus inventory

> 0 to 6 times SDE plus inventory

> 0 to 5 times EBIT

> 0 to 4 times EBITDA

> Depending on the franchise, makes three to six times EBITDA plus real estate and hard assets

> Blue Sky—two to four times EBIT Earnings

> Total transaction value in the industry currently ranges from two to four times pretax earnings

> Blue Sky—two to three times net profit or new unit sales (most recent year) times average front-end gross profit per unit

> Hard assets at cost—new parts, FF&E– Book + 50 percent depreciation,

> Blue Sky—3 times recast earnings

> The goodwill component of the sale price of an auto dealership (franchised only) normally falls within the range of two to six percent of gross revenues. Where added to the assets or book value of the business, this is a reliable method of determining price.

> Goodwill = 1 to 3 times pretax earnings (recast)

> Parts = current returnable parts

> FF&E = book value + one-half depreciation

> New Vehicles = net dealer cost

> Used Cars = as agreed

Pricing Tips

- "Net pretax profit posted strong gains, with the typical store generating $785,855 in 2011."In 2011, total dealership net profit before tax as a percent of sales was 2.3 percent, up from 2.1 percent in 2010."

  Source: NADA Industry Analysis Division, 2012

- "Service and Parts performance are key to successful operations. Profits from those departments should cover most expenses."
- "FFE should be at book value plus 50% depreciation."
- "Adjust rent to fair market"
- "At least 5% to 10% profit, EBIT and location are still the key."
- "Earnings multiple, new car PV multiple, new unit sales multiple"
- "Real estate is critical for any purchase."
- "The two most important characteristics are brands sold and location within a market. Competing outlets affect value. Market analysis, including measuring consumer demand in the area, is critical. Facility age is also a factor."
- "The brand is the key factor when buying or selling a dealership; Toyota and Honda are about the most difficult to buy and make the highest profits."
- "New auto dealerships usually have 4 profit centers, parts, used cars, F&I, and service. New car sales typically have very little margin. Ask the dealer about their absorption ratio (an industry term that indicates how much of their back-end is absorbing their overhead). Any new buyer would have to be approved by the manufacturer (Ford, GM, Toyota, etc.) Key people: used car manager, parts manager, service manager."
- "Depends on franchise and area of the country. Generally requires 400 per vehicle and up."
- "The health of the brand is vital."
- "Blue sky is a key factor in pricing. Real estate is very important, or a long-term lease with options for renewal is a must."
- "Watch for phantom profits in both car sales and warranty sales. Some dealers miss proper submission of warranty and rebate claims. Profits can be overstated as a result."
- "The current value is two to four times net profit of the most recent year. However, the new car franchises that are bringing up to five times net profit are Honda, Toyota and Mercedes Benz."
- "The two most important characteristics are brands sold, and location within a market. Competing outlets also affect value. Market analysis, including measuring consumer demand in the area, is critical. Facility age is also a factor."
- "Adjusted book value + blue sky is calculated as a multiple of adjusted pretax earnings. These multiples vary with the popularity of franchise, consolidated acquisition trends, vehicle market location, historical performance, etc."
- "FF&E—Priced at book price + one-half accumulated depreciation. Parts inventory = as inventoried—current returnable parts. Used cars—take or leave. New Vehicles—dealer net less holdback."
- "Other pricing methods include: (1) application of industry averages for gross profit as percentage of sales to the total revenues of the dealership being evaluated; (2) assessing financial data and applying appropriate multiples to recast net profit; (3) projection of potential based on industry average penetration statistics times appropriate multiples."
- "The goodwill of an auto dealership can generally be valued at one year's

pretax profit plus the dealer's salary and benefits, plus any adjustments from normalizing the financial statement against standard industry operating data."

Expert Comments

"New-car profits are weak. In fact, the used cars they generate (trades) are the lifeblood of a new-car dealership."

"Current economy shows how this industry is changing and more difficult to make a profit."

"Further consolidations or brand eliminations by OEMs will have significant impact on dealers. Brand risk is high."

"Difficult to enter, and profits have been declining over the past 3 years; many dealers are in the red."

Benchmark Data

Statistics (New Car Dealers)

Number of Establishments	17,024
Average Profit Margin	2.3%
Revenue per Employee	$663,000
Average Number of Employees	48
Average Wages per Employee	$50,574

Source: IBISWorld, June 2012

Products and Services Segmentation

New vehicles	52.8%
Used vehicles	33.1%
Parts and services	14.1%

Source: IBISWorld, June 2012

Industry Costs

Profit	2.3%
Wages	8.1%
Purchases	84.2%
Depreciation	0.3%
Marketing	1.7%
Rent & Utilities	2.4%
Other	1.0%

Source: IBISWorld, June 2012

Number of Enterprises by Number of Employees

Employees	Total
1 to 4	16.1%
5 to 9	7.1%
10 to 19	13.9%

Source: IBISWorld, June 2012

- "Salespeople should average at least 10 units each per month."
- "Used cars must be at least twice the sales of new cars to be profitable."
- "The number of new car dealerships for 2012 was 17,540 compared to 17,700 for 2011."

Source: 2012 National Auto Dealers Association (NADA) Data

Profile of dealerships' service and parts operations, 2012

Total service and parts sales	$4,593,905
Total gross profit as percent of service and parts sales	46.09%
Total net profit as percent of service and parts sales	7.07%
Total number of repair orders written	14,140
Total service and parts sales per customer repair order	$241
Total service and parts sales per warranty repair order	$250
Number of technicians (including body)	15
Number of service bays (excluding body)	19
Total parts inventory	$294,214
Average customer mechanical labor rate	$95

Source: NADA Industry Analysis Division, 2012

- "A sales manager should be generating $45,000 or more per month in gross profit."
- "% net profit to gross profit"
- "Some on the list sell just 35 vehicles a year, he said. Before the recessionary collapse last year, dealerships were averaging more than 650 new-vehicle sales a year, according to the dealers' main trade group, the National Automobile Dealers Association.
- "Sageworks, which collects and analyzes data from accounting firms show that used-car dealerships have a much higher profit margin than new-car dealerships: 3.19% to 5.67% the past four years, vs. 0.41% to 0.66% for new-car dealerships in the same period."
- "The key benchmark is new car sales per population in the primary market area."
- "Profit is around 2.75 to 3.25 percent of sales. Payroll should not exceed 41 percent of gross profit."
- "Each sales manager should be creating $55,000 to $70,000 per month in gross profit on his or her sales efforts. Everything else being at normal levels, the store will make a good profit, whether a large or small store. This is a very good benchmark."
- "Cost of Goods + Payroll/Labor Costs—88 percent"
- "Occupancy Cost—Total rent factor should not exceed 1 percent of gross sales."
- "Occupancy Cost—$300 to $400 per new car sold per year."
- "Profit (estimated)—3 percent of sales"
- "Number of new units sold, and number of units in operation, are important metrics."

Average Dealership Profile— 2011

Total Dealership Sales	$34,744,897
Total Dealership Gross	$4,992,196
Total Dealership Expense	$4,206,341
Net Profit before Taxes	$785,855
Average Net worth	$2,807,638
Net profit as % of net worth	28.0%

Source: 2012 National Auto Dealers Association (NADA) Data

Major expenses for the average dealership in 2011

Payroll	$2,610,000
Advertising	$363,168
Rent and equivalent	$403,990

Source: 2012 National Auto Dealers Association (NADA) Data

Share of total dealership sales dollars in 2011

New Vehicle 54.4%
Used Vehicle 32.4%
Service and Parts 13.2%

Source: 2012 National Auto Dealers Association (NADA) Data

Expenses as a Percentage of Annual Sales

Cost of goods .... 75% to 80%
Payroll/labor Costs .... 08% to 10% of gross profit
Occupancy .... 10% of gross profit
Profit (estimated pretax) .... 01.5% to 03%

Industry Trend

- "New-car sales should increase during 2012 slightly. Dealers should focus on parts and service sales and customer retention. Dealers must control advertising costs to be profitable."
- "The better run dealerships will survive and grow."
- "Some growth"
- "Better sales over the next 3 years as the economy improves."

Seller Financing:

- "3 years—very small percentage of selling price is carried."
- "Seller financing occurs in less than 30 percent of our transactions and does not normally extend beyond a five-year term."
- "5 years—only goodwill is seller-financed."

Questions:

- "How many insurance contracts do they have and what percentage of the gross income are they?"
- "What is your parts obsolescence percentage? CSI Scores?"
- "Staff that will stay on? Building lease if not owned. Franchise ratings and CSI ratings."
- "New car planning volume" s
- "Employee retention figures. Years at this location, age of equipment."
- "Are you ready to sell for market value?"
- "Is financing in place for new and used sales? Do you have a floor plan? Does the factory have any future plans for your facility—new or larger?"
- "Employee retention is key at this time with the downturn in the economy and sales."
- "Manufacturers' planning and future products. Market penetration figures and where do you stand with the manufacturer. Total registrations for your area."
- "Age of key personnel? What is the absorption ratio? Can I see your claims history? Who finances the new and used inventory? If this is a multiple-franchise operation under one roof, discover if the manufacturers are pushing for the dealership to split the franchise out into separate facilities."
- "Sales trends; consumer satisfaction survey results; recent market studies commissioned by manufacturer; facility standards adopted by manufacturer"
- "How many family members on the payroll? What dollar amount of personal items is being deducted from the financial statement?"

Resources

Websites
- www.wardsauto.com

Trade Publications
- AutomotiveNews : www.autonews.com

Associations
- National Automobile Dealers Association: www.nada.org
- American International Automobile Dealers: www.aiada.org

Auto Dealers—Used Cars		
SIC 5511-03	NAICS 441120	Number of Businesses/Units 147,231

Rules of Thumb

➢ Wholesale book value of cars; no goodwill; add parts, fixtures & equipment

Benchmark Data

Statistics (Used Car Dealers)

Number of Establishments	147,231
Average Profit Margin	4.6%
Revenue per Employee	$306,900
Average Number of Employees	2
Average Wages per Employee	$22,110

Source: IBISWorld, May 2012

Products and Services Segmentation

Used vehicles	37.2%
Parts and services	29.5%
Financing and insurance	27.6%
Other	5.7%

Source: IBISWorld, May 2012

Industry Costs

Profit	4.6%
Wages	7.4%
Purchases	59.5%
Depreciation	1.0%
Marketing	2.5%
Rent & Utilities	3.5%
Other	21.5%

Source: IBISWorld, May 2012

Market Share

CarMax Inc.	14.0%

Source: IBISWorld, May 2012

- Share of total dealership sales dollars: Used vehicles 32.4%

Source: National Automobile Dealers Association (NADA), 2012 NADA Data

- Some Industry Statistics
  Retail price: 50% are $5,000 to $10,000
  Average price: $8,875 to $10,000
  Average monthly inventory: 31.50 autos
  Average age of cars sold: 60% 3 to 5 years
  Approximately 350 cars sold annually by independent dealers
  Dealers: # of independent dealers in U.S.: 37,717
  Source: CNW Marketing Research, www.niada.com 2012

Industry Trend

- "'Used cars for dealers now are not as profitable, Richard Arca, pricing manager at Edmunds.com, told Auto Remarketing Wednesday. Arca elaborated about how two crucial dealership variables are tightening tremendously— wholesale supply especially of compact models and used-vehicle retail margins as prices climb more toward new-vehicle levels. "Financial data from the National Automobile Dealers Association back up Arca's assertion. March figures show gross profit as a percentage of a used-vehicle's price slid from 14.23 percent down to 12.96 percent year-over-year. That drop left dealers getting $2.149 in gross profit per used unit in March, down from $2,222 a year earlier."
  Source: "Weary Dealers Could Finally See Relief from Rising Gas Prices, Tight Fuel-Efficient Inventory"
by Nick Zulovich, www.worlddealer.wordpress.com. May 19, 2011

Questions

- General Questions What types of sales transactions did you have for the year under examination?
  a. Any sales at auctions? If yes, which?
  b. Any sales to wholesalers? If yes, which?
  c. Any sales to other dealers? If yes, which?
  d. Any consignment sales? If yes, describe.
  e. Any scrap sales? If yes, describe.
  f. Any in-house dealer financing sales?
  g. Any third-party financing sales?
  h. Did you have any other types of sales transactions?
  i. Did you have any sales that resulted in a loss on the sale? If yes, describe the nature of these sales.
  j. What sales did you have to relatives or family friends during the year? Identify.

Resources

Associations

- National Independent Automobile Dealers Association (ADA) : www.niada.com

Auto Detailing (See also Car Wash/Coin Operated and Full Service)		
SIC 7542-03	NAICS 811192	Number of Businesses/Units 14,000

Rules of Thumb

➢ 40 to 45 percent of annual sales plus inventory

Benchmark Data

Detailer Type	% of Total
Freestanding	37
Car Wash Combo	44
Mobile Services	11
Other Combo	8

Source:"Detailing Survey 2011—Results from Auto Laundry News," www.carwashmag.com. This is a very informative site—and publication—for Car Washes and Auto Detail—all sites should be this good.

Operating Costs as Percentage of Revenue

Rent	12.5%
Equipment/Supplies/Maintenance	6.4%
Chemicals (incl. soap, wax, compound, etc.)	7.8%
Labor	35.1%
Utilities (incl. water/sewer)	5.3%
Advertising & Promotion	5.3%
Insurance	3.8%
Customer Claims	1.0%

Source: "Detailing Survey 2011—Results from Auto Laundry News," www.carwashmag.com.

Average Monthly Gross Income (Detail Services Only)

Freestanding	$10,286
Car Wash Combo	$11,284
Mobile Service	$6,200

Source: "Detailing Survey 2011—Results from Auto Laundry News," www.carwashmag.com.

Retail	Free-standing
Complete Interior/Exterior Detail	$174.60
Interior Detail Only	$93.65
Exterior Detail Only	$96.77

Source: "Detailing Survey 2011—Results from Auto Laundry News," www.carwashmag.com.

- Average Gross Revenue Per Car (Car Wash Sales Only) $13.89
  Average Number of Cars Washed Per Month   3,348

  Source: "Detailing Survey 2011— Results from Auto Laundry News," www.carwashmag.com.

Average Number of Cars Detailed Annually

Freestanding	1,187
Car Wash Combo	2,375
Mobile Service	490

Source:"Detailing Survey 2011— Results from Auto Laundry News," www.carwashmag.com.

Daily Traffic Count

5,000–10,000	43%
10,001–20,000	17%
20,001–30,000	18%
30,001–40,000	10%
40,001–50,000	06%
More than 50,000	06%

Source: "Detailing Survey 2011— Results from Auto Laundry News," www.carwashmag.com.

- "A skilled detailer, who is working hard but not rushing, can probably complete a car in about 4 to 4.5 hours and make it look great. The average car would be only a few years old, be a mid-size, and be in average cosmetic condition with no major scratches or blemishes, and no major stains or excessive dirt on the interior."

Source: www.dealermarkclicks.com

Resources

Websites
- www.moderncarcare.com

Auto Glass Repair/Replacement

SIC 5231-10	NAICS 811122	Number of Businesses/Units 2,400

Rules of Thumb

➢ 45 to 50 percent of annual sales plus inventory

➢ 1.8 times SDE plus inventory

Benchmark Data

Statistics (Auto Glass Repair & Replacement Franchises)

Number of Establishments	2,025
Average Profit Margin	5.5%
Revenue per Employee	$127,500
Average Number of Employees	4
Average Wages per Employee	$34,217

Source: IBISWorld, August 2012

Products and Services Segmentation

Windshield repair	65%
Windshield replacement	24%
Window repair	7%
Window replacement	4%

Source: IBISWorld, August 2012

Major Market Segmentation

Households	45%
Commercial clients	25%
Insurance companies	18%
Other	12%

Source: IBISWorld, August 2012

Industry Costs

Profit	5.5%
Wages	26.8%
Purchases	53.2%
Depreciation	1.3%
Marketing	2.8%
Rent & Utilities	1.5%
Other	8.9%

Source: IBISWorld, August 2012

Market Share

Glass Doctor	18.0%
Novus Glass	15.1%
Super Glass	5.3%

Source: IBISWorld, August 2012

Industry Trend

- "A number of factors are impairing the ability of independent auto-glass-replacement shops to compete with large chains. Johnson Auto Glass and Trim Shop Vice President Dan Johnson said those factors include rising prices for replacement auto glass, lower reimbursements from insurance companies and efforts to steer insured parties away from independent auto-glass-replacement companies."

Source: "Business Tougher for Independent Auto-Glass-Replacement Companies" by Dan Heath,
www.pressrepublican.com

Resources

Trade Publications

- Glass Magazine—an informative site with archived articles of past issues: www.glassmagazine.com

Associations

- National Glass Association (NGA): www.glass.org
- National Windshield Repair Association—good site with an excellent overview of the industry: http://nwraassociation.org/

Auto Lube/Oil Change (See also All Tune & Lube, Grease Monkey, Jiffy Lube)

SIC 7549-03	NAICS 811191	Number of Businesses/Units 10,571

Rules of Thumb

- ➢ 40 percent of annual sales (tune-up) plus inventory
- ➢ 3 times EBIT (tune-up)
- ➢ 45 percent of annual sales (only auto lube businesses) plus inventory
- ➢ 1.5 to 2.25 times SDE plus inventory

Pricing Tips

- "There are two different service and working environments applicable to this business. The first being an oil and lube facility only, no service work is performed. The second being a tune-up business, performs oil and lube, in addition to service work, brakes, tune-ups, smog inspection, etc.

  "The first auto lube business generally shows a greater multiple, 2.5 SDE, while the auto tune-up business described above normally shows a 2.0 SDE.

  "The reasoning for the difference in the multiples above is the first business described is generally in a low-tech environment, with non-specialized training and employee wages are lower in comparison to specialized standards in this industry. In addition, most owners have multiple locations. The owner is mostly absentee in this operation and a manager is trained to perform all facets of operation and office functions as required. Demand is also higher.

"The second business described above requires a higher skilled employee (usually certified) and in most states the employees need to be tested. In addition the owner needs to be involved in the everyday functions of the operation, if only as an administrator. Most have a manager in place as well.

"Critical factors affecting business value are as follows: franchise vs. independent, manager and staff, customer base and vehicle count per day, average ticket per day, lease terms, equipment leased, owner's participation and location."

Above figures are plus inventory.

Benchmark Data

Statistics (Oil Change Services)

Number of Establishments	10,571
Average Profit Margin	11%
Revenue per Employee	$81,400
Average Number of Employees	7.4
Average Wages per Employee	$20,723

Source: IBISWorld, August 2012

Products and Services Segmentation

Oil changes	58.4%
Tire rotations	17.5%
Cabin air filter services	10.5%
Transmission flush services	8.5%
Other	58.4%

Source: IBISWorld, August 2012

Industry Costs

Profit	11.0%
Wages	26.1%
Purchases	38.2%
Depreciation	2.0%
Marketing	3.0%
Rent & Utilities	8.0%
Other	11.7%

Source: IBISWorld, August 2012

Market Share

Shell	19.7%

Source: IBISWorld, August 2012

Expenses as a percentage of annual sales (Auto/Lube--Repair Services)

Cost of Goods	24% to 30% (average 27%)
Payroll Costs	22% to 26% (with manager 26%)
Occupancy	10% to 16%
Royalty Fees (franchise)	4% to 8%
Profit (estimated pretax)	14% to 23%

Source: "Results from the Auto Laundry News—Fast-Lube Survey, 2011

Service	Average Price
Standard Multi-point Fast Lube/Oil Change	$35.45
Synthetic Oil Change	$65.31
Re-Refined Oil Change	$38.41
Transmission Fluid Drain/Flush	$105.56
Brake fluid Drain/Flush	$54.19
Power Steering Fluid Drain/Flush	$54.19
Differential Fluid Drain/Flush	$45.28
Radiator Flush/Fill	$75.39
Fuel-Injection cleaning	$65.95
Wheel Rotation	$19.57
Air-Conditioning Service	$92.84
Fast-Lube Revenue Average Gross Per Car	$50.10

Operating Expenses (Lube Only) as Percentage of Monthly Lube Revenues

Rent	11.1
Materials	34.6
Facility Maintenance	4.0
Labor	23.5
Utilities	2.4
Insurance	2.8
Customer Claims	0.8
Advertising/Promotions	2.0

Major Business Categories

Car Wash	57%
Freestanding Lube	26%
Auto Repair	15%
Other	2%

- Labor Costs
  Average Wage Per Hour Per Employee
    - ✓ 7% Paid Minimum Wage to $8.00 per hour
    - ✓ 72% Paid $8.00 to $10.00 per hour
    - ✓ 21% Paid over $10.00 per hour
- Average Number of Fast Lubes/Oil Changes per Location for the Year
  Freestanding: 12,184 With Car Wash: 12,506 With Auto Repair: 9,766
  Source: All of the above, except IBISWorld surveys are from the Auto Laundry News Fast-Lube Survey.
  This is a great publication and excellent web site.
- Tune-Up Services "Average sales volume per bay (single) $13K/mo. If you have eight bays the sales volume should be $100K per month if you have the proper equipment, mechanics and car count."

Industry Trend

- "To that end, we estimate that as of March 1, 2011 there were approximately 16,716 fast-lube facilities in operation, an increase of 185 facilities or 1.1 percent."
  Source: "All Shook Up" by Garrett McKinnon, National Oil & Lube News, 2011
- "Other pertinent figures that help define the fast-lube industry:
    - ✓ The average fast-lube customer changes his or her motor oil every 4,419 miles.
    - ✓ Between 2008 and 2010, only 3 percent of installed customers extended

their oil change intervals. (Source: Frost & Sullivan)

✓ In 2010, 75.4 percent of all automotive service events were attributed to the installed market. (Source: IMR Inc.)

✓ The average age of U.S. passenger cars and light trucks stands at 10.2 years, and U.S. drivers are keeping their vehicles an average of nearly 50 months, a 10 percent increase from 2008." (Source: R. L. Polk)

Source: "All Shook Up" by Garrett McKinnon, National Oil & Lube News, 2011

- "The most recent National Oil & Lube News report (2010) indicated that there was actually a decrease in the number of quick-lube operations doing business in the U.S. The report cites two possible reasons for this stagnation in the quick-lube market, one being a poor economy, and the other being an upward trend in the number of auto repair shops, tire installation locations and dealerships offering quick-lube service.

"The five largest U.S. fast-lube chains all saw store totals remain the same or decline over the past year; as the economy increased, competition constricted growth, according to the National Oil & Lube News' 2010 Tops in the Industry Ranking.

"NOLN published its annual lists of the largest fast-lube chains and other oil change providers in its March 2010 issue. Jiffy Lube remained atop the fast-lube chains with 1,976 stores, down 1 percent from 1,999 stores in 2008. The other largest fast-lube chains included Pennzoil 10-Minute Oil Change (887 stores, same as in 2008); Valvoline Instant Oil Change (850, same as in 2008); Texaco Xpress Lube (450, down 9 percent); and Kwik Kar (386, same as in 2008).

"Walmart Tire & Lube Express, classified as an 'oil-change plus' shop, again topped all oil change lists with 2,524 total U.S. stores. Rounding out the top five in the category were Bridgestone Retail Operations (2,112 stores), Goodyear Gemini Automotive Care (1,908), Midas Auto Service Experts (1,578) and TBC Retail Group (1,200). Bridgestone and TBC now represent groupings of several shop brands operated by a single company."

Source: www.motoroilbible.com/blog/quick-lube-oil-change

Seller Financing
- "4 years"

Resources

Trade Publications
- AutoInc.: www.autoinc.org

Associations
- Automotive Service Association: www.asashop.org

Auto Mufflers (See Also Midas & Meineke)		
SIC 7533-01	NAICS 811112	Number of Businesses/Units 15,200

Rules of Thumb

➤ 35 to 40 percent of annual sales plus inventory

➤ 1 to 1.5 times SDE plus inventory

Auto Parts and Accessories—Retail Stores

SIC 5531-11	NAICS 441310	Number of Businesses/Units 40,000

Rules of Thumb

➢ 40 percent of annual sales plus inventory

Pricing Tips

- "New cost of fixtures and equipment plus inventory at wholesale cost, nothing for goodwill. The inventory should turn over 4–6 times per year."

Benchmark Data

Statistics (Auto Parts Stores)

Number of Establishments	40,525
Average Profit Margin	7.1%
Revenue per Employee	$129,800
Average Number of Employees	8
Average Wages per Employee	$26,436

Source: IBISWorld, March 2012

Products and Services Segmentation

Accessories	33.3%
Maintenance parts	24.0%
Critical parts	23.3%
Performance parts	19.4%

Source: IBISWorld, March 2012

Major Market Segmentation

DIY customers	70%
Commercial and public sector customers	30%

Source: IBISWorld, March 2012

Industry Costs

Profit	7.1%
Wages	20.6%
Purchases	61.0%
Depreciation	3.0%
Marketing	1.3%
Rent & Utilities	2.0%
Other	5.0%

Source: IBISWorld, March 2012

Market Share

AutoZone Inc.	20.0%
Advance Auto Parts Inc.	15.3%
Genuine Parts Company	15.1%
O'Reilly Automotive Inc.	14.4%

Source: IBISWorld, March 2012

Key Statistics	Advanced Auto Parts	AutoZone	O'Reilly Automotive
No. of Stores	3,420	4,439	3,421
Avg sq. ft. per store	7,300	6,500	7,000
Sales Per Store	$1,595	$1,575	$1,424
Sales Per Sq. Ft.	$218	$239	$202

Note: Although the above chart represents only three chains of successful auto parts stores, the figures are relevant.

Source: "Auto Parts Retailers: Don't Hit the Brakes Just Yet" by Morningstore, July 12, 2010.

www.seeking alpha.com

Total stores in the U.S.	3,592
Average store size	6,350 sq. ft.
Average per store sales	$1,573,000
Inventory turnover	1.81
Average net sales per store sq. ft.	$248

Expenses as a Percentage of Annual Sales

Cost of goods:	61.3%
Payroll/labor Costs:	19.9%
Occupancy:	03.4%
Profit (estimated pretax):	05.3%

Resources

Associations

- Automotive Aftermarket Industry Association: www.aftermarket.org

Auto Rental

SIC 7514-01	NAICS 532111	Number of Businesses/Units 17,019

Rules of Thumb

➢ 45 percent of annual sales plus inventory

➢ Number of cars times $1,000

Pricing Tips

- "Reservation system, and national sales efforts, are critical. Many airport locations receive 70% or more of their business from this source. Off-airport locations are different; they can survive on local advertising as well as national."

Benchmark Data

Statistics (Car Rental)

Number of Establishments	17,019
Average Profit Margin	3.5%
Revenue per Employee	$253,680
Average Number of Employees	7
Average Wages per Employee	$37,062

Source: IBISWorld, July 2012

Products and Services Segmentation

Leisure car rental	41%
Business car rental	34%
Car leasing	19%
Car sharing	06%

Source: IBISWorld, July 2012

Major Market Segmentation

Off-airport market	35%
Business travelers at airports	30%
Leisure travelers at airports	35%

Source: IBISWorld, July 2012

Industry Costs

Profit	3.5%
Wages	14.8%
Purchases	31.1%
Depreciation	18.0%
Marketing	3.3%
Rent & Utilities	7.0%
Other	22.3%

Source: IBISWorld, July 2012

Market Share

Enterprise Rent-A-Car Company	39.3%
Hertz Global Holdings Inc.	18.9%
Avis Budget Group Inc.	18.5%
Dollar Thrifty Automotive Group Inc.	5.0%

Source: IBISWorld, July 2012

2011 U.S. Car Rental Market

Company	U.S. Cars in Service	#U.S. Locations
Enterprise Holdings (Includes Alamo Rent A Car, Enterprise Rent-A-Car, National Car Rental)	920,861	6,187
Hertz (Includes Advantage Rent-A-Car)	320,000	2,500
Avis Budget Group	285,000	2,300
Dollar Thrifty Automotive Group	118,000	445
U-Save Auto Rental System Inc.	11,500	325
Fox Rent A Car	11,000	13
Payless Car Rental System Inc.	10,000	32
ACE Rent A Car	9,000	90
Zipcar	7,400	128
Rent-A-Wreck of America	5,500	181
Triangle Rent-A-Car	4,200	28
Affordable/Sensible	3,300	179
Independents	55,000	5,350
Total	1,760,761	17,758

Source: ARN, Fact Book 2012

- "Income comes from two sources: operating income from rental and add-on services (such as CDW); and resale of vehicles (if the risk has not been assumed by the OEM in the fleet agreement). Accounting treatment (depreciation schedules for vehicles) can distort these sources."

Expenses as a Percentage of Annual Sales

Cost of goods	82%
Payroll/labor Costs	08% to 10%
Occupancy	04%
Profit (estimated pretax)	06%

Industry Trend

- "Increasing transparency of pricing with Internet travel sites. Increasing use of 'yield management' in pricing. Regulatory scrutiny of merged entities."

Questions

- "Relationships with franchisor; license agreement and royalty rate"

Auto Repair (Auto Service Centers)

SIC 7514-01	NAICS 811111	Number of Businesses/Units 210,970

Rules of Thumb

➤ 3.25 times SDE plus inventory plus work in process at cost

➤ 35% to 45% of annual sales plus inventory

➤ 1 to 2.5 times SDE plus inventory, ($75,000 to $100,000 SDE)

➤ 3 times SDE plus inventory ($150,000 + SDE)

➤ 1.5 to 2 times EBIT

➤ 2.5 to 2.75 times EBITDA

Pricing Tips

- "Pricing tips in this industry are normally based on SDE. Approx. 85% of all auto centers generate less than $1MM per year in revenues. The pricing tip for this is 2 to 2.5x SDE; if the business is generating less than $300k per year the multiple drops to 1.25 to 1.5x SDCF. All multiples above are plus inv. at cost."

"Lower if owner is main technician and fewer employees. Higher if owner runs business and has techs that do the work."

1. "Look at how much income is earned by the owner turning wrenches. The higher the percentage of business brought in by the owner's own efforts, the lower the multiple.

2. "Look at the parts sales to service sales ratio. Businesses with higher labor sales will sell for a higher multiple of sales number than those with lower service and higher parts sales."

"Look at the tire sales to mechanical sale ratio. Businesses with higher sale of mechanical services will sell for a higher multiple of sales than those with lower service sales and higher tire sales. Reason is the Gross Profit the business will produce given variables mentioned above."

- Auto Service Centers (minimum 4 bays), most service centers need minimum 8 bays to show higher revenues and strong cash flow.

Index	Owner's Cash Flow (SDE)
1.0 x to	$50K + SDE (approx. $400K annual sales)
2.0 x to	$100K + SDE (approx. $700 annual sales)
2.25-2.85 x to	$250K + SDE (approx. $1M+ annual sales)

"Above figures are all plus inventory. It's important to note that there should be a manager in place for the multiples shown."

"The above multiples take into account the FF&E (approx. $75K + for most auto service centers). Manager in place and willing to stay after the transaction closes is critical for buyers with no prior experience."

- "Takes longer to sell due to limited pool of buyers, and the buyers can get better deals."

- "With the economy slowing down, auto repair shop owners are getting 2 times SDE + inventory instead of 2.5 times SDE + inventory."

- "Many auto centers with sales revenues under $500k per year have closed their doors due to little or no profit. Consumers are driving less due to the high price of gas and this directly affects sales revenues. Rents continue to escalate and it becomes increasingly more difficult to find good managers or top-line techs. Major auto dealerships are also becoming more aggressive in their service departments and have taken some of the sales revenues away from the independent auto centers. Conversely the auto centers with sales exceeding $1 million per year continue to show good profits and will benefit from the smaller auto centers who close their doors. The above multiples do not include inventory, at cost; the multiples do include equipment, FF&E."

- "Rent can be added to the SDE if the seller also owns the building and is selling the building with the business. If the seller hires too many employees, it is sometimes possible to show the buyer why the business can be run with fewer employees, and add the soon-to-be-terminated employee's salary to the SDE."

- "Sometimes I will use 2.5 times SDE. This depends on if the business is located on a prime corner, how much equipment the business has, and how new the equipment is. A shop that has a very low SDE, or possibly is losing money, is able to sell for between $100K to $135K just for its location, built out, and equipment."

- "Smaller auto centers can be the most difficult to sell due to the very personal nature of the business. It is very helpful if the owner stays for 1 to 2 months to ease the buyer into the business especially creating a comfort level with the customers."

- "Most auto repair businesses carry very little inventory, so it's included in the selling price; however, if the business does carry a large inventory it is very often in addition to the selling price."

- "1. Owner's participation (tech or administrative). 2. Family members. 3. Equipment age. 4. Client core base. 5. Computer & software in place."

- "It is a labor-intensive business, the labor being specialized mechanics who have to be managed well, as mechanics can be lured away by car dealerships for a better wage."

- "It's important to note that there should be a manager in place for the higher multiples."

- "A very good automotive repair business is difficult to replicate because of the time necessary to build a customer base. Today's automotive technicians are very skilled people and very difficult to replace."

Expert Comments

"Competition is high, but if you have a good location, clean facilities and do a good job you can be successful in this industry."

"The industry has shifted since 2008; many smaller shops are closing as the larger auto centers are taking up a lot of the slack. In addition major auto dealerships are providing free oil changes and inspection for the first three years of purchasing a new vehicle."

"Cars are becoming increasingly complex. Qualified mechanics can be tough to find. Owner needs to have knowledge base or be able to retain quality techs to survive."

"There are a lot of car dealerships going out as well as a number of smaller automotive shops. People are keeping their cars longer due to the current economic climate. This gives way for more repair business with fewer competitors."

"Location is a prime factor that can dictate how successful a shop is and also dictates how much you can push the limits on valuation. The industry trend is going towards fewer cars being worked on, but higher average ROs [repair order]."

"It is easy to take over a shop even with little automotive experience. There is never a lack of work in this industry since all cars break down and need maintenance."

Benchmark Data

Auto Repair (Auto Mechanics)

Number of Establishments	210,970
Average Profit Margin	2.7%
Revenue per Employee	$98,800
Average Number of Employees	3
Average Wages per Employee	$29,420

Source: IBISWorld, March 2012

Products and Services Segmentation

General automotive repairs	41.2%
Brake repairs, front end repairs and wheel alignment	16.9%
Gasoline engine repairs	16.9%
Other repairs	14.1%
Transmission repairs	10.9%

Source: IBISWorld, March 2012

Industry Costs

Profit	2.7%
Wages	29.8%
Purchases	58.9%
Depreciation	1.6%
Marketing	1.8%
Rent & Utilities	4.1%
Other	1.1%

Source: IBISWorld, March 2012

- One experienced and successful industry expert has provided the following breakdown for Auto Repair:

Profit	14% to 22%
Wages	27%
Purchases	35% to 40%
Depreciation	1.6%
Marketing	1.8%
Rent $ Utilities	7% to 12%
Other	3%

- "The successful shop generates $150k per bay."
- "Profit should be approximately 17% profit of annual revenues once the business attains $55,000 per month in revenues; once the business attains $80,000 per month in revenues, the percentage goes to approximately 20% bottom line profit to sales."

Number of operational bays at a facility

3 or under	12.2%
4–6	44.5%
7–9	22.3%
10 or more	21%

- "91.3% are family-owned businesses
- "98.5% are independent

"Estimated Gross Annual Sales for 2011

Under $100K	.04%
$100K–$250K	5.6%
$250K–$500K	21.5%
$500K–$750K	20.8%
$750K–$1M	18.1%
$1M–$1.5M	16.8%
$1.5M–$2M	7.3%
Over $2M	.05%"

Average Ticket (Top 3 Responses)

$200–$250	18.1%
$250–$300	21.7%
$300–$350	17.4%

Source: "How's Your Business 2011, Mechanical" www.autoinc.org December 2011,
Excellent site—full of great information.

- Collision
  Number of operational bays at a facility:

5 or under	7.7%
5–10	22.1%
11–16	27.8%
17–22	18.3%
23–29	12.5%
30 or more	11.5%

- "$98 per hour labor rate, 35 percent on parts cost, mechanics paid on piece work versus hourly."
- "In this industry each tech (mechanic) should generate in total sales, $20k to $23k per month, this includes parts and labor on each vehicle for the month."
- "Sales per mechanic should be $12,000-18,000 per month if they write up their own estimates and order their own parts. For a mechanic that purely turns wrenches they should produce $20,000–$30,000 in monthly volume"
- "70 percent (173 million) of out-of-warranty vehicles are repaired at independent shops."
- "The majority of independent mechanical service shops continue to be family-owned (94 percent), independent (00 percent) businesses that have been in

operation an average of 25 years. Bay count has averaged seven per shop for the past 10 years, fluctuating only marginally."

- "Tire stores that do approximately 30% in service business will produce gross profits of 45%–55%. Businesses that produce 40%–50% of their business from mechanical repairs can get their gross profit up to 55%–60%."

- "Estimated average annual sales is $475,000."

- "The largest number of respondents (40 percent) have three to five service bays, with 29 percent reporting six to eight bays. Thirteen percent have nine to 11 bays and 10 percent have 12 or more bays. The average number of technicians these businesses employ is four. The most used method of compensating mechanical repair technicians is an hourly wage pay structure as noted by 40 percent of the respondents. Nineteen percent pay based on a percentage of the flat rate, while 10 percent pay their technicians a salary. The least used pay structure, according to the study, is a salary plus commission."

  Source: "How's Your Business?" by Monica Buchholz, ASA Vice President of Communications, Automotive Service Association, www.asashop.com

- "While the average number of ROs per shop was down by 3.4 percent in 2008, the average RO value was up 3 percent. This $8 average increase to $267 compared to $259 in 2007 helps offset the loss of volume. So while an average mechanical repair shop did fewer jobs, each job was worth more. The financial impact was less dramatic than the numbers might first suggest. Looking closer, ASA shop average RO value was 18.7 percent higher than the national average. ASA shop RO value was $317 in 2008, compared to the industry average of $267."

  Source: AutoInc.online edition, Automotive Service Association, www.asashop.org

- "Almost every auto repair shop is experiencing falling revenues in 2009, so a good shop is one that is less affected than others."

- "$400–$450 per sq. ft."

- "I'm finding that an average repair order of $500 to $550 is common for areas with higher incomes. In the lower income areas, average RO ranges from $300 to $350."

- "Margin on parts and labor should be 60% (which is a 2.5 markup). Average RO [Repair Order] of a good shop should be between $350 to $450. Auto technicians should be paid on a flat rate system, not hourly. There should be a lot of marketing efforts geared towards making repeat sales from existing customers."

- "Gross sales per year $300K–$400K is needed to at least survive and break even."

- "Average work order of $400 with a car count of at least 30 per week"

- "$98,000 annual sales per employee (technician). Typical garage has two employees + the owner-operator, who may or may not work the bays."

Expenses as a Percentage of Annual Sales

Cost of goods	30% to 40%
Payroll/labor Costs	25% to 30%
Occupancy	08% to 12%
Profit (estimated pretax)	12% to 18%

Industry Trend

- "Great upward potential as there are a lot of car dealerships going out as well as a number of smaller automotive shops. People are keeping their cars longer due to current economic climate. This gives way for more repair business with fewer competitors. You must have competent technicians and be able to instill trust with your customers."

- "More than 130,000 independent repair shops, conveniently located in most every community nationwide, have access to parts for all vehicles, as well as the required professional technicians, tools and equipment.

- "Independent repair businesses account for more than 70 percent of vehicle service and repair, compared to 28 percent of non-warranty repairs by new car dealerships. Even before the rash of dealership closings, the number of dealerships and their share of the service and repair market have gradually declined each year since 2000, according to AAIA."

Source: "Consumers Should Not Stress Out if Their Dealership Closes,"
Automotive Aftermarket Industry Association (AAIA), June 4, 2009

- "Increasing in mid-income demographics. Holding steady in high income."
- "Shops are getting bigger and mom and pops are slowly reducing, which might increase the cost of repair"
- "The turnover for mom and pops is high."
- "Specialized repair and/or large chains taking over"
- "Auto repair businesses should still be good to be into. With high oil prices and the push to find alternative fuels, etc., it is questionable where the industry will end up. I believe the industry will be strong for at least 10 more years."
- **Updates in the Auto Service Center Market**

"Over the last several years, I've seen some pretty dramatic changes in the market- place in regards to auto service centers. More business owners are calling to list, and hopefully exit, their current business. Some business owners have been in their business 15 to 25 years and are calling it quits.

"Many auto service centers that show $450K in sales revenues or less are more than likely to close their doors. The margin vs. the expense ratio has narrowed to such a degree that it is no longer equitable for these owners to open their doors if they're doing less than $450K per year, unless they own the building; even then, the business profits are minimal in most cases.

"Why the sudden change? From my personal observation there has been a major influx of new vehicles on the roads. From SUVs, sedans to coupes, all makes and models. In addition the dealerships and auto makers are providing free services on oil changes, tune-ups, etc. for the first 40,000 miles.

"What does this all mean for the average auto center? Fewer older models on the road and less opportunity to service late-model vehicles. Most of my core auto center business owners are down from 5% to 30% in sales over the last couple of years.

"My final observation will show that for at least 3 to 5 more years and/or until the marketplace has a slowdown on new-vehicle sales, the demand and multiples will be down for this type of business.

"How does this affect the multiples? With less demand for this type of business and more auto centers on the market, the multiples will normally go down from their past levels."

- "I've reduced the rule of thumb above from 2.3 x SDE to 1.8 x SDE."
- "Good growth due to the amount of vehicles on the road. As interest rates rise, fewer people purchase new cars, but rather repair them."
- "Specializing in the type of service and types of cars, vans, etc."
- "The smaller shops are having a very difficult time keeping mechanics and

often are a training program for dealers. Dealerships are trying every way they can to keep the service business, and technology is getting more complex. Specialty shops seem to be doing well. Drugs and alcohol are a very serious problem. There are a lot of old cars, and the need will always be there. I think the trend is for shops to become larger; smaller ones, especially where the owner is a mechanic, are fading fast, and difficult to sell to a non-experienced buyer. Mechanics in general do not have money to buy, and many [of these smaller shops] will end up as asset sales or for FF&E value."

Seller Financing:

- "The norm is for three to five years, with a 30 to 35% seller carry back, at 6% interest per annum"
- "Three to five years at 5.5%–7% interest. Make sure business cash flows and do balloon payment at end of term if need be."

Questions:

- "What is your hourly rate? How long have you been in business? How large is your customer base? Do you do foreign and domestic vehicles? How many fleet accounts do you have? Do you have accounts payable or are you on a cash basis?"
- "What are your average dollars per repair order and average hours per repair order? How many techs do you have? How many bays and lifts do you have? Where do you find your technicians? Where do you buy your parts? Do you replace engines and transmissions or sub them out? Are your technicians ASE certified? Do you have a quick lube station? Do you do emissions testing? Do you do pre-purchase inspections?"
- "What duties does the Seller perform on a day-to-day basis? Any family members involved in the business? Does the business have a stable mgr. and at least two key mechanics?"
- "Competition, reputation, role they play, history and competency of employees, condition of equipment. Any new equipment needed to keep up with technology? Are customer names and addresses in a data base? Commercial accounts and average outstanding receivables."
- "Do due diligence on reputation of business and be sure to get an agreement for warranty liability issues in purchase agreement. You don't want to have to pay for the seller's warranty-coverage issues."
- "What is your average repair order (RO) and average weekly car count? A good mechanical repair shop generally has an average weekly car count of 50 or more. A lube shop would have much higher car counts."
- "Profit margins on parts should be 55% to 60% average."

Resources

Associations

- Automotive Service Association—an excellent site for both auto services/collision businesses: www.asashop.org

Auto Service Stations (See Gas Stations)		
SIC 5541-01	NAICS 811111	

Auto Tire Stores

SIC 5531-23	NAICS 441320	Number of Businesses/Units 12,500

Rules of Thumb

➤ 1 to 3 times SDE plus inventory

Pricing Tips

- Auto Tire Centers (minimum 4 bays, the average tire & service center has 4 to 6 bays) Franchise; Big O Tire, Goodyear, Firestone, Tire Pros, etc.

Index		Owner's Cash Flow (SDE)
1.5 x	to	$50K + inv.
1.5–2 x	to	$75K + inv.
2–2.5 x	to	$100k + inv. (sales normally exceed $800K)
3 x	from	$125k - $250k + inv. (sales exceed $1 + million)

- "Rule of thumb for independent tire center: deduct 10% from above figure."
- "Successful retail tire dealers turn their tire inventories at least seven times a year, according to Norm Gaither, president of Dealer Strategic Planning Inc. The best way to determine tire inventory turns 'is to take the annual cost of sales and divide them by the average inventory,' he says."

  Source: "Independent tire dealers dominate," Modern Tire Dealer, January 2012
- "This business has shown some growth but has been affected by the price of oil per barrel. Tire prices have gone up as well as the other normal business expenses, i.e., rent, utilities, parts and labor costs have increased and these are four main variables. As such the owner needs to increase his hourly labor rate and product costs to offset these increases."
- "A product name identity on the business as shown above does generate a greater multiple as shown. If the business does not have a name identity or management in place, you will need to reduce the multiple by 10%. The above multiples do not include inventory, at cost; the multiples do include equipment, FF&E."

Benchmark Data

Statistics (Tire Dealers)

Number of Establishments	17,281
Average Profit Margin	3.2%
Revenue per Employee	$205,500
Average Number of Employees	9
Average Wages per Employee	$37,887

Source: IBISWorld, July 2012

Products and Services Segmentation

Automotive services	44.0%
Passenger car and light-truck tires	37.5%
Medium and heavy truck tires	8.8%
Automotive parts	7.5%
Farm tires	1.2%
Off-road tires	1.0%

Source: IBISWorld, July 2012

Major Market Segmentation

Drivers who purchase ordinary brands	66.2%
Trucking companies	15.8%
Drivers who purchase luxury brands	15.0%
Farmers	1.8%
Construction and mining companies	1.2%

Source: IBISWorld, July 2012

Industry Costs

Profit	3.2%
Wages	18.5%
Purchases	71.4%
Depreciation	0.8%
Marketing	1.0%
Rent & Utilities	1.9%
Other	3.2%

Source: IBISWorld, July 2012

- "Single-store owners make up 68% of the 30,000 independent retail, wholesale and commercial tire dealer locations in the U.S. In 2011, more than ever, the midsize dealers, both retail and wholesale, felt profitability pressure brought on by the combination of a struggling economy and the aggression of the larger retailers targeting them."

  Source: "Independent tire dealers dominate," Modern Tire Dealer, January 2012

- "According to DesRosiers Automotive Consultants Inc., oil changes drive the aftermarket, particularly tire sales. If the (car dealer) or independent does the oil change, they get the tire work, and it doesn't matter what age of vehicle they service," says President Dennis DesRosiers. Some 80% of independent tire dealers offer oil and lube service. They average 133 jobs a month. A typical tire dealer handles 11.4 different brands, which is in line with what dealers on the Modern Tire Dealer 100 list offer. He or she sells an average of 15 to 16 tires a day per outlet."

  Source: "Independent tire dealers dominate," Modern Tire Dealer, January 2012

- "Some 80% of independent tire dealers offer oil and lube service. They average 133 jobs a month.

  "The advertised cost of a standard oil (synthetic blend), lube and filter was $20.55, up 2% from last year ($20.16) and 21% from five years ago.

  "Service 2011—Oil change $20.55"

  Source: "Independent tire dealers dominate," Modern Tire Dealer, January 2012

- "Tires and tire sizes: A typical tire dealer handles 11.4 different brands, which is in line with what dealers on the Modern Tire Dealer 100 List offer. He or she sells an average of 15 to 16 tires a day per outlet."

  Source: "Independent tire dealers dominate," Modern Tire Dealer, January 2012
  A very informative site—and publication.

- "U.S. Consumer Tire Retail Market (Based on retail sales)
  Distribution channel 2011

Independent tire dealers	61.0%
Mass merchandisers	14.0%
Warehouse clubs	8.5%
Tire company-owned stores	7.5%
Auto dealerships	6.5%
Miscellaneous outlets	2.5%"

  Source: "Independent tire dealers dominate," Modern Tire Dealer, January 2012

Expenses as a Percentage of Annual Sales

Cost of goods	36% to 43%
Payroll/labor Costs	24% to 28%
Occupancy	09% to 15%
Profit (estimated pretax)	13% to 20%

Seller Financing:

- "5 to 7 years, on average "

Resources

Trade Publications

- Tire Business : www.tirebusiness.comModern Tire Dealer—a great Web site, one of the best : www.moderntiredealer.com

Auto Towing (See Towing Companies)

SIC 7549-01	NAICS 488410	

Auto Transmission Centers (See also AAMCO Transmission Centers)

SIC 7537-01	NAICS 811113	Number of Businesses/Units 17,000

Rules of Thumb

➤ 35 percent of annual sales includes inventory

➤ 1.5 to 2 times SDE includes inventory (as the SDE increases so will the multiple, i.e., SDE $50,000 the multiple will be 1.5 times, SDE $200,000 the multiple will be 2 times—all include inventory)

➤ 3 times EBITDA

➤ Rule of thumb—deduct 20 percent for independent centers.

Pricing Tips

- Auto Transmission Centers
  e.g., Franchise, Cottman, Sparky's, AAMCO

Index	Owner's Cash Flow (SDE)
1.0 x to	$50K + SDE
1.5-2.0 x to	$100K + SDE
2.0-2.25 x to	$150K + SDE (sales normally exceed $800K)

- "2 X Discretionary Earnings; 20 X Average last 16 weeks' sales; 16 X Average last 16 weeks plus Equipment"

- "Ratio of general auto repair to transmission services. Ratio of retail to commercial accounts. Concentration of business in commercial accounts. Average invoice amount. Seasonality. Reason for sale."

- "The industry is changing because of the improved reliability of transmissions, increased incorporation of electronics that make it difficult to determine if there is a transmission or an engine problem. The slowdown in new car sales has resulted in special deals from the manufacturers through dealers to provide extended warranty and incentives to trade in old and fuel inefficient cars.

Many shops including AAMCO are reacting by adding full auto repair. This has disrupted the 'model' of the classic shop's proforma by having to address added specialty labor. Competition from auto repair and even 'lube/tunes' are adding transmission repair; and rather than refer to specialty transmission shops, buy finished transmissions from third party and dealers. Pricing for a franchised shop, which in the recent past has shown sign of breakeven (typically $8,000 to $10,000/week), I try not to go below what it would cost to start a new franchise and reach breakeven ($200,000); but without profits to support debt service, the buyer pool is difficult."

- "Inventory in most transmission businesses can be excessive, discount the total amount from 20% to 40% as most owners have obsolete or outdated inventory."

Expert Comments

"People keeping cars longer is a positive. Parts Distributors are consolidating and fixing prices. Technology and the economy are encouraging total car repair which destroys classic parts and labor models."

"Reliability of transmissions, longer warranties, technology. competition from auto repair & dealers selling remanufactured transmissions."

The economy, technology, and associated competition from car dealerships"

Benchmark Data

- "Rent above 8–10% is a flag. Parts costing less than 15% indicates use of used parts. Part costs above 30% indicates skimming or high concentration general auto service. High concentration of fleet business versus retail may indicate the goodwill is tied to one owner or a key employee. and might not transfer."
- "Parts cost not to exceed 22%, and if less than 14%, a flag."
- "$3,500 to $4,000 per shop employee. Parts cost lower than 15% indicates used parts being used. High parts cost indicates high warranty costs, and/or skimming. High ratio of commercial sales to retail sales indicates a personal relationship that may not be transferable. Average invoice less than $1,000 on transmission repairs is an indication of a poor manager. Ratio of major to minor repairs should be high."
- "Estimated Average Annual Sales/Unit—$600,000"

Expenses as a Percentage of Annual Sales

Cost of goods	24%
Payroll/labor Costs	20% to 25%
Occupancy	08% to 12%
Profit (estimated pretax)	10% to 20%

Industry Trend

- "Better but trending toward franchises and large independents in major market—full-service auto repair with emphasis on diagnostics."

Seller Financing:

- "3 to 6.5 years"
- "50% down, 5 years better if 10 year ammortized with a 3–5 year balloon."

Questions

- "Reason for sale? Reason for sale again? Get specifics on employee function, pay rate and longevity. Get details on manager. What about warranty
- repairs? Ratio—retail to commercial concentration of sales? Rent and terms of lease?"
- "Why are you selling? What are the sales trends for last few years? How stable is the manager if ownership changes? What is the percentage of transmission service to general auto repair? How are your employees compensated? What is the ratio of retail/walk-in versus commercial? What is ratio of major to minor repairs? What is the average invoice for a major? What is percentage of warranty returns (comebacks)? Do your expenses include Workman's comp or alternative insurance?"
- "What does the owner do? Analyze weekly sales reports, if available; they provide a real insight as to what is going on. How many techs on payroll? A typical shop has three—a builder and two mechanics. What are they paid, and how is the manager compensated? Ratio of major repairs to minor, ratio retail to commercial accounts, look at 'comebacks.'"

Resources

Trade Publications

- Gears Magazine : www.gearsmagazine.com

Associations

- Automatic Transmission Rebuilders Association (ATRA): www.atra.com

Auto/Wrecking/Recyclers/Dismantlers/Scrap/Salvage Yards

(Auto parts—used & rebuilt)

SIC 5015-02	NAICS 441310	Number of Businesses/Units 2,023

Rules of Thumb

➢ "Values are based on the following: 3-6x earnings land and improvements vehicle and parts inventory, discounted based anticipated time to liquidate Goodwill such as customers, strategic location, and permitting can be fairly significant."

Pricing Tips

- "But in the scrap business the capital is your metal in the yard, and that's a commodity, which means the value can change. Indeed, the scrap business is a commodity founded on other commodities—the price of steel, the cost of shipping, and the relative values of currencies—which makes scrap especially sensitive to changes in the national and global economy."

  Source: "American Scrap" by John Seabrook, *The New Yorker*, January 14, 2008

Expert Comments

"Self-service auto recycling is the trend, due to lower personnel costs".

Benchmark Data

Statistics (Used Car Parts Wholesaling)

Number of Establishments	2,023
Average Profit Margin	3.5%
Revenue per Employee	$17,300
Average Number of Employees	8
Average Wages per Employee	$33,188

Source: IBISWorld, April 2012

Products and Services Segmentation

General auto recycling	55%
Parts remanufacturing	35%
Specialized motor vehicle dismantling and parts sales	10%

Source: IBISWorld, April 2012

Major Market Segmentation

Do-it-yourself customers	47%
Auto parts retail chains	30%
Independent auto parts dealers	14%
Automotive mechanics	9%

Source: IBISWorld, April 2012

Industry Costs

Profit	3.5%
Wages	17.2%
Purchases	66.4%
Depreciation	0.6%
Marketing	1.0%
Rent & Utilities	5.0%
Other	6.3%

Source: IBISWorld, April 2012

Market Share

Remy International Inc.	12.4%
Motorcar Parts of America Inc.	5.8%

Source: IBISWorld, April 2012

- "For self-service yards, 50% of all customers entering the yard typically make a purchase, and that purchase averages approximately $25-30 nationally."

Expenses as a Percentage of Annual Sales

Cost of goods	40% to 50%
Payroll/labor Costs	10%
Occupancy	14%
Profit (estimated pretax)	25%

Industry Trend

- Vehicles in operation—scrappage, by year
- "Net scrappage—the difference between sales and the growth of the light-vehicle population—produced a gain of 939,850 units added to an estimated 11.5 million in 2011, yielding an increase of nearly a million vehicles on the

road in 2011. Combined with stronger new car sales and continued economic growth, this boosted the average of cars and trucks in use, increasing new-vehicle sales in 2011 and beyond."

Source: "Vehicles in Operation and Scrappage," NADA Data 2012, www.nada.org

Seller Financing

- "6 years for self-service yards, and 12 years for full-service yards."

Questions

- "Are they able to pitch the sale of their yard to at least ten potential buyers?"

Resources

Associations

- Automotive Recyclers Association of New York: www.arany.com
- Automotive Recyclers Association: www.a-r-a.org

Aviation and Aerospace

Rules of Thumb

➢ 80 percent of annual sales

➢ 3.8 times SDE

➢ 4 times EBIT

➢ 5 times EBITDA

Pricing Tips

- "Must use both inventory and sales."

Expenses as a Percentage of Annual Sales

Cost of goods	20%
Payroll/labor Costs	50%
Occupancy	10%
Profit (estimated pretax)	20%

Industry Trend

- "Very high growth"

Bagel Shops (See also Bakeries and Bagel Franchises)

SIC 546101	NAICS 722211	Number of Businesses/Units 7,800

Rules of Thumb

➢ 30 to 35 percent of annual sales plus inventory

➢ 2.5 SDE plus inventory

Pricing Tips

- "Generally worth 1/3 of gross sales volume, with a decent rent. Higher rent or upcoming increase will lower price."
- "Rent a large factor; hand-rolled or frozen product?"

Expert Comments

"Easy to duplicate. Setup cost expensive. Most shopping centers already have a bagel shop."

Benchmark Data

- For additional Benchmark Information see also Restaurants—Limited Service
- "Bagels averaged $296 per store per week nationally during this 52-week span, a 0.7 percent increase from the previous year. Historically, bagels have increased sales since 2006; however, they saw a slight decline in average dollar sales in 2010.

  "Category Breakdown Unchanged:

  ✓ Regular Bagels: 29.5%

  ✓ Assorted/Variety Bulk Bagels: 53.1%

  ✓ Gourmet/Large Bagels: 12.4%

  ✓ Mini/Bite/Chunk Bagels: 3.8%

  ✓ Other Bagels: 1.2%"

  Source: "Bagels resume growth pattern after 2010 stall," Perishables Group, Inc, Chicago, Kelli Beckel@perishablesgroup.com

- "Rent and payroll the most important factors"

- Estimated annual 2011 unit sales for Bruegger's Bagel Bakery: $675,000. Estimated 2011 annual sales for Einstein Brothers: $700,000.

  Source: Nation's Restaurant News, June and July, 2012, www.nrn.com If you are involved in any way with the restaurant industry, you have to subscribe to Nation's Restaurant News.

Expenses as a Percentage of Annual Sales

Cost of goods	10%
Payroll/labor Costs	25%
Occupancy	20%
Profit (estimated pretax)	20%

Resources

Associations

- Independent Bakers Association: www.bakingnetwork.com

Bait and Tackle Shops (See also Sporting Goods Stores)

SIC 594-33	NAICS 451110	Number of Businesses/Units 9,000

Rules of Thumb

> 30 percent of annual sales plus inventory

Benchmark Data

- For Benchmark information see Sporting Goods

Bakeries (See also Bakeries—Commercial and Food Stores/Specialty)

SIC 5461-02	NAICS 445291	Number of Businesses/Units 29,000

Rules of Thumb

> 40 to 45 percent of annual sales plus inventory

> 2 times SDE plus inventory

Pricing Tips

- "Receivables; years in business; scope of market; new 'state-of-art' equipment vs. old."

Benchmark Data

Expenses as a percentage of annual sales

Cost of goods sold (Food)	05% to 10%
Payroll/Labor Costs	30% to 35%
Occupancy Cost	06% to 08%
Other Overhead	10% to 15%
Profit (estimated)	20%+

- "About one-third of bakers reported no change in customer counts, and only 14 percent claimed fewer customers, with an average decrease of 13 percent. The average number of customers visiting a retail bakery on a given day is also up. On the busiest days, an average of 258 customers are served, up from 225 in 2009. Even slow days have seen an uptick in customers coming through the door—105 in 2011 compared to 86 in 2009.

  "The median sale per customer rose 50 cents in the last two years, to $13."

- "Today's retail bakery almost cannot exist without some sort of presence on the Internet or social media websites. Nearly three-quarters of bakeries have their own websites, up from 65 percent in 2009. However, online ordering is taking a backseat to information. Only 27 percent of bakeries' Websitesare able to process orders, down from almost one-third in 2009.

  "Social media, which was barely on the radar two years ago, is playing a large role in many bakeries' marketing plans. Almost two-thirds of bakeries have a presence on a social media website, and of those nearly all are on Facebook (99 percent). Twitter comes in a distant second, with one-third of bakeries using it."

Percentage of average full-line retail bakery's dollar sales (2011)

Custom-decorated cakes	14%
Upscale dessert cakes/tortes	4%
Wedding cakes	9%
All-occasion decorated cakes	9%
Cookies	9%
Crusty bread/rolls	10%
Other bread/rolls	8%
Yeast-raised donuts	3%
Cake donuts	1%
Danish	2%
Muffins	4%
Puff pastry	3%
Pies	6%
Bagels	4%
Scones	2%
Cupcakes	5%
Other bakery items	6%

Source: "Retail Bakery Survey 2011: Optimism reigns supreme" by Katherine Martin, chief editor, modern-baking.com/bakery management

- "Percentage of full-line retail bakery operators offering the following items:
  1. Sodas, juices, teas 61%
  2. Conventional coffee service 56%
  3. Sandwiches 45%
  4. On-site dining 31%
  5. Espresso, other gourmet coffee 30%
  6. Other deli (salads, cheeses, etc.) 30%"

  Note: Figures above are approximate.
- For additional Benchmark Information see Food Stores — Specialty

Resources

Trade Publications
- Modern Baking: www.modern-baking.com

Associations
- Independent Bakers Association: www.independentbaker.net/
independentbakersassociation

Bakeries — Commercial (See also Bakeries)

SIC 5149-02	NAICS 311812	Number of Businesses/Units 6,000

Rules of Thumb

➢ 50 percent of annual sales plus inventory

➢ 1.5 to 2 times SDE plus inventory

Pricing Tips

- "Age & sophistication of equipment; convenience of bakery to major transportation hubs allowing for plentiful pool of employees."

- "Gross sales . . . what portion is from retail sales & how much from wholesale; inquire as to the amount of 'bags of flour' purchased weekly; loaves of bread sold weekly."
- "10–12 times the weekly sales"
- "The SDE multiplier is subject to increase or decrease based on the age and type of equipment. Further, large commercial bakeries require specialized human resources which may be the seller(s) whose expertise will need to be replaced. Oftentimes sellers minimize the difficulty in replacing their expertise, but this should be carefully evaluated and valuation adjustments made accordingly."
- "Be careful to check if one or two customers comprise a high percentage of the bakery's revenues."
- "Don't be fooled by the owner's overstatement of the value of the equipment. Most bakery equipment is valued at between 10% and 25% of replacement cost new. The larger equipment requires riggers to move it. The dismantling and re-installation of ovens requires specialized skill and knowledge."
- "Price dependent on the scope of distribution; whether they sell retail as well; their receivables, plus value of depreciated equipment (which in most cases is not worth much) and any product inventory kept in-house (flour and sugar are not cheap)."
- "Receivables are very important since they determine the amount of start-up capital needed. It was the cause of the demise of many a big wholesaler in New York."
- "Price will vary greatly depending on the volume and types of labor-saving equipment. This is an industry where payroll can be significantly reduced by machinery. Commercial contracts with restaurants, hotels, etc. are also a source of value."

Expert Comments

"This industry over the past several years has been under a tremendous squeeze on profitability. Price of flour & other needed ingredients has been most volatile, yet the market place has been most resistant to price increases...thus profit margins (& profit) have been reduced!!!"

"Commercial bakeries are generally a high risk/high competition business; and a large upfront outlay with common long-term collectibles. Most smaller bakeries almost always limit their amount of wholesale business because it necessitates longer working hours & more manpower—all to sell products at a lower profit than retail. The tremendous increase in flour prices has adversely affected this business as well. This increasing cost of flour & basic utilities, including fuel, makes entry & existence in this industry perilous."

"The bakery business traditionally produces much of its product at night so it can be delivered fresh in the morning. This limits the human resources available to work in the industry. While 'mom & pop' bakeries continue to do well, mid-size (sales $750K–$2.5M) companies are experiencing shrinking margins due to increased health care costs and pressure from larger, highly automated competitors."

"This is an old industry. Many of these businesses are passed from one generation to the next. This does not create an environment for growth or innovation. Ease of replication is influenced by high asset cost to enter this industry."

"Industry is declining due to eating habits of population. Cost of entry is very high due to equipment cost, unless used equipment is purchased. Marketability is limited by the size of the marketplace of professional bakers. In some parts of the U.S., facilities tend to be old. Competition is growing a bit due to the business education of young professional bakers."

"Price dependent on the scope of distribution; whether they sell retail as well; their receivables, plus value of depreciated equipment (which in most cases is not worth much) and any product inventory kept in-house (flour and sugar are not cheap)."

"Receivables are very important since they determine the amount of start-up capital needed. It was the cause of the demise of many a big wholesaler in New York."

"Price will vary greatly depending on the volume and types of labor-saving equipment. This is an industry where payroll can be significantly reduced by machinery. Commercial contracts with restaurants, hotels, etc. are also a source of value."

Benchmark Data

- "Cost of goods should be no more than 20% TOPS . . . just as rent should be no more than 10% of sales."
- "22%–25% cost of goods"
- "Direct cost of goods varies significantly from product to product. There is no little commonality between a bread bakery and a cake and pastry bakery. A well-run facility with reasonable Market Share should result in an SDE of 15%–20% of Gross Revenues."
- "Difficult to measure since many of these businesses operate from facilities that are old and much larger than required with new highly automated equipment available."

Expenses as a Percentage of Annual Sales

Cost of goods	25% to 28%
Payroll/labor Costs	30% to 40%
Occupancy	15% to 18%
Profit (estimated pretax)	15% to 18%

Industry Trend

- "Many smaller bakeries will be taken over by larger competitors. With less competition wholesale prices on bakery products will jump tremendously."
- "As obesity becomes more of an issue, I anticipate a slight decline in the industry."
- "Fewer and fewer competitors . . . with a growing trend toward baking artisan products."
- "There will be less & less competition, with a few giants controlling the market!"

Seller Financing

- "6 to 7 years"

Questions

- "Ask for flour and water bills, cost/price list of major items carried, aging of receivables & payables; see gas/electric bills; determine age and condition of equipment."
- "Is location of any importance to sales . . . if so how long is lease?"
- "Review and interview key customers—evaluate equipment carefully—check for expansion opportunity."

Bakery and Restaurant (See Bakeries & Restaurants)

	NAICS 722211	

Rules of Thumb

➤ 30 to 35 percent of annual sales plus inventory

Banks—Commercial

SIC 6021-01	NAICS 522110	Number of Businesses/Units 85,389

Rules of Thumb

➤ 1 to 2 times Book Value

➤ 350% of Annual Gross Sales includes inventory

➤ 15 times SDE includes inventory

➤ 15 times EBIT

Expert Comments

"The post-recession regulatory environment has burdened smaller community banks with compliance issues that are forcing many of them to consolidate in order to achieve the necessary economies of scale required to enable compliance."

Benchmark Data

Statistics (Commercial Banking)

Number of Establishments	85,389
Average Profit Margin	19.7%
Revenue per Employee	$321,300
Average Number of Employees	23.2
Average Wages per Employee	$84,477

Source: IBISWorld, August 2012

Products and Services Segmentation

Real estate loans	36%
Depository Services	34%
Loans to individuals	13%
Commercial loans	11.7%
Other loans	5.3%

Source: IBISWorld, August 2012

Major Market Segmentation

Retail customers	56%
Corporate clients	39%
Other clients	05%

Source: IBISWorld, August 2012

Industry Costs

Profit	19.7%
Wages	26.3%
Purchases	3.5%
Marketing	2.4%
Rent & Utilities	6.7%
Other	41.4%

Source: IBISWorld, August 2012

Market Share

Wells Fargo	12.8%
JPMorgan Chase & Co.	10.0%
Bank of America	6.1%
Citigroup Inc.	5.3%

- "1.5 to 2 X Book Value (Capital) for a well-run, CAMELS rated 1 bank. In some cases where an extraordinary benefit would result for a buyer such as securing a strategic location or customer/ loan base, a higher price could be common but in cases where no such forces exist to influence market value, the 1.5 to 2 times book multiplier is a good rule of thumb."

Expenses as a Percentage of Annual Sales

Cost of goods	25%
Payroll/labor Costs	35%
Occupancy	05% to 10%
Profit (estimated pretax)	25%

Industry Trend
- "Consolidation of smaller banks, high scrutiny of risk in making loans, lower profit due to building up of capital and reserves."

Questions
- "Are you now or have you ever been involved in banking? How much liquid capital do you have to invest? Have you spoken with any bank regulatory authorities about your plans to acquire a bank?"

Barbecue Restaurants (See also Restaurants)		
	NAICS 722211	Number of Businesses/Units 3,500

Rules of Thumb
➢ 30 percent of annual sales plus inventory

Benchmark Data
- Estimated Annual Sales: Sonny's Real Pit Bar-B-Q: $1.5 million; Smokey Bones Bar & Fire Grill: $2.5 million

Barber Shops (See also Beauty Salons)

SIC 7241-01	NAICS 812111	Number of Businesses/Units 50,000

Rules of Thumb

➤ 10 to 25 percent of SDE plus inventory; add $1500 per chair

Bars (See also Cocktail Lounges)

SIC 5813-01	NAICS 722410	Number of Businesses/Units 65,224

Rules of Thumb

➤ 35% to 45% percent times annual sales—business only plus inventory

➤ 2 to 2.5 times SDE plus inventory

➤ 2 to 2.5 times EBIT

➤ 2 to 2.5 times EBITDA

➤ 4 times monthly sales + game revenue (net) plus inventory

➤ 4 times monthly sales + liquor license and inventory

Pricing Tips

- "Competition, number of available licenses in town, previous violations"
- "Top-line method is used due to the perception of a cash business. This is changing and it is much more difficult to sell bars without documented earnings."
- "Understand the value of liquor license and percentages of alcohol vs. food." "Due to the 'cash' nature of this type of business, it is often difficult to asses value based on presented financials, so you must often use alternate methods besides cash flow."
- "Main variable is the fair market value of the liquor permit, as some areas have a high number of available permits which results in the permit having no, or limited, additional value, while in other areas limited number of available permits may cause the permit to have a substantial value. One will need to research type of permit and its availability and if in fact a market exists for the permit itself. I have seen liquor permits being sold for as high as $150,000, which obviously impacts the value of the business."
- "The location, lease rate, and restrictions on the conditional use permit or liquor license will largely impact any given operation's value. As some licenses are valued at $75K plus, there is always some 'floor' value regardless of profitability."
- "Factor in liquor license, understand what equipment is actually leased, make sure the restaurant is up to code and salable before investing time."
- "Location, lease, and liquor license dictate the value of a bar. The concept is usually changed with a new buyer, and a significant investment is made to improve the premises."
- "Recently in the Denver market we have seen 50 percent of sales as a rule of thumb; more if easily operated (fewer employees)."
- "You really need to understand if the liquor and beer costs are in line and how much the establishment is selling versus food."

- "Drinking places, or bars or taverns, are always in high demand. The most important factors in assessing the value of the business are the location and the lease (how long remains), when and at what rate will the options be exercised, etc."
- "Discretionary cash flow can be very different from deal to deal. There is one very important DCF item that should be identified: Does the bar or taproom have any vending? (Examples of this are video poker, tobacco, juke box, pool tables, etc;) If the answer is 'Yes,' then the next question should be, is there a vendor arrangement, or does the seller own the machines? A vendor arrangement means that the vendor owns the machines and collects a portion of the proceeds. If the seller owns the machines, the seller collects all of the proceeds, and can use these funds to reduce their COGS and labor considerably. In each case, (with the seller as owner or the vendor as owner of machines) OFF BALANCE SHEET seller financing or vendor financing can be a very powerful source of funds. There are a few little things that can alter the valuation in a bar or taproom. Generally, these types of establishments derive a lot of revenue from draft beer. (COGS for draft beer 25%–30%, gross profit 70%–75%). If the establishment is operating on an antiquated draft system, glasses may not appear clean, spouts look discolored, . . . this could warrant a discount. Most states require that draft system/draft lines are cleaned weekly. A potential buyer should ask for vendor beer invoices to determine the 'popular' products of the establishment. This is important if the buyer has a potential age group in mind as the primary patrons. This is a forward cash flow assumption that should be acknowledged. If vendor beer invoices are not made available, check the trash dumpster on a regular basis, it is an excellent source of information. If liquor is being served, the pouring routine should be observed. Measured shot or free pour can materially change COGS. 750ML bottle yields 26 ounces, which is 14 shots at a 1.75oz free pour, and 21 shots at a 1.25oz measured shot. This difference could be the cost of 1.5 bottles. (Generally these establishments sell mostly beer/draft beer, but this scenario should be included in forward cash flow assumptions.)"
- "You have to factor in the location, lease term or property sale, equipment and the ease of someone taking over without having to put a lot of funds in."
- "$ for $ of gross if property is included. Value of liquor license included in price."
- "Unreported cash is always an issue with these types of businesses. Any value placed on cash sales should be significantly discounted since these sales are not recognized by lending institutions and sellers need not be compensated or rewarded for illegal, unreported funds."
- "Never trust the books. Check sales tax returns, bank statements, etc. Also, check the price points and compare to the actual COGS. Are the comps legitimate on the P&L? Are COGS high due to the owner skimming, or are they giving the house away? We never address a value to skimming and never represent it to buyers. Experienced buyers will recast the financials using their own labor percentage, etc."
- "Location is key to success....as is longevity for resale unless major renovations will occur. Location needs to have sufficient parking."
- "It is easier to go through the receipts of the business than go through returns."
- "Lease terms a huge factor; ratio of food to liquor drinks; current market wants light food, less than 25%"
- "Value and type of liquor license is always a key consideration. Ownership of

real estate is always a big plus. Many buyers are looking for real estate as part of the purchase."

- "Location, value of lease, liquor license value, willingness of seller to hold note, cooperation of seller to supply necessary financial information, beware of 'red' flags."
- "+/- value of the liquor license
  +/- lease value
  +/- location
  +/- seller financing"
- "Is the seller reporting all income? What is seller's pour cost? Is seller hands-on owner?"

Expert Comments

"True bars (without food) are becoming less profitable. Bars in good, dense, urban locations are still strong but suburban bars are struggling. Stronger drunk driving laws, smoking bans, etc. have contributed. Plus full-service restaurants with bars have cut into some of the business."

"These businesses are highly marketable due to the public demand (and dream) of owning their own bar. The difficulty of obtaining new permits adds significant value to existing operations."

"Location, location, location. It is still the dream of many to be a 'bar owner.' A clean and well-maintained place always sells quicker than a 'dive.'"

"Bar sales are declining in general, due to smoking bans, new liquor laws and competition from restaurants with bars."

"Limited liquor license availability is a significant barrier to entry in some markets."

"Neighborhood bars seem to be popular despite a good or bad economy. Sometimes the closer to home the better with tougher DUI laws."

"Smoking ban hit many establishments hard in 06. Also, heavy liquor enforcement (over-serving, etc.)"

"Competition may keep a bar from succeeding initially; and, conversely, a competitive environment indicates a good area for customers and traffic. The fact that bars and nightclubs are extremely trendy could lead to significant profit declines after the 'buzz' has worn off."

"I think it is easier to open a bar versus a restaurant. There is a lot of competition so it is important that operators are constantly running promotions and keeping up to date with trends."

"Loss of smoking in bars and taverns has cut revenue in some cases by as much as 25%. Many smaller places unable to compete for the local business anymore."

"Bars and restaurants have always been highly competitive, risky, and potentially profitable endeavors, and extremely attractive to the majority of buyers within a market, yet they also tend to rely on contemporary trends within the area, and few can sustain consistent growth beyond the 'buzz' factor."

"I think the competition is intense for the local neighborhood places, brought on by the chain-type concepts opening up in suburban markets. Some of the rent factors make it cost-prohibitive for the local venue to compete. Neighborhood bars are always a popular pick since it is a recession-proof business."

"Lots of taverns, one on each corner. Liquor license may be the majority of the value."

"Must buy an existing liquor license in New Jersey, no new licenses available."

"Location is key to success...as is longevity for resale, unless major renovations will occur. Location needs to have sufficient parking."

Benchmark Data
- For Benchmark data see Bars and Nightclubs.

Statistics (Karaoke Bars)

Number of Establishments	1,055
Average Profit Margin	$64.100
Average Number of Employees	6
Average Wages per Employee	$12,563

Source: IBISWorld, April 2012

Industry Costs

Profit	2.5%
Wages	19.8%
Purchases	42%
Depreciation	4.5%
Marketing	1.5%
Rent & Utilities	6.5%
Other	23.2%

Source: IBISWorld, April 2012

Products and Services Segmentation

Alcohol and other drinks	58%
Cover and song charges	21%
Food	16%
Other	5%

Source: IBISWorld, April 2012

- "Total occupancy costs of 10% or less."
- "There is no greater markup than that of liquor."
- "Annual sales of $1,000 per square foot is a great general benchmark for a successful bar!"
- "Small easily operated bars are the most desirable. Rent at 10%–12% (or less) of sales help."
- "If the food costs can be kept down low 30's, reasonable rent, the place should be making money."
- "Benchmark Data vary widely with markets and types of establishments; food costs tend to be 25%–33%; however, productivity per square foot is a function of size and location (and subsequent lease rate)."

- "Serving alcohol should be an extremely profitable endeavor, with average pour costs running as low as 16 percent for liquor, 21 percent for draft beer, 25 percent for bottled beer, and 28 percent for wine."

  Source: "10 Tips for Small Bar Owners" www.nightclub.com/NCB March 2008

- "Rent should be 6% to 8% of gross sales. Liquor much more profit than food."
- "Most important factor is to have a rent factor (rent as a percentage of gross sales) in the 6% to 8% range. This is the first thing which I look at, and, far and away, it's the most important, as the only way to 'fix' it is to increase sales."
- "Successful restaurants should maintain their liquor costs at 15%, beer costs at 25%, and wine costs under 35%."
- "Hard to say. Still a very high percentage of 'bad books.' Any neighborhood bar (without food) that has an occupancy cost of ten percent or less is a great benchmark. Of course, skim or bad books skews the numbers."
- "Cost to sell a draft beer—25% to 30% of price of beer; cost to sell a bottled beer— 27% to 32% of price of beer; cost to sell liquor, 750ML bottle 20 shots poured (Avg)— 25% to 35% of price of bottle. Quick and dirty benchmark for bar and taproom, COGS beer and liquor 30%."
- "Successful bars and nightclubs can usually generate up to $5,000 per well on a good night."
- "Cost of goods should be below 28% of sales in a tavern/bar with little or no food. Payroll should be less than 20%."
- "The key is profitability. See if the seller can back up their statements. It is the bottom line. See if they have systems implemented to reduce loss. It is always helpful knowing they have controls in place."
- "Lite food is a plus"
- "$327 sales per sq. ft. in a bar generating $850,000 in sales with a 5% net profit"
- "Food costs in the 40s %—too high. Beer costs in the mid-20s % and under 30%—good."
- "Twenty-eight percent COGS is at the high end; some operators can be in the low 20s depending on the price points. Labor can be significantly lower or higher depending if the state has a tip credit for minimum wage. Ten percent to the bottom line is only a rule of thumb."

Expenses as a Percentage of Annual Sales

Cost of goods	20% to 25%
Payroll/labor Costs	20% to 25%
Occupancy	06% to 10%
Profit (estimated pretax)	10% to 20%

Industry Trend

- "Most bars are improving on their food to drive more bar business."
- "Food introduction may help the mom and pops."
- "Flavored vodkas, spirits, organic"
- "These businesses will continue to thrive through good times and bad, though they will see some decrease during recessionary periods."
- "Increasing costs and increasing competition from chains"
- "More bars, more craft beers, wines from different regions. I think we will see more pub-type concepts."

- "Increased governmental regulation, e.g., smoking bans"
- "More wine bars, tapas bars; drinking is always popular. More pricey drinks."
- "Liquor licenses in certain areas where there are high concentrations of establishments within major cities have become extremely difficult to obtain, thus driving the value of those licenses very high."
- "Smaller locations seem to be taking a smaller and smaller share of the existing business."
- "Diminished demand for bars due to influence of major chains with large bar followings and promotions"

Seller Financing

- "3 to 7 years"

Questions

- "Length of time employees have been at work, number of employees, tax audits? Recent violations?"
- "Violations, invoices for purchases, customer count and sales"
- "Unpaid taxes? Liquor license violations? Police runs?"
- "Please provide me with a copy of the permit or conditional use permit, as provided by the city and the state Alcohol Control Board."
- "The variance between the internal books and records versus the tax returns. Purchase invoice availability."
- "Liquor license violations, amount of revenue generated from games/ amusements on a weekly basis, # of 'cash' employees"
- "What conditions have been placed on the license restricting the hours, use, or entertainment associated with the license?"
- "Scrutinize happy hour, comps, etc. Many buyers think they can increase sales by eliminating giveaways which usually does not work. Ask to see all liquor invoices and cash receipts from liquor purchases."
- "For the tax returns, why they are selling? Cooperation is key in this business. Bars are difficult to sell when there are unreported sales, weak returns. Many of the sellers in our market will not hold notes."
- "Discretionary Cash Flow should be evaluated very carefully. There can be a huge difference from deal to deal."
- "How much cash revenue is not reported? Are there any conditions on the license or permits? What type of entertainment is specifically included in the permit for entertainment?"
- "Is the seller reporting all income? What is seller's pour cost? Is seller hands-on owner?"

Resources

Trade Publications

- Bar Confidential: Running a Successful Bar by Bob Johnson : www.barproducts.com

Bars — Adult Only (Adult Clubs/Nightclubs)

SIC 5813-01	NAICS 722410	

Rules of Thumb

> ➤ 100 percent of annual sales includes inventory
>
> ➤ 3.25 to 5 times SDE includes inventory

Pricing Tips

- "The industry has experienced a shake-out of weaker performing clubs beeng swallowed by larger operators as they become available. Although we have experienced recessionary forces, as the entire industry has, the Adult Club industry by and large has been more resilient than mainstream bars and nightclubs to the effects of discretionary dollar competition and distribution. The more troubling aspects are more related to legal issues of Independent Contractor Status and the efforts of the Citizens for Community Values (CCV)."

- "Adult clubs are of course cash heavy operations. Verifying internal ratios of cost can lead to a back-ended method of providing gross cash flow."

- "A true EBITDA + owner's compensation recast is a necessity . . . "

- "The best thumbnail is SDE. It stands up well to real-world numbers on the sales prices. Real estate, inventory, FFE all should be considered separately as add backs to total sale price. Some states allow the sale of inventory alcohol to the buyer, some do not. MAI appraisals do well for real estate. FFE is a 'swag' and over 3 years old stuff ought to write down to 10%–20% of initial cost."

Expert Comments

"The economy REALLY hits discretionary earnings spending . . ."

"Clubs took a hit this year and last year that was, in essence, an acceleration of a downward trend for the last 2 years . . . I do see signs of stabilization and stronger sales, as well as better customer #'s in certain markets . . "

"Adult clubs are a distinctive subset of alcoholic establishments."

"Conservative nibblings at the edges of law have served to limit growth of the industry. There has been a generalized effort on the part of the larger chains and owners to absorb reasonably priced clubs in targeted areas. Past the big and midsized players, the single and small operators struggle to maintain a stable cash flow with controlled labor costs, dancers, and stable legal environments."

Benchmark Data

- "SDE x 2.5–3.5 = possible sale price."
- "Should be reporting an SDE in neighborhood of 23%–26% or higher."
- "Rick's and its competitors benefit as well from what may well be a unique aspect of their business model. The entertainment that brings folks in the door is actually a moneymaker: Dancers pay to work there as independent contractors (how much depends on location and shifts, with some shifts costing several hundred dollars) and get paid from tips. That keeps overhead and

salary and benefit expenses low.

- "There are basically three revenue streams, in addition to the fees from dancers: cover charges, which can top $20; food and drinks; and services, which include the renting of private rooms. A customer may pay the club $400 to $500 for a spell in one of those rooms."
"Rent: <10%; liquor cost: 15%"
- "No more than 8 percent of gross income for rent"
- "Every club is different in its immediate area, and its state by state environment."

Expenses as a Percentage of Annual Sales

Cost of goods	17% to 23%
Payroll/labor Costs	n/a
Occupancy	<10%
Profit (estimated pretax)	20%

Industry Trend

- "Markets have remained relatively stable throughout the U.S. with the exception of the Las Vegas market. Stable; but more concentration of clubs under a few chains." "Like so many other 'sin' categories, the business seems to be resistant to economic downturns, especially as the customer base keeps expanding."
- "This industry is facing a slight decrease in profit margins: a constriction of the industry growth rate due to local government interference."

Questions

- "What violations have been charged? Is the owner aware of ANY pending litigation or legislation (either local or state) which will have a negative impact? There are others but the rest are more site specific."
- "How would he replace the Cash Flow of this business with something comparable?"
- "Why is he/she selling? What is wrong with this picture? I have yet to have an owner list a club with me because he woke up one morning, said, 'Gee, I think I'll let someone else make a bunch of money off my club, and I'll finance it to him on easy terms, too!' Inevitably, if someone wants to sell, there is usually a serious reason that is MATERIAL! Caveat Emptor, and make sure that both buyer and seller BOTH have their own individual attorneys."

Bars — **Nightclubs** (See also Bars)	
NAICS 722410	Number of Businesses/Units 9,400

Rules of Thumb

➢ 40 percent of annual sales

➢ 2.5 times SDE plus inventory

➢ 3 times EBIT

➢ 2 times EBITDA

Pricing Tips

- "The conditions or potential restrictions on the liquor license are paramount. Are there abbreviated hours, are happy hours or door fees allowed, what is the security guard-to-patron ratio, does a significant percentage of sales need to be derived by food sales, etc."

- "Buyers of nightclubs are generally going to implement their own concept and theme. Sellers rarely seek to sell when they are at the peak of their game, but when revenues begin to slide. The lifespan of a 'hot' club rarely lasts beyond 3 to 4 years, so at that point an owner may need to give the business a 'face lift' or sell it to a new owner who will implement a new theme. That in mind, value based on cash flow becomes less relevant since a new owner's investment will be the same regardless."

- "Hot nightclubs generally have a two to three year lifespan. Fortunately, this is generally more a function of promoters than the physical location. Unfortunately, this takes the critical success factors somewhat out of owner's hands, as it is often difficult for management teams doing 'In-House' promotion to adjust to ever-changing trends."

Expert Comments

"This industry is highly volatile as trends are constantly changing. Also, clubs on the Strip in Las Vegas, in Hollywood or in South Beach are significantly different from main street America."

Benchmark Data

Statistics (Bars & Nightclubs)

Number of Establishments	65,885
Average Profit Margin	3.6%
Revenue per Employee	$64,100
Average Number of Employees	5.6%
Average Wages per Employee	$12,558

Source: IBISWorld, June 2012

Products and Services Segmentation

Sale of beer and ale	42%
Sale of distilled spirits drinks	30.6%
Sale of meals/non-alcoholic beverages	11.2%
Other-accommodation, cigarettes, rentals and packaged liquor	7.8%
Sale of wine drinks	7.1%
Gaming/slot machine receipts	1.3%

Source: IBISWorld, June 2012

Industry Costs

Profit	3.6%
Wages	19.8%
Purchases	44.0%
Depreciation	3.2%
Marketing	1.2%
Rent & Utilities	6.5%
Other	21.7%

Source: IBISWorld, June 2012

- "Successful bars and nightclubs should sell at least $4,000 to $5,000 per well on weekends and busy nights."
- "While such Benchmark Data work with typical bars, these vary widely with nightclubs."

Expenses as a Percentage of Annual Sales

Cost of goods	25%
Payroll/labor Costs	30%
Occupancy	15%
Profit (estimated pretax)	20%

Industry Trend

- "There will always be a market for such venues, and buyers willing to pay premiums to A+ locations for venues."

Questions

- "Original invoices for liquor sales, and, with your fingers crossed, door counts per night."

Resources

Associations
- National Club Industry Association of America, NCIAA: www.nciaa.com

Bars with Slot Machines (See also Casinos/Casino Hotels)		
	NAICS 722410	

Rules of Thumb

➢ 3 times SDE plus inventory

Pricing Tips

- "Drinks are free to slot players. Pay close attention to <u>only</u> the net, providing other operating costs are in line."

Expenses as a Percentage of Annual Sales

Cost of goods	32%
Payroll/labor Costs	30%
Occupancy	10%
Profit (estimated pretax)	17% (estimated)

Seller Financing

- "Where the debt service does not exceed 35 percent of the SDE."

Baseball Teams (professional)		
SIC 7997-08	NAICS 711211	

Pricing Tips

- The average value of a big league baseball team is $523 million.

  Source: *Forbes* magazine

- Average Annual Revenue—$7 Billion
  Average Annual Salary—$2.5 Million

  Source: www.statisticbrain.com/professional-sports

Benchmark Data

Statistics (Sports Franchises)

Number of Establishments	823
Average Profit Margin	07%
Revenue per Employee	$445,800
Average Number of Employees	64
Average Wages per Employee	$285,299

Source: IBISWorld, March 2012

Products and Services Segmentation

Ticket sales	38%
Broadcasting and other media rights	31%
Advertising	12.5%
Other	11.5%
Concessions	3.5%
Licensing of rights to use property	2%
Merchandise sales	1.5%

Source: IBISWorld, March 2012

Industry Costs

Profit	7.0%
Wages	63.0%
Purchases	10.0%
Depreciation	5.0%
Marketing	7.8%
Rent & Utilities	6.0%
Other	1.2%

Source: IBISWorld, March 2012

Major US team sport revenue

League	Share of industry revenue (%)
NFL	37.4
MLB	28.7
NBA	18.7
NHL	13.9
Other	1.3

Source: *Forbes*.com

Basketball Teams (professional)

SIC 7941-03	NAICS 711211	

Pricing Tips

- The National Basketball Association's (NBA) New York Knicks is valued at approximately $655 million, while the Milwaukee Bucks are valued at approximately $258 million.

  Source: *Forbes* magazine

- The Average Annual Revenue is approximately $3.8 Billion.

Source: www.statisticbrain.com/professional-sports

Benchmark Data

- Note: For more information see Benchmark Data under Baseball Teams

		Franchise
Baskin-Robbins Ice Cream (See also Ice Cream/Yogurt Shops)		
Approx. Total Investment		A net worth of at least $250,000
Estimated Annual Sales/Unit		$195,000
SIC 2024-98	NAICS 722213	Number of Businesses/Units 6,000
Rules of Thumb		
➢ 45 to 50 percent of annual sales plus inventory		

Resources

Websites
- www.baskinrobbins.com

		Franchise
Batteries Plus		
Approx. Total Investment		$174,100 to $348,700
Estimated Annual Sales/Unit		Not Available
	NAICS 441310	Number of Businesses/Units 485
Rules of Thumb		
➢ 30 to 35 percent of annual sales plus inventory		

Resources

Websites
- www.batteriesplus.com

Beauty Salons (See also Barber Shops, Nail Salons, & Hair Care)		
SIC 7231-06	NAICS 812112	Number of Businesses/Units 1,078,141
Rules of Thumb		
➢ 35 percent of annual revenues; add fixtures, equipment & inventory		
➢ 2 times SDE plus inventory		
➢ 4 times monthly sales plus inventory		
➢ 2.5 times EBIT		

Pricing Tips

- "25% to 35% of annual sales"
- "Whether the operators are W-2 or #1099—and also how the chemical product costs are debited."
- "What percentage of the gross sales is generated by a service generating owner and how may the change in ownership shift the owner's income? The most effective pricing point is utilizing the SDE."
- "Check reason(s) for empty stations—turnover? Are stations rented?"
- "1. Check on chair rental versus commissioned stylist. 2. Check on staff turnover. It can be very high. 3. Reputation and location very important."
- " . . . installation of beauty shops in today's market costs from $2,000 to $2,200 per station (verify), but selling price is usually about $1,500 to $2,000 per station. The ultramodern shops usually have a considerable amount of tenant's improvements which should be taken into consideration . . . Rents are from $50 to $75 per station or the operators rent a station and retain a portion or all of the commissions earned . . . with resulting loss of goodwill value. Other approaches: (1) is to price the salon at 20 percent of gross sales, (2) 1–1.5 times recasted cash flow, or (3) 35 percent of gross sales plus equipment & inventory."

Expert Comments

"The beauty industry is as old as mankind and essentially a replenishment industry, the resale possibilities are endless, rebranding is the next frontier."

"Location and marketing are big factors in the success of a salon."

"Highly competitive industry with a fair level of risk. Can be easily replicated. Location, location, location."

"Levels of competition are high due to market saturation. The beauty industry needs education and direction to avoid the pitfalls of market saturation."

"Market saturation has occurred likely due to the creative nature of the salon professional wanting to expand yet not completing the necessary business market research. The risks are considered low because of the small monetary initial investment. The beauty industry trends will always grow due to vanity and fashion."

"Fair amount of turnover, but fair amount of buyers."

Benchmark Data

Statistics (Hair & Nail Salons)

Number of Establishments	1,078,141
Average Profit Margin	5.5%
Revenue per Employee	$28,100
Average Number of Employees	1
Average Wages per Employee	$14,101

Source: IBISWorld, April 2012

Products and Services Segmentation

Haircutting services 42.8%
Hair coloring services 18.1%
Other hair care services... 13.1%
Nail care services 10.2%
Other beauty care services... 5.7%
Merchandise sales.. 5.4%
Skin care services... 4.7%

Source: IBISWorld, April 2012

Industry Costs

Profit 5.5%
Wages.. 50.1%
Purchases.. 30.2%
Depreciation... 2.2%
Marketing 2.4%
Rent & Utilities 8.2%
Other.. 1.4%

Source: IBISWorld, April 2012

Market Share

Regis Corporation... 5.0%

Source: IBISWorld, April 2012

Establishments by Employment Size

Number of Employees ....Share
1 to 4... 63.5%
5 to 9... 21.5%
10 to 19... 10.9%

Source: IBISWorld, April 2012

- "If seller earns commission credits, do not include them in the owner's benefit—just what is earned as solely an owner."
- "A successful salon's gross sales should average $1000 per week per employee."
- "Full-time operators should produce a minimum of $50,000 annual gross revenue."

Expenses as a Percentage of Annual Sales

Cost of goods... 12%
Payroll/labor Costs... 60%
Occupancy .... 10% to 20%
Profit (estimated pretax) .... 10% to 15%

Industry Trend

- "More and more foreign buyers and growth in chain operations."
- "Growing trend with the Baby Boomers being more concerned with aging and graying."
- "Mainstream beauty services will continue. Natural processes for beauty treatments. Minor cosmetic surgery/treatments will interchange with spa and salon services. Male client services are increasing."

Seller Financing

- "3 to 5 years"

Questions

- "What percentage of the gross sales is generated by the seller?"

Resources

Trade Publications

- Modern Salon: www.modernsalon.com

Bed & Breakfasts (See also Inns)		
SIC 7011-07	NAICS 721191	Number of Businesses/Units 4,564

Rules of Thumb

➤ 550 percent of annual sales includes inventory and real estate

➤ 4.2 times gross room sales for small B&Bs (less than eight rooms); a little higher for dinner-service inns, 4.5; these are for businesses as opposed to real-estate-driven small properties

➤ 8 times SDE includes inventory and real estate

Pricing Tips

- "The larger inns are selling for 8 (w/o seller financing) to 10 times (w/seller financing) adjusted net operating income. The base real estate value of the smaller B&B contributes to a large part of the value. In small, supplemental income B&Bs, their value is typically $25,000 to $50,000 more than the base real estate value as a house or other real estate use. There are probably more supplemental income B&Bs than cash flow inns of the $20K+ U.S. B&Bs. Gross Rent Multiplier is in the 5 to 6 range. Midwest value is usually $80K to $100K/guestroom; 8 to 10 times operating income prior to debt based on the degree of seller financing. Smaller (less than seven rooms), non-urban B&Bs may not have any net cash flow and are typically sold for slightly above real estate value."

- "Smaller B&Bs (fewer than 8 rooms) are usually real-estate driven."

- "$50,000 to $100,000 per guest room. In the Midwest, the year-round larger inns are selling from $80,000 to $100,000 per guestroom. 3 times net operating income + $20,000 to $40,000 for the aesthetics & tax benefits + value of real estate & furnishings."

Expert Comments

"B&B buyers must make both a lifestyle & financial purchase decision. Innkeeping is one of the few businesses that you want to live where you work! For the past 5+ years, we have had smaller B&Bs sold/converted back to homes than we've had homes being converted to inns! Start-ups are more difficult to accomplish today versus the mid- 1980's primarily due to rising real estate values, high conversion cost, zoning restrictions, tougher lending practices, & a lack of market. demand for innkeeping (during a strong economy). Some of the smaller inns in less popular areas were converted to alternative uses and a minority of inns closed for avoidance of taxes from capital gains and depreciation recapture."

Benchmark Data

Statistics (Bed & Breakfast & Hostel Accommodations)

Number of Establishments	4,564
Average Profit Margin	20%
Revenue per Employee	$74,600
Average Number of Employees	4.6
Average Wages per Employee	$19,084

Source: IBISWorld, August 2012

Products and Services Segmentation

Bed & Breakfast	69%
Other—including Hostels	31%

Source: IBISWorld, August 2012

Major Market Segmentation

Vacation travelers	58.2%
Family travelers	21.8%
Business travelers	12%
Other—including meetings	8%

Source: IBISWorld, August 2012

Industry Costs

Profit	20.0%
Wages	25.6%
Purchases	15.0%
Depreciation	2.5%
Marketing	2.5%
Rent & Utilities	14.5%
Other	19.9%

Source: IBISWorld, August 2012

- "There are more small B&Bs becoming homes vs. homes becoming B&Bs. Most new innkeepers are replacing an income, and the supplemental income B&Bs tend to sell as homes. The larger, more profitable inns, that are within 3 hrs. driving of a metro area, are doing better than ever due to closer & quicker getaway travel patterns."

- "B&B buyers must make both a lifestyle & financial purchase decision. Innkeeping is one of the few businesses in which you want to live where you work! For the past 5+ years, we have had smaller B&Bs sold/converted back to homes than we've had homes being converted to inns! Start-ups are more difficult to accomplish today versus the mid-1980's primarily due to rising real estate values, high conversion cost, zoning restrictions, tougher lending practices, & a lack of market demand for innkeeping (during a strong economy). Some of the smaller inns in less popular areas were converted to alternative uses and a minority of inns closed for avoidance of taxes from capital gains & depreciation recapture."

- "The smaller the inn and lower the business income, the more the real estate value factor weighs heavily in the formula. The larger the inn and the higher the business income, the less this factor affects total value. Many of the larger inns have been selling in the 8 to 10 capitalization rate of net income, less any needed repairs, and up to a 20% discount if seller financing is not involved. Payroll/labor costs 12% to 15% with working owner; profit (estimated) 40% to 45% of sales"

- "The larger inns are selling for 8 (w/o seller financing) to 10 times (w/seller financing) adjusted net operating income. The base real estate value of the smaller B&B contributes to a large part of the value. In small, supplemental income B&Bs, their value is typically $25,000 to $50,000 more than the base real estate value as a house or other real estate use. There are probably more supplemental income B&Bs than cash flow inns of the 20K+ U.S. B&Bs."

- Profit (estimated) 40% to 45% of sales"

- "Many resort inns within three hours of a metro area can produce occupancy in the 40% to 50% range. Urban inns can produce 50% to 80% occupancy. Most non-urban inns below seven guestrooms provide to only supplemental income. It's kind of like owning a duplex; you can live in a better location & house than you could otherwise afford, but you don't give up your day job. About 50% of the U.S. B&Bs are this size."

- "Bed and Breakfast/Country Inn Statistics—The data below is from Studies and Surveys done by www.innkeeping.org—a very informative site.

Performance (in medians)

- ✓ Occupancy Rate   43.7%
- ✓ Average Daily Rate $150
- ✓ Revenue per Available Room $58

About the Inns

Some interesting data from an Industry *Study of Innkeeping Operations and Finance* from the Professional Association of Innkeepers International (PAII).

- ✓ 72% of B&Bs are run by couples
- ✓ 79% of innkeepers live on premises
- ✓ The typical B&B has between 4 and 11 rooms, with 6 guest rooms or suites being the average
- ✓ The average B&B has been open for 15 years
- ✓ The average age of the oldest part of a B&B building is 107 years
- ✓ 29% of B&Bs were in rural locations, 23% were urban, 5% suburban, and 43% were village
- ✓ 94% of rooms have private baths
- ✓ 36% have achieved an "historical designation" by a local, state or national historic preservation organization
- ✓ 5,700 square feet is the average size for a B&B
- ✓ 93% offer free high speed wireless Internet
- ✓ Most B&Bs provide the following in common areas: Internet, magazines, hot/cold beverages, board games, fireplace, refrigerator, newspapers, telephone, cookies/cakes/candies/fruit, fresh flowers, and televisions.
- ✓ Most B&Bs provide the following in guest rooms: Internet, television, luxury bed/linens, premium branded toiletries, robes, fireplaces, magazines and jetted tubs.

Expenses as a Percentage of Annual Sales

Cost of goods	15%
Payroll/labor Costs	10%
Occupancy	10%
Profit (estimated pretax)	10%

Industry Trend
- "B&Bs primarily cater to affluent, baby boomer travelers. That market appears to be growing. This is also the market that the next generation of innkeepers is coming from."

Seller Financing
- "7 years"
- "Seller is often 2nd 10 percent of sales price, 20-year term, 7-year balloon."
- "5 to 8 years; partial financing."

Questions
- "Can you show me how your B&B will work for me financially and in lifestyle?"

Resources
Websites
- www.innsforsale.com
- www.bedandbreakfast.com

Associations
- Professional Association of Innkeepers International—a wonderful site, lots of good information: www.innkeeping.org

Bedding and Mattress Shops (Retail)

SIC 5712-09	NAICS 442110	Number of Businesses/Units 8,326

Rules of Thumb
➢ 35 percent of annual sales plus inventory

Pricing Tips
- "More retail locations equal more favorable manufacturer pricing."

Expert Comments
"Bedding continues to be a needed product and the consumer now has a perceived need for enhanced comfort and a better night's rest."

Benchmark Data
Statistics (Bed and Mattress Stores)

Number of Establishments	8,326
Average Profit Margin	1.5%
Revenue per Employee	$237,700
Average Number of Employees	5.3
Average Wages per Employee	$30,073

Source: IBISWorld, July 2012

Products and Services Segmentation

Traditional mattresses	49.3%
Specialty mattresses	23.1%
Frames and box springs	19%
Other, including bedding and pillows	8.6%

Source: IBISWorld, July 2012

Industry Costs

Profit	1.5%
Wages	13.0%
Purchases	59.4%
Depreciation	0.5%
Marketing	6.7%
Rent & Utilities	7.0%
Other	11.9%

Source: IBISWorld, July 2012

- **Major Players**
  - ✓ Mattress Firm
  - ✓ Select Comfort
  - ✓ Sleepy's

Source: IBISWorld, July 2012

- "Increased ticket % for same store sales for the same month as opposed to previous year."

Expenses as a Percentage of Annual Sales

Cost of goods	25%
Payroll/labor Costs	10%
Occupancy	20%
Profit (estimated pretax)	45%

Industry Trend

- "Mattress Firm has completed its acquisition of fellow Top 100 retailer Mattress Giant, adding approximately 180 stores in seven markets in Florida and Texas.

  "The deal, valued at about $47 million, makes Mattress Firm the nation's largest specialty bedding retailer with more than 1,000 company-owned and franchised stores.

  "The deal effectively ends Mattress Giant's presence as a bedding retailer. The company once had more than 300 stores in a dozen states. Last year, it sold 55 stores to Mattress Firm and another 67 stores to Hicksville, NY–based Sleepy's."

  Source: "Mattress Firm completes Giant Acquisition" by Larry Thomas,
  Furniture Today, www.furnituretoday.com May 3, 2012

- "Bedding specialty stores, a fast-growing channel of distribution, may gain even more ground on their competition. Furniture stores, meanwhile, may lose share.

  "The question about mattress shopping plans produced findings suggesting more growth ahead for the bedding specialty store channel, which had a 42% share of the mattress distribution pie in 2009, the last year.

  "Furniture/Today examined bedding distribution trends. Ahead of that report, the Furniture/Today-HGTV Mattress Survey may portend some big changes in the offing. The survey found that 46% of consumers plan to shop for bedding first at a bedding specialty store, if price is not a consideration."

Source: "Survey: Bedding Stores Poised to Gain Ground" by David Perry, *Furniture Today*, March 29, 2011

Questions

- "What is the reason for selling? Where do you stand in terms of your relationships with the major bedding suppliers? What customer service issues might be pending?"

Resources

Trade Publications
- Bedding Today: www.furnituretoday.com/

Beef 'O' Brady's Family Sports Pubs		Franchise
Approx. Total Investment		$206,500 to $826,500
Estimated Annual Sales/Unit		$900,000
	NAICS 722410	Number of Businesses/Units 216

Rules of Thumb

➤ 22 percent of annual sales plus inventory

Resources

Websites
- www.beefobradys.com

Beer & Wine Stores – Retail (See also Liquor Stores)		
SIC 5921-04	NAICS 445310	

Rules of Thumb

➤ 4 times monthly sales plus inventory

Benchmark Data

- For Benchmark data see Liquor Stores

Beer Distributorships/Wholesalers		
SIC 5181-01	NAICS 422810	Number of Businesses/Units 2,013

Rules of Thumb

➤ $5.00 to $15 per case sold over the last 12 months; add hard assets & inventory. Multiple per case is dependent on brands sold—the popular ones command the higher multiples.

> ➤ "These types of distributing businesses are usually sold for the price of inventory at cost, plus the rolling stock, plus the land and improvements, if these are part of the sale, plus $1.00 for each case delivered per year, plus $1.50 for each keg delivered per year."

Pricing Tips

- "The two most important characteristics are (1) the brands carried, and (2) the territory.
- "Brands vary considerably in market sales, and also vary regionally. Territories that are densely populated tend to be serviced more efficiently."
- 1 U.S. BBL (beer barrel) = 31 U.S. gallons = 13.778 = 24/12-oz. cases

Expert Comments

"Franchise restrictions are important constraints on resale."

Benchmark Data

Statistics (Beer Wholesaling)

Number of Establishments	1,693
Average Profit Margin	16.1%
Revenue per Employee	$542,400
Average Number of Employees	64
Average Wages per Employee	$47,472

Source: IBISWorld, March 2012

Products and Services Segmentation

Cans of beer and ale (12 oz.)	45.8%
Cases of bottled beer and ale	38.3%
Cans of beer and ale (not 12 oz.)	9.1%
Beer and ale barrels and kegs	5.2%
Other malt beverages and brewing products	1.6%

Source: IBISWorld, March 2012

Major Market Segmentation

Eating and drinking places	39%
Retail liquor stores	23%
Other (including casinos)	18%
Food stores	15%
Hotels and motels	05%

Source: IBISWorld, March 2012

Industry Costs

Profit	16.1%
Wages	8.8%
Purchases	45.4%
Depreciation	0.7%
Marketing	2.0%
Rent & Utilities	1.5%
Other	25.5%

Source: IBISWorld, March 2012

Establishments by Employment Size

Number of Employees ....Percentage
Less than 20 ....45%

Source: IBISWorld, March 2012

- "Market values for beer distributors tend to be discussed as a multiple of cases sold in the past 12 months. These often vary from $5 to $15 per case sold, for well-established brands and successful operations. Struggling brands and operations can be priced less. There is no comparable metric for wine or spirits."

Industry Trend

- "The 'three-tier' system set up in most states after Prohibition is being challenged, at least on the edges, by interstate shipping of wine. Legal developments in this area will affect the value of wine distributors, although not beer distributors, over the next few years. Once you have a good operation in a decent area, this business will keep producing cash. Remember, the beer and wine business is over 2,000 years old."

Resources

Websites
- www.beerinstitute.org

Trade Publications
- Beer Marketer's Insights: www.beerinsights.com

Associations
- The National Beer Wholesalers Association (NBWA)—an informative Web site: www.nbwa.org

Beer Taverns — Beer & Wine (See also Bars, Brew Pubs)

	NAICS 722410	

Rules of Thumb

➢ 6 times monthly sales plus inventory

➢ 1 to 1.5 times annual EBIT

➢ 55 percent of annual sales plus inventory

Pricing Tips

- "There are 1,980 ounces in a keg, less 10 percent waste, about 1,700 net ounces per keg. If there are 12 ounces (net) in a glass of beer, divide 12 ounces into 1,700 net ounces per keg to determine cost and number of glasses that should be poured from that keg. Determine what a 12-ounce glass of beer is selling for, then multiply that times the number of glasses that is poured from the keg. This will give you the total gross per keg."

Resources

Websites
- www.beerinstitute.org

	Franchise
Ben & Jerry's (See also Ice Cream/Yogurt Shops)	

Approx. Total Investment	$175,250 to $451,250
Estimated Annual Sales/Unit	$300,000

SIC 2024-98	NAICS 722213	Number of Businesses/Units 810

Rules of Thumb

> ➢ 35 to 40 percent of annual sales plus inventory

Benchmark Data

- Estimated Annual Sales (2011):
  - ✓ Cold Stone Creamery: $325,000;
  - ✓ Friendly's Ice Cream: $1.2 million;
  - ✓ Baskin Robbins: $225,000

	Franchise
Between Rounds Bakery Sandwich Cafe	

Approx. Total Investment	$283,000 to $381,000
Estimated Annual Sales/Unit	Not Available

SIC 5461-01	NAICS 722211	Number of Businesses/Units 5

Rules of Thumb

> ➢ 40 to 45 percent of annual sales plus inventory

Resources

Websites

- www.betweenroundsbagels.com

Bicycle Shops	

SIC 5941-41	NAICS 451110	Number of Businesses/Units 4,065

Rules of Thumb

> ➢ 20 percent of annual sales plus inventory
> ➢ 1.5 times SDE plus inventory

Pricing Tips

- "If shops don't repair as well as sell, they could lose most of their income. Need to have mechanic in store!"

Benchmark Data

Statistics (Bicycle Dealership and Repair)

Number of Establishments... 4,065
Average Profit Margin 4.1%
Revenue per Employee .... n/a
Average Number of Employees 6
Average Wages per Employee $46,712

Source: IBISWorld, March 2012

Products and Services Segmentation

Mountain bikes.. 30%
Hybrid bikes 21%
Other bikes 20.5%
Road bikes.. 19%
Bicycle parts and accessories 05%
Repair and maintenance services 4.5%

Source: IBISWorld, March 2012

Industry Costs

Profit 4.1%
Wages... 19.7%
Purchases... 60.0%
Depreciation.. 2.0%
Marketing 5.5%
Rent & Utilities 4.0%
Other... 4.7%

Source: IBISWorld, March 2012

Market Share

Dick's Sporting Goods Inc... 16.0%

Source: IBISWorld, March 2012

- "According to recent research from the NBDA (2011), the average specialty bicycle retailer had gross annual sales of $866,817 up from an average of $550,000 in 2005. The typical specialty bicycle retailer did business from a store about 5,000 square feet in size. 84% of them had one location, and 92.8% had no more than two locations.

  "The average bicycle dealer's revenue was 47.4% bicycles, 35.5% parts and accessories, 10.7% bicycle repair, 0.8% bicycle rental, 1.9% fitness equipment and 3.5% 'other.' The average store sells approximately 650 bicycles per year, carries five bicycle brands (though not all in great depth), and numerous accessories brands. Recent trends are toward consolidation with retailers carrying fewer bicycle brands, sometimes at the urging of their suppliers who want more representation for their products. Gross margins on bicycles average about 37%, though the break-even point has been shown to be 38.6% for the average store (the average 'cost of doing business'). Margins on hardgoods are generally higher than those for bicycles (48% gross margin)."

  Source: "The Professional Dealer," Industry Overview, National Bicycle Dealers Association,
www.nbda.com—an excellent and informative site.

- "The approximately 4,200 specialty bicycle retailers commanded approximately 14% of the bicycle market in terms of unit sales in 2010, but 44% of the dollars, a dominant dollar share. Dealer price points generally start at around $200, with the average at $524, though prices can range into the thousands. While the number of specialty bicycle stores has declined in recent years due to consolidation, they are responsible for approximately the same amount of business through these fewer (but larger) stores today."

Source: Industry Overview, National Bicycle Dealers Association, www.nbda.com

Annual Gross Sales

More than $2 million	5%
$1.5 to $1.99 million	3%
$1 to $1.499 million	7%
$500,000 to $999,000	20%
Less than $500,000	65%

Source: "Want to Start a Bike Shop." Published by the National Bicycle Dealers

- Here are the average expenses for specialty bicycle retailers from the National Bicycle Dealers Association (NBDA) article "Want to Start a Bike Shop." While the data may be a bit dated, the percentages are still fairly accurate and a good guideline.

Expenses as a percentage of annual sales:

Payroll Expenses	20.5%
Occupancy	7.7%
Advertising/Promotion	3%
Auto/Delivery	0.5%
Depreciation	0.9%
Insurance	0.8%
Licenses/Other Taxes	0.5%
Professional Services	0.5%
Office Supplies/Postage	1.2%
Telephone	0.6%
Travel/Entertainment	0.4%
Other	1.3%
Total Operating Expenses	37.7%
Net Income Before Tax	4.2%
Gross Margin on Bicycle Sales	36%
Gross Margin on Clothing Sales	43%
Gross Margin on Other Equipment	48.1%

Industry Trend

- "While the number of physical stores has clearly declined, specialty bicycle retailers still sold approximately 3.1 million bicycles in 2011—a historically healthy number. This leads to the conclusion that the stores are becoming larger on average, with similar sales volume through fewer stores."

Source: "A Look at the Bicycle Industry's Vital Statistics," National Bicycle Dealers Association, Industry Overview 2011

- "2011 was a solid year for the U.S. bicycle industry, with direct effect sales of $6 billion, including retail sales of bicycles, related parts and accessories, through all channels of distribution.

"The size of the industry has remained remarkably stable since 2003, with sales between $5.8 billion and $6.1 billion each year (the exception being 2009). For comparison purposes, we have projected the industry at $5.3 billion in 2002, $5.4 billion in 2003, $5.8 billion in 2004, $6.1 billion in 2005 (an all-time high), $5.8 billion in 2006, $6.0 billion in 2007, $6.0 billion in 2008, $5.6 billion in 2009, $6 billion in 2010, and $6 billion in 2011."

Source: "A Look at the Bicycle Industry's Vital Statistics," The NBDA Statpak, www.nbda.com

Resources

Trade Publications
- Outspoken: Published by the NBDA Bicycle Retailer & Industry News—an informative site: www.bicycleretailer.com

Associations
- National Bicycle Dealers Association (NBDA): www.nbda.com
- Bicycle Product Suppliers Association—excellent site, well worth visiting: www.bpsa.org

Big Apple Bagels	Franchise
Approximate Total Investment	$254,300 to $379,628
Estimated Annual Sales/Unit	$350,000
NAICS 722211	Number of Businesses/Units 100

Rules of Thumb
- 35 to 40 percent of annual sales plus inventory
- Note: See also Bagel Shops

Resources

Websites
- www.babcorp.com

Big City Burrito	Franchise
NAICS 722211	

Rules of Thumb
- 50%–55% of annual sales plus inventory

Big O Tires (See also Auto Tire Stores)	Franchise
Approx. Total Investment	$247,500 to $958,300
Estimated Annual Sales/Unit	Not Available
NAICS 441320	Number of Businesses/Units 470

Rules of Thumb
- 35 percent of annual sales plus inventory

Resources

Websites
- www.bigotires.com

Billboard Advertising Companies (Outdoor Advertising)		
SIC 7312-01	NAICS 541850	Number of Businesses/Units 2,115

Rules of Thumb

➢ 12 times EBITDA

➢ 500 percent of annual sales

Pricing Tips

- "Billboards are bought and sold based on multiples of Net Revenue and Cash Flow, so these are the most common methods of valuation."
- "Values of billboard companies tend to be higher in large metropolitan areas, and lower in rural areas. Prices tend to be between 3 x and 6 x annual revenue."
- "EBITDA is normally 45% to 50%. Cap rates tend to be very low, usually more like real estate than an operating business. Acquirers prefer long-term leases at low rates for existing billboard locations."

"Billboard companies are usually worth surprisingly high prices in the market. Buyers and sellers rely almost exclusively on market multiples that are widely recognized as the best measures of fair market value. Discount rates and capitalization rates in this industry are more closely aligned with real estate yields than returns on operating businesses."

Source: "Appraising Billboard Companies" by Jeffrey P. Wright, ASA, CFA, *Business Valuation Review*

Expert Comments

"Industry growing, difficult to build new billboards"

"Revenue growth is up, while other advertising media are experiencing trouble. City, county and state rules controlling new billboard construction continue to tighten."

Benchmark Data

Statistics (Billboard & Outdoor Advertising)

Number of Establishments	2,655
Average Profit Margin	9.3%
Revenue per Employee	$263,500
Average Number of Employees	11
Average Wages per Employee	$44,797

Source: IBISWorld, May 2012

Products and Services Segmentation

Billboard advertising (bulletins)	50.3%
Street furniture and other urban fixture displays	13.6%
Billboard advertising (posters)	13.0%
Alternative and other leased displays	12.4%
Transit displays	10.7%

Source: IBISWorld, May 2012

Major Market Segmentation

Other	29.2%
Amusement and miscellaneous companies	16.6%
Finance, insurance and real estate companies	12.6%
Public transportation, hotels and resorts	9.6%
Retailers	8.4%
Communications companies	8.2%
Restaurants	8.2%
Media and advertising companies	7.2%

Source: IBISWorld, May 2012

Industry Costs

Profit	9.3%
Wages	17.2%
Purchases	6.0%
Depreciation	18.0%
Marketing	3.0%
Rent & Utilities	35.5%
Other	11.0%

Source: IBISWorld, May 2012

Market Share

CC Media Holdings Inc.	17.1%
Lamar Advertising Company	16.5%
CBS Corporation	15.1%

Source: IBISWorld, May 2012

Enterprises by Employment Size

No. of Employees	No. of Enterprises	Share
0 to 4	1,505	70.0%
5 to 9	279	13.0%
10 to 19	174	8.1%

Source: IBISWorld, May 2012

- "Achieving cash flow margins of 35% or higher"
- "Net revenue multiples range from 3 to 8 times, and cash flow multiples range from 7 to 18 times."
- "Occupancy cost = 20%
  Profit (estimated pretax) = 20%"
- "EBITDA margins are very high in this industry, usually around 45% to 50%. Fixed expenses normally represent a rather high percentage of fixed expenses, with 75% to 85% typical for larger companies. This includes site leases, taxes & licensing, lighting, vehicles, and to some degree labor. Workers must be employees to change advertising even if ad revenue is not strong. Variable expenses include a small number of items like printing and sales commissions."

    Source: "Appraising Billboard Companies" by Jeffrey P. Wright, ASA, CFA, *Business Valuation Review*

Expenses as a Percentage of Annual Sales

Cost of goods	05%
Payroll/labor Costs	05%
Occupancy	10%
Profit (estimated pretax)	45%

Industry Trend

- "Stabilization, should weather the recession better than other media."

Seller Financing

- "5 years"

Questions

- "Net revenue, cash flow, lease costs and occupancy levels"

Resources

Trade Publications

- BPS Outdoor: www.bpsoutdoor.com

Billiards (See also American Poolplayers Association)		
SIC 7999-12	NAICS 339920	Number of Businesses/Units 3,000

Rules of Thumb

➢ 50 percent of annual sales plus inventory

Benchmark Data

- "According to the 2012 *USA Sports Participation Survey—Billiards*, conducted by the Sporting Goods Manufacturers Association (SGMA):
  - ✓ There are 36,831,000 Billiards/Pool participants in the U.S.
  - ✓ There are 12,132,000 core (13+/year) Billiards/Pool participants in the U.S.
  - ✓ 65% of all Billiards/Pool participants and 68% of core (13+/year) Billiards/Pool participants are male.
  - ✓ 59% of all Billiards/Pool participants and 55% of core (13+/year) Billiards/Pool
  - ✓ participants are between ages 25 and 54.
  - ✓ 57% of all Billiards/Pool participants have a household income of under $75,000 per year.
  - ✓ 42% of all Billiards/Pool participants reside in a market size of 2,000,000+
  - ✓ 42% of all Billiards/Pool participants have a college degree or higher.

Source: Billiard Congress of America, www.home.bca-pool.com

Resources

Websites

- www.bca-pool.com

		Franchise
Blackjack Pizza (See also Pizza Shops)		
Approx. Total Investment		Not Available
Estimated Annual Sales/Unit		Not Available
SIC 5812-22	NAICS 722211	Number of Businesses/Units 45

Rules of Thumb

➢ 40% percent of annual sales plus inventory

➢ 3 to 4 times SDE (15% discount for cash) plus inventory

Resources

Websites

- www.blackjackpizza.com

	Franchise

Blimpie — America's Sub Shop (See also Sandwich Shops & Franchises)	
Approx. Total Investment	$60,000 to $200,000
Estimated Annual Sales/Unit	$185,000

SIC 5812-19	NAICS 722211	Number of Businesses/Units 920

Rules of Thumb

➢ 45 to 50 percent of annual sales plus inventory

Benchmark Data

- For Benchmark data see Sandwich Shops

Resources

Websites

- www.kahalamgmt.com

Boat Dealers (See also Marinas)	
SIC 5551-04	NAICS 441222	Number of Businesses/Units 40,458

Rules of Thumb

➢ 2 to 3 times SDE includes used boat inventory, parts and FF&E

➢ "Most dealerships finance their new boat inventory with flooring companies which are now requiring some type of industry background and/or experience. In most cases the new owner will take over the financing arrangements with the flooring companies for all current and future new boat inventory. The multiple can vary depending."

Pricing Tips

- "Boat dealerships in the Pacific Northwest typically sell for 2–3 times SDE which includes used boat inventory, parts and FF&E."

Benchmark Data

Statistics (Boat Dealership and Repair)

Number of Establishments	40,458
Average Profit Margin	1.8%
Revenue per Employee	$182,200
Average Number of Employees	2
Average Wages per Employee	$23,450

Source: IBISWorld, April 2012

Products and Services Segmentation

New boats.. 56.3%
Boat repairs and maintenance.. 19.0%
Other.. 14.0%
Used boats.. 10.7%

Source: IBISWorld, April 2012

Industry Costs

Profit 1.8%
Wages... 13.1%
Purchases... 69.5%
Depreciation.. 0.6%
Marketing.. 1.0%
Rent & Utilities 4.5%
Other.. 9.5%

Source: IBISWorld, April 2012

Market Share

MarineMax Inc. 3.9%

Source: IBISWorld, April 2012

- "Ninety-five percent of the 12.4 million registered boats in the U.S. in 2011 were less than 26 feet."

Source: National Marine Manufacturers Association, www.nmma.org, May 2012

Industry Trend

- "Leading a recovery are sales of aluminum power boats (primarily fishing and pontoon boats), which were up four percent in 2011. There were 77,150 aluminum power boats sold in 2011. The top ten states for aluminum power boat retail sales were (in order of highest to lowest): Texas, Minnesota, Michigan, Louisiana, Wisconsin, Florida, Alabama, Missouri, Arkansas and Illinois."

Source: National Marine Manufacturers Association, www.nmma.org, May 2012

Resources

Associations
- National Marine Manufacturers Association (NMMA): www.nmma.org

		Franchise
Boba Loca Specialty Drinks		
	NAICS 722213	Number of Businesses/Units 25

Rules of Thumb

➤ 30 percent of annual sales plus inventory

Resources

Websites
- www.bobaloca.com

Book & Stationery Stores (See also Book Stores)

SIC 5942-01	NAICS 451211	

Pricing Tips
- "Fixtures and equipment value plus inventory at wholesale cost, plus one-half year's net profit"

Book Stores — Adult

SIC 5942-01	NAICS 451211	

Rules of Thumb
➤ 100 percent of annual sales includes inventory

Pricing Tips
- "Half down at closing; other half financed and used to prove gross sales (a kind of earnout schedule)."

Expert Comments
"Internet retail is driving down profits."

Benchmark Data
- "1,000 SF should equal $200k–$250k in gross sales."

Expenses as a Percentage of Annual Sales

Cost of goods	20%
Payroll/labor Costs	n/a
Occupancy	12%
Profit (estimated pretax)	40%

Industry Trend
- "Slight drop but steady in some markets."

Book Stores—Christian (See also Book Stores—New)

SIC 5942-11	NAICS 451211	Number of Businesses/Units 3,600

Rules of Thumb
➤ 15 percent of annual sales plus inventory

Industry Trend
- "According to reports, online sales were up as much as 33 percent on Cyber Monday this year, sounding a positive note for the dismal economy. But owners of local stores and boutiques that do not offer online shopping say its boom has had a negative effect on their bottom line.
- "The Bible and Book Center in Baton Rouge, La., is just one of countless shops that are struggling against the Internet this Christmas. Opened in 1959, the family-owned Christian bookstore is a landmark in the Capitol city. But now

this long-established mom-and-pop shop is in danger."

Source: "Christian Book Store Struggles in Internet Culture" by Erika McManus, www.Fox News, December 05, 2011

Resources

Associations

- Christian Book Association: www.cbaonline.org

Book Stores — New		
SIC 5942-01	NAICS 451211	Number of Businesses/Units 30,400

Rules of Thumb

➤ 15 to 20 percent of annual sales plus inventory

➤ 1.5 to 2 SDE plus inventory

Pricing Tips

- "Gross margin, occupancy costs, diversity of products (non-book items), frequency of community events are all important factors when considering the price of a book store."

Expert Comments

"While the future of book stores is widely considered bleak, consumers love their local book store and, with the proper strategy, a buyer can be found."

Benchmark Data

Statistics (Book Stores)

Number of Establishments	27,366
Average Profit Margin	1.3%
Revenue per Employee	$100,700
Average Number of Employees	6
Average Wages per Employee	$13,405

Source: IBISWorld, May 2012

Products and Services Segmentation

Other merchandise	35.0%
Trade books	32.4%
Textbooks	22.1%
Religious books	4.1%
Magazines and newspapers	2.9%
Paperback books	2.5%
Other books	1.0%

Source: IBISWorld, May 2012

Industry Costs

Profit	1.3%
Wages	12.8%
Purchases	70.1%
Depreciation	3.3%
Marketing	4.0%
Rent & Utilities	2.4%
Other	6.1%

Source: IBISWorld, May 2012

Market Share

Barnes & Noble Inc.	35.4%
Follett Higher Education Group	8.1%

Source: IBISWorld, May 2012

- "Inventory turns of 3-4 times should be realized. Non-book sales should be at least 20% of overall sales. Store should be doing at least one event per week."

- "And though this would be the company's (Border's book stores) last year of profitability, it continued to expand, building huge stores of 25,000 and 30,000 square feet right into the Internet boom. Sales per square foot in its superstores plummeted from an average of $261 in 1997 to $173 by 2009. Borders even purchased a stationery company, Paperchase, in 2004, as handwritten correspondence withered. And then there's the company's entry into digital books: If you didn't know Borders had an e-reader called Kobo, you're not alone."

Source: *Bloomberg Businessweek*, November 14, 2011

Expenses as a Percentage of Annual Sales

Cost of goods	30% to 35%
Payroll/labor Costs	20% to 25%
Occupancy	06% to 10%
Profit (estimated pretax)	02% to 04%

Industry Trend

- "As Barnes & Noble fights for its future, the publishing industry holds its breath."

- "Several iterations later, the Nook and, by extension, Barnes & Noble, at times seem the only things standing between traditional book publishers and oblivion."

- "These are trying times for almost everyone in the book business. Since 2002, the United States lost roughly 500 independent bookstores—nearly one out of five. About 650 bookstores vanished when Borders went out of business last year."

- "Independents account for less than 10 percent of business, and Target, Walmart and the like carry far smaller selections than traditional bookstores."

Source: "The Bookstore's Last Stand" by Julie Bosman, *New York Times*, January 29, 2012

- "Brick-and-mortar bookstores are closing faster than you can say 'Kindle Fire.' But from Worcester to Truro, bookstores are resurfacing in an unexpected place: the town library.

   "Storage closets, refurbished basements, and forgotten areas of library buildings are now home to little shops with hundreds of used books, many of them in tiptop condition, available for sale. For less than the price of a shipping charge from Amazon, readers are helping their libraries buy museum passes, screen films, put on lectures, and offer other programs."

Source: "Hard Cover, Soft Sell" by Kathleen Pierce, *Boston Globe*, February 28, 2012

- "Over the past three decades, independent bookstores have faced a series of competitive threats. First, came the rise of chain bookstores, followed by the explosive growth of online giant Amazon.com. But when chain bookstore Borders filed for bankruptcy a year ago, independent booksellers in the Bay Area did not sigh with relief, nor did they toast to the newfound power and glory of the indie. That's because there's a new threat in town: e-books.

"In 2011, sales of print books in the United States dropped 9 percent from the previous year, according to Nielsen BookScan. E-book revenue, meanwhile, grew an astonishing 1,274 percent from 2008 to 2010, according to a Bookstats study.

"Amazon is the biggest seller of e-books, and controls the largest percentage of the e-book market. In fact, it now sells more e-books than print books—105 e-books for every 100 print books sold. Yet e-books represented only 5.2 percent of Indie Commerce sales at independent bookstores last year. More ominously for independent booksellers, e-books have become increasingly popular for readers between the ages of forty and sixty—the traditional bookstore demographic."

Source: "The New Threat to Independent Bookstores" by Holly MsDede, www.eastbayexpress.com

- "More and more, college students go buy the e-books."
- "Online textbooks are a growing—and cheaper—alternative for many college students.

  ✓ Hardcover price (new) $151.40

  ✓ Hardcover price (used) $113.55

  ✓ Hardcover rental price $71.15

  ✓ e-book purchase price $83.90

  ✓ e-book 180-day rental price $65.60"

Source: *Boston Globe*, September 1, 2011, National Association of College Stores

- "Textbook Rentals Up to 80% Off—High quality, Return them free when you're done.

  Huge Selection of Used Textbooks

  Free Express Shipping on New Textbooks."

Source: A recent ad for Barnes & Noble in an online ad, August 2012

- "Successful book stores will continue to be an important part of their communities. Consumers will realize the value of supporting their local business."
- "Or in the case of Brookline Booksmith, trying a little bit of everything. The 49-year-old store now sells Google e-books online, holds on average five events a week with authors, and may invest in an in-store printing press."

Source: "Bookstores forced to turn a page" by Kaivan Mangouri, *Boston Globe*, June 25, 2011

Questions

- "Sales trends, community standing, online sales, web site condition, staffing quality"

Resources

Trade Publications

- Independent Bookselling Today—This site offers good information on opening a bookstore: www.pazbookbiz.com
- Publishers Weekly: www.publishersweekly.com

Associations

- American Booksellers Association: www.bookweb.org
- Christian Booksellers Association: www.cbaonline.org

Book Stores—Rare and Used (See also Book Stores)		
SIC 5932-01	NAICS 453310	Number of Businesses/Units 5,000

Rules of Thumb

> ➤ 10 to 15 percent of annual sales plus inventory. In the case of rare books, the cost of the inventory would be based on some form of wholesale value or less the booksellers standard markup.

Pricing Tips

- "Used book stores seem to be a vanishing business. Many owners of these stores have closed them and now offer their books online. Rare book stores would have the same multiple as used stores, perhaps a bit higher. The real value is the inventory."

- "In response to your question about a pricing rule of thumb [We had emailed our request for this to Susan Spiegel of Book Hunter Press, and perhaps the leading authority on used bookstores in the U.S.], I'm not aware of any, but I doubt that even if one existed it would be helpful. But then, I must confess that I haven't been involved in buying or selling a business.

  "The reason for my skepticism: even among just-open shops, there is such a wide, wide range of inventory, that the same pricing mechanism could not automatically be used for all shops. Two shops may each have 10,000 books— but very, very different books in terms of wholesale or retail value.

  "The inventory in new bookstores is pretty homogeneous; this is not the case in a used bookstore. Even within a given store, there could be a range of value in the inventory with mass market paperbacks selling at one price point and hard-to-find hardcovers selling for $25-50+.

  "Stores with vastly different size inventories can have the same gross sales, depending on what types of books they are selling. In my humble judgment, one would have to arrive at a selling price based on the value of the inventory for that particular store, as well as that store's sales records.

  "One problem is that most dealers have only a small portion of their inventory computerized. And I have no idea of what type of pencil and paper records they keep for tax purposes on the cost of what they've bought.

  "Open shops that have gone out of business have disposed of their inventory in several different ways. Assuming that they can't sell the business to someone else who will continue it as a used bookstore (usually the first choice), some sell off their inventory to another, larger dealer. This may or may not involve donating the undesirable volumes to a library.

- "Some dealers close their shops, sell off a portion of their inventory, and continue selling online with a smaller inventory, often, but not always, in a specialty area/s."

Source: Susan Spiegel, Book Hunter Press

Benchmark Data

- "Three quarters of the dealers [open shops] sold an average of more than 200 books per month with 23% selling 200–499 books, followed closely by 21% selling 500–999 books a month. Sixteen percent of the open shops sold 2,000 or more books per month.

"For shops in the most frequent open-shop size category (25,000–44,999 volumes), 31% of the dealers sold an average of 500–999 volumes per month, followed by 28% selling 200–499 volumes. Only 8% of the dealers within this size category sold fewer than 200 books per month and, at the other extreme, 16% sold 2,000 books or more."

Note: A bit dated, but still valuable information and probably still very accurate.

Source: A Portrait of the U.S. Used Book Market, published by Book Hunter Press.

Industry Trend

- "Lahaina—Not only is Maui losing more of its new bookstores, the island's last remaining commercial used-book store has closed.

- "JoAnn Carroll said she closed Old Lahaina Book Emporium in Mariner's Alley last week after 15 years of selling and swapping books in Wailuku and Lahaina. She said two factors led her to shut down.

- "The economy is so bad, she said, many local people could no longer afford even used books. Customers would buy books, read them, then swap them for more books. 'I was turning into a lending library,' she said. The Lahaina location had proven to be much busier than her shop on North Market Street, she said, because of tourist traffic. But while she continued to get traffic, she didn't continue to get buyers. 'They would come in and say, 'I love your shop, but I just downloaded 20 books" into an e-reader, she said."

Source: "Last commercial used book store on Maui shuts down" by Harry Eagar,
The Maui News, July 22, 2011

Resources

Websites

- www.bookhunterpress.com

Bookkeeping Services (See Accounting)		
	NAICS 541219	Number of Businesses/Units 25,750

Bottled Gas (See Liquefied Petroleum Gas)		
SIC 5172-08	NAICS 422710	

Bowling Centers		
SIC 7933-01	NAICS 713950	Number of Businesses/Units 3,757

Rules of Thumb

➢ 180 to 200 percent of annual sales plus inventory

➢ 4 to 6 times SDE plus inventory

➢ 5 to 6 times EBITDA

Pricing Tips

- "Physical condition and updated equipment are critical factors. If real estate is leased, multiples are 4 to 5."

B - Rules of Thumb

- "$40,000 to $60,000 per lane for older centers. Newer centers up to $80,000 per lane (price must fit cash flow)."
- "Needed capital expenditures are a deduction."
- "Larger centers, metro markets and facilities in top physical condition each attract higher prices. Smaller centers, those in rural markets and/or those in need of capital get lower prices."
- "Necessary capital expenditures are deducted. Location/market are critical factors."
- "Physical condition of facility important. Demographics of market important."
- "Important: updated appearance and new amenities."
- "Maybe 2 times sales"
- "Revenues over $35,000/lane a plus. Location, physical condition and appearance are big factors."

Expert Comments

"Location is critical factor. Demographics, access, size of population base are important."

"Bowling generally does well in tough times; cheap recreation close to home."

"High barrier to entry due to equipment and real estate costs. Business has trended down for last 15 years due to decline in popularity of league bowling. Location is important, but many centers have closed due to real estate having higher and better use as something else."

"Location and quality of facility are critical. Revenue trends are also important."

"Bowling centers are expensive to build."

"Historical trend, i.e., stability of performance, very important. Competition is not very important."

"Bowling is a social equalizer. How fabulous can any one person be when everyone's wearing the same shoes?"

Source: Patrick Lyons bowling center owner, *Boston Globe*

Benchmark Data

Statistics (Bowling Alleys)

Number of Establishments	3,757
Average Profit Margin	6.7%
Revenue per Employee	$28,200
Average Number of Employees	21
Average Wages per Employee	$14,314

Source: IBISWorld, October 2011 (The latest available)

Products and Services Segmentation

Ten pin bowling activities	68%
Food, beverage and merchandise sales	24%
Non-bowling games	8%

Source: IBISWorld, October 2011

Major Market Segmentation

League bowlers 54%
Open bowlers.. 30%
Special event bowlers.. 16%
Source: IBISWorld, October 2011

Industry Costs

Profit 6.7%
Rent 8.0%
Utilities 3.0%
Depreciation... 5.3%
Other... 12.8%
Wages... 34.2%
Purchases... 30.0%
Source: IBISWorld, October 2011

Market Share

AMF Bowling Worldwide Inc. 13.5%
Brunswick Corporation... 10.2%
Source: IBISWorld, October 2011

Gross Revenues per Lane per Year

Excellent .... $40,000 or more
Good .... $35,000 to $40,000
Average .... $29,000 to $34,000
Inadequate ....$28,000 or less

Target Costs vs. Cost of Goods

Target Costs	Cost of Goods
Bar	28%-30% of total bar revenues
	22%-25% of liquor revenues
	28%-30% or draft beer revenues
	30%-33& of cans, bottles revenues
Supplies	03%
Food/Beverages	30% of total food/beverage revenues
Pro-Shop	60%-65% of total pro shop revenues
Vending, Other	60% of total vending revenues

Controllable Expenses
Payroll- Bowling ....30% of lineage revenues
Payroll-Bar .... 20% of bar revenues
Payroll-Food .... 25%-30% of snack bar revenues
Total Payroll .... 25%-28% of total revenues
Payroll Taxes ....13% of total payroll
Employee Benefits .... 5%-7% of total payroll
Total Employee Costs .... 28%-33% of total revenues
Advertising & Promotion ....3% of total revenues
Repair, Maintenance & Supplies ....5%-6% of total revenues*
Utilities .... 5%-7% of total revenues
*Varies with age and condition of center, building and equipment

Operating Income** as % of Total Revenues

Above Average	Average	Below Average
30%-33%	25%–28%	20%–22%

**Operating Income is defined as the funds generated by an operation before interest, real estate rent, non-recurring expenses, principal payments, capital improvements, depreciation and owner's salaries (above normal limits) and fringe benefits.

Courtesy: Sandy Hansell & Associates, Bowling's Only Full-Service Brokers, Appraisers & Financial Advisors. (800) 222-9131. September 2012

- "Sales in excess of $35,000 per lane."

Expenses as a Percentage of Annual Sales

Cost of goods	30% to 35%
Payroll/labor Costs	30%
Occupancy	10% to 20%
Profit (estimated pretax)	20% to 30%

Industry Trend

- "Well-run, well-promoted centers should do well—not much new competition"
- "Flat or declining revenues. Bowling is dependent upon customer's disposable income."
- "But even as alleys lost their mainstay league players they saw small but steady gains in the number of casual bowlers, according to the BPAA. To keep them coming, 500 centers nationwide spiffed up their digs. Others made over their menus and started to offer alternate game options, including laser tag, sand volleyball and salsa lessons.
- "'In past recessions, bowling did well because it is relatively affordable,' said Michael Mazek, editor of Bowling Center Management magazine. 'This one was different because people didn't want to spend on gas and travel. Bowling centers are becoming more interested in alternative revenue options, to make it more of a one-stop-shop.'"

Source: "Bowling alleys strike up new ways to attract customers," by Eleanor Goldberg, Medill News Service, www.maketwatch.com

Seller Financing

- "15 years with 5–10 year call; not done very often, mostly all-cash sales"
- "Usually bank financed"

Questions

- "Physical condition, necessary cap x, condition of equipment, life of lanes"
- "1. List of competitors and size of their facilities (# of lanes). 2. Population within market area. 3. Age and condition of roof and HVAC. 4. Age and condition of bowling equipment, especially pinsetters and lanes. 5. Is bowling equipment owned or leased?"
- "How much ready cash on hand? Experience in bowling?"
- "Why selling?"
- "1. League bowler count; 2. Recent facility/equipment upgrades; 3. Demographics within five miles."
- "Recent upgrades to facility, league schedule"
- "Are you open 365 days/yr?"

Resources

Trade Publications
- International Bowling Industry magazine: www.bowlingindustry.com

Associations
- Bowling Proprietors Association of America : www.bpaa.com

Franchise

Bresler's Ice Cream and Yogurt Shops

	NAICS 722213	Number of Businesses/Units 500

Rules of Thumb

➢ 35 to 40 percent of annual sales plus inventory

Brew Pubs (See Bars, Beer Taverns, & Breweries)

	NAICS 722410

Rules of Thumb

➢ 40 percent of annual sales plus inventory

Bridal Shops

SIC 5621-04	NAICS 448190	Number of Businesses/Units 7,500

Rules of Thumb

➢ 10 to 15 percent of annual sales plus inventory

Benchmark Data

Statistics (Lingerie, Swimwear & Bridal Stores)

Number of Establishments	40,305
Average Profit Margin	3.0%
Revenue per Employee	$104,100
Average Number of Employees	3
Average Wages per Employee	$17,279

Source: IBISWorld, August 2012

Products and Services Segmentation

Lingerie	40%
Swimwear	20%
Bridal gowns	15%
Other	15%
Uniforms	10%

Source: IBISWorld, August 2012

Industry Costs

Profit	3.0%
Wages	16.6%
Purchases	62.4%
Depreciation	1.3%
Marketing	6.9%
Rent & Utilities	6.4%
Other	3.4%

Source: IBISWorld, August 2012

Market Share

Limited Brands Inc.	51.1%

Source: IBISWorld, August 2012

- "Marriage: Average cost of a wedding increased 21.9 percent in the first half of 2010 to $23,867, up from $19,581 in 2009."

Source: *Bloomberg Businessweek*

Industry Trend

- "With stores like J.Crew offering a bridal collection and now Urban Outfitters, it seems some retailers are looking to tap into a market that is ready to flourish. With wedding season here, IBISWorld looks at what's really going on within this industry and where it may be headed.

  "'In 2010, the wedding industry will remain a difficult market with high unemployment and continued discomfort coming out of the worst recession in many years,' explained Toon van Beeck, senior analyst with IBISWorld.' Couples will continue to put off wedding plans this year, but 2011 is expected to be much stronger, as the economy will be in a better position than it is now or was in 2009. It's for this reason, companies like Urban Outfitters may be aiming to capitalize on a strong rebounding wedding market, with a number of couples looking to 2011 and 2012 to tie the knot'."

Source: "IBISWorld: Industry Insight: Retailers Say "I Do" To The Bridal Industry" June 2010

Franchise

Bruster's Real Ice Cream

Approx. Total Investment	Approximately $350,000
	Number of Businesses/Units 245

Rules of Thumb

➢ 40 to 45 percent of annual sales plus inventory

Resources

Websites

- www.brusters.com

Franchise

Budget Blinds

Approx. Total Investment		$89,240 to $173,070
Estimated Annual Sales/Unit		$700,000
	NAICS 442291	Number of Businesses/Units 811

Rules of Thumb

➢ 2 times annual EBIT plus inventory & equipment

➢ 50 to 55 percent of annual sales plus inventory

Resources

Websites

- www.budget-blinds-franchise.com

Building Inspection (See Home Inspection)

Building Materials (See also Lumberyards, Home Centers)

SIC 5211-26	NAICS 444110	

Rules of Thumb

➤ 40 percent of annual sales includes inventory

➤ 4 to 6 times EBIT

➤ 3 to 3.5 times SDE includes inventory

➤ 4 to 6 times EBITDA

Pricing Tips

- "NO MARKET for these businesses under current economy, hence low value . . . BV or less . . . "

- "These comments would apply to lumberyards dealing with contractors, sometimes called 'ProYards,' not home centers (DIY business) . . . if profits (EBT) are 5%–10% of sales, the business would likely sell for 1.5 times book value; less profitable lumberyards sell for book value, or in an asset sale. In an asset sale, if profits are above 5% EBT, use lesser of cost or market on the inventory and FMV on equipment and real estate used in the business, plus one year's EBT for goodwill/non-compete."

- "A store that does 30% to 50% of its sales in lumber and building materials is classified as a home center. If sales of lumber and building materials is over 60% of total sales, it is a lumberyard. A home center with sales between $2,000,000 and $5,000,000 should have SDE/total sales of at least 12%. Stores under 10% will sell for about 20% less. Stores with SDE/total sales over 14% are top performers and can be sold for as much as 4.0 times SDE or more."

- "As to a rule of thumb estimate of value, we see that most reasonably profitable businesses (5 percent EBT [earnings before taxes] on sales) in this industry sell for Fair Market Value on all the assets, including real estate, inventory and equipment, plus up to a year's EBT in the form of a goodwill non-compete agreement. Marginally profitable businesses sell for Fair Market Value of Assets only, and extremely profitable businesses, those with 5 percent to 10 percent EBT on sales, bring premium prices, FMV of assets plus up to 2 times EBT in goodwill/non-compete, etc. Key factors are earnings, inventory and accounts receivable turnover. Competition, profits and niche determine salability."

- "Many are sold on net asset value."

- "If sales $1.5 million to $20 million, and if operating net profit 0 to 5 percent, on sales, before tax, likely sell for fair market value; if 5 to10 percent, on sales, before tax will likely sell for 1.5 to 2 times annual net before tax + fair market value of assets."

Expert Comments

"The new housing market is vital to the 'PRO' type lumberyard, and new construction is terribly low"

"Very capital intensive . . . low ROI . . . fluctuates with economy and housing starts"

"Home centers and lumberyards are very capital intensive which keeps the potential for new competition at a minimum. Big boxes, however, can be fatal. A home center that is well merchandised, well staffed, and conveniently located can survive a big box hit. Typically the store's sales will return to normal one year after a big box moves into its market."

"Lot of risk to credit, plus housing ups and downs"

Benchmark Data

- "EBIT of 5.0% is good"

Expenses as a Percentage of Annual Sales

Cost of goods	75%
Payroll/labor Costs	10% to 15%
Occupancy	02% to 05%
Profit (estimated pretax)	03% to 05%

Industry Trend

- "Tough; with housing starts down, could force attrition"

Seller Financing

- "Buyers are sophisticated and well financed. It is rare to have seller financing of any kind."

Resources

Trade Publications

- ProSales Magazine: www.prosalesmagazine.com

Associations

- NorthAmerican Retail Hardware Association: www.nrha.org

	Franchise
Burger King	
Estimated Annual Sales/Unit	$1,120,000
NAICS 722211	Number of Businesses/Units 8,200 U.S. stores

Rules of Thumb

➢ 40 percent of annual sales plus inventory

Industry Trend

- "Burger King plans to complete the rollout of Cinnabon's Minibon product to more than 7,000 restaurants across the United States by September, the company said Tuesday."

  Source:"Burger King rolls out Minibon nationally" by Lisa Jennings, nrn.com/article, April 24, 2012

Resources

Websites
- www.burgerking.com

Bus Companies (Charter & Rental)	
(See also Ground Transportation Companies)	
SIC 4142-01 NAICS 485510	Number of Businesses/Units 7,000

Rules of Thumb

➢ 35 percent of revenues plus asset value of buses plus inventory

Benchmark Data

Statistics (Scheduled and Charter Bus Services)

Number of Establishments	7,487
Average Profit Margin	6.7%
Revenue per Employee	$107,900
Average Number of Employees	7
Average Wages per Employee	$26,444

Source: IBISWorld, July 2012

Products and Services Segmentation

Scheduled bus services—interurban transit	40.5%
Long-distance charter bus services	25.6%
Local charter bus services	24.4%
Scheduled bus services—rural transit	9.5%

Source: IBISWorld, July 2012

Major Market Segmentation

Private consumers—local	55%
Private consumers—long-distance	40%
Business travel	5%

Source: IBISWorld, July 2012

Industry Costs

Profit	6.7%
Wages	25.3%
Purchases	39.7%
Depreciation	6.2%
Marketing	3.3%
Rent & Utilities	7.9%
Other	10.9%

Source: IBISWorld, July 2012

Market Share

FirstGroup PLC	19.1%
Stagecoach Group	11.2%

Source: IBISWorld, July 2012

Statistics (Public School Bus Services)

Number of Establishments	11,409
Average Profit Margin	6.5%
Revenue per Employee	$52,600
Average Number of Employees	19.6
Average Wages per Employee	$18,365

Source: IBISWorld, September 2011

Products and Services Segmentation

Public school business for elementary and middle school students	68.9%
Public school busing for high school students	20.7%
School busing for private schools	5.0%
Other transportation and services	2.8%
Employee...bus services	2.6%

Source: IBISWorld, September 2011

Major Market Segmentation

Public elementary and middle schools	65.7%
Public high schools	26.2%
Private schools	5.1%
Other	3.0%

Source: IBISWorld, September 2011

Industry Costs

Profit	6.5%
Rent	2.6%
Utilities	3.2%
Depreciation	8.0%
Other	25.1%
Wages	35.3%
Purchases	19.3%

Source: IBISWorld, September 2011

How many coaches are in your fleet?

Fewer than 10	74.4%
10 to 24	17.9%
24 to 49	4.2%
50 to 99	2.4%
100 or more	1.1%"

- Carrier Revenue per Motorcoach, Averages
  Motorcoach Fleet Size

20 or more	$196,281
Less than 19	$248,062
Total	$159,275

Source: Motorcoach Census, American Bus Association (the latest available)

- "It is important to note that the motorcoach industry provides an average of 745 million passenger trips annually which is comparable to the domestic airlines and 25 times more than Amtrak."

Average number of vehicles in fleet	13
Median number of vehicles in fleet	9
Median annual cost per vehicle for licensing	$510
Median monthly cost of insurance per vehicle	$638

Median monthly finance payment per vehicle.. $2,500
Median overall percentage profit margin for 2009 .... 7%
Average hourly wage for drivers (excluding benefits)... $13.13
Average of company revenue that goes to labor costs.. 26%
Operators who maintain their fleets in-house 71%
Outsource their maintenance... 29$

Source: "Charger & Tour: Industry Stays Solid in Tough Year" April 30, 2010 www.lctmag.com

Seller Financing

- "3 years"

Resources

Trade Publications

- Bus Ride Magazine—another interesting site: www.busride.com

Associations

- American Bus Association: www.buses.org—a very informative site, and their magazine, Destinations, is also very informative

- United Motorcoach Association—also an informative site: www.uma.org

Business Brokerage Offices (See also Real Estate)		
SIC 7389-22	NAICS 531210	Number of Businesses/Units 3,000

Rules of Thumb

➢ If you were to sell your business brokerage business, what multiple of SDE would you expect to sell it for?

Average 2.4 for 2010

Average 2.1 for 2011

Source: 2010 and 2011 Business Brokerage Press Survey of the Business Brokerage Profession

➢ 50 percent of annual sales plus inventory

➢ 2 times SDE plus inventory

➢ 3 to 5 times EBITDA

Pricing Tips

- "Look at cash flow not annual gross sales. Bottom line is what the business is making; EBITDA."

- "Trends are important."

- "There have been sales reported at 2 times SDE. If owner is active in production, then his or her production must be subtracted, unless they will be staying for a period of time. Even then, some discount must be applied to his or her sales, because after selling, their production will most likely drop off."

- "One school of thought on pricing a business brokerage office is to pay for fixed assets, and a certain amount for each year with the same phone number, as there is a goodwill factor for it. A ballpark figure might be $10,000 per year (area code change doesn't count). Then the 'house's' portion of the commissions received on the listings purchased by the new owner would be split between the new owner and the selling owner. For example: Take a $10,000 fee; the selling agent would receive $2,500, the listing agent would receive $2,500 and the remaining $5,000 would be split 50/50. This is one way to handle an earnout. This method would apply to all listings at the time of sale and one renewal period. Deals in progress would be handled as follows: Offers signed both ways would belong to the selling owner and sales signed one way would belong to the new owner."

Expert Comments

"There seems to be a 'falling' out of the part-time business broker leaving the space open to full-time professionals"

Benchmark Data

- For additional Benchmark data see Real Estate Offices
- "Must understand owner's role and recast out personal production."
- What were your firm's approximate gross commissions for 2010 (Business brokerage activities only)? $456,835.
    - ✓ Office Average—$567,240
    - ✓ Sole Practitioner—$250,623
    - ✓ M & A Office—$845,928
      Source: *2011 Business Brokerage Press Survey of the Business Brokerage Profession*

Industry Trend

- "Increased business transactions with boomers nearing retirement or being laid off from corporate jobs."
- "Recovery?"

Resources

Associations
- International Business Brokers Association (IBBA): www.ibba.org

Butcher Markets (See Meat Markets)

Call Centers (Telemarketing)		
SIC 7389-12	NAICS 561421	Number of Businesses/Units 17,324

Rules of Thumb

➤ 10 to 12 times current monthly billings for larger services; may require earnout

➤ 5 to 7 times current monthly billings for smaller services; may require earn-out

Pricing Tips

- "Annual rate increases are recommended. One of the most important formulas I use in evaluating a business is determining profitability, which comes down to your rate structure. I recently sold a medical service for over 14 times monthly billing, and the reason it sold for that multiple was the way the services were priced. It was very profitable, averaging $365 per client. The service had only 140 accounts but billed over $50K per month producing a net profit margin of over 38%. Do not increase your rates just before selling your business to boost your monthly billing. A potential buyer will want to see a reasonable conversion history for the rate increase. I would also recommend going to a 28-day billing structure. This will give you an additional one month's billing per year, which should increase cash flow and your annual revenue.

- "Buyers are interested in businesses with a good profit margin of at least 20% or better, advanced equipment with updated software, management in place and a history of growth."

Source: Steve Michaels, TAS Marketing, tas@tasmarketing.com

Benchmark Data

Statistics (Telemarketing & Call Centers)

Number of Establishments	17,324
Average Profit Margin	5.5%
Revenue per Employee	$47,900
Average Number of Employees	25
Average Wages per Employee	$23,978

Source: IBISWorld, March 2012

Products and Services Segmentation

Telemarketing	64.3%
Customer service and technical support	23.1%
Other	6.8%
Debt collection	4.0%
Fundraising	1.8%

Source: IBISWorld, March 2012

Major Market Segmentation

Other industries	26%
Retail	21%
Banking and finance	18%
Telecommunications and IT	17%
Manufacturing	10%
Travel and entertainment	8%

Source: IBISWorld, March 2012

Industry Costs

Profit	5.5%
Wages	50.4%
Purchases	12.7%
Depreciation	4.5%
Marketing	2.5%
Rent & Utilities	5.3%
Other	19.1%

Source: IBISWorld, March 2012

Market Share

Convergys Corporation	10.0%
West Corporation	5.8%

Source: IBISWorld, March 2012

Enterprises by Employment Size

Number of Employees	Number of Enterprises	Share
0 to 4	1,487	36.6%
5 to 9	543	13.4%
10 to 19	672	16.5%

Source: IBISWorld, February 2012

- "A well-run answering service can generate a 30% profit. Your labor should run you around 40%, with 10% going to phones and taxes, and 20% for administration. Utilizing a voice mail system along with faxing and email for message delivery should reduce your labor by at least 10% to 15%."
- "The teleservices industry is exploding with growth potential. As of the beginning of 2009, there were 2700 telephone answering services nationwide billing $1.5 billion per year with over 1.4 million customers using 44,000 employees. That works out to an average TAS billing of $555,555 per year with 518 customers billing $89.00 per month.

  "Agents take approximately 41 calls per hour at 43 seconds each. The average revenue per minute is $1.09 and the revenue per call is $1.08."

  Source: TAS Services, www.tasmarketing.com. TAS is a business brokerage firm specializing in telephone answering services and related businesses. They have an excellent and very informative Web site.

- "You don't think of call center jobs as high-paying jobs; in fact, you tend to think of them as low-paying jobs that are often shipped overseas. But there are a few positions, including call-center analysts, who oversee quality and assurance and train the representatives, and the director of the call center who can make six figures. One listing on Indeed.com for a six-figure job as a QA Call Center Analyst in Chantilly, VA, requires that the person be bilingual—in English and Spanish. Call Center Directors, meanwhile, have a median salary of $121,000, according to HTTP://www.salary.com."

  Source: "Surprising Six-Figure Jobs" by Cindy Perman, finance.yahoo.com/career-work May 19, 2011

Industry Trend

- "There will always be the need to take and deliver information over the telephone, whether it be an answering service finding a doctor during an emergency or a call center that can complete an entire sales transaction over the phone or the Internet."

  Source: Steve Michaels, TAS Marketing, tas@tasmarketing.com

Resources

Associations
- International Customer Management Institute: www.icmi.com

Camera Stores		
SIC 5946-01	NAICS 443130	Number of Businesses/Units 2,653

Rules of Thumb

➢ 10 to 15 percent of annual revenues plus fixtures, equipment & inventory

Benchmark Data

Statistics (Camera Stores)

Number of Establishments	2,653
Average Profit Margin	9.7%
Revenue per Employee	$337,600
Average Number of Employees	3
Average Wages per Employee	$24,059

Source: IBISWorld, May 2012

Products and Services Segmentation

Cameras	45.2%
Photographic equipment and supplies	28%
Computer hardware, software and supplies	11.3%
Audio equipment	8.3%
Other merchandise	5.3%
Video cameras and gaming consoles	1.7%
Repairs	0.2%

Source: IBISWorld, May 2012

Industry Costs

Profit	9.7%
Wages	7.4%
Purchases	74.7%
Depreciation	0.6%
Marketing	1.7%
Rent & Utilities	3.6%
Other	2.3%

Source: IBISWorld, May 2012

Market Share

Ritz Camera & Image	17.9%

Source: IBISWorld, May 2012

Establishments by Employment Size

Number of Employees	Share
1 to 4	47.8%
5 to 9	41.0%
10 to 19	8.3%

Source: IBISWorld, May 2012

Resources

Associations
- Photo Marketing Association (PMAI)—good site: www.pmai.org

	Franchise
Camille's Sidewalk Cafe	
Approx. Total Investment	$223,500 to $589,500

SIC 5812-14	NAICS 722211	Number of Businesses/Units 84

Rules of Thumb

➢ 30 to 35 percent of annual sales plus inventory

Resources

Websites
- www.camillescafe.com

Campgrounds (See also RV Parks)	
SIC 7033-01	NAICS 721211	Number of Businesses/Units 13,453

Rules of Thumb

➢ 8.5 times EBITDA

➢ 3.8 times SDE (after cost of merchandise for store)

➢ 8.5 times SDE; add store inventory

➢ "The above always includes real estate and, 90 percent of the time, owner financing. Real estate value may be much higher than the value as a campground. Rules of Thumb generally do not apply to the 'low end' or to large RV resorts."

Benchmark Data

Statistics (Campgrounds & RV Parks)

Number of Establishments	13,453
Average Profit Margin	30%
Revenue per Employee	$111,200
Average Number of Employees	3
Average Wages per Employee	$24,827

Source: IBISWorld, June 2012

Products and Services Segmentation

Recreational and vacation camps (except campgrounds)	50.1%
RV parks and campgrounds	49.9%

Source: IBISWorld, June 2012

Industry Costs

Profit	30.0%
Wages	22.5%
Purchases	5.2%
Depreciation	2.5%
Marketing	1.1%
Rent & Utilities	8.9%
Other	29.8%

Source: IBISWorld, June 2012

- "When we look at rules of thumb, the following would apply to the 'typical campground' with a camp store and average amenities:
- "Registration income (site rental only) x 4.5
- "Gross profit (after cost of goods for the store) x 3.5
- "Adjusted net income (SDE) x 7.5
- "Multiply each one out and see if they come out reasonably close. If they are within $50,000 or so, they really mean something. If they are way off, it can mean some of the following: If the GP multiple is much higher than the RI, it is positive because they have strong store sales. If the GP multiple is lower, they are probably doing a bad job in the store or they are eating too much inventory (literally).
- "Obviously the net is very important, but I would tend to place a great deal of importance on the GP. This gives credit to strong store sales, good registration fees and the overall ability of the park to produce revenue. It also shows a picture before bad management. We know that a properly run park should net 40 percent to the bottom line, or they are not good managers. (Could be a good opportunity for the new owner.)
- "The net income multiple will float with interest rates. Since most are sold on a contract, the multiple goes up when interest rates are down. As in any business, you really need to understand how the adjustments were made. It is very normal for some owners to work very long hours with not enough employees. This is a pace that wore them out, and that is why they are selling.
- "When we look at the above multiples, I would qualify it with the following:
- "This is assuming that the park has modern utilities (some 50 amp service, most 30 amp), a good source of water and sewer (city services best). The sites need to be large enough for newer modern RVs with wide roads and level sites, and many pull-thru sites. The buildings need to be in good repair and include a game room, laundry and convenience store."

Expenses as a Percentage of Annual Sales

Cost of goods	10%
Payroll/labor Costs	10%
Occupancy	40%
Profit (estimated pretax)	40%

Industry Trend

- "Campgrounds across the country are increasingly investing in park model cabins with bathrooms and kitchens with full-size appliances in an effort to better accommodate family reunions and other large groups that include people who don't have an RV or would otherwise prefer not to spend the night in a tent, said William Garpow, executive director of the Recreational Park Trailer Industry Association.

- "But park operators also realize that rental accommodations enable them to significantly increase their business base. Esther Osborne, whose father founded Marble Quarry RV Park 32 years ago, has seen the difference park model cabins and other rental accommodations can have a campground's business base. 'It used to be more about clubs and older people that came in here,' she said. 'But now (with the rental accommodations) we're getting a huge mix with a lot of families with children.'
- "'And park model cabins and cottages have quickly become the rental accommodation product of choice for many of the nation's campgrounds, largely because these units are attractive, factory built units that can be set up on existing RV sites, Garpow said.'"

Source: "Campgrounds find they can host family reunions and other large groups…,"
ARVC Press Release, May 13, 2010

Resources

Associations
- National Association of RV Parks and Campgrounds (ARVC): www.arvc.org

Camps		
SIC 7032-03	NAICS 721214	Number of Businesses/Units 3,026

Rules of Thumb

➤ 2 times annual sales plus inventory

➤ 5 to 8 times SDE plus inventory

Benchmark Data

Statistics (Summer Camps)

Number of Establishments	3,026
Average Profit Margin	22%
Revenue per Employee	$108,900
Average Number of Employees	7
Average Wages per Employee	$30,894

Source: IBISWorld, June 2012

Products and Services Segmentation

Overnight recreational camp tuition or fees	85.2%
Other services	8.4%
Food items prepared for immediate consumption	2.8%
Room or unit accommodation for travelers and others	2.7%
Membership dues and fees	0.9%

Source: IBISWorld, June 2012

Major Market Segmentation

Children aged 9 years and younger	45.7%
Adolescents aged 10 to 19	41.3%
Adults	13%

Source: IBISWorld, June 2012

Industry Costs

Profit	22.0%
Wages	28.5%
Purchases	33.0%
Depreciation	2.5%
Marketing	5.0%
Rent & Utilities	2.0%
Other	7.0%

Source: IBISWorld, June 2012

- Enrollment Trends: Key Points
    - ✓ 74% resident camps & 26% day camps
    - ✓ 34% independent not for profit, 20% agency, faith-based, and independent for profit
    - ✓ 75% co-ed
    - ✓ 25% 1-300 campers
    - ✓ 34% 300-650 campers
    - ✓ 33% 650-2000 campers
    - ✓ Over 80% of respondents felt their enrollment of returning campers has stayed the same as last year and 30% say they have more returning campers than last year (up from 20% in 2010).

    Source: "2011 Enrollment Outlook," 2011 Survey: American Camp Association

- Resident Camp Report Highlights

    "The nature of the ownership/sponsorship of residential camps is varied with relatively even distribution across four categories: independent nonprofits (28%); agencies (26&); religious organizations (24%); and independent-for-profit operations (19%)."

    "The typical ACA day camp, according to the survey, was thirty-five years old, and 78 percent had been operating for at least a decade. Nearly half (46 percent) of all day camps were agency-sponsored, and the YMCA was the most common sponsoring organization. Just under a third (34 percent) of all day camps responding were YMCA camps. Just over 70 percent of all day camps own their own property, but while 99 percent have programs in the summer, only 34 percent use their facilities in the spring, and only a quarter have fall or winter programs. This seasonality of the business is one issue that may continue to be a concern if year-round schooling increases in popularity."

- "Day Camp Report Highlights

    The highest proportions of day camps are affiliated with independent nonprofits (36%) and agencies (25%).

    The typical (median) day camp director is a thirty-six-year-old, white female with a bachelor's degree. However, there is quite a bit of variation among this population based on each of the demographic attributes.

    The typical (median) day camp director has held his/her current position for five years and long-term tenures are rare.

    Seventy-nine percent of day camps that currently employ a camp director indicated that their camp directors are employed on a year-round basis. For these day camps, the median annual camp director salary (before taxes and deductions) was $38,300."

    Source: "ACA Camp Research," American Camp Association, Resident Camp Report Highlights

- The nature of the ownership/sponsorship of residential camps is varied, with relatively even distribution across four categories: independent nonprofits

(28%); agencies (26%); religious organizations (24%); and independent for-profit operations (19%).

The typical (median) residential camp director is a forty-three-year-old, white male with a bachelor's degree. However, there is quite a bit of variation among this population based on each of the demographic attributes.

The typical (median) residential camp director has held his/her current position for seven years. Thirty-six percent have relatively longer tenures of ten years or more.

Seventy-eight percent of residential camps that currently employ a camp director indicated that their camp directors are employed on a year-round, full-time basis. For these residential camps the median annual camp director salary (before taxes and deductions) was $43,000.

Note: The above figures are from 2007, but the latest available.

Source: "ACA Camp Research," American Camp Association

- "Gross Revenues—Residential Camps
  Respondents to the survey were asked to report an estimated gross revenue in their current fiscal year from all sources. The average for residential camps was $961,000 and the median was $540,000. Approximately 13 percent of camps reported estimated total gross revenues of over $2 million. and 16 percent estimate between $1 million and $1.9 million. At the other end of the spectrum, 8 percent of camps estimate gross revenues of under $100,000 for the year. New England residential camps reported the highest estimated total gross revenues, at $1.2 million. Mid-Atlantic residential camps reported the next highest median estimated revenues, at $624,000, followed by Southern camps ($560,000); Mid-America camps $400,000); and Western camps ($331,000).

- "Residential Camp Expenses and Profitability
  Labor is the largest expense for residential camps according to the respondents, accounting for 40 percent of outlays. The next single largest expense reported was food, at 11.4 percent of expenses, and program items and supplies, at 8.3 percent of all costs. Maintenance and insurance were the next largest expenses. Overall, average estimated expenses reported by residential camps were $896,000, with a median of $530,000. Independent for-profit camps have the highest expenses of all camp types, with average outlays of nearly $1.4 million. This was substantially higher than independent nonprofits (955,000); agency-sponsored residential camps ($782,000); or religious-sponsored residential respondents ($638,000). New England camps have estimated median expenses that are over $350,000 higher than those of residential camps in any other region."

Note: The figures above are for 2006 and although a bit dated, they still are interesting Benchmark Data.

Source: "ACA Camp Research," American Camp Association

Expenses as a Percentage of Annual Sales

Cost of goods	05% to 10%
Payroll/labor Costs	25%
Occupancy	10% to 20%
Profit (estimated pretax)	20%

Industry Trend

- "Where the wealthy send their children for the summer. The end of June marks the beginning of an annual migration, as school-aged kids, especially on the Eastern Seaboard, pack off for sleepaway camp. But as with many things, there are summer camps and then there are elite summer camps—the ones that cost $10,000 or more for a seven-week session.

  "What do these camps offer that others don't? The short answer is beautiful locations and top-notch facilities. Camp purists point to the Maine camps as the most traditional, sought-after experiences, mostly because of Maine's abundant wilderness and pristine lakes and beaches, but there are equally expensive camps in the Adirondacks, New Hampshire and Pennsylvania."

  Source: "America's Priciest Summer Camps" by Liz Moyer, June 15. 2010, *Forbes*, www.*forbes*.com

Resources

Associations

- American Camp Association: www.acacamps.org
- National Camp Association—an excellent and informative site: www. summercamp.org

Candy Stores		
SIC 5441-01	NAICS 445292	Number of Businesses/Units 7,500

Rules of Thumb

➤ 30 to 35 percent of annual sales plus inventory

➤ 1.7 times SDE plus inventory

Benchmark Data

- See Food Stores—Specialty for Benchmark Information

Resources

Trade Publications

- Candy Industry magazine—an excellent and informative site: www. candyindustry.com
- National Confectioners Association of the United States: www.candyusa.com

Car Washes — Coin Operated/Self-Service		
(See also Car Washes—Full-Serve/Exterior)		
SIC 7542-05	NAICS 811192	Number of Businesses/Units 14,616

Rules of Thumb

➤ Operations less than five years old generally sell for cost of original real estate, equipment, and improvement cost, plus negotiated figure 2 to 3 times EBIT.

➤ 4 times annual gross sales—"A good place to start"

Pricing Tips

- "Total cash business. Passive investment, almost labor free."
- "90 percent of self-service car washes will have combination of self-service and automatic bays."
- "98 percent of self-service/automatic car washes are sold with real estate, equipment and assets."
- "Nearly impossible to sell business only"
- "Takes 5 years to build new operation—gross annual sales volume to maturity."

Benchmark Data

Statistics (Car Wash and Auto Detailing)

Number of Establishments	14,616
Average Profit Margin	4.0%
Revenue per Employee	$45,300
Average Number of Employees	10
Average Wages per Employee	$15.011

Source: IBISWorld, May 2011

Products and Services Segmentation (2011)

Conveyor car washes	46.6%
Detailing	18.3%
Hand washing	13.7%
Self-service bays	12.9%
In-bay automatic car washes	8.5%

Source: IBISWorld, May 2011

Industry Costs

Profit	4.0%
Rent	8.1%
Utilities	11.9%
Depreciation	3.6%
Other	17.9%
Wages	33.5%
Purchases	21.0%

Source: IBISWorld, May 2011

Operating Costs   (per month as a percentage of total revenues)

Rent	18.3%
Equipment & Bldg. Maintenance	8.7%
Chemicals (soaps, waxes, etc.)	10.4%
Labor	10.9%
Utilities (incl. water/sewer)	14.3%
Advertising & Promotion	1.5%
Insurance	2.5%
Customer Claims	0.8%

- Average Daily Traffic Count at Best Site — 24,273
- Average Gross Revenue per In-Bay Customer — $7.72
- Average Monthly Gross Income per Self-Serve Bay — $1,709
- Average Number of Cars Washed Annually per Automatic — 17,076
- Average Gross per Car — $15.00

- Self-Serve Statistics for a single operation (Wand or Coin-op Style)
  - ✓ Average monthly revenue per bay — $1,489
  - ✓ Average percent of time bay is in use — 10%
  - ✓ Average annual revenue for a 2-bay operation — $41,000

Attendant (2010)

Full-time	14%
Part-time	36%
None	50%

Expenses (operating Costs as Percentage of Total Monthly Revenues)

Electricity	6.0%
Fuel (Gas, Oil, Etc.)	4.6%
Water	3.9%
Sewer	3.9%
Chemicals	5.8%
Vending Products	2.2%
Softener Salt	1.5%
Collection	1.7%
Lot Sweeping	2.3%
Attendant labor	12.9%
Bookkeeping	1.5%
Replacement Parts (Normal wear and tear)	4.4%
Replacement Parts (Vandalism)	1.1%
Vehicle Damage	0.5%
Refunds	0.5%
Pit Pumping	1.1%
Advertising & Promo	1.8%

Respondents Operating an In-Bay Automatic on Their Coin-Op Location

No	53%
Yes	47%

- "The average monthly gross income per bay was $1,275
- "The average monthly gross income per vacuum was $184"
- "Average monthly gross income and expense (2010) (average monthly gross income per automatic — $4,903; (average monthly expense per automatic — $1,790."

Source: "Self-Service Survey 2011— Results from Auto Laundry News,"

- www.carwashmag.com. This is a very informative site—and publication—for Car Washes and Auto Detail—all sites should be this good.
- "Competition in this industry is high."
- "Volatility medium (revenue fluctuations between 3 and 10 points.)"
- "The life cycle stage is growth."
- "There are no major players in this industry."
- Self-Serve Units
  - ✓ "Self-serve equipment cost is between $8,000 and $10,000 per bay.
  - ✓ Building costs are approximately $17,000 per bay.
  - ✓ Once opened, you can expect immediate cash flow.
  - ✓ Approximate monthly income is $1200–$1600 per bay.
  - ✓ The estimated income for an automatic unit is approximately $4800 per month.
  - ✓ Operating expenses are 17–20%, not including debt service."

Source: Magic Wand Car Wash, www.magiccarwash.com
(This information is a bit dated, but quite informative.)

- "The typical self-service facility:
    - ✓ Has five wand-bays and five vacuums;
    - ✓ Serves an estimated market population of 30,000 to 40,000 people;
    - ✓ Has an estimated 10-mile market radius;
    - ✓ Competes against two other self-service carwashes; and
    - ✓ Is open 7 days per week and 24 hours per day.
    - ✓ Produces average monthly revenue of $1,330 per wand-bay ($1,500 to $2,500 for new facilities), $176 per vacuum, and $395 for all merchandise vending.
    - ✓ Has average operating expenses between 25 percent and 40 percent of gross sales.
    - ✓ Pays an average debt service (principal and interest) of 26 percent of gross sales."

Source: Magic Wand Car Wash, www.magiccarwash.com
Again, this information is dated and we couldn't locate more current data, but still of interest.)

"ProForma-Annual

	Good Site Revenue		Better Site Revenue	
Wand-Bays	$90,000		$150,000	
Vacuums	$12.000		$20,000	
Vending	$5,400		$9,480	
Gross Revenue	$107,400		$179,480	

	Low Side	High Side	Low Side	High Side
Operating Exp.	$26,850	$42,960	$44,870	$71,792
Gross Margin	$80,550	$64,440	$134,610	$107,688
Debt Service	$27,924	$27,924	$46,665	$46,665
Profit*	$52,626	$36,516	$87,945	$61,023
*before depreciation and tax	49%	34%	49%	34%"

Resources

Associations

- International Carwash Association: www.carwash.org

Car Washes — Full Service/Exterior

SIC 7542-01	NAICS 811192	Number of Businesses/Units 14,616

Rules of Thumb

- ➢ .80 to 1 times annual sales plus inventory
- ➢ 3.75 to 4.75 times EBITDA

Pricing Tips

- "The value of a car wash varies greatly from the East Coast to the West Coast. Weather conditions dictate the value vs. sales and earnings, as the West Coast sees more sunshine and therefore more revenues on average."

- New Exterior-Only Wash Built Within the Past Year
  - ✓ Average purchase price of the new property (land only) $813,000
  - ✓ Average monthly rent (too few responses)
  - ✓ Average cost of improvements (bldg., landscaping, etc.) $1,550,000
  - ✓ Average cost of equipment $787,500

  Source: "Auto Laundry News," 2012 Survey, www.carwashmag.com

- "Plus economic value of the land, plus inventory not attached to the carwash tunnel"
- "Mace Security International Inc. has closed on the sale of Classic Car Wash in Lubbock, Texas, for $650,000 and entered into agreements to sell its remaining Lubbock carwash for $1.7 million and a carwash in Arlington, Texas, for $2.1 million, according to a company press release.

  "The company completed the sale of Classic Car Wash on June 2. The facility had a book value of $430,000 and was debt free, company officials said.

  "Mace agreed to sell Crystal Falls Car Wash in Lubbock on May 24. After a debt payment of $770,000 and sale closing costs, the company expects to net approximately $900,000 from the deal, officials said. The unnamed buyer has 45 days to perform a feasibility study and up to six months to remove existing underground storage tanks and obtain necessary environmental clearance, the release said.

  "The buyer made a $25,000 escrow deposit that is payable to Mace under certain default conditions.

  "The sales agreement for the Arlington carwash occurred June 1. The facility has a book value of $2 million, with outstanding debt of approximately $820,000. The unnamed buyer was given 90 days to close on the deal, although provisions allow up to three more 30-day extension periods with additional escrow deposits of $10,000 required for each extension requested."

  Source: "Mace Sells Texas Carwash, Agrees to Terms on Two Others," June 22, 2010, www.moderncarcare.com/hotnews

- "Mostly sold with real estate and is a cash business and not easy to verify income numbers."
- "Tax returns are not easily available and estimating is generally the rule; therefore using water bills, etc. to figure out the sales is one common method."
- "95 percent of car washes sold with real estate, equipment and assets. Very seldom sold with business only."
- "Car washing is a total cash business—strongest figure to be used is Gross Annual Sales in determining strength of business."
- "Key factors include current market conditions, owner salary, benefits, condition of equipment… these are just some of the typical costs and items buyers and sellers negotiate over."
- "4 times SDE without land"
- "2 times SDE + land & equipment"

Expert Comments

"A good high-volume car wash, $500k plus in annual sales with a good lease, brings forth a desirable business and good profit picture. The industry has slowed down some as the economy continues to struggle along with per household spending."

"Good weather brings forth more sales; summer is generally a better season than winter. There is some seasonality in this business; best time to purchase is early summer or late spring. Have working capital and cash flow in reserve for the winter months."

Southern California market is saturated. Slow economy and increased labor costs are driving avg. performing full-service carwashes out of business. Express washes (fully automated, min. labor) are the new-trend car washes"

"Location, marketing, management, and visual appeal"

"In some areas replication is easy, and in others it's difficult due to the local restrictions on the usability of water and recycling it, plus the traffic problems."

"Expensive to build a new full-service facility."

Benchmark Data
Statistics (Car Wash and Auto Detailing)

Number of Establishments	14,616
Average Profit Margin	3.9%
Revenue per Employee	$45,100
Average Number of Employees	10
Average Wages per Employee	$15,031

Source: IBISWorld, May 2012

Products and Services Segmentation

Conveyor car washes	46.6%
Detailing	18.3%
Hand washing	13.7%
Self-service bays	12.9%
In-bay automatic car washes	8.5%

Source: IBISWorld, May 2012

Industry Costs

Profit	3.9%
Wages	34.1%
Purchases	21.0%
Depreciation	3.6%
Marketing	1.7%
Rent & Utilities	20.0%
Other	15.7%

Source: IBISWorld, May 2012

Operating Costs (As a percentage of total revenues)

Rent	18.5%
Equipment & Bldg. Maintenance	4.2%
Chemicals	6.0%
Labor—Exterior	23.1%
Labor—Full-Service	35.8%
Utilities	8.3%
Insurance	4.4%
Advertising & Promotion	2.9%
Equipment on Lease	2.0%
Customer Claims	0.9%

Source: Survey 2011—Results from Auto Laundry News, www.carwashmag.com. This is a very informative site—and publication—for Car Washes and Auto Detail; all sites should be this good.

	Average Daily Traffic Count	Average Annual Wash Volume	Average Monthly Impulse Sales
Full-Service	34,000	63,000	$1,895
	32,000	61,000	$644

Extra Services at Full-Service Sites (2011)

	Average Price	% of Operators Offering Services
Detail	$138.56	81%
Upholstery Cleaning	$49.56	74%
Quick Lube	$35.98	24%
Carpet Shampoo	$36.78	81%
Exterior Vinyl Protectant	$9.99	60%
Interior Vinyl Protectant	$9.67	60%
Wax and Hand Buff	$73.87	76%
Wax and Machine Buff	$88.12	67%

Operating Costs (2011) (As a percentage of total revenues)

Rent	12.4%
Equipment & Bldg. Maintenance	4.3%
Chemicals	6.6%
Labor Exterior	21.7%
Labor Full-Service	35.5%
Utilities	7.4%
Insurance	2.7%
Advertising & Promotion	2.2%
Equipment on Lease	0%
Customer Claims	0.7%

- Average Cost per Hour per Employee (2011)
  - ✓ 40% Paid Minimum Wage to $8 per hour
  - ✓ 48% Paid $8.00 to $10.00 per hour
  - ✓ 12% Paid over $10.00 per hour

    Source: Survey 2011—Results from Auto Laundry News, www.carwashmag.com.

- Tunnel Carwash Statistics for a single operation
  - ✓ Average number of cars washed per year—45,750
  - ✓ Average price per carwash—$15
  - ✓ Average annual revenue—$686,250
- "Standard Industry 25% EBITDA NET in full service car wash tunnel business."
- "Car washes typically have lower numbers if tied in with a gas station and will do much higher numbers if it's a stand-alone drive-thru."
- "Majority are sold with real estate."
- "$300 per sq. ft. is very good."
- "The average full-service operator spends $277,234 on its on-line labor, and employs a staff of 32 persons. Compare that to the exterior/flex operators, who spend only $108,119 to keep an average staff of 14 employees busy at the wash."

    Source: *Professional Carwashing & Detailing*, June 2007. This is dated but still interesting.

- "A typical full-service car wash on average costs $2.5 million to open — a price tag that leaves many potential franchisees to think long and hard before committing to a concept, slowing down expansion."
- "Exactly how much water is used depends on the type of wash. Self-service

washes typically use 10 to 12 gallons for a single wash. Conveyor washes use 20 to 25 gallons and express exterior washes in which the car doesn't move require as much as 35 gallons on a single vehicle, said Mark Thorsby, executive director of the International Carwash Association. Some systems claim to be able to recycle close to 100 percent of that water."

Source: *Franchise Times*, September 2007. Dated, but probably still in the ballpark.

- Tunnel Car Wash
  According to industry trade magazines, the national average for traffic entering a tunnel car wash is .76%. Based on this figure, an area traffic count of 30,000 vehicles per day would result in approximately 228 cars entering your business. While regional differences may affect your average revenue per wash, the national average wash generates $9.75 per car.
- Based on the above figures:
  228 Vehicles Per Day X $9.75 Per Vehicle = $2,223.00 Per Day is the projected average income. If your facility is open 320 days per year, then your gross revenue from a single site will be approximately $711,360.00 per annum.
- The following guidelines are listed for the additional costs.

Item	Percent of Gross	Cost
Supplies	6.0%	$42,681.00
Utilities	7.5%	$53,352.00
Variable Expenses	5.5%	$39,124.80
Fixed Expenses	29.8%	$211,985.00
Labor	32.0%	$227,635.20
Subtotal	80.8%	$574,778.00

- Therefore, you could assume that the gross profit generated from one typical self-serve site would be:
  $711,360.00 - $574,778.00 = $136,582.00
- "Car washes usually run at 1/3 profit from gross. Example: $90,000 gross = $30,000 net."
- For additional Car Wash Benchmark data, see Car Washes—Coin Operated/ Self- Serve

Expenses as a Percentage of Annual Sales

Cost of goods..05%
Payroll/labor Costs...42.5%
Occupancy..10%
Profit (estimated pretax) 25%

Industry Trend

- "Below avg. Will improve with economy and the sell-off of underperforming locations, as well as automation of the carwash tunnel, and marketing."
- "Automation"
- "The number of car washes being built is growing slowly."

Seller Financing

- "Seller will generally carry 30–35% over five to seven years at 6% interest per annum."
- "20 percent down, 80 percent financing, 20 year amortization"

Questions

- "How many vehicles per month do they do, summer vs. winter and the average ticket on each vehicle. Any environmental issues? The length of the lease and the rent factor. Is there at least one mgr.?"

- "You need to ask the Seller the name of the equipment, the age of the equipment. Is the car wash brush or brushless, any problems with the system?"
- "Provable Gross and Net. Is all labor on the books. What percentage of gross income is cash. Average monthly car count and ticket price, all sources of income"
- "Water bills, proof of car counts and any other paperwork proving the stated numbers"
- "Are you clear with employees and are they all registered? Is there ground contamination? How are the tax records?"

Resources

Associations
- International Carwash Association: www.carwash.org

Car X Auto Service	Franchise
Approx. Total Investment	$214,000 to $326,000
Estimated Annual Sales/Unit	$750,000
NAICS 811111	Number of Businesses/Units 170

Rules of Thumb
➤ 35 to 40 percent of annual sales plus inventory

Resources
Websites
- www.carx.com

Card Shops (See Gift Shops/Hallmark Gift Shops)		
SIC 5947-10	NAICS 453220	Number of Businesses/Units 74,531

Rules of Thumb
➤ [Note: We debated whether to leave card shops as a stand-alone business, but there are few, if any, pure card shops. However, card shops still have a SIC and a NAICS number, so someone feels that they are still a stand-alone business. On the other hand, we have seen few gift shops that didn't have cards. In either event, we suspect that the rule of thumb would be about the same.]

Benchmark Data

Statistics (Gift Shops & Card Stores)

Number of Establishments	74,531
Average Profit Margin	3.4%
Revenue per Employee	$65,000
Average Number of Employees	3
Average Wages per Employee	$12,210

Source: IBISWorld, March 2012

Products and Services Segmentation

Souvenirs	31.5%
Cards	19.5%
Collectible gifts	17.6%
Novelties	13.4%
Holiday and seasonal decorations	8.2%
Party supplies	6.8%
Gift wrap	3.0%

Source: IBISWorld, March 2012

Industry Costs

Profit	3.4%
Wages	18.8%
Purchases	64.5%
Depreciation	1.9%
Marketing	2.1%
Rent & Utilities	4.9%
Other	4.4%

Source: IBISWorld, March 2012

Market Share

Amscan Holdings Inc.	7.8%

Source: IBISWorld, March 2012

	Franchise
Carl's Jr. Restaurants	
Approx. Total Investment	$1,315,000 to $1,860,000
Estimated Annual Sales/Unit	$1,250,000
SIC 5812-06 NAICS 722211	Number of Businesses/Units 1,290

Rules of Thumb

➢ 40 percent of annual sales plus inventory

Carpet Cleaning	
SIC 7217-04 NAICS 561740	Number of Businesses/Units 39,736

Rules of Thumb

➢ 50 to 55 percent of annual revenue plus inventory

➢ 1.8 times SDE plus inventory

Benchmark Data

Statistics (Carpet Cleaning)

Number of Establishments	39,736
Average Profit Margin	6.6%
Revenue per Employee	$54,800
Average Number of Employees	1.7
Average Wages per Employee	$19,753

Source: IBISWorld, October 2012

Products and Services Segmentation

Residential carpet and upholstery cleaning	51.5%
Commercial carpet and upholstery cleaning	20.1%
Other	15.4%
Offsite cleaning services	11.5%
Ventilation duct cleaning	1.5%

Source: IBISWorld, October 2012

Industry Costs

Profit	6.6%
Wages	35.9%
Purchases	20.7%
Depreciation	1.5%
Marketing	4.6%
Rent & Utilities	5.0%
Other	25.7%

Source: IBISWorld, October 2012

Market Share

ServiceMaster	9.9%
Chem-Dry Inc.	6.9%

Source: IBISWorld, October 2012

Resources

Websites
- www.carpet-rug.org

Associations
- Professional Association of Cleaning & Restoration: www.pcuca.org
- Restoration Industry Association: www.restorationindustry.org

---

Carpet/Floor Coverings

SIC 5713-05	NAICS 442210	Number of Businesses/Units 12,082

Rules of Thumb

➢ 20 percent of annual sales plus inventory

Benchmark Data

Statistics (Floor Covering Stores)

Number of Establishments	12,082
Average Profit Margin	2.0%
Revenue per Employee	$182,000
Average Number of Employees	7.5
Average Wages per Employee	$38,098

Source: IBISWorld, July 2012

Products and Services Segmentation

Carpets and rugs	58%
Ceramic tiles	16.5%
Hardwood	15.5%
Laminate	5%
Stone	5%

Source: IBISWorld, July 2012

Major Market Segmentation

Do-it-yourself consumers	40%
Do-it-for-me consumers	35%
Contractors	25%

Source: IBISWorld, July 2012

Market Share

CCA Global	50.0%

Source: IBISWorld, July 2012

Industry Costs

Profit	2.0%
Wages	21.3%
Purchases	65.0%
Depreciation	1.5%
Utilities	1.5%
Rent	4.5%
Other	4.2%

Source: IBISWorld, July 2012

Resources

Trade Publications

- Floor Covering Weekly: www.floorcoveringweekly.com

	Franchise
Cartridge World	
Approx. Total Investment	$130,000 to $204,000
NAICS 424120	Number of Businesses/Units 1,700

Rules of Thumb

➤ 30 to 35 percent of annual sales plus inventory

Resources

Websites

- www.cartridgeworld.com

	Franchise
Carvel Ice Cream Bakery (See also Ice Cream/Yogurt Shops)	
Approx. Total Investment	$351,000 to $354,500
Estimated Annual Sales/Unit	Not Available
SIC 2024-98	NAICS 722213	Number of Businesses/Units 450

Rules of Thumb

➤ 55 percent of annual sales or 20 to 25 times the number of gallons of liquid ice cream mix purchased plus inventory

➤ 2.25 to 2.5 times SDE plus inventory

Pricing Tips

- "Typically [priced] at $30 per gallon of ice cream mix used. Therefore, a 5,000-gallon store, which grosses approximately $250,000 would sell for $150,000 to $160,000 with SDE at about $65,000. The $150,000–$175,000 equates to approximately 60% of gross. Stores with disproportionate rental expense would be closer to 50% of gross or 2 times SDE. The exception is for the very few higher volume stores, above 8,000. These would sell for closer to $40 per gallon with SDE of 2.5."
- "Some franchised ice cream businesses with a positive history, updated facilities and verifiable sales numbers will move to 2.5 SDE. Conversely, a short lease and less than five years on franchise agreement will result in less than 2 times SDE."
- "Location drives price higher and typically has higher returns on product usage, therefore more profit. Free standing buildings with volume in excess of 10,000 gallons, rule of thumb would be 60 percent of annual sales, with average lease of 7 years remaining."

Benchmark Data

- "Food cost percentage typically is equal to SDE unless rent is above $25 per sq. ft."

Expenses as a Percentage of Annual Sales

Cost of goods:	26%
Payroll/labor Costs:	21%
Occupancy:	11%
Profit (estimated pretax):	25%

Seller Financing

- "3 to 5 years"

Resources

Websites

- www.carvel.com

Casinos/Casino Hotels		
SIC 7993-02	NAICS 713210	Number of Businesses/Units 779

Rules of Thumb

➢ Las Vegas Strip average: 8.1 times EBITDA

➢ Indian Gaming management contracts: 30 to 40 percent net (this is pulled from the top in "Operating Income" and should be calculated before debt service). 5 to 7 percent of gross used to be standard for Indian Gaming contracts. The NIGC must approve all contracts and agreements between management and tribal nations. The NIGC (National Indian Gaming Commission) is an independent federal regulatory agency of the United States. Management cannot own any part of the Indian casino. Contracts are typically five years with options to renew. The tribe will be responsible for paying down the debt service.

Pricing Tips

- "Casinos Only: Annual Revenue less than $3,000,000: 2.25 to 2.75 times verifiable annual cash flow (I would use a weighted average of the past three time periods). If the 'casino' doesn't own the slot machines, then the multiple would be less.

  "Annual Revenue $3,000,000 to $10,000,000: 2.75 to 3.25 times verifiable annual cash flow (I would use a weighted average of the past three time periods). If the 'casino' doesn't own the slot machines, then the multiple would be less.

  "Annual revenue over $10,000,000 (but not over $25,000,000): 3.00 to 4.00 times verifiable annual cash flow (I would use a weighted average of the past three time periods). If the 'casino' doesn't own the slot machines, then the multiple would be less."

- Remember the Buyer must get a gaming license. In Nevada, that could run: 6-7 months and $5,000 in cost for a 'Restricted License'. This allows the licensee to operate not more than 15 slot machines (not table games, etc.). This is common in what we call 'Tavern Licenses.'"

- "Circus Circus is a lower-rent property, and analysts and executives say budget properties are suffering as customers upgrade to well-appointed resorts that are offering deep discounts. If tourists can pay just a little bit more to stay at a more luxurious, newer hotel, they do it. The industry has a name for this trend: price compression.

  "MGM's Excalibur also is a budget property and, like Circus Circus, tends to attract cost-conscious adults with children. Both hotels have about 4,000 rooms. But when it comes to earnings and losses, this is a tale of two cities. Excalibur is more centrally located on the Strip, with more walk-by traffic and proximity to higher-end hotels, and it posted operating income of $8.4 million in the fourth quarter. That's within striking distance of the $8.9 million earned by neighboring Mandalay Bay, a much larger and more luxurious property that includes The Hotel, an upscale hotel expansion.

  "For 2009, Excalibur posted $48 million in operating income. That's down from $84 million the prior year but was better than Monte Carlo, New York-New York and Luxor, which are more expensive properties with higher-end amenities.

  "Circus Circus and Excalibur earned vastly different amounts of a key profit indicator called EBITDA—earnings before interest, taxes, depreciation and amortization. By this measure, Excalibur earned $72.1 million against Circus Circus' $27.1 million. Excalibur's EBITDA fell 35 percent, which is more within the range suffered by other major casinos in the recession. Circus Circus' EBITDA, however, fell by 52 percent."

  Source: "Empty lots hurt nearby casinos on the Strip's north end" by Liz Benston, April 5, 2010, www.lasvegassun.com/news

Benchmark Data

Hotel Casinos

Statistics (Casino Hotels)

Number of Establishments	305
Average Profit Margin	8.2%
Revenue per Employee	$136,400
Average Number of Employees	1,288
Average Wages per Employee	$34,455

Source: IBISWorld, February 2012

Products and Services Segmentation

Gaming tables and slot machines	66.9%
Accommodations	12.6%
Meals and non-alcoholic drinks	10.7%
Other	6.7%
Alcoholic drinks	3.1%

Source: IBISWorld, February 2012

Industry Costs

Profit	8.2%
Wages	25.4%
Purchases	8.0%
Depreciation	6.5%
Utilities	2.0%
Rent	2.0%
Other	47.9%

Source: IBISWorld, February 2012

Market Share

Caesars Entertainment Corporation	16.6%
MGM Resorts International	15.6%
Las Vegas Sands Corporation	3.9%

Source: IBISWorld, February 2012

Non-Hotel Casinos
Statistics (Non-Hotel Casinos)

Number of Establishments	474
Average Profit Margin	15.9%
Revenue per Employee	$22,800
Average Number of Employees	275
Average Wages per Employee	$29,871

Source: IBISWorld, March 2012

Products and Services Segmentation

On-premises gaming (riverboat and barge casinos)	69.3%
Off-track betting (riverboat and barge casinos)	14.7%
Cruise casinos	7.0%
Food and non-alcoholic beverages (riverboat and barge casinos)	4.8%
Alcoholic beverages (riverboat and barge casinos)	2.2%
Arcades and video games (riverboat and barge casinos)	2.0%

Source: IBISWorld, March 2012

Industry Costs

Profit	15.9%
Wages	23.5%
Purchases	5.0%
Depreciation	6.5%
Marketing	8.5%
Rent & Utilities	3.5%
Other	37.1%

Source: IBISWorld, March 2012

Market Share

Penn National Gaming Inc.	17.0%
Isle of Capri Casinos, Inc.	6.3%
Caesars Entertainment Corporation	6.0%

Source: IBISWorld, March 2012

Distribution of employer establishments by staff size

Employees	Establishments	Share of total (%)
1 to 4	83	16.3%
5 to 9	74	14.6%

Source: IBISWorld, January 2011

Las Vegas Strip Casinos

Revenues by Department	% of total
Gaming	38.2%
Rooms	24.0%
Food	15.4%
Beverage	6.6%
Other	15.8%
Total	100%
Occupancy Rate:	91.12%

Source: 2011 *Nevada Gaming Abstract*. Carson City: Nevada Gaming Control Board, 2012

- "With an average wage of approximately $70,500, the sector's employees earned significantly more than the U.S. median income of $43,460 (Bureau of Labor Statistics)."
- "The importance of the gaming machines produced by the equipment manufacturing sector cannot be overlooked, as polling consistently shows that slot machines are the most popular game on the casino floors. Currently, there are more than 854,000 gaming machines in 39 states nationwide, with Nevada (186,914), California (67,752), and Oklahoma (62,322) being home to the most."

Source: *2011 AGA Survey of Casino Entertainment*

- The opening of a new casino in Philadelphia, along with the reclassification of properties in suburban Philadelphia and Pittsburgh, led to the inclusion of the two cities on the list of top earning casino markets for the first time.
- Profile of Casino Visitors: Forms of Gambling Participated in During the Last 12 Months, 2010

Playing the lottery	49%
Casino gambling	25%
Playing poker	12%
Wagering on a race	9%
Internet gambling	1%

Source: *2011 AGA Survey of Casino Entertainment*

Industry Trend
- Breakdown of Global Casino Gaming Market

	2009	2014
U.S.	57%	43%
Europe, Middle East & Africa	17%	13%
Asia Pacific	22%	41%
Canada	04%	03%

Source: www.thesmokingjacket.com/entertainment/vital-statistics December 2011

Resources

Websites
- www.naspl.org
- www.igcouncil.org

Associations
- American Gaming Association: www.americangaming.org
- National Indian Gaming Association: www.indiangaming.org

Caterers/Catering		
SIC 5812-12	NAICS 722320	Number of Businesses/Units 9,375

Rules of Thumb
➢ 35 to 40 percent of annual sales plus inventory

Benchmark Data

Statistics (Caterers)

Number of Establishments	9,375
Average Profit Margin	4.5%
Revenue per Employee	$58,800
Average Number of Employees	12
Average Wages per Employee	$17,723

Source: IBISWorld, April 2012

Products and Services Segmentation

Wedding catering	22%
Corporate functions and product launch catering	20%
Birthday catering	15%
Catering for other parties	15%
Engagement catering	12%
Seminars and conference catering	11%
Retirement party catering	5%

Source: IBISWorld, April 2012

Industry Costs

Profit	4.5%
Wages	30.3%
Purchases	47.0%
Depreciation	1.0%
Marketing	1.5%
Rent & Utilities	6.0%
Other	9.7%

Source: IBISWorld, April 2012

Resources

Trade Publications
- Cater Source Journal: www.catersource.com

Associations
- International Caterers Association: www.internationalcaterers.org
- The National Association of Catering Executives (NACE): www.nace.net

Catering Trucks (See also Routes, Ice Cream Trucks, Food Trucks)		
	NAICS 722330	Number of Businesses/Units 4,157

Rules of Thumb
➢ 40 percent of annual sales plus inventory

Benchmark Data

Statistics (Street Vendors)

Number of Establishments	4,157
Average Profit Margin	23%
Revenue per Employee	$95,900
Average Number of Employees	3.9
Average Wages per Employee	$17,136

Source: IBISWorld, August 2012

Products and Services Segmentation

Traditional street vendors	45%
Mobile food preparation vehicles	37%
Industrial catering vehicles	18%

Source: IBISWorld, August 2012

Major Market Segmentation

Street locations and corners	55%
Other locations, venues and events	18%
Industrial or construction worksites	15%
Shopping malls	12%

Source: IBISWorld, August 2012

Industry Costs

Profit	23.0%
Wages	17.8%
Purchases	27.0%
Depreciation	5.0%
Marketing	0.5%
Rent & Utilities	3.4%
Other	23.3%

Source: IBISWorld, August 2012

- "This type of business will be largely cash intensive, since most individuals purchasing items from a mobile vendor pay in cash. Accordingly, gross receipts will be the main focus for the examination. The examiner will expect to see large cash deposits to the business bank account. To verify all cash is deposited or accounted for, the examiner must analyze the markup percentage. The examiner should expect to see a consistent markup percentage of about 100% on cold foods sold and about 200% on hot foods sold. For example, if an item is purchased for $0.50, it will generally sell for $1 or more."

Source: Internal Revenue Service Retail Industry Audit Technique Guide (ATG)

Cellular Telephone Stores
NAICS 443112

Rules of Thumb

➢ 40 percent of annual revenues plus inventory

➢ "Most cell-phone stores receive a small percentage of the usage fees based on the sale of the plan purchased by the customer with the telephone."

Resources

Associations
- Cellular Telecommunications & Internet Association (CTIA): www.ctia.org

Cemeteries		
SIC 6553-02	NAICS 812220	Number of Businesses/Units 8,608

Rules of Thumb

➢ 6 times SDE includes real estate

➢ 8 times EBIT includes real estate

➢ 6 times EBITDA includes real estate

Pricing Tips
- "Valuations will vary depending on the strategic fit of the buyer. A local funeral home is generally the best strategic fit and should, therefore, be willing to pay the most."

Benchmark Data

Statistics (Cemetery Services)
Number of Establishments	8,608
Average Profit Margin	8.8%
Revenue per Employee	$89,800
Average Number of Employees	4.5
Average Wages per Employee	$35,463

Source: IBISWorld, July 2012

Products and Services Segmentation
Sale of graves, plots and other spaces	39.1%
Internment	21.7%
Merchandise sales	18.8%
Cremation	13.1%
Cemetery maintenance services	3.7%
Pre-burial services	3.3%
Other	0.3%

Source: IBISWorld, July 2012

Industry Costs
Profit	8.8%
Wages	39.0%
Purchases	14.0%
Depreciation	2.2%
Marketing	5.0%
Rent & Utilities	5.1%
Other	25.9%

Source: IBISWorld, July 2012

Market Share
SCI	22.1%
Stewart Enterprises Inc.	7.2%
StoneMor	6.8%

Source: IBISWorld, July 2012

Questions

- "Trust fund information is critical. What are the liabilities? Are they properly funded? Is there a successful sales organization/program in place?"

	Franchise
CertaPro Painters	
Approx. Total Investment	$129,000 to $154,000

SIC 1721-01	NAICS 238320	Number of Businesses/Units 365

Rules of Thumb

➤ 45 percent of annual sales plus inventory

Resources

Websites
- www.certapro-franchise.com

Check Cashing Services (See also Pay Day Loans & Ace Cash Express)		
SIC 6099-03	NAICS 522390	Number of Businesses/Units 61,500

Rules of Thumb

➤ 75 percent of annual revenues

➤ 2 times SDE

Pricing Tips

- "The check cashing business is growing; every state has its own rules and regulations. Lease terms and whether a franchise or independent will affect pricing."

Benchmark Data

- See Payday Loans for additional Benchmark data.

Services/Products Offerings & Volumes

Check Cashing	96%
Money Orders	96%
Money Transfers	96%
Bill Payments	96%
Prepaid Debit Cards	88%
Payday Advances	58%
Travelers Checks	4%
Installment Loans	25%
Other Financial Products	63%

Source: Financial Service Centers of America, www.fisca.org

- "Check cashing should provide the owner with 1% of total gross sales as owner's discretionary income."

Expenses as a Percentage of Annual Sales

Cost of goods	99%
Payroll/labor Costs	01%
Occupancy	01%
Profit (estimated pretax)	01%

Industry Trend

- "A new FDIC report found that nationally, 17 million adults are unbanked. An additional 43 million adults are under banked. You are unbanked if you don't have a checking or savings account. The FDIC defined underbanked households as those that have a checking or savings account but use nonbank money orders, check-cashing services, payday loans, rent-to-own agreements, or pawnshops at least once or twice a year."

  Source: *Boston Sunday Globe*, "The Color of Money" by Michelle Singletary, December 6, 2009

- "Walmart (NYSE: WMT) today celebrated the grand opening of its 1000th Walmart MoneyCenter and announced plans to add Walmart MoneyCenters in 500 additional stores this year. The 1000th Walmart MoneyCenter, located in Chalmette, LA., gives customers affordable solutions on basic money services, including the Walmart MoneyCard.

  "'Walmart MoneyCenters are a cornerstone of our business and were specially created to give customers a welcoming environment where they can save when they cash checks, pay bills and transfer money,' said Jane Thompson, president, Walmart Financial Services. 'Customers ask when their stores will get a Walmart MoneyCenter, so we are delighted to announce the expansion into approximately 500 more stores.'

  With the anticipated expansion into 500 more stores this year, there will be Walmart MoneyCenters in approximately 40 percent of Walmart's 3,763 stores nationwide."

  Source: "Walmart Opens 1000th Walmart MoneyCenter, Announces 500 more for 2010,"
  March 16, 2010, www.walmartstores.com/pressroom

Resources

Websites

- www.fisca.org

	Franchise
Cheeburger Cheeburger Restaurants	
Approx. Total Investment	$400,000 to $600,000

SIC 5812-19	NAICS 722211	Number of Businesses/Units 45

Rules of Thumb

➤ 35 to 40 percent plus inventory

Resources

Websites

- www.cheeburger.com

Chemical Product and Preparations Manufacturing

(See Manufacturing—Chemical)

Franchise

Chester's International (Fried Chicken)

Approx. Total Investment		$60,000 to $400,400
Estimated Annual Sales/Unit		Not Available
	NAICS 722211	Number of Businesses/Units 50

Rules of Thumb

➤ 35 to 40 percent of annual sales plus inventory

Resources

Websites
- www.chestersinternational.com

Chicken Restaurants and Food-To-Go

(See also Restaurants—Limited Service)

	NAICS 722110	

Rules of Thumb

➤ 30 to 35 percent of annual sales plus inventory

Pricing Tips
- Chesters International—35% to 40% of annual sales
  Chick-fil-A—60% to 70% of annual sales (estimated annual sales—$2.5 million)
  KFC—30% to 35% (estimated annual sales—$925,000)

Franchise

Chick-fil-A

Approx. Total Investment		See below
Estimated Annual Sales/Unit		$2,500,500
SIC 5812-06	NAICS 722211	Number of Businesses/Units 1,600

Rules of Thumb

➤ 60 to 70 percent of annual sales plus inventory

Benchmark Data
- "Cathy, 86, credits the company's success to 975 franchisees and 600 employees who are unusually dedicated in an industry known for grumpy operators and high turnover among hourly workers. The turnover among

Chick-fil-A operators is a low 5% a year. Among hourly workers turnover is 60%, compared with 107% for the industry, We tell applicants, 'If you don't intend to be here for life, you needn't apply,' says Cathy, who opened his first restaurant in 1946."

Source: "The Cult of Chick-fil-A" by Emily Schmall, *Forbes*, July 23, 2007

- "The company asks operators to pay just $5,000 as an initial franchise fee. KFC, for example, demands $25,000 and a net worth of $1 million.Chick-fil-A pays for the land, the construction and the equipment. It then rents everything to the franchise for 15% of the restaurant's sales plus 50% of the pretax profit remaining. Operators, who are discouraged from running more than a few restaurants, take home $100,000 a year on average from a single outlet. A solo Bojangles' franchisee can expect to earn $330,000 (EBITDA) on sales of $1.7 million."

Source: The Cult of Chick-fil-A" by Emily Schmall, *Forbes*, July 23, 2007

Resources

Websites
- www.chick-fil-a.com

Child Care Centers (See Day Care Centers)

Children's and Infants' Clothing Stores

(See also Clothing Stores & Family Clothing Stores)

	NAICS 448130	Number of Businesses/Units 15,004

Rules of Thumb

➢ 25 to 30 percent of annual sales plus inventory

Benchmark Data

Statistics (Children's & Infants' Clothing Stores)

Number of Establishment	15,004
Average Profit Margin	3.6%
Revenue per Employee	$89,700
Average Number of Employees	8
Average Wages per Employee	$10,707

Source: IBISWorld, July 2012

Products and Services Segmentation

Girls' clothing	36.3%
Infants' and toddlers' clothing	36.0%
Boys' clothing	25.8%
Other	1.9%

Source: IBISWorld, July 2012

Industry Costs

Profit	3.6%
Wages	11.8%
Purchases	48.9%
Depreciation	2.4%
Marketing	14.2%
Rent & Utilities	11.3%
Other	7.8%

Source: IBISWorld, July 2012

Market Share

Toys 'R' Us Inc.	30.2%
The Children's Place Retail Stores Inc.	15.2%
The Gymboree Corporation	12.6%
Carter's Inc.	10.8%
Dressbarn Inc.	10.5%

Source: IBISWorld, July 2012

Chinese Restaurants (See Restaurants-Asian & Restaurants)

	NAICS 722110	Number of Businesses/Units 26,000

Rules of Thumb

➤ 30 percent of annual sales plus inventory

Chiropractic Practices

SIC 8041-01	NAICS 621310	Number of Businesses/Units 61,148

Rules of Thumb

➤ 55 to 60 percent of annual sales includes inventory

➤ 1 to 2.5 times SDE includes inventory

➤ 1.5 to 2 times EBITDA

Pricing Tips

- "Beware historical pricing data now that the Affordable Care Act ("Obamacare") has passed, as Medicare and many following PPOs with migrate to Accountable Care Organizations, losing patients to DC practices. Cash practices are worth more than insurance based practices. Otherwise, pricing is now similar to insurance-based medical practices."

"In addition to a thorough statistical analysis, other factors to consider when determining fair market value of an established practice include a compilation and assessment of the following:

  ✓ Office location, appearance, accessibility, visibility, equipment and layout
  ✓ Staff profile
  ✓ Gross and net income
  ✓ Accounts receivable
  ✓ Payor provider profile
  ✓ HMO/PPO affiliations
  ✓ Referral alliances

✓ Active patient list

✓ Office procedures (overall practice philosophy, consultation, examinations, report of findings, adjusting techniques and ancillary care.)

- "Only after a comprehensive review and evaluation of all of these factors can we look beyond the practice finances and statistics and determine a fair market value."

Source: www.chiroequity.com

- "Typically solo practice grosses $250k–$350k and will sell 50%-70%. Many substandard, low-grossing practices that will sell for much lower multiples. Some practices have almost no tangible assets ($10k–$20k);others have quite a bit of expensive equipment and possibly a lot of nutraceutical inventory."

- "Depends on hours worked. Value of equipment can vary considerably depending on techniques/technology. Equipment value for solo practice may range from $20k to $150k+ so this can affect value quite a bit. Price usually does not include A/R and sold as asset sale."

- "Cash practice is worth more than insured practice."

- "Normal selling range about 60% to 70% of gross income. Typical solo practice grosses $250k to $350k/year."

- "It is my personal belief that chiropractic market values are overheated, as practice sales are occurring that are difficult to support with earnings. Some lenders are leaving the market for the same reason, due to high & increasing rates of default on loans to buyers. I find that values of [3-4x (SDE minus one owner's market rate salary for work performed)] can be supported by earnings, the income approach to valuation, and the principle of substitution. On the other hand, there are demonstrated sales far above this level."

- "Pricing varies widely by location and type of practice, cash or insurance-dominated. Insurance reimbursement is still trending downward; Medicare is planning further reductions which other insurance companies will follow. Statistics are similar to medical family practice."

- "Are you and the doctor a compatible personality match? Is the personality of the selling doctor vivacious and outgoing, while the 'new' doctor is a little reserved? Is your chiropractic technique compatible with the seller's? Every instance of non-compatibility may mean one fewer patient will remain with you.

- "With compatibility being addressed, I value the practice and goodwill to be equal to one-year net income. This figure will be corrected based upon a few factors:

✓ Blend of patient financial classes

✓ Insurance dependency/non-dependency

✓ Selling doctor's philosophy (pain practice/wellness practice)

✓ Percentage of actual overhead (high overhead lowers value)

- "Purchasing a practice is a very smart thing to do. I would always look for a practice to buy rather than start fresh."

Source: From an article by Bruce A. Parker, D.C. in *Today's Chiropractic*.
For more information, go to www.bruceparkerconsulting.com.

Expert Comments

"Chiropractic is an easier specialty to get into than allopathic medicine, so competition is higher, and they are outside of the allopathic referral patterns so commonly have to do more marketing."

"Lots of competition but increasing need by baby boomers. Restrictive health insurance plans often don't cover chiro, so rate of self-pay is higher than medicine or dentistry."

"Practice income can be heavily influenced by state regulation of Personal Injury/Workers Comp laws. Many states have changed laws in last 10 years which drastically reduced practice incomes (by 50%–70%) as chiropractic stopped being reimbursed by insurance. Hard to finance. Most lenders shy away from chiro deals. Many buyers have less than ideal credit."

"Hard to finance relative to other health care practices. Easy startup with low cost."

"Insured practices subject to more risk"

"Lots of competition in some locales. High loan default rate. Low cost/barrier to entry. Many buyers have bad credit history."

"Insurance reimbursement is on the decline in many sectors, especially Medicare and WorkComp. Past 10 years' increasing values during hot economy are likely to be unsupportable in event of an economic downturn which will reduce patients' cash expenditures."

Benchmark Data

Statistics (Chiropractors)

Number of Establishments	61,148
Average Profit Margin	27.5%
Revenue per Employee	$90,000
Average Number of Employees	2
Average Wages per Employee	$26,258

Source: IBISWorld, June 2012

Products and Services Segmentation

Manual manipulation for back pain	25%
Extremity manipulating and adjusting	20%
Rehabilitation	20%
Non-manual procedures for back pain	15%
Manual manipulation for neck pain	11%
Non-manual procedures for neck pain	09%

Source: IBISWorld, June 2012

Major Market Segmentation

Private health insurance	42%
Patients paying out-of-pocket	28%
Property or casualty and auto insurance	14%
Medicare	08%
Workers' compensation	05%
Other	02%
Medicaid	01%

Source: IBISWorld, June 2012

Industry Costs

Profit	27.5%
Wages	28.7%
Purchases	5.5%
Depreciation	2.5%
Marketing	6.0%
Rent & Utilities	11.0%
Other	18.8%

Source: IBISWorld, June 2012

C - Rules of Thumb

- "There are many subspecialty modalities, often described by chiropractors as 'straights' versus 'mixers', i.e., straights do just spinal manipulation, mixed add other modalities; so Benchmark Data vary."
- "Chiropractors reported an average annual salary of $115,513 and an average total compensation of $123,375. While average total compensation has been higher in recent years, the average salary for DCs is the highest it has been since 1998 when the average salary was $131,200.

  "Though average billings and collections were right on par with last year, the average reimbursement rate was nearly 7 percent points higher (66 percent and 59 percent, respectively). Average billings for DCs were $523,014 compared to $541,396 last year.

  "Average collections were $345,247 compared to $323,421 last year."
- "Sees 122.5 patients each week; has a patient-visit average (PVA) of 26.8; attracts 6.1 new patients each week; and sees patients 31.4 hours a week."
- "Average Expenses
  - ✓ Advertising $9,966
  - ✓ Malpractice insurance $2,413
  - ✓ Office lease/mortgage (yr.) $24,114"

  Source: *Chiropractic Economics*, May 31, 2011—a very valuable site.
- "65%–75% overhead"

Components of Chiropractic Practice

Direct patient care	52.9%
Documentation	18.9%
Patient education	15.1%
Business management	13.2%

Source: National Board of Chiropractic Examiners

Reimbursement Categories, Managed Care, and Referral

Private Insurance	21.5%
Private pay/cash	21.2%
Managed care	19.4%
Personal injury	13.6%
Medicare	10.8%
Workers' Comp	07.8%
Pro Bono	03.9%
Medicaid	01.8%

Source: National Board of Chiropractic Examiners

Expenses as a Percentage of Annual Sales

Cost of goods:	06% to 10%
Payroll/labor Costs:	05% to 15%
Occupancy:	04% to 07%
Profit (estimated pretax):	25% to 50%

Industry Trend

- "High provider saturation keeps values up due to difficulty getting patients from scratch"
- "Up as boomers' health deteriorates"
- "Ancillary product revenue is increasing trend (nutrition, pillows, ointments, orthotics, exercise, etc.)."

Seller Financing

- "2–5 years"

Questions

- "Source of new patients, wait list, insurance impact, ancillary services or providers, ratio of established and returning patients ("once a back patient; always a back patient")"
- "State and federal compliance at all levels of business, clinical, billing, collections, labor, etc."
- "Any regulation/law changes in recent years (or planned) that may significantly impact revenue? % income from professional services versus product sales. Hours worked, number of patient visits/week, payer mix/insurance reimbursement."
- "School of practice, ancillary services"
- "# FTE DCs? # hours worked/week for each DC? Modalities offered? Practice focus? i.e., personal injury, wellness, workers comp, rehab, etc. Any recent/ pending legislation affecting practice income/insurance reimbursement? Payer mix? Ancillaries offered and % income (e.g., pillows, nutritionals, orthotics, creams, wraps, etc.)"
- "If the buyer is not a licensed chiropractor, the buyer should inquire of the state if a non-chiropractor is allowed to own a chiropractic practice or employ a chiropractor in that state."
- "Is the practice set up to support the way you want to work? If you want to run a family practice, and most of the clientele are work-related injury or PI (personal injury) patients, you will have to start from scratch to attract families to your practice. If your technique is notably different from the previous doctor's, you will have a difficult time transitioning the patients."
- "Is the practice located in the right place? If the practice is in a town you want to move to and live in for a long time, you can proceed knowing that you will be buying a business you can stay with for years. If the practice is not exactly where you want to be located, you will probably be better off finding a town you like and starting your own practice."
- "Is a practice broker involved? Most practice brokers are reputable, and they can help smooth the way toward a sale. But remember that the broker works for the seller—not the buyer—and the broker's objective is to get top dollar, as this determines the size of the sales commission. Hire your own CPA and attorney and verify everything the broker says."
- "Is the price reasonable? Many doctors will inflate the prices of their practices for two reasons: 1. They want to get paid for their years of work, and 2. They have been counting on using the proceeds of the practice sale to fund their retirement.
- "A practice in which the doctor has only been working a few days a week might seem like a steal, but if the selling doctor won't come down in price, you could end up paying too much for the practice."
- "Can you get a non-compete from the doctor? The last thing you want is to buy a practice and have the selling doctor open up down the street and take back all of his or her former patients. Some states (like California) do not uphold non-compete agreements, and you will have to pay a reasonable amount of money for a non-compete as part of the purchase price."
- "If you don't think you can get a good non-compete, or you don't think it will be upheld in court, the practice may not be for you. Make sure that you know the actual reason the doctor is selling. If your instincts tell you that you're not getting the whole story, be cautious."

- "How long will it take you to make a living from the practice? If the price is too high, if there is no strong patient base, or if you are going to have to start effectively from scratch, you might be better off going down the street and opening your own practice.
- "Finally, trust your instincts. If the offer sounds too good to be true, it probably is. If everything looks great and you have a good feeling about the practice and the location, it could be a wonderful lifelong investment for you."
- Jean Murray, PhD, has been counseling small business owners since 1974 and is currently helping chiropractic students and graduates who want to start their own practices.

Resources

Trade Publications
- *Chiropractic Economics*: www.chiroeco.com
- *Today's Chiropractic*: www.todayschiropractic.com

Associations
- American Chiropractic Association: www.acatoday.org
- National Board of Chiropractic Examiners—an excellent site: www.nbce.org

---

Cigar Stores (See Tobacco Stores)

Closet Factory	Franchise
Approx. Total Investment	$182,500 to $310,000

	NAICS 238390	Number of Businesses/Units 48

Rules of Thumb
➢ 55 percent of annual sales plus inventory

Resources

Websites
- www.closetfactory.com

Closets by Design	Franchise
Approx. Total Investment	$124,900 to $278,400
Estimated Annual Sales/Unit	Not Available

SIC 1521-20	NAICS 238390	Number of Businesses/Units 34

Rules of Thumb
➢ 45 percent of annual sales plus inventory

Resources

Websites

- www.closetsbydesign.com

Clothing Stores — Retail		
SIC 5699-77	NAICS 448140	Number of Businesses/Units 45,793

Rules of Thumb

> ➢ 40 to 45 percent of annual sales includes inventory
> ➢ 2.4 to 2.8 times SDE includes inventory

Benchmark Data

Statistics (Family Clothing Stores)

Number of Establishments	45,793
Average Profit Margin	6.8%
Revenue per Employee	$142,300
Average Number of Employees	14
Average Wages per Employee	$15,621

Source: IBISWorld, May 2012

Products and Services Segmentation

Women's casual wear	32.6%
Men's casual wear	17.4%
Women's formal wear	13.4%
Other women's wear	13.1%
Men's formal wear	8.8%
Children's wear	7.5%
Other men's wear	7.2%

Source: IBISWorld, May 2012

Industry Costs

Profit	6.8%
Wages	11.0%
Purchases	62.3%
Depreciation	2.3%
Marketing	7.6%
Rent & Utilities	6.2%
Other	3.8%

Source: IBISWorld, May 2012

Market Share

The Gap Inc.	12.5%
The TJX Companies Inc.	12.0%
Ross Stores Inc.	9.4%

Source: IBISWorld, May 2012

Expenses as a percentage of annual sales

Cost of goods sold	46% to 52%
Payroll/Labor costs	14% to 18%
Occupancy costs	6% to 10%
Profit (estimated pretax)	12% to 15%

Seller Financing

- "5 to 10 years"

Clothing Stores — Used

(See also Retail Stores, Used Goods, Consignment Shops)

SIC 5932-05	NAICS 453310	Number of Businesses/Units 20,000

Rules of Thumb

➢ 20 percent of annual sales plus inventory unless it is on consignment

Benchmark Data

▪ For Benchmark data see Used Goods

Resources

Associations

▪ The Association of Resale Professionals (NARTS)—a good site: www.narts.org

Cocktail Lounges (See also Bars)

SIC 5813-03	NAICS 722410	Number of Businesses/Units 10,000

Rules of Thumb

➢ 40 percent of annual sales plus inventory

➢ 3 to 4 times monthly sales; add license (where applicable) and plus inventory

➢ 1.5 to 2 times SDE; add fixtures, equipment and inventory

➢ $ for $ of gross sales if property is included, 40 percent of annual sales for business only plus inventory

Benchmark Data

▪ "Sales price 2½ to 3 times the annual liquor sales. Rent should never exceed 6 percent of the gross sales."

▪ "When buying liquor, only purchase what you can sell. Ignoring this simple rule has put many bars out of business...The only way to maintain a profitable operation is to establish a firm system of liquor control, and usage, that lets you know, to the penny, exactly how much each drink costs, and how much liquor is poured...Each dollar tied up in inventory is a dollar not working for you. And cash flow is the name of the game. So keep your inventory lean.... If you sell one-ounce drinks for $2 each, a quart bottle can generate 32 drinks, and $64 in revenues. If the quart bottle costs you $12, your gross profit will be $52. Subtract about $15 to cover labor and overhead, and you should clear $37.... However, if your bartender 'free pours' liquor, and his shots average 1 1/2 ounces, the number of drinks you get from a quart will be cut from 32 to 21. This will cut your revenue from $64 to $42. And your gross profit will fall from $52 to $30. And, if your bartender also gives away 4 free drinks out of the same bottle, your gross profit will drop to $22, minus your $15 in labor and overhead, which will leave you with just $7. That's why your liquor should be guarded like cash."

Source: "Eleven Tips to Owning a Profitable Bar," Specialty Group, Pittsburgh, PA

▪ For additional Benchmark data see Bars

Expenses as a Percentage of Annual Sales

Cost of goods	Food—30% to 40%; Beverages—18% to 22%
Payroll/labor Costs	25%
Occupancy	08%
Profit (estimated pretax)	10%

Industry Trend

- "Demand for this type of business seems to be declining."

Coffee Shops

(See also Restaurants—Limited Service & Coffee Shops (Specialty))

SIC 5812-28	NAICS 722213	Number of Businesses/Units 18,500

Rules of Thumb

➤ 3.5 to 4 times monthly sales plus inventory

➤ 35 to 40 percent of annual sales plus inventory

➤ 2 to 2.2 times SDE plus inventory

Pricing Tips

- "Trend of sales; owner's compensation including benefits, net profit, lease terms"

Expert Comments

"Ease of entry; unsophisticated owner/operators; personal use of products"

Benchmark Data

- "Food costs should not exceed 30%–33% of sales."

Expenses as a Percentage of Annual Sales

Cost of goods:	28% to 32%
Payroll/labor Costs:	25%
Occupancy:	08% to 12%
Profit (estimated pretax):	16% to 20%

Industry Trend

- "Frequent openings, frequent closings. Independents lose out to franchises."

Questions

- "Why are you selling? What problems have you had with employees, landlord, vendors, municipal officials, etc.? Do company records show all income (unlikely)?"

Resources

Websites

- www.coffeeuniverse.com

Associations
- Specialty Coffee Association of America: www.scaa.org

Coffee Shops (Specialty) (See also Coffee Shops)		
SIC 5812-28	NAICS 722213	Number of Businesses/Units 15,500

Rules of Thumb

➢ 40 percent of annual sales includes inventory

➢ 2.2 times SDE includes inventory

➢ 3 times EBIT

➢ 2.5 times EBITDA

Pricing Tips

- "The value of a coffee house is repeat business from a loyal customer base. Ensure that all vendor contracts will convey or transfer."
- "Recognize that profitability is key to determining overall value of the operation. A well-run, mature coffee house can net to the owner in excess of 20 percent of gross revenue."

Expert Comments

"While it is relatively easy to start a coffee house business, especially in relation to other types of food establishments, it can be a higher risk type of business due to the perceived simplicity of the business. Historically, specialty coffee establishments have participated in a high-growth industry segment and consequently have greater than average interest from potential buyers who are looking for a business."

"Opening a coffee house is relatively easy relative to other food and beverage businesses, however understanding the unique dynamics of the coffee house business can be a challenge. Is your location on the correct side of the road? Is your wholesale coffee pricing and quality up to par? How are you going to differentiate your location from the ubiquitous Starbucks?"

Benchmark Data

- For Benchmark data see Restaurants — Limited Service and Coffee Shops
- "Specialty coffees represent 37% of U.S. coffee cups and are considered the highest quality in the world.
- "The retail value of the U.S. coffee market is estimated at $30–32 billion dollars, with specialty comprising approximately a 37% volume share but nearly 50% value share.
- "40% of 18–24 year olds said they drink coffee daily, up from 31% in 2010 and on par with 2009's 40%, while 54% of 25–39 year olds said they drink coffee daily, up from 44% in 2010 and on par with 2009's 53%.
- "58% of consumers aged 18+ drank coffee yesterday, compared with 56% in 2010 59% in 2009, and 60% in 2008."

- Peet's Coffee & Tea Shops: estimated annual sales: $800,000
  Starbuck's Coffee Shops: estimated annual sales: $800,000
  Caribou Coffee Shops: estimated annual sales: $500,000
- "Facts and Statistics about Coffee Consumption in the United States
  - ✓ The average coffee cup size is nine ounces.
  - ✓ The average price for an espresso-based drink is $2.45.
  - ✓ The average price for a cup of brewed coffee is $1.38.
  - ✓ 35% of coffee drinkers prefer their coffee black.
  - ✓ 65% of coffee consumption takes place during breakfast hours.
  - ✓ Seattle has 10 times more coffee stores per 100,000 residents than the United States has overall.
  - ✓ The United States imports more than $4 billion dollars of coffee each year."

  Source: "Facts and Statistics about Coffee Consumption in the United States" by Carson Adley, May 11, 2010
- "Drink COGS should not be higher than 28% inclusive of all paper-goods costs."
- Dollar Size of Market

  Retail Sales Estimates Year End 2006—and Adjusted for inflation 2012.

  Coffee Cafes: (beverage retailers with seating)

  15,500 locations averaging $550,500 in annual sales (Adjusted for inflation 2012— $629,085)

  Coffee Kiosks: (beverage retailers without seating)

  3,600 locations averaging $300,000 in annual sales (Adjusted for inflation 2012—$342,826)

  Coffee Carts: (mobile beverage retailers)

  2,900 locations averaging $140,000 in annual sales (Adjusted for inflation 2012—$159,985))

  Coffee Bean Roaster/Retailers: (roasting on premises)

  1,900 locations averaging $925,000 in annual sales (Adjusted for inflation 2012—$1,057,047)

  Source: Specialty Coffee Association of America, www.scaa.org

Expenses as a Percentage of Annual Sales

Cost of goods:	28%
Payroll/labor Costs:	25%
Occupancy:	10%
Profit (estimated pretax):	20%

Seller Financing

- 3 years

Questions

- "What is your average ticket sale? What marketing efforts are currently in place? Have you measured customer loyalty? Are your employees cross trained?"

Resources

Websites
- www.coffeeuniverse.com
- www.virtualcoffee.com

Associations
- Specialty Coffee Association of America: www.scaa.org
- National Coffee Association of USA: www.ncausa.org

Coin Laundries

SIC 7215-01	NAICS 812310	Number of Businesses/Units 22,848

Rules of Thumb

➢ 100 percent of annual sales plus inventory

➢ 1 to 1½ times annual sales plus inventory

➢ 3 to 5 times SDE includes inventory (higher multiple for newer equipment and long lease)

➢ 4 to 5 times SDE plus inventory—assumes long-term lease (10+ years) and newer equipment (3–5 years old).

➢ 5 to 6 times EBIT

➢ 5 to 6 times EBITDA

➢ "Generally 2.5 to 5.0 times annual SDE; depends on various parts of the U.S. California, for example, sells between 4 and 5 times SDE, whereas in Nebraska it's 1.5 to 2.5 times SDE."

Pricing Tips

- "It is fair to say that a 10% misrepresentation as to gross sales can impact the overall value of a coin-laundry business by some 20%, and maybe considerably more; therefore, you must ask the right questions, and be able to assess the accuracy of the answers.

  "One ill-advised means of independent verification, which is commonly promoted by coin-laundry touts (both on-line and as half-learned authors of books on the subject), is the comparison of claimed revenue to water usage.

  "I consider it ill-advised for several reasons: Firstly, it is a relatively inexpensive method by which a seller can perpetrate a fraud by simply running-off water. Secondly, issues such as leaking water and mineral deposits within water meter mechanisms (water meter maintenance tends to be neglected by water providers) can significantly affect the accuracy of an analysis. Thirdly, many commercial washers now offer surreptitious programing which can significantly impact water usage (e.g., Wascomat 'Generation 6' washers can be adjusted to utilize 1.2 to 1.9 gallons of water per lb. of laundry—a maximum differential of 58.3%!)."

  Source: An excellent article by Gary Ruff, an industry consultant who is also an attorney.
Gary Ruff can be reached via his informative Web site: www.laundromatadvisor.com
or at (212) 696-8502 or (631) 389-280, He maintains two offices;
if you need advice or legal services in the coin laundry business—he knows his stuff.

- "Depending on the location, competition and most of all the lease, % of rent to sales and age of equipment."
- "Coin laundries normally sell for a multiple of their net earnings. The multiple may vary between three and five times the net cash flow, depending on several valuation factors. The following primary factors establish market value:
  - ✓ The net earnings before debt service, after adjustments for depreciation and any other nonstandard items including owner salary or payroll costs in services.
  - ✓ The terms and conditions of the real estate interest (lease), particularly length; frequency and amount of increases; expense provisions; and overall ratio of rent to gross income.
  - ✓ The age, condition and utilization of the equipment, and leasehold improvements; the physical attributes of the real property in which the coin laundry is located, particularly entrances/exits, street visibility and parking.
  - ✓ Existing conditions, including vend price structure in the local marketplace.
  - ✓ The demographic profile in the general area or region
  - ✓ Replacement cost and land usage issues.
- This resale market standard assumes an owner/operator scenario, with no allocation for outside management fees. Marketing time for store sales averages 60 to 90 days, depending on price, financing terms and the quality and quantity of stores available at the time of sale. Coin laundry listings are generally offered by business brokers who charge a sales commission of 8 percent to 10 percent. Many coin laundry distributors also act as brokers. The accepted standard of useful life for commercial coin laundry equipment is as follows:
  - ✓ Topload Washers (12 lbs. to 14 lbs.): 5–8 years
  - ✓ Frontload Washers (18 lbs. to 50 lbs.): 10–15 years
  - ✓ Dryers (30 lbs. to 60 lbs.):15–20 years
  - ✓ Heating Systems: 10–15 years
  - ✓ Coin Changers: 10–15 years"

  Source: Laundry Industry Overview, Coin Laundry Association, www.coinlaundry.org, an excellent and informative site.

- One Industry Expert has reported that a review showed that several hundred sales were for 80 percent of the asset value of the laundry.
- "You must buy value; which means you need to understand exactly what you are buying, being very careful not to pay too much. One of several major keys to price is gross sales. In fact, it is fair to say that a 10% misrepresentation as to gross sales can impact the overall value of a coin-laundry business by some 20%, and maybe considerably more; therefore, you must ask the right questions, and be able to assess the accuracy of the answers.
  "Determine the age and condition of the equipment. Inspect the water heating systems, as this is many times the most expensive single component to replace. These two observations will go a far way in determining an asking price, or variance from the standard of 100% of gross revenue as an asking price. Another great metric is determining water usage. Quite often water companies will sell water in HCF or Hundred Cubic Feet Units. 7.48 gallons of water is equal to one cubic foot of water, so 748 gallons of water equals a Hundred Cubic Feet. A standard top loader uses 30 gallons of water, and

the 30 and 50 pound units are multiples of the top loader. The dryer revenue should equal at least half of the washer revenue, up to 100% of the washer revenue."

- "Rising utility costs are an issue. I would recommend an analysis of the cost per wash and dry load, to insure a reasonable profit per turn."

- "Location is very important. Good locations are in densely populated areas with high percentage renters and low-to-mid income."

- "Population demographics within 1-mile radius should show high percentage renters (50+%), low-to-mid income, limited competition, larger family size."

- "The most difficult evaluation is the age and condition of the equipment. Industry-wide there seems to be a reluctance to replace equipment near to or at the end of the life cycle. As a result many owners decide to sell rather than improve. The buyer then faces the realization that within a short time frame an investment in equipment will be necessary. That has to factor into the equation of value, particularly in this category, since the equipment is the primary revenue generator. Refurbished or used equipment is an option here, and some is reasonably priced. Replacement of some of the equipment, or the equivalent value in credit in the offer to purchase or sales agreement, may need to be considered in order to facilitate a sale."

- "Coin laundry business is predictable. It does not jump up and down or respond to marketing as quickly as, say, a restaurant would. Having said that, the flat trend, old but functional equipment and slightly run-down interiors, get about 5 times the SDE; the newer equipment, crisp and clean interior with slight uptick in historical volume trend, tends to get high multiples. The annual sales number around $180,000 seems to be almost magical. Over that amount of annual sales, demand is huge, since they can be flowing around $100,000+ in profits."

- "Depending upon the market or location of the Laundromat, pricing can actually range between 1 and 1.5 times gross annual sales."

- "The good news is that, although banks want buyers to meet the same requirements for existing laundries, they can purchase a lower risk opportunity that requires less cash, because existing laundries, in most all cases, cost far less for the investor.

  "Existing laundries often have leaseholds grandfathered in, so buyers end up paying three to four times the net cash flow for an up-and-running business and save tons of money. Let's say that a laundry has a net cash flow of $75,000. You'll likely pay $225,000 to $300,000, and the bank would need 30% of these numbers. This saves more than two-thirds of the cash out of pocket compared to the new laundry scenario.

  "Fortunately, the current state of our economy has not affected the fact that people need to cover the bare necessities such as eating and washing clothes. Many of my customers have maintained their margins, and others who aggressively execute their marketing plans are actually seeing increases in revenue."

  Source: "New vs. Existing Stores: Starting a Coin Laundry in a Tough Economy" by Robert J. Renteria, WashPro USA, www.american coinop.com

- "If you lose your lease, it is very expensive to set up in a new location: machine pad construction (far more expensive if there is a basement); sufficient gas supply for dryers; lawful wastewater egress; plumbing (including sufficient water supply); three-phase and single-phase electrical layouts; dryer venting system; flooring, ceiling, and counter space. Accordingly, laundromats need to have a long and easily assignable lease."

Source: Gary Ruff, www.laundromatadvisor.com.

- "Location and demographics. It's important to study the surrounding area for city planned changes or housing changes that may affect business performance."
- "Larger multiplier number used for newer equipment & long-term lease"
- "Age of equipment a huge factor in price determining. Fold and wash service available?"
- "They typically sell for 100% to 125% of the annual sales. Location, age of machines, total appearance very important."
- "Typically laundries sell for between 55 and 65 times monthly net."
- "Net Income should = 1/3 of Gross Income. Sales price is 5+ x Net"
- "Coin-operated laundries typical based on a 20% return on capital"
- "Try and achieve a 25% return on capital; not including owner's salary."
- "Utility costs are the single largest operating expense in a coin laundry."

Source: Coin Laundry Association

- "Higher multiplier for businesses with newer equipment (3–4 years) and long-term lease (10+ years) increase business value."
- "Here are the steps used to calculate how many times the washers would have to be used to use all the water reflected in the water bill: (1) Get the water bills for the last year, (2) Since water bills are usually in cu. ft., you will have to figure out how many gallons of water were used (there are approximately 7.5 gallons per cu. ft.), (3) Find out how many gallons of water the particular washer type uses, (4) Calculate how many times the washers have to be used to use all the water based on the bill. That should give you the number of washes. Multiply that by the cost per wash. The national average for 'turns' is (5)—the number of times the washer is used. Dryer income is generally half that used of washer income, and vending income can produce 10 percent of total. Historically, laundries have been priced to sell at some multiple of their annual gross. Primarily because of tradition, this multiple varies from one section of the country to another, but normally it's within the 90 percent to 150 percent range. Variations on the annual gross formula include such rules of thumb as 12 to 18 times monthly gross, or three to five times annual net income (before taxes)."

Expert Comments

"Larger, bigger stores 5-10,000 sq. ft. with more services and larger washers and dryers. More 'card' stores."

"The ratings have remained consistent for many years, which helps to exemplify the fact that this category remains a good option for many business prospects. It remains a category which allows for owner flexibility. And in many instances it can be a business operated part time. The category facilitates a need that will not change; competition is moderate; risk is very reasonable; and profit, while not huge, is predictable and consistent."

"Competition in this category is not a significant concern, as most of the establishments have found their population niche. Therefore the amount of risk is not significant relevant to new Laundromats opening. At the same time the amount of growth is limited by the same geographic and population element, and so while the business is consistent, the potential for growth is limited. Locations are usually in economic areas that would support this type of business, and the facilities for the most part are average. Marketability spreads quickly by word of mouth. So, if you have a clean store with working machines and good lighting, you can be assured to be in the game. The trend in the industry has been and will remain consistent. While card-operated and automated machines have made some inroads, basic coin operation still leads the pack. While not difficult to replicate, the cost of replication is significant. And therefore the calculated return on the investment is long term."

"The coin-ops have seen more and more new ones pop open in recent years in northern California; and at the same time, ease of operation is making them a bit more lucrative for a time-pressed buyer who wants some cash flow, but does not want to be tied down to a business."

"Simple business to run, and location is important and should be based on demographics."

"Costly to set up a new store. Parking."

"Everybody found a place to do their laundry last week. To get that market, you have to provide a better place to do their laundry."

"If you've got a lease and you can't assign it to somebody else when you sell it, then it's going to cost you a lot of money."

Source: "The Coin Laundry Lease" by Bob Nieman, *The Journal*, March 2003

"Coin-op laundries typically are recession proof."

"Not difficult business to start, remodel or sell. Many potential buyers are looking for this type of business."

Benchmark Data
Statistics

Number of Establishments	22,848
Average Profit Margin	3.1%
Revenue per Employee	n/a
Average Number of Employees	2
Average Wages per Employee	$15,718

Source: IBISWorld, May 2012

Products and Services Segmentation

Washer services	55.2%
Dryer services	33%
Self-service dry cleaning	5.3%
Other	5.2%
Commercial laundry services	1.3%

Source: IBISWorld, May 2012

Major Market Segmentation

Renters using laundromats	38.6%
Renters using on-site laundry facilities	22.4%
Commercial, industrial, service industries and routes	16.9%
Colleges and universities	13.1%
Homeowners	9%

Source: IBISWorld, May 2012

Industry Costs

Profit	3.1%
Wages	17.7%
Purchases	23.0%
Depreciation	4.0%
Marketing	2.0%
Rent & Utilities	23.2%
Other	27.0%

Source: IBISWorld, May 2012

Market Share

Coinmach Corporation	12.8%
Mac-Gray Corporation	7.3%

Source: IBISWorld, May 2012

Enterprises by Employment Size

Number of Employees	Share
1 to 4	90.4%
5 to 9	6.4%
10 to 19	2.0%

Source: IBISWorld, May 2012

- "Average store 2500 sq. ft. utilities 25- 35% payroll 10% occupancy costs 25% gross profit 40%"

- "Coin laundries can range in market value from $50,000 to more than $1 million, and can generate cash flow between $15,000 and $200,000 per year. Business hours typically run from 6 a.m. to 10 p.m. The stores usually occupy 1,000 to 5,000 square feet of retail space, with the 2002 average being 2,260 square feet. New coin laundries are valued based on actual construction and equipment costs, while existing coin laundries are valued based primarily on revenues. Coin laundries are perfect examples of passive income generators. Coin laundries are also referred to as coin-op laundries, coin-operated laundries or Laundromats."

- "Dryer income is usually expressed as a percentage of overall income. Generally, dryer income varies between forty and sixty percent of total washer income. Income and expense percentages may vary significantly for stores offering additional services such as drycleaning and fluff and fold."

  Source: Laundry Industry Overview, Coin Laundry Association, www.coinlaundry.org, an excellent and informative site.

- "Average store size is 2000 square feet, though some larger stores or 5000+ square feet are located in densely populated areas."

- Utilities 25 % (can be higher depending on area)

  Payroll/Labor 8% to 10%

  Occupancy Cost 25%

  Profit (estimated) 35%

- "Rent-to-gross ratio should be no more than 25%. Labor costs run a minimum of 10% of monthly gross."

- "Location dependent on population demographics."

- "Coin laundries need a gross profit margin of 50 percent."

Expenses as a Percentage of Annual Sales

Cost of goods:... 0%
Payroll/labor Costs:...09% to 12%
Occupancy:.. 14% to 25% (40% to 55% including utilities)
Profit (estimated pretax): ....25% to 35%

Industry Trend

- "The trend will continue to pace or follow history. The need or demand for the industry is not changing, so I would conclude a bright future."
- "Large facilities will drive out smaller facilities. Successful operations will provide a wide range of services and customer assistance including pickup and delivery."
- "The economy has definitely slowed down the progress of new laundries, but this is just more reason to look into finding an existing coin laundry that is already generating cash flow. Finance companies have tightened their requirements for investors in new coin laundries, and unless buyers have an excessive cash reserve to float the business during the ramp-up, it will be almost impossible to build a new coin laundry in 2009 and beyond."

  Source: "New vs. Existing Stores: Starting a Coin Laundry in a Tough Economy" by Robert J. Renteria, WashPro USA, www.american coinop.com
- "Opportunity in areas of population growth and upgrading older, rundown stores."
- "Rising cost of utilities."
- "Laundromats adding some other services: children's play areas, sales of ancillary items, video rentals and more."
- "More amenities are being added to supplement the wash and dry revenues"
- "Changing from cash operations to debit card operations"
- "Great potential for growing areas, especially in dense population areas with large numbers of renters"

Seller Financing

- "5 to 10 years"
- Financing of new stores according to a survey conducted by the Coin Laundry Association:
    - ✓ 27% local bank
    - ✓ 17% equipment manufacturer
    - ✓ 05% independent financing
    - ✓ 12% SBA
    - ✓ 41% family & friends

Questions

- "#1 why are you selling. If you can find out the real reason, you have a clear shot at success !!. What is the crime rate in the immediate area. Who does the maintenance, how old are the machines. Do you know of a new laundromat being build or planned. Water, sewer, electric and gas bills for 2 years Can you work with the landlord. What other services could you provide, wash & fold, dry cleaning, vending machines, atm, shoe repair, soaps and supplies, spot cleaning service, shoe shine, tanning beds, fax & internet connection, more."
- "Area crime rate. Review utility bills. New development in trade area. New competition in trade area."

- "I would request copies of utility bills for at least 12 months. Request model numbers and age of washers and dryers, and ask for maintenance records. Especially request information on water heating systems, as this is probably the one single point of failure that can easily be the most costly repair item."
- "Who does the maintenance?"
- "Are you aware of any new laundries opening up in the surrounding areas?"
- "Age & condition of equipment. Is equipment mix suitable for market area? Are they taking in wash & fold or dry cleaning? Is store attended? Easy loading and parking? Environmental compliance and local government fees and restrictions? Length of increase value of business. Typically, the lease should be at least 10 years or more."
- "Why are you selling? Review utility bills for previous 3 years. Any new housing developments in the area?"

Resources

Trade Publications
- American Laundry News: www.americanlaundrynews.com

Associations
- Coin Laundry Association—good site: www.coinlaundry.org

	Franchise
Cold Stone Creamery (See also Ice Cream/Yogurt Shops)	
Approx. Total Investment	$294,250 to $438,850
Estimated Annual Sales/Unit	$325,000

SIC 2024-98	NAICS 722213	Number of Businesses/Units 1,100

Rules of Thumb
> 30 percent of annual sales plus inventory

> 1.5 to 2 times SDE plus inventory

Pricing Tips
- "Review the dollars paid to managers and management staff. The SDE can be greatly affected for the owner/operator. Margins are large for Cold Stone Creamery product sales. Overhead, such as rent and salaries, is typically disproportionate."

Expert Comments

"Product is unique, large machinery investment is required, thus difficult to duplicate without industry knowledge and sizeable investment ($250,000) in equipment."

Benchmark Data
- "Food cost is low at 20%, rent is typically above 10% since it is location dependent. Leases must be at least 15 years to provide value and time for ROI long term."

Expenses as a Percentage of Annual Sales

Cost of goods:.. 20%
Payroll/labor Costs.. 22%
Occupancy:.. 12%
Profit (estimated pretax): 22%

Questions

- "Will you finance, how is the store managed, do you have a production staff, separate from your counter staff? Are there any wholesale or outside accounts?"

Resources

Websites

- www.kahalamgmt.com

Collectibles Stores (See also Used Goods)		
SIC 5947-05	NAICS 453220	

Benchmark Data

- For Benchmark Information see Retail Stores—Small Specialty

Industry Trend

- "Although hard sales data have been difficult to come by, the general consensus in the industry is that after a down period, sales of collectibles are slowly on the upswing."

Source: "Crazy About Collectibles" by Randall G. Mielke, www.giftshopmag.com

Collection Agencies		
SIC 7322-01	NAICS 561440	Number of Businesses/Units 9,446

Rules of Thumb

➢ For agencies with revenues of $1 million +, 75 percent to 125 percent of annual revenues

➢ 100 percent of annual revenues includes inventory

➢ 3.5 to 6 times EBIDTA

Pricing Tips

- "Collection agencies are typically priced on a recast EBITDA income stream which includes earnings before interest, taxes, depreciation, and amortization and should add shareholders' salaries, perks and non-recurring expenses and then subtract a replacement salary for the shareholders. The valuation multiple typically ranges between 4 and 6 times EBITDA. The primary determinant of the multiple is the size of the company."
- "Adjustments are made for non-recurring expenses to arrive at adjusted EBITDA."

- "Collection agencies typically sell based on four to six times EBITDA. The size of the company is the greatest determinant of how large the multiple is."
- "Debt collection agencies have contracts with clients that are usually only for 30 days or less. In addition, client concentration is a major force as well."

Expert Comments

"Sustainability of profits is important."

"This is a service business with 30-day cancellation contracts with clients."

"Collection agencies typically have 30-day contracts with clients, whereby a client can pull back accounts in 30 days if performance is not meeting expectations."

Benchmark Data

Statistics (Debt Collection Agencies)

Number of Establishments	9,446
Average Profit Margin	7.4%
Revenue per Employee	$91,400
Average Number of Employees	15
Average Wages per Employee	$38,649

Source: IBISWorld, June 2012

Products and Services Segmentation

Contingent-fee servicing	52.1%
Portfolio acquisition	32.1%
Fixed-fee servicing	10.3%
Collateral recovery and repossession services	3.1%
Credit rating services	2.4%

Source: IBISWorld, June 2012

Major Market Segmentation

Consumer receivables	34.6%
Mortgage receivables	28.2%
Business receivables	21.6%
Other personal receivables	15.6%

Source: IBISWorld, June 2012

Industry Costs

Profit	7.4%
Wages	41.7%
Depreciation	2.0%
Marketing	1.2%
Rent & Utilities	5.1%
Other	42.6%

Source: IBISWorld, June 2012

Market Share

NCO Group Inc.	9.1%

Source: IBISWorld, June 2012

- Some Benchmark Data from the ACA International
  - ✓ The average collection "recovery rate" was 17.6% and the median was 16.2%.
  - ✓ The average commission rate was 28.9% and the median was 28.1%.
- "$70k per employee"
- "Sales per collector in successful collection agencies typically exceed 3–4X the collector's compensation on a monthly basis."
- "EBITDA should equal 20% or more of revenues."
- "50% of revenues are employee cost."

Expenses as a Percentage of Annual Sales

Cost of goods:	10%
Payroll/labor Costs:	40% to 50%
Occupancy:	05% to 10% (Varies by area)
Profit (estimated pretax):	15% to 20%

Industry Trend

- "Profitability should rise as unemployment improves."

Questions

- "Tenure of existing clients, percent of revenues from clients, any change in commission rates and placement volumes, tenure of the collection staff and management, pipeline of business opportunities."

Resources

Trade Publications

- Collection Advisor: www.collectionadvisor.com

Associations

- International Association of Commercial Collectors: www.commercialcollector.com

Comic Book Stores		
SIC 5942-05	NAICS 451211	Number of Businesses/Units 2,000

Rules of Thumb

➢ 12 to 15 percent of annual sales plus inventory

Benchmark Data

- "That's Entertainment also offers video games, toys, and other collectibles, but new comics, which arrive once a week, are a big part of business. The store stocks some 600 new titles a month at about $3 an issue. Many customers visit not only to pick up the latest adventures of their favorite heroes, but to hang out."

  Source: "Holy Internet, Batman" by John Dyer, *Boston Globe*, June 24, 2011
- "It's difficult to say what average sales are because very few stock only comics. We would guess that the average store turns $150,000 to $200,000 in comics, but again, that is not likely to be all that any of them sell."

Industry Trend

- "Worcester, MA—for nearly 40 years, Paul Howley has made his living by selling comic books. That's Entertainment, his flagship store, employs 20 people and sells more than $500,000 a year in glossy new comics. He displays them stacked floor to ceiling, encouraging customers to browse."

  Source: "Holy Internet, Batman" by John Dyer, *Boston Globe*, June 24, 2011

- "'We used to sit between Tower Records and WordsWorth Books—it was media city—and with those gone, foot traffic patterns are different,' Davis says. 'Like any bookstore we're facing online competition. There's illegal downloading. And our customer base is graying. There used to be all these 12-year-old boys running around in here, and that's a rarity now. The male adolescent fantasy has moved from comics to video games."

Community Newspapers

(See Publishers—Newspapers/Weeklies, Community Papers)

Computer Consulting

SIC 7379-05	NAICS 541512	

Rules of Thumb

➢ 50 to 65 percent of annual sales plus inventory

Pricing Tips

- Note: Many consulting businesses are one-man operations or are headed by someone who has the contacts and may basically be "the business." This person may be the goodwill, and without his or her presence the business may not be worth much. If this person stays while the business is slowly being transferred and an earnout is in place, the value may still be there.

Benchmark Data

Statistics (IT Consulting)

Number of Establishments	455,918
Average Profit Margin	7.5%
Revenue per Employee	$189,300
Average Number of Employees	4
Average Wages per Employee	$79,094

Source: IBISWorld, April 2012

Products and Services Segmentation

Computer systems design, development, and integration	36.3%
Computer application design and development	25.8%
Other services	17.0%
IT technical support services	10.1%
IT computer and network management services	6.0%
IT technical consulting services	4.8%

Source: IBISWorld, April 2012

Industry Costs

Profit	7.5%
Wages	41.7%
Purchases	18.8%
Depreciation	1.1%
Marketing	3.5%
Rent & Utilities	8.6%
Other	18.8%

Source: IBISWorld, April 2012

Market Share

International Business Machines Corporation	4.2%
Hewlett-Packard Company	3.2%

Source: IBISWorld, April 2012

Establishments by Employment Size

Number of Employees	Share
1 to 4	73.0%
5 to 9	10.6%
10 to 19	7.4%

Source: IBISWorld, April 2012

- "Of those that run multi-person businesses, most have fewer than three owners. Corporations have two to three non-owner employees.
  "Almost 90% of firms earned $500,000 or less, while 4.4% earned a million or more.
- "75% of ICCA Consultants have over 15 years of experience in their field."
  Source: Independent Computer Consultants Association, (ICCA), www.icca.org

Resources

Associations
- TechServe Alliance: www.techservealliance.org/
- Independent Computer Consultant Association: www.icca.org

Computer Programming Services—Custom
(See also Computer Consulting)

SIC 7371-02	NAICS 541511	Number of Businesses/Units 71,000

Pricing Tips

- "Traditional methods use some multiple of revenues for valuation; however, this is fraught with problems. Growth in revenues is a key aspect, prized in establishing higher value. Earnings are not unimportant, although high-growth companies may be more attractive even without earnings. Look for stability or managed growth in operations.
  "Because software companies must be nimble to respond to market actions, and are vulnerable to loss of key persons, control premiums (and lack of control discounts) and discounts for illiquidity are typically enhanced in this industry."

Industry Trend
- "Down—foreign competition at lower hourly rates is moving programming services jobs overseas."

Questions
- "1) Productivity of current workforce 2) Projects ongoing and anticipated 3) Strategic advantages of this business over the competition."

Computer Services		
SIC 7378-01	NAICS 811212	Number of Businesses/Units 58,000

Rules of Thumb

➤ 55 percent of annual sales, plus fixtures, equipment and inventory

Benchmark Data

Statistics (Electronic & Computer Repair Services)
Number of Establishments.. 60,237
Average Profit Margin.. 5.4%
Revenue per Employee $116,600
Average Number of Employees.. 3
Average Wages per Employee $54,398

Source: IBISWorld, February 2012

Products and Services Segmentation
Computer and office equipment repairs.. 39.7%
Other electronic equipment (including medical equipment) repairs.................... 36.8%
Communications equipment repairs 12.9%
Consumer electronics (including radio, TV and VCR) repairs 10.6%

Source: IBISWorld, February 2012

Major Market Segmentation
Small and medium businesses (SMBs)... 51.6%
Large companies 25.7%
Individuals... 10.9%
State and local governments 6.7%
Federal government.. 5.1%

Source: IBISWorld, February 2012

Industry Costs
Profit 5.4%
Wages.. 46.2%
Purchases 30.0%
Depreciation.. 2.3%
Utilities 3.1%
Rent 5.0%
Other.. 8.0%

Source: IBISWorld, February 2012

Computer Stores		
SIC 5734-07	NAICS 443120	Number of Businesses/Units 20,000

Rules of Thumb

➤ 30 percent of annual sales plus inventory

Benchmark Data

Statistics (Computer Stores)

Number of Establishments	18,442
Average Profit Margin	4.4%
Revenue per Employee	$209,300
Average Number of Employees	5
Average Wages per Employee	$29,501

Source: IBISWorld, January 2012

Products and Services Segmentation

Laptop computers	35%
Desktop computers	32%
Printers, scanners and supplies	11%
Peripherals and other hardware	10%
Software	8%
Storage devices	4%

Source: IBISWorld, January 2012

Major Market Segmentation

Households	59.2%
Businesses	22.3%
Educational institutes	12.5%
The government	6.0%

Source: IBISWorld, January 2012

Industry Costs

Profit	4.4%
Wages	13.4%
Purchases	73.3%
Depreciation	1.0%
Utilities	1.0%
Rent	2.3%
Other	4.6%

Source: IBISWorld, January 2012

- The top 3 players account for 76% of industry revenue:
    - ✓ Best Buy Co., Inc.
    - ✓ Apple Computer, Inc.
    - ✓ Fry's Electronics, Inc.

Source: IBISWorld, January 2012

Computer Systems Design		
SIC 7373-98	NAICS 541512	

Rules of Thumb

➤ 50 percent of annual sales plus inventory

➤ 2 to 4 times SDE plus inventory

➤ 3 to 6 times EBIT

➤ 3 to 7 times EBITDA

Pricing Tips

- "Very work-force intensive. Make sure the business can prosper without the owner. Contracts are important."
- "System design firms are often classified as 'programming' firms. More work is being done by temporary employment firms, renting IT professional staff."
- "Highly variable valuations. Biggest component of valuation is the management structure. Midmarket companies with excellent management structure can get very good multiples but a small operation which is highly owner driven may get very little. Having contracts with large customers can improve valuation significantly."

Expert Comments

"Talented people can easily leave and start their own gig. Contracts with a very wide customer base can be very important. Corporate clients are more valuable than consumer clients."

"Design firms are being acquired by the large consulting houses. May be attractive for strategic reasons, such as industry niches and/or package familiarity."

"Highly knowledge driven industry. Risk can be very high depending on the importance of the role played by the current owner. If the owner's role is non-critical, then the business can be very lucrative."

Benchmark Data

- "$100,000 or more per employee"
- "$100,000 or more in revenues per technician and $200,000 or more per engineer"
- "Revenue and profit growth is more important than stability of earnings. Sales per employee is a key metric."

Expenses as a Percentage of Annual Sales

Cost of goods:	20%
Payroll/labor Costs:	50% to 55%%
Occupancy:	05%
Profit (estimated pretax):	20%

Industry Trend

- "Continuing growth as technology and tools become indispensable for businesses and individuals."
- "Consolidating"

Questions

- "Reasons for the exit. Strategic growth plans. Customer retention plans. Employee specific compensation issues."
- "Who is (are) the key employee(s) who drives the sales. Are there any critical technical roles?"

Concrete Bulk Plants (Ready-Mix)

SIC 5032-30	NAICS 32732	Number of Businesses/Units 5,783

Rules of Thumb

➤ 30 to 35 percent of SDE plus fixtures, equipment and inventory

Benchmark Data

Statistics (Ready-Mix Concrete Manufacturing)

Number of Establishments	5,783
Average Profit Margin	3.5%
Revenue per Employee	$252,200
Average Number of Employees	16
Average Wages per Employee	$53,828

Source: IBISWorld, March 2012

Products and Services Segmentation

Ready-mix concrete (various strengths and attributes)	84.7%
Contract work	10.3%
Steel concrete	5.0%

Source: IBISWorld, March 2012

Major Market Segmentation

Non-residential building market	35%
Residential building market	35%
Highway, street, bridge and tunnel construction market	20%
Other public works and infrastructure construction	10%

Source: IBISWorld, March 2012

Industry Costs

Profit	3.5%
Wages	21.4%
Purchases	52.8%
Depreciation	3.8%
Marketing	1.0%
Rent & Utilities	5.9%
Other	11.6%

Source: IBISWorld, March 2012

Establishments by Employment Size

Number of Employees	Share
1 to 4	28.62%
5 to 9	19.20%
10 to 19	25.56%

Source: IBISWorld, March 2012

	Franchise
Conroy's Flowers	
Approx. Total Investment	Not Available
Estimated Annual Sales/Unit	Not Available

SIC 5992-01	NAICS 453110	Number of Businesses/Units 50

Rules of Thumb

➤ 45 to 50 percent of annual sales plus inventory

Resources

Websites
- www.conroysflowers.com

Consignment Shops

(See also Resale Shops, Clothing Stores—Used, & Used Goods)

SIC 5932-04	NAICS 453310	Number of Businesses/Units 40,000

Rules of Thumb

➤ 15 to 20 percent of annual sales

➤ Note: Consignment shops are just that. They very seldom purchase inventory; rather, they place it on the sales floor and have agreements with the owner regarding price, and generally a schedule in which the price is reduced every month or so for a set period of time. After this period, the goods are usually returned to the owner. The shop works on essentially a commission or fee only if the goods sell.

Benchmark Data

- For additional Benchmark data see Used Goods
- "What sells: clothing, bookcases, cookbooks, costume jewelry, kitchen gadgets, golf clubs

  "What doesn't sell: collectible dolls, fur coats, large paintings, vintage dinnerware, needlepoint art"

  Source: National Association of Resale and Thrift Shops
- "Consignment policies tend to vary among stores and online sites, but most will take items they like and then divvy up profits with the seller, who can get as much as 70 percent of a sale. On the buying end, consumers are paying less than 50 percent of the retail cost for many items."

  Source: "The Rich Discover Consignment Shops," *Newsweek*, March 24, 2009, www.*newsweek*.com

Industry Trend

- "The new wave of consignment shops features stylish fashions, jewelry and furniture—all in good condition and at lower-than-retail prices."

  Source: "Back in style: Consignment stores' business booming," www.thetimesnews.com May 15, 2011

Construction — Buildings

	NAICS 236	

Rules of Thumb

➤ 20 to 30 percent of annual sales plus inventory

➤ 1 to 2 times SDE plus inventory

➤ 1 to 3 times EBITDA

Pricing Tips

- "With very small companies with 1 or 2 employees the norm lately has been to look at FMV of assets as bottom line for pricing purposes."

- "Value in Construction trades business is dependent on many factors not normally associated with small business valuation."
- "In many instances in a challenging economy it is not unusual to sell one of these companies for the fair market value of their assets."

Expert Comments

"Small companies have been hit real hard in the economic downturn we have been in for the last few years."

"Make sure you understand the sales and marketing side of the business and how feasible it will be to remove the owner from the business without a serious decline in new and referral business."

Benchmark Data

Statistics (Home Builders)

Number of Establishments	390,374
Average Profit Margin	17.5%
Revenue per Employee	$266,500
Average Number of Employees	2.1
Average Wages per Employee	$100,186

Source: IBISWorld, July 2012

Products and Services Segmentation

General contracting	61.4%
Construction management services	21.4%
Subcontracting	6.2%
Other	6%
Remodeling	5%

Source: IBISWorld, July 2012

Major Market Segmentation

Private-sector clients (property developers)	65%
Private-sector clients (households)	30%

- "In the final analysis, a construction business should always be worth the FMV of its hard assets."

Expenses as a Percentage of Annual Sales

Cost of goods	20% to 30%
Payroll/labor Costs	25%
Occupancy	05% to 10%
Profit (estimated pretax)	25% to 45%

Industry Trend

- "The surviving companies will be slow to recover."
- "Stagnant"

Questions

- "What would happen to this company if we plucked you out of here today for 1-3 months? Would the business operate effectively?"

Construction — Electrical	
NAICS 238210	Number of Businesses/Units 205,090

Rules of Thumb

➤ 2 times SDE plus inventory

Pricing Tips

▪ "Strong order book is essential. Wide range of customers."

Expert Comments

"Underpricing of bids is a serious risk but may be used to increase order book in preparation for sale. Good demand for sound business. Location is relatively unimportant."

Benchmark Data

Statistics (Electricians)

Number of Establishments	205,090
Average Profit Margin	3.0%
Revenue per Employee	$131,600
Average Number of Employees	4.3
Average Wages per Employee	$48,300

Source: IBISWorld, June 2012

Products and Services Segmentation

Electric power installation and servicing (including lighting)	70%
Telecommunication installation	10%
Other construction services	09%
Fire and security system services	06%
Electronic control system installation	05%

Source: IBISWorld, June 2012

Major Market Segmentation

Single-family homes	36.4%
Commercial buildings	28.5%
Industrial buildings	14%
Institutional buildings	10.5%
Apartment buildings	5.6%
Non-building construction	5%

Source: IBISWorld, June 2012

Industry Costs

Profit	3.0%
Wages	43.8%
Purchases	36.0%
Depreciation	0.5%
Rent & Utilities	3.0
Other	13.7

Source: IBISWorld, June 2012

Expenses as a Percentage of Annual Sales

Cost of goods	50%
Payroll/labor Costs	30%
Occupancy	n/a
Profit (estimated pretax)	06%

Industry Trend

- "Directly dependent on construction industry but can work related areas if necessary to cover slack period."

Questions

- "1. Details of job costing, current and bids 2. List of staff, experience, and time with business 3. Usual financial and due diligence."

Construction — Excavation (site preparation)	
NAICS 238910	Number of Businesses/Units 35,796

Rules of Thumb

➢ 25 percent of annual sales plus inventory

➢ 2.2 times SDE plus inventory

➢ 1.8 times EBIT

➢ 2 times EBITDA

Pricing Tips

- "Adjust for age/condition of equipment."

Expert Comments

"Due to the economy, construction and site prep companies are declining."

Benchmark Data

Statistics (Excavators)

Number of Establishments	35,796
Average Profit Margin	8.3%
Revenue per Employee	42,000
Average Number of Employees	7.3
Average Wages per Employee	46,257

Source: IBISWorld, May 2012

Products and Services Segmentation

Earthmoving, excavation, land clearing and trench digging	50%
Deep foundation construction	20%
Nonbuilding construction excavation	13%
Land improvement, earth retention, sharing and stabilization	10%
Other nonbuilding excavation	07%

Source: IBISWorld, May 2012

Major Market Segmentation

Residential building market	40%
Non-residential building market	35%
Nonbuilding construction market	25%

Source: IBISWorld, May 2012

Industry Costs

Profit	8.3%
Wages	42.0%
Purchases	26.6%
Depreciation	8.8%
Marketing	0.9%
Rent & Utilities	10.1%
Other	3.3%

Source: IBISWorld, May 2012

Expenses as a Percentage of Annual Sales

Cost of goods:	25%
Payroll/labor Costs:	40%
Occupancy:	10%
Profit (estimated pretax):	25%

Industry Trend
- "The construction industry is tied to the economic recovery."

Questions
- "Customer lists, future contracts, condition of equipment and any lawsuits?"

Construction — Heating & AC (See HVAC)

Construction — In General

	NAICS 23	

Rules of Thumb

➢ 20 to 25 percent of annual sales plus inventory

➢ 1 to 2 times SDE plus inventory

➢ 1.5 times EBIT

➢ 2 to 3 times EBITDA

➢ Note: "Some construction firms own significant equipment and some are run from storefronts, so rules of thumb are misleading. The business history is very important, as is the value of signed contracts to be completed, and understanding how a company bills its work in progress. Accounts receivable can average over 45 days, increasing the working capital required and decreasing the business value. Once again rules of thumb are not very useful."

Pricing Tips
- "Many times businesses in this sector will end up selling for the fair market value of their assets not including cash, receivables, or investments. When pricing these businesses you must consider the fair market value of the assets."
- "Good supply of buyers for firms doing over a million dollars in EBIT with 20 percent or better profit margins. Smaller ones are fairly difficult, and the best practice is to merge with larger company that doesn't have a presence in that

area. Important for owner to stay after transaction. Individual to individual transactions are the most difficult."

- "Determining the sale price of a contracting or service-related business is difficult at best. One must consider how dependent the business is on the ongoing involvement of the owner, does the business have an established client base that produces repeat business that will continue post acquisition, does the business have a systematic sales and marketing function that will continue to produce new business without the owner present, and, does the fair market value of the equipment exceed the rule of thumb price?"

- "Stock vs. assets, employment agreements."

- "Construction companies are relatively hard to sell, with the exception of ones that have been established many years and enjoy an established name and reputation. These should be [priced at] depreciated value of fixtures and equipment and rolling stock, plus 10 percent of the sale price for goodwill, plus 25 percent of the part of the business period which has already been contracted for."

Expert Comments

"Construction and service-related businesses have a low cost of entry and require a minimum investment to start. Many of these businesses are centered around the owner's reputation and do not have a sales and marketing plan in place to develop new sales on a regular basis."

"Very competitive business, easy to enter, high profit margins, significant risk."

"Because of the many categories in construction, I generally applied the average value. Construction companies are difficult to sell and relatively difficult to replicate because of capital requirements."

"It takes a special buyer to take on a contracting or service-related business. Your most likely buyer on some occasions might be a competitor from another market that wants entrance into your market. In some fields the fact that a contractor is Union is actually a plus because the contractor only needs to have the journeymen on payroll when they are on the job, and therefore ongoing payroll costs are reduced and profit is increased. Additionally, the Union contractors get a significant amount of support from the Union that translates into additional business and growth opportunities."

Benchmark Data

Statistics (Home Builders)

Number of Establishments	390,374
Average Profit Margin	17.5%
Revenue per Employee	$266,500
Average Number of Employees	2.1
Average Wages per Employee	$100,186

Source: IBISWorld, July 2012

Products and Services Segmentation

General contracting	61.4%
Construction management services	21.4%
Subcontracting	6.2%
Other	6%
Remodeling	5%

Source: IBISWorld, July 2012

Major Market Segmentation

Private-sector clients (property developers)	65%
Private-sector clients (household)	30%
Federally funded projects	2.5%
State or locally funded projects	2.5%

Source: IBISWorld, July 2012

Industry Costs

Profit	17.5%
Wages	37.2%
Purchases	37.0%
Depreciation	1.0%
Marketing	0.6%
Rent & Utilities	1.3%
Other	5.4%

Source: IBISWorld, July 2012

Statistics (Municipal Building Construction)

Number of Establishments	16,091
Average Profit Margin	9.0%
Revenue per Employee	$650,300
Average Number of Employees	13.8
Average Wages per Employee	$372,317

Source: IBISWorld, May 2012

Products and Services Segmentation

General contracting services	67%
Construction management services	11.5%
Remodeling contracting services	11.5%
Other construction activities	10%

Source: IBISWorld, May 2012

Major Market Segmentation

Educational building construction	57.8%
Healthcare building construction	25.5%
Public safety facilities construction	7.8%
Recreational building construction	5.5%
Religious building...construction	3.4%

Source: IBISWorld, May 2012

Industry Costs

Profit	9.0%
Wages	59.4%
Purchases	18.3%
Depreciation	1.5%
Marketing	2.2%
Rent & Utilities	3.4%
Other	6.2%

Source: IBISWorld, May 2012

- "Many service-related contracting businesses will charge at least 2 times their direct costs as their hourly fee for service."

Expenses as a Percentage of Annual Sales

Cost of goods	25%
Payroll/labor Costs	30% to 40%
Occupancy	05% to 10%
Profit (estimated pretax)	25%

Industry Trend
- "This sector is closely tied to the ups and downs of the general economy."

Seller Financing
- "5 to 7 years, however SBA loans up to 10 years can be obtained"

Questions
- "If for some reason you were unable to work for the next 6–12 months, what would happen to this business? Where do you get your business from? What systems do you have in place to generate new sales?"
- "How do you secure new work?"

Resources

Websites
- www.contractorsforsale.com

Associations
- National Association of Home Builders: www.nahb.com

Construction — Specialty Trades		
SIC 1799-99	NAICS	

Rules of Thumb
➤ 1 to 2 times EBITDA

Pricing Tips
- "When pricing a construction or service-related contracting business, one must take many factors into consideration."

Expert Comments
"This is a highly competitive business that is typically dependent on the owner's goodwill."

Benchmark Data
- "Service businesses will set hourly rates at 2 to 3 times their direct cost per employee per hour to cover overhead and markups."

Expenses as a Percentage of Annual Sales

Cost of goods	25%
Payroll/labor Costs	40%
Occupancy	10%
Profit (estimated pretax)	25%

Industry Trend
- "This sector will improve as the economy improves."

Questions
- "How do you get new jobs? Do you have a sales and marketing plan that generates new work on a consistent basis?"

Consulting (See Sales Consulting)

Contract Manufacturing (See also Job Shops & Machine Shops)

SIC 3999-06	NAICS 332710	Number of Businesses/Units 2,700

Rules of Thumb

> ➤ 3 to 4 times EBITDA plus reasonable owner's compensation
>
> ➤ 2 to 4 times SDE plus inventory

Pricing Tips

- "4 x EBITDA is just a rule of thumb. A range of 3 x to 8 x is realistic depending on a range of factors (history, custom concentration, future prospects, etc."

Expert Comments

"Competition is high and the key to gross profit margins is using technology to be low- cost manufacturer."

Benchmark Data

Expenses as a Percentage of Annual Sales

Cost of goods	45%
Payroll/labor Costs	20%
Occupancy	15%
Profit (estimated pretax)	20%

Industry Trend

- "The industry will continue to improve as U.S. manufacturers become more competitive."

Seller Financing

- "5 years max with a due on sale provision."

Questions

- "Customer concentration and who has technical skill to operate"
- "Discuss the outlook for the company. What opportunities exist for the buyer and why the seller isn't pursuing them."

Contractors— Masonry

SIC 1741-01	NAICS 238140	Number of Businesses/Units 95,573

Rules of Thumb

> ➤ 27 percent of annual sales includes inventory
>
> ➤ 1 to 2 times SDE includes inventory

Pricing Tips

- "Commercial masonry is worth more than residential masonry."
- "Home masonry will go for 1X SDE, and B2B will go for 1.5X SDE."

Expert Comments

"Relationships with your builders helps getting the contracts for work"

"The industry is changing to foreigners and they are bidding lower to get jobs."

"When home building is doing well, so is this industry; when the home building industry slows down, so does this industry."

Benchmark Data

Statistics (Masonry)

Number of Establishments	95,573
Average Profit Margin	2.8%
Revenue per Employee	$104,000
Average Number of Employees	2.9
Average Wages per Employee	$31,638

Source: IBISWorld, June 2012

Products and Services Segmentation

Masonry contracting using brick or block	66%
Other (including work with concrete, marble and granite)	16%
Pointing, cleaning, and caulking	6%
Refractory contracting	6%
Stone contracting	6%

Source: IBISWorld, June 2012

Major Market Segmentation

Residential construction market	45%
Commercial construction market	32%
Municipal construction market	18%
Other	5%

Source: IBISWorld, June 2012

Industry Costs

Profit	2.8%
Wages	30.5%
Purchases	43.4%
Depreciation	2.0%
Marketing	0.1%
Rent & Utilities	4.5%
Other	16.7%

Source: IBISWorld, June 2012

- "They estimate that they charge $2.00 per brick and built a very profitable company doing so."
- "Non-union is more salable than union."

Expenses as a Percentage of Annual Sales

Cost of goods: 20%
Payroll/labor Costs: 50%
Occupancy: .... 10% to 15%
Profit (estimated pretax): .... 15% to 20%

Industry Trend

- "Flat"
- "With economy, slowdown on home construction"

Questions

- "What % of bids do they get?"
- "Union or non-union labor?"
- "Relationships to the customers, are the contracts assignable, and when will you introduce the buyer to customers before closing?"
- "Make sure they have good foremen in place to run the crews going forward with a new buyer."
- "Understand the builders' contracts in place."

Convenience Stores

(See also Convenience Stores with Gas, Gas Stations w/Convenience Stores/Mini Marts)

SIC 5411-03	NAICS 445120	Number of Businesses/Units 67,921

Rules of Thumb

➤ 10 to 20 percent of annual sales plus inventory

➤ 2 to 2.5 times SDE plus inventory

➤ 2 to 3 times EBITDA plus inventory—C-store only

➤ 6 to 8 times EBITDA plus inventory—real estate + business

➤ 5 times EBITDA less cosmetic renovation to receive a national brand of fuel; inventory is separate and above

➤ See General Information below for definitions of each type store

➤ Kiosk—1 to 2 times EBITDA plus real estate & fixtures & equipment

➤ Mini-Convenience—2 to 3 times EBITDA plus real estate & fixtures & equipment

➤ Limited-Selection Convenience Store—2 to 3 times EBITDA plus real estate & fixtures & equipment

➤ Traditional Convenience Store—3 to 4 times EBITDA includes real estate & fixtures & equipment less inventory

➤ Expanded Convenience Store—4 to 5 times EBITDA includes real estate & fixtures & equipment less inventory

➤ Hyper-Convenience Store—same as Expanded Convenience Store

Pricing Tips

- "Stores doing less than $50,000 per month inside sales are not in high demand and bring next to nothing in today's market. Those doing $50k+ per month inside bring 2x's EBIT or more. Gas volume (outside sales in gallons) is less important due to low margins but can still draw customers who may spend money inside if gas is priced competitively."

- "Average price is between 2 and 3 times SDE, 3 to 5 times when real estate is involved. Business with nominal revenue, average under $1,000 per day in sales, is actually buying a job and sale price is 1 or 1.5 times, definitely under 2 times of SDE."
- "Always check the profit margins carefully other than overall sales."
- "Location of business. Competition in the immediate area. Types of products sold. Lottery commissions helpful."
- "Or you can do the Korean way of a rule of thumb, which Korean store owners typically approach in pricing: 20 x average weekly sales."
- One industry expert reported: "Should strive for an overall 'weighted' inside gross profit margin of 30 percent. Included in this margin, you should attempt to get a margin between 50 percent and 60 percent for deli sales. Outside gasoline/fuel sales margins will vary all over the place depending on competition. You're in the ballpark, generally, if you get a bottom line profit of between 6.5 percent and 7.0 percent of total sales after taxes, depreciation and amortization."
- "Interstate location more desirable"
- "(1) Gas included, (2) Location, (3) Owner works, (4) Beer and wine license, (5) Franchise or independent"
- "Location and brand of gasoline very important"
- "(1) Age and condition of petroleum equipment is important, (2) Environmental issues must be dealt with prior to closing. Phase I and II reports required."
- "An up-to-date current property appraisal is helpful. Also, there is software available for measuring the potential value and potential revenue/gallonages of a new-build location, or for measuring the investment value of an existing location based on the gallonage, inside sales, quick food sales, and car wash sales."
- "Usually valued at 3 to 4 times the monthly gross depending upon age of the structure, a new versus mature business, location, etc. This price would not include the real estate or inventory, but would include the fixtures and equipment at market value. The value of the food inventory for a super market is about $12 per sq. ft."
- "The buyers/jobbers and lenders all accept the 5 times EBITDA."
- "Beer and wine license a plus; good deli counter a plus; 3,000+ sq. ft; ample parking; easy in-out; extra storage; good corner location, ample inventory."
- "High sales volume with profit important; need loss leaders, especially milk and bread; good personnel; customer service important; open early morning; clean facility."

Expert Comments

"Inside profit margins are not as sensitive as in other food operations. Folks shop for convenience, not price."

"Convenience stores in general have significantly dropped in price over the past few years. Demand for good stores is still very high but inside sales and rent are the most significant factors in deciding price and desirability."

"The fact that this is mostly a cash business, relatively less risky, easy to learn and replicate make this business appealing to many people. Some areas are obviously saturated and avoidable. In general, the industry is very marketable if and only if: seller has substantiating books and records for current 3 years and that daily inside sales are minimum $1,000–$1,500 (excluding extraneous revenues). Importance of location, traffic count and trading area demographic to this industry is no different than to any other retail business. Industry growth has been very stable."

"C-Stores depend more on inside sales now because of high gas prices."

"Easy to start up a convenience store location. Some areas are saturated with this type of business."

Benchmark Data
Statistics (Convenience Stores)

Number of Establishments	67.921
Average Profit Margin	1.5%
Revenue per Employee	$355,600
Average Number of Employees	2.5
Average Wages per Employee	$29,794

Source: IBISWorld, July 2012

Products and Services Segmentation

Cigarettes and other tobacco products	32.5%
Groceries and other products	25%
Nonalcoholic beverages	16.5%
Alcoholic beverages	16%
Food service products	10%

Source: IBISWorld, July 2012

Market Share

7-Eleven Inc.	18.8%
Alimentation CoucheTard Inc.	7.3%

Source: IBISWorld, July 2012

- "Again, most stores need to do $50k+ inside per month or more. Those doing $100K per month inside sales are in very high demand."
- "Convenience stores sell the majority of gasoline purchased in the country— 80% of all fuel sold in the United States in 2011. Of the 148,126 convenience stores in the United States, 120,950 sell motor fuels (82%)."

Source: www.nacsonline.com

- Sheetz stores: estimated annual sales—$1 million
  WaWa stores: estimated annual sales—$900,000
  Casey's General stores: estimated annual sales—$300,000
  7—11 stores: estimated annual sales—$275,000
  Circle K stores: estimated annual sales—$148,000
  Note: The above figures are just those for the 2011 food service portion of the total estimated annual sales.
- "Of the consumers polled in the online panel, 82 percent said they purchase prepared foods from a convenience store at least once a month, and 52 percent said they do so at least once per week, Timothy Powell, a Technomic

director of research and a consultant who leads the C-store foodservice program, said in a statement.

"'Convenience stores are increasingly falling into the same consideration set as fast-food restaurants,' said Powell. 'This really speaks to the enhanced foodservice offerings in convenience stores as well as evolving consumer behaviors.'

"Among chains that have pursued growth through C-store locations are Chester's Chicken of Birmingham, Alabama; Pizza Pro of Cabot, Arkansas; and Subway of Milford, Connecticut. Denver-based Quiznos, which in recent years has seen large-scale closures of conventional franchised restaurants, in 2011 opened in more than 200 C-stores."

Source: "An inconvenient truth" by alan.liddle@penton.com, *Nation's Restaurant News*, December 19, 2011

- "With the U.S. Census Bureau data showing the U.S. population at 308.7 million, there is one convenience per approximately every 2,100 residents."

Source: "U.S. Convenience Store Count," http://www.nacsonline.com/, January 24, 2011

- "Attractive offerings have a 30%+ gross profit margin on inside sales"
- "The 144,000 convenience stores in the U.S. have annual sales that put the industry in the same ballpark as grocery, restaurants and non-prescription drug stores.

"In an (economic) downturn, the longer you have to think about a purchase, the less likely you are to make it,' Lenard said. Convenience stores allow for quick decisions.

"Beer Sales: Nearly 80 percent of convenience stores sell beer, accounting for nearly one-third of all beer purchased in the United States, about 93 percent of which is sold cold. In fact, the U.S. convenience store industry sells more than 2 billion gallons of beer a year—roughly one-third of all the beer purchased in the United States.

"Candy Sales: Candy is a high-impulse item in convenience stores. In fact, many shoppers (49 percent) report that their candy purchases were unplanned, according to global research firm Envirosell.

"Coffee Sales: More than three out of four adult Americans say that they drink coffee either daily or regularly, according to the National Coffee Association, and convenience stores are one of the preferred destinations for coffee drinkers. Consumers stop to buy coffee more than they fill up their cars, providing convenience stores with a great opportunity to build loyalty and repeat sales.

"Technology: The integration of technology into convenience stores continues at a fast pace. Over the past decade, the convenience store industry has gone from being a technology laggard to a technology leader in using new technologies to deliver convenience.

"While such operating features are not a required condition of membership, convenience stores have the following characteristics:

- ✓ While building size may vary significantly, typically the size will be less than 5,000 square feet;
- ✓ Off-street parking and/or convenient pedestrian access;
- ✓ Extended hours of operation with many open 24 hours, seven days a week;
- ✓ Convenience stores stock at least 500 SKUs; and
- ✓ Product mix includes grocery type items, and also includes items from the following groups: beverages, snacks (including confectionery) and tobacco.

- "The percentage of one-store operators, true mom-and-pop stores, continues to climb. The percentage of one-store operators topped 50 percent for the first time in 2001. Today, that percentage is 62.3 percent. The states with highest percentage of one-store operators are Washington (78 percent), Georgia (74 percent), Louisiana (71 percent), Mississippi (71 percent) and New Jersey (71 percent). In Washington DC, 78 percent of convenience stores are one-store operations.

  "The average convenience store has a sales area of 2,768 square feet. New stores average about 2,800 square feet of sales area and about 1,900 square feet of non-sales area—a nod to retailers recognizing the importance of creating destinations within the store that require additional space—whether coffee islands, food service areas with seating, or financial services kiosks. Convenience stores also have expanded their offerings over the last few years, with stores becoming part supermarket, restaurant, gas station and even a bank or drug store. (NACS State of the Industry data)

  "The convenience store industry is America's primary source for fuel. Convenience stores sell an estimated 80 percent of the gasoline purchased in the United States. Of the 144,875 convenience stores in the United States, 79 percent (114,673 stores) sell gas. In 6 states, at least 95 percent of convenience stores sell gas: North Dakota, Wyoming, Nebraska, Iowa, South Dakota and Kansas.

  "More stores are seeking to become restaurants that happen to sell gas. The convenience store industry is a destination for on-the-go meals. The average store has more than $20,000 a month in food service sales. This includes prepared food ($11,600 per month), hot dispensed beverages—like coffee ($6,900 per month), commissary packaged sandwiches ($2,900 per month), cold dispensed beverages ($2,200 per month), and frozen dispensed beverages ($2,000 per month).

  "Consumers are embracing convenience stores like never before. An average store selling fuel has around 1,100 customers per day, or more than 400,000 per year. Cumulatively, the U.S. convenience store industry alone serves nearly 160 million customers per day, and 58 billion customers every year."
  Source: "Fact Sheets: U.S. Convenience Store Count," www.nacsonline.com 2010

- "Utilities led the increases on direct-store operating expenses, up 8.1% to reach $3,965 per store per month, followed by repairs and maintenance, up 6.3%. The largest operating expense was wages and benefits, up 2.4% to reach $18,245 per store per month. Here, with unemployment high, retailers have a chance to reshuffle the personnel deck. 'It's a great time to have controlled turnover in the c-store,' said Duskiewicz, 'and get the right people on the bus.'"

- "Deli/Sandwiches; prepared food to go is the plus which can put one store ahead of another provided it is done right."

- "Average range of gross profit (GP) is 20% to 35% excluding gasoline revenue."

- "Two out of three (65 percent) of all convenience stores offer food prepared on site, and 91 percent offer commissary/packaged products."

- "Should strive for average 30 per cent 'weighted' inside margin on merchandise sales."

- "Rental less than $15 per square foot can make all the difference in a successful convenience store business."

- "C-stores annual sales $767,000; food service annual sales $115,000"

- "High volume, easier to sell. Small stores under $25,000 month, very hard to sell."
- "Secondary Income (about 1.7% of total sales; $250,000 = $4,250 and at $150,000 = $2,550)"
- "Rebates & Allowances
  Product Placement Fees
  Special Promotions
  Pay Phones
  Car Vacuums/Air/Water
  ATMs
  Money Orders
  Lottery
  Prepaid Cards"

Source: "How to Evaluate a Listing or Sale in the C-Store Industry," a presentation by Jim Town,
Business Evaluation & Appraisals, Inc.

Expenses as a Percentage of Annual Sales

Cost of goods..60% or less—Good Store
Payroll/labor Costs..20% +/- (Owner operator will lower)
Occupancy...07% to 15% +/- (Rent or Mortgage Payment)
Profit (estimated pretax) .....10% to 15% Gasoline Profit Should Cover Rent/Mortgage

Industry Trend

- "The convenience retailing industry continues to be dominated by single-store operators, accounting for 62.7 percent of stores. The growth of one-store operations mirrored the overall growth in store count. The industry increased by 1,800 stores overall, the number of one-store operations increased by 1,766. Texas once again led in terms of overall stores, with 14,466 stores, nearly one-tenth of all U.S. convenience stores. California was ranked number two in store count at 10,581, followed by Florida at 9,348."

Source: "U.S. Convenience Store Count," www.nacsonline.com, January 24, 2011

- "Foodservice at Convenience Stores: While convenience stores have offered fresh, prepared foods for years, it is only over the last decade that the trend has accelerated. The result is that convenience stores have continued to evolve from gas stations that happen to sell food to restaurants that happen to sell gas."
- "Beer Sales: Nearly 80 percent of convenience stores sell beer, accounting for nearly one-third of all beer purchased in the United States, about 93 percent of which is sold cold. In fact, the U.S. convenience store industry sells more than 2 billion gallons of beer a year—roughly one-third of all the beer purchased in the United States."

Source: www.nacsonline.com

- "When it comes to convenience retailing in the United States, small operators, according to the NACS/TDLinx 2010 Convenience Industry Store Count, own approximately 62 percent of all stores, or about 90,000 locations. These stores bear names like Push 'Em Station, Sooner Superette and Lovely Food Mart, with new Americans owning a considerable number of these independent locations.

  "A decade ago, single stores made up half of the U.S. convenience industry, but over the last five years, the increase in the number of small operators had outpaced the overall growth rate in the convenience retailing industry. There are two reasons for this. The wave of mergers and acquisitions among midsize and large chains over the past decade often resulted in the divestiture of the less profitable locations, many of which were, and continue to be, picked up by small operators.

"Another reason: Major oil companies have preferred to focus on their core business in lieu of running convenience store operations, and over the past few years, several have sold off company-owned stores. Many of those stores have ended up in the hands of independent retailers."

Source: "Small Is Big," National Association of Convenience Stores Magazine, February 2010

- "Steady trend in convenience stores. Still a valuable service to small communities."

Seller Financing

- "5 years all due and payable with 15-year amortization"
- "5 to 7 years"

Questions

- "Do you have accurate books so I can go to a bank for a loan?"

- "Any previous environmental issue, current leak test result, 3 years' tax return, lease agreement. Do you want to sell or test the market?"

- "Ask for 3 years of tax returns. Don't base buy decision on under-the-table numbers."

- "Amount of gross that's tobacco related. Lottery sales, any employee or customer thefts?"

- "Location, location, location; traffic count and number of rooftops dictate the best locations, along with traffic patterns, red lights, curb cut access, etc. Age and condition of petroleum and other equipment are important; environmental issues must be dealt with prior to closing. Phase I and II reports are almost always required for financing and property transfer. What is the mixture of sales? How do your sales break down concerning gas, merchandise/cigarettes, beer, grill, deli? Have all of your EPA requirements been completed? How many robberies have you had since you bought the store? Do you have key people? Who supplies your gasoline? Who owns the gasoline equipment? Who is your wholesaler that supplies the majority of your groceries? Are there any convenience stores being built within two miles of the store?"

Resources

Websites
- www.csnews.com

Associations
- National Association of Convenience Stores—excellent site, lots of valuable information: www.nacsonline.com

Convenience Stores with Gas

(See also Convenience Stores, Gas Stations w/Convenience Stores/Mini Marts)

SIC 5411-03	NAICS 447110	

Rules of Thumb

➢ Note: The information that follows is also in C-Stores with Gas. It is a confusing issue, and perhaps there is no difference between a C-store with gas and a gas station with a C-store, but many experts still feel that there is. So here goes, again: Convenience stores with gas—these operations are more convenience stores than gas stations such as a 7-Eleven or Circle K. Gas stations with convenience stores (mini-marts)— these operations are more gas stations than convenience stores, such as Mobil, Shell and Exxon gas stations that have convenience stores. In many cases, the garages and stations themselves have been retrofitted to be convenience stores. These operations may include a car wash.

➢ 20 to 25 percent of annual sales plus inventory

➢ 2 to 2.5 times SDE plus inventory. 3.5 times SDE would be for SDE of $300,000+ on a consistent basis.

➢ 1 to 2.5 SDE (with service bays) plus inventory.

➢ 2.25 to 3.75 times EBITDA (business only) higher multiples as EBITDA increases.

➢ 5 to 6 times SDE includes real estate

➢ 5 to 7 times EBITDA includes real estate

➢ "3.0 to 3.5 times EBITDA—including the real estate is a good rule of thumb for convenience stores with gas. 2.0 to 3.5 times EBITDA for leased sites. Current and future requirements from oil companies are reducing the overall number of stations across the country. Before you purchase any gas station make sure you ask the oil company what the future is of that particular site. Age and condition of the petroleum equipment and environmental issues are important considerations in selling these businesses. A Phase I & II are required for both purchased and leased sites if a loan is required through a bank or the SBA (very difficult in this environment).

➢ Convenience Store with Gas, e.g., Circle K, Citgo

Index (multiple)		SDE	Gals/Mo
1.0x	to	$50K+	50K
2.25x	to	$90K+	75K+
2.75x	to	$150K+	100K+

The above value multiples do not include inventory (at cost).

➢ "7-Eleven convenience stores without gas are primarily controlled by the parent company (51%), thus your profit picture is relatively lower than the businesses shown above and therefore your multiples will be lower as well."

Pricing Tips

- "Convenience stores are priced one of two ways. With real estate and without real estate. The pricing for without real estate is generally between 2-3 times the stores EBITDA. And if the store has real estate included in the sale then the multiple is generally between 5-6 times the stores EBITDA depending on the quality of the assets. Both of these rules of thumb exclude inventory."

- "Factors impacting value include: Location, Fuel Supply Contract and Length, Age of Tanks & Pumps, Environmental Issues, Liquor License"

- "The multiples used to be higher, however due to market conditions they have come down approximately 20% in the last two years. The eroding profit margin, measured as cents per gallon, has tightened up in the marketplace since then, resulting in the gas station owner being forced to look for volumes and margins elsewhere in the station. The snack shop/convenience store section has stepped up to the plate and accounts for about 80% of the profits, while the other 20% and all of the gasoline margin goes towards the costs of employees and such. Depending on the rent or the mortgage structure, the 80% figures adjust up or down. Do not let the huge sales volumes fool you; measure the gallons times the margin, and not the millions in actual sales/revenue figures."

- "In 2005, the investment required to open a new convenience store, which includes land, building, total equipment and inventory, was $2.85 million for new urban stores, and $1.92 million for new rural stores (in areas of less than 50,000 population). Of that, more than one-third of the investment was for equipment and technology at urban stores ($1.13 million), and at rural stores ($821,000)."

  Source: National Association of Convenience Stores, 2012. This is a wonderful site. It is full of informative and interesting articles.

- "2-3 Times SDE, Sales Under $ 350,000 a year, you have bought a long hour job."

- "2 to 3 x SDE or 3–3.5x EBIT are the best; the percentage of annual gross sales doesn't reflect a fair price."

- "3 to 5 times EBITDA including the real estate. Margins are getting squeezed in some areas, therefore must be taken into consideration."

- "Gross sales is not a good factor in pricing, since the profit margin varies between gas and grocery sales."

- "3 to 4 times EBITDA including the real estate is a common rule. Location, traffic count, brand, and population are important considerations."

- "It has nothing to do with total sales volume or revenue. It does have everything to do with average gallons sold, and margins per gallon; volatility in industry requires you map out gallons and margins per month for last 2 years. Majors tend to have flat fixed margins, minors and unbranded markets move between 2–4 cents to high of 25%–30% margins."

- "Multiple of 2x SDE is mid-point of the range 1.75-2.25x SDE, and does not include the real estate. May be priced separately and added to SDE multiple, or 'digested' in the business valuation by a higher range of multiples. Real estate valuations may be considered by the same 3 Arizona markets, but should also consider the class of property, i.e., A, B & C. The full range when including real estate is approx. 5X SDE for a C-class property in rural AZ, to 14x for a Class-A property in Phoenix metro."

- "Dealer stations in our market sell for 2.2 to 2.5 post due diligence SDE for the business only. I value gas stations with the land by starting with SDE and deducting the buyer's required income for managing the station and any necessary reserves, and then I capitalize that amount by what I feel is the market cap rate. This is basically a real estate approach to the value."

- "Fewer and fewer stations surviving in today's competitive market."

- "2 or 3 times net SDE—most stores have horrible records; proof of numbers is thru gas receipts and store invoices. Gallons per month, pool margin, inside sales, other income and do the tanks meet 2009 standards."

- "Factors that most influence value are volume of gasoline sales, location, length, C-store versus service bays, traffic count and major brand identity."

- "Age of tanks; does station have canopy (is it cantilever or mech. attached); is it clean (environment); location, location, location."

- "The geographical site/location is key to a buyer in many offers and subsequent sells. Near freeways or interstates, high visibility corner locations or locations near major malls all come with a premium price tag."

- "The length of lease, the type of fuel supply contract (whether there is a contract with a major oil company or the buyer may purchase fuel on the open market) and the age and condition of the equipment will determine whether the site comes in at the low or high end of the range."

- "Sales and the gross profit on items like tobacco is indicative of the net"

- "Convenience stores can be valued in several different ways. If a convenience store does not include real estate and you are selling the business only then generally the rule of thumb would be 2-3 times EBITDA (net income) as long as the lease for the facility is reasonable. If the convenience store includes real estate the rule of thumb is generally 4-6 times EBITDA. Consolidators usually pay around 4-5 times EBITDA, but if the unit is well located and the assets are in good condition and if it was being sold to another jobber or independent then you can expect to get more based on these qualities at least an additional 10%-20% more."

- "3 to 5 times EBITDA including the real estate is a general rule. Location, traffic count, brand, population are all important considerations."

- "Consider what is included in the gross sales, i.e., does the figure include high-volume items such as lottery sales that have a small profit yield? When being provided sales figures that show high increases and an upward trend, look for the cause. An example would be the recent escalation in gasoline prices. On paper the increase will appear to be increased sales when in reality the apparent increase might be a static number of sales. I find it is better to alert the prospective buyer to these issues and increase your credibility as a transaction facilitator who treats both sides fairly."

- Influence Factors
"Factors that have a direct bearing of value in today are market. Store sales should be greater than $30K per month (do not include lottery sales) to be considered above average. What percentage is gross profit on average? The rent is a straight fee or a percentage of sales. Things to add into the value of this business: volume is greater than $40K per month; gross profit should be a minimum of 30 percent; appearance; part of a large gas station and/or car wash; long-term lease. Things to subtract in this business: volume is below $25K per month; gross profit is below 27 percent; major competition in the neighborhood; virtual free standing without a gas station or car wash."

Expert Comments

"Lots of turnover with bad stores, hard to find good profitable, clean stores". "Major oil companies are getting out of owning properties and managing labor. More and more foreign buyers are coming into the marketplace. Oil companies primarily want to be in the fuel supply business as their core profit driver."

"Stand-alone gasoline stations are dwindling in number. Most stations have some other profit center like a car wash, convenience store, service garage, or lube center." "A gas station is not easy to replicate by any means, with all the environmental regulations and what have you. The profit trend is definitely downwards, with non-branded or independent owners who primarily buy product on the open spot market being hammered the most. The branded market seems to want to try to chase non-branded independents out of the market with their pricing on racks."

"Risk in the gas station business is mostly systemic relating to the overall economy. Pricing risk of fuel involves international political risks affecting supply, etc. Demand risk relates to the current economic recession/depression. Difficulty of replication stems from financing for ground-up projects —available exclusively at this time from private sources; no institutional money for construction."

"With the way the economy is now, it's very tough to generate a decent profit out of a gas station. Customers looking for cheaper gas, cheaper groceries, increased use of credit cards—all this affects the business; and with the big oil companies like Racetrac and QT opening stores every day, they are affecting independent gas stations big time."

"It is getting very expensive to build a new ground-up facility. Average does cost close to $ 2 million, therefore it is costly to replicate. Not to mention the uphill battle with most urban zoning requirements which causes lengthy delays and adds to the soft costs." "Gas stations are very tough businesses; with increasing gas prices and increasing big corporate stores like QT and Racetrac , competition will always be high."

"Competition might be a business killer; risky business; the profit trend is almost the same, didn't change much; the location and the facility condition affects the business on a large scale; the marketability of this business is high due to a large supply of buyers; this industry will always be in demand even with the presence of big corporate stations like Racetrac and QT still growing."

"Gas stations and car washes are becoming more available in the listing base and not selling nearly as quickly as in the past. Financing is difficult to acquire as the main reason, also the drop in profitability along with rising rent factors are making gas stations less appealing. Some independent stations choose to close rather than face environmental upgrades. Profit trends downward on gasoline, with gas profit paying some to most of costs only. Marts/snack shops/stores are major moneymaking factors,"

"Very competitive industry today with the hyper markets, grocery stores, and big box retailers all getting into the convenience store industry. Location is everything with traffic count, population, and highway access critical to success."

"Hard to replicate due to site work needed and tank cost"

"The facts that this is cash business, relatively less risky, easy to learn and replicate make this business appealing to many people. Some areas are obviously saturated and avoidable. In general, the industry is very marketable if and only if the seller has substantiating books and records for 3 years and that daily inside sales are minimum $1,000–$1,500 (excluding extraneous revenues). However, the recent downturn economy affected the storewide 10% to 25% revenue down ubiquitously."

"Downturned economy affects this industry. 10% to 30% revenue is down from the previous year. We see more closed down c-stores this year than any other year. High gasoline price, high cigarette price obviously added to the tough economy."

"Expand the inside variety, sales, and profit, and depend less on the gas margins over which you have limited control."

"There is a relatively high degree of competition in the industry, but yearly cash flows are fairly predictable, so the risk involved is environmental risk. Even this risk, though, has been mitigated in the recent past by fuel equipment upgrades and state-funded insurance plans for gas stations. Profitability has declined as fuel has been recognized as a commodity, and price and location matter as much as brand. Also, most cars do not need the premium gasoline, which normally commands a higher margin. Convenience stores have replaced many of the old service stations, and big-box retailers like Wal-Mart and Home Depot have entered into the market and taken away Market Share   and therefore profitability from the traditional retailers. Many gas station sites are in excellent retail locations with high traffic count and good retail and residential back-up. Because the cash flows are predictable, the more modern sites are very marketable, while the older sites with environmental issues and dated equipment are far less marketable. The industry continues to grow at a slow pace, with sales up year on year but the number of locations declining (so sales per location continue to increase). Once controls are in place with one site, this business is fairly easy to replicate. Cash controls and employee retention are paramount issues."

"The convenience store industry is going through a cycle now, because of low fuel margins and increased credit card fees thereby forcing a lot of middle-of-the-road operators to depart from the business. There is a move for consolidation within the industry. At the present time there are about 140,000 convenience stores in the United States with only a minority of them owned by major oil companies. There is still an opportunity for an owner operator to be profitable as long as he can control his labor and have sufficient inside sales and not depend on fuel."

"C-Stores are marketable if they are priced fairly. Up-to-date equipment, EPA compliance and motivation (reflected in the pricing) have a major influence on marketability. Good records to document sales both inside and outside are important factors too."

"A larger location is better. A full liquor license is harder to obtain. Tobacco products have a high cost and low profit. Higher rent costs."

"A convenience store is not too difficult to open by itself, especially if it's without gasoline. Convenience stores come in all kinds of formats: corner stores, main street, highway exits, inside malls, inside airports, inside college campuses, etc. Location is very important to get the walk-in traffic."

"High profit margin with varied merchandise and lots of smaller profit centers: cell phones, phone cards, money orders, lottery, Western Union, bill payment centers, deli, ATM, copy center, etc."

Benchmark Data

- "Inside sales with 30% or more margins will do good with sales over $50k for an owner operator."
- "The U.S. convenience store industry has 148,000-plus stores that account for more than $680 billion in sales.
- "U.S. Convenience Store Count: The U.S. convenience store count increased to a record 148,126 stores as of December 31, 2011, a 1.2 percent increase (1,785 stores) from the year prior, according to the latest NACS/Nielsen Convenience Industry Store Count.
- "Convenience stores sell approximately 80 percent of the gasoline purchased in the United States each year.
- "Motor Fuel Sales: Convenience stores sell the majority of gasoline purchased in the country—80 percent of all fuel sold in the United States in 2011. Of the 148,126 convenience stores in the United States, 120,950 sell motor fuels.
- "The industry has a number of critical issues, including outrageous credit card fees, gasoline retailing misperceptions, debit card holds and more.
- "Credit Card Fees a Growing Challenge for Convenience Stores: While convenience stores sought to rein in most of their expenses in 2008, a significant expense continued to grow: credit/debit card fees. In 2008, these fees again surpassed industry pretax profits, and are expected to grow even more in the coming years.
- "Beer Sales: Nearly 80 percent of convenience stores sell beer, accounting for nearly one-third of all beer purchased in the United States, about 93 percent of which is sold cold. In fact, the U.S. convenience store industry sells more than 2 billion gallons of beer a year—roughly one-third of all the beer purchased in the United States.
- "Candy Sales: Candy is a high-impulse item in convenience stores. In fact, many shoppers (49 percent) report that their candy purchases were unplanned, according to global research firm Envirosell.
- "Coffee Sales: More than three out of four adult Americans say that they drink coffee either daily or regularly, according to the National Coffee Association, and convenience stores are one of the preferred destinations for coffee drinkers. Consumers stop to buy coffee more than they fill up their cars, providing convenience stores with a great opportunity to build loyalty and repeat sales.
- "Technology: The integration of technology into convenience stores continues at a fast pace. Over the past decade, the convenience store industry has gone from being a technology laggard to a technology leader in using new technologies to deliver convenience."

Source: National Association of Convenience Stores, 2012.

- "The percentage of one-store operators, true 'mom-and-pop' stores, continues to climb. The percentage of one-store operations are Washington(78 percent), Georgia(78), Alabama(76), Connecticut(73), and Mississippi(72). In Washington, DC, 80 percent of convenience stores are one-store operations."

  Source: National Association of Convenience Stores, 2012.

Expenses Based on Sales

Fuel sales	1.3 million gallons, $3.08 million
Gross profit margin	6.9%
In-store sales	$1.081 million
Gross profit margin	29.5%
Pretax profit	$42,196, or 1.2 percent of revenue

- "A good store should do a minimum of $750,000 to $1,000,000 in yearly sales plus lottery, and be at least 3,000 sq. ft. It should have a good deli counter and liquor, and a large parking lot with easy in and out. A free-standing building is better with extra storage."
- "Gross profit % of in store sales should be in the 30%–35% range; gasoline is almost a lost leader in many markets."
- "Determining Benchmark Data is very difficult because there are many factors that make a successful operation. Similarly, it is difficult to determine percentages of gross sales for various items, mainly because the gas prices fluctuate so much. An operation may have revenues of $3.5 million one year and $5 million the next year, without a material change in gas or store sales."
- "$480 per sq. ft. approx."
- "Factors that influence price and things to look for: Store sales should be greater than 30K per month to be considered a good business. When addressing the sales, do not add in the lottery sales. What percentage is the gross profit on average? The rent is a straight fee or a percentage of sales. Things to add into the value of this business: volume is greater than $40K per month, gross profit should be a minimum of 30 percent, appearance, part of a large gas station and/or car wash. Things to subtract in this business: volume is below $25K per month, gross profit is below 27 percent, competition in the neighborhood, part of a small gas station; e.g., Circle K or 7-Eleven, location, appearance."
- For additional Benchmark data see Convenience Stores and Gas Stations with Convenience Stores

Expenses as a Percentage of Annual Sales

Cost of goods:	70% or less — Good Store
Payroll/labor Costs:	20% +/- (Owner-operator will lower)
Occupancy:	05% to 07%
Profit (estimated pretax):	06% to 12%

Industry Trend

- "7-Eleven once again holds the top position on Convenience Store News' Top 100 Convenience Stores list. The Dallas-based division of the Japanese C-store giant, 7-Eleven, operated 6,727 stores, as of April 2011, almost 2,000 more than its runner-up, Shell. However, despite adding more than 200 net new stores over the past year (not including the recently announced pending acquisition of 188 Wilson Farms stores in western New York), 7-Eleven's total store count represents less than 12 percent of the total 57,721 stores operated by the Top 100."

Source: Convenience Store News, May 2011

- "Research has shown that 70 to 75 percent of consumers at the pump do not enter the store. 'That's huge. That's a lot of people who buy gas and nothing else,' he said, adding that 95 percent of the consumers who use credit cards never enter the convenience store."

Source: "NACStech: C-Stores Strive to Reach Consumers at the Pump," www.retailtechnology.csnews.com May 17, 2011

- "Rutter's Farm Stores, most of which are also gas stations, are scattered throughout Pennsylvania and have become a model for mixing traditional family values with the latest and greatest technology trends. The average store is just 11 years old and about 5,300 sq.ft.—or about 50% more than the size of an average convenience store of about 3,500 sq. ft. 'We're a grocery store, and we're a fast-food restaurant, and we're a gas station, and we're a little casino that sells lottery, and we're a little bank that sells money orders,' explains Scott Hartman, president and CEO. 'We're so many different things all under one roof.'"

Source: "Customers don't want to go anywhere else," www.candyindustry.com, April 25, 2011

- "While convenience stores have offered fresh, prepared foods for years, it is only over the last decade that the trend has accelerated. The reason is two-fold:
  - ✓ More and more time-starved consumers want on-the-go meal solutions, and
  - ✓ Retailers have found that foodservice can deliver new customers inside the store, and at a higher profit level than for items like gas, which has razor-thin profit margins. The result is that convenience stores have continued to evolve from gas stations that happen to sell food to restaurants that happen to sell gas. The overall convenience store foodservice category includes: food prepared on-site, commissary/packaged sandwiches, hot dispensed beverages, cold dispenses beverages, and frozen dispensed beverages."

Source: "Nacsonline.com/Nacs" September 1, 2010

- "Recent spiraling downward profits have weeded out significant numbers of weak businesses. Tight money, in turn, affects and lessens the overall asking price as well as the final price of stores. Fewer closings and they often take longer."

- "Overall convenience store industry profits rose 54 percent in 2008 to reach $5.2 billion, reversing a two-year decline where profits dropped 42 percent over that period. Industry sales jumped 8.1 percent to reach $624.1 billion, with both motor fuels sales (up 10.1 percent to $450.2 billion) and in-store sales (up 3.2 percent to $173.9 billion) showing growth.

"The convenience store industry sells an estimated 80 percent of the fuels purchased in the United States, and motor fuels sales continue to dominate industry revenues, accounting for 74.5% of all sales dollars, in examining same-firm sales data. However, overall fuel gallons sold declined 2.4 percent because of low gross margins the industry faced during the first three quarters of 2008.

"Credit card fees continue to be the industry's top pain point, surging another 10.5 percent in 2008 to reach a record $8.4 billion—nearly three times the level just five years ago."

Source: "Convenience Store Sales, Profits Showed Gains in 2008," www.nacsonline.com, April 7, 2009

- "Labor intensive, long hours, and there is competition"
- "Very competitive industry with shrinking fuel margins forcing all profits to come from the inside sale of groceries, food, cigarettes and other items."
- "The trend is towards much bigger stores with multiple fueling locations. The big box retailers and grocery stores are also jumping into this business."

Seller Financing
- 20 year amortization. 1-2 percentage points over current bank rate to give Buyer an incentive to go get a loan. 3-5 year balloon."
- "SBA and bank loans have become increasingly more difficult due to economic conditions and type of business"
- "7 years, on average 6 percent interest per annum."
- "As much as 50 percent of sales price could be financed—3 to 5 years typical."
- "Franchise—3 to 5 years (5 to 10 percent)"
- "4 to 7 years 6% interest"
- "Property—10 to 15 years (8 to 11 percent)"
- "7% to 8% interest"

Questions
- "Why are you selling? What are his gas margins after credit card fees? Is there any outstanding lawsuits or environmental issues?"
- "5 years' financial and gas sales history; phase I & II environmental reports"
- "Crime history, employee turnover and rent."
- "What are the future plans for this business per the oil company(supplier)?"
- "Any new competition? Security & safety? Road construction? Introduction to vendors."
- "Gallons history, margins history, both for last four years; plot against spot prices to see how tight street pricing gets on that street."
- "The quality of their historical financial statements, including both income statements and balance sheets. This is both for prospective buyer due diligence and lender requirements."
- "As much paperwork as possible to get to the truth"
- "Status of the underground tanks"
- "Some key questions a buyer would want to ask the current owner: if the oil company owns the property or if the land is leased to the oil company. The value of the business will be less if the land is leased from another entity. The reason is that when the lease expires, even if there are options, the oil company may decide not to renew. Make sure the oil company owns the property; worst case make sure the lease for the station runs at least for another 10 years (when the oil company does not own the land). Buyers should also be concerned about the types of tanks that are underground—are they steel or fiberglass? If the owner has steel tanks, find out why the tanks have not been replaced with fiberglass. Ask the current owner if there have been any leaks or contamination. If the answer is yes, find out when and to what extent. Has the problem been corrected?"
- "One should also find out who is responsible for any and all contamination that lies above or below the surface of the site (dealer or oil company or landlord). Always require, in an offer to purchase agreement, a clause that states that the buyer will perform as part of the due diligence a Phase I report by an

accredited environmental or chemical engineer who has a license to do so, with the results approved to the buyer's satisfaction. If a Phase II or III report is required, it is strongly suggested that it be done as well."

- "How many gallons per year does the site sell? What is the margin? What are the store sales excluding lottery sales? What are the lottery sales? Any additional revenue streams? How old is the equipment?"

- "Be sure to ask the seller if he has signed a fuel purchase agreement with a jobber or oil company. Is the seller getting any rebates from the jobber or oil company? Is the seller getting any hold-back money from his cigarette suppliers? Are there any additional state or local or city taxes that are an add-on up and beyond what your competitors pay? And then the big one: What is the environmental status of the property? Are there any outstanding environmental issues? Does the state that the property is located in have a cleanup fund? Most states have an insurance fund that has a deductible from $10,000 to $50,000.However, some states do not have a fund and the owner of the property is required to buy separate insurance. This is a must to find out. You can sell the store and have everything done and won't be able to get the deal financed because of environmental issues. Be careful. Find all of this out first before you get into the deal too far."

- "Do you have tax returns for the past 3 years? Do your P&L's agree with the tax returns? Have you had any fuel contamination issues? If so, are they resolved? What is the pool margin (profit over the rack price)?"

Resources

Associations
- National Association of Convenience Stores—excellent site, lots of valuable information: www.nacsonline.com

Cost Cutters Family Hair Care		Franchise
Approx. Total Investment		$94,495 to $210,295
Estimated Annual Sales/Unit		Not Available
SIC 7241-01	NAICS 812112	Number of Businesses/Units 850

Rules of Thumb

➢ 55 to 60 percent of annual sales plus inventory

Country Inns (See Bed and Breakfasts)

Country/General Stores	
SIC 5399-02	NAICS 452990

Rules of Thumb

➢ 20 percent of annual sales plus inventory

Coupon Books		
	NAICS 541870	

Rules of Thumb

➤ 2 to 4 times EBITDA

Seller Financing

▪ "Not usually seller financed. If financed, 2 to 3 years."

Courier Services (See Delivery Services)		
SIC 4215-01	NAICS 492110	Number of Businesses/Units 2,600

Court Reporting Services		
SIC 7338-01	NAICS 561492	Number of Businesses/Units 170,900

Rules of Thumb

➤ 30 to 35 percent of annual revenues includes inventory

Benchmark Data

▪ Court Reporting Services in the U.S. (The report below is the latest available)

Statistics (Court Reporting Services)

Number of Enterprises	170,905
Average Wages per Employee	$23,647
Average Profit Margin	4.0%
Average Revenue of Enterprise	$106,258

Source: IBISWorld, August 2009 (last available)

Share of employer establishments by employment size, 2005

Employment Size	Share (%)
1 to 4 Employees	71.3

Source: IBISWorld, August 2009

Item	Cost
Profit	4%
Rent	n/a
Utilities	n/a
Depreciation	4%
Other	54.4%
Wages	37.6%
Purchases	n/a

Source: IBISWorld, August 2009

▪ "There are no major players in this industry."

Source: IBISWorld, August 2009

- IBISWorld has discontinued updating this business. We have left the last report, as it still contains information of interest.

"Although pay varies by specialty, experience, and certification, the median annual earnings for wage and salary court reporters were $49,710 in May 2008. At the low end, reporters earned less than $25,360, and the most highly compensated pulled in more than $83,500, according to the U.S. Bureau of Labor Statistics. Aside from a salary, official court reporters earn a per-page fee for transcripts."

Source: "Court Reporter" by U.S News Staff, December 28, 2009, www.money.usnews.com

Industry Trend

- "Of the more than 50,000 court reporters in the United States, more than 70 percent work outside of the courtroom, according to the National Court Reporters Association.

- "The Department of Labor's Bureau of Labor Statistics projects that jobs in this field will grow more than 18 percent between 2008 and 2018—a good deal faster than the average for all occupations."

Resources

Associations

- The U.S. Court Reporters Association: www.uscra.org
- American Association of Electronic Reporters and Transcribers: www.aaert.org
  National Court Reporters Association: www.ncraonline.org

	Franchise
Coverall Health-Based Cleaning Systems (Commercial Cleaning)	
Approx. Total Investment	$10,576 to $37,150
Estimated Annual Sales/Unit	Not Available
NAICS 561720	Number of Businesses/Units 9,350

Rules of Thumb

➤ 2 to 3 times monthly volume

➤ Master/Area developer—sell for 3 to 5 times earnings plus some blue sky for size and potential of market (some cases).

➤ 4 times EBITDA

Pricing Tips

- "The four basic components of determining the value and price of a Master Franchise of Coverall include the collective principal amount of Franchisee Notes outstanding, the value of the exclusive rights to the population territory inclusive of the number of businesses with 5 or more employees, the value of the business structure (number of commercial accounts serviced and the number of franchisees) and the cash flow of the territory."

Expenses as a Percentage of Annual Sales

Cost of goods:..	80%
Payroll/labor Costs:..	04%
Occupancy:...	01%
Profit (estimated pretax):	10%

Resources

Websites

- www.coverall.com

	Franchise
Culligan International — Franchise/Dealership	
Approx. Total Investment	$104,500 to $695,000
Estimated Annual Sales/Unit	Not Available
NAICS 422490	Number of Businesses/Units 650

Rules of Thumb

➢ 80 to 120 percent of gross annual sales—dependent on several things: market size, current penetration rental base, water quality, etc.

Industry Trend

- "International Company (Culligan), the world's leading innovator and provider of water treatment and filtration systems for more than 70 years, announced the sale of its vended water business owned and operated by Culligan Store Solutions, LLC (CSS), to Primo Water Corporation (Primo), a leader in retail water exchange and retail sales of water dispensers. The sale price is $105M, and the transaction is expected to close later this year."

Source: www.Culligan.com. June 7, 2010

Seller Financing

- "Frequently 7 to 10 years."

Resources

Websites

- www.culligan.com

	Franchise
Curves for Women (See also Fitness Centers)	
Approx. Total Investment	$39,170 +
Estimated Annual Sales/Unit	Not Available
SIC 7299-06	NAICS 713940	Number of Businesses/Units 9,000

Rules of Thumb

➢ 1.5 times SDE plus inventory

➢ 30 percent of annual sales plus inventory

Pricing Tips

- "1.5 to 2 times SDE. The number of monthly check drafts and club size and location are important value factors along with membership trends."
- "Most clubs need 175–200 members to break even. 90% EFT is typical."

Expert Comments

"Acquisitions of existing franchises are generally excellent investments as a result of expected return on investment, market potential, and ongoing franchisor investment and research in the fitness industry."

"Other franchisors using the '30-minute-circuit' program have entered the marketplace with very mixed results. Current Curves locations have closed in market areas which were saturated."

Benchmark Data

- "1.5 employees per $100K sales"
- "It takes about 125 members to break even."
- "Usually owner-operated facilities are run at minimal expenses."

Expenses as a Percentage of Annual Sales

Cost of goods:	05%
Payroll/labor Costs:	20% to 25%
Occupancy:	10% to 15%
Profit (estimated pretax):	25% to 30%

Seller Financing

- "3 years"

Questions

- "What was your highest membership number? Review monthly membership history for last 3–5 years. Why do members join your club? Why do/don't they renew yearly membership? Explain club safety/parking lot issues if any. Review lease. Any complaints from adjoining tenants concerning music/noise issues? What are the nearest Curves Clubs to you? Other competing franchise clubs?"
- "Why are you selling the business? Is this a franchise? How long have you owned it? Are there any local market conditions affecting the business?"

Dairy Drive-Thru

	NAICS 722213	

Rules of Thumb

➤ 25 percent of annual sales plus inventory

	Franchise

Dairy Queen

Approx. Total Investment	$345,000 to $1,600,000
Estimated Annual Sales/Unit	$820,000

SIC 2024-98	NAICS 722211	Number of Businesses/Units 5,900

Rules of Thumb

➤ Price = 1.1 to 1.2 times annual sales for stores w/real estate

➤ Price = .45 times sales for leased facility. Rent = variable item

➤ "Walk-up"— two windows with real estate—1.24 (+/-) times annual sales

➤ Without real estate —.5 (+/-) times annual sales

➤ Full Brazier— with real estate—1.15 (+/-) times annual sales

➤ Without real estate—.5 (+/-) annual sales"

Pricing Tips

▪ "Dairy Queens: With Real Estate = 1.1X sales. IDQ leaning toward 'Corporate' type ownership, moving away from 'Ma & Pa' owners."

Expert Comments

"Many players in this market"

Benchmark Data

▪ "Dairy Queen 'Grill & Chills' are doing pretty well. Very high 'entry' cost of $1.5 million +/-, which requires $2 million sales to be profitable."

Expenses as a Percentage of Annual Sales

Cost of goods:	31%
Payroll/labor Costs	25%
Occupancy:	08%
Profit (estimated pretax)	15%

Seller Financing

▪ "Rarely seller financed."
▪ "5 years with balloon payment."
▪ "SBA financing—17 to 18 years with real estate; 7 to 10 years without real estate."

Questions

- Questions to ask seller: "Leased facility—rent important; owned facility—loan & taxes important"

Resources

Websites
- www.dairyqueen.com

Data Processing Services

SIC 7374-01	NAICS 541513	Number of Businesses/Units 49,627

Rules of Thumb

➤ 15 percent of annual sales plus inventory

➤ 2.2 times SDE plus inventory

➤ 2 times EBIT

➤ 2.2 times EBITDA

Pricing Tips

- "A proprietary software component could raise the multiple to as much as 10 x."

Benchmark Data

Statistics (Data Processing & Hosting Services)

Number of Establishments	49,627
Average Profit Margin	12%
Revenue per Employee	$391,100
Average Number of Employees	4
Average Wages per Employee	$71,888

Source: IBISWorld, May 2012

Products and Services Segmentation

Business process management and data processing	23.8%
Application service provisioning	18.3%
Data storage and management services	12.4%
IT technical support services	7.6%
IT computer network and network management services	7.4%
Other services	25.3%

Source: IBISWorld, May 2012

Major Market Segmentation

Financial firms	16%
Resellers	26%
Government firms	12%
Content providers	7%
Non-financial enterprises	39%

Source: IBISWorld, May 2012

Industry Costs

Profit	12.0%
Wages	18.7%
Purchases	4.2%
Depreciation	12.4%
Marketing	3.0%
Rent and Utilities	9.0%
Other	40.7%

Source: IBISWorld, May 2012

Market Share

Hewlett-Packard Company	15.6%
International Business Machines Corp.	14.1%

Source: IBISWorld, May 2012

- "Location is NOT important. Skill sets and experience of employees is the key to larger contracts. Annual maintenance contracts based on number of 'seats' is more valuable than service contracts."

Expenses as a Percentage of Annual Sales

Cost of goods:	n/a
Payroll/labor Costs:	35%
Occupancy:	n/a
Profit (estimated pretax)	40%

Industry Trend

- "More maintenance contracts vs. service contracts"

Questions

- "Ask for resumes of employees and meeting with a few top customers during due diligence."

Dating Services

SIC 7299-26	NAICS 812990	Number of Businesses/Units 3,745

Rules of Thumb

➢ 30 to 35 percent of annual sales

Benchmark Data

Dating Services

Number of Establishments	3,745
Average Profit Margin	19%

Source: IBISWorld, September 2012

Products and Services Segmentation

Online dating	58.2%
Matchmakers	15.2%
Mobile dating	10.5%
Singles events	8.3%
Other	7.8%

Source: IBISWorld, September 2012

Industry Costs

Profit	19.0%
Wages	26.8%
Purchases	11.7%
Depreciation	2.1%
Marketing	10.0%
Rent & Utilities	5.3%
Other	25.1%

Source: IBISWorld, September 2012

Market Share

InterActive Corp	23.7%
EHarmony	13.6%

Source: IBISWorld, September 2012

Industry Trend

- "When it comes to looking for love, online dating is the place to look. Research by Stanford University shows that online dating is quickly displacing offline venues as the preferred medium for meeting people to date. According to Stanford sociologist Michael Rosenfeld, the biggest groups likely to go online for love are gays, lesbians, and middle-aged heterosexuals. Those groups, particularly, have abandoned traditional means of meeting people to date like through friends, family, or local outlets."

  Source: "Online Dating Gaining in Popularity for Meeting a Potential Partner." February, 2010. www.onlinedatingmagazine.com.

- "California Attorney General Kamala D. Harris released a joint statement with Match, eHarmony, and Spark Networks (operator of dating sites like JDate and Christian Mingle) to announce the partnership and encourage other dating sites to implement similar policies.

- "The sites will cross reference prospective clients with national sex offender registries and provide an abuse reporting system. Anyone who is a registered sex offender will be barred from the online dating services.

- "Online dating services garnered 40 million users in 2011. Americans have spent over $1 billion on membership fees."

  Source: "Online dating services to screen future clients" by Chenda Ngak, www.cbsnews.com

Resources

Trade Publications

- Online Dating Magazine: www.onlinedatingmagazine.com

Day Care Centers/Adult (See also Assisted Living, Nursing Homes)	
SIC 8322-10	NAICS 624120	Number of Businesses/Units 3,800

Rules of Thumb

➤ 70 to 75 percent of annual sales

Pricing Tips

- "A higher price can be justified if the mix of clients is more private pay than Medicaid reimbursement or paid by other government programs. Additional revenue and profit and thus value/price can be obtained by adding services such as bathing, in home care service and transportation."

Expert Comments

"The time to reach breakeven is relatively long as this is still a relatively new segment of senior healthcare. The majority of adult day care centers are run by non-profit entities. The challenge for adult day care owners is to build a payer mix that is not dependent upon governmental programs (i.e., Medicaid) and to focus on the private pay client. Unlike the in home non-medical care business, this is a 'bricks & mortar' investment with significant initial build out cost but has a staffing model that is perfect for an absentee owner or an owner/operator."

Benchmark Data

- "Private-pay daily rates were obtained for adult day services. Adult day services national average daily rates increased by 4.5% from $67 in 2010 to $70 in 2011."
- "The typical adult day care center is about 5,000 sq. ft. and has an equivalent full- time staff of about 9. The average annual sales per square foot is thus about $160, and the average annual sales per employee is about $90,000."
- "More than 150,000 individuals receive care and services at an adult day center."

Source: www.leadingage.org/facts 2011

- "Adult day care is becoming increasingly important in the burgeoning elder-care business.
    - ✓ Individual facilities day demand is growing 5%–15% a year.
    - ✓ Adult day care serves at least 400,000 people nationally, by some estimates.
    - ✓ The average cost is around $61 a day. A home health aide could run about $152 for an eight-hour day.
    - ✓ Services can include physical therapy, exercise and grooming.
- "Adult day services provide health, social, and therapeutic activities in a supportive group environment for individuals with cognitive and/or functional impairments.
- Some are freestanding centers or programs; others are affiliated with a facility or organization such as a nursing home, assisted living community, senior center, or rehabilitation facility."

Source: "Market Survey of Long-Term Care Costs," Met Life, October 2011

Expenses as a Percentage of Annual Sales

Cost of goods:	0
Payroll/labor Costs:	25%
Occupancy:	20%
Profit (estimated pretax)	20%

Industry Trend

- "And although most adult day care centers are still operated as part of a larger organization like a skilled nursing home or medical center, they are gaining in popularity with entrepreneurs, as well as companies that are developing chains.
- "A look at the numbers helps to explain why. Although there are more than 3,500 adult day centers providing care for 150,000 people, the National Adult Day Services Association estimates that more than 5,400 are needed.

- "With the portion of the population 65 and over expected to grow to 20 percent by 2030 from 12.4 percent, demand is projected to skyrocket."

  Source: *New York Times*, March 29, 2007

Seller Financing

- Yes, usually for three (3) years.

Questions

- "What is your capacity and current loading? What is your payer mix? Do you provide any benefits to your employees? Is your occupancy cost above or below market? Are you a franchise? Is the owner the operator or an absentee owner? Do you also provide in home care services in addition to your base adult day care offering?"

Resources

Associations

- National Adult Day Services Association: www.nadsa.org

Day Care Centers/Children (See also Schools)		
SIC 8351-01	NAICS 624410	Number of Businesses/Units 868,903

Rules of Thumb

➢ 50 to 55 percent of annual sales includes inventory

➢ 2 to 3 times SDE includes inventory

➢ 2.5 to 3 times EBIT

➢ 3 to 4 times EBITDA

➢ 2 times SDE includes inventory. Most childcare centers are acquired with the real estate. The 2 multiple of SDE is after the debt service required to buy the real estate.

➢ Depending on the size of the facility (licensed capacity), location, and demographics of the area, the rule of thumb is:

➢ Center Size
<40	1 to times SDE
40 to 85	2 to 3 times (depending on expansion possibilities) SDE
100+	3 to 4 times SDE

➢ "Pricing ranges from 1.5 to 4 times EBITDA depending upon the size (licensed) of the facility. The larger the facility, generally the higher the multiple."

➢ "Two times cash flow for smaller centers (licensed for under 75). Up to four times cash flow for larger centers (licensed for 100 +)."

Pricing Tips

- "State regulations play a major role in the valuation of a child care business. As a general rule, higher degree of regulation often leads to higher quality of child care and lower business value due to cost of regulatory compliance. Child care market rates are not keeping pace with the cost to meet state regulations."

- "Competition, and location, ease of access, and capacity of center important"
- "State quality/star ratings and licensed capacity are drivers influencing multiplier; rarely gets above 3.75 multiple unless licensed for over 160 children and has earnings to support debt service after director salary(s)"
- "Larger the better. Better multiples if licensed for over 100 kids."
- "Multiple of 2 to 2.5"
- "Size is a factor: the larger the facility, the higher the multiplier. Less than 50 (multiple 2); over 100 (multiple 3)."
- "For a quick check you can use license cap times area sales ($10,000 a kid times 100 kids= X)"
- "State laws, regulations and market rate have large impact on price."
- "Site location is critical; curb cuts and ease of access in/out of center is very important; proper side of road for traffic flow during rush hour; tenure of center, tenure of teachers and their level of secondary education; strong director/mgr very important; quality centers with consistent earnings achieve price points in the higher end of the price range than other centers."
- "Based on gross sale, is 2 to 3 times sales. Based on lic. capacity, it runs $10,000 to $14,000 per child."
- "Size matters. Licensed capacity less than 75 expect a 2 1/2 to 3 times EBITDA, over 100 expect a 4 +/- EBITDA multiple."
- "The larger the business, the higher the multiple of earnings. A 4X multiple is the maximum for a large center (licensed for 100+). Smaller businesses, depending upon how well they are maintained, can achieve 2.5 times SDCF."
- "Price is a direct effect of cash flow. The amount the business provides the seller needs to cover debit service and provide a return to the buyer. Banks look for a debit service ratio of 1.25 to 1.50. Price is also determined by the number of students and the income they provide to the school. For example, childcare centers sell from $10,000 per child (license cap) to as low as $6000 per child. Price is also sometimes 2 times gross income."
- "Much of the value of a child care center is based upon number of children enrolled, gross revenues, net operating income and what percent of revenues are subsidized by the state."

Expert Comments

"Replication more difficult in states with high regulatory compliance"

"It would take 6–12 months to start from ground up, dealing with DCF licensure, health department, fire department, etc."

"Be careful to make sure that the seller isn't being taxed twice on any reimbursements from any governmental agencies."

"Recession means less children in childcare centers, and more at home with unemployed parent."

"There are numerous governmental agencies to deal with in transferring ownership of a center. It can take anywhere from a few weeks to a few months from the time of the offer until the deal actually closes."

"While it is relatively easy to replicate a child-care business, value can be created in a center that has a track record and has been in existence for decades."

"If no one is watching the children, it doesn't matter how many different jobs are created because people will not be able to work."

Source: Jen Wohl, National Economic Development and Law Center

"Lots of competition"

"With parents losing jobs, the kid count will go down."

"Economy has heavily impacted enrollment & earnings; values are down, but 'multiples' are down overall, as there are lots of centers available for sale."

"High cost of entry—some states have high regulations".

"Cleanliness of facilities is important to the perception of the parents."

"A center with real estate is desired by buyers. Current modern facilities maintain value."

"Newer facilities will command a higher service cost. Make sure the educational program keeps pace with changes in the educational sector. Some businesses have dual licenses and are licensed by the Department of Education."

"Very expensive to start a medium to large center from the ground up"

"Many variables here; location is key factor; strong operators/directors can achieve 22%—28% EBITDA depending on location, state & federal programs, level of income in area, etc."

"Depending upon growth rate of young population base, the better the curriculum the more difficult the business is to replicate."

"Risk is increasing due to over-competition in some markets, high entry cost due to real estate cost and regulations."

"Although some child care business can be 'relatively easily' duplicated (with know-how), the better programs are tough to duplicate the educational curriculum and track record (if they have been around for 20+ years)."

"Good childcare will always be needed and sought out by parents. The truest test of value in this business is going to be the premium you can establish for a 'quality' program with many years of history and a strong reputation for the caring of children as opposed to a "business operation."

"In most states, the laws and regulations governing child care centers are very complex. Many of these laws and regulations have a direct impact on the bottom line, i.e. requiring a certain minimum student to teacher ratio. These complex regulations have created a very high barrier to entry into the child care industry. And, compliance with regulations has, over the years, turned profitable centers into unprofitable, virtually impossible to sell centers."

"Other than 'occupancy costs' all other expenses are pretty proportional to enrollment or gross revenues and are easily managed as such. If rent can be tied to enrollment, then risk is greatly reduced (example: 10% of gross receipts for rent)."

"$1,000 to $2,500 per licensed child capacity depending on the success of current business"

"Attractors are: good location, appealing type of building, low or fixed rent , high current enrollment, high historic enrollment, low staff turnover rate, very good reputation, many years in service, several program types. Detractors are pretty much the opposite."

"Real estate can be the largest value in a day-care transaction. Rent should be adjusted to reflect Fair Market Value (FMV) rent based on a) comparable information available or, b) a percentage of the real estate appraisal value and, c) cross-checked by making sure, if financed, that the rent will cover the debt services (and a return on the down payment)."

"Industry is very competitive and regulated in California. Almost impossible to move existing business to alternate location if facility lease is not renewable. License to operate not transferable to buyers."

Benchmark Data

Statistics (Day Care)

Number of Establishments	868,903
Average Profit Margin	6%
Revenue per Employee	$27,200
Average Number of employees	2
Average Wages per Employee	$13,534

Source: IBISWorld, July 2012

Products and Services Segmentation

Child care centers	65%
Nanny and babysitting services	20%
Family day care services	15%

Source: IBISWorld, July 2012

Industry Costs

Profit	6.0%
Wages	47.9%
Purchases	10.5%
Depreciation	1.1%
Marketing	2.0%
Rent & Utilities	6.0%
Other	26.5%

Source: IBISWorld, July 2012

The People

Number of residents	301,461,533
Number of families with children younger than age 18	34,883,550
Number of single-parent headed families with children younger than age 18	10,779,688
Number of families with children younger than age 18, below poverty level	5,802,201

Source: National Association of Child Care Resource and Referral Agencies (NACCRRA)
March 2011, NACCRRA and the State of California

Children Under 6 with Parents in the Labor Force

In two-parent families, both parents in labor force	8,971,157
In single-parent families, parent in the labor force	5,856,354
Total children younger than age 6 needing child care, as parents work	14,827,511

Source: National Association of Child Care Resource and Referral Agencies (NACCRRA)
March 2011, NACCRRA and the State of California

Child Care Costs, Family Incomes

Average, annual fees paid for full-time center care for an infant .... $4,620–$18,773
Average, annual fees paid for full-time care
    for an infant in a family child-care home ....$4,620–$11,940
Average, annual fees paid for full-time care
    for a 4-year-old in a family child-care home....................................$3,780–$11,475
Median annual family income of single parent (female headed)
    families with children younger than age 18... $24,244
Cost of full-time care for an infant in a center,
    as percent of median income for single parent (female headed)
    families with children younger than age 18..25.4%–52.5%

Source: National Association of Child Care Resource and Referral Agencies (NACCRRA)
March 2011, NACCRRA and the State of California

Child Care Supply

Number of centers 118,598
Number of nationally accredited child care centers...11,493
Percent of child care centers that are accredited 9.8%
Number of child care homes.. 231,556

Source: National Association of Child Care Resource and Referral Agencies (NACCRRA)
March 2011, NACCRRA and the State of California

- "Benchmark Data are only accurate if for the same state, licensed size or rating scale. It is not possible to accurately compare child care businesses located in different states operating under different laws and regulations."
- Workforce and Training U.S.
  Average annual income for full-time, year-round child care provider—$20,940
  Source: National Association of Child Care Resource and Referral Agencies (NACCRRA)
  March 2011, NACCRRA and the State of California
- "But costs are high here, too. According to the National Association of Child Care Resource and Referral Agencies, a network of more than 700 child-care resource centers, Massachusetts has the highest average day-care costs in the nation: The price tag to place one infant in day care for a year averages $18,773, or 18 percent of the average two-parent family's wages and a whopping 67 percent of the average single mom's pay. (A 4-year-old's care costs $13,158, also a national high.) At the top of the scale, parents around Boston can shell out as much as $2,500 a month on one infant's care—more than a month's worth of food, sometimes even more than rent or a mortgage payment. Over 12 months, they'll spend more than the cost of a school year at a state college.
  "Even a chain with centers around North America and the UK, like Watertown-based Bright Horizons Family Solutions, which has economies of scale and corporate clients, showed only modest profits in its last financial statements made as a public company (it was taken private by Bain Capital in 2008, but a company representative confirms that current profits aren't impressive, either). Much of the company's revenue, up to 80 percent, goes right out the door to teachers' wages and benefits. Insurance, rent, maintenance, taxes, heating and cooling bills, cleaning supplies, snacks, and—yes—buying toothbrushes takes care of the rest."
  Source: "The Countdown Begins, by Melissa Schorr, *Boston Globe Magazine*, December 10, 2010
- "Small centers (under 100) need to have an owner/operator to realize a profit. Over 100 and it can be run by an absentee owner. Any rent above $10–$12 a square foot is too much."
- "Approximately 2.3 million individuals earn a living caring for and educating children under age 5 in the United States, of which about 1.2 million are

providing child care in formal settings, such as child-care centers or family child-care homes. The remaining 1.1 million caregivers are paid relatives, friends, or neighbors.

Provider Setting	Number of Workers	Percent of Workers
Center-Based Staff	550,000	24%
Family Child Care Home Providers	650,000	28%
Paid Relatives	804,000	34%
Paid Non-Relatives	298,000	13%
Total	2,301,000	100%

- "Child-care providers earn an average wage of only $9.46 an hour. With average salaries of $19,670 a year for child-care workers, many individuals holding these jobs do not earn very much more than the 2007 federal poverty level of $17,170 annually for a family of three."

Source: "Child Care Workforce," www.naccrra.org

- "According to the report, in 2008, the average price of full-time care for an infant in a center was as high as $15,895 a year. For a 4-year-old in a center, parents paid up to $11,680 a year for full-time care. Parents of school-age children paid up to $10,720 a year for part-time care in a center. Average prices for full-time care in a family child care home were as much as $10,324 for infants, $9,805 for a 4-year-old, and $7,124 for a school-age child. Additionally, the report found that average monthly child-care fees for an infant were higher than the amount that families spend on food each month. In every state, monthly child-care fees for two children at any age exceeded the median rent cost, and were nearly as high as, or even higher than, the average monthly mortgage payment."

Source: "Parents and the High Price of Child Care: 2009 Update," www.naccrra.org

- "Labor is 35% to 50% of revenue."
- "41%–45% payroll for North Carolina centers with 4- or 5-star ratings."
- "Minimum $1,000 net profit per full-time enrollment to $3,000."
- "States license based upon square footage per child. Physical layout combined with rent is a large factor in determining profitability of a business."
- "Depends on area, but we've sold schools based on Lic Cap $10,000 to $16,000 per child."
- "Each state varies between $5,000—$10,000/student fees."
- "Labor expense of 35% to 45% is good."
- "20%–24% EBITDA; Strong, tenured director and teachers, high education level of staff, good visibility; payroll costs 43%–48% of sales."
- "Easier to sell small and large centers, harder to sell medium-size centers."
- "10% net operating profit"
- "In order to make a reasonable owner operator income, in most states, a center will need to have a licensure and enrollment of 75 children or more. Additionally, most the regional and national chains will not consider a center with less than a 125 enrollment/licensure and would prefer more than 200."
- "EBITDA should range from $1,000 to $2,000 per licensed child, providing owner operates a compliant business. Salaries below 40 percent of sales should be investigated to ascertain the operation is [being] legally operated. Salaries above 45 percent of sales could indicate (a) inefficiency in the physical facility layout, (b) too many employees, or (c) lots of long-term employees (some turnover of staff is expected in the industry, and can actually help the earnings of the business)."

- "Signs of a bad day care center:
"A so-so reputation—If other parents aren't thrilled with the center, it's best to keep looking. Loose rules—If a home daycare doesn't have rules and organization, it's not likely to be right for you. Keep looking. A curriculum in hiding—Your child needs age-appropriate activities to encourage his development. If the center doesn't offer them, move on. An unqualified staff—If a center is understaffed, it's not for you.
"The National Association for the Education of Children (NAEYC) has set these guidelines: For babies, the ratio is one caregiver for every three children if a group has six infants, one for every four if a group has eight babies. For toddlers (12 to 24 months), the ratio is 1:3 for six children, 1:4 for eight children or kids, and 1:4 for children. For children between 24 and 36 months, the ratio should be 1:4 for a group of eight, 1.5 for a group of ten, and 1:6 for a group of 12. When you tour the facility, watch carefully to see whether babies are tended to quickly or if the staff, overworked and overwhelmed, lets them wail. An under-compensated staff—If the staff's training isn't up to snuff, they seem overworked, or they don't stick around very long, the center isn't for you. Dirty, unsafe facilities—If the center seems dingy, cramped, or dangerous, move on. An expired license—A license isn't everything, but if a center doesn't have one, it's not for you."

Source: www.family.msn.com

Expenses as a Percentage of Annual Sales

Cost of goods:	10%
Payroll/labor Costs:	40% to 50%
Occupancy:	10% to 20%
Profit (estimated pretax)	10% to 15%

Industry Trend

- "Increased regulation and decreased profits"
"As unemployment shrinks, centers will improve"
- "Better, cleaner centers will do well, while dirtier centers with bad management will close their doors."
- "The industry will grow, but at a slower pace."
- "Continued growth, especially in some ethnic groups. Pricing schedules will not increase due to economy. Parents will seek out alternative, less expensive child care options."
- "More regulation"
- "Depending upon the demographic area, some consolidation"
- "Number of centers will stay flat. Cost to open is high."
- "Solid growth; education requirements becoming more important and required"
- "Growing industry, but it costs more to set up center because of real estate cost."
- "Stable to modest growth depending upon the demographic area"
- "Regional and national chains will continue buyouts."

Seller Financing

- "Three to five years w/o RE 15–20 years with RE"
- "Most are 90 percent SBA financed."
- "Business only—7 to 10 years."

Questions

- "Numerous questions related to compliance with county and state laws and regulations. Percent private to public pay. Compliance records. Teacher and staff qualifications."
- "Are you on the food program? Subsidized care? Gold Seal?"
- "Any lawsuits or complaints filed?"
- "Tell me about staff turnover, infractions reported to licensing agencies (and cures for infractions), inspection report violations and new or threatened competitors."
- "Does the provider have a contract with the children's parents? If yes, ask for the contract. Does the provider have a rate schedule? Is the same schedule used for all children or do some have a special rate? Determine which children have a different rate and the amount. If the provider does not have the rate schedule for the year in question, ask for the current rate schedule and then ask how it differed in the tax year under exam. Does the provider furnish year-end statements to the parents as to how much they paid in the tax year?"
- "Any state subsidies? Review price schedule. Listing of all licenses—NAEYC accredited? Any claims against center? Confirm enrollment counts. Discuss curriculum. Education/experience of staff."
- "What local, state & gov. programs are you getting funding from & how much per age group... then go & verify from the state & counties how much of this money you will NOT be getting during the 6–8 month probationary period post closing & what the risks are of losing this funding ST & LT. Be sure you properly calculate this loss into your working capital needs & be prepared for it post closing. Consult with state & verify playground has adequate square footage for licensed capacity stipulated on license (they do not always match)."
- "What are employees and staff turnover rates? Provide a list of complaints with the licensing authority, and their resolution."
- "Are there any infractions against the business? Have they been resolved? And, how so?"
- "Always confirm enrollment numbers and review last 12 months' trend, etc, verify payment process & bank deposits; get copies of all records and complaints from the state and review with owner (many claims are unfounded)"
- "Licensing compliance, working ratios, teacher education qualifications, rates in terms of competition, private pay vs. government-supported care."
- "Are they in compliance with the regulating authority, and what are the most recent violations? Are there any lawsuits threatened or pending?"
- "Are children state subsidized?"
- "Last price increase, capacity of school, number of children, ages of children"
- "1. Waiting lists—a good sign of quality. 2. Enrollment schedules—try to understand these. 3. How are they hitting their numbers. 4. The quality of staff—age and training. 5. Community reputation—check several sources."
- "Why do they want to sell? What is the current capacity of the school? What are the current gross income and expenses of the school?"
- "Enrollment by age group, % government funded. License number. Do they own the real estate? Employee count, education level, credentials, experience, pay rate."
- "Make sure the labor cost is in line with industry standards, and inquire as to deviations to make sure the facility is staffed properly (legally). Child care is a state-regulated business which mandates child-to-staff ratios. Look at the

demographics in the area, as birth rates have an impact on future business. Location of the facility near affordable housing (which turns over) is a benefit. Rules of thumb based on gross sales can be misleading, as they do not incorporate operating-cost efficiencies."

Resources

Trade Publications
- Child Care Owner: www.childcareowner.com

Associations
- National Association for the Education of Young Children: www.naeyc.org
- National Association for Family Child Care: www.nafcc.org
- National Child Care Association: www.nccanet.org/
- Association for Early Learning Leaders: www.naccp.org

Deck the Walls		Franchise
Approx. Total Investment		$112,541 to $201,087
Estimated Annual Sales/Unit		Not Available
	NAICS 442299	Number of Businesses/Units 50

Rules of Thumb
➢ 35 percent of annual sales plus inventory

Resources

Websites
- www.dtwfraninfo.com

Del Taco		Franchise
Approx. Total Investment		$582,700 to $1,107,500
Estimated Annual Sales/Unit		$1,120,000
	NAICS 722211	Number of Businesses/Units 525

Rules of Thumb
➢ 75 percent of annual sales plus inventory

Resources

Websites
- www.deltacofranchise.com

Delicatessens (See also Restaurants)

SIC 5812-09	NAICS 445110	Number of Businesses/Units 41,000

Rules of Thumb

➢ 40 percent of annual sales plus inventory

➢ 2 times SDE plus inventory

➢ "It the deli is open five days a week, it's 50 percent of annual sales; if it's open six days a week, it's 40 percent of annual sales; and, if it's open seven days a week it's 30 percent of annual sales."

➢ Retail 40 percent of annual sales plus inventory

➢ Industrial 50 percent of annual sales plus inventory

➢ Office Buildings 50 percent of annual sales plus inventory

Pricing Tips

▪ "It's important to recognize the distinction between sandwich shops and a real delicatessen. A real deli sells cold cuts plus many other traditional deli items; it usually does make and sell sandwiches, but it represents only a portion of their business. A sandwich shop is like a Subway or Quizno's."

Resources

Associations

▪ International Dairy-Deli-Bakery Association: www.iddba.org

Delivery Services

SIC 4212-05	NAICS 492210	Number of Businesses/Units 191,879

Rules of Thumb

➢ 70 percent of annual sales plus inventory (if any)

➢ 2 times EBITDA for businesses under $1 million

➢ 3 times EBITDA for businesses from $1 to $5 million

➢ 4 times EBITDA for businesses over $5 million

Benchmark Data

Statistics (Courier and Local Delivery Services)

Number of Establishments	191,879
Average Profit Margin	6.9%
Revenue per Employee	$112,200
Average Number of Employees	4
Average Wages per Employee	$32,721

Source: IBISWorld, August 2012

Products and Services Segmentation

Ground deliveries	55.5%
Domestic air transit deliveries	29%
International air transit deliveries	8.5%
Messengers and local deliveries	7%

Source: IBISWorld, August 2012

Major Market Segmentation

Households	20%
Finance and insurance	15%
Other	15%
Government departments	10%
Healthcare	10%
Retail trade	30%

Source: IBISWorld, August 2012

Industry Costs

Profit	6.9%
Wages	28.8%
Purchases	23.4%
Depreciation	5.5%
Marketing	2.5%
Rent & Utilities	8.9%
Other	24.0%

Source: IBISWorld, August 2012

Market Share

United Parcel Service Inc.	42.0%
FedEx Corporation	25.0%

Source: IBISWorld, August 2012

Resources

Associations
- Express Delivery & Logistics Association: www.expressassociation.org

---

Dental Laboratories

SIC 8072-01	NAICS 339116	Number of Businesses/Units 12,000

Rules of Thumb

➢ 45 percent of annual sales plus inventory

➢ 1 times SDE plus equipment and inventory

➢ 2 times SDE includes equipment & inventory

Benchmark Data

Total Industry 2007

Lab Sales	$8 billion
Average Sales per Laboratory	$666,000 per year
# of Labs	12,089 (5,000 of which are sole proprietors)
# of Dental Technicians (U.S.)	53,000

Note: The above information is a bit dated, but still informative.

- "Let's start with the premise that for most laboratories labor is the largest single cost item, typically running between 45% and 60% of revenues. Keep this important concept in mind. Increasing the productivity of your technicians is not just the number of units you ship to clients. It requires increasing output without increasing the time the technicians spend working. If they build 40 units of porcelain in a 40-hour week, building 50 units in a 50-hour week is not increased productivity. It's actually worse because you are now paying overtime. Increasing productivity requires producing 45 units in that 40-hour week. If you are a crown and bridge lab, your goal should be to produce 3.75 complete finished units per technician per day. Removable labs should shoot for 3.25 units. A five-technician crown and bridge lab should average 18.75 per day."

Source: "Higher Productivity = Bigger Profits" by Chuck Yenker,
www.dentalproductsreport.com, March 2010

- "Industry Asks FDA to Improve Regulation of Dental Restorations to Protect Patient Safety in $5.5 billion U.S. dental-restoration products industry. Most domestic dental laboratories are exempt from registering with the FDA, and most typically employ just 3.5 people."

Source: National Association of Dental
Laboratories and www.businesswire.com

Dental Practices

SIC 8021-01	NAICS 621210	Number of Businesses/Units 172,082

Rules of Thumb

➤ 50 percent of annual sales includes inventory

➤ 1.3 to 1.8 times SDE includes inventory

➤ 4 times EBIT

➤ 4 to 5 times EBITDA

➤ 50 to 70 percent of annual collections subject to how weighted practice is towards managed care versus private fee for service (cash pay) and condition of equipment

Pricing Tips

- "Age of equipment, quality of three-party payer contracts, quality of location in terms of patients."
- "Specialty practices are a little riskier. Home offices can be difficult to sell."
- "What should I scrutinize when looking at a practice?
- Look at the gross production of the office to determine if you can produce or have produced that amount of dentistry. Also look to see if collections are close to the level of production, what the overall overhead of the office is and what makes up that overhead. For the physical office, look to be sure the location is in an area that will support your vision of your practice and that the building is in good condition. Within the office, note the quality and age of the equipment and whether anything is in major disrepair. Eventually, you will review patient charts and reports to verify statistics like new patient flow and the amount of active patients. You will want to get some idea of what kind of treatment patients are accustomed to and what has been done for them. Despite the importance of working equipment, do not over-emphasize its value. You are primarily purchasing goodwill, or the ongoing patient flow and production of the office. Equipment is easily, and affordably, replaceable. A quality patient base, skilled staff and working office systems are not."

Source: Buying a Practice—FAQs, www.towniecentral.com/Dentaltown/Article

- "Procedurally, in determining the value of a practice we review at least three years of financial information, including tax returns and profit and loss statements. The value of a dental practice is ultimately a function of the previous year of cash flow.

Specifically, you should be most interested in their net income of the practice after normalizing expenses and factoring out owner's compensation, whether that compensation be cash (actual income) or non-cash (expenses paid for the owner by the practice, or amortization, depreciation, etc.) With the true office overhead identified in this manner, a purchaser is able to evaluate the performance of the practice as a business, determining what he or she can afford to pay and make a reasonable living (after paying the debt service)."

Source: "Selling a Practice: FAQs" by Greg Auerbach, MBA,
Originally published in the September 2010 issue of Dental Town Magazine.

- "Specialty practices are a little riskier especially if they depend a lot on referring dentists."
- "Specialties receive much higher multiples and are in greater demand."
- "Solo practice should be grossing at least $500K–$700K. If less, probably an underperforming practice. Amount of hygiene (i.e., teeth cleaning) revenue can affect profitability. Value of equipment can vary, as some equipment is quite expensive (e.g., CEREC or digital radiography)."
- "Specialty will dictate above or below average multiple"
- "Average general dentistry px sells for 60%–65% of gross, with +/- 25% standard deviation."
- "The average new dental start-up office (2,000 square feet with 5–6 treatment rooms, 2 fully equipped to start) costs between $450,000 and $550,000 to complete. The cost also includes some working capital and marketing allowances.

  "Would the cost of purchasing an existing dental office rival or exceed the cost of a start-up? Would you have to replace outdated equipment? What can you do to enhance your chances for selling your practice?

  "A 'must' purchase is the *American Dental Association's Valuing a Practice: A Guide for Dentists.* http://www.adacatalog.org/. Read it, learn it and memorize it!

  "According to *Valuing a Practice*, a practice is likely to sell for between 40% and 65% of the average last 3 years of gross income.

  "Many factors can either raise or lower the value. Find out what these factors are."

Source: Before You Pull the Trigger... by Gordon Osterhaus Jr., DDS May 2006,
American Dental Association. (This is a bit dated, but still useful information.)

- "It varies by specialty, with prosthodontia being lowest, followed by perio and pedo. Endo is highest."
- "It depends upon the dental specialty, practice style, patient mix, clinical staff, payer mix, location, referral patterns, and many other factors specific to the practice."
- "Mathematical approach—Simple math can be used to check the alleged number of active patients for reasonableness. Divide the yearly collections (as verified by tax returns) by the number given for patient files. This will give you the average income per patient for the year. In many regions, you can expect this number to be between $285 and $385. If your answer to this math problem is less than that, there may be more patient files than reported. A higher answer indicates fewer patient files. The seller should explain any deviations from the average yearly collections per patient. The fee schedule may be high, driving the average up. A high average also might indicate that patients want

quality dentistry that simply costs more. Either of these explanations means good news. But, a lower average may indicate the patient base does not desire good dentistry or that the patients just cannot afford it. Although there may be more patients in terms of actual numbers in the latter situation, you'll have to work harder to get the gross collections desired. Until the law changes, use any method available to find out all you can about the patient base. The exact restrictions of the Patient Privacy Act and its impact on information available to a practice buyer are yet to be determined. We recommend that you watch for updated information from the ADA as further developments on this legislation unfold."

Source: *Practice Transitions* by Dr. Gene McCormick and Bob Fitzgerald, CPA, www.dentalsales.com

- "How much managed care or third-party pay versus fee for service; number of actual patients; quality of staff; condition of equipment; any expansion possible"
- "A lot depends on the number of patients that are in a practice, the location of the practice, the type of medicine/dentistry that is being done, the overhead, the lease, etc."
- "Specialty practices are somewhat more risky and for the same numbers will generally sell for a little less. For a partnership, the price may be skewed depending on how income is split."
- "Managed care brings down value, while private fee practices have highest value."

Expert Comments

"Dental practices are most marketable in desirable suburban areas and least in rural areas. Good profit for time practicing, typically 40% to 45% of gross, depending on practice."

"Fewer dentists from schools, trend to aggregate dental practices."

"Easier to get into than medicine, less risky, less regulated. Recession has big influence on customer spending. Rural markets are underserved."

"More baby boomers, more demand. Easy to obtain start-up finance. But still buyers for good practices in desirable locations"

"Fee-for-service or insurance-based practice will cause multiples and marketability to increase/decrease."

"Much better market than for medicine"

"100% financing available. Start-up money available too. Plenty of buyers. Growth 14%."

Benchmark Data

Statistics (Dentists)

Number of Establishments	172,082
Average Profit Margin	17.1%
Revenue per Employee	$122,600
Average Number of Employees	5
Average Wages per Employee	$47,38

Source: IBISWorld, May 2012

Products and Services Segmentation

Cleanings and oral hygiene treatment	18%
Oral surgery, emergencies and other care treatments	8.5%
Fluoride and sealant applications	8%
Periodontal disease treatments	4.5%
Prosthodontics and orthodontics treatments	3%
Examinations	20%
Radiographs	20%
Caries treatments	18%

Source: IBISWorld, May 2012

Industry Costs

Profit	17.1%
Wages	38.5%
Purchases	10.7%
Depreciation	7.5%
Marketing	0.5%
Rent & Utilities	9.5%
Other	16.2%

Source: IBISWorld, May 2012

- "Review your overhead percentages:
    - ✓ Salary ratios: Overall 20-24%
    - ✓ Lab: 8–10%
    - ✓ Dental supplies: 5–6%
    - ✓ Facility: 4–6% for renters; 5–8% for owners
    - ✓ General administrative: 6–10%
    - ✓ Marketing: 2–5%
    - ✓ Doctor salary: 20–25%
    - ✓ Retirement, reinvestment, and capital expenditures: 20–25%
      Source: "12 ways to control the overhead monster" by Linda Drevenstedt, RDH, MS, Devenstedt Consulting, LLC, April 2012

- "If you move your overhead to 55% during these tough times, think of the opportunity when times become better. Many dentists continue to operate under the old rules with an overhead of 75%. When your production drops 20%, your overhead is now 90%. With just a 10% drop in production, that is a 30% to 40% drop in net. Pressure mounts to pay bills and continue your chosen lifestyle. There are better choices with much less pressure.
  "Net return is a choice. It takes a strong plan and action to make 55% happen. Tough decisions are required. If net is the thing creating the most frustration, do something about it."
    Source: "Refocus to 55% overhead: by Bill Blatchford, DDS, www.dentaleconomics.com, May 1, 2011

- "A highly profitable practice will have a 40 percent to 50 percent profit margin. A practice that hovers at a 30 percent profit margin is doing something wrong. Inefficient staffing, poor production, or too many unnecessary expenses can be the culprits."
    Source: The Snyder Group, www.snydergroup.net

- "3 operatories, 1–2 hygienists"
- "$500 per patient billing and higher desirable"
- "Profitable enterprise with 35% to bottom line"
- "As % of gross: Staff Wages 20%–25%; Lab 7%–9%; Supplies 6%–7%; Rent 4%–6%; others typically 3% or less."
- "About 30% of revenue should be hygiene. Need about 1200–1500 active patients/year to sustain one full-time dentist"

- "65% to 75% overhead"
- "Gross over $500,000 is a successful practice"
- "Avg. sole general dentistry practice gross is about $735K. Avg. about 3.8 lay staff per FTE DDS. Non-DDS staff expense about 29%, rent 4%-7%, laboratory expense 7%, monthly charges in A/R 1.2, hygienist income should be about 30% of revenue, associate DDS compensation usually about 30% of production. "

Expenses as a Percentage of Annual Sales

Cost of goods:	10%
Payroll/labor Costs:	30% to 40%
Occupancy:	04% to 07%
Profit (estimated pretax)	30%

Industry Trend

- "As the economy improves, patients will do more dentistry."
- "The ADA is taking steps to increase dialogue with large group practices and gather information regarding this rapidly expanding career option. This sector of the dental workforce has experienced significant growth in a relatively short period of time. According to the ADA Health Policy Resources Center, in just two years the number of large dental group practices has risen 25 percent. For now, it's still a small piece of the overall dental delivery system pie. In a 2008 sampling frame, the Health Policy Resources Center concluded that solo dentist practices account for 92 percent of all dental practices, and very large group practices with 20 or more dentists make up only 3 percent. However, in analyzing its data on individual dentists, the HPRC has concluded that the rate of solo practitioners is falling. In 2010, 69 percent of dentists were solo practitioners compared to 76 percent in 2006."

Source: "ADA explores growth of large group practices" by Karen Fox, ADA News Staff, April 2012, www.ada.org

- "Increasing due to the Health Care Reform allowing millions of disadvantaged persons in"
- "Dentistry remains a good profession. Excellent profit potential for those willing to work hard. Technology and new cosmetic procedures should keep productivity and demand high."
- "Growing demand. Trend to add more ancillary services (i.e., teeth whitening, cosmetics) to improve profitability."
- "Dependent on insurance coverage allocated to dental practices"
- "Improvements in technology, quality of materials, and education of consumers regarding services available and transparency in pricing will continue to accelerate."
- "Stable"
- "More female dentists"
- "Employment of dentists is projected to grow about as fast as average for all occupations through 2014."

Source: www.stats.bls.gov/oco/print/ocos072.htm

- "Many dentists will be wanting to transition their practices."
- "Strong for adult specialties as baby boomers age. Much dentistry is elective, and a general economic slowdown could quickly affect dentistry."

Seller Financing

- "Very good 3rd-party financing available—sometimes even 100 percent."
- "Bank financing is readily available. Terms are usually 100% of the price plus working capital over 7 to 10 years."

Questions

- "Why selling? What type of practice do you have (e.g. types of procedures)? What plans do you participate with? Number of treatment rooms?"
- "Ask about: What are the revenues comprised of? What 3rd party payer sources exist? Age and condition of equipment. How they market."
- "Besides all the typical questions, how many active patients do they have; do they want to stay on or leave; and if they own the real estate (50%–60% do), do they want to rent or sell it."
- "Are billing practices compliant? Any staffing issues, personal or professional?"
- "Age of practice and equipment, demographics of practice, call-back programs, average annual billing per patient."
- "Type of practice, hours worked, amount of hygiene revenue, number of operatories, type of procedures commonly performed, payer mix, insurance contracts"
- "Many! Ask for operations data including number and types of procedures performed, demographics of patients, management systems and reports available in the practice, payer issues, regulatory requirements, technology issues, etc."
- "Patient lists, recall rates, hygiene rates"
- "# FTE dentists? gross receipts? # lay staff? hygienist income as % of gross? # right-handed operatories vs. # left-handed operatories."
- "What type of procedures performed on patients? Type of insurance accepted?"

Resources

Trade Publications

- Dental Economics: www.dentaleconomics.com

Associations

- American Dental Association: www.ada.org

Detective Agencies (See Investigative Services)		
SIC 7381-04	NAICS 561611	

Diagnostic Imaging Centers		
	NAICS 621512	Number of Businesses/Units 6,602

Rules of Thumb

➢ 100 percent of annual sales includes inventory

➢ 3.25 times SDE includes inventory

➢ 4 times EBIT

➢ 5 times EBITDA

Pricing Tips

- "May be necessary to include A/R in the price for working capital needs. Age and type of equipment very important."

Expert Comments

"Highly competitive and constant change taking place with reimbursement rates via Medicare."

Benchmark Data

Statistics (Diagnostic Imaging Centers)

Number of Establishments	6,602
Average Profit Margin	12.3%
Revenue per Employee	$246,200
Average Number of Employees	13.9
Average Wages per Employee	$69,379

Source: IBISWorld, September 2012

Products and Services Segmentation

Computed tomography scans and x-rays	35%
Sonography imaging	25%
Magnetic resonance imaging scans	20%
Positronemission tomography scans	20%

Source: IBISWorld, September 2012

Major Market Segmentation

Private insurance payments	40%
Medicare and Medicaid payments	25%
Other	11.5%
Hospital payments	10%
Health practitioner payments	8%
Out-of-pocket payments	5.5%

Source: IBISWorld, September 2012

Industry Costs

Profit	12.3%
Wages	29.1%
Purchases	41.9%
Depreciation	8.0%
Marketing	1.0%
Rent & Utilities	6.5%
Other	1.2%

Source: IBISWorld, September 2012

Expenses as a Percentage of Annual Sales

Cost of goods:	10%
Payroll/labor Costs:	25%
Occupancy:	05% to 10%
Profit (estimated pretax)	40%

Industry Trend

- "Uncertainty. While the need for scans (CT, MRI, X-ray) will continue to go up, reimbursements will likely fall."

Dialysis Centers

	NAICS 621492	Number of Businesses/Units 29,440

Rules of Thumb

➤ 5 to 10 times EBITDA

Pricing Tips

- "Patient mix (types of payer sources) is key; geography is also important given differences in reimbursement in different areas and regulations."

Benchmark Data

Statistics (Emergency & Other Outpatient Care Centers)

Number of Establishments	29,440
Average Profit Margin	8.7%
Revenue per Employee	$185,600
Average Number of Employees	16
Average Wages per Employee	$61,840

Source: IBISWorld, July 2012

Products and Services Segmentation

Kidney dialysis centers	21%
Freestanding ambulatory surgical and emergency centers	20%
HMO medical centers	9%
Other outpatient care centers	50%

Source: IBISWorld, July 2012

Major Market Segmentation

Medicare	25%
Other	16%
Medicaid	10.5%
Patients (out-of-pocket)	6.5%
Other Government	4.5%
Private Insurance	37.5%

Source: IBISWorld, July 2012

Industry Costs

Profit	8.7%
Wages	33.1%
Purchases	25.0%
Depreciation	4.0%
Marketing	2.5%
Rent & Utilities	3.5%
Other	23.2%

Source: IBISWorld, July 2012

Market Share

Fresenius Medical Care Aktiengesellschaft	8.8%
DaVita Inc.	8.4%

Source: IBISWorld, July 2012

- "Often owners will hear estimates based on amounts 'per patient' which can be inaccurate, as they may be based on very different types of programs in different areas with different payer groups."

Industry Trend

- "Dresner Partners, a leading FINRA-registered, middle-market investment bank and IMAP member, advised Dialysis Corporation of America, Inc. (DCA) (NASDAQ: DCAI) on its recently completed sale to U.S. Renal Care, Inc. (USRC). Headquartered in Linthicum, Maryland, DCA is a leading regional provider of outpatient dialysis services in the eastern and midwestern U.S., operating 37 dialysis centers and 11 acute programs across seven states. With the acquisition, Plano, Texas-based USRC will operate 84 dialysis facilities as well as home and acute programs across nine states, providing care to roughly 5,500 End Stage Renal Disease (ESRD) patients in Arkansas, Georgia, Maryland, New Jersey, Ohio, Pennsylvania, South Carolina, Texas, and Virginia. The $110.25 million transaction, announced on April 14th, was completed on June 3rd."

  Source: "Dresner Partners Advises Dialysis Corporation" by Marketwire, www.sys-com., June 9, 2010

- "Going through new update on conditions of participation and reimbursement changes over time, but still a very solid area given the long-term relationship with patients and relatively predictable cash flow"

Questions

- "Whether they are the medical director, and what relationships they have with patient referral sources, whether they would continue to work in the unit post transaction, etc."

Dick's Wings & Grill		Franchise
	NAICS 722211	Number of Businesses/Units 20

Rules of Thumb

➤ 35 percent of annual sales

Resources

Websites
- www.dickswingsandgrill.com

Diners (See Restaurants)		
	NAICS 722110	

Rules of Thumb

➤ 30 to 35 percent of annual sales plus inventory

Direct Mail – Advertising		
(See also Advertising Material Distribution Services)		
SIC 7331-05	NAICS 541860	Number of Businesses/Units 3,178

Rules of Thumb

➤ 40 to 50 percent of annual revenues plus inventory

➤ 2 to 2.5 times SDE not including inventory

Pricing Tips

- "Valpak used to be the gold standard for this industry at a multiple of 3. Considering new technology and the economy most have been selling at 2 X SDE or slightly less."
- "Valpak is the definite leader in this industry but technology and the Internet have hurt their multiple. Where I used to get 3 x SDE, I am currently realizing between 2.25 and 2.5 SDE"

Expert Comments

"On-line coupon technology has hurt this industry."

"Marketability is high. Location and facilities are solid because this biz thrives in metropolitan areas and can be run out of your home."

Benchmark Data

Statistics (Direct Mail Advertising)

Number of Establishments	3,178
Average Profit Margin	6.5%
Revenue per Employee	$190,800
Average Number of Employees	22
Average Wages per Employee	$49,361

Source: IBISWorld, July 2012

Products and Services Segmentation

Full direct mail services	49.3%
Lettershop services	21%
Printing and fulfillment services	17.4%
Other services	8.1%
Mailing list support services	4.2%

Source: IBISWorld, July 2012

Major Market Segmentation

Finance, banking and insurance institutions	20%
Other	20%
Restaurants and travel companies	15%
Business-to-business market	12%
Retail stores	33%

Source: IBISWorld, July 2012

Industry Costs

Profit	6.5%
Wages	26.0%
Purchases	27.5%
Depreciation	2.9%
Marketing	1.0%
Rent & Utilities	9.5%
Other	26.6%

Source: IBISWorld, July 2012

Enterprises by Employment Size

# of employees	# of enterprises	Share (%)
0 to 4	1,542	50.8
5 to 9	442	14.5
10 to 19	434	14.3

Source: IBISWorld, July 2012

Market Share

Valassis Communications Inc.	10.6%
Harte-Hanks Inc.	6.8%

Source: IBISWorld, July 2012

Expenses as a Percentage of Annual Sales

Cost of goods:	65%
Payroll/labor Costs:	05% to 10%
Occupancy:	05%
Profit (estimated pretax)	20% to 25%

Industry Trend

- "Key client objectives for 2012 were customer retention, ranked number one in the survey, followed closely by customer acquisition and customer profitability. Nearly nine of 10 respondents declared direct marketing as the medium best equipped for reaching their marketing objectives.
  "Key findings include: Direct mail ranked number one (88%) planned marketing channels for 2012, followed by web/micro-site, email, and social media. Two-thirds (64%) of respondents use social media as part of their marketing plan."

  Source: "Direct Mail the Top Channel for Some of America's Best Known Companies,"
  www.printinthemix.com, Fast Facts, March 2012

- "Continuing decline unless they can integrate current technology."
- "This industry will go through a shakeout because of the Internet, with only the industry leaders surviving."

Questions

- "How many recurring agreements are in place? How large is your biggest client?"
- "How many active clients? What is your average net profit?"

Resources

Associations

- Direct Marketing Association: www.the-dma.org

Direct Selling Businesses	
SIC 5963-98 NAICS 4543	Number of Businesses/Units 879,394

Rules of Thumb

➢ 4.5 to 5 times EBITDA

Benchmark Data

Statistics (Direct Selling Companies)

Number of Establishments	879,394
Average Profit Margin	6.1%
Revenue per Employee	$40,400
Average Number of Employees	1
Average Wages per Employee	$6,525

Source: IBISWorld, August 2012

Products and Services Segmentation

Wellness products	22.8%
Personal care products	21.3%
Other products and services	18.4%
Clothing and accessories	10.3%
Leisure and educational products	3.3%
Home and family care products	23.9%

Source: IBISWorld, August 2012

Industry Costs

Profit	6.1%
Wages	16.4%
Purchases	62.7%
Depreciation	0.5%
Marketing	4.0%
Rent and Utilities	0.4%
Other	9.9%

Source: IBISWorld, August 2012

Establishments by Employment Size

# of Employees	Share (%)
1 to 4	68.3
5 to 9	16.8
10 to 19	9.6%

Source: IBISWorld, August 2012

Market Share

Alticor Inc.	16.0%

Source: IBISWorld, August 2012

Expenses as a Percentage of Annual Sales

Cost of goods:	60%
Payroll/labor Costs:	01%
Occupancy:	01%
Profit (estimated pretax)	10%

	Franchise

Discovery Computers (Canada)

SIC 5734-07	NAICS 443120	Number of Businesses/Units 6

Rules of Thumb

➢ 50 percent of annual sales plus inventory

Pricing Tips

- One store sold for $495,000

Resources

Websites

- www.discoverycomputers.com

Display Advertising (See Billboards)

Distribution/Wholesale — Electrical Products

	NAICS 421610	Number of Businesses/Units 10,892

Rules of Thumb

➤ 35 percent of annual revenues plus inventory

Pricing Tips

- "This category includes electrical components which tend to sell for less than the above figure which is the other category included in this entry—electrical equipment."

Benchmark Data

Statistics (Electrical Equipment Wholesaling)

Number of Establishments	10,892
Average Profit Margin	3.5%
Revenue per Employee	$871,900
Average Number of Employees	6.8
Average Wages per Employee	$59,184

Source: IBISWorld, June 2012

Products and Services Segmentation

Lighting fixtures	15.2%
Relay and industrial controls	12%
Motors and generators	11%
Power and distribution transformers	10%
Switchgear and switchboard apparatus	10%
Other	24.8%
Wiring and cables	17%

Source: IBISWorld, June 2012

Major Market Segmentation

Electrical contractors	35.4%
Private and public power utilities	20%
Other	5.6%
Industrial users	39%

Source: IBISWorld, June 2012

Industry Costs

Profit	3.5%
Wages	6.9%
Purchases	81.5%
Depreciation	0.7%
Marketing	1.3%
Rent & Utilities	2.0%
Other	4.1%

Source: IBISWorld, June 2012

Market Share

WESCO International Inc.	5.0%
Graybar Electric Company Inc.	4.0%

Source: IBISWorld, June 2012

Distribution/Wholesale — Grocery Products/Full Line

SIC 5141-05	NAICS 424990	Number of Businesses/Units 2,987

Rules of Thumb

➢ 3 to 4 times SDE

➢ 4 times EBIT

➢ 4 to 4.5 times EBITDA

Pricing Tips

- "Use 25%–30% of GPM [gross profit margin] times 4 to arrive at goodwill price including all F F & E. To this number, add the dollar amount of net working capital to be included in the sale."

Expert Comments

"All of the above factors influence the purchase price as indicated."

Benchmark Data

Statistics (Grocery Wholesaling)

Number of Establishments	2,987
Average Profit Margin	1.5%
Revenue per Employee	$880,700
Average Number of Employees	39
Average Wages per Employee	$61,556

Source: IBISWorld, June 2012

Products and Services Segmentation

Specialty food	16%
Canned food	15%
Fresh meat	11%
Frozen food	11%
Household items	9%
Other	8%
Beverages	3%
Other grocery products	27%

Source: IBISWorld, June 2012

Major Market Segmentation

Food service outlets	25%
Other wholesalers	11.4%
Federal, state and local government bodies	3.4%
Businesses and households	3.1%
Supermarkets and other grocery retailers	57.1%

Source: IBISWorld, June 2012

Industry Costs

Profit	1.5%
Wages	6.8%
Purchases	80.0%
Depreciation	0.5%
Marketing	1.1%
Rent & Utilities	1.6%
Other	8.5%

Source: IBISWorld, June 2012

Market Share

C&S Wholesale Grocers Inc.	19.8%
Wakefern Food Corporation	9.1%
Supervalu Inc.	7.6%

Source: IBISWorld, June 2012

- "$285,000–$300,000 sales per employee would be a good benchmark for a successful wholesale distributor."
- The top 3 players account for 34% of industry revenue:
    - ✓ C&S Wholesale Grocers, Inc.
    - ✓ Supervalu Inc.
    - ✓ Wakefern Food Corporation."

Source: IBISWorld, August 2010

Expenses as a Percentage of Annual Sales

Cost of goods	80% to 83%
Payroll/labor Costs	12%
Occupancy	05%
Profit (estimated pretax)	07% to 08%

Questions
- "Stability of gross profit margins?"

Distribution/Wholesale — In General

(See also Wholesale Distribution—In General)

	NAICS 423610	

Rules of Thumb

➢ 2 to 3 times SDE plus inventory

➢ 50 percent of annual sales plus inventory

Pricing Tips
- "Distribution companies that are profitable with a strong history and diversified customer base can command high multiples"

Expert Comments

"Easy to replicate, lots of competition"

Benchmark Data
- "High margins for the most part"

Expenses as a Percentage of Annual Sales

Cost of goods:	70%
Payroll/labor Costs:	15%
Occupancy:	05%
Profit (estimated pretax)	10%

Industry Trend
- "Growing industry, particularly over the Internet"

Questions

- "What other products or lines can they distribute, are there any restrictions given by current suppliers?"

Distribution/Wholesale — Industrial Supplies	
NAICS 423840	Number of Businesses/Units 8,700

Rules of Thumb

➤ 50 percent of annual revenues plus inventory

Benchmark Data

Statistics (Industrial Supplies Wholesaling)

Number of Establishments	5,227
Average Profit Margin	5.9%
Revenue per Employee	$691,100
Average Number of Employees	9
Average Wages per Employee	$57,329

Source: IBISWorld, May 2012

Products and Services Segmentation

Mechanical power-transmission supplies	20%
Industrial containers and supplies	17%
Industrial valves and fittings	13%
Welding supplies (excluding gasses)	7%
Miscellaneous supplies	43%

Source: IBISWorld, May 2012

Major Market Segmentation

Other wholesalers for resale	21.3%
Businesses for end use	10.8%
Retailers for resale	8.5%
Other	8.3%
Contractors	5.2%
Industrial users for production inputs	45.9%

Source: IBISWorld, May 2012

Industry Costs

Profit	5.9%
Wages	8.4%
Purchases	70.8%
Depreciation	0.5%
Marketing	1.0%
Rent & Utilities	3.8%
Other	9.6%

Source: IBISWorld, May 2012

Distribution/Wholesale — Janitorial	
NAICS 423850	Number of Businesses/Units 3,598

Rules of Thumb

➤ 30 to 40 percent of annual sales plus inventory

Benchmark Data

Statistics (Cleaning & Maintenance Supplies Distributors)

Number of Establishments	3,598
Average Profit Margin	14.8%
Revenue per Employee	$306,800
Average Number of Employees	11.2
Average Wages per Employee	$49,574

Source: IBISWorld, October 2012

Products and Services Segmentation

Paper and plastics products	51.9%
Chemical supplies	30.4%
Janitorial supplies and accessories	10.2%
Power equipment	6.1%
Other janitorial products	1.4%

Source: IBISWorld, October 2012

Major Market Segmentation

Janitorial service companies	26.8%
Industrial buildings	17.3%
Schools, colleges and universities	15.5%
Healthcare centers	13.3%
Retail outlets, hotels, restaurants and recreational buildings	9.8%
Commercial buildings	9%
Government buildings	8.3%

Source: IBISWorld, October 2012

Industry Costs

Profit	14.8%
Wages	16.3%
Purchases	57.2%
Depreciation	2.8%
Marketing	2.1%
Rent & Utilities	3.2%
Other	3.6%

Source: IBISWorld, October 2012

Distribution/Wholesale — Medical Equipment & Supplies	
NAICS 42145	Number of Businesses/Units 9,000

Rules of Thumb

➤ 50 percent of annual revenues plus inventory

Pricing Tips

- "Pricing on medical equipment tends to be a higher percentage of sales than medical supplies. While the percentage of annual sales price might be a bit higher than the multiple in the Rule of Thumb above, the price based on percentage of annual sales for medical supplies could be lower."

Benchmark Data

Statistics (Medical Supplies Wholesaling)

Number of Establishments	9,484
Average Profit Margin	5.2%
Revenue per Employee	$848,000
Average Number of Employees	20
Average Wages per Employee	$92,630

Source: IBISWorld, June 2012

Products and Services Segmentation

Electromedical equipment	28.8%
Orthopedic devices and hospital supplies	29.7%
Dental equipment	3.9%
In vitro diagnostic substances and devices	9.5%
Surgical and medical instruments	28.1%

Source: IBISWorld, June 2012

Major Market Segmentation

Veterinarians	27.0%
Clinics	22.0%
Dentists	10.5%
Alternate care providers	9.5%
Hospitals	31.0%

Source: IBISWorld, June 2012

Industry Costs

Profit	5.2%
Wages	11.1%
Purchases	63.0%
Depreciation	2.0%
Marketing	2.0%
Rent & Utilities	7.0%
Other	9.7%

Source: IBISWorld, June 2012

Market Share

Cardinal Health Inc.	6.2%
Owens & Minor Inc.	6.0%

Source: IBISWorld, June 2012

Distribution/Wholesale — Tools

	NAICS 423171	

Rules of Thumb

➢ 55 percent of annual sales includes inventory

➢ 3.7 times SDE includes inventory

Pricing Tips

▪ "Higher multiples for the higher net profit industries"

Expert Comments

"Location is not typically important since there is not much drop in traffic."

Benchmark Data

Statistics (Tool and Hardware Wholesaling)

Number of Establishments	5,380
Average Profit Margin	4.3%
Revenue per Employee	$417,800
Average Number of Employees	15
Average Wages per Employee	$51,020

Source: IBISWorld, May 2012

Products and Services Segmentation

Bolts, nuts, rivets and other fasteners (excludes nails)	42.1%
Hand tools and power tools	34.3%
Others	17.5%
Cutlery	6.1%

Source: IBISWorld, May 2012

Major Market Segmentation

Retailers	39.6%
Wholesale establishments for resale	23.8%
Building contractors and heavy construction	15.2%
Manufacturing and mining industries	11.3%
Businesses for end use	4.9%
Other	2%
Repair shops	1.5%
Government bodies	1.7%

Source: IBISWorld, May 2012

Industry Costs

Profit	4.3%
Wages	12.5%
Purchases	72.2%
Depreciation	2.9%
Marketing	1.4%
Rent & Utilities	2.9%
Other	3.8%

Source: IBISWorld, May 2012

Market Share

Stanley Black & Decker Inc.	17.4%
True Value Company	4.8%

Source: IBISWorld, May 2012

- "Very hands-on with the key customers. Must maintain knowledge of the products they need to service their clients."

Expenses as a Percentage of Annual Sales

Cost of goods	74%
Payroll/labor Costs	08%
Occupancy	01%
Profit (estimated pretax)	15%

Industry Trend
- "Good"

Questions
- "Do you need a mechanical background or inclination to be successful?"

Document Destruction	
	NAICS 561990	

Rules of Thumb

> 150 percent of annual sales includes inventory
> 4 times SDE includes inventory
> 6 times EBIT
> 6 times EBITDA

Pricing Tips

- "Prices range from 1.25 to 2.0 times gross revenues"
- "Mobile shredding operations include price adjustments to compensate for the age of the fleet."

Expert Comments

"High revenue growth rates have attracted new market competition."

"This is a high growth industry, with low technology requirements and relatively few barriers to entry."

Benchmark Data

- "Well-run businesses can generate $250K–$300K revenue per vehicle in fleet."
- "EBITDA margins should exceed 30% for mobile operations and 35% for plant-based operations."

Expenses as a Percentage of Annual Sales

Cost of goods:.. 40%
Payroll/labor Costs:... 25%
Occupancy:.. 05%
Profit (estimated pretax) 30%

Industry Trend

- "Industry revenues should continue to grow. Consolidation has reduced the number of larger independently owned businesses."
- "Revenue trends exceed 20% growth due to heightened awareness of confidentiality and identity theft concerns. Many state regulations require shredding of confidential information."
- "Shredding Ahead: business booms as market demands document destruction"
  Source: www.ezy-waysecurityshredding.com.au

Questions

- "Age of fleet and the output of plant facilities are important. Industry standard equipment is a must."
  "What % of the business is recurring versus one-time purge service revenues? Is the service provided on-site at the customer location via a mobile shredding truck or destroyed in a plant environment off-site?"

Dog Kennels (See also Pet Grooming)

SIC 0752-05	NAICS 812910	Number of Businesses/Units 9,000

Rules of Thumb

➢ 1 times annual sales plus inventory

➢ 2 to 3 times SDE plus inventory

➢ 2.7 times EBIT

Pricing Tips

- "Multiplier can be anything from 1 to 3.5, most sold comps support a range of 2 to 3. Issues affecting multiplier selection are: longevity, occupancy rates for boarding kennels (similar to hotel/motel analysis), seller involvement, financing ability, state of facilities, location, etc. Grooming salons are in the 1 to 2 times multiplier; if seller is the groomer and no staff, there is no business goodwill."

- "Careful consideration of multiplier of 'add backs,' revenue trend, geographic location."

- "American Boarding Kennel Association (ABKA) uses 1 to 1.5 times gross sales PLUS real estate. These transactions can be very real estate intensive and often business does not support debt service. That needs to be taken into consideration when pricing. Location and zoning influence pricing considerably."

- "Multiplier depends largely on 1) type of facility (old/new), 2) geographic area (how difficult is licensing and zoning), 3) growth of business in the past 5 years, 4) how involved/important is the seller in the operation, 5) how large is real estate component (if high, price gets inflated, so business is priced for less)."

- "One way of calculating the market value of a boarding kennel would be to figure the present market value of just the real estate and add to that 1 or 1½ times the annual gross. Now, the difference between 1 and 1½ times would be determined by the area. For example, if the kennel is in a growing area, you would be more inclined to go 1½ times. If the kennel is in an area that is static, and there is reason to feel that the kennel will continue to do more business, then you could use one times the annual gross."

Expert Comments

"Competitors not only include other facility (i.e., real estate) based businesses, but an animal owner's friends, relatives, etc. that often 'watch the pet' cheaper. In home petsitters are gaining popularity, so they need to be considered in competition analysis. 'Barriers to entry' include zoning and land use laws, which are getting stricter raising the value of existing, properly zoned facilities. Industry itself continues to grow and has survived the recession fairly well. Very marketable business, but lots of unqualified buyers. Risk can be high, especially to a buyer with no prior industry experience. Lending can be challenge due to mixed-use properties. Seller's personal goodwill needs to be measured carefully against real business goodwill; high customer loyalty to seller causing a risk for buyer. If seller is the groomer, buyer can expect the grooming income to diminish drastically upon purchase. Often a real estate holding company (owned by the seller as well) owns the real estate and the business (operating company owned by the seller) pays rent to the holding company. When recasting, it's imperative to substitute that rent for Fair Market Rent in the area; sometimes this leads to an add-back, sometimes to a deduction. The business must be valued based on SDE that INCLUDES occupancy cost. One can't add back all the rent and then value based on that SDE; there is a cost for the real estate the business uses to generate income."

"Multiplier depends on the following factors: 1. Geographic location (determines marketability and desirability) 2. Seller's role and risk assessment of transfer 3. Historical revenue trends 4.Type and age of facility (older facilities are less desirable/not many buyers willing to buy 5. Real estate value (if high, business will most likely not generate enough to support debt service, hence fetches a lower valuation to still stay within a price range that it can actually be sold)."

"Dog daycares are experiencing heavy growth and thus competition, easy to replicate. Older boarding kennels with outdated facilities are difficult to market/sell, resort styles attract more buyers. Industry is growing, profit margins are historically high and continue as such. Zoning restrictions are growing limiting entry in some states. The smaller the business, the higher the risk for new owner. Customers tend to be very loyal to the owner, and do not deal with change in ownership well. Grooming salons are very high risk, as most customers will leave with the seller. The less the seller is involved in the business, the lower the risk. This is a personal service industry, and needs to be assessed as such."

"Barriers to entry depend largely on zoning and licensing. In some states it's very easy, some states very restrictive. Seller is the highest risk for buyer due to the personal nature of the business. Lots of interested buyers, financing the deal can be difficult. Industry growing as a whole; the trend is more toward the resort style/ communal play facilities. Older facilities are hard to market, small buyer pool."

Benchmark Data

- For additional Benchmark data see Pet Grooming
- "Occupancy! A successful facility should have a year-round occupancy level of at least 50%. Per-run revenue can be measured; but, as many facilities also provide grooming and daycare services, not a reliable benchmark. Payroll below 40% of Gross Income. Overall, SDE should be close to, or above, 30% of Gross Income."
- "Boarding kennels: Year-round occupancy should be minimum of 50%, preferably over 55%. Avg. annual income per run/enclosure around $3500. Dog daycares: average number of dogs per day around 1 dog per 75 SF of (inside) area."
- "Analyze like a hotel, based on occupancy. Statistically, a decent operation should have at least a 50% occupancy (yearly). SDE should be 24% to 30% of gross sales, if business well managed."
- "Another set of numbers you might find useful is this: the average kennel occupancy nationwide is 55.9 percent; the average income per run is $2.902 annually. Now these numbers can have some significance in helping people figure out how much a kennel should be making. For example, if you have 100 runs that are occupied 55.9 percent of the time, you can figure that the kennel would be doing average business. Multiply that by the daily charge

for customers. The numbers should come out somewhere near what the present owners say they are grossing for the year on boarding. If they say they are making a lot more than that, it means that they are claiming that they have more than 55.9 percent occupancy. And that would merit some further investigation."

- Estimated Sales of Boarding Facilities in the U.S.

Size of Kennels (dog runs)	Average Gross Income
Small (under 50; average–27)	$134,000
Medium (50–99; average–69)	$339,000
Large (100+; average–137)	$654,500
Avg. Annual Income per Dog Run	$2,902
Avg. Dog Occupancy	55%
Avg. Days' Stay per Dog	6.5

- Dog Kennel Expenses

Size of Kennels (see above for size)

Expenses (As a % of gross sales)	Small	Medium	Large
Payroll	30.63%	49.95%	26.37%
Employee Benefits	1.33	1.22	1.56
Auto/Truck	1.93	0.94	1.38
Travel & Entertainment	0.31	0.36	0.33
Kennel Insurance	2.02	1.26	1.08
Repairs & Maintenance	4.01	2.50	1.93
Office Supplies	1.18	0.89	1.29
Utilities	2.61	2.34	2.81
Telephone	1.48	0.89	0.54
Yellow Page Ads	1.69	1.29	1.60
Other Advertising	2.15	0.95	1.11
Office & Administration	0.75	0.67	1.68
Professional Services	0.82	0.61	0.77
Veterinary Expenses	1.44	0.43	0.43
Licenses	0.39	0.31	0.10
Other	3.97	3.91	4.00

The above are recent estimates. Not all kennels have all of the services above. The information was furnished by the American Boarding Kennel Association (ABKA).

Source: www.kennelsource.com March 22, 2005
(The figures are a bit dated; the latest we could find, but still informative.)

Expenses as a Percentage of Annual Sales

Cost of goods:	03%
Payroll/labor Costs:	40%
Occupancy:	17%
Profit (estimated pretax)	30%

Industry Trend

- "Industry continues to grow, new services are being added. Customers spend more and more money on their pets, that have been elevated to a family member status."
- "Growth, more franchises, more 'resort' style facilities, more competition."

Questions

- "1. What are your day to day duties at the business? (how much does the customer base rely on the seller) 2. Verify zoning and land use from the county department directly. 3. How much of the income do you produce personally (grooming, training, etc.)? 4. Staff and what level of authority do they have? 5. How do you think the clientele will react when they learn that you've sold? 6. Get confirmation on any septic, well, etc. issues. 7. Which licenses are required (besides regular business license) to operate?"

- "1. Determine if a successful kennel or not. 2. Pricing in comparison to competition and how often they are raised (industry notorious for not raising prices regularly) 3. Real estate issues: septic, water, inspections, set-backs, neighbors, noise ordinances, etc."

- "How involved is seller in day-to-day operations and with clients? License/ zoning/inspections. Relationship with neighbors and veterinary clinics. Longevity of staff. If grooming is a part of the business, is it a groomer or the seller doing the work? How does the facility stand out from the competition in the area?"

Resources

Associations
- National Association of Professional Pet Sitters: www.petsitters.org
- Pet Care Services Association: www.petcareservices.org

		Franchise
Dollar Discount Stores (See Dollar Stores)		
Approx. Total Investment		$99,000 to $195,000
Estimated Annual Sales/Unit		Not Available
	NAICS 452990	Number of Businesses/Units 140

Rules of Thumb

➢ 20 percent of annual sales plus inventory

Benchmark Data
- For Benchmark data see Dollar Stores

Dollar Stores		
	NAICS 452990	Number of Businesses/Units 39,923

Rules of Thumb

➢ 15 to 20 percent of annual sales plus inventory

➢ 2 to 2.5 times SDE plus inventory

➢ 2 to 2.5 times EBITDA

➢ 1.5 to 2 times EBIT

Pricing Tips
- "With the increase in competition, margins must be looked into carefully."
- "Sells easily, as mom-and-pops are moving in, and it's day hours only."
- "Very competitive market. More diversification and the astute marketers are moving to the $1–$5 spread."

- "There seems to be a downward pressure on profitability but the dollar stores are expanding into higher priced and higher margin items."

Expert Comments

"Stores do better in a down economy."

"Not too difficult to replicate; needs a large amount of inventory; the larger the store, the better the variety and the sales."

"Dollar stores are starting to become 1- to 5-dollar stores with items in that price range."

"Easy to replicate and possible margin squeeze"

Benchmark Data

Statistics (Dollar and Variety Stores)

Number of Establishments	39,923
Average Profit Margin	2.8%
Revenue per Employee	$190,700
Average Number of Employees	9.4
Average Wages per Employee	$17,845

Source: IBISWorld, April 2012

Products and Services Segmentation

Consumables	62.2%
Household products	13.5%
Apparel and accessories	12.6%
Other	11.7%

Source: IBISWorld, April 2012

Industry Costs

Profit	2.8%
Wages	9.6%
Purchases	62.3%
Depreciation	1.2%
Marketing	3.8%
Rent and Utilities	4.7%
Other	15.8%

Source: IBISWorld, April 2012

Market Share

Dollar General Corporation	28.7%
Family Dollar Stores	15.9%
Dollar Tree Stores Inc.	12.5%
Big Lots Inc.	9.5%

Source: IBISWorld, April 2012

- "But Dollar Tree and its deep discounting cousins Dollar General and Family Dollar, which offer about 25% to 30% of their merchandise for a buck and keep the bulk of it under $10, are no longer pushing just garage-sale junk. At Dollar General, for example, about 70% of the products are consumables like dry goods, drinks, paper towels, toothpaste and diapers.
"This is stuff people need, priced attractively to draw traffic to the stores. Eight years ago, about 60% of Dollar General's product assortment consisted of consumables. And now about 78% of those products are national brands: Tide, Bounty, Crest, Coca-Cola, Cheerios.

"At the end of 2007, Dollar General sold $165 per sq. ft. (0.09 sq m) of real estate. By end of the second quarter of this year, sales jumped to $199 per sq. ft., a 21% increase.

"Dollar Tree stores are 8,580 sq. ft. (797 sq m) on average: Walmart discount stores average 108,000 sq. ft. (10,033 sq m), while the Supercenters are some 185,000 sq. ft. (17,187 sq m). The small box stores offer a narrower selection of items, holding inventory costs down."

Source: "The Buck Shops Here" by Sean Gregory/Charlotte, Time Magazine, January 2011

- "Good ones do over $550 per sq. ft."
- "$400-600 sq. ft."
- "Dollar stores—a label they picked up because many of their products sell for $1 or less—are soaring at a time traditional retailers have been sucked into the market downdraft. This year, shares of department store chain Macy's are down 62%, and drugstore chain Walgreen (WAG) is down 38%. Shares of Circuit City (CC) plunged 60% on Monday alone when the consumer electronics retailer filed for bankruptcy protection.

"Family Dollar, for instance, now gets 61% of its revenue from consumables, which includes food as well as paper, candy, snacks, and pet food. Half of 99 Cents Only's revenue comes from food, says James Ragan of Crowell Weedon. 'People will be shopping for food no matter what,' he says.

Source: "Dollar stores' stocks defying the economic downturn" by Matt Krantz, USA Today.
www.dollarstoremerchandise.com

Expenses as a Percentage of Annual Sales

Cost of goods:	70% to 75%
Payroll/labor Costs:	15% to 17%
Occupancy:	10%
Profit (estimated pretax)	20% to 25%

Industry Trend

- "They fall short of Wal-Mart or a full-scale neighborhood grocer, and are markedly less pricey than your corner convenience store. Dollar General, the largest dollar store chain in the U.S., recently (March 30) opened its 10,000 store in Merced, CA. The Tennessee-based chain added 63 units in the space of roughly two months, which sounds like a lot, but is actually a little off the pace the company needs to achieve the 625 new stores slated to open this year.

"Going forward, DG needs to average 1.8 new stores per day to hit its new-store expansion target of 625 units and seven percent square footage growth by the end of its fiscal 2013. And then DG needs to maintain or possibly accelerate that pace over the coming fifteen years, as Dollar General claims the U.S. market is capable of supporting upwards of 20,000 stores.

"Family Dollar, the second largest chain operates around 7,100 stores and like Dollar General, the aggressive growth plans include a net new 450 to 500 stores this year. The real estate strategies for Dollar General and Family Dollar are similar in that the sites they occupy are typically along primary arteries near the low-income transit routes. This site selection strategy provides these two leading chains with impulse-oriented visits aimed to attract convenience minded consumers.

"Dollar Tree is the third largest dollar chain with around 4,350 stores. The Chesapeake, VA–based chain operates a differentiated real estate strategy in that the stores are typically located near a major discounter like Wal-Mart or Target. The products are virtually the same as Dollar General and Family Dollar; however, Dollar Tree is a little larger selling space (of around 10,000 square feet) versus the 8,000 to 9,000 square foot stores operated by the larger peers."

Source: "Dollar Stores Take on Walmart, and are Starting to Win," by Brad Thomas, contributor, *Forbes*, April, 2012, www.buckstore.com/dollar-store-news

- "Brown will stock items that can be found in most dollar stores—food, household products, hardware, baby needs, health and beauty aids, party supplies, toys, pet items and pharmaceuticals—plus services his competitors don't supply. Those include Internet access; DVD rentals; photo processing; balloons; bill-paying centers; fax, copy and print services; and lottery ticket sales.

  "Brown said 85 percent of his merchandise will sell for $1; nothing will be over $1.50. 'People are pinching every penny they can,' he said. 'That is one of the reasons I started this.'"

- "Gentry, Ark.—Walmart Stores opened its first Walmart Express, its answer to the growing threat of dollar stores. The 15,000-square-foot store, one-tenth the size of a Walmart superstore, is to carry everything consumers might need on the spur of the moment, from milk and eggs to DVDs."

- "Dollar stores have shown the biggest gain in shopper visits over the last year out of all the retailers that sell basic consumer goods, according to market research data. Manufacturers are racing to package more affordable versions of products common at those stores, and other budget retailers, feeling the loss of customers, are trying to duplicate their success."

  Source: www.buckstore.com, February 28, 2011

- "Dollar stores—they used to be known for racks of worthless trinkets spread out among some semi-useful bathroom and kitchen supplies, but today these thrifty behemoths have managed to expand their inventory and clientele enough to become one of America's strongest industries. So much for the era of luxury."

  Source: "How America Learned to Love the Dollar Store" by Tal Pinchevsky

- "Next to supercenters, dollar stores remain the fastest growing channel among food, drug, and mass retailing. No-frills stores, low prices, and a small, easy-to-shop and easy-to-access format gives shoppers a convenient option to big box discount retailers, like Wal-Mart. 'Dollar stores combine pricing power, efficient operations, and small stores to make the model work,' comments Skrovan."

  Source: www.retailindustry.about.com/od/seg_dollar_stores/a/bl

Questions

- "Tax returns and all invoices"
- "Paperwork, and sit and observe"
- "Margins and vendor contacts"

Resources

Websites
- www.buckstore.com/dollar-store-news/

Franchise

Domino's Pizza (See also Pizza Shops)

Approx. Total Investment	$119,950 to $461,700
Estimated Annual Sales/Unit	$700,000

SIC 5812-22	NAICS 722211	Number of Businesses/Units 9,000

Rules of Thumb

➤ 45 percent of the first $400K in annual sales, 50 percent of the next $100K ($400 to $500K) in annual sales, then 55 percent of the next $250K of annual sales (from $500 to $750K)

Resources

Websites

- www.dominosbiz.com

Donut Shops (See also Dunkin' Donuts)

SIC 5461-05	NAICS 722213	Number of Businesses/Units 18,717

Rules of Thumb

➤ 45 to 50 percent of annual sales plus inventory (and can go much higher for a great store)

➤ 2 to 2.5 times SDE plus inventory

Pricing Tips

- "Higher coffee sales (60 percent of sales) produce higher value. Very low coffee sales produce lower values."
- "Length & cost of lease? Retail vs. wholesale business? Percentage of business that is coffee (the higher the percentage of coffee sales, the higher the price)"

Benchmark Data

- For Additional Benchmark Information see Restaurants — Limited Service

Statistics (Doughnut Stores)

Number of Establishments	18,717
Average Profit Margin	3.8%
Revenue per Employee	$84,200
Average Number of Employees	8
Average Wages per Employee	$14,459

Source: IBISWorld, June 2012

Products and Services Segmentation

Doughnuts in bulk	27.1%
Other beverages	21%
Yeast doughnuts	15.7%
Coffee	14%
Other items	09%
Other doughnuts	7.8%
Mini doughnuts and doughnuts holes	5.4%

Source: IBISWorld, June 2012

Industry Costs

Profit	3.8%
Wages	17.4%
Purchases	37.1%
Depreciation	2.0%
Marketing	4.5%
Rent & Utilities	5.9%
Other	29.3%

Source: IBISWorld, June 2012

- "The store needs to be located on the morning side of traffic flow in order to do a high volume and to minimize ... risk of failure. The donut business is not an absentee business."

Source: The Donut Factory

Expenses as a Percentage of Annual Sales

Cost of goods:	21% food (+ 4.2% paper goods)
Payroll/labor Costs:	20% to 23%
Occupancy:	10%
Profit (estimated pretax)	0

	Franchise
Dr. Vinyl	
Approx. Total Investment	$25,000 to $50,000
Estimated Annual Sales/Unit	Not Available
NAICS 325211	Number of Businesses/Units 220

Rules of Thumb

➢ 70 percent of annual sales plus inventory

Resources

Websites
- www.drvinyl.com

	Franchise
Dream Dinners	
Approx. Total Investment	$254,900 to $337,600
	Number of Businesses/Units 105

Rules of Thumb

➢ 40 percent of annual sales plus inventory

➢ Note: As of October 12, 2012, this company's web site stated that they "are not offering franchises at this time."

Resources

Websites
- www.dreamdinners.com

Drive-in Restaurants (See also Restaurants)

	NAICS 722211	

Rules of Thumb

➤ 40 to 45 percent of annual sales plus inventory

➤ 5 to 6 times monthly sales plus inventory

Drive-In Theaters

	NAICS 512132	Number of Businesses/Units 380

Rules of Thumb

➤ 2 percent of annual sales plus equipment and real estate

Benchmark Data

- "Cohen says he nets 20% on revenue of $800,000. But that's not really a profit so much as pay for working 65-hour weeks, eight months a year. Drive-ins fork over 50% to 60% of ticket sales (on first-run titles) to movie studios, usually a break from the typical of indoor theaters. Just as at the multiplex, the bulk of drive-in gross profit comes from popcorn and soft drinks. The outdoor theaters get revenue only on dry nights in warm weather, crimping their ability to cover fixed costs like property taxes and equipment depreciation.

  "Starting a drive-in from nothing might cost you $500,000 for a single-screen projector, land rearranging (to give cars something of the pitch you get at an indoor theater) and buildings for concessions and bathrooms. You'll need at least 10 acres of land, with the right kind of zoning. That's enough for hundreds of cars. "As a result Floyd hopes he will bring in $350,000 in revenue this year and finally eke out a small profit. Last year his $310,000 gross disappeared this way: $75,200 for movie rentals, $51,600 for food, $45,000 for 17 seasonal employees, $43,500 for taxes and $41,000 for other operating costs. He would have cleared a few bucks if not for that damned mortgage."

  Source: "Under the Stars" by Allison Fass, *Forbes*, June 4, 2007 (Dated, but informative)

Industry Trend

- "And with more than half the cinema screens in America already converted to digital, experts believe 35 mm prints could disappear altogether within two or three years. The industry says digital leads to a quicker turnover of movies, greater choice for consumers, and the promise of 3D and other special features.

  "But hundreds of small independent cinemas, in the US and around the world, have already decided they cannot afford to buy the equipment needed, say industry sources. The death of the drive-in—if that is what is happening—is likely to be felt more keenly in the US than in a country like the UK, where the concept never really got out of first gear."

  Source: "Drive-in cinemas: Will they survive the digital age?" by Brian Wheeler, BBC News, uditoa.org/news, December 2011

Resources

Associations

- United Drive-in Theatre Owners Association:
  www.driveintheatre-ownersassociation.org

Driving Schools (Instruction)

SIC 8299-02	NAICS 611692	Number of Businesses/Units 114,382

Rules of Thumb

➤ 1 times SDE plus fair market value of fixed assets

➤ 40 to 45 percent of annual sales plus fair market value of fixed assets

Benchmark Data

Statistics (Driving Schools)

Number of Establishments	114,382
Average Profit Margin	9.5%
Revenue per Employee	$38,100
Average Number of Employees	2.1
Average Wages per Employee	$21,228

Source: IBISWorld, July 2012

Products and Services Segmentation

Exam preparation and tutoring	49.5%
Other schools	40.3%
Driving schools	10.2%

Source: IBISWorld, July 2012

Industry Costs

Profit	9.5%
Wages	54.4%
Purchases	14.8%
Depreciation	3.1%
Marketing	6.7%
Rent & Utilities	3.0%
Other	8.5%

Source: IBISWorld, July 2012

Drug Stores (See Pharmacies)

Franchise

Dry Clean USA (See also Dry Cleaning)

Approx. Total Investment	$350,000 to $$500,000

SIC 7212-01	NAICS 812320	Number of Businesses/Units 464

Rules of Thumb

➤ 55 percent of annual sales plus inventory

Resources

Websites

▪ www.drycleanusa.com

Dry Cleaners

SIC 7212-01	NAICS 812320	Number of Businesses/Units 41,454

Rules of Thumb

➤ 70 to 80 percent of sales plus inventory. Plants with on-site laundry equipment will get a higher multiple. Plants with over-the-counter sales of $35,000 will receive higher multiples.

➤ 2.5 to 3 times SDE plus inventory

➤ 2 to 3 times EBIT

➤ 2.5 to 3 times EBITDA

➤ 2 times SDE for a poor unit, 2.5 times SDE for a "so-so" business, 3 times SDE for a good store, 3.5 times SDE for a "hot" unit with a good lease & equipment, 4 times SDE for a real "winner."

➤ "70% of annual gross sales if equipment is under five years old. If equipment is between six and 10 years old, it will be 60% of annual gross sales. If equipment is over 11 years old, it will be between 40% and 50% of the annual gross sales."

➤ "Purchase price ranges from 70% of annual sales to 100%. Single stores with full garment pricing (no discounts, no coupons) & having monthly retail sales over $35,000 will achieve the higher multiple. Retail pick-up stores (no equipment) 25% to 50% of annual sales."

➤ "One can get 3 times cash flow (SDE) if the owner is a manager and does not perform a specific job such as counter, dry cleaner or presser. If the owner does perform a specific job, such as dry cleaner, etc., the cash flow should include the owner's salary and the business would be valued at 2.5 times that cash flow."

➤ "Dollar for dollar (100 percent of sales) on a plant that has dry cleaning equipment and a single-buck or double-buck shirt unit, assuming all sales are over-the-counter, not from pick-up stores or hotels or other cleaners. 75 percent of sales for plant w/o shirt unit, & 50 percent of sales on pick-up stores, assuming sales are $125,000 or more."

➤ "75 to 100 percent of annual gross sales for complete retail plants, must be able to verify. Pick-ups (drop stores) go for 30 to 50 percent of annual gross sales. Routes vary greatly, but can sell for 25 to 50 percent of actual paid gross sales."

Pricing Tips

▪ "Dry cleaners under $500,000 in sales sell dollar for dollar to sales. Higher volume dry cleaners can command a premium up to 20%–25%."

▪ "Break down gross sales between pickup stores, route sales, and wholesale accounts."

▪ "If the equipment is over 5 years old, the SDE multiplier should be 2 times."

▪ "Agency work not of any value, keeps employees busy."

▪ "The larger dry cleaners sell for a premium and earn a larger percent SDE. The smaller dry cleaners <$250k do not command a premium price and also earn a smaller percent of SDE."

- "The multiple used can be as much as 3 times if the owner just manages the business and does not perform any specific duties."
- "If the equipment is under five years old, use one (1) times SDE plus what equipment is valued as a going concern."
- "100%–110% of yearly gross, depending on equipment condition, age, etc., competition, and location."
- "If the dry cleaner does its own shirts in-house with its own shirt equipment, the price can be 3 x SDE or 100% of gross sales. The value based on gross sales is assumed that all the sales come over the counter and not from an outside agency, such as hotels, tailor shops, or other dry cleaners and office convenience stores."
- "100% of gross sales is used as a guideline for a plant that processes its own shirts and all income is from over-the-counter sales. If the dry cleaner sends out its shirts, then we use a price based on 75% of gross sales."
- "Sixty percent (60%) of annual gross sales if equipment is over 10 years old. Eighty-five percent (85%) of annual gross sales if equipment is under 5 years old."
- "Make sure that the dry cleaning machinery, boilers and shirt laundry equipment are modern and in good condition; check on any current, ongoing, or past environmental issues. Make sure that the landlord will continue to rent space for a plant operation; get good books and records information to be able to get a firm grasp on the operation."
- "Make sure you know where sales are coming from—over-the-counter or wholesale, etc."
- "If equipment is under 5 years old, the price can be 80 to 90 percent of gross sales; if equipment is 6 to 10 years old, the price can be between 70 and 80 percent of gross sales; and if the equipment is 11 to 20 years old, the price can be 50 to 70 percent of gross sales."
- "The most common rule of thumb for determining the marketing price used by sellers and buyers (and brokers!) is still one times the annual gross sales for a full plant, and 50 percent of annual gross sales for a pickup store. The actual selling price is then a percentage up or down from that starting point (usually down), depending on specific features of the business. The more important features are the type and length of the lease; type, age and condition of equipment; ability to verify actual annual gross sales; and the location. Due to environmental issues, the most important feature is a lease that allows for dry cleaning with perc or petroleum on the premises and at least 10 years of term (five years with five-year option to renew). Most sellers today want to be 'cashed out' and outside financing is available. Many buyers feel that if they are paying cash with outside financing (usually with higher interest rates), then the seller should discount his selling price. Often when outside financing is available, the seller will still be required to provide a small promissory note to make up the difference between the agreed selling price, down payment, and funds provided by the lender."
- "'A business is worth what a buyer is willing to pay for it and what the seller is willing to sell it for.' We hear this a lot and cannot argue with this wisdom. The majority of dry cleaners are small cash businesses and family owned and operated. Many cannot provide substantial financial information with accurate cash flow/net profit figures. Consequently, buying decisions are based more on the buyer's approval of the location and equipment. If the contingencies for sales verification and satisfactory lease are met, then buyers can feel comfortable with the simple multiple of gross sales method. Depending on

the variables present with each business, most desirable plants are selling for 75–99 percent of verifiable gross sales. Pickup stores are selling for 20–50 percent of sales, and routes can go for 15–40 percent."

- "Dry cleaners and laundries nationwide sold for 60 to 80 percent of gross sales; the variation in percent is based on the age of the equipment."

- "Dry cleaning plants without laundry equipment have been selling for 75 to 85 percent of annual net total sales. Dry cleaning plants with laundry equipment have been selling for 85 to 100 percent of annual net sales. Also, selling price ranges from 2.65 to 3.5 x discretionary cash flow earnings before owner's compensation and debt service."

- "In pricing a dry cleaning plant today, the single most important consideration is the premises' lease. How long is it, and does it allow dry cleaning on the premises? Many new shopping centers will not allow dry cleaning with 'perc'; if this is the case, then processing must be done elsewhere, involving more expense. Not having the ability to dry clean does affect the value of a location. The ideal dry cleaning situation which would demand the highest value on the market would be as follows: (1) A strong retail location with a drive-thru;. (2) No previous contamination problems; (3) Permission to use dry cleaning machine and chemicals on the premises; (4) At least 5 years' lease, with a 5-year option to renew; (5) New EPA-approved dry cleaning machine with proper installation and spill containment tray; (6) Good shirt pressing equipment; (7) Good gas-fired boiler. Anything less than the above would reduce the price accordingly from the one times annual gross sales rule of thumb."

- "Value added: Retail over-the-counter vs. wholesale & drop-store income. Shirt equipment in-house. Shirt volume & pricing to equal general dry cleaning margin. All equipment to meet environmental regulations. Seller financing vs. all cash & SBA financing. Is payroll under 30 percent of gross sales? Is shirt volume no more than 20 percent of gross volume?"

- "If equipment is under 5 years old and store is all retail, 70–80 percent of annual gross. Decreases to 50 percent if equipment is over 5 years old. "

- The traditional buyers' method:
  "The long-held mind set is that buyers will generally pay for a "perfect" dry cleaning business dollar for dollar on retail over the counter sales; $.75 on a dollar for sales from a pickup outlet or a route under the same ownership as the plant; and $.50 on a dollar for wholesale work performed for outside businesses."

  "The immigrant buyers' method:
  Immigrant buyers often look at prices as multiples of weekly gross sales. Typically: 50 times weekly sales for retail, approx. 30 times weekly sales for pickup stores and routes (owned and operated by the seller). Immigrant buyers often have little interest in wholesale businesses and may not be willing to pay for this type of sales."

Expert Comments

"Dry cleaning is changing the business model. More and more smaller >$200,000 dry cleaners are going out of business and larger dry cleaners <$500,000, more centrally located are becoming the new business model."

"Dry cleaners under $400,000 easy to replicate, dry cleaners over $750,000 very difficult to replicate, dry cleaners over $1 million, very very difficult to replicate"

"There are many, many dry cleaners but most tend to remain mom and pop shops. In order to stand out they must do more volume, a home delivery service, or contract work with large corporations."

"Good business, especially if the family of the owner is part of the mix."

"Competition from DISCOUNT cleaners hurts the profit."

"There are many, many dry cleaners and it is a very competitive industry. It is not hard to set up a dry cleaning plant, but a very successful one that has a good location is the trick!"

"These dry cleaning plants are very expensive to start up. The cost of the equipment and the cost of installation make it very difficult to replicate easily."

"Much more competition in dry cleaning, new discount dry cleaners, and larger volume dry cleaning plants."

"Discount dry cleaners are flooding most markets. The discount cleaners and laundries are not money-makers and have very poor quality control. When they come into a market, they hurt the professional cleaners and laundries."

"Some markets have many discount cleaners."

"Historic Profit Trend: Profit is down due to fixed expenses going up, such as rent, employment. Also, competition from discount cleaners."

"Dry cleaning is a long-term business with not a lot of drastic ups and downs."

Benchmark Data

Statistics (Dry Cleaners)

Number of Establishments	41,454
Average Profit Margin	5.8%
Revenue per Employee	$53,400
Average Number of Employees	4
Average Wages per Employee	$17,605

Source: IBISWorld, October 2012

Products and Services Segmentation

Dry cleaning services	68.1%
Commercial laundry services	15.9%
Reselling services	9.4%
Other	4.7%
Maintenance and repair	1.9%

Source: IBISWorld, October 2012

Industry Costs

Profit	5.8%
Wages	33.1%
Purchases	20.0%
Depreciation	2.9%
Marketing	3.5%
Rent & Utilities	17.7%
Other	17.0%

Source: IBISWorld, October 2012

- "There are 2 types of dry cleaners: full price and discount. Full price dry cleaners can be smaller, 2,000 sq. ft. or less, discount dry cleaners need to be 3,000 sq. ft. or more. Sales per sq. ft. depend on full price or discount, supplies usually run between 5% - 8%, depending on the business model."
- "Payroll costs paralleled regional gains and losses, with operators in the Northeast reporting an average increase of 0.5% over last April, and those in the South adding 0.8%. In the Midwest, payrolls were off 0.3%, and operators in the West reported the deepest payroll cut, 4.2%. While 43.2% of operators left payrolls unchanged, drycleaners nationwide are paying an average of 1.0% less this year."

Source: "StatShot: Sales Gain Steam in Northeast, South" by Ian P. Murphy, May 24, 2011, www.americandrycleaner.com

- "Labor percentage should be at least 36% to 40% for an absentee owner."
- "Location with drive-thru"
- "Keep agency work to a minimum."
- "Large dry cleaners—$750,000 annual sales, avg. 3,000 sq. ft."
- "Each employee presser should generate between $1,300 and $1,800 of sales per week."
- "Supply costs (hangers, bags, cleaning solvent, etc.): approx. 6% to 8% of gross sales. Payroll costs for an owner-operated store: 30% to 35% of gross sales. SDE profit: approx. 25% to 32%."
- "Valuation can be as high as 100% of gross sales if it is a full operating plant (with a shirt unit). Valuation can be 75% of gross sales if only does dry cleaning and sends shirts out to be cleaned. Valuation can be based on 3 times SDE if owner manages only and 2.5 times SDE if the owner helps in production (such as dry cleaner or presser)."
- "A plant should generate at least $300k per year to be successful."

Expenses as a Percentage of Annual Sales

Cost of goods	30%
Payroll/labor Costs	25% (lower figure with owner working full time)
Occupancy	11% to 15% + R.E. Taxes & C.A.M. (top locations MA)
Profit (estimated pretax)	15% to 25%

Industry Trend

- "Most dry cleaners rue the trend that has seen many dress codes shifts to business casual, and more than three-quarters of respondents (76.1%) to this month's AmericanDrycleaner.com *Wire* survey say the ongoing movement toward casual clothing in the workplace has had a major impact on the industry.

"Approximately 22% say the business casual dress code has had a 'minor impact,' and 2.2% say it has had no impact.

"What impact has casual clothing had on overall drycleaning sales volume in the last few years? Roughly 43% say their sales have decreased substantially (more than 5%) each year, and 31.8% say theirs has decreased slowly (0-5%).

"Nearly 14% say their sales have been flat. Sales have increased slowly (0-5%) each year for 6.8% of respondents, and 4.5% say their sales have increased substantially (more than 5%).

"So, what if anything, has your plant done to respond to this trend? Among *Wire* survey respondents, 53.3% have explored new sidelines to fill excess plant capacity, and 46.7% have targeted casual clothing as a source of business."

Source: "Survey: Business Casual Dress Code Still Dampening Drycleaning Sales," by Bruce Beggs, www.americandrycleaner.com April 2012.

- "The trend for dry cleaning is leaning toward bigger dry cleaners more centrally located.

  "Operators were slightly more pessimistic about growth returning to drycleaning. Asked, 'Do you think drycleaning is experiencing or will soon experience renewed demand?' 45.1% said 'No,' 31.9% said 'Not Sure,' and 23.1% said 'Yes.'

  "'About 95% of clothing on [the] market is wash-and-wear,' one operator points out. 'Even silk and wool is washable. I see a very dim future for the industry due to this fact. Plus, people are saving money wherever they can—drycleaning is one of the first items to get crossed off the list.'"

  Source: "Recovery Slow to Reach Drycleaners, Survey Says" by Ian P. Murphy, April 13, 2011, www.americandrycleaner.com

- "Larger, higher volume cleaners rather than the small mom & pop shops"

- "Last month, our company received more than 30 calls from operators who do not have routes, but are thinking about getting in to it. It was amazing to hear the discouragement of those whose businesses have dropped 10, 20 or 30 percent in the last four years. Some owners were hoping to sell out and retire by 2010 while others bought in to the industry, not realizing that the profit margins were not quite what they expected. A few were also multi-generational owners whose parents are handcuffing them, preventing routes. Well, whatever the case may be, all I can do is wish some of them Godspeed.

  "This is why I am considering 2010 crunch time. Routes are becoming essential for surviving. They provide a stability insurance policy for your future. If you are a young owner, your future depends on it. If you are wishing to sell, buyers now, more than ever, look at the size of your route. No matter what, it is time to decide where you want to be in 2012. For those who are doing well in routes, do not get comfortable and do not allow your staff to be comfortable, either. This may be the biggest mistake successful owners tend to make. They believe that their sales are never going to slide and they put the delivery service on auto-pilot. They hire cheaper drivers, sell less and expect growth. I would say that 40 percent of our business has come from this category."

  Source: James Peuster, The Route Pro www.natclo.com/1006/peuster.htm.

- "The economic downturn has contributed to at least a 20 percent drop in dry-cleaning volume since September, said Alan Spielvogel, director of technical services for the 3,000-member National Drycleaning Association."

  Source: "Dry-cleaning down 20 percent nationwide" by Stephanie Esters, *Kalamazoo Gazette*, January 7, 2009, www.mlive.com

- "Stable"

- "Down maybe 10% now, Always a good business if rent is low and location is surrounded by residential."

- "More small dry cleaners are consolidating into larger, more efficient operations."

- "Larger, more centralized cleaners, either discount cleaners or high-end with many services. Mom-and-pop cleaners phasing out."

- "The dry cleaning business is a service business, and a good owner-operator will have no problem in growing its sales."

- "In metropolitan areas, business will decline. In high-income areas, it will grow."

- "The low-end cleaner, who depends only on retail from a single shop, may have a difficult time making it in the larger cities due to fierce competition and discounters. Cleaners will have to learn how to move beyond retail and get into a network of pickup stores, commercial accounts, routes or other activities out their back doors to make it."

- "Will continue to be a basic service, but discounters and immigrant population sweat shops affect profit picture of industry."

Seller Financing

- "Seller, 2 to 5 years and 8 to 12 percent interest; banks/lenders, 3 to 7 years and 2 to 5 points over prime with sufficient collateral, often a second position lien on a home if real estate is not included with the business."
- "5 to 10 years"
- "Sellers have not been keen to offer seller financing. Typical transaction is bank financed for all cash to the seller. Sometimes we can get sellers to carry back 10 to 15 percent of the purchase, subordinate to the bank."
- "Sellers on the east coast have to hold paper 99 percent of the time—usually 50 to 80 percent financed for 5 to 10 years."

Questions

- "The age of the boiler and the dry cleaning machine. Anything newer than 10 years is good."
- "How has his business been trending in the last 3 years?"
- "Contamination from PERC"
- "What is your competition?"
- "Monthly sales important, any environmental issues, will landlord renew lease?"
- "Make sure that the drycleaning machine, boiler and shirt laundry equipment are modern and in good condition; check on any current, ongoing or past environmental issues; make sure that the landlord will continue to rent space for a plant operation; get good books & records information to be able to get a firm grasp on the operation."
- "Where do the gross sales come from: over-the-counter, pick-up stores, hotels, other dry cleaners, etc."
- "Is he a discounter? How old are the major pieces of equipment: boiler, dry cleaning machine and shirt unit?"
- "How long has the business been established? How old is the equipment? Has the property been checked for environmental? If yes, can a Phase One Environmental Study be provided?"
- "How can you verify your actual sales? What is your lease, concerning assignments? Has the property been tested for environmental problems? How old is your equipment? Are you willing to do all or part of the financing? Is it possible for the buyer to observe the business during business hours? Are sales: retail, from owned pickup, commercial accounts, wholesale to other cleaners, delivery routes, or other? Check lease, equipment, prices and environmental compliance. Dry cleaning machines type: perc or hydrocarbon? Garment pricing. Advertising/coupon programs if any. Environmental problems? Landlord lease transferability issues? Will the landlord allow an on-site operating plant to continue within its premises? Does owner have environmental insurance? Does landlord require environmental insurance? Age, condition & capacity of equipment?"

Resources

Trade Publications
- National Clothesline: www.natclo.com
- American Dry Cleaner: www.americandrycleaner.com

Associations
- Dry Cleaning and Laundry Institute: www.ifi.org

Dry Cleaning Pickup Outlets/Stores (See also Dry Cleaning)

SIC 7212-01	NAICS 812320	

Rules of Thumb

➢ 25 to 50 percent of annual sales

➢ 30 times weekly sales

Dry Cleaning Routes (See also Dry Cleaning)

SIC 7212-01	NAICS 812320	

Rules of Thumb

➢ 15 to 40 percent of annual revenues

		Franchise

Dunkin' Donuts

Approx. Total Investment		$240,100 to $1,667,750
Estimated Annual Sales/Unit		$860,000
SIC 5812-06	NAICS 722213	Number of Businesses/Units 9,000

Rules of Thumb

➢ 60 to 100 percent of annual sales plus inventory

➢ 4 times SDE plus inventory

➢ 5 times EBITDA

➢ "Prices typically run 5 times EBITDA on groups of 3 or larger. Rule of thumb which is still very strong in the marketplace is about 1.25 times annual sales in very high coffee sale areas of New England. It is closer to 1 times sales in the Mid-Atlantic where coffee sales are still very good, but not so high as in New England. Where coffee sales are much less, values run about .75 times annual sales.

➢ "These numbers can be affected (up and down) by unusually low or high rents, and/or the requirement to undergo a major remodel in the near future."

Pricing Tips
- "The higher values are ascribed to units with a greater percentage of coffee sales."

- "Dunkin' Donuts minimum cash required is $750,000 with a net worth of at least $1,500,000. Minimum 5-store development required."

Source: Dunkin' Donuts

- "The value is decreased if the unit or units require substantial remodeling in less than 4–5 years."
- "Sufficient length of leases and franchise agreements, percentage of businesses coming from coffee/beverages."

Expert Comments

"It is a well-known franchise, but there is stiff competition from Starbucks and McDonald's."

"The marketability is not as high as one would expect for such a profitable and growing business. The reason is that the franchisor has very strict requirements to approve a buyer."

Benchmark Data

- "Food cost can be in the low 20's, as well as labor costs."
- "Food costs 20% to 24% or less, depending on business mix."

Expenses as a Percentage of Annual Sales

Cost of goods:	23% to 24% + 4% supplies (paper)
Payroll/labor Costs:	22%
Occupancy:	08% to 10%
Profit (estimated pretax)	15% to 20%

Industry Trend

- "Dunkin' Donuts plans to double its locations in the United States over the next 20 years, the company announced Wednesday.
  "The coffee and doughnut chain currently operates nearly 7,000 stores nationwide. Each new store adds an average of 20 to 25 new employees, both full and part-time a Dunkin spokeswoman said."

  Source: "Dunkin' Donuts to double U.S. locations" by Annalyn Censky @CNNMoney
- "Consolidation to players with larger networks of multi-unit operations"

Seller Financing

- "7 years—usually are bank/SBA financed."

Questions

- "When are remodels due? Lease details are critical, and length of time remaining on the franchise agreements. Does the seller have expansion rights in adjacent areas?"
- "What percent of sales is beverages?"

Resources

Websites

- www.dunkinfranchising.com

E-Commerce (Electronic Shopping)		
SIC 5731-24	NAICS 454111	Number of Businesses/Units 55,743

Rules of Thumb

➤ 30 percent of annual sales includes inventory

➤ 2 to 4 times SDE includes inventory

➤ 3 to 6 times EBITDA

Pricing Tips

- "Always prepare and research the specific industry/product being sold online and the more niche related the product or service the higher multiple. Buyers love niche related online stores."
- "Prices vary depending on age of business...at least three years is excellent...12 months is usually necessary."
- "A business with little or no inventory will be more valuable and easier to sell. Many buyers are looking for a business which can supplement their current career. The ease with which a buyer can learn and run the online business is a big factor."
- "Must understand and quantify Internet traffic, search engine rankings (organic vs. ppc), and which sites they sell product through (i.e., eBay, Amazon, internal Website, etc.)"
- "2.5–4x is the range, with the value changing based on barriers to entry such as vendor relationships, natural search positions, years in business, revenue size in general, etc."
- "Often times the business is the inventory, so it's included."
- "Length of time in business, barriers to entry, product offerings, etc. All would up the multiple (or lower it if the aforementioned are weak)."
- "The gross sales are usually not applicable to determine value because of low expenses."
- "Length of time in business, quality of vendor contracts if applicable, website technology, members, search engine rankings, etc."
- "Natural search results and third-party rankings (e.g., Google) can play a significant role as an asset."

Expert Comments

"Internet storefronts can easily be replicated. Finding a good source for product will always help reduce risk."

"The business will be more valuable if it is harder to replicate."

"E-Commerce is growing and the use of the Internet continues to be an integral part of more retail shopping experiences."

"Online shopping continues to grow, but so does the competition, so being able to differentiate oneself is a major coup."

"A unique product with aggressive marketing will usually succeed."

"Risk is relatively low and competition quite high unless niche based as most are that we see. Location has little to no impact. Industry trends can have a major impact but not always good or bad per se. Replication is an issue sometimes, and lastly, marketability—that's in the eye of the beholder so to speak."

"Most adult Americans already shop online, so how many more people can try it?"

Source: *New York Times National Edition*

Benchmark Data

Statistics (E-Commerce & Online)

Number of Establishments	55,743
Average Profit Margin	6.8%
Revenue per Employee	$1,301,900
Average Number of Employees	3.3
Average Wages per Employee	$43,406

Source: IBISWorld, June 2012

Products and Services Segmentation

Clothing, footwear, accessories and jewelry	14.8%
Sporting goods, toys, hobby items and games	13.8%
Furniture and home appliances	7.2%
Medication and cosmetics	6.5%
Office equipment and supplies	5.5%
Food, beverages and pet food	4.5%
Computers and TVs	24.5%
Other merchandise	23.2%

Source: IBISWorld, June 2012

Industry Costs

Profit	6.8%
Wages	3.6%
Purchases	61.9%
Depreciation	1.3%
Marketing	4.6%
Rent & Utilities	0.9%
Other	20.9%

Source: IBISWorld, June 2012

Enterprises by Employment Size

# of Employees	Share (%)
1 to 4	50.9
5 to 9	1.8
10 to 19	1.0

Source: IBISWorld, June 2012

Market Share

Amazon.com Inc.	9.0%

Source: IBISWorld, June 2012

- Sales: Online retail sales have grown $28.3 billion in the past 4 years.

Marketing

Ask	2.18%
Bing	9.43%
Yahoo	14.96%
Google	71.40%

- Internet: In the last decade, the number of households with Internet access has grown 29% in the U.S.

Internet

2000	55%
2008	82%
2009	85%
2010	84%

Source: www.internetretailer.com/trends/

- "Because of the low overhead and ease of operations, many of these businesses have returns of 30%–40%."
- "Average conversion rate would be anything around 1% (that is 1% of all visits turn into orders). Anything over 2% is excellent."
- "Sales per square foot is the key. Sales divided by the square foot."
- "10% net and above is quite good, certainly subject to the industry."

Expenses as a Percentage of Annual Sales

Cost of goods:	20% to 50%
Payroll/labor Costs:	0% to 50%
Occupancy:	0% to 10%
Profit (estimated pretax)	50% to 60%

Industry Trend

- "Unlimited growth potential for the next 3-5 years."
- "Online shoppers in the United States will spend $327 billion in 2016, up 45% from $226 billion this year and 62% from $202 billion in 2011, according to a projection released today by Forrester Research Inc. In 2016, e-retail will account for 9% of total retail sales, up from 7% in both 2012 and 2011, according to the report, 'US Online Retail Forecast, 2011 to 2016,' by Forrester analyst Sucharita Mulpuru. That represents a compound annual growth rate of 10.1% over the five-year forecast period.

  "The steady growth in the number of web shoppers also is helping to boost e-commerce sales. Forrester says that 192 million U.S. consumers will shop online in 2016, up 15% from 167 million in 2012. But the bigger factor in driving e-commerce growth is that each shopper will spend more on average, the report says. U.S. consumers in 2016 will each spend an average of $1,738 online, up 44% from $1,207 in 2012.

  "Many consumers will prefer the web to bricks-and-mortar retailers in large part because of online deals, the report says—70% of holiday shoppers last year said they made purchases online rather than in stores because online retailers offered better deals."

  Source: "E-retail spending to increase 62% by 2016" by Thad Rueter, Senior Editor

- "Computers and electronics represent nearly 42% of the sales on Amazon. com.

  Source: www.internetretailer.com 2012

- "Ten years ago, the e-commerce channel of distribution did not exist. Today, it is a very sophisticated model that is changing the competitive landscape. The tools of e-commerce are rapidly becoming the new Benchmark Data of excellence, especially in the area of customer service. It is estimated that the e-commerce channel will reach $300 billion by the end of 2012 in the United States alone."

  Source: "Is Technology Changing Direct Selling? App-solutely," www.directsellingnews.com, May 2011

Seller Financing

- 2-5 years

Questions

- "What kind of accounting software they use? How much do you spend per month on internet advertising and what kind of advertising? i.e., Google ad words, Facebook, twitter, Does someone handle their SEO for them and website updating?"
- "1. Last 12 months' Income/expenses/net or Profit/loss Statements for each month. How can you best verify these numbers? Plan to do this with tax returns, merchant account records, CPA or audited financials, bank records etc. 2. Breakout your sales and expenses into the major components of income and show any major trends 3. Proforma/Projected (your best estimate) next 12 months sales/expenses and the business plan to explain these projected results. 4. How many employees and your total time and involvement. 5. Have you included your salary or the salary of someone to take your place in the expenses? 6. Could anyone do this with training for a month from you or is industry know-how too important? 7. How long has this business been on the web? 8. What is the traffic to your site? List exclusives per month and page views or your best measure of merit for traffic. How can you verify these numbers? Provide password for any traffic statistics verification by third party. 9. If not with high traffic, how do you get your customers? List the means and associated advertising cost and effectiveness such as conversion rates, etc. 10. List the assets that you are selling to include websites, domain names, customer lists, inventory (at wholesale price plus shipping to new owner's location), unique software, proprietary business processes or systems, intellectual property to include: inventions, literary and artistic works, and symbols, names, images, designs, copyrights, trademarks, patents, and related rights. Also list unique website content. List any licensing involved and how this would be handled with a transfer of business ownership. 11. What has been your growth or lack thereof in the past three years? What are the prospects for growth and how would a new owner do this? Why have you not done this? 12. What/who is your major competition? What is your position in Market Share relative to this competition? How are you different from the competition? 13. Do you require all cash or would you take a promissory note for some significant portion of the sale price? 14. What type of training would you be able to provide? 15. Would you consider a consulting or employment contract for 6 to 12 months or longer if requested by a buyer? 16. Why are you selling?"
- "Does the seller inventory the product? Who does the credit card processing and what are their fees? Who does the Web hosting and how much traffic can the Web site handle? How do you maintain your Internet rankings? What are you doing to increase your Web presence?"
- "Why selling? What will you do next (non-compete issues)? How would you grow the business? Other areas of marketing they have not done (affiliate, etc.)."
- "How easy is it for a buyer to learn the business?"
- "Any repeat business? Percentage of revenue budgeted for advertising?"

Resources

Trade Publications
- Internet Retailer: www.internetretailer.com
- E-Commerce Times: www.ecommercetimes.com/

Eagle Transmission Shop

(See also AAMCO Transmissions, Auto Transmission Centers, etc.)

Approx. Total Investment	$194,000 to $292,500

SIC 7537-01	NAICS 811113	Number of Businesses/Units 25

Rules of Thumb

➢ 40 percent of annual sales

➢ 2.5 times SDE

Benchmark Data

- "Cost to get to break even is the same as AAMCO—approx. $200,000 (this is my targeted bottom sale price)."
- "Franchises with an owner overseeing a manager in the expenses are still selling for 2.5 to 3 X SDE."
- "Franchised shops with SDE of at least $100,000 with high percentage retail are very marketable."
- "Franchised shops that historically are not breaking even with a manager in the expenses are very hard to sell."
- "If the location seems OK, the price seems to bottom out at about $125,000. Small independents are getting more and more difficult."

Resources

Websites
- www.eagletransmission.com

Electric Motor Repair

SIC 7694	NAICS 811310	

Rules of Thumb

➢ 33 percent of annual sales plus inventory

➢ 3 times SDE plus inventory

➢ 5 times EBIT

➢ 4 times EBITDA

Pricing Tips

- "Condition of equipment and customer concentration are significant factors."
- "Industry is always a mix of repair of customer motors and resale of new

motors and related products. Rule of thumb for pricing is one-third of annual repair sales plus 15% of annual product sales, plus inventory. Most successful buyers for smaller businesses in the industry have electric motor background. Condition of equipment and extent of machine shop tools is important."

Expert Comments

"This is a mature industry. The repair market (higher margins) is stable to declining slightly as increased costs force higher horsepower standard motors to be replaced (lower margins) rather than repaired. Other technological factors and the shift to more offshore manufacturing have resulted in no net growth and eroding profits. Successful shops have either good niche customer markets and/or services or a long-term approach to partnering with customers to reduce customer's motor operating costs. Sales growth for individual companies usually comes from taking sales away from competitors."

Benchmark Data

- $150,000 sales per employee is an average for companies with approximately 2/3 repair, 1/3 new sales.

Expenses as a Percentage of Annual Sales

Cost of goods:	25%
Payroll/labor Costs:	25%
Occupancy:	10%
Profit (estimated pretax)	05%

Industry Trend

- "Repair lags general industry trends. Emphasis on power generation and distribution including wind energy."

Questions

- "Technical strengths of shop employees? Concentration of customers? Where is future growth coming from?"
- "Buyer needs to establish the repeatability and retainability of current customers after change in ownership."

Electrical Contracting (See Construction — Electrical)

Embroidery Services/Shops

SIC 7389-42	NAICS 314999	

Rules of Thumb

➢ 55 to 60 percent of annual sales plus inventory

Employment Agencies (See Recruiting Agencies)

Engineering Services

NAICS 54133	Number of Businesses/Units 156,398

Rules of Thumb

➤ 40 to 45 percent of annual revenues; add value of fixtures & equipment; may require earnout

Benchmark Data

Statistics (Engineering Services)

Number of Establishments	156,398
Average Profit Margin	6.5%
Revenue per Employee	$189,900
Average Number of Employees	6.7
Average Wages per Employee	$82,397

Source: IBISWorld, June 2012

Products and Services Segmentation

Commercial, public and institutional projects	13.5%
Municipal utility projects	12%
Miscellaneous federal government projects	10%
Project management services	10%
Residential building projects	7.5%
Industrial and manufacturing plant and process projects	17%
Transportation projects	15.5%
Other	14.5%

Source: IBISWorld, June 2012

Major Market Segmentation

Energy and gas companies	20%
Utilities, mining and industrial companies	17.5%
The government	15%
Construction companies	47.5%

Source: IBISWorld, June 2012

Industry Costs

Profit	6.5%
Wages	45.5%
Purchases	20.0%
Depreciation	2.5%
Marketing	0.2%
Rent and Utilities	9.0%
Other	16.3%

Source: IBISWorld, June 2012

Market Share

URS	4.6%
Fluor	4.0%

Source: IBISWorld, June 2012

	Franchise

Environment Control (Commercial Cleaning Services)

Approx. Total Investment	$55,000
NAICS 561720	Number of Businesses/Units 53

Rules of Thumb

➤ 42 percent of annual sales plus inventory

Pricing Tips

- The firm has 53 units in 19 states. Go to their Web site for more information: www.environmentcontrol.com
- How much can I expect to earn?
- The great thing about owning a business is you earn exactly what you are worth. You no longer have to wait for annual performance evaluations or periodic raises; your income is in direct proportion to your efforts.
- We cannot predict how much you will earn, but we do know about our current franchise owners. Here is a summary of their annual earnings.*
    - ✓ 12% over $200,000
    - ✓ 41% over $100,000
    - ✓ 12% over $75,000
    - ✓ 5% over $50,000
    - ✓ 21% over $25,000
    - ✓ 9% under $25,000

    These figures are for 12 months ending March 2010 and include all owners with at least one year as an owner.

Resources

Websites
- www.environmentcontrol.com

Environmental Testing		
	NAICS 541380	

Rules of Thumb

➤ 60 percent of annual sales plus inventory

➤ 2 to 2.5 times SDE plus inventory

Pricing Tips

- "SDE must at least be equal to new debt service using a 1.5 ratio, owner's salary and any capex requirements, or it's priced too high."
- "Be sure the accounting is on the accrual method so there is no confusion as to how values are arrived at."

Expert Comments

"Owner and his contacts are more the driving, networking force than the location or the facilities."

Benchmark Data

- "It can be a roll-up-your-sleeves kind of business."

Expenses as a Percentage of Annual Sales

Cost of goods:.. 02%
Payroll/labor Costs:... 30%
Occupancy:... 03%
Profit (estimated pretax) 16%

Industry Trend

- "Steady, but RE activities have big influence."

Questions

- "Why did you get in the business and why are you getting out at this time?"

Equipment & Party Rental/General Rental (See Rental Centers)

Event Companies

SIC 7389-44	NAICS 812990	Number of Businesses/Units 356,293

Rules of Thumb

➢ 3 times EBITDA plus asset value.

Pricing Tips

- "Are there events on the books going forward? How many repeat clients?"

Benchmark Data

Statistics (Trade Show and Conference Planning)

Number of Establishments... 20,836
Average Profit Margin 18.9%
Revenue per Employee $135,400
Average Number of Employees 4.8
Average Wages per Employee $32,896

Source: IBISWorld, March 2012

Products and Services Segmentation

Planning conventions, conferences and related activities 43%
Planning trade shows and related activities.. 39%
Planning other special events and related activities... 18%

Source: IBISWorld, March 2012

Major Market Segmentation

Retail sector.. 15.8%
Business and communications industries.. 13.6%
Other.. 11.4%
Consumers 11.0%
Food industries 7.0%
Education industries 4.6%
Manufacturing sector 18.6%
Healthcare, engineering and science industries.. 18.0%

Source: IBISWorld, March 2012

Industry Costs

Profit	18.9%
Wages	24.4%
Purchases	20.0%
Depreciation	2.9%
Marketing	17.0%
Rent & Utilities	7.5%
Other	9.3%

Source: IBISWorld, March 2012

Market Share

The Freeman Companies	10.2%
Viad Corporation	7.7%

Source: IBISWorld, March 2012

Statistics (Party & Event Planners)

Number of Establishments	335,457
Average Profit Margin	15.7%
Revenue per Employee	$18,300
Average Number of Employees	1.1
Average Wages per Employee	$7,096

Source: IBISWorld, June 2012

Products and Services Segmentation

Corporate social events	30%
Other	20%
Birthday parties	16%
Weddings	34%

Source: IBISWorld, June 2012

Industry Costs

Profit	15.7%
Wages	38.0%
Purchases	23.4%
Depreciation	1.2%
Marketing	16.2%
Rent & Utilities	1.9%
Other	3.6%

Source: IBISWorld, June 2012

Industry Trend

- "AIG and new administration in U.S. have made it fashionable not to have extravagant affairs and corporate conferences."

Seller Financing

- 2 ½ years

Fabric Stores		
SIC 5949-02	NAICS 45113	Number of Businesses/Units 18,566

Rules of Thumb

➢ 3 times monthly sales plus inventory

Benchmark Data

Statistics (Fabric, Craft & Sewing Supplies)

Number of Establishments.. 18,566
Average Profit Margin 1.9%
Revenue per Employee $72,900
Average Number of Employees 3.3
Average Wages per Employee $9,831

Source: IBISWorld, June 2012

Products and Services Segmentation

Fabrics 40%
Sewing and craft supplies.. 33%
Other.. 12%
Seasonal decorations 8%
Fabric home décor... 7%

Source: IBISWorld, June 2012

Industry Costs

Profit 1.9%
Wages.. 13.8%
Purchases 64.3%
Depreciation 2.2%
Marketing 2.0%
Rent & Utilities 3.0%
Other... 12.8%

Source: IBISWorld, June 2012

Market Share

Jo-Ann Stores 26.0%
Michaels Stores 13.7%
Hobby Lobby Stores Inc. 9.6%
Hancock Fabrics Inc. 6.8%

Source: IBISWorld, June 2012

Industry Trend

- "Question: What happened to fabric stores? Answer: Good women's clothes made from beautiful fabrics became cheaper as more people were making money on cheap labor, so there was less sewing going on. Also, a lot of stores that have gone were family-run businesses. The younger generation had no interest in continuing to run them."

- "My goal is to create a drop-in-sewing café here. This idea started in Paris. Customers come in and sew for $10 an hour. They'll bring in their existing clothes that they want to change. I'll be there to help them do it."

Source: "It's in her life's fabric" by Sam Allis, *Boston Globe*, August 7, 2010

Resources

Websites

- www.fabshopnet.com

Family Clothing Stores (See also Clothing Stores, Women's Clothing)		
SIC 5136	NAICS 448190	Number of Businesses/Units 40,500

Rules of Thumb

➢ .75 to 1.5 times SDE plus inventory

Pricing Tips

- Women's Apparel— "try 23 percent of annual sales + inventory and/or 1.1 times SDE."

Benchmark Data

Statistics (Family Clothing Stores)

Number of Establishments	40,875
Average Profit Margin	4.6%
Revenue per Employee	$141,000
Average Number of Employees	16
Average Wages per Employee	$13,444

Source: IBISWorld, June 2011

Products and Services Segmentation

Women's casual wear	32.6%
Men's casual wear	17.4%
Women's formal wear	13.4%
Other women's wear	13.1%
Men's formal wear	8.8%
Children's wear	7.5%
Other men's wear	7.2%

Source: IBISWorld, June 2011

Industry Costs

Profit	4.6%
Rent	5.0%
Utilities	1.2%
Depreciation	2.2%
Other	11.7%
Wages	9.5%
Purchases	65.8%

Source: IBISWorld, June 2011

Family Entertainment Centers

	NAICS 713120	

Rules of Thumb

➤ 3 times EBITDA

		Franchise

Fantastic Sam's

Approx. Total Investment		$115,000 to $228,600
	NAICS 812112	Number of Businesses/Units 1,240

Rules of Thumb

➤ 35 to 40 percent of annual sales plus inventory

Resources

Websites

- www.fantasticsams.com

Fast Food (See also Restaurants—Limited Service)

	NAICS 722211	

Rules of Thumb

> 35 to 45 percent of annual sales plus inventory

Resources

Websites
- www.nrn.com

Associations
- National Restaurant Association: www.restaurant.org

Franchise

Fast Signs

Approx. Total Investment		$168,985 to $295,103
Estimated Annual Sales/Unit		Not Available
SIC 3993-02	NAICS 541890	Number of Businesses/Units 529

Rules of Thumb

> 42 to 46 percent of annual sales plus inventory

Resources

Websites
- www.fastsigns.com

Franchise

Fast-Fix Jewelry and Watch Repairs

Approx. Total Investment		$166,325 to $307,750
SIC 7631-01 & 7631-02	NAICS 811490	Number of Businesses/Units 163

Rules of Thumb

> 80 to 85 percent of annual sales plus inventory

Resources

Websites
- www.fastfix.com

Franchise

FastFrame

Approx. Total Investment		$105,800 to $150,300
SIC 7699-15	NAICS 442299	Number of Businesses/Units 300

Rules of Thumb

> 32 percent of annual sales

		Franchise
FasTrac Kids		
Approx. Total Investment		$78,455 to $210,155
Estimated Annual Sales/Unit		Not Available
	NAICS	Number of Businesses/Units 300

Rules of Thumb

➢ 45 percent of annual sales plus inventory

FedEx (Ground)		
	NAICS 492210	

Rules of Thumb

➢ 65 to 70 percent of annual sales

➢ 1.4 times SDE

Resources

Websites
- www.fedex.com

Film Companies (See Audio & Film Companies)

Fine Dining (See Restaurants)		
	NAICS 722110	

Rules of Thumb

➢ 30 to 35 percent of annual sales plus inventory

Benchmark Data
- For Benchmark data see Restaurants—Full Service

Fire Suppression Systems Sales & Services		
	NAICS 238220	

Rules of Thumb

➢ 80 percent of annual sales plus inventory

➢ 2.2 times SDE plus inventory

Pricing Tips
- "Business does not have to be profitable to obtain price, but must have good accounts, preferably with contracts in place."

- "The value of the customers can depend on whether the owner is the primary contact or the employees."
- "Most of these businesses are small and run by family. There are larger companies that are actively seeking to roll up smaller companies. Their primary interest is retaining the current customers and the pricing of the products and services. They are more focused on gross sales than SDE or EBITDA."

Expert Comments

"Location of the business is not important as long as it is central to its customer base. In general these are not retail businesses and do not have walk-in traffic. They test/service/refill fire extinguishers and do installation and service of fire suppression systems. This has been a 'mom-and-pop' industry with businesses that have revenues of less than $1 million. There are several companies like Simplex Grinnell who are big players. It is an industry that is ripe for roll-up to increase revenues by adding customers, and consolidation is occurring in many markets."

Benchmark Data

- "Typical Benchmark Data are sales per customer. These range from $100 to a $1,000 per year. Customer concentrations can be of big concern. A large quantity of smaller companies and customers that represent less than 5% of revenue are preferred."

Expenses as a Percentage of Annual Sales

Cost of goods:	20%
Payroll/labor Costs:	24%
Occupancy:	05% to 06%%
Profit (estimated pretax)	15%

Industry Trend

- "Smaller businesses will be purchased by larger businesses."
- "Increasing NFPA requirements for portable extinguishers is driving the sale of new models with an opportunity to increase service. Businesses have to stay compliant with NFPA standards for insurance purposes."

Questions

- "Revenue per customer? Are there contracts in place for service? Employees interact with customers, so questions about their capabilities are important. Ask questions about relationships with local fire marshals and fire departments which can be very important. You want them on your side because they are often the enforcement arm for fire safety compliance."
- "Questions about customer concentration. There should be lots of small accounts as measured by revenue ($500–$1,000 per year). Large accounts suggest risk in transfer for the buyer."

Resources

Associations

- National Fire Protection Association: www.nfpa.org
- National Fire Sprinkler Association: www.nfsa.org

Franchise

Firestone Tire Stores (See also Auto Tire Stores)

	NAICS 441320	Number of Businesses/Units 1,500

Rules of Thumb

➤ 35 percent of annual sales plus inventory

Fish & Seafood Markets

	NAICS 445220	Number of Businesses/Units 3,822

Rules of Thumb

➤ 20 to 25 percent of annual sales plus inventory

Benchmark Data

Statistics (Fish and Seafood Markets)

Number of Establishments	3,822
Average Profit Margin	7.0%
Revenue per Employee	$186,600
Average Number of Employees	3.0
Average Wages per Employee	$21,586

Source: IBISWorld, December 2011

Products and Services Segmentation

Fresh and frozen fish and shellfish	69%
Canned fish and shellfish	26%
Cured fish and shellfish	5%

Source: IBISWorld, December 2011

Major Market Segmentation

Consumers	65.5%
Single-location restaurants	27.2%
Chain restaurants	7.3%

Source: IBISWorld, December 2011

Industry Costs

Profit	7.0%
Rent	2.0%
Utilities	1.0%
Depreciation	2.0%
Other	4.7%
Wages	11.3%
Purchases	72.0%

Source: IBISWorld, December 2011

Fitness Centers (See also Racquet Sports Clubs)

SIC 7991-01	NAICS 71394	Number of Businesses/Units 33,527

Rules of Thumb

➤ 70 to 100 percent of annual sales plus inventory

➤ 2 times SDE plus inventory

> ➤ 3 times EBITDA
>
> ➤ "One year's annual revenues; usually reduced (or pro-rated) by memberships
>
> ➤ already contracted and paid for"
>
> ➤ "The clubs today have the electronic transfer money systems . . . One rule of thumb would be ten times the monthly amount . . . so if the club has $10,000 a month going through the electronic transfer, then the price would be $100,000 plus the value of the equipment . . . taking into consideration that the lease has sufficient time on it . . . most clubs today have $30,000 and up on the electronic transfer money. If there is 10 years on the lease, added value can be given for that."

Pricing Tips

- "What condition is the equipment in? Is the lease within market rents?"
- "Paid-in-full memberships are often subtracted from purchase price."
- "Fitness and/or health centers historically have been priced at 10 times the Electronic Transfer Money. Example: If the club has $15,000 a month on the electronic transfer money, times 10 equals $150,000 plus value of equipment. Equipment can be about $100,000 (depreciated), plus a ten-year lease is added value . . . so market price would be on or about $300,000.00 to $350,000.00 depending on condition of the facility . . . naturally all of this would be assuming the $15,000 cash flow covers the net, plus . . . "

Major franchise companies in the fitness business

Name	# of Units	Approximate Investment
Anytime Fitness	1,500	N/A
Bally Fitness	420	$1 million–$2.5 million
Contours Express	315	$34,000–$49,000
Curves	9,000	$39,170-$44,595
Gold's Gym	770	$895,000–$1 million
Snap Fitness	1,900	$77,000 to $242,000

Expert Comments

"The industry is still growing and there is more competition all the time. Membership rates per capita are still rising and many niche players are filling market needs."

"There are a few big publicly held competitors in the marketplace which have a big effect on market areas that are densely populated. There are increasing numbers of franchise systems filling niche areas of the fitness industry. Though there is more competition, health club membership enrollment by the general population is still well below 20% nationwide. This, coupled with the increasing awareness of the need for regular exercise, bodes well for continued industry growth."

"The average rate of memberships per capita continues to grow in the U.S. Obesity is a major health concern which employers and insurance companies are starting to battle by providing health club membership assistance. Full-service clubs are but one choice in a market that continues to grow with clubs that focus on niches of the industry (i.e. women only, children's performance, 24/7 convenience clubs, etc.)."

"Amount of competition: With local municipalities putting in tax funded health centers, consumers have a wide choice of facilities to choose from these days. Amount of risk: A club that has a profitable history will continue to survive in spite of increased competition if they have created a loyal clientele by providing personal service. Historical profit trend: Awareness of the healthy benefits exercise affords people is more and more mainstream. Location and Facilities: The older clubs (i.e,. the 30,000 s.f. clubs of the 70's and 80's) were usually well-constructed single-use facilities that age well. Newer clubs tend to be very small, personal training facilities or extremely large facilities with everything you can think of for exercise and family activities. Marketability: This is a very sexy, attractive industry that many buyers can see themselves involved in on a day to day basis. Many times, there is real estate involved in the transaction which makes lending a bit simpler. Industry trend: More general awareness of the health benefits of exercise are driving club membership numbers. Health insurance companies are now offering health club membership programs that pay the membership fees for Senior citizens in an effort to reduce their costs. Ease of replication: It is cost prohibitive to create a club building like they used to be constructed. On the other hand, it is relatively easy to lease a retail strip center space and fill it with leased equipment."

"Profitability is concurrent with owner experience in the field. Employee sales and management training programs are important to the success of this business. It is an entity of its own that cannot be learned in MBA programs."

Benchmark Data

Statistics (Gym, Health & Fitness Clubs)

Number of Establishments	33,527
Average Profit Margin	8.4%
Revenue per Employee	$45,200
Average Number of Employees	17.1
Average Wages per Employee	$13,889

Source: IBISWorld, July 2012

Products and Services Segmentation

Gyms and fitness centers	65%
Other	10%
Dance centers	7%
Swimming pools	7%
Ice and roller rinks	6%
Tennis centers	5%

Source: IBISWorld, July 2012

Industry Costs

Profit	8.4%
Wages	29.9%
Purchases	20.0%
Depreciation	7.5%
Marketing	10.0%
Rent & Utilities	15.5%
Other	8.7%

Source: IBISWorld, July 2012

- "28 percent of respondents said they plan to expand their facilities in 2011. Multi-club respondents (41 percent) are more likely to expand than those who own a single club (25 percent).
  "A majority of clubs (64 percent) have personal training as a source of non-dues revenue. All other sources had less than 50 percent of respondents using them.
  "Consumers plan to spend an average of $131 per month in 2011 for a gym membership: most (94 percent) say this is the same or more than they spent last year, according to a survey by American Express. Likewise, the majority intend to spend the same or more on personal trainers (73 percent) and specialty fitness programs, such as Pilates or boot camp classes (71 percent)."
  Source: "2011 State of the Health Club Industry Survey," www.clubindustry.com
- "42 percent of club members attend their clubs less than 50 days per year."
  Source: "U.S. Health Club Industry Records Solid Performance in 2009,"
  The International Health, Racquet & Sportsclub Association (IHRSA), March 31, 2010
- "Profit of 10%–20%, membership attrition rate of 30% is average."
- "Membership retention approximately 65%; revenue per member: $700+; indoor s.f./member: 13.5; revenue/ indoor s.f. $45; non-dues revenue of 20% of total revenue."
- "Estimated median of $655,000 in revenue per club"
- "Estimated median of 9 full-time and 34 part-time employees per club"
- "Based on a median payroll cost of 41% of total revenue"
  Source: International Health, Racquet & Sportsclub Association (IHRSA)
- "The average fitness company has annual revenues of $500,000 or less with about 15 employees."

U.S. IHRSA Member Clubs	5,400
U.S. Health Club Members in IHRSA Clubs	11 million
Total U.S. Industry Revenues for 2008	$19.1 billion
Total U.S. Industry Payroll and Benefits	$8.2 billion

Expenses as a Percentage of Annual Sales

Cost of goods:	0% to 10%
Payroll/labor Costs:	20% to 25%
Occupancy:	10% to 15%
Profit (estimated pretax)	15% to 20%

Industry Trend

- "LA Fitness, one of the largest gym chains in the country, has become an even more dominant player in the health club industry. The Irvine company last week took over 171 Bally Total Fitness locations in 16 states, including about 40 in Southern California, marking one of the biggest deals by a gym chain in recent years. The $153-million purchase, which gives LA fitness more than 500 locations nationwide, is a smart move, experts said."
  Source: "LA Fitness pumps up with acquisition" by Ricardo Lopez, articles.latimes.com, December 10, 2011
- "Some franchise clubs are growing at the rate of one club per day."
- "In an online survey of more than 38,000 people conducted for SGMA by Sports Marketing Surveys, 36 percent of respondents said they planned to spend more in joining or rejoining health clubs over the next 12 months. The figure is up 23 percent from last year.
  "The report also gave some insight to what fitness activities could be most popular as more people join and rejoin health clubs. Using a variety of market

data, SGMA researchers predicted the growth potential for 20 sports and fitness activities. Of traditional club-centered activities, squash and yoga showed the greatest potential for growth, with projected rises of 52 percent and 42 percent, respectively, by 2015. High impact (35 percent) and step (33 percent) aerobics, running (31 percent), cardio kickboxing (26 percent) and group stationary cycling (22 percent) rounded out the list."

Source: "2011 State of the Health Club Industry Survey," www.clubindustry.com

- "28 percent of respondents said they plan to expand their facilities in 2011.
- Multi-club respondents (41 percent) are more likely to expand than those who own a single club (25 percent).
- More than one-third (38 percent) of respondents plan to renovate their facilities in 2011.
- One in five respondents said they will add a facility in 2011. One-third of multi-club respondents plan to add at least one facility in 2011.
- The turnover of membership is proportional between single-club and multi-club respondents.
- The primary ways that members learn about a club are the Web site (76 percent), a member referral campaign (67 percent) and in the neighborhood/drive-by (58 percent).
- The majority of clubs (60 percent) will focus on direct referrals from current members for their marketing efforts in 2011.
- A majority of clubs (64 percent) have personal training as a source of non-dues revenue. All other sources had less than 50 percent of respondents using them.
- Respondents expect revenue to increase 5 percent in 2011 compared to 2010.
- 3 out of 4 respondents expect to keep their prices the same in 2011 for dues (76 percent) and non-dues (76 percent).
- 71 percent of respondents expect to increase their programming in 2011, with group exercise (58 percent) group training (54 percent) and personal training (51 percent) being the most common programs to be added or increased."

Source: "2011 State of the Health Club Industry Survey," www.clubindustry.com

Questions

- "Match bank statements with monthly remits and request supervised access to the membership software."
- "What is the attrition level? How many members are on long-term contracts? Request the monthly remit amounts for trailing 12 month period."
- "Do you know of or have you heard of any rumors about any potential competition coming within 15 miles of this club? Why selling?"
- "Does the company buy or lease its exercise and weight equipment? Leasing is very common. How many members are there on average? It should be about 3,000. What is the referral rate for new members? It should be about 75%–80%. What is the member attrition rate? It is usually about 30%–37%."

Resources

Websites

- www.clubindustry.com

Associations

- International Health, Racquet & Sportsclub Association: www.ihrsa.org

Floor Coverings (See Carpet Stores)

	Franchise

Floppy's Mouse Club (See also Schools)

SIC 8243-01	NAICS 611420	

Rules of Thumb

➤ 70 percent of annual sales plus inventory

Resources

Websites
- www.floppysmouseclub.com
- www.mouseclubusa.com

Flower Shops (Florists)

SIC 5992-01	NAICS 453110	Number of Businesses/Units 37,446

Rules of Thumb

➤ 30 to 35 percent of annual sales includes inventory

➤ 2 times EBITDA

Pricing Tips

- "Review the Profit and Loss Statement to determine if wire service revenues and expenses (FTD, Teleflora, etc.) are tracked on separate line items to ensure that the sales are not overstated and cost of goods is not understated."

- "A premium should be given for stores with a significant number of commercial accounts (especially if there is a credit card on file for ease of billing) which helps protect revenues from big box stores that also sell flowers and plants."

- "Florists with a significant number of weekly or house accounts are very attractive in the marketplace and can command slightly higher multiples. Below market rent can also justify higher multiples. Conversely, shops located near grocery stores with large floral departments or near big box discounters should expect lower multiples."

Expert Comments

"Owning a flower shop continues to be a desirable lifestyle business for creative entrepreneurs who wish to provide an artistic and meaningful contribution to their community."

"The floral industry has been deeply affected by the economy and online 'orders.' Grocery stores and discount warehouses have also taken Market Share from retail florists."

Benchmark Data

Statistics (Florists)

Number of Establishments	37,446
Average Profit Margin	1.2%
Revenue per Employee	$60,200
Average Number of Employees	3
Average Wages per Employee	$16,334

Source: IBISWorld, February 2012

Products and Services Segmentation

Arranged cut flowers	52.5%
Indoor potted plants	14%
Giftware	12.5%
Unarranged cut flowers	12%
Other	6%
Outdoor nursery plants	3%

Source: IBISWorld, February 2012

Industry Costs

Profit	1.2%
Wages	25.6%
Purchases	49.5%
Depreciation	1.9%
Utilities	2.4%
Rent	4.9%
Other	14.5%

Source: IBISWorld, February 2012

Establishments by Employment Size

Number of Employees	Share of Establishments
0 to 4	86.8%
5 to 9	9.2%
10 to 19	3.0%

Source: IBISWorld, February 2012

Statistics (Flower Shops Online)

Number of Establishments	6,135
Average Profit Margin	1.3%
Revenue per Employee	$77,800
Average Number of Employees	4.7
Average Wages per Employee	$26,015

Source: IBISWorld, February 2012

Products and Services Segmentation

Flower sales	63.5%
Gift basket and other delivery sales	19%
Plant sales	10.5%
Floral network services	7%

Source: IBISWorld, February 2012

Industry Costs

Profit	1.3%
Wages	34.3%
Purchases	38.5%
Depreciation	3.7%
Marketing	15.4%
Rent & Utilities	5.3%
Other	1.5%

Source: IBISWorld, February 2012

Market Share

1-800-flowers.com Inc.	23.2%
FTD	14.8%
Provide Commerce Inc.	12.6%
Teleflora LLC	12.6%

Source: IBISWorld, February 2012

- "Average Sales per establishment—$320,000"

  Source: U.S. Economic Census, Retail Trade, 2007

- "Weddings: account for approximately 10% of retail florists' business.

- "Sympathy: accounts for approximately 22% of retail florists' business. Corporate sales: makes up approximately 17–22% of retail florists' sales."

  Source: Floriculture Industry Overview/Society of American Florists

- "Indeed, the flower shop accounts for the bulk of Nielsen's revenues, but sales of gifts and home décor are growing and now account for about 15 percent to 20 percent to 25 percent of the total."

  Source: "Nielsen's Florist & Garden Shop: 2011 Retail Florist of the Year" by Shelley Urban, www.floristsreview.com

- "For a florist to be profitable, the rent should not exceed 15% of gross sales."

- "Local business is generally more profitable than wire-service-generated income."

Expenses as a Percentage of Annual Sales

Cost of goods:	33%
Payroll/labor Costs:	20%
Occupancy:	10%
Profit (estimated pretax)	20%

Industry Trend

- "Floral Departments ranked 6th in growth among all supermarket departments.

- "Floral department sales at supermarkets: $779.3 m in 2010. <0.18% of total supermarket sales."

  Source: *Progressive Grocer*. September 2012

- "I am concerned about the rapid decline in the number of retail florists in the U.S. and the perilous financial condition of many of those who remain in business.

  "Offshore production of cut flowers began in the late 1970s. By 1979, after occasionally receiving flowers that were grown in Colombia, I decided to go see what was taking place. I traveled to Bogota and Medellin in 1979, where I saw that the world of flower retailing was about to change drastically. Royer's immediately initiated direct shipments of cut flowers from Colombia. By 1982, we had sold our greenhouses, which had been fulfilling 80 percent of our needs for cut flowers and plants.

  "Flower growing was quickly becoming an international business and was gravitating to countries with ideal year-round conditions and low wages. As cargo planes grew larger, and as airport refrigeration and handling facilities improved, the advantages of buying from offshore producers grew proportionally.

- "During the 1980s and '90s, virtually all cut-flower greenhouses on the East Coast were idled, and growers across the country felt the impact.

  "Grocery stores entered the floral marketplace. The large volume of offshore flowers entering the U.S. made it possible, for the first time, for supermarkets to obtain a consistent supply of low-cost flowers to stock floral departments. By the mid-1970s, many progressive supermarkets began to experiment with floral departments, and the vast majority of supermarkets quickly followed. Supermarkets soon owned a 10 percent share of the retail floral market. "We are still reeling from the effects of a recession, which has much to do with the decline, but it is only part of the story. Sales declines for other types of retailers have averaged less than 10 percent, and anecdotal evidence indicates that many florists have experienced declines of 15 percent and more. My sources report that wire service membership is down 20 percent in 2009 alone, and florists have seen their share of the overall floral market decline from nearly 100 percent to less than 50 percent over three decades. Currently, Internet competition continues to gain Market Share and further reduce the florists' share."

Source: "What has happened to our industry?," by Kenneth R. Royer, AAF, www.floristsreview.com

Seller Financing

- "2 to 5 years"

Questions

- "Percentage of local business versus wire service?"

Resources

Websites
- www.aboutflowers.com

Trade Publications
- Florists' Review: www.floristsreview.com

Associations
- Wholesale Florist & Florist Supplier Association: www.wffsa.org
- Society of American Florists—for members only: www.safnow.org

Food Processing & Distribution		
	NAICS 233310	

Rules of Thumb

➤ Processing:
  Branded—5 to 7 times EBIT
  Non-Branded—4.5 to 6 times EBIT

➤ Distribution:
  Branded and Non-Branded—4 to 5 times EBIT

Pricing Tips
- "Rate of growth; gross margins—higher is better; customer concentration—high is a threat; management continuity, high synergies."

Food Service — Contractor

	NAICS 722310	Number of Businesses/Units 21,862

Rules of Thumb

➤ 40 to 55 percent of annual sales plus inventory

➤ 2.5 times SDE plus inventory

Pricing Tips

- "Location, location, location. We like to use a rule of thumb that there will be 1 person for every 200 sf of building space, and then we will calculate a frequency rate depending on the building usage and the location of the unit in the building. If you do not break down the number of people and frequency usage and calculate an average sale 50% less than industry average (because you will sell a lot of snacks and drinks if the frequency percentage is high), you will not get a true customer count; and that is the important number in the metrics formula, as well as if there is more than one building in the office complex."

- "A better operator can create 25% to 40% more sales quickly. You can still sell potential in this industry."

Expert Comments

"Bigger players working into smaller locations to try to catch both markets in a way the independents cannot"

"The secret is out: the big players are looking for the prime locations. as well as marketing to the employees like never before, and the customers are much more demanding of quality."

"The positive in this area of food service used to be low competition, but there are many lunch delivery and catering operations fighting for this market. The building owners used to see a restaurant in their building as an amenity; now they see it as a revenue source, so the occupancy costs have jumped and will continue to rise until the building owners need tenants or have to keep employees happy."

Benchmark Data

Statistics (Food Service Contractors)

Number of Establishments	21,862
Average Profit Margin	5.1%
Revenue per Employee	$79,500
Average Number of Employees	19.4
Average Wages per Employee	$21,734

Source: IBISWorld, March 2012

Products and Services Segmentation

Food and nonalcoholic drinks served on premises	63.3%
Food and nonalcoholic drinks served off premises	31.7%
Other	2.6%
Alcoholic drinks served on premises	2.2%
Renting public rooms and arenas (e.g. meeting or convention rooms)	0.2%

Source: IBISWorld, March 2012

Major Market Segmentation

Colleges and universities	32%
Manufacturing, industrial and mining industries	25%
Recreation, leisure and sports industries	20%
Government and healthcare	13%
Airlines and airports	10%

Source: IBISWorld, March 2012

Industry Costs

Profit	5.1%
Wages	27.8%
Purchases	44.0%
Depreciation	1.2%
Marketing	2.0%
Rent & Utilities	5.5%
Other	14.4

Source: IBISWorld, March 2012

Market Share

Compass Group	34.8%
Aramark Corporation	29.2%
Sodexo	26.3%
Delaware North	6.7%

Source: IBISWorld, March 2012

- "You cannot have an occupancy cost over 10% and keep your margins. You should also get all the food service in and around the complex like vending, sales meeting luncheons, etc. Food cost will be higher than average because there is normally not enough space for a full cooking setup operation that can be run by as few people as possible in the down time."

Expenses as a Percentage of Annual Sales

Cost of goods:	35% to 37%
Payroll/labor Costs:	16% to 19%
Occupancy:	07% to 10%
Profit (estimated pretax)	15% to 20%

Industry Trend

- "This industry has nice potential over the next few years as landlords struggle to fill empty office & industrial space, but the secret is out so there will be more operators interested in these smaller spaces."
- "Bigger players working into smaller locations to try to catch both markets in a way the independents cannot."

Questions

- "#1) The lease is very important (get a copy and read it slowly). #2) Agreement with company is very important (get a copy and read it slowly). #3) What are the sales trends for the last 2 years? #4) What improvements or repairs are needed? #5) Count the people in the building. #6) Get information on employees. #7) Make a spreadsheet of the compatible operations. #8) Outside setting is a big value. If they don't have it, can you add outside set? #9) Do you like the food they sell? #10) What equipment will you need and is there room for it? #12) Make sure the common areas are kept up nicely. #13) How many hours does the owner work? #14) Call health department for inspection ASAP. #15) Can you increase the hours? #16) Equipment age is important. #17) When is the last time seller had a price increase?"

- "Finance as long as the lease; need to know customer counts & average check and number of people in the complex"

Food Service Equipment and Supplies

NAICS 423440	

Rules of Thumb

➢ 45 percent of annual sales plus inventory

➢ 2.5 times SDE plus inventory

➢ 4.5 to 5 times EBIT

➢ 5 to 6 times EBITDA

Pricing Tips

- "10 times EBITDA for dealerships"
- "All assets saleable? Obsolete equipment?"

Benchmark Data

- "40% + gross margins"
- "$200,000/employee"

Expenses as a Percentage of Annual Sales

Cost of goods:.. 30%
Payroll/labor Costs:.. 30%
Occupancy:...05% to 07%
Profit (estimated pretax) 10%

Industry Trend

- "The industry is consolidating, thus the margins are decreasing."

Resources

Trade Publications

- Food Service Equipment & Supplies Magazine: www.fesmag.com
- Foodservice Equipment Reports: www.fermag.com

Food Stores (See Grocery Stores—Small to Medium Size)

Food Stores — Specialty

NAICS 44529	Number of Businesses/Units 48,380

Rules of Thumb

➢ Food Stores—Specialty consists of several types of retail food stores including:

➢ Candy Stores—30 to 35 percent of annual sales plus inventory

➢ Bakeries—40 to 45 percent of annual sales plus inventory

➢ Dairy Stores—25 percent of annual sales plus inventory

➢ Other—35 to 40 percent of annual sales plus inventory

Pricing Tips

- "This category also includes the following retail businesses: confectionery products, gourmet foods, organic and health foods, packaged nuts, spices and soft drinks.
- "In general, these businesses will sell for 30 to 35 percent plus inventory."

Benchmark Data

Statistics (Specialty Food Stores)

Number of Establishments	48,380
Average Profit Margin	3.5%
Revenue per Employee	$69,600
Average Number of Employees	3
Average Wages per Employee	$9,973

Source: IBISWorld, May 2012

Products and Services Segmentation

Bakery products	30%
Other foods	30%
Candy	25%
Dairy products	10%
Coffee and tea	5%

Source: IBISWorld, July 2012

Industry Costs

Profit	3.5%
Wages	14.4%
Purchases	50.2%
Depreciation	1.9%
Marketing	4.0%
Rent & Utilities	7.0%
Other	19.0%

Source: IBISWorld, July 2012

Industry Trend

- "Some Highlights
    - ✓ Natural food stores are the fastest growing retail channel, boasting a sales increase of 19.8 percent between 2009 and 2011.
    - ✓ Cheese and Cheese Alternatives is the largest specialty food category, at $3.44 billion.
    - ✓ Manufacturers say that specialty food stores and natural supermarkets are the fastest growing retail channels for specialty foods.
    - ✓ The average transaction size for specialty food stores was $41.49 in 2011, up 11.4 percent over 2010.
    - ✓ Three-quarters of retailers say that local is the most influential product claim today and two-thirds report the claim will grow the most in the next three years.
    - ✓ Retailers say the fastest emerging cuisine is Latin; importers report that Eastern European and Indian are growing."

Source: "Specialty Food Industry at a Glance," The State of the Specialty Food Industry 2012, www.specialtyfood.com

Resources

Websites

- www.specialtyfood.com

Food Trucks		
	NAICS 722330	

Rules of Thumb

➤ 25 to 30 percent of annual sales plus inventory

Pricing Tips

- "A big difference between food trucks and catering trucks is that the food truck is many times named after a restaurant or recognizable chef. This is often difficult to transfer and most likely neither the restaurant or chef will be willing to allow a stranger to operate under their name. In other words a good portion of the value (and goodwill) is the name. If franchises such as Chili's or one of the steakhouse franchises get into the food truck business—that would be transferable with franchisor approval. Some food trucks do not use a well-known name, but rather specialize, such as the grilled cheese sandwich truck that did so well on a TV show. A food truck specializing in a particular food category would be transferable, again with permission."
- "Food trucks might be a fad, but they may also be a very successful business model."
- FOOD TRUCKS

  Pros

  1. The growth of the mobile restaurant unit is a long term trend (Source: NRA) 2. Excellent marketing tool for an existing restaurant 3. A throwback to the Good Humor Man and the "Roach Coach". 4. A positive option in a commercial neighborhood with no restaurants nearby. 5. Similar to the open air markets in Europe. 6. Ease of entry and lower start-up cost at $70,000–$120,000 for a new truck. 7. Can be a positive contribution to the less affluent community 8. An affordable dining alternative for college students.

  Cons

  1. Not fair to existing restaurant owners who have to pay rent, taxes, etc. and have had to adhere to strict building codes, especially sanitation (5 sinks, etc.) with the Board of Health. 2. Sanitation codes need to be strictly enforced—temperatures, hygiene, etc. 3. The business is very weather dependent—New England vs. Florida

  Food trucks are a brand new industry. According to a recent article in the *Boston Globe*, Boston currently has over 40 mobile eateries operating in the city, with up to 60 more being added next spring. Entrepreneur Ron Sarni (Sarni's Cleaners) is a leading advocate and leases ready to go trucks to mobile chefs. He also founded the Boston Area Food Truck Association to help candidates navigate the red tape.

  Source: Charles Perkins, The Boston Restaurant Group, Boston, MA, 2011

Benchmark Data

- (For additional Benchmark data see Catering Trucks)
- "Since 2009, the number of trucks listed on the Roaming Hunger website has grown 710 percent, to more than 2,300, Resnick said. And food truck growth is anticipated to grow another 260 percent by 2014, he said.
- "Success depends on many factors, he added, but among them are differentiated branding, a reasonably sized menu, a good selection of sales locations, a strong social media presence and patience when it comes to growth.

"'These brands are being built very slowly,' Resnick said. Many have found success in teaming with other operators to provide informal food-truck malls and also by joining the growing number of local food truck associations, which can now be found in such cities as Chicago, New York and Philadelphia, and such regions as Southern California and the District of Columbia

"In addition, Resnick said, food trucks need to develop a catering program to expand the meal occasions and revenue-stream stability. With regular catering income, a truck can better survive the rough road of inclement weather and other business drawbacks. 'Catering is what's going to pay your bills,' he said.

"Because they already face at least four regulatory hurdles, including health permits, business licensing, parking restrictions and zoning laws, food trucks with alcohol beverage sales have been few and far between. 'If you could figure out the drive-thru daiquiri truck, I think you could do pretty well,' Resnick said with a laugh."

Source: "Food Trucks: Possibilities and pitfalls to consider" by Ron Ruggles, nrn.com, May 6, 2012

- "Underemployed chefs and spunky small-business owners have realized that food trucks are an ideal first business—even in tough economic times. At $50,000 to $100,000, their start-up costs are about a tenth of what it might cost to open a bricks-and-mortar restaurant in high-rent cities, says Matt Geller, CEO of the Southern California Mobile Food Vendors Association (SoCalMFVA), one of the first trade associations organized for food truck owners.)"

Source: "Costco members pave the way for success with gourmet food trucks" by Teri Cettina, The Costco Connection, July 2012

- "It might be hard to argue. Grilled cheese has been popular since at least the 1930s, when an open-faced version served at Sunday supper was referred to as a 'cheese dream.' Last year, 195 million servings of grilled cheese were ordered at U.S. restaurants, according to NPD Group, a market research company. On a good day, Roxy's sells upward of 400 sandwiches, sometimes in just a few hours, for about $7 each.

- "Melanson, 39, was in the prep kitchen in Jamaica Plain early in the morning before heading for the SoWa market. While roasting three large pans of sliced mangos for the daily special, he talked about how he wasn't fazed by 'The Great Food Truck Race.'"

Source: "Cheesy does it" by Jialu Chen, *Boston Globe*, August 16, 2011

Industry Trend

- "Under pressure to protect bricks-and-mortar restaurants from increased competition, several big cities are starting to apply the brakes on a rising tide of food-truck vendors with fully loaded kitchens.

- "Boston, Chicago, St. Louis and Seattle are among the cities enacting laws that restrict where food trucks can serve customers in proximity to their rivals and for how long. Some food-truck operators argue that they shouldn't be punished for offering an innovative service, especially since many cities already allow restaurants to open up alongside one another."

Source: "Street Fight: Food Trucks vs. Restaurants" by Sarah E. Needleman, online.wsj.com August 2012

- "Food trucks appear to be more than just a passing fad. 'I believe they're here to stay and will keep growing in the years ahead,' says Annika Stensson, a spokesperson for the National Restaurant Association. In a 2011 survey by the trade association, almost six out of 10 respondents (59 percent) said they would be likely to visit a food truck if a favorite restaurant offered one, up from 47 percent a year ago."

Source: "Costco members pave the way for success with gourmet food trucks" by Teri Cettina, The Costco Connection, July 2012

- "Thirty percent of the chefs said that mobile food trucks and pop-up restaurants will be the hottest operational trend in 2011; 18 percent said restaurants with gardens will be the top trend, and 17 percent said social media marketing."

- "Aramark Rolls out Ballpark Food Truck

  Denver—Aramark rolled out its first ballpark food truck in July—and then just left it there. It's an immovable feast, at least for now.
  "The Wok in the Park food truck, selling Asian-inspired noodle bowls, was introduced in the outfield concourse at Coors Field here, home of Major League Baseball's Colorado Rockies. David Freireich, spokesman for Aramark, said the Coors Field food team 'thought it would be a good opportunity to take something that is popular and trendy on the streets and bring it into the ballpark.'

  "Freireich said the fully operational truck will remain parked for the remainder of the season. 'However, it is licensed to travel throughout Denver, so there is a strong possibility that it could appear at festivals or go up to a curb during lunch hour' after the season is over, he said.
  "Aramark will watch Wok in the Park closely, Freireich added, and may expand the truck idea to other sports venues."

  Source: Article by Ron Ruggless, *Nation's Restaurant News*, August 8, 2011

- "Food Trucks Gaining Momentum, New Research Finds

  Food trucks are one of the hottest trends in the restaurant industry right now, and consumers are showing increasing interest in mobile foodservice, new research by the National Restaurant Association confirms.

  "The new research, a consumer survey conducted last month, found that nearly six out of ten (59 percent) American adults say they would be likely to visit a food truck if their favorite restaurant offered one, up from 47 percent just one year ago.

  "'Our research shows that in just one year, the number of consumers who say they would be likely to visit a food truck has increased significantly. We also found that food trucks have a more noticeable presence in communities in the West and Northeast than in other parts of the United States,' said Hudson Riehle, senior vice president of the Research and Knowledge Group for the National Restaurant Association.
  "'Though food trucks are often equated with chefs and entrepreneurs, they also present opportunities for operators of established restaurants to expand their operations and presence, as a majority of consumers say they would visit a food truck run by their favorite restaurant. Mobile foodservice can be a good way to extend an existing restaurant brand beyond the four walls of the establishment,' Riehle said.
  "In addition, the survey found that nearly one-fifth (18 percent) of consumers saw a food truck in their community this summer, and more than one-quarter (28 percent) of those who saw a food truck made a purchase.

  "When asked how they typically found the food truck they visited, 73 percent said they just saw it on the street, and 54 percent said they selected it from an area where food trucks typically gather, 39 percent found out from a friend, and 13 percent found it through social media."

  Source:www.restaurant.org/nranewsblog/2011

Franchise
Foot Solutions (See also Shoe Stores)

Approx. Total Investment	$200,000 to $225,000

	NAICS 448210	Number of Businesses/Units 200

Rules of Thumb

➤ 60 to 65 percent of annual sales plus inventory

Resources

Websites
- www.footsolutions.com

Football Teams (Professional)	
SIC 7941-05 NAICS 711211	Number of Businesses/Units 31

Rules of Thumb

➤ The value of the Washington Redskins of the NFL is approximately $1 billion while the value of the Arizona Cardinals is roughly half of that figure.

Source: *Forbes* magazine

➤ Average Annual Revenue — $9 Billion

➤ Average Annual Salary — $1.75 Million

Source: www.statisticbrain.com/professional-sports

Pricing Tips

- Revenue and operating income are for the 2009 season and net of revenue sharing and stadium debt service. Value of team based on current stadium deal (unless new stadium is pending), without deduction for debt (other than stadium debt). Earnings before interest, taxes, depreciation and amortization (EBITDA).
- Note: We have found that *Forbes* tackles some pretty interesting valuation issues (no pun intended).

Benchmark Data

- For Benchmark data for professional sports teams see Baseball

Franchise
Framing & Art Centre (See also Picture Framing)

Approx. Total Investment	$118,200 to $179,400

SIC 5999-27	NAICS 442299	Number of Businesses/Units 51

Rules of Thumb

➤ 60 percent of annual sales plus inventory

Benchmark Data

- For Benchmark data see Picture Framing

Resources

Websites

- www.framingartcentre.com

Franchise Food Businesses (See Franchises)

| | NAICS 722 | |

Rules of Thumb

➤ (This category is dominated by McDonald's, Burger King, Wendy's, KFC, Domino's, Pizza Hut, Arby's, Dairy Queen, Taco Bell & Denny's—others are Subway, Blimpie's, Baskin Robbins & Schlotzsky's)

➤ 52 to 60 percent of annual sales plus inventory

➤ 2.5 SDE plus inventory

➤ 4 times EBIT

➤ 3.5 times EBITDA

➤ Asset value plus 1 year's SDE plus inventory

Pricing Tips

- "Establish seller-adjusted cash flow and multiply times 2.5 to 3.5"
- "The multiples are a bit above the level for the industry in which the franchisee participates."
- "Stability of income, down payment & quality of franchisor"
- "Labor costs typically represent 15 to 20 percent of gross food sales. Food costs generally run from 28 percent to a high 40 percent for red meat on the menu. Pizza shops run about 28 to 30 percent. Rent should not exceed 10 percent."
- "Check the franchise agreement. Who pays transfer and training fees? Does the franchisor have the first right to purchase the business? Will the transition require the facilities to be upgraded to franchisor's current standards? If yes, the upgrade cost can be substantial."

Expert Comments

"All of the above factors influence pricing."

Benchmark Data

- "$600 to $800 per sq. ft. is respectable."

Expenses as a Percentage of Annual Sales

Cost of goods:	30%
Payroll/labor Costs:	19%
Occupancy:	07%
Profit (estimated pretax)	22%

Industry Trend

- "Food-related concepts represent the single largest category of franchise business opportunities, with more than 151,000 quick service restaurants, 61,000 retail food businesses and 36,000 full-service restaurant locations among the nation's 750,000 franchise establishments, according to the International Franchise Association.

  "And it doesn't look like the eateries are about to push back from the table soon. These businesses are forecast to add locations in 2012 at the rate of 2.6 percent for quick service, 0.9 percent for retail food, and 2.1 percent for full-service restaurants, easily outpacing the industry's 1.9 percent overall average unit growth rate, the IFA reported."

  Source: "Restaurant Franchises Are Cooking" by Mark Henricks, Special Advertising Section, INC magazine, April, 2012

Seller Financing

- "5 to7 years; however, SBA loans up to 10 years can be obtained."

Franchises		
		Number of Businesses/Units 784,000 +

Rules of Thumb

- ➤ We have listed franchises with a "quick" rule of thumb, or range, usually expressed as a percentage of sales. For many of them we have based it on quite a few actual sales; others may have been based on just a few; and in some cases just one where we felt it was appropriate. They can be a good starting point for pricing the business.

- ➤ Many of the franchises are well known while others are very new with just several units. By the time this goes to press, some of the franchises may have folded, sold or merged. We try to keep this as up-to-date as possible. We could use your help. To contribute to our ever-growing list, just go to our Web site and click on Franchise Update and complete the form that will show up and email to us at tom@bbpinc.com and also if you find that a franchise has disappeared or merged, etc., please let us know. Obviously the big changes such as Mail Boxes to UPS Stores will be caught by us or by our researchers (hopefully).

  Keep in mind that rules of thumb are just that. Every business is different and rules of thumb will never take the place of a business valuation or even an opinion of value. But, they will give you a quick ballpark idea of what the business might sell for everything else being equal. A rule of thumb will tell you whether a seller is in the ballpark when he or she tells you what they think their business is worth or what they want to sell it for.

- ➤ For up-to-date information and for those companies where the number of units is not shown, track down their Web site. Read the footnotes where indicated. Also, additional information is usually available under its own listing in this Guide. We have listed every franchise listed below, and others where information was available, by itself alphabetically by name within the Rules of Thumb section. In some cases, there is the Estimated Annual Sales per Unit and the Approximate Total Investment.

➢ Remember, that rules of thumb are not intended to create a specific value or to be used for an appraisal. They supply a quick "ballpark" price range. They can provide a starting point for pricing a business or a sanity check after performing an informal valuation. Read the How to Use Section of the Guide, in the front, to gain some insight on how to make some adjustments to make the rule of thumb a bit more accurate.

➢ Several other factors can greatly influence the selling price of a franchise. One is the question of the transfer fee levied by the franchisor and who pays it. This amount can be substantial, so find out the information on this prior to going to market. The second is the franchisor requiring a major change in outside appearance and a change in the interior of the unit — or both. This should also be investigated before attempting to sell it. The costs involved in either requirement can be substantial.

Name of Franchise (Notes)	Selling Price as a % of Sales
AAMCO Transmission	40%–45%
A & W Restaurants	40%–50%
Ace Cash Express	1.25
Ace Hardware stores (1)	45%
Adam and Eve	40%
Andy on Call	25%
Aero Colours	75%
All Tune & Lube	20%–25%
AlphaGraphics	60%–65%
Allegra Printing	70%
American Poolplayers Association (APA) (2)	1.4 SDE
Arctic Circle	50%
Atlanta Bread Company	25%–30%
Baskin-Robbins Ice Cream	46%–56%
Batteries Plus	30%–35%
Beef O'Brady's	22%
Ben & Jerry's	35%–40%
Between Rounds Bagel Deli & Bakery (3)	
Big Apple Bagels	42%
Big City Burrito	55%–60%
Big O Tires	35%
Black Jack Pizza	55%–60%
Blimpies	50%
Boba Loca	30%
Bresler's Ice Cream	35%–40%
Bruster's Ice Cream	50%
Budget Blinds (4)	45%–50%
Burger King	40%
Camille's Sidewalk Café	30%–35%
Carl's Jr.	40%–50%
Cartridge World	30%–35%
Carvel Ice Cream/Restaurants	60%
Car X Auto Service	35%–40%
CertaPro Painters	45%
Chester's International	45%
Cheeburger Cheeburger	35%–40%
Chick-Fil-A	60%–70%
Closets by Design	50%
Closet Factory	62%
Cold Stone Creamery	30%–35%
Conroy's Flowers	55%–60%

Cost Cutter's Family Hair.. 57%
Coverall North America (5) .... 2–3 times mo. sales
Culligan Dealerships.. 80%–120%
Curves for Women (6).. 2.0 SDE
Dairy Queen.. 45%–50%
Deck the Walls 35%–40%
Del Taco 90%
Dick's Wings and Grill 35%
Dollar Discount Stores 20%
Domino's Pizza 50%–55%
Dream Dinners.. 45%
Dr. Vinyl... 75%
Dry Cleaners USA.. 55%
Dunkin' Donuts (7) 75%–80%
Eagle Transmission Shops (8).. 40%
Environment Control 42%
Fantastic Sam's (9) 35%–40%
Fast Fix (Jewelry) 80%–85%
Fast Frame 32%
• FasTrac Kids.. 45%–50%
Fast Signs.. 42%–46%
FedEx Ground .... 65%–70 %
Firestone Tire Stores 35%
Floppy's Mouse Club 70%–75%
Foot Solutions .... 60%—65%
Friendly Computers 30%
Framing & Art Centre 60%
• Friendly Computers 35%–40%
Friendly's Restaurant... 40%
Geeks on Call 60%
General Nutrition Centers 40%
Godfather's Pizza 28%
Goin' Postal... 30%–35%
Goodyear Store (Business Opportunity).. 35%
Grease Monkey International... 58%
Great Clips... 1–1.5 SDE
Great Harvest Bread Co. (10)
Great Steak & Potato... 55%–60%
Grout Doctor 89%
Hallmark Cards 40%
Harley-Davidson Motors (11) 87%
Heavenly Hams 48%
Home Helpers 35%
Home Team Inspection 36%
Honest 1 Auto Care 70%–75%
House Doctor.. 24%
Hungry Howie's Pizza & Subs 35%–40%
• Huntington Learning Center... 60%
i9 Sports.. 65%–70%
Iceberg Drive Inn 40%–45%
Jani-King... 26%
Jersey Mike's Subs 50%
Jiffy Lube.. 50%
Jimmy John's... 65%–70%
Johnny Rockets 80%–90%
Jon Smith Subs.. 20%
Juice It Up... 24%
Kentucky Fried Chicken (KFC) 30%–35%
Kwik Kopy (printing)... 50%–60%

Kumon Math & Reading Centers	45%–50%
La Estancia	35%–40%
Lady of America	45%–50%
Laptop Xchange	85%–90%
Lenny's Subs	15%
Liberty Tax Service	40%
Li'l Dino Subs (12)	64%
Little Caesar's Pizza	55%
Logan Farms (honey-glazed hams)	30%
MAACO Auto Paint	40%
MaggieMoo's Ice Cream (13)	32%
Maid Brigade	45%
Mail Boxes, Etc. (See UPS Stores)	40%–45%
Mama Fu's	30%
Marble Slab Creamery	45%–50%
Martinizing	60%
McGruff's Safe Kids ID System	52%
Meineke Car Care Center	30%–35%
Merry Maids	45%
Midas Muffler	35%–40%
Minuteman Press	65%
Molly Maid	40%
Money Mailer	40%–45%
Mountain Mike's Pizza	27%
Moto Photo	72%
Mr. Gatti's Pizza	25%–30%
Mr. Jim's Pizza	35%–40 %
Mr. Payroll	1.3%
Mr. Rooter Plumbing (14)	
Mrs. Fields Cookies	68%
Murphy's Deli	50%
Music Go Around	40%
My Favorite Muffin	30%–35%
Nathan's Famous	100%
Nature's Way Café	45%
Natural Chicken Grill	25%–30%
New York Pizzeria	35%–40%
Obee's Soup/Salad/Subs	55%–60%
Oil X Change	30%
Once Upon A Child	25%
Orange Julius	32%
Original Italian Pie	35%–40%
OXXO Dry Cleaners	65%
Pak Mail	50%
Panera Bread	35%–40%
Papa John's Pizza (15)	
Papa Murphy's Pizza	35%–40%
Parcel Plus	25%
Petland	57%
Pillar to Post—Home Inspection	40%
Pizza by George	50%
Pizza Factory (16)	35%
Pizza Inn	47%
Planet Beach	35%–40%
Play It Again Sports	40%–45%
Precision Tune Auto Care	36%
Pump It Up	30%
Purrfect Auto	50%–55%
Quaker State Lube	50%

Quizno's Classic Subs (17) 25%–30%
Red Robin Gourmet Burgers 32%
Renaissance Executive Forums 75%
Rocky Mountain Chocolate Factory 65%–70%
Rita's–Ices, Cones, Shakes 80%–130%
Roly Poly Sandwiches 34%
Safe Ship 40%
Samurai Sam's Teriyaki Grill 50%
Sarpino's Pizza 50%
Sears Carpet & Upholstery Care 30%
Senior Helpers .... 40% to 45%
ServiceMaster Clean 55%–60%
Serv Pro 90%
Shell Rapid Lube (Business Opportunity) 50%
Signarama 55%–60%
Sir Speedy (printing) (18) 55%–60%
Smart Box 48%
Smoothie King 40%–45%
• Snap Fitness 40%
Soup Man (Original) 30%
Subway (19) .... 65%–70 %
SuperCoups 40%–45%
Superior Inspection 1.3%
Swisher (restroom hygiene service) 75%
Taco John's 31%
Tan USA 60%–65%
TCBY 40%–45%
The Maids 40%–45%
Togo's Eatery 60%–65%
Topz Healthy Burgers 40%
Tropical Smoothie Café .... 50%—55%
Two Men and a Truck 43%
U Save (auto rental) (20) 10%–15%
UPS Stores 40%–45%
Valpak Mailers .... 3 SDE
Valvoline Instant Oil Change 50%
We the People 86%
Wild Birds Unlimited 30%–35%
Wine Kitz (Canada) 55%
Wingstop Restaurants 33%
Wireless Toyz 45%–50%
Worldwide Express 50%–55%
Your Office USA 60%
You've Got Maids 60%
Ziebart International (auto services) 42%
Zoo Health Club 20%

(1) Sales seem to indicate that smaller sales bring a higher multiple (50% +) than stores with sales over a million, which seem to bring lower multiples. Price is plus inventory which may be the cause of lower multiples for larger stores. (2) $1,000 to $1,800 per team in sales; selling price - $2,000 to $2,500 per team (3) 3–4 times earnings (4) 2 times annual EBIT, plus inventory & equipment(5) Master/Area developer—Sell for 3 to 5 times earnings plus some blue sky for size and potential of market (some cases).(6) Prices for Curves for Women seem to be all over the place. Some sales have been reported at 75+% of sales. One sale reported was 1.31 times sales for four units. (7) In … Dunkin Donuts shops now sell for 75–125% of annual sales, depending mainly on geography. It's about 125% in New England, 100% of sales in the Mid-Atlantic States, and lower in the South and Midwest. There really is not a Dunkin' Donuts market in the West. A sale in Colorado was reported that sold for 22% of sales. (8) Eagle is a Texas-based franchise

www.eagletransmission.com. They are the strongest transmission franchise in the Dallas area with 21 locations and are a minor player in Houston and Austin. The attraction is the royalties at 4% in Dallas and 6% Houston and Austin, and the training is "hands on" locally. (9) These stores sell for maximum 2 times SDE versus $120,000 to $150,000 + for new. 10 to 12 sales have been reported at 2 times SDE for absentee owner stores (most are) and 2 times SDE + manager's salary of owner operated.(10) 3.3 – 3.4 times SDE (11) Netted $2,100,000 and seller retained 20% of ownership. (12) One sold for 80% of sales, but it was located in an office building with vending rights. (13) One MaggieMoo's Ice Cream & Treatery sale was reported at 92%, three years old, great location, growth at 15% approx. a year; but only 15% down payment (14) 1–4 times SDE plus hard assets. The number between 1–4 depends on several factors such as the owner operating a truck, etc. (15) The only sale reported of Papa John's was a 3-store chain which sold for $475,000 with $150,000 down and grossed $1,191,700. (16) Pizza factory has approximately140 units in the 10 Western States. (17) Quiznos, which has struggled as a higher-priced alternative to Subway, has closed an estimated 1,000 of its U.S. shops (the company won't confirm the number) and has begun putting mini-stores in gas stations in a bid to boost sales. April 2011, www.msn.com (18) One sale was reported at 70% of sales. (19) "As a former multi-unit Subway franchisee and a Development Agent, now a business broker Subway stores, there are many different formulas I have seen. 30 to 40 weeks' sales, or 60 to 70% of sales is a popular one. Actual sales price depends on supply and demand and is closer to 70% of sales in So. CA." "On stores with gross sales of $300,000 to $500,000, multiple of 40% of annual sales. On stores with sales of $500,000+, multiple of 50% of annual sales. Franchisor would like 30% as a down payment on resales." "I would suggest for Subway, in New England and maybe all of New England, due to the high number of pizza restaurants, Subways tend to sell for a much lower of percentage of sales than 47%—sometimes as low as 20– 25%." (20) Price does not include cost of vehicles, and revenues do not include auto sales.

Pricing Tips

- Pricing the franchise resale obviously depends on the franchise. Is the franchise value added or—as in some cases—value subtracted? Does franchising add value to the business or would the same business— independent of a franchise label—bring as high a price in the marketplace? When calculating a multiple of annual sales, is it before subtracting the royalty fees, or are they included in the annual sales? After all, 6 percent of just $500,000 in annual revenues is $30,000, but just $12,000 at 40 percent of annual sales. The $12,000 probably doesn't have much of an impact on pricing unless the sales are really astronomical.

- McDonald's has always been the franchise that everyone compares others to, but that has changed recently. However, it probably hasn't hurt the price of a McDonald's—it is still a very strong brand. One disadvantage of franchising is that, like Burger King, the company gets sold several times, and the direction of the new owners can play havoc with operational support, advertising and growth of the company. In most cases, franchisees have no control over this. The strength of a franchise is the success of the brand name and the reputation created in the marketplace. Many franchises have been able to create that brand-identity and awareness to add a lot of value to the price of one of the units. And, if you want to buy a very popular franchise in a particular geographical marketplace, you have to pay the going rate.

- Some prospective business buyers like the security and the support of a franchise. Still others want the independence of owning and controlling their own business. Buying an independent business provides just that. No answering to the franchisor, no royalties and no heavy advertising fees, no forced purchasing from certain suppliers—and no politics. Owning your own independent business also allows you to expand, change, add or delete products and/or services. Independent businesses can be very quick to adjust to changes. Franchises, especially large ones, are very cumbersome and slow to adapt to new trends and ideas.

- The choice is a personal one. Some very strong independent operators have chosen, after years of independence, to buy a franchise, while some franchisees felt stifled and changed to an independent business.

- As for pricing a franchise, we don't see much of a difference between an independent business and the franchised one, except for the very big players, where the franchise label probably adds a lot of value, maybe 10 to 20 percent, based on the same gross. On the other hand, the fledging franchise with just a few units has some real problems on the resale side. If it's fairly new, there are plenty of new units available, the name doesn't really mean anything yet, and the age old question is asked—why is the business for sale? In cases like this, the percentage multiples might be reduced by the same figure as is added for the well-known brand name—most likely lower.

- Despite what the franchise industry would like us to believe, not all franchises are successful. What has always struck us as strange is the buyer who is very number- oriented and turns down a very good business due to some slight anomaly in the financial statement from two years ago, and who will be the same buyer who purchased a franchise (a new one) where he has seen no books and records and has no idea whether the location will work out or not.

Source: The Business Broker

- Key Considerations When Pricing a Franchise

"Lease Terms—If the lease doesn't contain a provision for at least 10 years remaining, the price can be affected accordingly.

"Franchise Rights—If there aren't at least 10 years left in the franchise agreement, a price adjustment downward should be made. This may not be applicable in those states where the franchisor may not terminate the agreement unless there is a default.

"Territorial Rights—If the franchise agreement does not provide for territorial rights, this could be a minus. In other words, if the franchisor can open additional units in the immediate area, the value of the existing franchise could be diminished. However, if the franchisee has additional territorial rights then the value may be increased.

"Business Mix—If the bulk of the sales is in low-profit items, value may be diminished; whereas if high profit items make up a substantial part of the business, value may be increased. Is there wholesale business? Do one or two customers make up a majority of the business? Business mix should be considered.

"Remodel Requirements—Does the franchise agreement state that the business has to be remodeled periodically? How often and how much remodeling? The value of the business may be reduced by the cost of the remodeling, depending on when it has to be done.

"Hours of Operation—Does the franchisor require specific hours and days open? Some franchisors, especially food related, donuts/convenience stores, may state that the business has to be open 24 hours a day, seven days a week. The shorter the hours, the better the price.

"Location—Obviously, the better and more desirable the location, the better the price.

"Cash Flow—The price of a small business may be based on its sales history rather than on reported profitability. Some businesses are just not operated efficiently from a cash management point of view. Certainly, strong cash flow benefits the price asked, but a poor cash flow coupled with strong historical sales does not necessarily detract from the price."

Excerpted from a presentation to the American Institute of Certified Public Accountants by Bernard Siegel, Siegel Business Services, Philadelphia, PA.

Questions

- "The same questions that apply to any business for sale, plus: Have you reached your financial expectations that you had when you purchased the franchise? How long have you owned the franchise? Have you had problems or issues with the franchisor? Has the franchisor provided the support and services they agreed to? How many new franchises have been sold in the past 2 years?"

Freight Forwarding		
SIC 4731-04	NAICS 488510	Number of Businesses/Units 18,561

Rules of Thumb

➢ 50 percent of annual sales

➢ 2.6 times SDE

Expert Comments

"Just sold a niche market, owner plus one employee freight forwarder, for $1.1 million at these figures."

Benchmark Data

Statistics (Freight Forwarding Brokerages & Agencies)

Number of Establishments	18,561
Average Profit Margin	6.3%
Revenue per Employee	$228,200
Average Number of Employees	12.7
Average Wages per Employee	$52,026

Source: IBISWorld, June 2012

Products and Services Segmentation

Agency and brokerage services	49.7%
Freight forwarding	43.8%
Other freight related services	5.3%
Process consulting	1.2%

Source: IBISWorld, June 2012

Major Market Segmentation

Manufacturers	62%
Importers and wholesalers	23%
Others	15%

Source: IBISWorld, June 2012

Industry Costs

Profit	6.3%
Wages	22.6%
Purchases	57.2%
Depreciation	1.9%
Marketing	2.0%
Rent & Utilities	5.1%
Other	4.9%

Source: IBISWorld, June 2012

Market Share

C.H. Robinson Worldwide Inc.	7.0%
Deutsche Post	5.7%
United Parcel Service	5.7%
Deutsche Bahn	4.8%

Source: IBISWorld, June 2012

- "The strategy has helped the cargo brokers, which act as middlemen between freight companies and manufacturers, to take a 35 percent share of boxed sea freight. That's still far short of their near-domination of air markets, where forwarders handle 95 percent of cargoes, leaving 'huge scope for expansion,' said Damian Brewer, an analyst at RBC Capital Markets in London."

Source: "K+N Pushes Maersk to One-Click Shipping in Ryanair Mold: Freight Markets" by Leigh Baldwin, June 22, 2011. www.Bloomberg.com/news

Industry Trend

- "Jean-Louis Demeulenaere, CEO of Geodis Group, said: 'Our aim is to, at least, double our freight forwarding business in the U.S. within the coming 5 years, based on external and organic growth.' One Source Logistics was founded mid-2003, offering truckload, LTL and air freight management with a 'best-in-class' Transportation Management System. It has developed a particular specialty for time-critical deliveries for the retail industry.

  "With Geodis Wilson it has developed new container Freight Stations at five major gateways into the U.S. at Atlanta, Chicago, Los Angeles, Miami and Newark."

Source:"Geodis Wilson bid to double US freight forwarding business," www.postandparcel.info, June 9, 2011

Questions

- "Do you need a customs license?

	Franchise
Friendly Computers	
Approx. Total Investment	$59,000 to $219,000
NAICS 811212	Number of Businesses/Units 80

Rules of Thumb

➤ 30 percent of annual sales plus inventory

Resources

Websites
- www.friendlycomputers.com

Friendly's Restaurant

	Franchise
Approx. Total Investment	$485,600 to $1,981,300
Estimated Annual Sales/Unit	$1,100,000
NAICS 722110	Number of Businesses/Units 380

Rules of Thumb

➢ 40 percent of annual sales plus inventory

➢ On or about October 4, 2011, Friendly's filed for bankruptcy and announced that they have closed at least 60 restaurants. Many of the units are company owned. Caution is advised in pricing these restaurants. This information is dated October 5, 2011.

Resources

Websites

▪ www.friendlys.com

Fruit & Vegetable Markets

NAICS 44523	Number of Businesses/Units 12,183

Rules of Thumb

➢ 35 to 40 percent of annual sales

Benchmark Data

Statistics (Fruit and Vegetable Markets)

Number of Establishments	12,183
Average Profit Margin	8.6%
Revenue per Employee	$126,600
Average Number of Employees	3
Average Wages per Employee	$20,696

Source: IBISWorld, August 2012

Products and Services Segmentation

Other vegetables	25%
Potatoes	21%
Other fruit	20%
Grapes	8%
Apples	7%
Lettuce	7%
Onions	7%
Oranges	5%

Source: IBISWorld, August 2012

Industry Costs

Profit	8.6%
Wages	16.2%
Purchases	65.7%
Depreciation	1.5%
Marketing	1.1%
Rent & Utilities	3.0%
Other	3.9%

Source: IBISWorld, August 2012

Fruits and Vegetables (Wholesale)

SIC 5148-01	NAICS 424480	Number of Businesses/Units 5,779

Rules of Thumb

➢ 25 percent of annual sales plus inventory

➢ .50 to 1 times SDE plus inventory

➢ .75 times EBIT

➢ .75 times EBITDA

Pricing Tips

- "How much commission/profit does wholesaler charge its customers per basket/box? It usually is about $2.50 to $3 per . . . anything less makes the wholesaler merely a shipping company."

- "Actual gross sales achieved is not an important analysis tool . . . since there is usually an inverse relationship between sales volume & amount of profit that may be achieved (for instance, the more a box of tomatoes costs, the less profit may be added on). Better to determine how many packages/boxes of product are handled weekly & what 'profit per unit' is achieved."

Expert Comments

"It is perhaps one of the least expensive businesses to start & operate, but just as easy to destroy without a strong paying customer base. One can grow this business through adding of multiple delivery trucks & yet not even have to rent warehouse space."

"It is perhaps one of the easiest businesses to start from 'scratch' . . . relatively easy to sell, with little downside risk."

Benchmark Data

Statistics (Fruit & Vegetable Wholesaling)

Number of Establishments	5,779
Average Profit Margin	3.4%
Revenue per Employee	$586,000
Average Number of Employees	22.5%
Average Wages per Employee	$35,201

Source: IBISWorld, March 2012

Products and Services Segmentation

Other vegetables	24.5%
Other fruit	22%
Potatoes	21.2%
Grapes	8%
Lettuce	6.6%
Onions	6.6%
Apples	6.4%
Oranges	4.7%

Source: IBISWorld, March 2012

Major Market Segmentation

Supermarkets and grocery stores	43.4%
Food service providers	33.2%
Institutional consumers	15.4%
Fruit and vegetable processors	8%

Source: IBISWorld, March 2012

Industry Costs

Profit	3.4%
Wages	6.0%
Purchases	76.4%
Depreciation	3.2%
Rent & Utilities	4.0%
Other	7.0%

Source: IBISWorld, March 2012

- "How much is profit per package/box? Is a buyer used?"
- "Is there adequate storage area for holding buy-in/specials?"

Expenses as a Percentage of Annual Sales

Cost of goods:	40% to 50%
Payroll/labor Costs:	30%
Occupancy:	10%
Profit (estimated pretax)	10% to 20%

Industry Trend

- "Smaller wholesalers either going out. . . or taking on additional food lines."
- "Large food distributors/club stores are a constant source of competition . . . so the only way to keep a customer base is through providing personalized service. This is the current & future trend."

Fuel Dealers (Wholesale)

	NAICS 424720	

Rules of Thumb

➤ 1.5 times SDE plus inventory

➤ 1.5 EBITDA

Pricing Tips

- "Wholesalers/distributors are large-volume, low-margin operators; therefore the price is 1–2 times EBITDA."

Benchmark Data

- "Typical wholesaler does $30 million in annual sales."

Resources

Trade Publications

- Butane Propane News: www.bpnews.com

Associations

- National Propane Gas Association: www.npga.org

Funeral Homes/Services

SIC 7261-02	NAICS 812210	Number of Businesses/Units 28,556

Rules of Thumb

➤ 200 percent of annual sales includes inventory and real estate

➤ 5 to 6 times SDE includes inventory and real estate; 4 times SDE without real estate

➤ Under 75 funerals per year, 3 to 4.5 times EBITDA; 75 to 150 funerals, 4 to 5 times EBITDA; and 150 + funerals, 4.5 to 6 times EBITDA

➤ 6 to 6.5 times EBITDA if real estate is included. If real estate is not included, long-term triple net lease is a must (8 to 10 percent of sales); purchase price would be 4 times EBITDA or approx. 1 times trailing 12 months sales.

➤ 6 times EBIT includes real estate

Pricing Tips

- "Valuations formulas are very difficult to use to obtain highest possible value. Knowing the highest value requires understanding how the business will fit into a buyer's operational strategy and what the buyer's costs will be to operate."

- "Real estate is typically included in sale and can help with collateral for financing."

- "Pricing is primarily dependent upon SDE along with the amount of real estate associated with the business. Multiples generally include all business assets, inventory and real estate."

- "5 to 6 times SDE is the common benchmark in the industry. The revenue multiple is less important but does fall within a normal range of 1.5 to 2.25 times revenue."

- "Funeral homes that are larger in size and have more traditional funeral services are slightly more valuable than the standard rules of thumb."

- "Valuations can be negatively affected by high cremations or eroding Market Share. Valuations can be positively affected by strong real estate values, high growth areas, or increasing Market Share."

- "There are a handful of general methods used to value funeral home businesses. For example, one rough rule of thumb is valuing the funeral home business at $10,000 per call. Of course, this method fails to account for average revenue per call. Obviously, a funeral home with 200 calls doing 90% traditional funerals is worth more than a 200 call firm with a 60% cremation rate."

- "Another valuation method that is employed is to multiply earnings before interest, taxes, depreciation and amortization (EBITA). Usually, a multiplier factor of from 1.8 to 3 is used. For example, if a firm had average earnings of $500,000 before interest, taxes, depreciation and amortization, under this method the firm would be worth anything from $900,000 to $1,500,000 depending on the multiplier that is used. The choice of which multiplier to employ may depend on the particular facts of the funeral home business such as whether its Market Share is increasing, how effective its pre-need program is, etc."

- "Amount of pre-need & how it is funded, volume trends; e.g., Market Share , change in business mix (at need versus pre-need & burial versus cremation. Is the owner staying in community or are there other plans?"

- "Funeral home values are driven by the projected cash flow of the business. Funeral homes that perform a large percentage of cremations are typically less profitable and therefore less valuable than businesses that perform more traditional funerals."

- "You need to understand the value or non-value of pre-needs."

- "Reduce purchase price by the amount of underfunded/unfunded trust funds. Size of market? Is real estate included? Number of services performed per year?"

Expert Comments

"Amount of Competition—number and type of competitors should be considered. Industry Risk—is generally low compared to other service industries. Historical Profit Trend—steady to decreasing depending on geographic location within U.S. Location and Facilities—important factors due to changing demographics in a particular market or facilities that no longer meet customer expectations. Marketability— generally a ready market of buyers for good quality businesses. Industry Trends— towards more cremation and higher service charges. Ease of Replication—high barriers to entry for starting up a full-service funeral home due to facility and equipment costs."

"Profits may be decreasing in some businesses as cremation services increase."

"Very high cost of entry into the market for a full-service funeral home. Discount operations can be started with less cash up front but this requires a much larger marketing outlay than a traditional operation. "Very high barriers to entry. Funeral home buyers are typically easy to find. Outside financing is a challenge."

Benchmark Data

Statistics (Funeral Homes)

Number of Establishments	28,556
Average profit Margin	13.5%
Revenue per Employee	$118,000
Average Number of Employees	4.1
Average Wages per Employee	$27,862

Source: IBISWorld, June 2012

Products and Services Segmentation

Traditional funeral services	38.9%
Caskets and other merchandise	25.1%
Cremation services	19.3%
Cash advances for funeral services	11.6%
Other funeral services	5.1%

Source: IBISWorld, June 2012

Industry Costs

Profit	13.5%
Wages	24.9%
Purchases	45.9%
Depreciation	2.4%
Marketing	2.1%
Rent & Utilities	5.2%
Other	6.0%

Source: IBISWorld, June 2012

Market Share

SCI	11.1%

Source: IBISWorld, June 2012

- 2010 U.S. Cremation Rate = 40.62%
  2010 Canadian Cremation Rate = 58.17%

  Source: 2010 NFDA General Price List Survey, www.nfda.org Cremation Facts—
  A bit dated, but the latest available and still of interest.

- "Average funeral expenses run $6,560.

  "Let's start with the most basic component of a traditional funeral. While the average cost of a metal casket is $2,295, Casket and Monument Discount sells metal caskets for $895. Wal-Mart offers caskets starting at $995.

  "Not everyone likes the idea of having their body stuffed in a box for eternity. They prefer cremation. That will spare you the cost of a casket, though you can rent one if you want to hold a viewing first. A viewing also entails embalming (up to $1,000, plus a few hundred dollars for dressing, cosmetics, and hair styling), something usually not required by law but considered necessary for a viewing."

  Source: "Funerals need not be a time for others to reap excess profit at your expense"
  by Andrew Meacham, *Boston Globe*, May 1, 2012

- "And, according to a survey by the National Funeral Directors Assn., women make up 60% of students in mortuary science school—up 71% from 12 years ago.

  "Typically need one licensed FD per 60–70 annual services. Licensed FD's typically earn approximately $45,000–$50,000 per year."

- "The days of the cookie-cutter funeral are fading. Staid remarks at a church or funeral home lectern are being supplemented with slide shows, and services are moving to golf or yacht clubs to reflect a person's life.

  "Nearly 41 percent of all U.S. deaths led to cremation last year, a big jump from about 15 percent in 1985, according to the Cremation association of North America.

  "Shop Around: Funeral costs vary widely. The average funeral cost about $6,500 in 2009, the latest figure from the National Funeral Directors Association."

  Source: "Times have changed in the funeral business, but it still pays to plan ahead"
  by Tom Murphy of the Associated Press, *Boston Globe*, December 20," 2011

Expenses as a Percentage of Annual Sales

Cost of goods:	20%
Payroll/labor Costs:	30%
Occupancy:	10% to 12%
Profit (estimated pretax)	30% to 35%

Industry Trend

- "Cremations will continue to increase. Average profits will likely decline."

Seller Financing

- "10–15 years"
- "15–20 percent of purchase price for 10 years"
- "7–10 years"

Questions

- "Ask about any new competitors."
- "Why is seller selling? How long has seller owned the business? How many competitors are there in the market? What are the demographics in the market? Are there any key employees in the business?"
- "Service mix varies considerably from region to region, has major impact on value of the business."
- "Check volume trends and average sales trends for at least 5 years."
- "Will he stay and help with the transition? Continuing former owner's goodwill is extremely important typically."

Resources

Associations
- National Funeral Directors Association: www.nfda.org

Furniture and Appliance Stores	
SIC Furniture Stores 5712-16	SIC Appliance Stores 5722-02
NAICS Furniture Stores 442110	NAICS Appliance Stores: 443111

Rules of Thumb

➢ 2 times monthly sales plus inventory

Pricing Tips

- Large privately held profitable furniture stores may bring as much as one times annual sales.

Benchmark Data

- "Industry average is about $325 in sales per sq. ft."

Furniture Refinishing		
SIC 7641-05	NAICS 811420	Number of Businesses/Units 23,897

Rules of Thumb

➢ 50 percent of annual sales plus inventory

Benchmark Data

Statistics (Furniture Repair & Reupholstery)

Number of Establishments.. 23,897
Average Profit Margin 5.0%
Revenue per Employee $49,000
Average Number of Employees 1.3
Average Wages per Employee $16,188

Source: IBISWorld, August 2012

Products and Services Segmentation

Office furniture repair 35%
Upholstery repair of household furniture.. 32%
Wooden household furniture repair... 24%
Other furniture repair services 9%

Source: IBISWorld, August 2012

Major Market Segmentation

Households.. 60%
Businesses 38%
Government 2%

Source: IBISWorld, August 2012

Industry Costs

Profit 5.0%
Wages... 32.9%
Purchases 31.0%
Depreciation 1.3%
Marketing 1.1%
Rent & Utilities 6.6%
Other... 22.1%

Source: IBISWorld, August 2012

Furniture Stores		
SIC 5712-16	NAICS 442110	Number of Businesses/Units 40,810

Rules of Thumb

➢ 60 percent of annual sales includes inventory

Pricing Tips

- "Analyze gross profit margin & ratio of repeat clientele to new customers."

Benchmark Data

Statistics (Furniture Store)

Number of Establishments.. 40,810
Average Profit Margin 0.9%
Revenue per Employee $229,400
Average Number of Employees 6.9
Average Wages per Employee $34,839

Source: IBISWorld, August 2012

Products and Services Segmentation

Living room furniture	43.7%
Bedroom furniture	29.4%
Dining room furniture	14.6%
Other furniture	12.3%

Source: IBISWorld, August 2012

Industry Costs

Profit	0.9%
Wages	14.9%
Purchases	56.4%
Depreciation	1.2%
Marketing	6.7%
Rent & Utilities	7.0%
Other	12.9%

Source: IBISWorld, August 2012

- "Just the Stats: Stationary upholstery accounted for 20% of furniture store sales in 2008 and accounted for 21% of selling space in furniture stores in 2008. Median best-selling price points for a leather stationary sofa, $1,199, and $799 for a fabric-covered sofa.

"Just the Stats: Master bedroom accounted for 11% of furniture store sales in 2008 and 12% of selling space in furniture stores in 2008. Median best-selling price point, $1,199.

"Just the Stats: Casual dining accounted for 11% of furniture store sales in 2008 and 14% of selling space in furniture stores in 2008. Median best-selling price points for dinette/casual dining (a table and four chairs), $699, unchanged from the year before. Average markup for table and four chairs, 1.83 times.

"Just the Stats: Formal dining accounted for 4% of furniture store sales for fiscal year 2008 and 5% of selling space in furniture stores in 2008. Median best-selling price points for a table and 4 chairs, $1,599.

Average markup for table and 4 chairs, 1.18 times."

Source: "Just the Stats," www.furnituretoday.com

Expenses as a Percentage of Annual Sales

Cost of goods:	30%
Payroll/labor Costs:	15%
Occupancy:	20%
Profit (estimated pretax)	35%

Questions

- "What is the reason for selling? Will the purchaser assume ownership of the client base? Is there already a fully functional Web site?"

Resources

Trade Publications

- Bedding Today: www.furnituretoday.com/

Garage Door Sales & Service

SIC 5211-02	NAICS 444190	Number of Businesses/Units 29,749

Rules of Thumb

➢ 25 percent of annual sales plus inventory

Benchmark Data

Statistics (Garage Door Installation)

Number of Establishments	29,749
Average Profit Margin	18.1%
Revenue per Employee	$75,400
Average Number of Employees	2
Average Wages per Employee	$26,400

Source: IBISWorld, October 2011

Products and Services Segmentation

Retrofits and upgrades	68%
Installation in new commercial construction	2%
Installation in new residential construction	10%
Repair and maintenance work	20%

Source: IBISWorld, October 2011

Major Market Segmentation

Homeowners	62%
Garage door merchants	26%
Construction firms	12%

Source: IBISWorld, October 2011

Industry Costs

Profit	18.1%
Rent	2.0%
Utilities	3.0%
Depreciation	2.3%
Other	14.4%
Wages	34.3%
Purchases	25.9%

Source: IBISWorld, October 2011

Garbage/Trash Collection (See also Waste Collection)

SIC 4953-02	NAICS 562111	Number of Businesses/Units 8,500

Rules of Thumb

➢ 1.5 to 2.5 times annual sales

Pricing Tips

- "In the larger cities, garbage routes are selling from $30 to $34 for each dollar taken in per month. Perimeter routes around the larger cities sell for $18 to $22 for each dollar taken in per month, with the smaller communities selling from $14 to $18 for each dollar taken in during the month. If the dump is owned by the garbage collector, you should also add the amount of the land and permit value."

Benchmark Data

Statistics (Waste Collection Services)

Number of Establishments	8,878
Average Profit Margin	9.4%
Revenue per Employee	$262,700
Average Number of Employees	20.7
Average Wages per Employee	$45,010

Source: IBISWorld, July 2012

Products and Services Segmentation

Other	30.1%
Non-residential waste collection services	28.2%
Residential waste collection services	21.7%
Transfer facility services	12.2%
Recyclable material collection services	7.8%

Source: IBISWorld, July 2012

Major Market Segmentation

Commercial and business firms	37%
Municipal government and individuals	32%
Industrial firms	19%
Construction and demolition firms	12%

Source: IBISWorld, July 2012

Industry Costs

Profit	9.4%
Wages	17.5%
Purchases	8.5%
Depreciation	10.5%
Marketing	1.0%
Rent & Utilities	3.0%
Other	50.1%

Source: IBISWorld, July 2012

Market Share

Waste Management	29.9%
Republic	18.1%

Source: IBISWorld, July 2012

Garden Centers/Nurseries

(See also Lawn Maintenance and Service, Landscape Services)

SIC 5261-04	NAICS 444220	Number of Businesses/Units 13,991

Rules of Thumb

➢ 25 percent of sales plus inventory

Benchmark Data

Statistics (Nursery and Garden Stores)

Number of Establishments	13,991
Average Profit Margin	1.6%
Revenue per Employee	$226,400
Average Number of Employees	8.4
Average Wages per Employee	$25,210

Source: IBISWorld, June 2012

Products and Services Segmentation

Equipment.. 48.8%
Grain and animal feed 16.7%
Chemicals 14.8%
Plants.. 10.6%
Tools and parts 5.4%
Other supplies.. 3.7%

Source: IBISWorld, June 2012

Major Market Segmentation

Baby boomers... 45%
Consumers aged 60 and up 26%
Consumers of all other ages 11%
Farmers 10%
Corporate entities 8%

Source: IBISWorld, June 2012

Industry Costs

Profit 1.6%
Wages... 11.3%
Purchases 72.6%
Depreciation 2.1%
Marketing 2.0%
Rent & Utilities 4.4%
Other 6.0%

Source: IBISWorld, June 2012

- What do you project for your 2011 sales as compared to this year?

Up more than 10 percent 8.7%
Up 15 to 10 percent 39.6%
Up 1 to 4 percent 30.2%
Flat... 16.1%
Down less than 5 percent 3.4%
Down 5 to 10 percent... 0.7%
Down more than 10 percent 1.3%

What are your top 3 areas of focus for 2011?

Increasing margins 58.7%
Better merchandising to increase sales....................................... 52.9%
Training employees for better customer service........................... 38.1%
Changing the facilities to create a better shopping environment... 35.5%
Improving my product mix.. 33.5%
Increase my marketing reach 29.0%
Hosting more events in the garden center.................................... 22.6%
Using my point-of-sales system to my advantage 14.2%
Having or increasing educational seminars in the store 13.5%
Attending more events for education and buying 1.9%

Source: *State of the Industry 2011*, Today's Garden Center, December 2010

- How many year-round employees does your organization have?

5 or fewer.. 55%
6 to 10 .... 20%
11 to 15 .... 10%
20 to 25 .... 3%
More than 25.. 12%

Source: www.todaysgardencenter.com/magazine

Industry Trend

- "What Will 2013 Bring?
- To sum up the past year for independent garden centers in one word it would

be RELIEF for many from the accumulated strain of bad weather and poor economy. Some have been treading water and others have been swimming forward. Both activities are strenuous and fatiguing. Those who have been treading water may stay alive to see another spring. Those who have been moving forward may be closer to a distant shore they cannot yet see."

Source: Sid Raisch is founder of Horticultural Advantage, a consulting firm to independent garden centers and service provider to The Garden Center Group. He created the Advantage Development System to help client companies increase effectiveness to earn greater profits. For more, go to AdvantageDevelopmentSystem.com

Questions

- Here are some key questions to get answered in analyzing garden centers:
- How many months are you open for business (determine season)? If not open all year, which months are you open?
- What method do you use to value your ending inventory (e.g., cost)?
- What makes up your inventory in the winter months?
- How are obsolete/damaged goods accounted for?
- What is your policy regarding returns and allowances for plants?
- Do you have a slow season? Which months? What other sources of income do you have during the slow season?
- Who are your major suppliers (any related parties)?
- What services do you provide? (Landscaping, lawn service, delivery, plant rental, etc.?)

Source: The above is excerpted from an IRS Audit Technique Guide (Market Segment Specialization Program—MSSAP).

Gas Stations — Full-and/or Self-Serve

(See also Convenience Stores with Gas)

SIC 5541-01	NAICS 447190	Number of Businesses/Units 18,059

Rules of Thumb

➢ Note: Some of the information that follows is also in C-Stores with Gas. It is a confusing issue, and perhaps there is no difference between a C-store with gas and a gas station with a C-store, but many experts still feel that there is. So here goes, again: Convenience stores with gas—these operations are more convenience stores than gas stations such as a 7-Eleven or Circle K. Gas stations with convenience stores (mini-marts)— these operations are more gas stations than convenience stores, such as Mobil, Shell and Exxon gas stations that have convenience stores. In many cases, the garages and stations themselves have been retrofitted to be convenience stores. These operations may include a car wash.

➢ 10 to 15 percent of annual sales plus inventory

➢ 2.5 to 3 times SDE plus inventory

➢ 2.5 to 3.0 times EBIT

➢ 2.5 to 3.5 times EBITDA (business only)

➢ 1.5 to 2.5 SDE (with service bays, business only) plus inventory

➢ 5 to 6 times SDE includes real estate

> ➤ 5 to 7 times EBITDA—business and real estate
>
> ➤ "4 to 6 times EBITDA including the real estate is a good rule of thumb for convenience stores with gas. 2 to 3.5 times EBITDA for leased sites. Age and condition of the petroleum equipment and environmental issues are important considerations in selling these businesses. A phase I & II report are required for both purchased and leased sites."

Pricing Tips

- "Buyers are looking for high volume gas stations, the norm is the higher the gasoline volume per month the more attractive the business becomes. That being said you also need to be aware of the margin on each gallon of gas sold. Find out if the tanks underground have been inspected in the last year and meet or exceed EPA and local standards. Ask if any leaks or hazardous waste has been found/detected on the premises in the last ten years. If the gas station has a convenience store associated the value is higher, if there is a car wash the value increases again."

- "Service Stations are more than dispensers of gasoline. The typical station has one or more of the following sources of revenue:
  - ✓ Gasoline
  - ✓ Diesel fuel
  - ✓ Sale of Vehicles
  - ✓ Car Wash
  - ✓ Mini-Markets
  - ✓ Lottery
  - ✓ Check Cashing
  - ✓ Propane
  - ✓ Scales
  - ✓ Repair Shops with or without Tow
  - ✓ Towing
  - ✓ Kerosene"

  Source: www.irs.gov/business/small/article

- "The multiples used to be as high as 4.5 to 5 times the SDE in 2003. The eroding profit margin, measured as cents per gallon, has tightened up in the marketplace since then, resulting in forcing the gas station owner to look for volumes and margins elsewhere in the station. The snack shop/convenience store section has stepped up to the plate and accounts for about 80% of the profits, while the other 20% and all of the gasoline margin goes towards the costs of employees and such. Depending on the rent or the mortgage structure, the 80% figures adjust up or down. Do not let the huge sales volumes fool you; measure the gallons times the margin, and not the millions in actual sales/revenue figures."

- "3 x SDE or 2–3 times EBIT are the best; the percentage of annual gross sales doesn't reflect a fair price."

- "3 to 4 times EBITDA including the real estate."

- "Margins are getting squeezed in some areas, therefore must be taken into consideration."

- "Gross sales is not a good factor in pricing, since the profit margin varies between gas and grocery sales."

- "3 to 4 times EBITDA including the real estate is a common rule. Location, traffic count, brand, and population are important considerations."
- "It has nothing to do with total sales volume or revenue. It does have everything to do with average gallons sold, and margins per gallon; volatility in industry requires you map out gallons and margins per month for last 2 years. Majors tend to have flat fixed margins, minors and unbranded markets move between 2–4 cents to high of 25%–30% margins."
- "Multiple of 2x SDE is mid-point of the range 1.75-2.25x SDE, and does not include the real estate. This range is applicable to Arizona statewide, and it narrows when considering 3 identifiable markets within AZ: Phoenix metro, Tucson metro, and rural. Real estate, when included, may be priced separately and added to SDE multiple, or 'digested' in the business valuation by a higher range of multiples. Real estate valuations may be considered by the same 3 Arizona markets, but should also consider the class of property, i.e., A, B & C. The full range when including real estate is approx. 5X SDE for a C-class property in rural AZ, to 14x for a Class-A property in Phoenix metro."
- "Dealer stations in our market sell for 2.2 to 2.5 post due diligence SDE for the business only. I value gas stations with the land by starting with SDE and deducting the buyer's required income for managing the station and any necessary reserves, and then I capitalize that amount by what I feel is the market cap rate. This is basically a real estate approach to the value."
- "Fewer and fewer stations surviving in today's competitive market."
- "2 or 3 times net SDE—most stores have horrible records . . . proof of numbers is through gas receipts and store invoices. Gallons per month, pool margin, inside sales, other income and do the tanks meet 2009 standards."
- "Factors that most influence value are: volume of gasoline sales, location, length, C-store versus service bays, traffic count and major brand identity."
- "Age of tanks; does station have canopy (is it cantilever or mech. attached); is it clean (environment); location, location, location."
- "The geographical site/location is key to a buyer in many offers and subsequent sells. Near freeways or interstates, high visibility corner locations or locations near major malls all come with a premium price tag to the buyer."
- "Stand-alone gas stations are dwindling in number as it is difficult to survive on just gasoline alone. Most stations are also service garages and/or have some other profit center to generate income."
- "Gas only: 2 to 2.5 times SDE plus inventory
  Gas with food market: 2.5 to 3 times SDE plus inventory
  Gas with car wash/food mart: 2.5 to 4 times SDE plus inventory
  Gas with garage/repair: 1.5 to 2 times SDE plus inventory"

Expert Comments

"With the consumer watching every penny, the inside store sales are declining, and rising gas prices are not helping either. A good combination of competitive gas prices, inside store markdown sale with cross merchandising will help the gas station owners move through these difficult times."

"Major oil companies are getting out of owning properties and managing labor. More and more newer immigrants are getting into locations as owners across the country. Oil companies primarily want to be in the fuel supply business as their core profit driver."

"Stand-alone gasoline stations are dwindling in number. Most stations have some other profit center like a service garage, or lube center etc."

"A gas station is not easy to replicate by any means, with all the environmental regulations and what have you. The profit trend is definitely downwards, with non-branded or independent owners who primarily buy product on the open spot market being hammered the most. The branded market seems to want to try to chase non-branded independents out of the market with their pricing on racks."

"Risk in the gas station business is mostly systemic relating to the overall economy. Pricing risk of fuel involves international political risks affecting supply, etc. Demand risk relates to the current economic recession/ depression. Difficulty of replication stems from financing for ground-up projects—available exclusively at this time from private sources; no institutional money for construction."

"With the way the economy is now, it's very tough to generate a decent profit out of a gas station, Customers looking for cheaper gas, cheaper groceries, increased use of credit cards—all this affects the business; and with the big oil companies like Racetrac and QT opening stores every day, they are affecting independent gas stations big time."

"It is getting very expensive to build a new ground-up facility. Average does cost close to $2 million, therefore it is not that easy to replicate. Not to mention the uphill battle with most urban zoning requirements which causes lengthy delays and adds to the soft costs."

"Gas stations are very tough businesses; with increasing gas prices and increasing big corporate stores like QT and Racetrac, competition will always be high."

"Competition might be a business killer; risky business; the profit trend is almost the same, didn't change much; the location and the facility condition affects the business on a large scale; the marketability of this business is high due to a large supply of buyers; this industry will always be in demand even with the presence of big corporate stations like Racetrac and QT still growing."

"Gas stations are easy to market, especially with the real estate. competition declining, since some stations choose to close rather than face environmental upgrades. Profit trends downward on gasoline, with gas profit paying some to most of costs only. Marts/snack shops/stores are major moneymaking factors,"

"Very competitive industry today with the hypermarkets, grocery stores, and big box retailers all getting into the convenience store industry. Location is everything with traffic count, population, and highway access critical to success."

"Hard to replicate due to site work needed and tank cost"

Benchmark Data

Statistics (Gas Stations)

Number of Establishments	18,059
Average Profit Margin	1.8%
Revenue per Employee	$793,500
Average Number of Employees	9.6
Average Wages per Employee	$21,032

Source: IBISWorld, July 2012

Products and Services Segmentation

Gas 56%
Diesel 34%
Automotive services (e.g. repairs and car washes) 5.5%
Automotive parts 2.5%
Non-automotive parts 2%

Source: IBISWorld, July 2012

Major Market Segmentation

Freight companies 56.4%
General public 8.9%
Public transportation and government vehicles 14.2%
Private transportation companies 20.5%

Source: IBISWorld, July 2012

Industry Costs

Profit 1.8%
Wages 2.7%
Purchases 80.0%
Depreciation 0.8%
Marketing 1.5%
Rent & Utilities 5.0%
Other 8.2%

Source: IBISWorld, October 2012

Market Share

Shell 10.0%
BP PLC 8.3%
Chevron Corporation 6.1%

Source: IBISWorld, July 2012

- "There were 157,393 total retail fueling outlets in the United States in 2011. This is a steep and steady decline since 1994, when the station count topped 202,800 sites. This count includes convenience stores, grocery stores, truck stops, traditional gas stations and low-volume locations like marinas. "U.S. retail (regular) gasoline prices averaged $3.53 in 2011. Compared to 2010, gasoline prices were 74 cents per gallon higher in 2011, largely because of the higher costs of crude oil (59 cents per gallon) and higher refinery margins (12 cents per gallon)."
- "If the gas station does 150k+ gallons per month with a gas margin of .20 cents or higher per gallon the convenience store is doing at least $45k per month, this would be recognized as a good opportunity."

Source: National Association of Convenience Stores

- "Good locations should do upwards of $400 per sq. ft."
- "The minimum acceptable inside store volumes are about $3.00 per 100 gallons. So, if the station does about 60,000 gallons of fuel, it must do a minimum of $18,000 in store sales to survive. The cigarettes category, the largest dollar sales and up to 38% of total inside sales volume, continues to suffer due to government regulations and increased taxation. The alternative category of water and energy drinks continues to suffer in first half of 2009, mainly due to economic forces."
- "Adding prepared meals in the store tends to increase the bottom line since these items have a high profit margin."
- "Crude-Oil Suppliers: 95 cents—Since the summer, crude's price per barrel has dropped more than 70%. Canada reaps the largest share of our crude-oil dollars Saudi Arabia and other OPEC nations produce 20% of the oil we consume.

G - Rules of Thumb

"Oil Companies: 23 cents—Large firms such as ExxonMobil and BP make money on oil drilling, refining and distribution. On average, big oil's after-tax profit equals a healthy 8% of the pump price, which is why the oil companies were raking it in when you paid more than $4 a gallon.

"Your state and city: 23 cents—These taxes, and the price you ultimately pay at the pump, vary widely. New Yorkers shell out 41 cents a gallon, while Georgians hand over only about 12 cents.

"The Feds: 18 cents—For now Washington's cut is fixed at this amount. Congressional commissions are urging lawmakers to increase the tax to pay for road projects.

"Service Stations: 10 cents—After paying expenses, station owners make a measly few cents of profit per gallon. High gas prices don't change that, since they increase the amount that stations pay in credit-card fees and shrink their margins. (Stations make most of their money selling coffee, snacks and the like.)"

Source: "Where Your Money Goes for a $1.68 &9/10 Gallon of Gas," *Money Magazine*, March 2009. Note: Numbers are U.S. averages as of December 2008. Breakdowns are estimates based on data from the Department of Energy, the Association of Pipelines, the American Petroleum, the Association for Convenience & Petroleum Retailing, and *Money* research.

- "$450–$500 per sq. ft."
- "Traditional Benchmark Data still are looked for when considering the early stage feasibility of buying an operating station: fuel volume (gals/mo.) and store sales without lottery. Given the complexity of the variables and trends, these have become less valid in assessing the future success of a gas station business. A better starting point I believe is the overall historical SDE. Capitalizing this to a price must consider the value of the real estate and the quality of the property, including location. Estimated pretax profit (below) is historically understated with private companies in AZ, hence the need to determine SDE. The number provided is representative of the pretax profit, but seldom a valid representation of the financial benefit accruing to the owner."
- "Auto repair facilities, not found too easily any more, are more profitable per square foot than markets. However, auto repairs must be run right, and carry a lot of headaches with them."
- "A good gas station should pump at least 1.2 million gas gallons yearly."
- "Gross profit per gallon is what generates the income."

Expenses as a Percentage of Annual Sales

Cost of goods:.. 75%
Payroll/labor Costs:.. 08% to 10%
Occupancy: .... 05% to 10%
Profit (estimated pretax) .... 03% to 05%

Industry Trend

- "The entire Gas and Oil industry is changing and evolving rapidly. Research continues as alternative sources of gasoline are evolving into forms of bio fuel, ethanol, propel, biodiesel, flex fuel E85, cellulose ethanol, shale, along with natural gas, electric and battery-charged vehicles becoming more prevalent. Agricultural waste and other non-edible plant products such as stalks, husks, woodchips and grasses are cellulosic fodder for advanced ethanol production. The structural components of plants, or cellulose, can be processed by enzymes or acetogens, broken down into sugars and fermented to produce alcohol-based fuels like ethanol. Since cellulose is not used for food, it's often an industry byproduct, and can be sourced from a variety of fast-growing plants; cellulosic-based ethanol is even more sustainable and energy-efficient than traditional ethanol." "I think in general we are passing the worst of the economic downturn, but being smart in keeping the regular customer will be a tough challenge."

- "With the downturn in the economy there is pressure to push the asking prices downward since cash & credit is tighter."
- "Steady growth. Even if the type of fuel changes from gasoline to another product it will be still sold through a fuel station of sorts, therefore the business model is stable."
- "Decline. Most stand-alone gasoline stations cannot survive without other profit centers."
- "In south Florida trend is to LARGER stores, 2000 sq feet or more. More food service inside the larger C-store; repair bays are history."

Seller Financing

- "3 years, on average 8 percent interest per annum."
- "As much as 50 percent of sales price could be financed—3 to 5 years typical."
- "Franchise—2 to 3 years (5 to 10 percent)"
- "Property—10 to 15 years (8 to 11 percent)"

Questions

- "5 years' financial and gallonage history; phase I & II environmental reports"
- "Any new competition? Security & safety? Road construction? Introduction to vendors."
- "Gallons history, margins history, both for last four years; plot against spot prices to see how tight street pricing gets on that street."
- "The quality of their historical financial statements, including both income statements and balance sheets. This is both for prospective buyer due diligence and lender requirements."
- "As much paperwork as possible to get to the truth"
- "Status of the underground tanks."
- "Some Key Questions

  A buyer would want to ask the current owner if the oil company owns the property or if the land is leased to the oil company. The value of the business will be less if the land is leased from another entity. The reason is that when the lease expires, even if there are options, the oil company may decide not to renew. Make sure the oil company owns the property; worst case make sure the lease for the station runs at least for another 10 years (when the oil company does not own the land). Buyers should also be concerned about the types of tanks that are underground—are they steel or fiberglass? If the owner has steel tanks, find out why the tanks have not been replaced with fiberglass. Ask the current owner if there have been any leaks or contamination. If the answer is yes, find out when and to what extent. Has the problem been corrected?"
- "One should also find out who is responsible for any and all contamination that lies above or below the surface of the site. Always require, in an offer to purchase agreement, a clause that states that the buyer will perform as part of the due diligence a Phase I report by an accredited environmental or chemical

engineer who has a license to do so, with the results approved to the buyer's satisfaction. If a Phase II or III report is required, it is strongly suggested that it be done as well."

Resources

Trade Publications
- National Petroleum News: www.npnweb.com

Gas Stations w/Convenience Stores/MiniMarts

(See also Gas Stations and Convenience Store w/gas)

SIC 5541-01	NAICS 447110	Number of Businesses/Units 92,100

Rules of Thumb

➢ Note: The information that follows is also in C-Stores with Gas. It is a confusing issue, and perhaps there is no difference between a C-store with gas and a gas station with a C-store, but many experts still feel that there is. So here goes, again: Convenience stores with gas—these operations are more convenience stores than gas stations such as a 7-Eleven or Circle K. Gas stations with convenience stores (mini-marts)— these operations are more gas stations than convenience stores, such as Mobil, Shell and Exxon gas stations that have convenience stores. In many cases, the garages and stations themselves have been retrofitted to be convenience stores. These operations may include a car wash.

➢ 20 to 25 percent of annual sales plus inventory

➢ 80 percent of annual sales with real estate plus inventory

➢ 4.0 to 4.5 times SDE plus inventory, when a full service car wash is included (min. $250k SDE)

➢ 4 to 5 SDE with mini-mart (minimum 800 sq. ft.), 200K gals/mo., with the mini-mart $35K+/mo

➢ 3 to 4 times EBIT

➢ 2.5 to 3.75 times EBITDA (business only)

➢ 4 times EBITDA

➢ 4 to 7 times EBITDA—business and real estate, with car wash or large convenience store included

➢ 7 times EBITDA with real estate

Pricing Tips
- "3 to 5 times EBITDA including the real estate is a general rule. Location, traffic count, population, are important considerations."
- "Buyers are looking for high volume gas stations, the norm is the higher the gasoline volume per month the more attractive the business becomes. That being said you also need to be aware of the margin on each gallon of gas sold. Find out if the tanks underground have been inspected in the last year and meet or exceed EPA and local standards. Ask if any leaks or hazardous waste has been found/detected on the premises in the last ten years. If the gas

station has a convenience store associated the value is higher, if there is a car wash the value increases again."

"The value of gas stations, at least in the Northeast, is impacted strongly by the age and viability of the underground storage tanks. These can cost $200,000 or more to replace and many single-walled tanks are required by the state governments to be removed from the ground. Another significant determinant of value is the fuel supply agreement. If the location is controlled by a fuel distributor or oil company, the business is usually worth less because a new owner will not have the ability to buy fuel on the open market."

- "The multiples used to be higher, however due to market conditions they have come down approx. 20% in the last two years. The eroding profit margin, measured as cents per gallon, has tightened up in the marketplace since then, resulting in forcing the gas station owner to look for volumes and margins elsewhere in the station. The snack shop/convenience store section has stepped up to the plate and accounts for about 80% of the profits, while the other 20% and all of the gasoline margin goes towards the costs of employees and such. Depending on the rent or the mortgage structure, the 80% figures adjust up or down. Do not let the huge sales volumes fool you; measure the gallons times the margin, and not the millions in actual sales/revenue figures."

- "2 to 3 x SDE are the best multiples; the percentage of annual gross sales doesn't reflect a fair price."

- "4 to 6 times EBITDA including the real estate."

- "Margins are getting squeezed in some areas, therefore must be taken into consideration."

- "Gross sales is not a good factor in pricing, since the profit margin varies between gas and grocery sales."

- "4 to 6 times EBITDA including the real estate is a common rule. Location, traffic count, brand, and population are important considerations."

- "It has nothing to do with total sales volume or revenue. It does have everything to do with average gallons sold, and margins per gallon; volatility in industry requires you map out gallons and margins per month for last 2 years. Majors tend to have flat fixed margins, minors and unbranded markets move between 2–4 cents to high of 25%–30% margins."

- "Multiple of 2x SDE is mid-point of the range 1.75-2.75x SDE, and does not include the real estate. may be priced separately and added to SDE multiple, or 'digested' in the business valuation by a higher range of multiples. Real estate valuations may be considered by the same 3 Arizona markets, but should also consider the class of property, i.e., A, B & C. The full range when including real estate is approx. 5X SDE for a C-class property in rural AZ, to 14x for a Class-A property in Phoenix metro." "Dealer stations in our market sell for 2.2 to 2.5 post due diligence SDE excluding property (California). I value gas stations with the land by starting with SDE and deducting the buyer's required income for managing the station and any necessary reserves, and then I capitalize that amount by what I feel is the market cap rate. This is basically a real estate approach to the value."

- "Factors that most influence value are: volume of gasoline sales, location, length, C-store versus service bays, traffic count and major brand identity."

- "Age of tanks; does station have canopy (is it cantilever or mech. attached); is it clean (environment); location, location, location."

- "The geographical site/location is key to a buyer in many offers and subsequent sells. Near freeways or interstates, high visibility corner locations or locations near major malls all come with a premium price tag."

- "4 to 6 times EBITDA including the real estate is a good rule of thumb for convenience stores with gas. 2 to 3.5 times EBITDA for leased sites. Current and future requirements from oil companies are reducing the overall number of stations across the country. Before you purchase any gas station make sure you ask the oil company what the future of that particular site is scheduled for in the future."

- "Age and condition of the petroleum equipment and environmental issues are important considerations in selling and buying these businesses. A phase I & II report are required for both purchased and leased sites. Standard SBA loans are becoming more challenging as we all are aware, find the bank or lending institution in your area who provides the best opportunity for a bank/SBA loan for gas stations and convenience stores."

- "This industry has gone through some major changes within the core structure from 5 or 10 years ago. Mergers and buy-outs have affected the competition in the market place. With only 4 majors now in the network we have seen a steady rise in consumer retail prices at the pumps. Along with the mergers and billion dollar buy-outs we have also noticed within the industry substantial increases in the franchisee rents as well as diminished profits."

- "Major oil companies (Exxon-Mobil, Chevron, BP, etc.) have greatly enhanced their profits over the last 2 to 3 years. If the trend continues, I foresee Federal controls of some degree, price caps versus the price per barrel of crude oil. Owner pool margins have increased in the last several years also, now averaging, .20 to .30 cents per gallon."

- "Average gallons pumped on a monthly basis (minimum 150K) are normally a good station. Another factor is the pool margin (minimum .20 cents per gallon is good)."
  "Conditions that can affect the overall value are gas stations with mechanical bays or gas only, short-term lease, oil company does not own the property, history of soil contamination, low sales volume, appearance, outdated equipment, poor geographical location."

- "Some factors that detract are small lot size and access issues."

- "The most valid pricing comes from capitalizing adjusted cash flow, or SDE. If the gas station acquisition includes the real estate, this either needs to be broken out and priced in addition to the business, or digested in the capitalization calculation. Severely reduced transaction volume, little or no new construction, and poorly defined interest rate scale to define risk (& CAP rates) due to government intermediation make the standard approaches to pricing uncertain."

- "Profit margin on gasoline should be more than 6 cents per gallon. Store gross margins will average 20% to 25%. Pricing is based on DE, not gross, since margins are small and reflective of competition."

- "Question: What are some of the unique issues involved in valuing a gas station/convenience store? Answer: There are several issues. These stores are special-purpose properties, and the underlying value includes the incremental value associated with the business enterprise, which is distinct from the value of the real estate. Bifurcating the real estate and business components is therefore a significant issue. Other important issues include:

✓ Fuel volumes
✓ Number and type of fuel dispensers and related payment technology
✓ Site location and visibility
✓ Condition and deferred maintenance
✓ Size
✓ Demographic and regional growth trends
✓ Branded versus unbranded
✓ Number and distance of competitors
✓ Traffic counts
✓ Diversification of revenue streams
✓ Ingress and egress
✓ Profitability and trends

It is important to conduct a site visit to properly understand the strengths and weaknesses of the subject location and ascertain the competitive threats. One issue that people don't really consider, but it's an important one, is ingress and egress and the barriers to access a location. The ease of being able to get in and out of the property is going to have an impact on the valuation because people want to get in and out quickly and don't want to be inconvenienced by required turning maneuvers, crossing traffic lanes, or having to make a U-turn. They would rather access a station that's in their direct path as opposed to maneuvering into another station.

"Question: How do you handle a gas station/convenience store with multiple revenue streams? Answer: The diversification of revenue lowers the overall risk profile of the gas station/convenience store and reduces the dependence on the lower-margin gas sales. The inside sales or the convenience store aspect typically has much higher margins than gas sales. The more revenue sources there are, the more diversification there is in the business, which helps lower the overall risk profile and related discount rate."

Source: "Special Issues to Consider When Valuing a Gas Station/Convenience Store" by Lynton Kotzin, CPA/ABV, CBA, ASA, CFA, and managing partner of Kotzin Valuation Partners, LLC

- "The age of the station plays a big part in the valuation. Buyers are wary of stations more than 10 years old, due to environmental risk and wear/tear on the facility."

- "Prices are higher if there is high gasoline volume and store sales and less competition. Highway sites, businesses with co-brands and businesses with excellent store sales score higher."

- "Normally 7 times EBITDA with real estate and 4–5 times without real estate in Midwest."

- "First the quality of the assets will always come into play. Are the building and the roof and the parking lot and the refrigeration equipment in good condition? Does the business have a fuel purchase agreement with its supplier and is it long term and what are the terms and costs of the agreement? And what is the environmental status of the property? Are there any known incidents on file or does there need to be a phase 1 or phase 2?"

- "3 to 5 times EBITDA including the real estate is a general rule. Location, traffic count, brand, population, and competition are all important considerations."

- "5–7 times with real estate for stores doing $70k+ inside and 70k+ gallons per month"

- "SDE should be at or about $100,000 before businesses will generate strong buyers' interest."

- "2 to 3 times EBITDA for business alone or 3 to 5 times business with property"
- "C-Stores with gas are still the staple of the small business which typically most immigrant communities seem to be purchasing due to the stability and ease of operation."
- "Gasoline volume and gasoline margin are key indicators of value; beer/wine license receives a higher price; store size greater than 1000 sq. ft. gets a higher price; length of time and type of fuel contract; franchised vs independent impacts price but depends on area."
- "Factors that increase the value include a long-term lease, no contract with a major oil company (so the buyer can negotiate his own contract), strong convenience store and/or strong co-brand. Factors that decrease the value include strong competition, lack of space for development, small lot size, full-service gasoline requirements."
- "The rule of thumb when valuing a convenience store with real estate is 5–6 x EBITDA; without real estate, it is 2–3 x EBITDA plus inventory. Questions to ask from the seller are: Is the store branded (Mobil, BP, Shell etc.) and if so how long is the contract to the brand? You need to know this, because the buyer may want to change the brand, and there will be a financial obligation to the brand to get out of the commitment."
- "3 to 5 times EBITDA including real estate; 2.0 to 3.5 times EBITDA for leased sites. Age and condition of petroleum equipment, and environmental issues are important considerations in selling these businesses. A phase I & II are required."
- "A business including real estate could command a 5 multiple of EBITDA. Multiples can be shaded by exclusivity, barriers to new competition, quality of the improvements, etc."
- "6–7 times EBITDA with the real estate included for a branded decent store doing over $50,000 inside sales and 50,000 gallons per month.
- "Individual operator buyers are looking for stores that are management run/ absentee owned where they can get in and run the stores themselves. This enables them to know what is walking in and out of the store, alleviate high payrolls, plus another 12% payroll tax, maybe some workers compensation, better be able to know about markups, etc. There are lots of buyers for these stores, which is driving price up versus the traditional EBITDA method of valuation."

Expert Comments

"Location, location, location; the industry is being dominated by National and Regional players with deep pockets."

"Competition in this industry is relatively high with a good number of oil companies actively advertising their product."

"Major oil companies are selling off their company-owned stations. More foreign buyers are coming into the marketplace. Oil companies primarily want to be in the fuel supply business as their core profit driver."

"Stand-alone gasoline stations (gas only) are dwindling in numbers. Most stations have some other profit center like a car wash, convenience store, food franchises, service garage, or lube center."

"A gas station is not easy to replicate by any means, with all the environmental regulations and what have you. The profit trend is definitely downwards, with non-branded or independent owners who primarily buy product on the open spot market being hammered the most. The branded market seems to want to try to chase non-branded independents out of the market with their pricing on racks."

"Risk in the gas station business is mostly systemic relating to the overall economy. Pricing risk of fuel involves international political risks affecting supply, etc. Demand risk relates to the current economic recession/ depression. Difficulty of replication stems from financing for ground-up projects —available exclusively at this time from private sources; no institutional money for construction."

"With the way the economy is now, it's very tough to generate a decent profit out of a gas station, Customers looking for cheaper gas, cheaper groceries, increased use of credit cards—all this affects the business; and with the big oil companies like Racetrac and QT opening stores every day, they are affecting independent gas stations big time."

"It is getting very expensive to build a new ground-up facility. Average cost $ 2+ million, therefore it is costly to replicate. Not to mention the uphill battle with most urban zoning requirements which causes lengthy delays and adds to the soft costs."

"Gas stations are becoming more challenging; with increases in gas prices and increases in big corporate stores like Costco and Wal-Mart, competition will always be high."

"Competition might be a business killer; risky business; the profit trend is almost the same, didn't change much; the location and the facility condition affects the business on a large scale; the marketability of this business is high due to a large supply of buyers; this industry will always be in demand even with the presence of big corporate stations like Racetrac and QT still growing."

"Gas stations and car washes are becoming more available in the listing base and not selling near as quickly as in the past. Financing is difficult to acquire as the main reason, also the drop in profitability along with rising rent factors are making gas stations less appealing. Some independent stations choose to close rather than face environmental upgrades. Profit trends downward on gasoline, with gas profit paying some to most of costs only. Marts/snack shops/stores are major moneymaking factors."

"Very competitive industry today with the hyper markets, grocery stores, and big box retailers all getting into the convenience store industry. Location is everything with traffic count, population, and highway access critical to success."

"Hard to replicate due to site work needed and tank cost"

"Good high-volume single stores are hard to find and they are usually older stores"

"Gas stations are perhaps the closest thing we have to perfect competition in the world. Prices are readily visible and there are almost always plenty of competitors to give the customer a choice. The risk level is relatively low because there are few fluctuations in volume from year to year. There is some risk in the fuel margin, as the margin is highly dependent on what the commodity market for fuel is doing. Profits remain steady in the fuel and in the stores, with the possibility for a little rise in profitability in the Northeast with the exit of two major oil companies (Shell and Mobil) from the retail business and the removal of some of their fuel price subsidies. Regulations continue to be a burden that erodes the profitability of the typical location, but the consolidation of the industry has somewhat offset that. Good gas stations are highly marketable— there is a seemingly endless supply of buyers, usually foreign-born (Indian, Pakistani, Lebanese, etc.). The industry is mature and consolidating, and gas will someday go away as a fuel source, so it is in a long and slow decline. The gas station/c-store model is fairly easy to replicate. Gas stations with service bays are not so easy to replicate."

"Location, location, and location is the major factor in determining success in this business."

"Barrier to entry in this business is high, as the same inventory of gas stations keeps changing hands and opening new gas stations is very difficult due to regulations."

"High competition, but owner operators can compete on service and quality of products."

"The recession (depression) of the last couple years has taken a significant number of stations out of the business—hence, less competition. Also, in AZ there hasn't been any significant construction of new units since the early 2000s. Increased risk stems primarily from a foggy horizon for economic recovery, which also speaks to the expected profit trends. Difficulty in new unit construction comes primarily from lack of financing - this is also a challenge for existing station acquisition, given that the historic profit trends for stations coming to market are trending down."

"Major chain operations are taking over the markets and hurting the small mom and pop gas station with pricing and quick service (# of gas pumps)."

"The gas station industry is consolidating and going through the same types of changes that are occurring with hardware stores, pharmacies and local general stores. These other types of stores are being challenged by stores like Home Depot, Walgreens and Wal-Mart. The small, local, full-service gas station is being supplanted by large Hess, Mobil, Exxon or Shell stations that have large convenience stores, car washes and co-brands. These large stores are able to pump a lot more volume than the older sites and therefore need less margin to survive. This is compounded by the fact that the larger stores have stronger ancillary revenues from their convenience stores and other revenue sources. A modern store is more easily marketable. The older sites are being transformed into other retail uses, like banks and coffee shops."

"Expensive to build a new store. Contamination issues are a major factor in marketability and financing."

"Large Gas/C-Store locations are the norm and become pretty difficult for most competitors to build easily."

"The convenience store industry is a very competitive industry with over

145,000 stores in the United States. Over the years the big box retailers entered the business with Walmart, K Mart, Costco and various other chains that work on a smaller margin. Although the industry is easy to enter with the building of a box and adding gasoline and grocery items, the American public still likes new things and continues to be attracted to the bright and shiny businesses. Plus the newer stores are larger in size and offerings of products such as fast food or other food items for the convenience store shopper. The selling of convenience stores is still very much alive with the building of new stores and the older ones being sold off to independent operators. Typical retail environment where an owner will be working many hours."

"There continues to be consolidation in the gas station arena. The number of gas stations is steadily declining even as the population grows. There are more sites with convenience stores, and gas stations are being affected by tough competition much in the same way as pharmacies and 'five and dime' stores have been in the last 10–15 years. Bigger, cleaner, more competitive stores continue to sprout up while tired old service stations continue to close."

"Location, Location, Location is the major factor in determining a store's success!"

"Margins fluctuate greatly; Majors are divesting their corporate stores; Circle K and Quik Trip are dominating the c-store industry in our state [Arizona]."

"The gas station industry continues to consolidate rapidly. With the exit of big oil companies like Chevron, Mobil and Shell from gasoline retail, we will likely see consolidation continue for three to five years and then possibly see the industry fragment slightly. Large multi-site operators will buy many of the major oil companies' locations, with some being left over for the smaller operators. Consolidation will continue to hurt the small mom & pop operation and help the large-volume highway and busy main thoroughfare locations."

"It costs nearly $2 million to build a new location. The soft costs are high also, as urban zoning laws can delay and add to the cost."

"Gas stations and C-stores have been in high demand and as a result prices paid have been exaggerated compared to many businesses. Some buyers try to buy low and then re-sell in 2–3 years and make their profit when they sell. Make sure to verify financials."

"This is a $570 billion annual gross sales yielding net over $5 billion profit industry. The trend indicates historically stable growth, easy to replicate and also relatively easy to market as long as seller has books and records to substantiate the operational profit. In general, success of store clearly depends on location, condition of gasoline equipment and fixtures, traffic count & patterns, demographic of immediate trading area. However one has to be cautious in selection of a business site. There are often victims of small stores facing dreadful competition with a big box gas store like Wawa or Sheetz. A retailer has to have crucial research, not limited to a county economic development agency, to find out any possible agenda for an incoming competitor in the area, prior to deciding to purchase a store."

"High barrier to entry due to amount of capital needed to build stations; large entry of foreign investors; often find sellers with inadequate financial statements."

"More competition and larger facilities. More local land restrictions. Higher land and building costs."

"Huge superstores make it hard to compete in large populations. Good stores are hiding in smaller communities with less competition. If you find a store in a good location, you can bet one of the big boys will also think it is a good location and soon join you. Make sure you are landlocked or closest to the Interstate."

"The convenience store industry is in turmoil due to entry of the big box retailers and the reduced profit margins on fuel sales. As with many other industries, people continue to build the newer, brighter, bigger, shiny stores and cannibalize the older ones. The big get bigger, and the weak get shoved out."

"Consolidation! But, newer and better sites are being built. Small operators are constantly buying and selling sites discarded by the majors and many are doing better than previously (when being run by larger corporations). Replication is easy, but the cost is prohibitive. Average build-up cost is $1.8 million to construct a new gas/C-store."

Benchmark Data

Statistics (Gas Stations with Convenience Stores)

Number of Establishments	92,200
Average Profit Margin	2.0%
Revenue per Employee	$495,100
Average Number of Employees	7.4
Average Wages per Employee	16,821

Source: IBISWorld, June 2012

Products and Services Segmentation

Gasoline	63%
Groceries	12%
Diesel	08%
Tobacco products	07%
Packaged alcoholic beverages	04%
Meals and snacks	03%

Source: IBISWorld, June 2012

Industry Costs

Profit	2.0%
Wages	3.5%
Purchases	82.5%
Depreciation	1.0%
Marketing	4.0%
Rent & Utilities	4.5%
Other	2.5%

Source: IBISWorld, June 2012

- "If the gas station does 150k+ gallons per month with a gas margin of .20cents or higher per gallon, the convenience store is doing at least $45k per month, this would be recognized as a good opportunity."

- "Motor fuels sales accounted for more than two-thirds of the convenience store industry's sales in 2010 (67%). However, because of low margins, motor fuels sales contributed less than one-third of total store gross margins dollars (26%)."
- "The average convenience store in 2010 sold roughly 124,000 gallons of motor fuels per month, which translates into approximately 4,000 gallons per day."
- "Gasoline gross profit is about ten cents on each gallon, convenience stores have 30% gross profit and car washes have about 80% gross profit. Gas stations with car washes are highly recommended to those buyers who do not want to buy a repair facility as part of the gas station."
- "100,000 gallons of gas sold per month is a minimum for a profitable station. $50,000+ per month is minimum for the convenience store sales."
- "Fuel margins in the Northeast average somewhere around 15 cents per gallon. Convenience store margins are around 25%–30%. A successful business can be measured by sales and margin. Any store with 1 million + gallons and $750,000 + in store sales (provided the rent is reasonable) is an attractive location."
- "Look at margins 28%–32% inside sales, 9 cents per gallon."
- "Gross profit % of instore sales should be in the 30%–35% range; gasoline is almost a lost leader in some markets."
- "C-store gross margins trend somewhere between 28% and 35%."
- "$500–$600 sq. ft."
- "Convenience stores that are in highly price-sensitive areas which are highly dependent on cigarette and beer pricing are higher risk. High margins are found in fountain drink and coffee sales; difficult for independents located close to Circle K's and 7 Elevens who offer fountain sales regularly."
- "Store performs less than $30,000 inside sales and less than 30,000 gallon gasoline sales per month—buyer is buying a job."
- "$400 per sq. ft. if they are good."
- "In the Northeast, gas sales of more than 1 million gallons and store sales of more than $500,000 per year indicate a moderately successful business."
- "Some sellers value stores close to 8–10x the inside sales per month."
- "Monthly stores sales greater than $60K/month; gasoline volume greater than 150,000 gallons a month with a weighted margin of 10 cents or more."
- "I don't really have such Benchmark Data, but in MA/New England a site will not likely get a second look if it does not pump over 1 million gallons and have over $400,000 in store sales."
- "Gross profit % of instore sales should be in the 30–35% range; gasoline is almost a loss leader in many markets. Fuel margins vary widely and can be from 5 cents to 15 cents/gallon depending on the market and cost pricing."
- "$250 to 280 per sq. ft."
- "A good gas station should pump at least 1.2 million gas gallons yearly, and take in $540,000 yearly in the Mart plus any lotto sales. Most higher sales gas stations will have a car wash and some type of food service."
- "The basic things to look for in a convenience store with fuel are the monthly gallons and then the inside sales. Gasoline has generally stopped being a profit generator due to the big box retailers getting into the business (Wal-Mart, Sam's, K-Mart etc.) so there isn't much profit in the fuel; however the more gallons a store does, generally the better the inside sales are. The gas has become the hook to get the people into the store."

- "Approx. $400 [in sales] per sq. ft."
- "High volume a must in today's stations; lower volume stations difficult to sell; repairs not as desirable."
- "$0.10 to $0.15 profit per gas gallon, 25% to 30% gross profit margin C-store; pump 120,000 to 150,000 gas gallons monthly minimum; $45,000 to $60,000 C-store + Lotto monthly minimum; $6,000 car wash monthly minimum; open 24/7; 1,200 sq. ft. C-store with food service."
- "Gas stations go upscale to lure customers, boost profits. The change comes at a crucial time for the nation's 138,000 convenience stores. At the same time profit margins are shrinking, the $395 billion industry is facing tough new competition from grocers adding fuel pumps and drug stores that offer more food than pharmaceuticals."
- "The economics of the transformation make sense. A good price on fuel might get people in the door once or twice a week. Great coffee, brick-oven pizza, and gelato could pull them in daily."

Expenses as a Percentage of Annual Sales

Cost of goods:	65% to 75%%
Payroll/labor Costs:	10% to 15%
Occupancy:	06% to 10%
Profit (estimated pretax)	05% to 10%%

Industry Trend

- "Lots of stores which sold in the last 3–5 years will be re-selling again as owners find it hard to profit, but they will find it hard to re-sell as well."
- "This will continue to be a very stable and attractive business for the next few years."
- "The trend is towards much bigger stores with multiple fueling locations. The older and smaller stores have a hard time competing with a new larger modern store."
- "Continuing down-to-flat."
- "Positive"
- "Bigger companies will force smaller companies out because they can buy cheaper and advertise more. Convenience hot/cold deli and fast food type items in stores will see growth. More of a one stop shop for all things fast and convenient."
- "St. Petersburg, FL—A new Rally filling station here stocks 100 beers including obscure microbrews. Its wine selection is worthy of a supermarket. And one staffer works the cappuccino bar while a full-time cook whips up made-to-order sandwiches, salads, soups and flatbread pizza, according to a report by the *St. Petersburg Times*. 'We cater to both Bubba and the BMW set,' said Mark Perreault, who runs the 12-pump, 1.5-acre site leased from Risser Oil Corp.
- "The up-market venture is a prime example of how gas station owners are grappling with the changes dogging this 'rough-and-tumble industry,' the newspaper reported.
  "The new Rally store, at 2200 Fourth St. N., includes a beer cave, cigar bar, some produce and a business plan to pump as much gas as all nine stations that once were within two miles. 'You make so little off gas and need so much traffic to get enough people inside the store that these mega-stations are becoming the future. The little guy just cannot do the volume,' said Bud Risser, a St. Petersburg wholesaler who sells 250 million gallons a year to the 80 gas

stations he controls, which sell a variety of brands from Spring Hill to Naples, FL.

"As the newspaper report noted, Hess and Racetrac have been on building sprees of 12 to 20 pump locations, while Wawa is signing deals to branch into Central Florida in 2012 with even bigger fresh food counters that hand-make so many hoagies that shoppers order by touch-screen. Other stations sell branded fast food such as Dunkin' Donuts, Subway, Quiznos and Taco Bell."

Source: "New Rally Location Follows Industry Trend of Bigger Stores," June 25, 2011 www.csnews.com

- "Mom-and-pop stations are being driven out of the market by the large chain operations. Oil company rents are becoming too high. Margins on gasoline are declining. Therefore, small stations are declining."

Seller Financing

- "Usually finance, 20- 25% for three years at 6% interest."
- SBA and bank loans have become increasingly more difficult due to economic conditions and type of business
- "7 to 10 years on average 6 percent interest VIR, per annum. As much as 50 percent of sales price could be financed by the Seller"
- SBA requires most Buyers to have experience and bring in at least 25% down Loans on Property—10 to 15 years (7 to 11% interest)

Questions

- "Why is he selling? What if any is the greatest concern owning a gas station? How is the oil company to work with? What does the Oil Company expect if I purchase this business?"
- "Has there ever been any contamination, gas leaks or EPA issues in the last 10 years. Who is responsible for any gasoline leaks from the underground tanks? What training is provided by the oil company prior to taking possession? Ask about the term of the lease and the rent moving forward."
- "What is the age and material of tanks? Is there contamination? Who is responsible for that? Is the site part of a state clean-up fund? What are the gallon sales? Fuel margin? Store sales and margin? Lottery sales and net lottery income? Any ancillary sales (air, vending, ATM, etc.)"
- "Will they participate in financing?"
- "How much is rent? What is the monthly gross profit? What is the pool margin on gas after credit card fees?
- "1. Gallons of gasoline sold/month. 2. What is the 'Pool Margin'? 3. Who sets the street price for the gasoline? 4. If seller owns the real estate, what does he pay for gasoline over RACK (wholesale)? 5. Seller is responsible to provide a current environmental survey on the property if seller owns RE. If property is leased from oil company, be sure they are responsible for environmental issues. 6. What will new rent be to a buyer?"
- "Gas volume, profit margin, store sales, lottery sales, rent. Length of lease is important, any zoning issues, any plans for the road to change, any new competition expected."
- "What is the fuel volume? Fuel margin? Store volume? Store margin? Credit card fees? Lottery sales? Ancillary income? How old is the equipment, especially the tanks? Is there environmental contamination? Who is responsible for contamination?"
- "Any new competition? Any road construction? Safety.etc.? More paperwork the better as it's easier to check & verify."

- "5 years' financials by profit center; petroleum equipment information; real estate appraisals; phase I & II environmental reports."
- "Everything about sales, income and the underground equipment"
- "Gasoline volume, cents per gallon margin (very important), store sales, store margin, lottery net income, ancillary income, environmental status, size, age and material of tanks, zoning, traffic count, competition."
- "How old are the storage tanks? What are they made of? Is there any environmental issue?
- "Audited financial statements? Environmental issues? New development in area—competitors?
- "Are there any environmental issues? Do you have a contract with a supplier? What is cost? Any rebates?"
- "5 years' financials by profit center; petroleum tank information; phase I & II reports."
- "A buyer would want to ask the current owner if the oil company owns the property or if the land is leased to the oil company. The value of the business will be less if the land is leased from another entity. The reason is that when the lease expires, even if there are options, the oil company may decide not to renew. Make sure the oil company owns the property; worst case make sure the lease for the station runs at least for another 10 years (when the oil company does not own the land). Buyers should also be concerned about the types of tanks that are underground—are they steel or fiberglass? If the owner has steel tanks, find out why the tanks have not been replaced with fiberglass. Ask the current owner if there have been any leaks or contamination. If the answer is yes, find out when and to what extent. Has the problem been corrected? One should also find out who is responsible for any and all contamination that lies above or below the surface of the site. Always require, in an offer to purchase agreement, a clause that states that the buyer will perform as part of the due diligence a Phase I report by an accredited environmental or chemical engineer who has a license to do so, with the results approved to the buyer's satisfaction. If a Phase II or III report is required, it is strongly suggested that it be done as well. "

Resources

Trade Publications

- Retail Business Review :
  www.conveniencestoresgasstations.retail-business-review.com

Associations

- Service Station Dealers of America: www.ssda-at.org

Gatti's (Pizza)	Franchise
Approx. Total Investment	$330,000 to $4,500,000
Estimated Annual Sales/Unit	$1,000,000

SIC 5812-22	NAICS 722211	Number of Businesses/Units 150

Rules of Thumb

➤ 30 to 35 percent of annual sales plus inventory

Resources

Websites
- www.gattispizza.com

Geeks on Call	Franchise
Approx. Total Investment	$53,350 to $82,150
Estimated Annual Sales/Unit	Not Available
NAICS 811212	Number of Businesses/Units 125

Rules of Thumb

➢ 60 percent of annual sales plus inventory

Resources

Websites
- www.geeksoncall.com

General Nutrition Centers		Franchise
Approx. Total Investment		$165,000 to $200,000
Estimated Annual Sales/Unit		Not Available
SIC 5499-04	NAICS 446191	Number of Businesses/Units 3,184

Rules of Thumb

➢ 40 percent of annual sales plus inventory

Resources

Websites
- www.gnc.com

Gift Shops (See also Card Shops & Hallmark Gift Shops)		
SIC 5947-12	NAICS 453220	Number of Businesses/Units 71,500

Rules of Thumb

➢ 35 percent of annual sales plus inventory

➢ 2.5 to 3 times SDE includes inventory

➢ 3 to 4 times EBITDA

➢ Inventory @ cost + FF&E + 1 to 2 times SDE

Pricing Tips

- "Inventory should be valued separately and include any costs associated with shipping inventory to the point of sale and preparing it for sale. Example: beads are bought in bulk. They are heavy and require extra costs to ship and require time and cost to re-package and weigh into smaller sellable units."
- "1. Location weighs heavily. 2. Products are very important in relation to value. Is the store a card + gift shop? Does it carry high-end American crafts and upscale gifts, gifts + toys? The mix is important along with profit margins."

Expert Comments

- "For smaller stores, unreported cash sales may exist. For larger stores, management, location and experienced buyers are key. Volume/type of products sold is very important. Merchandise buyers can make or break profitability, image, etc."
- "Relatively easy to get into a craft business but difficult to obtain and maintain profitability. Smaller independently owned stores tend to be operated by owners with a passion for the craft rather than a passion for business."

Benchmark Data

- For additional Benchmark data see Card Shops
- "Gross sales benchmark of $125K per employee"
- "Rent at 10% of GAS (Gross Annual Sales); Sales per Square Foot at $150–$175; Sales per Employee at $75,000–$125,000; Advertising at 3%–4% of GAS."
- "Small store sales are usually $200–$300 per sq. ft.; larger stores $300–$500 per sq. ft. Small stores should average $125,000 per employee."
- "Move Over Hallmark. Walmart is the Nation's Top Source for Gifts."

Source: www.findarticles.com

Expenses as a Percentage of Annual Sales

Cost of goods:	50% to 55%
Payroll/labor Costs:	08% to 15% (larger stores)
Occupancy:	06% to 08%/mall stores 08% to 12%
Profit (estimated pretax)	20% to 25% for sole proprietor; 05% to 10% for larger stores

Industry Trend

- "I don't have the statistics, but I believe there are fewer gift shops in business every year. The successfully operated gift stores appear to be in tourist locations and affluent communities. It is extremely difficult to secure unique gift products to sell, and many gift products are available at major retailers and discounters nationally at often discounted prices, making it virtually impossible for small stores to compete."
- "Survival is extremely difficult."
- "Large stores have survived recession, etc. Small stores are becoming extinct due to rising costs, difficulty in obtaining knowledgeable/motivated employees, the inability to buy with volume discount, difficulty moving old inventory, poor buying decisions."

Seller Financing

- "3 to 7 years"

Questions

- "Any unusual trends, seasonal or one-time hot selling items included in gross sales revenue? Explain the competition in detail. Discuss thoroughly the theft and/or shrinkage issues. Any convictions recently? Who is really responsible for purchasing duties?"
- "For small stores—What are your cash sales and are any expenses paid with cash? What do you 'love' and 'hate' about owning this store? Both answers may surprise you!! "

Resources

Associations

- Craft and Hobby Association—a good site: www.craftandhobby.org

	Franchise
Godfather's Pizza	
Approx. Total Investment	$100,000 to $300,000 depending on business model
Estimated Annual Sales/Unit	$384,000

SIC 5812-22	NAICS 722211	Number of Businesses/Units 600

Rules of Thumb

➢ 25 to 30 percent of annual sales

Resources

Websites

- www.godfatherspizza.com

	Franchise
Goin' Postal (See also Mail and Parcel Centers)	
Approx. Total Investment	$46,865 to $133,115

SIC 7331-01	NAICS 561431	Number of Businesses/Units 260

Rules of Thumb

➢ 30 to 35 percent of annual sales plus inventory

Resources

Websites

- www.goinpostal.com

Golf Carts — Sales & Service (See also Golf Courses & Golf Shops)		
SIC 5571-02	NAICS 441229	Number of Businesses/Units 1,500

Rules of Thumb

➢ 25 to 30 percent of annual sales plus inventory

Golf Courses

SIC Private: 7997-06 Public: 7992-01 NAICS 713910

Number of Businesses/Units 11,945

Rules of Thumb

➤ Rule of Thumb (Private): 2.5 to 5 times SDE plus inventory

➤ Rule of Thumb (Public): Net income multipliers—8 to 11, typically 9 to 10

➤ 4 times golf related income (green fees, golf carts, driving range—does not include pro shop or food & beverage)

Pricing Tips

- " ... I learned you don't make money just selling green fees. You make money selling big-ticket items: clubs, clothes, bags, lessons, and most important, real estate around the course. We offered none of those, so we scraped by, selling food and beverages, liquor, and cart rentals. I'd always hated power carts on golf courses, until I became a golf-course owner. They're unhealthy to customers, but extremely healthy to the bottom line."

  Source: "Dreams For Sale" by Matthew Rudy, *Businessweek*, November 10, 2008

- "Fourth, I finally realized that golf is part of the hospitality industry and that I'm a terrible host. I'm not a people person. I don't schmooze well. Our green fees were $17 weekdays, $22 weekends; and when an elderly man demanded his 'senior discount,' I snapped that I was practically giving away the golf as it was, and I'd be damned if I'd let the AARP crowd bankrupt me."

- "Real estate value big determinant in price of a golf course"

- "Personal property + equipment (FF&E) usually accounts for 3 to 10 percent of the purchase price depending on the amount of equipment leased and type of operation (daily fee vs. private). From 4 to 7 percent of price is typical."

- "Profit estimated—40 percent."

- "Due to weather-related conditions, a 5-year average for cash flow should be used— capital reserves of 5 percent should always be accounted for."

- "Add to price for additional assets such as development land. Also check rounds of golf, P&L and type of facilities."

- "Be careful to look at non-golf income for 'normal' distribution."

Benchmark Data

Statistics (Golf Courses & Country Clubs)

Number of Establishments	11,945
Average Profit Margin	2.0%
Revenue per Employee	$68,900
Average Number of Employees	27.8
Average Wages per Employee	27,855

Source: IBISWorld, June 2012

Products and Services Segmentation

Memberships	39%
Golf course green use	25%
Food and beverages	21%
Other sales and services	8%
Equipment rentals and sales	7%

Source: IBISWorld, July 2012

Industry Costs

Profit	2.0%
Wages	40.0%
Purchases	43.0%
Depreciation	6.8%
Marketing	1.0%
Rent & Utilities	4.0%
Other	3.2%

Source: IBISWorld, July 2012

- "Meadow Creek's pitch at a chic yet almost minimalist décor is also proving an attractive alternative for events such as weddings and banquets. So much so that even with 26,000 rounds a year and a weekday rack rate of $55 with cart, food-and-beverage sales account for a full 35 percent of club revenues."

Source: "The Right Tempo" by Trent Bouts, June 2011. www.golfbusiness.com

Expenses as a Percentage of Annual Sales

Cost of goods:	20%
Payroll/labor Costs:	45%
Occupancy:	15%
Profit (estimated pretax)	20%

Industry Trend

- "25.7 million Americans (age 6+) played at least one round of golf in 2011. That represents a national golf participation rate of 9.0% for the year. Golf remains one of the most popular participation sports in this country.

- "The good news is that the year-over-year reduction of 400K golfers is smaller than what we've seen in the past three years of the great recession. For reference, we lost one million golfers from 2009 to 2010 and 1.5 million between 2008 and 2009. We suspect this reduced net outflow is yet another sign that we are bouncing along the bottom of the trough and on the verge of a modest recovery. Based on past NGF research, this pattern would be similar to how golf rebounded when the country emerged from previous recessions.

- By rounds:
    - ✓ 6.8 million Avid golfers (25+ rounds annually and incl. in the Core number below)
    - ✓ 14.4 million Core golfers (8+ rounds annually)
    - ✓ 11.3 million Occasional golfers (fewer than 8 rounds annually)

Source: "2011 U.S. Golf Participation Flat with Previous Year," www.clubnewsmaker.net

- "About GolfNow.com

GolfNow.com is the Internet's largest and most comprehensive online tee time reservation service. Since its launch in 2001, GolfNow.com has expanded to more than 80 markets in North America and the UK and now provides tee time access to more than 3,100 courses for more than 1.1 million registered users. The site's demand-based Dynamic Pricing Engine puts operators in complete control of their tee sheets and pricing. GolfNow.com is powered by Golf Channel, which is seen in 83 million homes in the U.S. The site is also supported by GolfChannel.com, the Internet's No. 1 golf destination. The service is part of GolfChannel.com's online platform of Internet sites designed to help the recreational player enjoy every aspect of the game."

Source: "Golf News for Tuesday, June 28, 2011," www.worldgolf.com

Seller Financing
- "5 to 7 years"
- "20 years"

Questions
- Questions to ask seller: "Is there adjoining acreage that could be used for golf community homes? This can greatly increase value of the golf course."

Resources

Websites
- www.golfcourseindustry.com

Trade Publications
- Golf Courses and Country Clubs: A Guide to Appraisal, Market Analysis, Development, and Financing by Arthur E. Gimmy, MAI, and Martin E. Benson, MAI, published by The Appraisal Institute: www.appraisalinstitute.org

Associations
- National Golf Course Owners Association: www.ngcoa.org

Golf Driving Ranges & Family Fun Centers
(See also Amusement Arcades)

SIC 7999-31	NAICS 713990	

Rules of Thumb
➢ See Amusement Arcades and IBISWorld chart below

Benchmark Data

Statistics (Golf Driving Ranges & Family Fun Centers)
Number of Establishments	95,300
Average Profit Margin	5.6%
Revenue per Employee	$52,100
Average Number of Employees	1.9
Average Wages per Employee	$16,24

Source: IBISWorld, July 2012

Products and Services Segmentation
Family fun centers	45%
Other	30%
Driving ranges	10%
Miniature golf centers	9%
Shooting ranges	6%

Source: IBISWorld, July 2012

Industry Costs
Profit	5.6%
Wages	30.5%
Purchases	26.0%
Depreciation	3.0%
Marketing	1.0%
Rent & Utilities	16.0%
Other	17.9%

Source: IBISWorld, July 2012

Market Share

CEC Entertainment Inc.	8.8%
Dave & Buster's Holdings Inc.	5.8%

Source: IBISWorld, July 2012

Golf Shops (See also Golf Courses)	
NAICS 451110	

Rules of Thumb

➢ 30 percent of annual sales plus inventory

Pricing Tips

- "The total number of off-course retail locations has shrunk by 25% in the last five years."

Source: "How Healthy is our Game?" by Matthew Rudy, *Businessweek*, May 26, 2008

Expert Comments

"Off-course retailers have been pressed hard by the big box retailers and the manufacturers."

Industry Trend

- "Smaller footprint and more niche service oriented retailers."
- "No matter what industry you are in . . . it has always been somewhat taboo for your supplier to compete head to head against you for sales by selling direct to the consumer. Imagine for a second that you own a golf store in your local town that sells golf equipment. Now imagine that one of the companies you buy equipment from which happens to be your #1 selling product in your store calls to inform you that they will be opening up their own store right across the street . . . selling the exact same thing you do. Your worst nightmare has just come true . . . you are beyond upset . . . but don't know what to do . . . and it gets worse. Not only is your supplier now your direct competitor right across the street . . . but they can control price and inventory however they see fit . . . which will most likely put you out of business and bury everything you have worked so hard to build. Don't think it can happen? Well it is. And not many people are talking about it. And taboo or not this seems to be the trend in many industries . . . look no further than Apple as a prime example. And the golf industry looks like the next one in line to follow suit."

Source: "How Will This Trend Impact the Golf Industry? June 2, 2011, www.mygolfspy.com

Questions

- "Is the seller willing to allow the buyer a 10% rejection on the inventory (or some other fixed amount)?"

Resources

Websites

- www.progolfed.com
- www.ngf.org

Goodyear Tire Stores (See Auto Tire Store)

	NAICS 441320	

Rules of Thumb

➢ 35 percent of annual sales plus inventory

Gourmet Shops (See also Food Stores—Specialty)

SIC 5499-20	NAICS 445299	Number of Businesses/Units 3,000

Rules of Thumb

➢ 20 percent of annual sales plus inventory

Benchmark Data

- For Benchmark data see Food Stores—Specialty

	Franchise
Grease Monkey (See Auto Lube/Tune-up & other Lube Franchises)	
Approx. Total Investment	$850,000 to $1,200,000
Estimated Annual Sales/Unit	Not Available
NAICS 811191	Number of Businesses/Units 247

Rules of Thumb

➢ 50 percent of annual sales plus inventory

Resources

Websites

- www.greasemonkeyshine.com

	Franchise
Great Clips	
Approx. Total Investment	$109,400 to $202,500
Estimated Annual Sales/Unit	Not Available
NAICS 812112	Number of Businesses/Units 2,800

Rules of Thumb

➢ 1 to 1.5 times SDE plus inventory

Benchmark Data

- "According to Goggins, (Vice-President of Development for Great Clips) the company's earnings claim shows franchisees spend $150,000 on average to open a salon, ringing up $306,000 annually. That nets them a tidy $54,000."

Resources

Websites
- www.greatclipsfranchise.com

Great Harvest Bread Company		Franchise
Approx. Total Investment		$148,677 to $461,294
Estimated Annual Sales/Unit		Not Available
	NAICS 722211	Number of Businesses/Units 200

Rules of Thumb
➢ 3.2 to 3.4 times SDE plus inventory

Resources

Websites
- www.greatharvest.com

Great Steak		Franchise
Approx. Total Investment		$153,050 to $456,000
Estimated Annual Sales/Unit		$425,000
SIC 5812-19	NAICS 722211	Number of Businesses/Units 161

Rules of Thumb
➢ 50 to 55 percent of annual sales plus inventory

Resources

Websites
- www.kahalamgmt.com

Green Businesses		
	NAICS 541620	

Pricing Tips

- "My expertise is in what I call an 'industry horizontal.' Environmentally sustainable businesses can exist in virtually any industry. I've sold a furniture company, a toy manufacturer, a retail store, a recycled product manufacturer, a body care product company, etc. The multiples and rules of thumb for those are the same as the industries they are a part of, the difference being that their environmental sustainability makes them value at the higher end of the range than average."

Industry Trend

- "Continued growth especially in sectors such as renewable energy and organic food products. Organic body care products and natural and organic clothing are up and coming in this space as well."

Grocery Stores – General

(See also Grocery Stores—Small to Medium Size & Supermarkets)

SIC 5411-05	NAICS 445110	

Number of Businesses/Units Supermarkets 64,063

Rules of Thumb

➤ 15 to 20 percent of annual sales plus inventory

➤ 2 to 3 times SDE; add fixtures, equipment plus inventory

➤ 3 times EBITDA

Pricing Tips

- "Location, demographics, and competition are the 3 biggest factors in pricing."
- "Always investigate the possibility of new competition."
- "Rent above 3% of sales, or a short-term lease will reduce value of business."
- "Buyer will pay a premium for stores that include real estate. Discretionary Earnings are far more important to buyers than gross sales."

Expert Comments

"Competition, employee costs, and the economy in general have decreased profitability."

"Great demand for larger, profitable stores with stable competition."

Benchmark Data

Statistics (Supermarkets and Grocery Stores)

Number of Establishments	64,063
Average Profit Margin	2.0%
Revenue per Employee	$212,100
Average Number of Employees	9.9
Average Wages per Employee	$20,940

Source: IBISWorld, June 2012

Products and Services Segmentation

Other food items	28%
Meat, fish, poultry and delicatessen items	17%
Other non-food items	15%
Drugs and health products	10%
Fruit and vegetables	10%
Dairy products	8%
Beverages (including alcohol)	7%
Frozen foods	5%

Source: IBISWorld, June 2012

Industry Costs

Profit	2.0%
Wages	9.7%
Purchases	72.0%
Depreciation	2.0%
Marketing	5.0%
Rent & Utilities	4.0%
Other	5.3%

Source: IBISWorld, June 2012

Market Share

Kroger	18.9%
Safeway	8.3%
Supervalu	6.2%

Source: IBISWorld, June 2012

- Supermarket Facts—Industry Overview 2010 — 2011

Number of employees	3.4 million
Total supermarket sales—2011	$584,369 billion
Number of supermarkets—2011 ($2 million or more in annual sales)	36,569
Net profit after taxes, 2011	1.09%
Median total store size in square feet— 2010	46,000
Median weekly sales per supermarket—2010	$466,011
Percentage of disposable income spent on food—	
USDA figure for 2010 food at home	5.5%
Food away from home	3.9%
Weekly sales per square foot of selling area—2010	$11.78
Sales per customer transaction—2010	$26.78
Sales per labor hour—2010	$166.55
Average # of trips per week consumers make to the supermarket—2012	2.2
Average # items carried in a supermarket in 2010	38,718

Source: "Supermarket Facts", Industry Overview 2010 — 2011, Food Marketing Institute

- "Sales/sf = $450-$600."
- "Sales per employee $223K."

Expenses as a Percentage of Annual Sales

Cost of goods:	74%
Payroll/labor Costs:	10%
Occupancy:	03%
Profit (estimated pretax)	02% to 03%

Industry Trend

- "The 'New' Food Store: Food stores to continue to get smaller (10,000–13,000 square feet) as the economy continues to sputter—with fewer employees, but more affordable mainstream prepared-food and service departments. These stores will be owned by both independents and chains, become pervasive in the hippest downtown areas of major cities where the new emerging workforce—and aging Baby Boomers—are moving."

Source: "Six of the 'New' Food Trends to Watch in 2011 by Phil Lempert, plempert@supermarketguru.com, wwwsupermarketnews.com/viewpoints

- "Slow or no growth in profitability"
- "Growth will only keep up with inflation in the short term."

Questions

- "What new competition would likely enter market?"

Resources

Websites
- www.gmabrands.com
- http://foodindustrycenter.umn.edu/
- www.progressivegrocer.com
- www.fmi.org

Associations
- National Grocers Association (NGA): www.nationalgrocers.org

---

Grocery Stores — Small to Medium Size
(See also Convenience Stores & Supermarkets)

SIC 5411-05	NAICS 445110	

Rules of Thumb

- ➢ 2 times SDE plus inventory
- ➢ 10% to 15% of annual sales plus inventory
- ➢ "Real estate, business, inventory (total package)—4 times recasted cash flow not including owner's salary." [EBIT]
- ➢ 3 times EBITDA
- ➢ "Rules of thumb only apply to stores that are currently profitable with no new competition on the horizon."

Pricing Tips

- "…Up to $2,000,000 gross sales…these stores are usually sold for fair market value of fixtures and equipment plus the inventory at retail cost less 27–36 percent. Rent should never exceed 2.5 percent of the gross sales. Markup of these small stores usually runs between 17 percent and 20 percent of wholesale cost. Or, value of business is 3 to 5 times weekly gross (per United Grocers), plus fixtures and equipment, plus inventory."
- "Larger stores have lower overall gross profits and tend to have more spoilage."
- "Breakeven sales approximately $160,000 year."
- Independents are operators of 11 stores or fewer, while chains have 11 or more stores.

Source: Food Industry Review, The Food Institute

Expert Comments

"Current or anticipated competition is the biggest factor in valuing or selling a grocery store."

"Larger gross sales easier to market"

"Easy to open a convenience store or grocery store—a lease and some shelving."

Benchmark Data

- For additional Benchmark data see Grocery Stores — General
- "I see margins of 27%–28% in smaller stores in rural areas."
- "Must have turnover, long lease, and good employees."
- "Rent should be below 5% of the gross sales."

Expenses as a Percentage of Annual Sales

Cost of goods:	70%
Payroll/labor Costs:	15%
Occupancy:	03% to 05%%
Profit (estimated pretax)	02.5%

Industry Trend

- "Slow steady growth"

Questions

- "Reason for sale. Is there a new competitor coming into the marketplace?"

Resources

Associations

- National Grocers Association: www.nationalgrocers.org

Ground Transportation Companies (Motorcoach/Limousine)		
(See also Bus Companies & Limousine Services)		
	NAICS 484110	Number of Businesses/Units 480

Rules of Thumb

➢ 3 times EBITDA plus vehicle value for small to midsize operations; 4 times EBITDA plus—for over 15 vehicles

Pricing Tips

- "Maintenance records? Facility?"
- "Who controls the groups? The quality of the drivers and how long have they been with the company? Are the groups preformed or do they sell into them? Condition of equipment counts."

Benchmark Data

Statistics (Airport Shuttle Operators)

Number of Establishments	480
Average Profit Margin	9.7%
Revenue per Employee	$8,100
Average Number of Employees	15.4%
Average Wages per Employee	20,562

Source: IBISWorld, December 2011

Major Market Segmentation

Short-haul consumers	55%
Long-haul consumers	40%
Business travelers	5%

Source: IBISWorld, December 2011

Products and Services Segmentation

Short-distance shuttle services 65.9%
Long-distance shuttle services 34.1%

Source: IBISWorld, December 2011

Industry Costs

Profit 9.7%
Rent 2.0%
Utilities 2.6%
Depreciation.. 8.2%
Other... 16.5%
Wages... 25.4%
Purchases... 35.6%

Source: IBISWorld, December 2011

		Franchise
Grout Doctor		
Approx. Total Investment		$20,405 to $39,915
Estimated Annual Sales/Unit		Not Available
	NAICS 811411	Number of Businesses/Units 73

Rules of Thumb

➤ 85 to 90 percent of annual sales plus inventory

Resources

Websites

- www.groutdoctor.com

Guard Services (See also Security Services/Systems & Alarm Companies)		
SIC 7381-02	NAICS 561612	Number of Businesses/Units 35,000

Rules of Thumb

➤ 30 percent of annual sales plus inventory

➤ 3 times SDE includes inventory

➤ 3 times EBITDA

Pricing Tips

- "Non-union are worth more"
- "If guards are 1099's, business is worth less."

Expert Comments

"As crime increases, so does security"

"It is easy to lose a client if you have to go to bid every year."

Benchmark Data

- For additional Benchmark data see Security Services/Systems
- "Cost is different for an armed guard, for an event security, or 24-hour security service."

Expenses as a Percentage of Annual Sales

Cost of goods:	05%
Payroll/labor Costs:	70%
Occupancy:	05% to 10%
Profit (estimated pretax)	15% to 20%

Industry Trend

- "5–10 growth a year"
- "Stable"

Questions

- "Most guard companies have major clients; explain anything over 20%, could become an earnout event."
- "Relationship to customers?"

Gun Shops and Supplies

SIC 5941-29	NAICS 451110	Number of Businesses/Units 8,700

Rules of Thumb

➢ 30 to 35 percent of annual sales plus inventory

Benchmark Data

- Note: The following information is for gun and ammunition manufacturing, but may have information to help in pricing Gun Shops.

Statistics (Guns & Ammunition Manufacturing)

Number of Establishments	516
Average Profit Margin	8.5%
Revenue per Employee	$317,100
Average Number of Employees	68.3
Average Wages per Employee	$82,745

Source: IBISWorld, April 2012

Products and Services Segmentation

Small arms	27%
Small arms ammunition	26%
Other ammunition	25%
Other ordnance and accessories	22%

Source: IBISWorld, April 2012

Major Market Segmentation

Civilians	60%
The military	25%
Law enforcement	15%

Source: IBISWorld, April 2012

Rules of Thumb - **H**

Industry Costs

Profit 8.5%
Wages.. 20.2%
Purchases 52.5%
Depreciation 4.0%
Marketing 1.5%
Rent & Utilities 6.5%
Other.. 6.8%

Source: IBISWorld, April 2012

Market Share

Alliant Techsystems Inc.. 12.5%
Freedom Group Inc... 7.0%

Source: IBISWorld, April 2012

Industry Trend

- "The guns and ammunition industry will experience its first decline in five years in 2010. Although Americans drastically cut back their spending during the recession, firearms and ammunition grew by an astounding 8.9 percent in 2009 alone. Prior to this year, growth was in the double digits in 2006 and 2008, and it was clear that this industry was flourishing in recent years. However, this thriving industry is expected to take a radical turn for the worse, declining by a whopping 5.7 percent in 2010, to $9.83 billion."

Source: "IBISWorld: Industry Insight: Gun Manufacturers," June 2010

Resources

Associations

- National Association of Federally Licensed Firearms Dealers: www.amfire.com
- National Shooting Sports Foundation: www.nssf.org

Hair Care		
	NAICS 812112	

Rules of Thumb

➢ 35 to 50 percent plus inventory (the more popular the franchise, generally, the higher the price, all other things being equal)

➢ 1 to 2 times SDE plus inventory

Benchmark Data

- For additional Benchmark data see Beauty Shops

	Franchise
Hallmark Gift Shops	
Approx. Total Investment	$250,000 to $500,000
NAICS 453220	Number of Businesses/Units 3,200

Rules of Thumb

➢ 40 percent of annual sales plus inventory

Pricing Tips

- "Inventory valuation is crucial; inventory should be no more than one third of annual volume. If it is more, then it is probably old and over-valued. Many stores have collectibles that are very slow moving, and very high in value. Unless inventory over-valuation is anticipated, deal can fall through because of this very contentious issue."

Expenses as a Percentage of Annual Sales

Cost of goods:	50%
Payroll/labor Costs:	12%
Occupancy:	max 14%
Profit (estimated pretax)	18%–20%

Resources

Websites
- www.hallmark.com

Hardware Stores		
SIC 5251-04	NAICS 444130	Number of Businesses/Units 17,081

Rules of Thumb

➢ 45 to 50 percent of annual sales plus inventory

➢ 3 to 3.5 times SDE plus inventory

➢ 3.5 times SDE including inventory

Pricing Tips

- "The above multipliers apply to average hardware stores with less than $600k in revenues that have an SDE profit margin (SDE/Sales) of 12%-20%. If the SDE margin is less than 12% the Revenue Multiple will be .46 and the Cash Flow Multiple will be 4.6. If the SDE profit margin is greater than 20% the Revenue Multiple will be .55 and the Cash Flow Multiple will be 3.0. The average store with revenues between $600k and $1,200k generally earns a Revenue Multiplier of .51 and a Cash Flow Multiplier of 4.3. However, the SDE profit margin must be between 11% and 16%. If it is below 11% the revenue multipliers are .48 and the Cash Flow multipliers are 4.7. If the SDE profit margin is more than 16% the Revenue multipliers are .54 and the Cash Flow Multipliers are 3.7. Stores with revenues from $1,200k to $2,000k earn Revenue Multipliers of .35 and Cash Flow Multipliers of 3.0 for SDE profit margins in the 9%-15% range. For stores with SDE profit margins less than 9%, the Revenue Multipliers will be .28 and the Cash Flow Multiplier will be 3.6. If the SDE Profit margins are greater than 15% the Revenue Multiplier will be .40 and the Cash Flow Multiplier will be 2.9. All the above multipliers include inventory."
- "Profitability of a store is a key driver to its value. Calculate the store's SDE% (SDE divided by total Sales). A store with revenues in the $1 million to $1.5 million range with an SDE% of 10% will see Revenue Multipliers of 35% (including inventory) and Cash Flow Multipliers of 3.40 (including inventory).

Stores with SDE% of 13% (the average for stores this size) will earn Revenue Multipliers of 42% and Cash Flow Multipliers of 3.40. Stores in the high range of profitability with SDE% of 18% will earn Revenue Multipliers of 53% and Cash Flow Multipliers of 3.0. Stores with sales under $1 million will earn somewhat lower multipliers. Stores with sales less than $700k will earn much lower multipliers. Stores under $700k can barely make a living for the owner. It is not uncommon to see a store with $500-600k in revenues, for example, being sold for the value of its inventory only."

- "1.9 times SDE plus inventory. Inventory, however, should be between 25% and 30% of Total Revenues. If inventory is more than 30%, the seller will not get full price on the surplus inventory."
- "Smaller stores with revenues less than $600,000 and SDE less than $100,000 are generally not worth much more than the value of their inventory."

Expert Comments

"Stores with revenues below $600k are very difficult to sell. Profits provide low incomes to the owner. Stores should be franchised to gain any advantage in this market."

"The presence of a Home Depot or Lowe's in a store's market intensifies competition. The store must seek niche markets ignored by the big boxes to survive. Customer service is a must. Even though competition may be intense in big box markets, small independent hardware stores can flourish when properly managed."

"Even though most stores have seen revenue declines, the demand for profitable stores is still strong."

"Stores in good locations will still bring premium prices. Rural locations are often insulated from the effects of big boxes."

"Franchised hardware stores continue to be in demand even though sales have declined. Buyers seem willing to forgive a slight downturn in sales this year, just because most stores are experiencing declines."

"Reasonably profitable hardware stores sell very quickly."

"Heavy industry consolidation by the big boxes means that small operators must be aligned with a major franchisor. Local dealer advertising groups are also a must. Plenty of help on the store floor, convenient parking, knowledgeable staff, and quick service are far more important to today's hardware shoppers than price. Therefore, small neighborhood stores that possess those characteristics will survive the big boxes quite well."

Benchmark Data

Statistics (Hardware Stores)

Number of Establishments	17,801
Average Profit Margin	1.6%
Revenue per Employee	$156,600
Average Number of Employees	8.1
Average Wages per Employee	$25,998

Source: IBISWorld, May 2012

Products and Services Segmentation

Hardware, tools, plumbing and electrical supplies..58.1%
Other..15.2%
Lawn, garden and farm supplies...10.8%
Paint and sundries...8.8%
Lumber and other building materials..7.1%

Source: IBISWorld, May 2012

Major Market Segmentation

Do-it-yourself Consumers 69.5%
Contractors 19%
Do-it-for-me...11.5%

Source: IBISWorld, May 2012

Industry Costs

Profit 1.6%
Wages..16.4%
Purchases 59.0%
Depreciation..1.2%
Marketing...3.1%
Rent & Utilities 3.3%
Other 15.4%

Source: IBISWorld, May 2012

- "Urban stores will see Gross Profit Margins in the 42% to 46% range. Rural stores have Gross Margins in the 38% to 41% range."
- "For stores in the $1 million to $1.5 million range, payroll on the average should be about 12% of Gross Revenues. However, payroll for stores in the rural areas can be in the 10%–11% range, and in the big cities payroll may be in the 13%–18% range."
- "Small stores doing less than $1,000,000 may generate $100/sq ft per year in sales. Profitable stores typically produce $150/sq ft to $200/sq ft."
- "Inventory around 2.0–2.5; Sales are $100–$150/ Sq Ft Best run stores with revenues in the $1 million to $1.5 million range can turn inventory at 3.0 times and sales at $200/ Sq Ft. Stores in rural areas have labor costs ranging 12–13% of sales and rent 4–5%; big cities pay 16–20% and rent is 7–10% of sales. The difference is in the gross profit margins. Rural stores are doing 38–41% and big city stores are doing 42–48%."
- "Annual sales per square foot for underperforming stores is typically under $100. A good store will be over $150 per square foot and a super store over $200. Stores with inventory less than $30 per square foot will be underperforming. $40 or more per square foot is a well stocked store (providing there is less than 10% obsolete or slow moving inventory). Ace Hardware stores must be rated as 'Vision 21 Compliant' by Ace Hardware Corporation. If not, Ace will require a buyer to pay for approximately $125,000 to $175,000 is upgrades. This cost will typically cut the selling of the business by up to $100,000. Activant Point of Sale computer is a must with Ace."
- "Should turn their inventory 2.5 to 3 times per year. Fixtures and equipment should not exceed 16 percent of the average stock carried per year. These stores are sold for fixtures and equipment at depreciated value plus the inventory at wholesale cost. Markup runs from 35 to 40 percent."
- Financial Profile of Hardware Stores
  Operating Profile

Average Size of Selling Area (sq. ft.) 8,555
Total Sales $1,290,226
Total Asset Investment.. $601,996
Total Inventory $372,635
Income Statement
Net Sales 100%
Cost of Goods Sold... 60.1%
Gross Margin 39.9%
Patronage Dividend/Purchase Rebate 1.3%
Total Gross Margin.. 41.2%
Total Expenses 39.5%
Gross Operating Profit.. 1.3%
Other Income 1.2%
Net Profit (before taxes) 2.9%

Source: "Retail D-I-Y Market Profile" by Don Tratensek and Chril Jensen issued by the
National Retail Hardware Association in *Hardware Retailing* 2006.

Sales per Sq. Ft. of Selling Area: $151
Total Sales per Employee: $143,358
Inventory per Sq. Ft. of Selling Area: $44
Net Sales to Total Inventory: ....3.5 times
Average size of Transaction: $15

Source: "Retail D-I-Y Market Profile" by Don Tratensek and Chril Jensen issued by the
National Retail Hardware Association in *Hardware Retailing* 2006.
All of the above data is the latest we could find, but it is still quite informative.

Expenses as a Percentage of Annual Sales

Cost of goods:...50% to 60%
Payroll/labor Costs:...12% to 15%
Occupancy:..05% to 08%
Profit (estimated pretax) ....01% to 03%

Industry Trend

- "Many stores are going out of business from the recession"
- "An antique armoire stocked with scented candles sits at the end of the aisle
  in this west Omaha hardware store, a few feet from the familiar white bag of
  Scotts lawn fertilizer. The armoire and candles are a testament to the growing
  purchasing power of women, as are other stylishly selected items around the
  store, in areas dedicated to home décor, children's birthdays and kitchen ware.
  "This True Value Hardware store has all the nuts and bolts (and fertilizer) of a
  typical hardware store, but with additional areas designed to draw women into
  widget land. Think Westlake meets Michael's after a brief fling with Yankee
  Candle.
  "'I wanted our customers, when they stepped in there, to know they were
  stepping into a different area,' said store co-owner Laura Castro, who designed
  the female-oriented areas of the store . . .'"

Source: "Retailers go after women by offering 'shopper-tainment'" by Robert Tysver,
World-Herald News Service, April 26, 2011

- "Sales and profits for stores located in markets that were high growth prior
  to 2007 have suffered significant declines in recent years. Market Value
  Multipliers for stores in these areas have declined as profits have declined."
- "Very stable industry growth. The next few years should see growth at about
  3% per year."
- "Computerization, renovation, innovation. Do or die."

Questions

- "How do you value your ending inventory on the books? Is there concealed inventory or understated inventory? How often do you do a physical inventory? Is your cash register point-of-sale system read barcodes? Is your inventory counts computerized? "

- "If an Ace Hardware store—are you Vision 21 compliant? Hardware wholesales (Ace, True Value, Do It Best) have operating Benchmark Data that they require their dealers to adhere to. These include store signage, decor, color schemes, updated computers, attendance at hardware shows, participation in advertising groups etc. These requirements are expensive. It is not uncommon that a buyer will have to pay to upgrade the store to those standards immediately after purchasing the store."

- "Is your computer database current? Are inventory counts accurate?"

Resources

Associations

- National Retail Hardware Association: www.nrha.org

Harley-Davidson Motorcycle Dealerships		
(See also Motorcycle Dealerships)		
SIC 5571-06	NAICS 441221	

Rules of Thumb

➢ "87% of annual sales. In this case the agency netted $2,100,000 and seller retained 20 percent of ownership."

➢ 3.5 SDE plus net assets plus inventory

➢ 1 to 6 times EBITDA

Benchmark Data

- For additional Benchmark data see Motorcycle Dealerships

Industry Trend

- "Harley-Davidson might be one of the best-known brands in the world, but it's perceived, at least in some circles, as the motorcycle of choice for aging baby boomers. Now the motorcycle giant confronts a double whammy: its aging customers are facing physical challenges that could keep them off their bikes for good, and financial troubles are stemming from the recent market meltdown. On top of that, luxury brand Harley is itself struggling to get through a broad, deep recession and credit crisis 'People walk through the front door looking to buy a bike because they want it, not because they need it,' says George Dennis, the dealership's business and finance manager. 'How many people have the disposable income to dump $20,000 on a Harley?' Bikers talk: What's so special?"

Source: Is Harley-Davidson Over the Hill?," www.moneycentral.msn.com, April, 2009

Questions

- "Why are you selling? What are the strengths and weaknesses of your business? Are there any add-backs? What is your reputation in the marketplace? What is the upside potential?"

Resources

Websites
- www.harley-davidson.com

Health & Safety Industries

Rules of Thumb

➤ 3 to 5.5 times EBIT (Distribution)

➤ 3 to 7 times EBIT (Manufacturing)

Health Clubs (See Fitness Centers & Racquet Sports Clubs)

SIC 7991-01	NAICS 713940	

Health Food Stores (See also General Nutrition Centers)

SIC 5499-01	NAICS 446190	Number of Businesses/Units 58,377

Rules of Thumb

➤ 1 to 1.5 times SDE plus inventory

➤ 40 percent of annual sales plus inventory

Benchmark Data

Statistics (Health Stores)

Number of Establishments	58,377
Average Profit Margin	5.8%
Revenue per Employee	$133,000
Average Number of Employees	2.2
Average Wages per Employee	$31,171

Source: IBISWorld, July 2012

Products and Services Segmentation

Vitamin and mineral supplements	30%
Orthopedic equipment	20%
First-aid products	19%
Convalescent care products	13%
Sports nutrition products	12%
Other	6%

Source: IBISWorld, July 2012

Industry Costs

Profit	5.8%
Wages	23.0%
Purchases	62.0%
Depreciation	1.5%
Marketing	2.0%
Rent & Utilities	5.0%
Other	0.7%

Source: IBISWorld, July 2012

Market Share

General Nutrition Centers 8.9%
Vitamin Shoppe... 5.1%

Source: IBISWorld, July 2012

Industry Trend

Breakdown of Products

	Sales in billions	Growth in 2003	Growth in 2004	Growth in 2005-2008
Functional Foods	$24.5	6.9%	7.6%	6-8%
Supplements	$20.3	5.7%	2.6%	3-5%
Natural/Organic Foods	$18.4	13.1%	13.2%	8-10%
Natural Personal Care	$5.5	8.7%	11.3%	10-12%

Source: *Nutrition Business Journal*

Resources

Associations

- National Association for the Specialty Food Trade: www.specialtyfood.com/

Hearing Aid Sales		
SIC 5999-79	NAICS 446199	Number of Businesses/Units 12,500

Rules of Thumb

➢ 70 to 80 percent of annual revenues plus inventory

➢ 4 times EBITDA

Pricing Tips

- "Larger practices will command the higher valuations. Particularly if the owner is absentee and trained dispensers are in place."
- "Transition agreements for long periods are common."

Expert Comments

"Market for audiology and hearing aids is expanding as baby boomers enter the market. Franchises such as Miracle Ear and Beltone reduce obstacles to entry and increase ease of replication."

Benchmark Data

- "Cost of Goods sold should not exceed 35%"
- "$300,000 per dispenser"

Expenses as a Percentage of Annual Sales

Cost of goods:.. 40%
Payroll/labor Costs:.. 20%
Occupancy: 05%
Profit (estimated pretax) 18%

Industry Trend

- "iData Research, a leading medical device market research agency, revealed that the U.S. hearing-aid and audiology device market was valued at over $5.7 billion in 2011.
- "The market, driven by technological advancements in cochlear implants, bone-anchored hearing-aids and the introduction of wireless Bluetooth capability from Starkey, GN Resound and cochlear America, is expected to touch almost $8 billion in annual sales by 2018."

Source: headsets.tmcnet.com

- "More than 28 million Americans have some degree of hearing loss, a number that could reach 78 million by 2030."

Source: Hearing Industries Association (HIA)

- "Growth with aging population"

Seller Financing

- 3 years

Questions

- "Is this business free from liens/encumbrances with vendors that would prohibit the sale of the practice?"
- "Are any loyalty agreements or right of first refusals in place?"

Resources

Trade Publications

- Audiology Online: www.audiologyonline.com

Associations

- Hearing Industries Association (HIA): www.hearing.org

Heating Contractors (See HVAC)		
		Number of Businesses/Units 46,800

Heating Oil Dealers		
	NAICS 454311	

Rules of Thumb

➤ 25 percent of annual sales plus inventory

➤ 2.5 times SDE plus inventory

➤ 3 to 3.5 times EBIT

➤ 3 to 4 times EBITDA.

Pricing Tips

- "Most of these businesses are bought on a retained gallonage basis, typically around 1 X gross profits plus assets. Location, customer mix, automatic vs. will call delivery are important issues. Impacted by weather."

- "There is slow turnover in this industry, as most dealers are 2nd or 3rd generation in the business."
- "Industry buyers used to price on the basis of gallons delivered, especially automatic gallons. They now price at 4 to 5.5 times EBITDA, based upon number of automatic vs. 'will call' customers, margins per gallon, location, competition from discounters, condition of equipment, etc."
- "Low margin, high risk business since there is credit risk involved."
- "Most industry buyers want to acquire on the basis of 'retained gallons,' where the buyer offers a limited amount of cash up front and pays only for customer gallons that actually get delivered over a period of time. This puts the risk on the Seller and often requires the Seller to remain in the business for some period. It also, however, allows the Seller to get top dollar for his business due to the 'no risk' nature of the deal to the Buyer. Industry buyer will also pay cash up front, but only for customers who are on some type of automatic delivery (automatic, service, and budget customers). These customers are less price sensitive and will typically stay through any transition in ownership."
- "Usually are sold for 6 to 6.5 cents per gallon the company pumped per year, plus the rolling stock, plus the inventory at cost, plus the cost of the real property in the event it is included in the sale. Usually a high volume low net profit type of business."
- "It depends on the amount of hard assets. Gross profits generally drive the value of these businesses. The higher the gross profit, the higher the value. Gross profit per gallon is a key ratio. Some things that detract from value are high real estate values (land & bldgs.), and other outdated petroleum bulk plants, & petroleum equipment. Any environmental problems are a concern."

Expert Comments

"Declining volume due to high prices, other cheaper fuel sources, image, weather, conservation, etc."

"Customer satisfaction/loyalty is inversely proportional to price of fuel oil."

"Mature industry with significant environmental regulations. Price spikes similar to summer of 2008 hurt the industry. Growth generally comes through acquisitions. More consolidation for the future."

"Competition is relatively high due to: 1. Discounters, 2. Overcapacity of oil to be delivered, trucks, personnel in a mild winter and every summer; 3. The consolidation in the industry."

"Replication is easy at an entry level if the entrant is near a distribution point and sells on a 'cash on delivery' basis. Otherwise, it takes years to develop a strong customer base on automatic delivery."

Benchmark Data

- "Less desirable companies (discounters) are very difficult to sell."
- "Gross profit per gallon is a good benchmark. Should exceed $.60/gallon in most markets and higher in metro areas."
- "EBITDA is the most common benchmark. Another would be number of automatic gallons x margin per gallon x a multiple of 1 to 1.5 but in the end, industry buyers will look at EBITDA."
- "Gross profit per gallon is a good benchmark. Should be in the $.50 to $.70 gallon range in rural markets, and higher in the metro areas."

- "Most successful full-service companies in Connecticut and Massachusetts target margins of 45 to 55 cents per gallon but 'discounters' will work on margins as low as 25 to 30 cents by keeping their overhead low, not delivering too far from a terminal, and not offering oil burner service, credit, automatic delivery, budget plans, etc."

Expenses as a Percentage of Annual Sales

Cost of goods:	60% to 70%
Payroll/labor Costs:	10% to 15%
Occupancy:	02% to 05%
Profit (estimated pretax)	05% to 10%

Industry Trend

- "Heating oil usage will decline based on increasing price, conversion to natural gas, and growth of alternative energy sources. The industry is consolidating, and many small businesses (<1,000 customers) are having a difficult time competing."
- "Slow decline as people move to other clean energy sources and conservation."
- "The industry is in the midst of consolidation, as larger companies employ economies of scale and best practices, placing great pressure on the 'mom and pop' companies started in the 50s and 60s."

Seller Financing

- "We typically get cash at closing for fixed assets, and finance the intangibles over 2 to 5 years."
- "2 or 3 years"
- "5 to 7 years"

Questions

- "5 years' financials and gallonage history; customer base breakdown by class of customer and type of delivery (automatic or will call); asset listing; phase I & II environmental reports."
- "How many gallons do you deliver? What are your average margins per gallon? How many gallons delivered are to automatic customers, service customers, budget plan customers, and 'will call' customers."
- "Three-year history of dollar sales, gallonage + gross profits. financials, # of customers by product, & type of dispatch (automatic vs. will call). Age and condition of equipment."

Resources

Websites

- www.api.org

Trade Publications

- Oil& Energy Magazine: www.nefi.com/oilandenergy/index.html

Associations

- Petroleum Marketers Association of America (PMAA): www.pmaa.org

		Franchise
Heavenly Ham		
Approx. Total Investment		Not Available
Estimated Annual Sales/Unit		Not Available
	NAICS 722211	Number of Businesses/Units 130

Rules of Thumb

➤ 30 to 35 percent of annual sales plus inventory

Resources

Websites
▪ www.heavenlyham.com

Heavy Equipment Sales & Service	
	NAICS 811310	

Rules of Thumb

➤ 50 percent of SDE plus fixtures, equipment and inventory

Hobby Shops (See also Toy Stores)		
SIC 5945-08	NAICS 451120	Number of Businesses/Units 21,409

Rules of Thumb

➤ The Hobby and Toy category in IBISWorld also includes: Craft Supplies, Hobby Goods, Traditional & Electric Games, and Magic Supplies (See Benchmark Data for percentages of each). The percentage of annual sales and the multiple of SDE would be about the same as listed below plus inventory.

➤ 20 percent of annual sales plus inventory

➤ 1.5 times SDE plus inventory

Pricing Tips

▪ "Don't buy too much inventory. In the hobby business, October through January are the busiest sales months while many find February, March, August and September are slower. When approaching a heavy selling season, you need to increase inventory. When it ends, you need to move whatever seasonal or outdated inventory that did not sell out the door as quickly as you can."

Source: www.nrhsa.org

Benchmark Data

Statistics (Hobby & Toy Stores)

Number of Establishments	21,409
Average Profit Margin	2%
Revenue per Employee	$121,200
Average Number of Employees	7
Average Wages per Employee	$14,298

Source: IBISWorld, July 2012

Products and Services Segmentation

Traditional toys	35%
Other toys and games	34%
Hobby and craft supplies	24%
Youth electronics	7%

Source: IBISWorld, July 2012

Industry Costs

Profit	2.0%
Wages	11.7%
Purchases	70.0%
Depreciation	1.6%
Marketing	1.1%
Rent & Utilities	3.7%
Other	9.9%

Source: IBISWorld, July 2012

Market Share

Toys 'R' Us Inc.	47.7%
Michaels Stores Inc.	21.9%
Jo-Ann Stores Inc.	13.2%

Source: IBISWorld, July 2012

- "The gross profit margin for the average hobby shop is around 35 percent, before expenses and taxes. Net profit margins are usually less than 10 percent."

Source: National Retail Hobby Stores Association

Resources

Trade Publications
- Model Retailer magazine: www.modelretailer.com

Associations
- National Retail Hobby Stores Association: www.nrhsa.org
- Craft & Hobby Association: www.hobby.org

Home Centers

(See also Building Materials/Lumberyards/Hardware Stores)

	NAICS 444110	Number of Businesses/Units 8,458

Rules of Thumb

➢ 40 to 45% percent of annual sales includes inventory

➢ 2 times SDE plus inventory

Pricing Tips

- "Home centers are a hybrid hardware/lumberyard. Typically they will do 50% lumber and 50% hardware. They focus primarily on the do-it-yourself customers, although they will also deal with the pro contractors. Home centers will usually have little higher prices in lumber than a pro lumberyard. However, they are usually in nicer locations and well-defined commercial areas. Lumberyards need much more yard space and therefore are often located in areas where acreage is cheap, i.e., in the more undeveloped areas. Home centers will usually have retail store space in the 10,000 to 20,000 sq ft range with a modest sized outdoor lumber area."

- "Sales indicate that smaller sales bring higher multiple than stores with sales over $1 million."

Expert Comments

"High capital investment keeps new competition out of the market, unless, of course, it is a big box."

"The high capital costs for inventory and fixtures and the lack of good locations are significant barriers to entry."

Benchmark Data

Statistics (Home Improvement Stores)

Number of Establishments	8,458
Average Profit Margin	4.2%
Revenue per Employee	$319,200
Average Number of Employees	60.01
Average Wages per Employee	$27,10

Source: IBISWorld, June 2012

Products and Services Segmentation

Lumber and other building and structural materials	29%
Tools, equipment, paint and flooring	20%
Lawn, garden and farm equipment supplies	14%
Household appliances, kitchen goods and housewares	12%
Plumbing fixtures and supplies	10%
Electrical supplies	9%
Hardware	3%
Other	3%

Source: IBISWorld, June 2012

Major Market Segmentation

Professional customers	40.8%
Do-it-yourself market	36.8%
Do-it-for-me market	22.4%

Source: IBISWorld, June 2012

Industry Costs

Profit	4.2%
Wages	8.3%
Purchases	69.6%
Depreciation	1.0%
Marketing	3.0%
Rent & Utilities	1.9%
Other	12.0%

Source: IBISWorld, June 2012

Market Share

Home Depot	40.8%
Lowe's	32.6%

Source: IBISWorld, June 2012

- "Sales per square foot of retail space should be greater than $250. Margins should be greater than 33%; payroll should be less than 17%–18% to be profitable. Must have well-defined marketing programs in place. Should have advertising greater than 2% of sales, preferably 3% or more."

- "A good home center may do $300–$400/sq ft per year in sales."

Expenses as a Percentage of Annual Sales

Cost of goods:	65% to 70%
Payroll/labor Costs:	13% to 15%
Occupancy:	05% to 06%
Profit (estimated pretax)	10% to 15%

Industry Trend

- "Home centers have been less impacted than lumberyards during the last two years. The primary reason is that profits come mostly from the hardware side of the business, which has been 'hit' less hard than lumber sales."

Questions

- "Does any one contractor represent more than 10% of your lumber business? This is a personality business. If the old owner goes, the customer might leave too."
- Are there any potential franchise or refurbishment costs that will be included in the sale?

Home Health Care — Care-Giving

(See also Home Health Care—Equipment and Supplies)

	NAICS 621610	Number of Businesses/Units 314,126

Rules of Thumb

- 50 percent of annual sales plus inventory
- 3 to 4 times SDE plus inventory
- 4 to 6 times EBIT
- 4 to 6 times EBITDA

Pricing Tips

- "Must be aware of reimbursement"
- "A good business should have at least a 20-point margin. If not, the business may be a lot more valuable to a seasoned acquirer than the numbers show."
- "Multiples can be higher for high-cash-flow companies due to high interest from acquirers."
- "Price the same as service industry in general."
- "Need to watch for employee and customer related litigation."

Expert Comments

"Nature of this industry breeds competition. but lack of necessary operational and marketing skills means that only a few gain the critical mass necessary. Successful companies need to be good at personal marketing and dealing with employees."

"It is easy to start a home health company but difficult to get past the critical point of $1–$2 million in sales. Businesses past that point see a lot less competition than the smaller ones."

"Service business with low asset base, competition is increasing due to ease of entry."

"The above ratings are for mid-market companies. For smaller companies, barriers to entry are minimal, and profit and growth trends are not as favorable."

Benchmark Data

Statistics (Home Care Providers)

Number of Establishments	314,126
Average Profit Margin	6.9%
Revenue per Employee	$49,000
Average Number of Employees	5
Average Wages per Employee	$25,361

Source: IBISWorld, June 2012

Products and Services Segmentation

Traditional home healthcare and home nursing care	61.6%
Home hospice	22.6%
Homemaker and personal services	6.8%
Other	6.3%
Home infusion therapy	1.3%
Rental medical equipment	1.1%
Home respiratory therapy	0.3%

Source: IBISWorld, June 2012

Major Market Segmentation

Medicare	41%
Medicaid	24%
State and local governments	15%
Out-of-pocket	10%
Private insurance	8%
Other	2%

Source: IBISWorld, July 2012

Industry Costs

Profit	6.9%
Wages	51.5%
Purchases	28.5%
Depreciation	3.0%
Rent & Utilities	2.0%
Other	8.1%

Source: IBISWorld, June 2012

Statistics (In-Home Senior Care Franchises)

Number of Establishments	7,783
Average Profit Margin	15.3%
Revenue per Employee	$116,500
Average Number of Employees	8
Average Wages per Employee	25,682

Source: IBISWorld, March 2012

Products and Services Segmentation

Homemaker and personal services	50%
Home hospice	22%
Other services	16%
Home nursing care	12%

Source: IBISWorld, March 2012

Industry Costs

Profit	15.3%
Wages	23.7%
Purchases	15.0%
Depreciation	2.0%
Marketing	4.5%
Rent & Utilities	6.5%
Other	33.0%

Source: IBISWorld, March 2012

Market Share

Home Instead Inc.	14.8%
Interim HealthCare Inc.	12.2%
Comfort Keepers	5.5%

Source: IBISWorld, March 2012

- "Cost can average $18 to $22 an hour for in-home care, with discounts in some cases for 24-hour care, for simple companion care, for veterans or for those belonging to groups like Power Over Parkinson's."

  Source: "No place like home: Health care industry booms" by Karen Walenga, *Green Valley News*, February 16, 2011.

- "The average hourly rate for a certified home health aid is $32.37."
- "The 2011 national average private-pay hourly rate for home health aides and homemaker/companion services remain unchanged from 2010 at $21 and $19 respectively."

  Source: 2011 MetLife Market Survey of Adult Day Services and Home Care Costs.

- "Homemakers or companions provide services that include light housekeeping, meal preparation, transportation, and companionship. This type of care is often appropriate for those with Alzheimer's disease or other forms of dementia who may be physically healthy but require supervision. Homemakers and companions are not trained to provide hands-on assistance with ADLs such as bathing and dressing."

  Source: 2011 MetLife Market Survey of Adult Day Services and Home Care Costs.

- "Profit margin should be 20% or more."
- "People intensive. Payroll can be about 60% of revenues, which also means that acquirer should be a good people manager."
- "Too much variance between different segments of the industry to generalize"
- "Number of customers, number of live-in situations, average billings per hour per employee."

Expenses as a Percentage of Annual Sales

Cost of goods:	05%
Payroll/labor Costs:	50% to 55%
Occupancy:	05%
Profit (estimated pretax)	20%

Industry Trend

- "Not-for-profit organizations manage 31% of all nursing homes in the United States."

  Source: www.aahsa.org (from Surveys conducted by Genworth Financial)

- "Growing, due to aging of population"
- "Excellent growth as baby boomers age and as people carry appropriate insurance"
- "Home Health Care Industry Focus"

"In 1994, approximately one in eight Americans was age 65 and older. But by 2030, one in five Americans will be a senior citizen. From 2010 to 2030, the number of baby boomers age 65 to 84 will grow by an estimated 80 percent while the population age 85 and older will grow by 48 percent. In addition, between 1994 and 2020, the nation's population of 85 years and older is projected to double to 7 million, and then increase to between 19 and 27 million by 2050."

"So it's easy to see why those in the home health care industry see another boom on the horizon—one of ever-increasing demand for services."

Source: www.missouribusiness.net/iag/focus

Questions

- "Who runs the operations (i.e., people) and will they be staying post acquisition?"

Home Health Care — Equipment and Supplies		
(See also Home Health Care Rental)		
SIC 8082-01	NAICS 532291	Number of Businesses/Units 21,000

Rules of Thumb

➢ 85 percent of annual sales plus inventory

➢ 4 times EBITDA excluding rental equipment depreciation

➢ 4 times EBIT

➢ 4 times SDE plus inventory

Pricing Tips

- "Know the payer source—% of Medicare. Know the product mix—# of respiratory patients. Know the referral concentration—# of referring physicians. Know the monthly new-patient setups."
- "Payer mix rental vs. sales"
- "Depends on type of contracts (Medicare-Medicaid, private pay, nursing home, etc.) and length of contracts."
- "The age of the equipment may make it subject to obsolescence. A careful inventory of equipment located in patient homes must be made and evaluated by an expert."
- "Multiples of EBITDA range from 3 to 5. Much of the pricing depends on product mix, e.g., respiratory, DME, infusion, sleep apnea, etc."
- "Competition is high because the market is huge and growing. Risk is low because established businesses have patient referral sources. Profits are slightly down due to more third-party 'paperwork' requirements. Marketability is high, since many large companies are growing by acquisition. Industry is growing due to an aging population."

Expert Comments

"Substantial pressure on margins due to Medicare implementing cost controls and national competitive bidding."

Benchmark Data

- See additional Benchmark data under Home Health Care (care-giving and nursing)
- "20% + EBITDA margins. Need to show annual growth in sales and profits. Stable referral sources."
- "Revenue % oxygen"

Expenses as a Percentage of Annual Sales

Cost of goods:	35%
Payroll/labor Costs:	20%
Occupancy:	05%
Profit (estimated pretax)	35%

Industry Trend

- "Continued consolidation due to competitive bidding."
- "Declining profits because of Medicare pricing pressures"

Questions

- "Any outstanding Medicare audits? Are they accredited?"

Resources

Websites

- www.hmenews.com

Home Health Care Rental (See also Home Health Care Equipment)		
SIC 5999-20	NAICS 532291	Number of Businesses/Units 3,960

Rules of Thumb

➢ 4 times EBITDA

Pricing Tips

- "Payor mix (Medicare, Medicaid, commercial, etc.). How many 'capped' patients?"

Expert Comments

"Industry demand is growing but margins continue to decline as CMS (Center for Medicare & Medicaid Services) reduces reimbursement to providers."

Benchmark Data

Statistics (Home Medical Equipment Rentals)

Number of Establishments	3,960
Average Profit Margin	20.5%
Revenue per Employee	$160,100
Average Number of Employees	9.4
Average Wages per Employee	$42,412

Source: IBISWorld, May 2012

Products and Services Segmentation

Durable medical equipment	30%
Oxygen and respiratory therapy equipment	70%

Source: IBISWorld, May 2012

Major Market Segmentation

Medicare	48%
Private insurance	16%
Medicaid	15%
State and local governments	9%
Out-of-pocket payers	7%
Other	5%

Source: IBISWorld, May 2012

Industry Costs

Profit	20.5%
Wages	26.4%
Purchases	39.3%
Depreciation	3.7%
Marketing	1.2%
Rent & Utilities	5.0%
Other	3.9%

Source: IBISWorld, May 2012

- "Historically, high O2 (oxygen concentrators), high Medicare businesses were preferred, but this has changed with reimbursement reductions and added legislation from CMS."

Expenses as a Percentage of Annual Sales

Cost of goods:	10%
Payroll/labor Costs:	20%
Occupancy:	04%
Profit (estimated pretax)	18%

Industry Trend

- "Continued pricing pressures and uncertainty of Medicare reimbursement rates. Implementation of competitive bidding will further erode profit margins."

Questions

- "How many O2 patients are 'capped?'"

	Franchise
Home Helpers	
Approx. Total Investment	$47,150 to $86,400
NAICS 621610	Number of Businesses/Units 658

Rules of Thumb

➢ 35 percent of annual sales plus inventory

Resources

Websites

- www.homehelpers.cc

Home Inspection

	NAICS 541350	Number of Businesses/Units 23,551

Rules of Thumb

➢ 45 percent of annual sales includes inventory

Benchmark Data

Statistics (Building Inspectors)

Number of Establishments	23,551
Average Profit Margin	19.2%
Revenue per Employee	$67,300
Average Number of Employees	1.4
Average Wages per Employee	$27,773

Source: IBISWorld, August 2012

Products and Services Segmentation

Home inspection services	45.8%
Specific element inspection services	31.6%
Commercial building inspection services	17.6%
Other	5%

Source: IBISWorld, August 2012

Major Market Segmentation

Home buyers and sellers	35.8%
Individuals seeking repairs or maintenance	23.7%
Commercial building construction market	16.8%
The government	13.7%
New home builders	10%

Source: IBISWorld, August 2012

Industry Costs

Profit	19.2%
Wages	41.2%
Purchases	7.9%
Depreciation	2.2%
Marketing	11.6%
Rent & Utilities	4.5%
Other	13.4%

Source: IBISWorld, August 2012

Statistics (Home Inspection Franchises)

Number of Establishments	2,414
Average Profit Margin	19.2%
Revenue per Employee	$48,000
Average Number of Employees	1.6
Average Wages per Employee	$19,814

Source: IBISWorld, August 2012

Products and Services Segmentation

General home inspections	68.9%
New construction inspections	21.5%
Other specialty inspections (e.g. infrared, radon, termite, energy)	9.6%

Source: IBISWorld, August 2012

Major Market Segmentation

Home buyers	29.5%
Home sellers	25.8%
Commercial and savings banks	20.6%
Other	13.3%
New Home Builders	10.8%

Source: IBISWorld, August 2012

Industry Costs

Profit	19.2%
Wages	41.2%
Purchases	7.2%
Depreciation	4.4%
Marketing	12.0%
Rent & Utilities	4.5%
Other	11.5%

Source: IBISWorld, August 2012

- "While it is difficult to scientifically predict your market potential, there are some general guidelines which you might find useful. As a rule of thumb, roughly 15,000 existing homes are sold annually per 1,000,000 population size, or 1.5%. Calculating the percentage of these homes, the percentage that are inspected can be as high as 95% in major cities and along the East and West coasts, and as low as 10%–25% in more rural areas. Try to obtain from local officials and real estate salespeople the figures for the population in your region and the percentage of homes there that are inspected. Then apply the following formula to estimate your current home inspection business opportunity: (Population x .015) x % of homes inspected = # of home inspections conducted per year.

- "For example, if (1) one million people live in your area and you determine that roughly (50%) fifty percent of the homes sold are inspected, then you can estimate that about (7,500) seven thousand five hundred inspections are conducted annually. This is a minimum figure, because it does not include inspections of newly built homes and, as the market and consumer awareness grow, the number of home inspections overall will grow as well.
"Now check your local Yellow Pages to determine the number of home inspectors working in your area, and divide the number of annual home inspections by that figure. Twenty (20) inspectors in our example above would mean that each inspector would average about three hundred seventy five (375) inspections per year. This is only a general picture, however, since multi-inspector firms account for a larger Market Share   , while part-time inspectors will do fewer. The average home inspection fee nationally is $240, and so a home inspector in this scenario could project to earn an annual gross income of $90,000. It is quite feasible, however, for well-trained inspectors to earn well over $100,000."

Source: International Society of Home Inspectors, http://www.ishionline.org/

Resources

Associations

- National Association of Home Inspectors—a good site: www.nahi.org
- International Society of Home Inspectors—an excellent site with lots of good information: www.ishionline.org

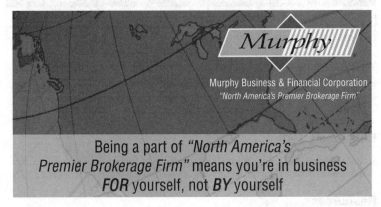

Murphy Business & Financial Corporation
"North America's Premier Brokerage Firm"

Being a part of *"North America's Premier Brokerage Firm"* means you're in business *FOR* yourself, not *BY* yourself

At Murphy Business, we provide the new or experienced business broker with the support required to build a successful business brokerage firm. "We allow the Business Broker to concentrate on what they do best, work with clients listing and selling businesses."

You will:

Spend most of your time with clients
Receive all necessary support and training
Run you own business in your local market
Take advantage of a proven lead generating system
Receive the benefits of being part of a larger organization
Much more!

Your Clients Will:

Benefit from our complete range of services:
Business Sales • Buyer Searches • Business Valuations • Business Consulting • Financing Assistance • Mergers & Acquisitions • Commercial Real Estate • Machinery & Equipment Appraisal & Brokerage

Home Nursing Agencies (See also Home Health Care—Care-Giving)

	NAICS 621610	

Rules of Thumb

➤ 4 times EBITDA

Pricing Tips

- "Multiples of EBITDA commonly used for home nursing agencies run from as low as 1 to 5 times 12 month trailing EBITDA."

Benchmark Data

- "With the aging of America, and the growing need for health care services, this is a growth industry. Low cost of entry equals a competitive environment."

Resources

Associations
- National Association for Home Care and Hospice: www.nahc.org

		Franchise

Home Team Inspection Service (See also Home Inspection)

Approx. Total Investment		$39,000 to $71,000
SIC 7389-96	NAICS 541350	Number of Businesses/Units 201

Rules of Thumb

➤ 35 percent of annual sales plus inventory

Benchmark Data

- For Benchmark data see Home Inspection

Resources

Websites
- www.hometeaminspection.com

Home-Based Businesses

Rules of Thumb

➤ The best way to price a home-based business is to first find out if the business is dependent on the owner. If so, it may be impossible to price as it may have little or no value. However, if the business is transferable it may have value. Prepare an SDE figure and then create a multiple (see Introduction for more information on SDE and a corresponding multiple) to arrive at an approximate price. If the business corresponds to a business listed in this Guide, see if the information there helps.

Industry Trend

- "After 37 years of following small and home business launches, the National Mail Order Association (NMOA) predicts a new explosion in people starting a business because of layoffs and fears of salary reductions. 53 percent of small (businesses with one or more owners but no paid employees) businesses in the U.S. are 'home- based' businesses."

Homeland Security

Rules of Thumb

- ➤ 100 percent of annual sales includes inventory
- ➤ 3.5 times SDE includes inventory
- ➤ "Defining a company as Homeland Security is tricky. Government contractors are typically more Homeland Security companies than traditional security companies. Since this industry is already in the hundreds of billions, and is expected to grow exponentially over the next decade, I would recommend a new category."

Pricing Tips

- "Funded contracts are worth a minimum of 1x revenue."
- "There is a tremendous difference between backlog and funded backlog. Funded backlog should receive a very high premium on that number. If customer is Federal Government, and you are supplying them with a unique technology, there is a tremendous amount of value, even after the life of the product, in parts. This will add longevity to any product pipeline."

Expert Comments

"As the government grows, the industry will grow exponentially."

"The Homeland Security industry is experiencing consolidation. Therefore competition is increasing in certain areas where companies have historically not seen any. Companies with proprietary technology, particularly technology currently being used by the government, are greatly increasing in value."

"The recent government funding for Homeland Security products has made this a growing industry for many years to come. Large Homeland Security contractors, many who are also defense contractors, are seeking small companies with patented products to be able to capture more government products."

"Location is irrelevant. It is important to have a plan for foreign sales."

Benchmark Data

- "A patented product with a history of orders can realize as much as 30x earnings."
- "Multiple of earnings for funded contracts is typically 7–8x's."
- "1 to 3 times revenue"

Expenses as a Percentage of Annual Sales

Cost of goods:	30%
Payroll/labor Costs:	20%
Occupancy:	10%
Profit (estimated pretax)	25%

Industry Trend

- "There is a steady demand for security products and technology for well into the future. The trend is clearly toward exponential growth."
- "Growing, but a lot going to the larger industry players."
- "This industry is experiencing exponential growth because of an insatiable demand from the customer base."

Questions

- "Can you export this service or technology? Are you an 8a company? How do you market this product? (Most do not, and have a few key contacts)."
- "How much of his orders are funded? How much is coming from GSA schedule? Can you see an invoice? Does the government pay him promptly?"
- "What is the amount of your funded backlog? How much of your equipment is rejected each year? Do you know how many pieces of your equipment are deployed and actively used? What patent or market protection do you have?"

Resources

Trade Publications

- Government Security News: www.gsnmagazine.com

Homes – Retirement

(See also Assisted Living Facilities & Nursing Homes)

SIC 8059-04	NAICS 623311	Number of Businesses/Units 25,300

Pricing Tips

- "Selling price is quite varied, from $2,000 to $3,000 + per bed, depending upon the number of beds. There is no hard and fast rule of thumb which will apply because of the condition of the real estate and whether or not there are quarters for the owner/operator and the size of the home."

	Franchise
Honest-1 Auto Care	
Approx. Total Investment	$174,200 to $292,500
	Number of Businesses/Units 25

Rules of Thumb

➢ 60 to 65 percent of annual sales plus inventory

Resources

Websites

- www.honest-1.com

Hospital Laundry—Supply (See also Uniform Rental)

	NAICS 812331	

Rules of Thumb

➤ 50 percent of annual sales plus inventory

Pricing Tips

▪ An industry expert states that for laundry with hospital contracts a rule of thumb is 50 percent of gross annual sales. This is because that market is a very competitive one.

Benchmark Data

▪ For additional Benchmark data see Uniform Rental
▪ The Textile Rental Services Association (TRSA) estimates the following costs that hospitals spend for on-premise laundry services:
  ✓ fringe benefits, taxes, insurance—12%
  ✓ fuel oil, natural gas—7%
  ✓ depreciation—2%
  ✓ maintenance—2%
  ✓ water and sewer—1%
  ✓ electricity—1%
  ✓ interest on investment, administration, and support—5%

Source: www.trsa.org

Resources

Associations
▪ Textile Rental Services Association (TRSA): www.trsa.org

Hotels & Motels (See also Motels)

SIC 7011-01	NAICS 721110	Number of Businesses/Units 49,967

Rules of Thumb

➤ 250 to 300 percent of annual sales plus inventory

➤ 8 times SDE

➤ 8 to 10 times EBITDA

➤ 2.0 to 3.5 times annual room revenues—average 2.5

➤ Outside corridors—2.0 to 2.5 times annual room revenues

➤ Inside corridors—2.5 to 3.0 times annual room revenues

➤ Seldom seen—3.5 times annual room revenues

Pricing Tips

▪ "Smaller, limited service property (100 rooms and less) buyers tend to value hotels based on annual room revenue (2.5-3 times) whereas larger, full service property buyers tend to value hotels on cap rates (9-12%)."

- "Key findings from the Hotel Transaction Almanac:
  - ✓ 31 percent of deals in 2011 involved distressed assets.
  - ✓ 35 percent of hotel acquisitions were by REITs.
  - ✓ The average room revenue multiplier was 4.2.
  - ✓ The average cap rate rose from 9.1 percent in 2010 to 10.5 percent in 2011."

  Source: Hotel Transaction Almanac, a report from STR Analytics and the Hotel Investment Barometer

- "After falling 31% in 2009, hotel values have risen 17% in 2010, 20% last year and HVS projects 17% increases this year and next."

  Source: "Hotel Transactions Set to Surge" by Eric Stoessel, www.ihonline.com

- "At least one person on the panel was willing to throw out a number. John O'Neill, a consultant and professor at Penn State University's School of Hospitality Management, said values per room will be down 2.2% by year end, citing results from the Penn State Index of U.S. Hotel Values."

  Source: "Hotel values expected to increase in 2011" by Patrick Mayock, HotelNewsNow.com
  www.hotelnewsnow.com

2011 value per room US $		% change
Luxury	$265,930	+6.4%
Upper Upscale	$141,474	+7.2%
Upscale	$96,549	+6.7%
Midscale w/ F&B	$54,975	+2.7%
Midscale w/o F&B	$63,651	+3.6%
Economy	$17,531	+11.0%
Total U.S.	$80,424	+7.5%

Source: Penn State Index of Hotel Values

- Determining value

  "While it's difficult to give broad-based advice on deriving value for any one particular hotel, O'Neill did share an automated valuation model to at least put you in the ballpark.

  - $42,873 (constant)

  + net operating income per room x 5.615

  + average daily rate c 615.039

  + number of rooms x 33.693

  + occupancy x 234.891

  = estimated value per room

  "O'Neill admitted the formula is a bit general, and property specifics should be taken into account when determining value. However, the above model is on average within a 10% range of the actual hotel sale price, compared to appraisals, which vary by only 5%.

  "Marling shared some of his general methodology as well:

  1. Determine normal NOI. While 'normal' is a relative term—especially in this era of the 'new normal'—Marling said the important thing is to be realistic. Don't simply assume you'll return to 2007 operating levels. Survey the demand drivers in your particular market, and draw reasonable conclusions about future performance.

  In doing so, factor in the cost to get to normal. If you've been putting off a property improvement plan or other capital expenditure, consider those costs in your valuation estimate.

  2. Determine cap rate—Once you get to normal, decide what your cap rate would be at that normal. It's often lower than you might think, Marling said. For a midscale asset, think in the range of 8% to 9%. For trophy assets, it might even be lower, at 6.5% to 7%.

3. This can be incredibly difficult to determine, given that ranges are so broad, Marling said. A cap rate can be anywhere from 7.5 to 15, and the resulting discount rate might be between 9% and 15%.

"'There's a huge, big range of values, and you just need to concentrate on the process each time,' he said."

- "Independent older properties: 1.5–2 times annual room revenue. Moderate franchise, 30–70 rooms: 2–3 times room revenue. Larger franchise properties, 70+ rooms: 4–5 times room revenue, but more often around a 10 cap rate."

- "Most independent, exterior-corridor properties will sell for 1.5–2.0 times gross sales, while franchise or flagged properties will sell for 3 times gross sales. In major metro markets with higher real estate values, these numbers will be pushed up."

- "Most franchise flagged properties ask between 3–4 times annual room revenue and end up getting 2.5–3 times, depending on improvements needed, condition and brand of property."

- "Hotels should be priced only after taking into consideration an ample FF&E Reserve of 4 to 5 percent of revenues (in addition to Repairs and Maintenance expense). Anticipate third-party financing of 60 to 70 percent of the purchase price and debt service coverage (1.25-1.5) can be proven. Some like to analyze based on ADR and Occupancy Rates and some base on times gross revenue only. Land lease or exterior corridor properties are going at 2x gross revenue and some interior franchise units may go as high as 3.5x."

- "Buyer pricing should always be done AFTER provision form FF&E Reserve of approximately 4%. Repairs & Maintenance and FF&E Reserve TOGETHER should total approximately 8–9% of total sales. Forget exterior corridor properties."

- "Usually use a rule of thumb from 2.0 to 3.0 of gross sales. In extreme cases, up to 3.5 for excellent franchised property. Age and condition of property as well as FF&E makes a difference. We use several approaches to actual valuation of a property. Adequate (approx 5%) for reserves. RevPAR (Revenue per Available Room) seems to be the thing today, not gross sales."

- "Hotels are based on many things, since you just don't buy a hotel business. You have real estate attached 100% of the time. Revenue per available room, occupancies, average daily rates play important parts. In general, a hotel would sell according to the amount of rooms built. In general, you could take revenue per available room per year and multiply that by number of rooms then multiply that number by anywhere from 3 to 10 to get a price; of course this would depend upon what type of flag the hotel was flying. Food and beverage operations both in hotels and free standing are similar. Basically a good rule of thumb is to take the replacement cost of the FF&E plus leasehold improvements, then add this amount to 50% of revenue or 3x seller's discretionary cash or bottom line after seller add-backs."

- "Most appraisers use only the land plus building, plus FF&E for total valuation. We prefer to consider all of these, but add a value for the going business based on the gross and net income."

- "Beach properties: 3 ½ to 5 times sales. Oceanfront: 4 to 5 times gross sales."

- "Some buyers and sellers prefer to use a cap rate to determine value while others prefer a dollar amount per room."

- "Whether or not the property is franchised, business hotel or resort can influence value."

- "Large capital investment on front end makes the property susceptible to new, better-located competition. Need ongoing reserve for replacement of FF&E."
- "Location and franchise make a great difference. Also, we must consider extended-stay motels."

Expert Comments

"Expensive to build new. Pie isn't getting any bigger with more properties taking a piece of the pie. Property value has decreased which makes property not worth as much as say 3–5 years ago."

"Constant upgrades and increased same class competition can strangle cash flow."

"The trend is toward limited service, manageable properties under 80 rooms, as they are able to be owner operated with limited staff, and the economy does not affect the properties as readily."

"There is a large pool of buyers for hotel properties but these buyers are discretionary and will not overpay. Good locations are nice but susceptible to newer, nicer developments which can hurt business. Mid-markets with median competition are favorable."

"There is a lot of competition in the hospitality industry. Many properties turn a mediocre profit, but the appreciation in property value is usually the benefit. Buy a property, maintain it for 3–5 years, sell it for a profit."

Benchmark Data

Statistics (Hotels and Motels)

Number of Establishments	49,967
Average Profit Margin	6.0%
Revenue per Employee	$88,400
Average Number of Employees	29.4
Average Wages per Employee	$23,568

Source: IBISWorld, March 2012

Products and Services Segmentation

Guest room rentals from hotels with 25 or more rooms	62.7%
Motels	6.2%
Food and alcohol sales from hotels with 25 or more rooms	12.5%
Conference room rentals from hotels with 25 or more rooms	4.2%
Other revenue from hotels with 25 or more rooms	4.2%
Hotels with fewer than 25 rooms and other accommodations	3.8%

Source: IBISWorld, March 2012

Major Market Segmentation

Business travelers	28.5%
Vacation travelers	25.7%
Conference travelers	25%
Personal or family travelers	20.8%

Source: IBISWorld, March 2012

Industry Costs

Profit	6.0%
Wages	26.8%
Purchases	38.1%
Depreciation	6.6%
Marketing	2.0%
Rent & Utilities	5.6%
Other	14.9%

Source: IBISWorld, March 2012

Statistics (Boutique Hotels)

Number of Establishments	2,076
Average Profit Margin	7.8%
Revenue per Employee	$88,400
Average Number of Employees	29.4
Average Wages per Employee	$31,424

Source: IBISWorld, March 2012

Products and Services Segmentation

Lodging	70.5%
Food	16.7%
Lounges	6.8%
Spa and wellness services	6%

Source: IBISWorld, March 2012

Major Market Segmentation

Business travelers	68%
Leisure travelers	29.3%
Other travelers	2.7%

Source: IBISWorld, March 2012

Industry Costs

Profit	7.8%
Wages	35.7%
Purchases	38.1%
Depreciation	6.0%
Marketing	1.0%
Rent & Utilities	5.6%
Other	5.8%

Source: IBISWorld, March 2012

Market Share

Marriott International	6.2%
Hilton Hotels	5.1%
Starwood	3.2%
Wyndham Worldwide Corporation	2.5%

Source: IBISWorld, March 2012

Hotel Statistics	Full-Service Hotels	Limited-Service Hotels
Average nightly occupancy	66%	68.4%
Average number of rooms per hotel	290	114
Average daily rate	$105.25	$86.82

Source: STR Global, www.statisticbrain.com /hotel-revenue-statistics, March 23, 2012

Average Hotel Revenue Statistics (Per Day)

	Full-Service Hotels	Limited-Service Hotels
Total Average Daily Revenue	$56,472	$22,679
Total Average Daily expenses	$41,768	$13,110
Total Average Daily Profit	$14,704	$9,569

Source: STR Global, www.statisticbrain.com /hotel-revenue-statistics, March 23, 2012

"2010 Hotel Food-And-Beverage Revenue"

Restaurant: 30.2%
Bar: 5.6%
Room Service: 4.4%
Mini Bar: 0.9%
Banquet: 41.0%
Public Room Rental: 3.0%
Audio Visual: 3.4%
Service Charges: 8.1%
Other: 3.4%

Source: Franchise Times, March 2012

2009 At-a-Glance Statistical Figures

Properties* 50,800
Guestrooms 4,762,095
Billions in sales $127.2
Revenue per available room (RevPAR) $53.50
Average occupancy rate 54.7%
*Based on properties with 15 or more rooms

Source: 2010 Lodging Profile—AH&LA, www.ahla.com

- "RevPar is what you need to look at, but most buyers still looking at annual sales. Look for new players coming into the market."
- "Hotels are valued differently as to who the buyer is. For owner-operator they may look at 2–3 times annual gross revenues, while investors will look at cap rates, and existing hospitality groups will look at Market Share and price per room costs for an acquisition versus the cost of building new."
- "2 to 3.5 x gross room revenue, $30,000 per room."
- "2.5–3 times annual room revenue for franchises properties and 1.5–2 times room revenue for daily independent; about 1.5 times for weekly hotels."

Expenses as a Percentage of Annual Sales

Cost of goods: .... 05% to 10%
Payroll/labor Costs: .... 25% to 30%
Occupancy: .... 50% to 60%
Profit (estimated pretax) .... 10% to 20%

Industry Trend

- "For 2011, the U.S. lodging industry posted pretax profits of $21.6 billion—up from $18 billion in 2010—and $137.5 billion in sales—up from $127.7 billion in 2010, according to the American Hotel & Lodging Association (AH&LA) Lodging Industry Profile (LIP), an annual statistical analysis of the industry. This $137.5 billion contributed to an overall $813 billion in tourism sales, with resident and international travelers' expenditures in the U.S. estimated at $2.2 billion/day; $92.8 million/hour; $1.5 million/minute; and $25,700/second."

Source: The American Hotel and Lodging Association (AH and LA) www.ahla.com July 2012

- "PKF Hospitality Research, LLC (PKF-HR) forecasts that the supply of hotel rooms in the United States will grow by 0.6% in 2012.

"That figure is less than half the long-run average annual rate of change for this measure. Concurrently, the demand for hotel rooms will increase by 2.2%, slightly above its long-run average.

"The greatest increases in supply are forecast for the upper-midscale (2.7%) and upscale (1.4%) chain-scale segments. Select-service, boutique, and extended-stay properties dominate the new properties entering these two segments; however, PKF-HR is projecting a 2.5% decrease in the supply of midscale hotel rooms.

"PKF-HR is forecasting a 4% increase in the number of occupied rooms at upper-midscale properties. Demand for upscale hotels is forecast to increase by 3 percent."

Source:" PKF: Modest Supply Growth Expected in 2012," PFK Hospitality Research, LLC, June 7, 2012

- "The amount of foreclosure will bring prices down, if buyers can afford to sell them. Disability law requiring handicap access to any swimming pool could be costly for owners."

- "The recovery of the U.S. lodging industry continues in a pattern established in the first quarter of 2010, with occupancy gains still outpacing gains in room rate. According to the June 2011 edition of *Hotel Horizons*, PKF Hospitality Research (PKF-HR) forecasts that the demand for U.S. hotel rooms in 2011 will increase a solid 4.9 percent, while the average daily room rate (ADR) paid by guests will rise a modest 2.4 percent.

"It won't be until 2013 that we see the majority of the 50 markets in our *Hotel Horizons* universe exceed their long-run occupancy rate. Accordingly, PKF-HR is forecasting that U.S. room rates beyond 2011 will grow at a greater pace: 5.5 percent in 2012 and another 5.8 percent in 2013.

"By controlling labor costs, hotel managers can offset the inefficient hotel revenue growth and achieve gains on the bottom-line. PKF-HR is projecting unit-level net operating income to increase 11.7 percent in 2011. Profit growth will be even greater in 2012 (17.9 percent) as room rates begin to drive RevPar."

Source: "PKF-HR: U.S. Demand growth outpacing ADR growth," July 6, 2011,
www.hospitalityworldnetwork.com

- "Consistent with Smith Travel Research's recent re-categorization of midscale hotels from Midscale with Food & Beverage and Midscale without Food & Beverage to Upper Midscale and Midscale, the Penn State Index of U.S. Hotel Values has re-categorized its classifications, as well. The Upper Midscale category includes such hotel brands as Comfort Suites, Hampton Inn, Holiday Inn and TownePlace Suites, while the Midscale segment includes Baymont, Howard Johnson, LaQuinta and Quality Inn.

"The Upper Midscale hotel segment is anticipated to register strong improvements in market value of approximately 11% in both 2011 and 2012. The Midscale Category is expected to show decent value increases of 7.6% and 10.9% in 2011 and 2012, respectively.

"The Economy segment is projected to record the strongest percentage increases in hotel values in 2011 and 2012 of 15.0% and 17.8%, respectively. The Luxury segment is anticipated to show the highest increases in value per room of approximately $24,500 and $36,400 in 2011 and 2012."

Source: "It Might Be Time to Buy Hotels" by John O'Neill, www.honline.com July 6, 2011

- "The pie is not getting any bigger, there are just more taking a bite out of it."
- "Trend is toward moderate priced property and extended stay with free perks like breakfast and wi-fi."

Seller Financing
- "Not usually seller financed currently"
- "20 years"
- "5 to 10 years"
- "20 to 30 year amortization, 5 year balloon."

Questions

- "ADR, occupancy, RevPar, punch list, recent inspection reports"
- "Punch list items for franchise. Capital expenditures. This can be huge."
- "Are there capital expense items that need attention? How much contracted room business do they have? How much room business do they have on the books and for how long a period of time? What was their last QA score if it is a franchise hotel? Do they know of any new highways being constructed in the future that may divert traffic to or away from the hotel? Any new competition coming up in the area?"

Resources

Websites

- www.hotelmanagement.net
- www.hotelbusiness.com
- www.lhonline.com

Trade Publications

- Lodging Magazine: www.lodgingmagazine.com
- Hotels and Motels: Valuations and Market Study, published by the Appraisal Institute : www.appraisalinstitute.org

	Franchise
House Doctors Handyman Professionals	
Approx. Total Investment	$70,000 to $120,000
Estimated Annual Sales/Unit	Not Available
NAICS 811411	Number of Businesses/Units 103

Rules of Thumb

➢ House Doctor is a handyman service specializing in minor home repairs

➢ 24 percent of annual sales plus inventory

Resources

Websites

- www.housedoctors.com

	Franchise
Hungry Howie's Pizza & Subs	
Approx. Total Investment	$225,000 to $358,000
Estimated Annual Sales/Unit	$484,000
NAICS 722211	Number of Businesses/Units 575

Rules of Thumb

➢ 35 percent of annual sales plus inventory

Benchmark Data
- For Benchmark data see Pizza Shops & Sandwich Shops

Resources

Websites
- www.hungryhowies.com

	Franchise
Huntington Learning Center	
Approx. Total Investment	$113,850 to $245,850
	Number of Businesses/Units 280

Rules of Thumb
➤ 60 percent of annual sales

Resources

Websites
- www.huntingtonfranchise.com

HVAC—Heating, Ventilating & Air Conditioning		
	NAICS 238220	Number of Businesses/Units 95,094

Rules of Thumb
➤ 25 to 30 percent of annual sales plus inventory

➤ 2 to 2.5 times SDE plus inventory

➤ 3 times EBIT

➤ 2.75 times EBITDA

Pricing Tips
- "Mix drives value. There is an enormous range of pricing based on the mix of business. Prices for these businesses range from under 10% of revenue to over 100% of revenue. This is an enormously fragmented industry and therefore every company mix, set of controls, recurring nature, and margins will drive value."
- "Biz mix is a critical value driver. Must evaluate the mix in order to price."

Expert Comments
"Competition: highly fragmented, over 50,000 contractors. Risk: a required recurring market. Historic profit trend: as varied as there are contractors. Location: proximity to market important, but not a driving factor as services provided off-site. Marketability: tough to carry sustainability based on typical owner influence. Growth: somewhat mature slow growth industry. Ease of replication: these businesses are easily replicated."

Benchmark Data

Statistics (Heating and Air Conditioning)

Number of Establishments	95,094
Average Profit Margin	5.4%
Revenue per Employee	$144,600
Average Number of Employees	4.7
Average Wages per Employee	$63,826

Source: IBISWorld, July 2012

Products and Services Segmentation

New construction HVAC installation	57%
HVAC maintenance and repairs	31%
HVAC upgrades and replacements	6.3%
Refrigeration system installations, maintenance and repairs	5.7%

Source: IBISWorld, July 2012

Major Market Segmentation

Single-family homes	25.9%
Other	13.5%
Healthcare and institutional buildings	13.3%
Educational buildings	12.6%
Manufacturing and industrial buildings	11.5%
Office buildings	11.1%
Retail	7%
Apartment buildings	5.1%

Source: IBISWorld, July 2012

Industry Costs

Profit	5.4%
Wages	45.4%
Purchases	38.1%
Depreciation	1.0%
Marketing	1.0%
Rent & Utilities	2.6%
Other	6.5%

Source: IBISWorld, July 2012

Expenses as a Percentage of Annual Sales

Cost of goods:	65%
Payroll/labor Costs:	22%
Occupancy:	03%
Profit (estimated pretax)	05%

Industry Trend

- "Here's what's happening:
    - ✓ Plumbing companies moving into the HVAC business
    - ✓ HVAC companies adding plumbing to their service offerings
    - ✓ Contractors adding specialty services to their businesses. Some examples include irrigation, lawn fertilization, water softeners, bottled water, geothermal market, water-well drilling
    - ✓ Business scope changes—large, residential new-construction contractors change to primarily commercial
    - ✓ Single-family home contractors beginning to do multi-family condos
    - ✓ Service and repair contractors entering the single-family market
    - ✓ Single-family specialists moving into multi-family construction

✓ Radiant work is becoming more marketable in upscale homes, particularly in the Northeast. It's used in just under 25% of homes in Canada, and the trend is moving south.

Source: "An Industry Forever Changing" by Eddie Hollub, *Contracting Business*; www.contractingbusiness.com

Resources

Trade Publications
- Air Conditioning Refrigeration News: www.achrnews.com

Associations
- Air Conditioning Contractors of America: www.acca.org

		Franchise
i9 Sports		
Approx. Total Investment		$44,900 to $69,900
	NAICS 713990	Number of Businesses/Units 132

Rules of Thumb

➢ 65 to 70 percent of annual sales plus inventory

Ice Cream Trucks (See also Catering Trucks)		
	NAICS 722330	

Rules of Thumb

➢ 1 times SDE plus fair market value of the truck(s) plus inventory

Pricing Tips

- "How much do you make selling ice cream? 'If it's raining outside, you can make as little as $3, but on a good day, you can earn $500. These days, though, the high gas prices are eating into my profit...'"

  Source: "Selling ice cream, bringing back memories" by Cindy Atoji Keene, *Boston Globe*, July 27, 2008

- "Today, ice cream trucks are owned by small regional companies that rent to independent drivers, or individuals who go it alone.

  "Some, including Tanner, buy a fleet and rent to drivers such as Phillips, who take home 35 percent of their daily sales—minus the $12 daily truck rental fee and gas costs. Tanner gets the other 65 percent to cover operational and stocking costs: He supplies 64 varieties of ice cream from various suppliers to every truck.

  "Phillips said that, so far, her best day netted more than $400 in sales. She's been working six days a week, now aiming for $500."

  Source: *Boston Globe*, Thursday August 18, 2005. Dated, but still informative.

Benchmark Data

- For Benchmark data see Catering Trucks

Resources

Websites
- www.icecreamtrucksuperstore.com

Associations
- International Dairy Foods Association: www.idfa.org
- International Association of Ice Cream Distributors and Vendors (IAICDV): www.iaicdv.org

Ice Cream/Yogurt Shops (See also Baskin-Robbins, Carvel, etc.)		
SIC 5812-03	NAICS 722213	Number of Businesses/Units 20,000

Rules of Thumb

- ➤ 60 percent of annual sales plus inventory
- ➤ 2.2. times SDE plus inventory (franchised only)
- ➤ 3 times EBIT
- ➤ 3 times EBITDA
- ➤ 15 to 20 times weekly sales (independent only)

Pricing Tips
- "Length of lease a major factor and property ownership desirable"
- "Condition of premises, age of equipment, and location of shopping center critical to resale value."
- "2.5 x SDE applies to franchised ice cream stores with minimum 8+ year lease remaining with transfer fee included in the price. If less than 8 year lease or if seller requires buyer pay transfer fee, appropriate modifications need to be made. Non franchised ice cream businesses sell at 15-20x weekly sales assuming condition and lease (8+) years are acceptable."
- "Franchised ice cream operations have consumed the marketplace, and independent stores are virtually unsellable. Well-run franchised operations have good resale value, although seasonal in many marketplaces."
- "These stores are usually sold for a little less than one half year's gross sales. If it is a franchise store, such as Dairy Queen, Arctic Circle, or A&W, 15 percent can be added to the asking price. Net profit usually runs from 18 percent to 22 percent. Lease on the property should not exceed 6 percent (upper limit) of gross profit."

Expert Comments

"Location-driven business with increasing competition in the marketplace. Co-branding is an ideal situation for this concept to offset the seasonality and utilize the facility to a greater degree."

"Franchised operations protect many of the negatives, but increasing availability of premium desserts and ice cream limit expansion possibilities."

Benchmark Data
- For Benchmark Information see Restaurants — Limited Service
- "Product cost is lower in many franchises who manufacture product on site. However, those franchises typically have higher labor costs."

- "Limit retail operations to 1200 s/f or less."

Expenses as a Percentage of Annual Sales

Cost of goods:	28%
Payroll/labor Costs:	22%
Occupancy:	10%
Profit (estimated pretax)	05%

Industry Trend

- "Dramatically increasing product costs will strain profitability, increase in number of franchised concepts will cause competition unseen in the marketplace in its history."
- "Exceedingly shared market with co-branded products (i.e., Dunkin/Baskin)."

Questions

- "Equipment servicing questions, employee history, historical sales"
- "Owner operated or absentee? Any wholesale accounts."
- "Sales by month to determine fluctuations; manager, if any, and salary, with benefits. Changes in product cost and related change in selling price of products. Sales trends, on a month-to-month basis. Must speak to company district manager, if a franchise, about his/her requirements of a new buyer."

Resources

Websites
- www.malcolmstogo.com

Associations
- International Dairy Foods Association: www.idfa.org

Ice Hockey Teams (Professional)

SIC 7997-05	NAICS 711211	

Rules of Thumb

➢ The average value of a National Hockey League team is $228 million. ". . . up 2% from last year, yet 14 teams saw their values decline amid struggles to sell tickets and sponsorships in a weak economy. More than half the league lost money last year."

Source: *Forbes*, December 20, 2010

Benchmark Data

- For Benchmark data for professional sports teams see Baseball Teams

Iceberg Drive Inn

	Franchise
Approx. Total Investment	$132,500 to $556,000
Estimated Annual Sales/Unit	Not Available

	NAICS 722211	Number of Businesses/Units 20

Rules of Thumb

➢ 40% to 45% of annual sales plus inventory

Resources

Websites
- www.icebergdriveinn.com

Incentive Companies

	NAICS 561520	

Rules of Thumb

➢ 3 to 5 times EBITDA—multiple expands as free cash flow number rises.

Pricing Tips
- "Is the future business under contract with cancellation clauses?
- "How many programs are on the books for the next 12 months? Are they serving various industries or concentrating on one sector? Diversity is better. Three types—travel, merchandise, debit card. Points tracking & redemption, etc. = big interest in online registration and digital offerings."

Industrial Safety and Health

Rules of Thumb

➢ Manufacturing—5 to 7 times recasted EBIT less debt

➢ Distribution—4 to 6 times recasted EBIT less debt

Information and Document Management Service Industries

	NAICS 5415	

Rules of Thumb

➢ 4 to 6 times normalized EBITDA

Information Technology Companies

	NAICS 541512	

Rules of Thumb

➢ 100 to 150 percent of annual sales

➢ 3 to 4 times SDE

➢ 4 times EBIT

➢ 4 to 6 times EBITDA

Pricing Tips
- "Might increase multiple if selling company has secured gov't contracts especially if in secured agency."
- "Consider any off-balance sheet value, i.e., IP, Gov't contracts, valued customer relationships, unique vendor relationships."

- "Multiples can run as high as 10 x for select software products."
- "An IT services company is defined as an organization with a business-to-business services model which may include competencies in custom application development, application implementation, application integration, systems integration application hosting and technology consulting."
- "Is there an SLA (Software License Agreement) for each type/copy of software being used? Are the SLA's assignable? Has the vendor given written permission to assign them and under what conditions? Has the company been reported to the Software Consortium as a company using unlicensed software? Is the technology based on open standards and/or proprietary? Is there a complete inventory list of all software and hardware being used in the business? What 3rd parties are hosting applications and providing IT Services?"
- "Off-balance sheet items such as: customer/client lists, developed technology, R&D yet to be commercialized, patents, proprietary products, future potential to grow the business."
- "Ask questions about client relationships that will remain, about product & market development, about other competitive advantages."

Expert Comments

"Historical profit trends are key. Also regarding the marketability is a factor if it has intellectual property value to sell."

"While many IT companies exist and there is lots of competition, this is a market of constant growth and low risk."

"If an IT services company has aligned with a leading technology provider, they frequently experience tremendous growth in business equity. I have seen the ownership of professional services companies sell their equity within just a few years and realize a return on investment multiple of 10 or higher."

Benchmark Data

- "Most important in the IT area would be sales growth trends"
- "Gross margin, utilization of consultants, percent recurring revenues"

Expenses as a Percentage of Annual Sales

Cost of goods:	05%
Payroll/labor Costs:	75%
Occupancy:	05% to 10%
Profit (estimated pretax)	15% to 20%

Industry Trend

- "Budgets are still growing for IT. Sales revenue should grow"
- "Steady but moderate growth. Demand for Information Technology is ever increasing. Growing demand for additional storage and retrieval of data."
- "Unique software products will always be in demand."

Seller Financing

- "3 years"

Questions

- "Why are they selling, revenue and earnings track record, size of customer's geographic footprint, who are their technology partners, etc...?"
- "Must have references and be able to demo product(s)"

Injection Molding		
	NAICS 333220	

Rules of Thumb

➢ 4.5 to 6 times EBITDA

Inns (See also Bed and Breakfasts)		
SIC 7011-02	NAICS 721191	Number of Businesses/Units 14,000

Pricing Tips

- "Inns & B & Bs (businesses as opposed to real-estate driven small properties—small is 3 rooms or less): 4.2 times gross room sales, a little higher for dinner service; 4.51 times room sales. Factors affecting price are area, size, style & owner's quarters. Dinner food service makes a property more difficult to sell. Everyone wants a B&B."
- "For motels & lodging, a commonly used rule of thumb is the GIM (Price/Gross Annual Income) which varies from 3.5 to 5.0. For these kinds of properties, a CAP rate of 10 percent is typical. More important is the cash flow for an inn to be economically feasible; the inn must have enough income to pay the expenses, debt service, and enough left over for the owners to live on."
- "On larger inns, use 8 (bank-financed) to 10 (seller-financed) cap rate on Net Operating Income (NOI) before debt & depreciation. For smaller inns, take the asset value of the underlying real estate & furnishings, add it to 3 times the net operating income and add $20K to $40K for the aesthetics & tax benefits. Work backward to see if NOI can support debt service and reduce accordingly."
- "Must have private baths now. Operating expense can range from $3K to $10K per room depending on occupancy and size of building. Income is usually $5K to $20K per guest room depending on location (occupancy & room rate) and amenities."
- "Leased [inn] properties priced at 30–60 percent of gross sales. Owned properties priced at 50 percent plus of gross sales."
- "Buyer should have a sense of good taste, common sense & hospitality ... cash flow is not great, it will mostly cover living expenses (mostly tax deductible) and there is real estate appreciation potential which you can retain tax free to the degree it is your primary residence. Future of business is excellent—has a great appeal to over-50, early-out, college-educated baby boomers; a lot of teachers. Buyer profile doesn't generalize to other typical businesses."
- "...In business w/leased property, monthly rent & terms of lease are a major factor. Food cost should be plus or minus 30 percent. Labor cost should be plus or minus 25 percent. Also, how much debt does the business have? How much do the owners pay themselves? How many hours do they work?"

Benchmark Data

- For additional Benchmark data see Bed and Breakfasts
- "Operating expenses 40 to 50 percent"
- "Is this a profitable business? You can make a living, but it can vary seasonally and depends on the location. Even a small property can be highly profitable if you have a high average rate (average income per occupied room in a given time period) or you offer more amenities or services, such as a restaurant.
  "How has the hotel business changed over the years? The level of customers' sophistication has risen as well as what they're seeking in a travel destination. The physical plant needs to match the guest expectations. Today, what guests have at home, they also want to see in a hotel, whether it's flat-screen TV, wireless everywhere, Keurig coffee makers, free-standing mirrors, granite countertops, or dual showerheads in the bathroom. We try to balance having amenities with retaining the classical architecture and feel of an 1899 building."

Source: "Running an inn isn't a simple life," by Debbie Lennon, proprietor, Kennebunkport Inn,
Boston Sunday Globe, May 23, 2010

Expenses as a Percentage of Annual Sales

Cost of goods	15% (food, cleaning supplies & linens)
Payroll/labor Costs	10% not including owner
Occupancy	07% to 10%
Profit (estimated pretax)	0

Seller Financing

- "Most large inns are seller financed., typically with 20 percent down and terms @ 9 percent, 30-year amortization with a 7-year balloon."
- "5 to 10 years"
- Some owner financing, full owner financing—20-year amortization, 5–10-year balloons, 7 years normal

Resources

Websites
- www.bb-4-sale.com

Associations
- Innkeeping.org: www.innkeeping.org,

Instant Print (See Print Shops)

	NAICS 323114	

Insurance Agencies/Brokerages

SIC 6411-12	NAICS 524210	Number of Businesses/Units 373,676

Rules of Thumb

- ➢ 125 to 150 percent of annual sales includes inventory
- ➢ 3 to 5 times SDE plus inventory
- ➢ 4 to 5 times EBIT
- ➢ 5 to 6 times EBITDA

> "A. Standard Multi-Lines Independent Insurance Agency

   a) under $1 million commission, Multiple of Gross Commission Income—
   1.25 to .85, depending on carriers represented.

   b) over $1 million commission and fee income, EBITDA, 3 to 9 times.

   B. Non-Standard Auto Insurance Agency. Insurance Commission Income,
   excluding add-on coverage's, times last year's retention, .2 to 1.0 times
   commission income.

   C. Surplus Lines Agency; .80 to 1.0 times commission."

> 100% of annual commissions; applies to multi-line agencies doing
   $100,000– $200,000 in gross commissions

> 1.0 to 1.5 times annual renewal commissions

> 1.5 times annual commissions (property & casualty)

> 2 times annual revenues (standard agency)

> "Agencies with more revenue ($1.5M + in commissions) are typically
   valued at 5–8 times EBITDA. This roughly translates into 1.5–2.0 + times
   commission revenues. Hard markets yield more contingent income and
   increased pricing on carrier premiums. EBITDA margins after recasting
   should come in between 15%–40% depending on size; any brokers above
   $2 million in commissions due to economies of scale issues."

Pricing Tips

- "Currently, we are seeing 2-3x's the commissions for sales of Allstate agencies.
  Reviewing the CSRP will help get insights into the business (such as retention
  rate)."

- "Don't confuse SDE with EBITDA with adjusted EBITDA. This is one of the
  biggest mistakes that I see made by other brokers. Many brokers also simply
  market an agency at 2 x revenue regardless of the quality of the book of
  business and available financing. There are many factors that can influence
  the market value such as the carriers, lines of business, client demographics
  and non-commission based income. Financing and deal terms are also
  critical to getting an agency sold and getting the highest price. Personal lines
  P&C agencies can be sold at fixed prices based on the low risk of a broad
  customer base. Commercial lines P&C and employee benefits agencies have
  larger accounts and are often structured with an earn-out or retention-based
  payment on large accounts. I have valued well over 100 insurance brokerage
  businesses and write articles for a national publication on the subject so please
  feel free to contact me if you have any questions."

- "Expected account retention by the buyer is critical. Loss ratios of less than
  50% are a significant plus. Smaller agencies are often sold as a book of
  business that will be combined with an existing agency, after which the seller's
  location may be shut down. These books of business are usually sold as a
  multiple of commissions, with the multiple perhaps as high as 2.0. Larger
  agencies are usually sold as a multiple of SDE, often including an earn out
  component that can bring the total price to 7.0 or higher in the event of stellar
  future performance (hard to achieve)."

- "Key factors to consider when adjusting the value of an agency are length
  of time the current owner is willing to stay on board, renewal retention, size

of book, and carriers represented. Buyers are willing to pay a premium for agencies where the current owner is willing to stay on for 2 or more years. Agencies with commission income over $2M will usually sell for multiples such of 2 to 3 times gross commission due to larger brokerage firms being potential buyers."

- "NON STANDARD AUTO: 1.10 times commission LARGE AGENCIES: 1.65 times commission"
- "Agencies with SDE of 25% or higher, after inclusion of the buyer's likely cost to hire a replacement for the departing seller, are likely to sell for higher multiples of commissions, and sometimes higher multiples of SDE as well."
- "The insurance brokerage industry is highly diverse and the valuation process can be complicated. Valuation multiples can range from <1 to 3 times commission revenue and 3.5 to 8 times EBITDA. Deal structures will also vary depending on the risk of the agency or book of business. "
- "Multiples vary greatly based on type of ins. agent: Standard, Non-Standard, Surplus Lines. Agencies with commission income over $1.5m will be higher multiple based on many operational factors and composition of client. Brokered business, non-standard auto, and agency finance are assigned lower multiples. Retention rates and industry concentration should be reviewed carefully. Insurance Company relationships are critical, requiring review of loss ratios with each company represented, special commission arrangements, possibility of contract cancellation. Degree of differentiation in level of service and breadth of services offered is key separators from the competition"
- "1 to 3 times annual commission for property & casualty books of business. Varies based on ratio of standard vs. non-standard business."
- "Expected retention by the BUYER is critical. Loss ratios are very important. Benefits business is very hard to value because of uncertainty regarding health care reform."
- "Start with the recasting. Determine the DE and adjusted EBITDA. Identify fixed expenses and opportunities for a strategic buyer to consolidate overhead. The average agency should have a DE/revenue of > 40%. If the prospect is not at that level, need to figure out why. Look at the risk factors: revenue history, carriers represented and commission rates, lines of insurance (personal, commercial, life/health; each also has subdivisions that are relevant), average renewals, average policy size and size existence of any large policies (greater than $10k premium), carrier loss ratios (should be under 50%), employment agreements with producers (potential for employee to walk with customers), etc. Contact third-party financing options and determine the amount and rate they will finance so you can look at debt service coverage (most deals happen with an ROIC > 40% so the terms may shift against the seller if you don't pre-arrange a reasonable deal structure). Low risk agencies (e.g. stable, standard personal lines) can be sold at fixed terms for higher multiples (typically > 4.5 x adjusted EBITDA). Higher risk (e.g. commercial lines with large accounts) may be structured with an earnout and lower price. Just like any business, the value is driven by the proforma earnings, risk and terms of the sale."
- "Seller expected to remain 12 to 36 months (earn-out) for max price."
- "Larger P&C agencies will sell for 6–7.5X pro-forma EBITDA to nationals. Smaller agencies will sell as books of business for 2–3X gross commissions."
- "Niche agencies often receive higher value compared to main street agency."
- "Range between 1x and 2.5x annual gross revenue. Higher percentage paid

for agencies with standard vs. non-standard business."

- "It is no longer a strong seller's market. Prices have come down, but there is no consensus by how much."
- "Multiples range from 1.5 to 2x the gross commissions and will depend on type of agency, i.e., preferred or sub-standard, as well as the quality of the carrier appointments."
- "Can range from 1 to 3 times gross commissions depending on profitability of agency."
- "Insurance agencies typically sell for a multiple of the premium income (gross sales) which can vary between 2 and 4 times this number but usually is 2 times since this multiple depends on many factors, such as the type of insurance markets the agency is appointed with, the retention rate of their policies, the commission earned on renewals for the existing book and how long this agency has been operating."
- "Standard agency= 2x annual commissions, Sub-standard agency =1x revenues."
- "Working capital adjustment 30 to 60 days."
- "Pricing for smaller agencies is often between 1.5 and 2.0 times annual commissions. Pricing is often between 6.0 and 7.0 times adjusted EBITDA."
- "P&C insurance agencies: 2X standard PL book, 1.75X sm comm book; 1.5X large account book; multiples may be higher or lower depending on financial Benchmark Data to peer groups."
- "Brokered Business—1.0 times commission. Non-Standard Auto (direct bill)—1.0 to 1.25, (agency bill/premium finance)—.5 to .8 times commission."
- "Length of time in business, reputation, possible cross-selling opportunities in the future, etc."
- "Working Capital Adjustment can be a big number"
- "Insurance Agency veterans still think in terms of valuing an agency at 1.5 to 2 times total premium and not necessarily on the Sellers Discretionary Earnings which is a more accurate way of determining if the agency is profitable."
- "Brand-name carriers, licensed personnel, revenue per client, revenue per employee, target accounts."
- "Seller is expected to provide Working Capital—90 to 120 days in company"
- "Pricing today is higher than it was 10 years ago. Typical pricing is 150% to 200% of annual commissions for smaller agencies, and 6 to7 times EBITDA for medium and larger agencies. Balance adjustments range between net zero to one-month's net working capital. Tax complications can be severe for a 'C' corporation, or an agency that has been a 'C' corporation any time during the prior ten years."
- "Agencies with volume above $1.5 million will sell closer to 8 times EBITDA and/or 1.5 to 2.0 times commission revenues. Direct-bill premiums have a value of 30% higher than agency-bill policies, better retention."
- "Insurance agencies sell for a multiple of annual commissions received by the Agency. That number can run from 1 to 4 with 2 being the most likely. Determining factors are lines of business sold (P&C commercial, P&C personal, life, health), carriers the agency is appointed with, size of the agency, loss ratios, retention rate and the diversity of clients."
- "The insurance products and companies represented by the agency are an important component of value. Commissions generated from the sale of securities sell at much lower multiples. An analysis of the client mix is

necessary to determine the nuances of valuation."

- "Persistency of policy renewals. Employee length of employment. Number of insurance companies represented."

- "Direct-bill policies have a value of 30% greater than agency-bill policies, due to retention. Personal lines have greater value than commercial lines due to the relationship with clients and commission to the producer. Agencies with state-of-the-art Internet-based management systems and transactional filing seem to generate greater revenue per employee."

- "Contract persistency is critical to the continuation of fees. The demographics of the clientele base should be carefully analyzed. The range of valuation multiples is very wide and varies by the type of revenue stream and how it's paid. Regulation violations by the owner can severely reduce the price."

- "Renewal (persistency) rate. Amount of assigned risk business. Any client that accounts for 5% of the gross revenue. Length of employment—present employees. Agency contracts with insurance companies. Lost ratio of book of business over past five years."

- "Ask if the property and casualty has standard and sub-standard, and if the percentage of each standard is 1.5 times annual commissions, but sub-standard is 1.0 times annual commissions."

- "Renegotiations of agency contracts by companies as a condition of approving the new agent destroy value and kill deals. The time is perhaps right, though, because the industry is at the point in its cycle when they want all the business they can get on almost any terms. Companies often have a 'pocket' buyer, who is the only buyer they will agree to. Approval often means acceptance of a reduced commission rate. Traditional agencies aren't worth the time and effort."

- "One interesting exception has come to my attention, and that is brokerage-based agencies that deal extensively in employee benefits, particularly employee group health insurance. The business tends to be high volume, stable, and consistently profitable. The contractual relationships that have been set up by many of the major HMOs etc. with brokers have volume and quality factors such that two agencies, each receiving $3 in revenue, if combined, may receive $12–$15. Beyond that, various sources have identified this as a fertile field for cross-selling opportunities and other incremental revenue."

Expert Comments

"'Risk' is generally considered a function of probable account retention. Small agencies with few potential local buyers must often be kept open post sale, lowering profits for the buyer and complicating finding suitable management for the location post sale. These agencies may sell for multiples of commissions as low as 1.0."

"Organic growth has been tough over these past four years especially for commercial agencies due to the weak economy and soft insurance market. Therefore, existing agencies are looking to grow more by acquisitions, which has of course created a strong demand in this industry."

"Nationwide, Allstate and State Farm are no longer a factor in the FI marketplace. Great opportunity for INDEPENDENT INSURANCE AGENCY."

"Many more buyers than sellers at a given time. Attractive for existing agencies to acquire other agencies rather than building organically through sales and promotion. It is also a faster way to grow."

"The insurance brokerage industry is very competitive, however there can be significant barriers of entry for new competition and the revenues are recurring."

"Florida insurance market is very limited to high-volume insurance agencies"

"Agency income is directly related to the economy so there has been downward pressure on commission income over the last 3 years."

"There is high buyer demand. Banks have been aggressive acquirers. The industry is going through consolidation. It is a good time to be a seller."

"Getting competitive contracts from carriers is very difficult for someone wanting to start an independent insurance agency from scratch."

"High competition locally and nationally for the industry. Industry stable but revenue impacted by regulation and natural disasters. The buying market is saturated with savvy, strategic buyers. The broker needs to understand the industry and market well."

"Changing market conditions for carriers."

"Property & liability agencies tend to be multigenerational and don't change hands frequently. It is difficult to start the business from scratch. Customers remain with the agency unless they are mistreated or they find a much lower price."

"Existing brokers choose to grow their business by purchasing mature books of business from retiring brokers."

"Insurance agencies are generally very marketable. One reason is the ease with which one agency can often be consolidated with another."

"Low barriers to entry, captive agents (Allstate and State Farm), and direct writers (Progressive and Geico) make competition very high."

"P&C personal lines independent agency competition is high due to direct writers Geico and Progressive, and profit margins continue to shrink due to carrier expense ratio pressures. Barriers to entry are relatively low if you buy into the industry, but high to start up a company from scratch due to appointment requirements by national carriers. Profitable and portable books of business are highly marketable at realistic multiples of EBITDA."

"Marginal agencies are hard to sell."

"It is currently a seller's market, making most agencies fairly easy to sell. Starting a new agency from scratch is difficult because getting favorable contracts from carriers is dependent on volume expectations."

"There is significant competition in selling insurance, and the easiest way to grow an agency is to acquire an existing, profitable book of business."

"Personal lines property/casualty premiums are increasing annually. Commercial lines property/casualty premiums are static or declining. Medical benefits premiums are increasing annually."

"Florida property markets are tight and carriers are NOT appointing. Casualty markets are wide open."

"There is significant competition in all product lines, but for entrenched agencies the opportunity lies in acquiring existing books of business that fit the focus of a particular agency."

"Since buyers are counting on the existing client base staying with the agency post sale, property & casualty agencies are generally quite salable regardless of the amount of competition in their market area. Independent agencies competing with them are quite often the buyer, and are able to achieve operating economies of scale that can make the acquisition quite a bit more profitable than proforma financial statements from the seller would indicate. For this reason, even a marginally profitable agency can often command a healthy multiple of revenue when sold. The most common concern of buyers is account retention post sale. Agencies with difficult accounts to retain will almost always sell for less. Account retention is so important that sales are often structured with a significant part of the price based on account retention post sale. It should be noted that starting an independent insurance agency today can be quite difficult, but combining an existing agency with another is often quite beneficial. The resulting profits can be greater than the sum of the parts." "Lot of competition in personal lines. Location is more important if the agency business is more personal lines. Commercial lines, location not much of a factor. What markets/contracts the agency has will limit them to the type of business the agency can focus on. Agencies are easy to sell to other agencies that want to expand. Larger insurance brokerages can absorb a book of business without much increase in overhead."

Benchmark Data

Statistics (Insurance Brokers and Agencies)

Number of Establishments	373,676
Average Profit Margin	10.3%
Revenue per Employee	$174,000
Average Number of Employees	2.5
Average Wages per Employee	$54,164

Source: IBISWorld, July 2012

Products and Services Segmentation

Personal P&C insurance	25.7%
Life and health insurance	21.6%
Other annuity and insurance	6.1%
Insurance administration and risk consulting	5.5%
Annuities	3%
Title insurance	2%
Commercial P&C insurance	36.1%

Source: IBISWorld, July 2012

Major Market Segmentation

Households	48.9%
Businesses	46.1%
The government	5%

Source: IBISWorld, July 2012

Industry Costs

Profit	10.3%
Wages	31.4%
Purchases	5.6%
Depreciation	0.7%
Marketing	1.7%
Rent & Utilities	3.6%
Other	46.7%

Source: IBISWorld, July 2012

Market Share

Marsh & McLennan	2.0%
Aon Corporation	1.4%
Arthur J. Gallagher & Co.	0.9%
Willis Group Holdings	0.7%

Source: IBISWorld, July 2012

- "$125-150k in revenue per CSR on personal lines. $200-300k in revenue per CSR on commercial lines."
- "Pertaining to personal lines P&C agencies, the agency should typically have one CSR per $125–$150k in revenue. Pertaining to commercial lines P&C agencies, the agency should typically have one CSR per $200k+ in revenue."
- "125,000 commission revenue per employee in larger commercial agency. Trends downward as agency size decreases."
- "An agency in the top quartile should be able to put a 25% EBITDA on the bottom line."
- "Average commission revenue per sales staff should be about $130k. Lower means underperforming or low commission rates. Higher means a well performing operation. Rent should be 5-6% of revenue. Total employee comp should be 30-40% of revenue on average. Anything significantly above or below should be investigated further to understand the abnormal productivity."
- "Best Practices: $159k/employee; $3,000 to $5,000 revenue/client"
- "$125,000 per employee"
- "Low loss ratio. High level of standard vs. non standard business 75%+."
- "Revenue per employee $125,000 to $150,000"
- "$100K revenue per employee"
- "Loss ratios of 60% or less"
- "Average Profit Margins approximately 9% to 10%."
- "Revenue per client—$3,000

  Revenue per employee—$100,000

  Profit for agency under $25,000 is 18%

  Profit for agency between $250,000 and $500,000 should be 30%

  Profit for agency between $1 and $2 million should be 40%

  Profit for agency between $2 and 5 million should be 50%"
- "275 sq. ft. per employee, $100,000 in commissions per full-time equivalent employee or above is good; producers with large books of business would be in the $400,000–$1 million + range in terms of commissions to the agency."
- "Personal lines P/C accounts should generate $3,000 to $5,000. Average annual premium revenue per employee should be $85,000 to $125,000. Owner Benefit: 30%–50% of gross income."

- "Loss ratios under 60%"
- "Most common Benchmark Data: revenue per employee, loss ratio, new business growth, retention rate or persistency, mix of business, # of lives."
- "$100k revenue per employee, occupancy cost should be between 8% and 12%."
- "Revenue per employee: $70 to $125.000. Revenue per client: $3,000 and up. Owner benefit: $250K commission—10% to 18%; $250 to $500K—30%; $500 to $2 million—40%; over $2 million—50%."
- "Payroll/labor cost listed below includes benefits. Revenue per full-time employee avg. $130,000."
- "$150,000 in revenue per producer"
- "Revenue of $100,000 per employee, Profit for agency selling $1 to $2 million should be around 40%, and $2 to $4 million around 50%. Payroll should be about 35% and average profit 25%."
- "Profit for agency between $250,000 and $500,000 should be 30%. Profit for agency between $1 and $2 million should be 40%. Profit for agency between $2 and $5 million should be 50%."
- "The most relevant benchmark is agency profit of 25% or more, adjusted to correct for excess owner compensation plus all the myriad ways an owner typically benefits financially from ownership."

Expenses as a Percentage of Annual Sales

Cost of goods	15%
Payroll/labor Costs:	35% to 50%
Occupancy:	05% to 10%
Profit (estimated pretax)	15% to 25%

Industry Trend

- "P&C—minimal growth; Health—shrinking competition and revenues due to reduced compensation rates under PPAC (Obama's healthcare law)."
- "Standard agencies' revenue will improve as business revenue increases. Small standard agencies will be relegated to small business. Consolidation will continue with regional brokers acquiring strong local standard agencies."
- "Continued industry consolidation."
- "The market will remain 'soft' for at least all of 2010, and quite possibly longer. This means renewal premiums for the same risk will be falling, thus putting pressure on agency commission revenue."
- "Shrinking margins due to the economy."
- "Florida property premiums increasing."
- "Flat"
- "More consolidation."
- "Consolidation and intense price competition from direct writers (do not work through independent agents)."
- "Good career path for young people. The insurance industry will continue to prosper. Service businesses will be desirable."
- "Average agencies will probably experience a steady decrease in value."
- "Profits are likely to decline, but not by as much as for many small businesses."
- "Hardening P&C pricing market will make agency profits higher. Tighter credit will continue to depress sales price of agencies."

- "Continued industry consolidation. Carriers want agents to write more business with them or risk the chance of being dropped."
- "Small agencies are under substantial pressure from insurance carriers to get bigger."
- "The insurance business will continue to be highly competitive and rest on the ability of the agency to service their clients at a high level. Rates are important, but service and keeping the clients satisfied is the way to grow an agency."
- "Consolidation of smaller agencies, selling more products; some insurance companies are selling direct, they should continue to grow. more and more customers using Internet to purchase insurance."

Seller Financing

- "Most sales have some component of an earnout based on retained business (future commissions). May make it necessary for seller to stay on for a period of time after sale to increase likelihood business will stay with new ownership."
- "Down payment—25 to 50 percent
- Balance—24 to 60 months, plus interest @ 2 percent over prime"
- "50% of gross commissions for 3 years"
- "3 to 5 years"
- "Sometimes owner financing on renewals. For instance, 1.50 times renewals. This can be tricky because buyer may take the cream of the crop and seller is left holding the bag."

Questions

- "For Allstate agencies, ask for the CSRP reports"
- "What insurance companies do you represent and what premium and loss ratio have you had with each for last 3 yrs? Employees and date of hire? Persistency? Top 10 clients and commission revenue from each? Copies of all producer agreements? Cash or accrual basis tax payer? Itemized list of commission receivables and premium payables?"
- "What is the product mix? (personal lines, commercial lines, benefits, and general description of any specialization). 'S' vs. 'C' corp status. Have tax issues been assessed? Will an asset sale generate tax issues for the seller? Are the employees subject to enforceable non-piracy agreements?"
- "Why are you selling?"
- "Do key employees have employment agreements and do they have covenants not to compete? How many insurance companies are represented and how long have you represented them? Have any insurance companies told you that their contract with you is going to be terminated? What % of business is auto-assigned risk and fair plan?"
- "What will you [current owner] do to help with account retention, post sale?"
- "What is your loss ratio. How much business is standard vs. non-standard. What is business mix personal vs. business."
- "Are you willing to do an earnout"
- "What are your loss ratios? What is your retention rate? What kind of business do you write? Who are your main carriers?"
- "Do your producers have vesting rights to their books of business?"

- "How many clients do you have? What is your year-to-year retention rate on these clients? What is the commission rate for renewals of existing policies?"
- "Size of book? Mix of book by product line? Expense ratio for agency? Loss ratio for P&C book? New business growth? Licenses held? Carrier appointments held? Written premium by carrier?"
- "Carriers represented, volume of premium/commission with carrier, loss ratio with carrier. Personnel staying after transaction and their importance."
- "Companies represented, percentage of cancellations with each carrier, the appointment with the carriers must be transferable, how long at same location, key employees: do they have a non-compete agreement in force now, or will they sign one before the sale?"
- "Will buyer inherit the client base, will seller give up the renewal and trail commissions of existing clients? What is the likelihood of existing clients canceling their contract after knowing that the ownership changed hands?"
- "Are your carriers A-rated?"
- "What do you want to do for the first 5 years after closing? Earnout reality check."
- "Copies of company's statements including production, loss ratios, possibility of transfer of appointments with insurance carriers, income taxes for last 3 years, how you get customers,"
- "How will you assist with account retention post sale?"
- "What carriers do you have contracts with? What is the mix of business/ personal/ commercial? Why are you selling? How many accounts are on the books? Who are your competitors? What do your customers like best about your operation?"

Resources

Websites
- www.iii.org
- www.independentagent.com

Trade Publications
- American Agent and Broker: www.propertycasualty360.com/American-Agent-Broker Associations
- American Association of Insurance Services: www.aaisonline.com
- The Council of Insurance Agents and Brokers: www.ciab.com/

Insurance Companies (in general)

(See also Insurance—Life and Property & Casualty)

NAICS 524210	

Rules of Thumb
➤ 1 to 2 times capital and surplus

Pricing Tips
- "A ton of information is required, beyond the company's financial statements and tax returns, such as reports submitted to the insurance department of the states the company does business in; actuarial reports on the adequacy of amounts in reserve to pay claims; rating of company by one or more insurers-

rating organizations; status of any significant lawsuits pending against the company; its reputation in the industry; and its relationship with its sales force. Just getting an opinion as to value involves hundreds of hours of document review and analysis."

Benchmark Data
- For Benchmark data see Life & Property and Casualty Insurance

Resources

Trade Publications
- Insurance Networking News: www.insurancenetworking.com

Insurance Companies—Life	
NAICS 524210	Number of Businesses/Units 8,276

Rules of Thumb
➢ 1 to 2.5 times capital and surplus

Benchmark Data

Statistics (Life Insurance & Annuities)
Number of Establishments.. 8,276
Average Profit Margin 4.7%
Revenue per Employee $2,686,300
Average Number of Employees.. 3.5
Average Wages per Employee $94,963

Source: IBISWorld, September 2012

Products and Services Segmentation
Individual annuity considerations... 33.5%
Group annuity considerations 18%
Group disability and LTC insurance.. 16%
Individual disability and LTC insurance 14%
Individual life insurance 14%
Group life insurance...
4%
Other.. 0.5%

Source: IBISWorld, September 2012

Industry Costs
Profit 4.7%
Wages.. 9.1%
Purchases.. 59.4%
Depreciation... 0.5%
Marketing 2.5%
Rent & Utilities 0.3%
Other.. 23.5%

Source: IBISWorld, September 2012

Market Share
MetLife Inc. 3.0%
Northwestern Mutual Life Insurance Company.. 2.9%
MassMutual Financial Group 2.2%

Source: IBISWorld, September 2012

Insurance Companies—Property & Casualty

(See also Insurance Agencies)

NAICS 524126	Number of Businesses/Units 5,098

Rules of Thumb

➢ ½ to 3 times capital and surplus

Pricing Tips

- "I have a Property & Casualty company for sale with stockholders' equity of $145 million; the asking price is 1.6 to 1.7 times stockholders' equity. Price dropped due to an adjustment in some bad risks that were eliminated."

Benchmark Data

Statistics (Property, Casualty and Direct Insurance)

Number of Establishments	5,098
Average Profit Margin	12.5%
Revenue per Employee	$752,200
Average Number of Employees	30.3
Average Wages per Employee	$82,726

Source: IBISWorld, July 2012

Products and Services Segmentation

Property and casualty insurance (P&C) personal	39.9%
Property and casualty insurance (P&C) commercial	37.6%
Reinsurance	8%
Workers' compensation insurance	5%
Other	3%
Title insurance	3%
Mortgage and financial guaranty insurance	2%
Medical malpractice insurance	1.5%

Source: IBISWorld, July 2012

Major Market Segmentation

Personal market	51.5%
Commercial market	40.5%
Other insurance carriers	8%

Source: IBISWorld, July 2012

Industry Costs

Profit	12.5%
Wages	10.4%
Purchases	0.4%
Depreciation	1.2%
Marketing	1.0%
Rent & Utilities	2.0%
Other	72.5%

Source: IBISWorld, July 2012

Market Share

State Farm	11.7%
Liberty Mutual Group Inc.	7.3%
Allstate Insurance Company	6.0%
The Travelers Companies Inc.	5.3%
American International Group Inc.	4.1%

Source: IBISWorld, July 2012

Internet Hosting — Colocation

Rules of Thumb
➢ 3 to 4 times EBITDA

Pricing Tips
▪ "Prices are down from 2 years ago."

Expert Comments
"Industry was growing by 50% per year prior to the economic downturn. Still growth in the industry."

Benchmark Data
▪ "Most are netting between 33% and 44% of gross income."

Expenses as a Percentage of Annual Sales
Cost of goods	n/a
Payroll/labor Costs	n/a
Occupancy	n/a
Profit (estimated pretax)	33%

Industry Trend
▪ "Massive growth"

Internet Publishing (See Publishing—Internet)

Internet Sales (See E-Commerce)

Investigative Services (See also Guard Services & Security Services)

	NAICS 561611	Number of Businesses/Units 8,000

Rules of Thumb
➢ 70 to 75 percent of annual sales

Benchmark Data
▪ For Benchmark data see Security Services

Investment Advice

	NAICS 523930	

Rules of Thumb
➢ 1.5 times SDE

➢ 1 times annual sales

Pricing Tips
▪ "Contract persistency is critical to the continuation of fees. The demographics

of the clientele base should be carefully analyzed. The range of valuation multiples is very wide and varies by the type of revenue stream and how it's paid. The numbers above are considered to be averages. Regulation violations by the owner can severely reduce the sales price."

Expert Comments

"Industry consolidation and company marketing efficiencies are promoting the move away from commissioned sales force."

Benchmark Data

Statistics (Financial Planning and Advice)

Number of Establishments	141,722
Average Profit Margin	16.8%
Revenue per Employee	$190,500
Average Number of Employees	2
Average Wages per Employee	$97,231

Source: IBISWorld, May 2011

Products and services segmentation (2011)

Individual and small business portfolio management	29.0%
Business and institutional portfolio management	23.0%
Financial planning services	21.0%
Other services	21.0%
Pension planning services	6.0%

Source: IBISWorld, May 2011

Industry Costs

Profit	16.8%
Rent	4.0%
Utilities	2.0%
Other	24.1%
Wages	53.1%

Source: IBISWorld, May 2011

	Franchise
Jani-King (See also Janitorial Services & Coverall)	
Approx. Total Investment	$8,170 to $74,000
Estimated Annual Sales/Unit	Not Available
NAICS 561720	Number of Businesses/Units 13,000

Rules of Thumb

➢ 25 to 30 percent of annual sales plus inventory

Resources

Websites

- www.janiking.com

Janitorial Services (See also Coverall & Jani-King)

SIC 7439-02	NAICS 561720	Number of Businesses/Units 785,216

Rules of Thumb

➤ 45 percent of annual sales plus inventory

➤ 1.5 times SDE plus inventory

➤ 1 times one month's billings; plus fixtures, equipment and inventory

➤ 4 times monthly billings; includes fixtures, equipment and inventory

Pricing Tips

▪ "Janitorial (Contract Cleaners)—1.5 times net, depending upon the amount of hired help. An industry evaluation is 3 to 5 times the monthly gross depending upon the equipment and the type of accounts; e.g., government vs. private . . . a very conservative approach which could vary widely on a monthly basis. Government contracts could offer more start-up security for a prospective purchaser."

Benchmark Data

Statistics (Janitorial Services)

Number of Establishments	785,216
Average Profit Margin	5.0%
Revenue per Employee	$28,300
Average Number of Employees	2.2
Average Wages per Employee	$14,152

Source: IBISWorld, July 2012

Products and Services Segmentation

Standard commercial cleaning	59%
Other commercial cleaning	18.6%
Other	10.8%
Residential cleaning	7%
Damage restoration cleaning	4.6%

Source: IBISWorld, July 2012

Major Market Segmentation

Offices	32%
Educational facilities	31.7%
Retail complexes	12.3%
Residences	7%
Government	6.2%
Industrial plants	6.1%
Healthcare facilities	4.7%

Source: IBISWorld, July 2012

Industry Costs

Profit	5.0%
Wages	49.9%
Purchases	26.0%
Depreciation	2.0%
Marketing	1.4%
Rent & Utilities	3.8%
Other	11.9%

Source: IBISWorld, July 2012

Market Share

ABM Industries Inc... 5.1%

Source: IBISWorld, July 2012

- "For contract janitorial services, average estimated gross sales skyrocketed to $4,153,450 [2004] from $1,418,527 in 2003. The median estimated 2004 gross sales was $550,000. Respondents who perform janitorial services reported charging an average of $0.31 per square foot."

- Benchmarking Survey Report

  This survey was conducted and produced by the research department at the CM B2B Trade Group, the parent of *CM/Cleaning & Maintenance* magazine. It is being sponsored as a service by P&G ProLine ™, Proctor & Gamble's complete line of floor care, carpet care, daily cleaner, and specialty cleaner products.

  The survey found the following averages of interior building area cleaned in square feet per FTE (full-time equivalent employee) per hour, with no obstructions:

  2–4 year college/university: 12,466
  Schools/districts (K–12): 11,388
  Private office building:... 10,853
  Government facility: 7,835
  Medical facilities:.. 5,931

  "Median square footage per FTE per hour was as follows:
  2–4 year college/university: 5,000
  Schools/districts (K–12): 4,000
  Private office building:... 4,500
  Government facility: 4,000
  Medical facilities:... 2,050"

  Source: "Benchmarking Survey: Which Facility Has Best Cleaning Production?" by Nicole Lemperle, Associate Editor, *CM Cleaning & Maintenance Management*.

Industry Trend

- "US demand to exceed $67 billion in 2013. US demand for commercial and residential cleaning services is forecast to reach $67 billion in 2013. Within the residential cleaning service market, the trend toward hiring professional cleaning services (particularly for interior cleaning and swimming pool cleaning) will continue to foster growth, although advances will decelerate over the short term, reflecting weaker gains in disposable personal income, which in turn will moderate growth prospects somewhat. Major growth drivers include increases in the number of dual income households and the aging of the 'baby-boomer' generation.

  "Interior building cleaning services to remain dominant.

  "Interior building cleaning services, which accounted for nearly three-fourths of total cleaning services revenues in 2008, will remain dominant going forward. Gains will derive primarily from expanding use of outside cleaning services in institutional and residential markets, with more moderate growth in the commercial, office and industrial sectors.

  "U.S. cleaning service firms to number 680,000 by 2013. The total number of cleaning service establishments in the U.S. is projected to increase to more than 680,000 by 2013, with total employment approaching 1.7 million. The majority of these companies will compete in the interior cleaning service segment of the industry, which now includes more than 500,000 establishments."

  Source: www.prnewswire.com

Resources

Trade Publications
- C M Cleaning & Maintenance Management—informative site based on the magazine: www.cmmonline.com

Associations
- Building Service Contractors Association International: www.bscai.org

	Franchise
Jersey Mike's Subs	
Approx. Total Investment	$150,082 to $519,970
Estimated Annual Sales/Unit	$530,000

SIC 5812-19	NAICS 722211	Number of Businesses/Units 500

Rules of Thumb
➢ 50 percent of annual sales plus inventory

Benchmark Data
- For Benchmark data see Sandwich Shops

Resources

Websites
- www.jerseymikes.com

Jewelry Stores		
SIC 5944-09	NAICS 448310	Number of Businesses/Units 58,703

Rules of Thumb
➢ 4 to 6 times EBIT if inventory included
➢ None—too inventory intensive

Pricing Tips
- "What return on assets would be expected if current owner left city?"
- "A destination upscale jeweler has a much better 'chance' of being sold as a going business."
- "Highly capital intensive—inventory on hand most critical in pricing"
- "Price is based on amount of inventory, current value, years in business, and profit of operations now and after sale is completed."
- "No magic formula—jewelry is a high-capital requirement for inventory and hiring personnel; trust & confidence of owners not readily transferable. Will seller sell without inventory—or one year's supply based on sales volume that is high enough to be attractive—example: annual sales of $500,000 with inventory at cost of $200,000 is attractive if business has growth and is currently profitable."

Benchmark Data

Statistics (Jewelry Stores)

Number of Establishments	58,703
Average Profit Margin	9.2%
Revenue per Employee	$177,600
Average Number of Employees	2
Average Wages per Employee	$29,554

Source: IBISWorld, August 2012

Products and Services Segmentation (2012)

Diamond Jewelry	48%
Watches	13.9%
Gold jewelry	10.6%
Other gemstone jewelry	8.8%
Other merchandise	8.3%
Loose gemstones, including diamonds and colored gemstones	5.7%
Pearl jewelry	3%
Platinum jewelry	1.7%

Source: IBISWorld, August 2012

Industry Costs

Profit	9.2%
Wages	16.3%
Purchases	55.9%
Depreciation	3.5%
Marketing	5.9%
Rent & Utilities	6.5%
Other	2.7%

Source: IBISWorld, August 2012

Market Share

Signet Group	10.4%
Tiffany	6.1%
Zale	5.2%

Source: IBISWorld, August 2012

Comparative Financial and Operating Ratios

High-Profit Versus Low-Profit Firms

Performance Measure	High-Profit Firms	Low-Profit Firms
EBIT to Total Assets	12.6%	-1.0%
Net Profit Before Taxes to Net Sales	6.5%	-1.9%
Asset Turnover (net sales/total assets)	1.5X	1.4X
Inventory Turnover	1.0X	1.0X
Sales Per Square Foot—Total	$413.03	$510.26
Sales per Full Time Employee	$232,432	$200,745
Sales Growth	-3.9%	-13.6%
Total Debt to Total Asset	54.3%	43.9%
Current Ratio	3.4	3.1
Sales Per Store	$961,296	$1,346,890
Store Size	2,362	2,200

Source: 2010 Jewelers of America Cost of Doing Business Report, sponsored by Jewelers of America and *National Jeweler's* America's best jeweler network

- "Sales in decline, profits improving— ...respondents reported a median overall sales decrease of 4.5%, a 1% greater decline than in 2008. For the second year, chains reported the steepest declines (-13.6%) and showed little change from 2008 (-13.2%). Independent high-end retailers had a decline of 7.5%, compared to -1.3% in 2008. The bright spots came from designer/artist/ custom jewelers, who had a median sales increase of 3.1%, up from -.8% in 2008, and mid-range retailers, whose -.9% median sales growth is up from – 5.5% in 2008.

"Industry profitability in 2009 held steady, with specialty jewelers experiencing a median 3.8% net profit as a percent of net sales versus 3.6% in 2008. In 2009, gross margins recovered across all store types, with 49.4% as the median overall gross margin, compared to 48.6% in 2008.

"*The 2010 Jewelers of America Cost of Doing Business Report* demonstrates that effective management is critical during economically challenging times, when even high-profit firms experienced - .9% sales growth on average. However the flat sales growth of high-profit firms looks favorable when compared to the 7.8% sales decline reported by low-profit firms.

"In 2009, high-profit stores reported almost 100% greater sales per store than their low-profit peers (an average of $2,122,998 compared to $1,478,504). They also reported a much greater ratio of earnings before interests and taxes (EBIT) to total assets: 16.4% on average compared to – 2% of low-profit firms. Higher operating expenses continue to be a downfall of low-profit firms, with their high-profit peers spending less on payroll, occupancy and advertising. In fact, high-profit retailers reported an average of 8.7% less on total operating expenses than low-profit firms.

"Distribution of sales—The distribution of sales remains relatively consistent year to year. In 2009, the diamond category (loose and set) remained the majority, with 46% of sales, down 3% from 2008. The next biggest product categories are colored stone jewelry (8% of sales) and karat gold (8%). Repair sales remain an important category, bringing in 10% of sales."

Source: "Jewelers of America Releases 2010 Cost of Doing Business Report," www.jewelers.org

Expenses as a Percentage of Annual Sales

Cost of goods	55% to 58%
Payroll/labor Costs	22%
Occupancy	N/A
Profit (estimated pretax)	06%

Industry Trend

- "For the second year in a row, *National Jeweler's* exclusive year-end survey showed that sales continue to rebound for retail jewelers, with 72 percent of respondents reporting gains in same-store sales in 2011. Of those nearly three-quarters of survey respondents who reported sales increases, 24 percent said their sales were up by more than 10 percent, while 20 percent reported sales climbed more than 20 percent year-over-year."

- "A total of 83 percent of jewelers reported that their same-store sales were flat or up in 2011, compared to 73 percent last year."

Source: "Exclusive Report: A strong year for jewelers" by Michelle Graff, www.nationaljeweler.com, February 6, 2012

Seller Financing

- Not seller financed—inventory too portable—high risk
- 3 years

Resources

Websites
- www.nationaljeweler.com

Trade Publications
- Instoremagazine: www.instoremag.com

Associations
- Jewelers of America (JA): www.jewelers.org

			Franchise
Jiffy Lube International			
Approx. Total Investment		$229,000 to $323,000	
	NAICS 811191	Number of Businesses/Units 2,032	

Rules of Thumb
➢ 45 to 50 percent of annual sales plus inventory

Benchmark Data

Resources

Websites
- www.jiffylube.com

			Franchise
Jimmy John's Gourmet Sandwiches			
Approx. Total Investment		$305,500 to $485,500	
Estimated Annual Sales/Unit		$820,000	
SIC 5812-19	NAICS 722211	Number of Businesses/Units 1,214	

Rules of Thumb
➢ 65 to 70 percent of annual sales plus inventory

Benchmark Data
- For Benchmark data see Sandwich Shops

Job Shops/Contract Manufacturing (See also Machine Shops)		
	NAICS 332710	

Rules of Thumb
➢ 1.5 to 2 times SDE plus inventory

➢ 3 to 5 times EBIT

➢ 3 to 4 times EBITDA

Pricing Tips

- "4 x EBITDA is just a rule of thumb. A range of 3 x to 8 x is realistic depending a range of factors (history, custom concentration, future prospects, etc.")
- "Best rule of thumb in this industry to use as a barometer is FMV of FFE&M plus 1X EBITDA."
- "Job shops with full range of capabilities (turning, milling, grinding, stamping, etc.) are more desirable."

Expert Comments

"Competition is high and the key to gross profit margins is using technology to be low-cost manufacturer."

"Recent influx of orders from OEM's has contributed to better backlog. Receivable aging improving and more shops able to get 33%–50% deposits. Not as much used equipment in the field as prior years. Competitive edge goes to automated shops with palletized tool changing machining centers, wire EDM, etc."

"In some cases, the machinery & equipment has a higher value than the business."

Benchmark Data

- For additional Benchmark data see Machine Shops
- "Most modern shops set up to have one employee service two machines."
- "Determine unused capacity. Buyers will want to determine potential without major capital investment."

Expenses as a Percentage of Annual Sales

Cost of goods:	40% to 50%
Payroll/labor Costs:	25% to 28%
Occupancy:	03% to 05%
Profit (estimated pretax)	12%

Industry Trend

- "The industry will continue to improve as US manufacturers become more competitive"
- "Shrinking market based on overseas competition, declining manufacturing base, high operating costs"
- "Lack of 'tradesmen' will require CAPEX for CNC equipment."

Questions

- "Discuss the outlook for the company. What opportunities exist for the buyer and why the seller isn't pursuing them."
- "Backlog, WIP, age, qualifications & tenure of staff, condition of equipment (look at line items for R&M closely to avoid machinery held together with band aids), need for CAPEX near and mid-term, etc.?"
- "Will the business be sustainable when owner leaves? Any known environmental issues?"

Franchise

Johnny Rockets

Approx. Total Investment		$636,500 to $875,000 total investment
Estimated Annual Sales/Unit		$950,000
	NAICS 722211	Number of Businesses/Units 289

Rules of Thumb

➢ 70 to 75 percent of annual sales plus inventory

Pricing Tips

- "Some have sold for 100 percent of sales."

Resources

Websites

- www.johnnyrockets.com

Franchise

Jon Smith Subs

	NAICS 722211	

Rules of Thumb

➢ 20 percent of annual sales plus inventory

Franchise

Juice It Up

Approx. Total Investment		$167,444 to $325,508
	NAICS 722213	Number of Businesses/Units 90

Rules of Thumb

➢ 20 to 25 percent of annual sales plus inventory

Resources

Websites

- www.juiceitup.com

Junk Yards (See Auto Wrecking, etc.)

Franchise

KFC (Kentucky Fried Chicken)

Approx. Total Investment	$1,300,000 to $2,500,000
Estimated Annual Sales/Unit	$915,000
NAICS 722211	Number of Businesses/Units 4,850

Rules of Thumb

➢ *Note: The figures on Approximate Total Investment if restaurant is a stand-alone building and would include all equipment, etc. Figures do not include land or lease costs.

➢ 30 to 35 percent of annual sales plus inventory

Franchise

Kumon Math & Reading Centers (See also Schools)

Approx. Total Investment	$67,763 to $145,320
Estimated Annual Sales/Unit	Not Available
NAICS 611691	Number of Businesses/Units 1,500

Rules of Thumb

➢ 80 to 90 percent of annual sales plus inventory

Franchise

Kwik Kopy Business Center (See also Quick Printing)

Approx. Total Investment	$185,000 to $220,000
Estimated Annual Sales/Unit	Not Available
NAICS 323114	Number of Businesses/Units 16

Rules of Thumb

➢ 50 to 60 percent of annual sales plus inventory

Franchise

Lady of America (See also Fitness Centers)

Approx. Total Investment	$187,500 to $455,000
	Number of Businesses/Units 200

Rules of Thumb

➢ 45 to 50 percent of annual sales plus inventory

Resources
Websites
▪ www.loafitnessforwomen.com

Land Surveying Services

SIC 8713-01	NAICS 541370	Number of Businesses/Units 19,007

Rules of Thumb

➢ 40 to 80 percent of annual fee revenues; plus fixtures, equipment and inventory; may require earnout

Benchmark Data

Statistics (Surveying and Mapping Services)

Number of Establishments	19,077
Average Profit Margin	3.3
Revenue per Employee	$91,100
Average Number of Employees	4
Average Wages per Employee	$45,339

Source: IBISWorld, December 2011

Products and Services Segmentation

Property line surveying (e.g. subdivision layout and design)	27.7%
Construction surveying	21.6%
Engineering and other services	16.9%
Topographical and planimetric surveying and mapping	15.9%
Geospatial photo processing from aircraft and satellites	10%
Subdivision layout and design services	7.9%

Source: IBISWorld, December 2011

Major Market Segmentation

Construction firms	25%
Federal government departments and agencies	20%
Land subdivision and development firms	20%
Professional technical firms	15%
City, county and state surveying offices	10%
Energy, utility and mining companies	10%

Source: IBISWorld, December 2011

Industry Costs

Profit	3.3%
Wages	50.1%
Purchases	11.5%
Depreciation	3.0%
Utilities	3.0%
Rent	5.0%
Other	24.1%

Source: IBISWorld, December 2011

Resources

Websites
- www.acsm.net

Trade Publications
- Professional Surveyor magazine: www.profsurv.com

Landscape Services (See also Lawn Maintenance & Service)

SIC 0782-04	NAICS 561730	Number of Businesses/Units 449,055

Rules of Thumb

- ➤ 45 to 50 percent of annual revenues plus inventory
- ➤ 1.5 times SDE; plus fixtures and equipment (except vehicles) & inventory
- ➤ 2 to 4 times EBITDA (may be higher for larger firms)

Pricing Tips

- "Multiples of EBITDA range from 2 to 6 depending on size, profitability and industry segment."
- "Landscape contractors need substantial capital investments for equipment. Startup costs of $100,000 are needed to compete in this industry. 'It's a difficult field unless you're a really large company' said Crabtree, who has been in the industry for over 15 years. Profit margins are typically 5%."

Source: www.urbanforest.org

Expert Comments

"Competition is fierce and ease of replication is as easy as owning a lawnmower and weed whacker. Much better once the company reaches several million in sales."

"Set yourself apart from the competition. Get long-term contracts. Focus on maintenance."

Benchmark Data

Statistics (Landscaping Services)

Number of Establishments	449,055
Average Profit Margin	5.7%
Revenue per Employee	$68,400
Average Number of Employees	2.1
Average Wages per Employee	$33,081

Source: IBISWorld, July 2012

Products and Services Segmentation

Lawn maintenance	40.8%
Basic landscape design and installation	20.8%
Lawn care	13.2%
Other	9.0%
Tree and ornamental care	7.1%
Snow and ice removal	4.9%
Irrigation	4.2%

Source: IBISWorld, July 2012

Major Market Segmentation

Residential market	55.3%
Commercial clients	36.2%
Government and institutional clients	8.5%

Source: IBISWorld, July 2012

Industry Costs

Profit	5.7%
Wages	48.1%
Purchases	25.1%
Depreciation	2.5%
Marketing	4.0%
Rent & Utilities	4.0%
Other	10.6%

Source: IBISWorld, July 2012

- "In the Lawn and Landscape Magazine Industry Overview 2011 survey respondents had business lines as follows: 63% single family residential, 25% commercial/industrial, 7% multi-family, and 5%."

Expenses as a Percentage of Annual Sales

Cost of goods	50%
Payroll/labor Costs	30%
Occupancy	05%
Profit (estimated pretax)	10% to 15%

Industry Trend

- "The Global Industry Analysts Report says 'the landscaping services market in the U.S. is expected to recover and is poised to reach U.S. $80.06 billion by 2015.'"

- "It's not just the big boys that are more optimistic about business conditions, According to a fall survey of Green Industry PRO readers, 58% expect maintenance sales to grow this year while 49% expect lawn care sales to grow. On the other hand, less than 10% expect maintenance and/or lawn care sales to dip.
  "Since 90% of landscape companies employ fewer than 20 people, we're talking about a lot of average-size companies that are feeling pretty good about their chances of remaining competitive."

  Source: "Slow but Steady" by Gregg Wartgow, Green Industry Pro, www.greenindustrypros.com

Seller Financing

- "Generally difficult to finance because of lack of assets."

Questions

- "Does the company have contracts with its clients? Are all employees legal? How many customers are built on relationships with the seller, and what will happen to them if he sells?

Resources

Websites
- www.landcarenetwork.org

Trade Publications
- Turf Magazine: www.turfmagazine.com
- Landscape Management: www.landscapemanagement.net
- Lawn and Landscape: www.lawnandlandscape.com

Associations
- Association of Professional Landscape Designers: www.apld.org

Language Translation (See Translation and Interpretation Services)		
		Number of Businesses/Units: 34,500

	Franchise

Laptop Xchange	
Approx. Total Investment	$183,750 to $267,800

		Number of Businesses/Units 5

Rules of Thumb

➢ 80 to 85 percent of annual sales plus inventory

Resources

Websites
▪ www.laptopxchange.com

Laundromats (See Coin Laundries)	
	NAICS 812310	

Law Firms	
SIC 8111-03	NAICS 541110	Number of Businesses/Units 425,250

Rules of Thumb

➢ 90 to 100 percent of annual fee revenue; firms specializing in estate work would approach 100 percent; may require earnout.

➢ 4 times SDE includes inventory

➢ 3.5 times EBIT

➢ 3.5 times EBITDA

Pricing Tips

▪ "A lot will depend upon the consultants, and how loyal they are to the firm."

▪ "Whether the multiplier is in the lower or the higher level of the range depends primarily on how much repeat business is expected, the nature of the law practice, the number of clients and the transferability of client relationships. If there is a great deal of repeat business and client loyalty that can be transferred, the multiplier will be higher. In the sale of a law practice, a portion of the clients will not stay with the practice by reason of the close personal relationship usually developed between client and attorney. This must be considered when determining the multiplier. The multiplier may then be raised or lowered depending on the stability of the flow of future revenue expected."

Source: "Valuing Professional Practices and Licenses"

Expert Comments

"It is difficult to replicate, as the good businesses have reputations built over many years."

Benchmark Data

Statistics (Law Firms)

Number of Establishments... 434,500
Average Profit Margin 19.4%
Revenue per Employee $38,700
Average Number of employees 3
Average Wages per Employee $79,991

Source: IBISWorld, May 2012

Products and Services Segmentation

Commercial law services 38%
Other services... 18%
Personal injury law services 18%
Intellectual property and trademark low services... 14%
Property law services.. 12

Source: IBISWorld, May 2012

Major Market Segmentation

Business and corporate clients.. 65%
Households.. 25%
Government and public clients 10

Source: IBISWorld, May 2012

Industry Costs

Profit 19.4%
Wages.. 38.6%
Purchases.. 2.0%
Depreciation... 1.6%
Marketing 7.0%
Rent & Utilities 12.7%
Other.. 18.7%

Source: IBISWorld, May 2012

Enterprises by Employment Size

No. of Employees	No. of enterprises	Share %
0 to 4	130,731	74.9
5 to 9	25,091	14.4
10 to 19	10,941	6.3
20 to 99	6,567	3.8
100 to 499	907	0.5
500+	218	0.1%
Total	174,455	100

Source: IBISWorld, May 2012

Statistics (Personal Injury Lawyers & Attorneys)

Number of Establishments... 46,623
Average Profit Margin 12.2%
Revenue per Employee $177,600
Average Number of Employees 3
Average Wages per Employee $78,205

Source: IBISWorld, March 2012

Products and Services Segmentation

Automobile accidents... 42.8%
Other personal injury cases 40.6%
Medical malpractice 16.6%

Source: IBISWorld, March 2012

Industry Costs

Profit	12.2%
Wages	44.0%
Purchases	2.0%
Depreciation	1.4%
Marketing	12.0%
Rent & Utilities	9.7%
Other	18.7%

Source: IBISWorld, March 2012

- "The high-tech revolution, globalization, and Wall Street's (dubious) expansion have generated still more demand for sophisticated legal services. In 1985 the 50 top-grossing firms had a combined revenue of $3.4 billion. If their collective top line had increased at the rate of inflation, it would have been the equivalent of $6.9 billion in 2010, Trotter notes. Instead, the figure rose to $48.4 billion.

  "Baker & McKenzie, the largest American-based firm with nearly 4,000 lawyers and a leverage ratio of 4.48 associates to each partner, ranks 79th in average per-partner profitability. Wachtell Lipton, with 231 attorneys and leverage of 1.69 to 1, ranks first in average per-partner profit, with $4.3 million."

  Source: "White Shoe Blues" by Paul M. Barrett, Bloomberg Businessweek, April 23 — April 29, 2012

Industry Trend

- "Fast growing. Litigation is becoming larger and larger, especially in the medical, accounting and technical fields."

- "The latest version of The American Lawyer's Summer Hiring Survey shows that large law firms extended 33 percent fewer job offers to their summer associates last year than they did the year before – a drop partially explained by the fact that summer classes were down across the board.

  "Among the 79 firms that responded to the survey, 1,791 summer associates received offers in 2010, compared to the 2,679 who got offers in 2009. Ffifty-six firms made fewer offers to summer associates last year than they had in 2009, 16 made more, and seven made the same number."

  Source: www.amlawdaily.typepad.com posted by Tom Huddleston, Jr., July 27, 2011

Questions

- "What is their backlog? Customer concentration?"

Lawn Maintenance & Service (See also Landscape Services)

SIC 0782-06	NAICS 561730	Number of Businesses/Units 39,000

Rules of Thumb

- ➤ 50 percent of annual sales plus inventory
- ➤ 2 to 2.75 times SDE plus inventory
- ➤ 2.5 to 3 times EBIT
- ➤ 3 to 3.5 times EBITDA

Pricing Tips

- "Depending on size 2 - 4 times EBITDA for large company could be higher"
- "The baseline multiple of SDE for commercial landscape maintenance

businesses is typically between 2.5 and 3 plus inventory. The range of the multiple depends on the customer concentration, type of customer, quality of equipment and management in place. Landscape construction and residential landscape maintenance businesses have much lower value compared to commercial landscape businesses. I have found that financial buyers typically pay more than strategic buyers since they are buying their way into the industry. The real value in landscape service companies relates to the recurring nature of the revenue including both the monthly maintenance fees and extras that are derived from the monthly maintenance customers."

- "The value in landscape service companies lies within the recurring revenue. Landscape maintenance companies have much higher value compared to companies that focus on landscape construction. I have found that financial buyers typically pay a lot more than strategic buyers since they are buying into the industry. 2.5 to 3.0 X SDE + inventory is typically where strong landscape service companies will sell for assuming that the majority of revenue is maintenance or extras tied to maintenance customers. Also, commercial accounts or HOA's have more value than residential customers."

- "Larger companies = higher value. Equipment Fair Market Value should be added to gross sales and SDE multiplier formulas."

Expert Comments

"Landscape maintenance companies are marketable since the industry has been impacted less compared to other businesses in the current economy. Their margins have been reduced, but businesses still need to maintain their properties."

"Generally difficult to finance because of lack of assets."

"Maintenance is fairly easy to learn"

"Easy entry, many small companies and large companies. Those that are professionally operated are successful."

Benchmark Data

- "50% gross profit or more"
- For additional Benchmark data see Landscape Services
- "Gross profit target of 40%+ is desirable"
- "$75K per employee"

Expenses as a Percentage of Annual Sales

Cost of goods	35% to 45%
Payroll/labor Costs	35% to 45%
Occupancy	02% to 05%
Profit (estimated pretax)	10% to 15%

Industry Trend

- "Continued pressure on gross profits due to customer budget issues, increasing fuel costs and workers comp rates."
- "Gross margins have been squeezed a bit due to the tightening of the economy. Industry will remain relatively strong as all commercial customers will continue to maintain their properties."
- "More smaller companies, easy entry."

Seller Financing

- "25% to 50% seller financing over 5 years"

Questions

- "What % of revenue is maintenance versus new construction? Maintenance has much more value. What is the % of revenue from commercial maintenance versus residential maintenance? Commercial maintenance has more value. What is the customer concentration? Who maintains the relationships with the customers? What is the quality and maintenance history on the vehicles and equipment."
- "What is the turnover of customers? How much business is the owner responsible for?"
- "What is your customer concentration? Who manages the customer accounts? Who holds the contractor's license? Will key employees agree to stay?"
- "Residential vs. commercial customers. Rates. Equipment. Staffing. Licenses."

Resources

Websites

- www.landcarenetwork.org
- www.lawnandlandscape.com

Associations

- American Nursery & Landscape Association: www.anla.org

		Franchise
Lenny's Subs		
Approx. Total Investment		$216,500 to $369,000
SIC 5812-06	NAICS 722211	Number of Businesses/Units 162

Rules of Thumb

➢ 15 to 20 percent of annual sales plus inventory

Resources

Websites

- www.lennyssubs.com

		Franchise
Li'l Dino Subs		
	NAICS 722211	Number of Businesses/Units 15

Rules of Thumb

➢ 64 percent of annual sales plus inventory

Pricing Tips

- "One sold for 80 percent of sales, but it was located in an office building with vending rights."

- Note: No record of this company as a franchise could be located through a computer search, but it has been included just as it has been for several years—just in case.

Benchmark Data

- For Benchmark data see Sandwich Shops

	Franchise
Liberty Tax Service (See also Accounting Firms/Tax Practices)	
Approx. Total Investment	$56,800 to $69,000
Estimated Annual Sales/Unit	Not Available
NAICS 541213	Number of Businesses/Units 3,631

Rules of Thumb

➤ 45 to 50 percent of annual sales plus inventory

Resources

Websites
- www.libertytaxfranchise.com

Limousine Services		
(See also Ground Transportation & Taxicab Businesses)		
SIC 4119-03	NAICS 485320	Number of Businesses/Units 137,306

Rules of Thumb

➤ 50 to 55 percent of annual revenues plus vehicles

➤ 2 to 2.5 times SDE plus vehicles

➤ 4 times EBITDA — companies with corporate accounts under contract plus vehicles.

➤ 3 times EBITDA plus vehicles

Pricing Tips

- "You need to look at Owner's Discretionary Cash Flow (also known as Seller's Discretionary Earnings). You also need to know whether the limousines are owned outright, financed or leased. Depreciation expense becomes an important consideration because the owned vehicles wear down rapidly and must be replaced to keep the business looking 'up to date.'"
- "The figure needs to be adjusted for the fair market value of the vehicles less the outstanding debt."
- Note: Depreciation is usually considered an "add-back" and is therefore part of the Seller's Discretionary Earnings/EBIT/EBITDA. However, in this type of business it should not be added back as it is a necessary business expense. Vehicles are the mainstay of the business and replacement is ongoing business.

Expert Comments

"No real barriers to entry. It is easy to finance vehicles and create a website."

"Any person can get started by buying one vehicle and building from there."

Benchmark Data

- Note: See Taxicab Businesses for additional Benchmark data
- "A profitable business should net 15% to 20% because the margins are high."
- "36% of operator revenue in 2009 was derived from business/corporate travel, a significant drop from 50% in 2008. With the meltdown/slowdown in the financial services and banking sectors, along with the crackdown on corporate business travel, this number is no surprise.

"The average gross revenue for respondents in 2009 was $1,057,488 (median was $374,500), down $284,000 from the average gross revenue in 2008. The median figure, which more accurately reflects the status of small to medium size companies, however, held steady.

"The number of operators reporting revenues of less than $100,000 rose from 1% in 2008 to 22.4% in 2009; those reporting revenues between $100,000 and $249,000 rose from 19% in 2008 to 25.9% in 2009. Meanwhile, those operators reporting annual revenues in categories between $250,000 and $2.9 million all fell by several percentage points, indicating that more of the larger operators got shoved down into lower revenue categories for 2009.

"Sedans, the daily workhorses of the chauffeured transportation sector, generated on average 40% of operator revenue in 2009, down from 48% in 2008. Meanwhile, revenue share from stretch limousines rose slightly, from 12% in 2008 to 13.8% in 2009. Revenue share from non-stretch SUVs climbed from 8% in 2008 to 9.9% in 2009. Revenue from limo, party, shuttle, and mini-buses generated about the same share of revenue for operators from year to year.

"Some of the more positive glimmers include: Although operator profits took a hit, they didn't completely tank as was the case in other retail and service sectors. The median operator profit margin for 2009 was 10%, down from 15% in 2008. Given the severity of the recession, any profit margin in two digits seems positive.

"48% of operators said they get reservations from third-party industry Web sites such as limos.com compared to 46% in 2008, a sign that online commerce continues to grow despite economic contraction.

"Average fleet sizes did not decline from 2008 to 2009, but median fleet size went down from 8 to 7."

Source: "2010–11 LCT Fact Book: Looks Like the Worst is Over," by Martin Romjue, April, 2010.
www.lctmag.com

Expenses as a Percentage of Annual Sales

Cost of goods	30% to 35% (Auto Purchases)
Payroll/labor Costs	25% to 35%
Occupancy	05% to 10%
Profit (estimated pretax)	10% to 20%

Industry Trend

- "If economy improves, the industry will improve. There will always be a demand for weddings, proms, special events, corporate executives, etc."
- "Declining due to the economy"

Seller Financing

- "Seller should expect 50% down and offer 10 year amortization with a 3 year balloon at 6% interest."

Questions

- "You will want to see the repair and maintenance records for all the vehicles. You will want to know if there have been any accidents. You will want to know if there is outstanding litigation or workmen's compensation issues. What background checks and drug tests are performed on new hires?"
- "Have all vehicles been properly maintained regularly?"
- "Look at the maintenance logs; have a mechanic check all vehicles."

Resources

Trade Publications
- Limousine, Charter, and Tour: www.lctmag.com

Associations
- National Limousine Association—the association has a study on this industry, but it is for members only. However, the site itself has a lot of excellent information and is well worth a visit: www.limo.org

Linen Services—Supply (See Uniform Rental)		
		Number of Businesses/Units 1,600

Resources

Associations
- Textile Rental Services Association of America (TRSA): www.trsa.org
- Western Textile Services Association: www.wtsa.org

Liquefied Petroleum Gas		
SIC 5984-01	NAICS 454312	Number of Businesses/Units 1,700

Rules of Thumb

- ➤ 130 percent of annual sales plus inventory
- ➤ 3 times SDE plus inventory
- ➤ 4 times EBIT
- ➤ 6 times EBITDA (Good double-check is 2.5 to 3.5 gross profit)

Pricing Tips

- "'The biggest factors are the quality of the company, the quality of the market and then we look at margins,' says Armentano, whose company seeks to acquire 3 to 5 million gallons annually. 'We want to buy a company that we know we can grow and prosper with.'"

  Source: John Armentano, vice president of acquisitions for Paraco Gas Corp. in Rye Brook, N.Y., "Winter Windfall" by Brian Richesson, www.lpgasmagazine.com May 1, 2010

- "Company ownership of tanks and cylinders at the customer's location is an important consideration. The higher the % of company ownership, the more valuable the company. High gross margin per gallon is also very important."
- "Multiple of gallons 1–2X; multiple of gross margin 1–2.5X; add value .for high number of company- owned lease tanks, relatively new trucks (less than 5 years), high percentage of residential accounts, backup management and infrastructure, current safety programs, current equipment/storage controls."
- "4 to 5 times EBITDA (Normalized Earnings). Some very attractive and growing markets will demand 6 times EBITDA—depends on the business and location."
- "Under 1 mm annual gallons—4.5 to 6.5 times EBITDA. Over 1 mm annual gallons—5.5 to 7.5 times EBITDA. Some use a multiple of annual gallons."
- "…Customer mix, market position, age & condition & efficiency of equipment. The bulk of the asset value is usually in field tanks at customer locations… A large number of residential customers is generally a plus."

Expert Comments

"Capital-intensive business; desirable alternative clean-burning fuel; larger national companies are aggressively looking for acquisition opportunities."

"Even though the barriers to entry are increasing, smaller companies' marketability is decreasing."

"The propane industry is very capital intensive in that most companies want to own and control the tanks at customer locations. For this reason, the business is difficult to enter. Price spikes and supply displacements are also issues during the peak winter months. There is a high level of technical expertise needed to install and service propane equipment. Drivers and technicians must pass rigorous training programs and DOT requirements."

"Extremely mature industry with little innovation"

Benchmark Data

- "Gross profit per gallon is a key factor. Average gp/gallon should now be exceeding $1.00/gallon in most areas."
- "The business is a delivery business, so the more efficient the delivery, aka gallons per bobtail, the higher the profit."
- "Gross profit per gallon is a key factor. A typical overall company gross profit range is now exceeding $1.00/gallon in many areas depending on a company's customer mix. Some areas of the country are significantly below this benchmark due to customer ownership of tanks in the field."
- "EBITDA per gallon greater than $0.15"
- "Can vary considerably by company, depending on customer mix between residential, commercial, farm & industrial type customer."

Expenses as a Percentage of Annual Sales

Cost of goods	40% to 50%
Payroll/labor Costs	15% to 25%
Occupancy	02% to 05%
Profit (estimated pretax)	15%

Industry Trend

- "Slow but steady growth in most areas as people shift away from heating oil. Propane is a viable clean-burning alternative fuel choice with many advantages over other fuels."
- "Growing"

Seller Financing

- "Typically cash at closing for fixed assets; intangibles are sometimes financed over five years."
- "Five years"

Questions

- "5 years' financials and gallonage history; gross profit per gallon by segment of business; complete list of assets including tank inventory, bulk plants, trucks, etc., real estate appraisal."
- "Customer concentration, competition, age of fleet, tenure/age of employees, reason for exit"
- "Company ownership of customer tanks & cylinders is an important consideration. Where the company owns most of the customer field equipment, and there are good gross profits, a much better value can be obtained."
- "Lease tank coverage, age of equipment, age and volume of bulk storage, type of customer base."

Resources

Websites

- www.propanecouncil.org

Trade Publications

- LP Gas Magazine: www.lpgasmagazine.com
- Butane/Propane News (BPN): www.bpnews.com

Associations

- National Propane Gas Association: www.npga.org

Liquor Stores/Package Stores (Beer, Wine & Liquor Stores)		
SIC 5921-02	NAICS 445310	Number of Businesses/Units 43,488

Rules of Thumb

➤ 40 to 45 percent of annual sales plus inventory

➤ 2 to 3 times SDE plus inventory

➤ 2.5 to 3.5 times EBITDA

➤ 3 times EBIT

Pricing Tips

- "This type of business sells for higher multiples in states where they restrict the number of licenses per town, such as in Massachusetts. In these areas large stores with over $1 Million in sales may sell for as much as 45% of sales or 4X SDE."
- "A healthy liquor store with appropriate inventory should net 15% to 20% for the owner. The following items are critical for success. 1. Location. 2. Competition. 3. Inventory level. 4. Product mix. 5. Hours. 6. Familiarity with customers."

- "The larger the cash flow, influences the multiple being utilized to price the business and ultimately influences the sell price. In addition, owner financing will aid in obtaining a higher multiple, with respect to the final sale price of the business. Owner operator stores, with less than $50-60,000 cash flow tend to fall into the 1-1.5 times multiple, for a beginning asking price. $75,000–$100,000 net discretionary cash flow, where the owner works less than 25 hours per week, a seller can expect to see a 2 times multiple or more when the business sells."
- "Other criteria needs to be considered, such as occupancy expense, gross profit, location etc."
- "Liquor stores are highly desired by buyers—particularly if they include real estate. The more inventory, the greater the value. If a big box competitor is already in place, and no new locations can open up, this is a positive if the store is making a profit."
- "Careful attention must be paid to product mix. Sometimes smaller stores selling 6 packs & nips will be more profitable than high-volume stores pumping out 30 packs all day. Check for % of wine sales as fine wines sell at better margins. A near auction atmosphere exists in the northeastern U.S. where 'new American' buyers will pay premium prices."
- "Competition in area, lease terms"
- "Location, product mix, profitability, lease, etc. have impact on asking price/value. Stores with over $1 million in sales and/or with real estate are more desirable."
- "Some buyers use 3–4 times monthly sales, and experienced buyers generally will use 1.5–2 times seller's discretionary earnings, contingent upon size of store, and years in business."
- "In Massachusetts, liquor stores are priced at 40%–50% of sales for stores doing over $750,000 in sales. Smaller stores sell for 30%–35% of sales. Massachusetts commands higher prices because of the cap on licenses issued per town. If the business owner is selling the real estate he may also get a higher multiple for the business."
- "Liquor stores will often sell for a price equivalent to 6 months' worth of sales."
- "1 to 2 times adjusted EBITDA + liquor license + FFE + inventory = asking price."
- "You must consider location, occupancy expense, product mix, gross profit and payroll."
- "As always, watch for high lease rates as a percentage of sales. Overall lease rates in excess of 8% depress multiples and pricing, all other factors being equal."
- "Licensing is a big issue in most states. Those states where licenses are hard to obtain (NJ for example) are worth more money. Businesses with real estate attached generally fetch a premium."
- "Asking prices have generally been increasing over the last few years due to demand. Location, GPM and payroll expense are key factors to consider when determining price."
- "Depending on fixed overhead expenses, to include the percentage of rent to gross sales, a formula of 3–5 times monthly sales will also be considered. Generally we take 3–5 of the formulas used and average them based on gross sales, cost of rent, current margins, and breakeven point for an owner operator, or investor."

- "Location is critical. Amount of competition is critical. Carrying a very large amount of inventory is necessary for success."
- "Pricing trend is up for stores doing $1 million plus. More buyers looking for RE also. May have to adjust COGS to industry standards."
- "I generally use 2–3 times SDC plus inventory plus any add-backs."
- "In general, liquor and convenience stores have been selling for prices equal to 6 months' sales."
- "I use 2 times SDE plus inventory at cost. Often times the price is 1 times SDE if there has been a decline in sales."
- "Pay close attention to inventory amount, turns, owner operated or use of employees, rent cost as a percentage of gross sales, margins on gross sales. 25%–28% will be closer to a true value. These areas listed will create various ranges when they are higher or lower than good working averages. Inventory should allow for 9–10 turns per year. Occupancy cost/sales should be no more than 7%–8% using the above ratios and multipliers."
- "Is store high volume because of lower margins? What percentage of store is fine wine? Is this percentage growing? Are there any other package goods licenses available in town? What is the town's position on awarding malt beverage and beer licenses? Is store on right-hand side of road heading home?"
- "Higher discount stores will sell for lower multiples, Lottery is an added bonus."
- "7 to 9 months of sales plus inventory is a general rule of thumb for a liquor store."
- "In NJ, generally speaking, many business brokers use 50 cents to a dollar in revenue to obtain price. I like basing price first off of SDE and then second off of location."
- "Total Gross sales, minus all expenses, add back owner's salary and any personal expenses paid for by the business=Seller's Discretionary Cash flow. Take that figure and start with a 2 multiple for a small store and increase in .25 increments for strong lease, increasing sales, high wine sales."
- "One must take into consideration location, occupancy expense, condition of assets, level of inventory, product mix, payroll expense, additional income from lotto/check cashing and GPM. (GPM must not include additional income)."
- "Buyers look at % of annual gross sales and SDE more so than EBIT or EBITDA."
- "The terms of the lease are very important. Discount stores worth less, wine stores worth more. As always, location, location, location."
- "Analyze last 3 years of income and expense information."

Expert Comments

"Some states restrict the number of licenses per town and in those states the licenses can be very valuable if the town does not have any more available."

"In most municipalities there are restrictions for opening new liquor stores. Additionally, liquor stores typically cannot be located with 1,000 feet of a school or church."

"Location is very important, for the businesses success. In addition, multiple locations, allowing for larger case quantity purchases, will provide a better pricing and profit model for an owner. Thus, a buyer should provide for ongoing working capital, to operate the store in order to take advantage of quantity case pricing. This is important, to the success and ongoing survival of the store, particularly if there is a large volume store close by, which is viewed as a competitor. Margins are shrinking in the industry at both the retail and wholesale levels. Hence, many small stores are struggling to survive, due to their occupancy cost being high, in relation to both their sales and margins. The lower margins drive the cost of occupancy up, which cannot be adjusted, when the owner is locked into a specific lease period. Hence, we are seeing many small operators, at best buying a job. When they get into the business and overlook the need, for additional working capital and potential negative cash flow for an extended period of time, when starting a store, from 'scratch'".

"Liquor stores with annual revenue of $1.5M and above are very much in demand."

"Liquor stores are controlled in that locations are limited. Any store must have $200,000 in inventory to be very successful and to take advantage of distributor discounts on large purchases."

"Most states place limits on number of licenses available increasing barrier to entry. The Great Recession has proven that while people continue to drink, those that may have habitually reached for top-shelf goods are lowering their reach to mid-priced brands. Distributors saw only a 2% increase in dollar volume in MA in 2010. Right side of the road preferable to capture homeward bound shoppers. Big box chains getting more & more licenses to sell alcohol as are smaller stores getting wine and malt beverage licenses."

"Must have good gross profit, lottery sales a plus."

"Liquor laws vary state to state and have a great bearing on competition, barrier to entry, marketability and profit trend. Colorado retailers, as an example, are facing legislative battles to stop grocery chains and convenience stores from selling full-strength beer and wine. Distributors are pressuring for changes to how sales tax is collected. Government in general is looking for ways to increase revenue through taxation changes. Conversely, liquor stores are perceived as recession resistant and therefore popular targets of acquisition. The public is more focused on a good shopping experience in stores. Customer service, presentation and cleanliness matter more now than ever before. SBA lending is difficult to find even for profitable stores."

"Increase in competition, especially larger stores."

"Recession-proof business. Location and selection and price say it all."

"Location and price are everything with a liquor store."

"Liquor stores continue to attract many buyers. Popular business to own. Long retail hours."

"In the Denver area, legislative pressure by grocery stores and convenience stores is having a detrimental impact on marketability."

"Profits have been flat or just below, largely due to the current economic situation, Demand has remained steady due to the Asian influence."

"Location, easy access, on a route home from work or near and/or within a major grocery chain are very important to gross sales and customer loyalty."

"Lease rates seem to be one of the most important factors for liquor stores, as are gross margins."

"Location, competition and inventory level are highly important. The most popular business listings are liquor stores."

"Fuel surcharges putting squeeze on profits. Some states have regulations limiting # of stores and limiting minimum selling prices. More C-stores getting beer & wine licenses. Demand remains high especially with 'New Americans.'"

"Ease of Replication—In most cases, creating a new liquor store is very hard. Unless someone has a license or can obtain an existing one, it is impossible to open a liquor store. Competition, for this reason, is not a major factor. Since the competitive set is already in place, potential buyers already know who they are up against."

"Competition is the key to the sale of a liquor store. If prices can be kept low, customer loyalty can be established and maintained."

"Visibility, Ease of in and out important, shopping center or strip center that offers grocery shopping as an additional opportunity for the customer to combine shopping for different purchases. Easy location to shop on the way home from work or Saturdays."

"'New Americans' have caused significant increase in prices of liquor stores. C-stores with beer & wine licenses are threatening full liquor stores. States that highly regulate this industry historically have driven profit margins down."

"Wine stores have a higher percentage of gross profit margin. Growing stores with great leases tend to sell for more money."

"Profit trends seem to be increasing due to more emphasis on wine sales. Ease of replicating difficult due to licensing issues. Marketability is high due to current demand."

"Many states regulate # of stores allowed. Careful for supermarkets getting beer & wine licenses. Industry trends flat with exception of wines and high-end vodkas. Smaller stores can be as profitable as mega stores if selling lots of singles, 6 packs, 100-250 ml. at higher margins than 30 pks. & 1.5L. Common belief is people tend to drink during good and bad times."

"Though these businesses can be easily replicated, the challenge to replicators is getting the liquor license by the city. Cities generally restrict the number of licenses in an area based on the number of citizens living in the area."

"In high-income areas, competition is based on discounts and specials."

Benchmark Data

Statistics (Beer, Wine & Liquor Stores)

Number of Establishments	43,488
Average Profit Margin	8.1%
Revenue per Employee	$276,000
Average Number of Employees	3.8%
Average Wages per Employee	$17,991

Source: IBISWorld, July 2012

Products and Services Segmentation

Liquor	21.1%
Wine	20.5%
Food	18.7%
Beer	17%
Other	9.9%
Tobacco products	7.3%
Soft drinks	5.5%

Source: IBISWorld, July 2012

Industry Costs

Profit	8.1%
Wages	6.6%
Purchases	69.2%
Depreciation	0.3%
Marketing	0.5%
Rent & Utilities	9.6%
Other	5.7%

Source: IBISWorld, July 2012

Percent of total Sales Tendered by Liquor Stores

Spirits and Liquors	40%
Beer	30%
Groceries, Cigarettes, Cigars	25%

- "Profit should be 15% to 20% for a $1.0 million store or above. This assumes 7 days a week operation, open until 11:00 p.m. six days a week, inventory level of $250,000, surveillance cameras, drug and background checks for employees, extensive selection of wine and liquor with reasonable selection of wines."
- "Product Costs should not exceed 80%, based on purchase, or sales volume. Smaller locations should keep product costs no more then 72-75%. Occupancy costs Are very critical to the operation, As well as the location."
- "Gross Profit 25-30%, occupancy expense 306%, payroll not to exceed 7%, wine sales making up of at least 40% of revenue and stores between 5-10,000 square feet."
- "Gross profit of 25% or more, employee costs of 8%–12% as a percentage of sales, POS/Inventory system in place, and appropriate mix of beer, wine and spirits, and margins reflective of the mix."
- "$250 per square foot annually"
- "20 to 25% gross income, stores that sale more beer profit % lower, stores that sale more wine profit % higher."
- "Good rule of thumb for operating expenses, in addition to rent, should not exceed $1,000. Margins for South Carolina should not be any lower than 20%. Rent, ideally, should not exceed 7% of annual gross sales."
- "Must be able to generate at least a 35% gross margin."
- "Gross profit should be between 23% and 28% and provide a minimum of $1 million in annual revenue."
- "$300,000–$500,000 per year gross sales, for a 1800–2400 square foot space."
- "Gross margins of 24% or better, overall occupancy costs of 6%–8%, good mix of beer, wine and liquor sales."
- "Successful stores are showing a GPM of 25% or better. Those stores are typically focusing on wine sales where margins are higher."

- "Watch for stores that sell singles and six-packs, as this is where the profits lie. Liquor stores should have tight control of inventory. The days of the profits being in cases of Scotch in the basement are gone."
- "Stores selling high volume in smaller quantities, i.e., 6-packs, 100 ml, wine, nips etc. will have much better GP than '30-pack stores.' Beware of stores that stock only 1 to show and 1 to go —probably haven't got the cash flow to buy best deal."
- "Occupancy costs must remain within 7% for a successful operation."
- "Benchmark Data: Location to populated neighborhoods, gross margins of 25% or better. 1–2 part time employees, owner operator, unless 3 units are owned by same owner."
- "Must have a rental amount less than 7% of gross sales to make money"
- "Rent expense between 3–6 percent of revenue, payroll 7 percent or less not including owner, SDE typically 10 percent of gross sales,"
- "Gross margins should be between 22%–28%. Higher wine sales will push the margins to the 28% range."
- "Gross margins should be at least 35%. Facility lease should be no more than 7%. Payroll expenses should be no more than 10%."
- "Sales per sf should be at least $25 per sf per month. Occupancy costs higher than 8% will decrease the value of the business, as this is one of the main cost components analyzed when valuing a liquor store."
- "Blended margins can be confusing without understanding product mix and demographics. POS systems [Point of Sale] a real pain with constant price changes but discourages employee theft."
- "Rental and employee cost are major factors in determining profitability of the store."
- "Business usually requires owner-operator to work in store for best results."
- "Gross margins should be between 20% and 25%."
- "Rental must be below 7% of gross."
- "Stores that sell more 6-packs, singles, pints, wine in 750s etc. will exhibit higher gross margins than high-volume stores selling 30-packs, wine in 1.5s or boxes."
- "Gross profit should be no less than 20% and 23% median."
- "Too many variables. Example: beer store; fine wine store, etc."
- "Know your marketplace—selling higher margin product like wine and beer area will tie up too much cash and not help the profits of the business."
- "Normal product mix in sales is 60% liquor and 40% wine."
- "Watch the gross profit levels. Must keep the rental figures below 7% of gross at all times."
- "Gross profit percentage is a huge factor. Is the store full markup or discount?"
- "Turn inventory 9 to 10 times a year."
- "Typically a store with normal margins needs to do $1 million + to sustain 6-figure earnings. Smaller stores need to do more business in higher margin goods like 6-packs, singles, nips, wine and high-end liquor to sustain a livable wage."
- "3,500 sq. ft., ample parking, easy in and out, free-standing building, prefer basement and/or extra storage, some food items, buying co-op with regular ads, pricing"
- "The typical store grosses about $350,000/year. Overall gross profit margins in

liquor stores generally are between 21 to 24 percent, the exceptions being very large (over $1,000,000/year) discount stores that operate on lower margins—and wine specialty stores."

Expenses as a Percentage of Annual Sales

Cost of goods	65% to 80%
Payroll/labor Cost	08% to 12%
Occupancy	08% to 10%
Profit (estimated pretax)	10% to 15%

Industry Trend

- "More supermarkets and discount stores, such as Costco, will obtain licenses to sell beer, wine and liquor. Smaller stores will sell their licenses to these larger stores or to multi-store owners."
- "More liquor store owners owning multiple stores versus one store/one owner. Families and chain stores are aggressively purchasing liquor stores."
- "The worse the economy gets, the better this business gets."
- "The market will remain to have high demand, primarily for stores with revenue of $1 million+.
- "Liquor stores always remain one of the most desired businesses to own, and cities limit the amount available due to population census controls."
- "Increased competition from big box stores. Independents have to concentrate on better beer & wine selections not carried by mass merchandisers. Stores regulated by state laws likely to see margins shrink."
- "Liquor stores are the most popular businesses. Those with real estate are in great demand."
- "Liquor stores continue to be strong businesses, primarily for the convenience consumers constantly strive for."
- "Should get stronger with poor economy"
- "Continued growth for the larger stores"
- "Industry giants getting larger. Mom-and-pop stores fading."

Seller Financing

- "Many stores can be bank financed but sometimes the seller will finance the inventory for 1 year."
- "5 years on business, 30 to 120 days on inventory"
- "I would suggest that the buyer pay 100% of the inventory cost plus put 50% down for the business. The seller can offer 6%, ten year amortization with a three year balloon."

Questions

- "1. Have you ever been robbed? If so, how did it turn out? 2. Who is your competition, how far away are they located, how long have they been there and what should cause a person to buy from you rather than from your competition? 3. Who are your distributors and what type special deals do they offer? 4. Have long has each employee been with you? 5. What percentage of your sales are liquor, wine and beer? 6. How much inventory do you have for liquor, wine and beer?"
- "1. Lease terms and amount 2. Sales By year, for last 3 years 3. Margins and net profit. 4. Provide Copies Of All invoices and bank statements, for a minimum of 2 years. 5. Will they be willing to owner finance a portion, of

the sale price. 6.Will they allow you to view the closing of the store each day, with regards to their bookkeeping, for 1-2 weeks. 7. Why are they selling the business. 8. What would they do to grow the business. 9. What 2 things do they not like about the business and how would they fix them, if they had the time and money. 10. How much time of a training period will the seller provide and would they be available, by phone, for additional support, up to one year, at an agreed upon day and time."

- "Has a big box competitor opened up in the last 12 months? Is one scheduled to open in the next 12 months? What is the mix of wine, hard liquor and beer?"
- "Blend of merchandise sales by wine, liquor and beer and by size of units sold. Special deals they receive from distributors. Under the table labor and vendors. Is there a co-op to buy at best price?"
- "Inventory turnover rate"
- "Closest competition, term of lease, payroll cost, how computer system controls inventory and ordering. Do they work on margins or markup? How do store margins compare to any stores within 2–3 miles? How did they arrive at selling price? How would they grow the business, and how long will they provide training and distance for a covenant not to compete?"
- "Is there an option on the property or is it owned by the seller? What competition is nearby? Are there any other licenses available in the town? Do you owe any back taxes or fees that would hold up the transfer of the liquor license?
- "What are your sales tax numbers and are you current?"
- "1. Can sales be demonstrated through tax returns and operating statements? 2. Product sales mix? 3. POS system in place? 4. How often is an inventory count done and how many turns per year? 5. Rent structure, terms, options, rate, NNN costs? 6. Competition in area, length of ownership of store."
- "Lease rate, term, options, NNN cost, assignability, product mix percentages, margin overall and for each category, operating entity type, length of time in business, why selling, knowledge of competition, inventory control systems in place."
- "Security/surveillance system in place? Theft/shrinkage."
- "How often do you order from your distributors? What is your markup on beer, wine and liquor? What percentage of your sales are beer, wine, liquor and other?"
- "How much income was derived from buying smart? Additional sources of revenue, if any and amount? Request copies of sales tax reports from state, to verify the numbers represented. How many suppliers are used and terms available if any? Has there been or is there any liquor store in the process of being opened in the area? What type of terms will the landlord provide, for a long-term lease with options? Does it justify being opened each day at 9:00 a.m. vs. 10:00 a.m. and what have the sales trends, by day, been during that extra hour? Obtain a certificate of good standing, from the state, relative to all taxes being paid and current, particularly the sales taxes. How does the buyer figure margins, markup, gross profit and/or product cost? Much confusion among individuals relative to this topic."
- "What is the mix of sales—wine, beer, liquor, cigarettes, misc.? What is the closest that a new competitor can open a store? How frequently are you receiving deliveries from distributors?"
- "Ask to review bank statements, sales tax reports and purchase invoices to confirm unreported cash sales."
- "Is there any distressed merchandise? Any rumors of new competition? Why are you selling?"

- "Rent, cost of goods sold, payroll, lottery commissions, inventory ordering, are they on POS?"
- "Besides the general questions that could be found on a Profit & Loss: What types of products do you sell the most of? What types of customers do you get? Do you sell smaller items mostly (6 packs, 12 packs, pints, shots, etc.) or larger items (30 packs, cases of beer large bottles, etc)? (this helps to decide gross margin)."
- "Why are they selling? Days and hours they work? Margins? Payroll paid off books? Case vs. broken-case pricing and what percentage of business is broken-case purchases? Cost of broken-case purchasing? Is this cost calculated before or after establishing margin on product sold? Also, any taxes paid on product purchases and are they, too, calculated before calculating margins or added on after this formula?"
- "How long in business. Length of lease, option to buy building. Recent competition in area."
- "What is your product mix by beer, wine, liquor and by sizes? What percentage of sales are cigarettes? Does your accountant include lottery sales in gross revenues? Why is there so much dust on your bottles? Will the wholesaler take back the 12 cases of Turkish Raki that have been 'on sale' for 4 years?"
- "What conditions are associated with this license?"
- "How long is the lease, is it assignable? Average gross markup of all products. What is the competition in the area? Percentage of sales of beer, wine, liquor and cigarettes? How much is the lottery commission annually?"
- "Area liquor store openings and closings in the last year?"
- "Distressed inventory(s), any new competition contemplated, product mix by department and size, general security questions, quality and turnover of employees, how many vendors per product?"
- "Percentage of sales in the different categories; such as wine, beer, liquor and misc.?"
- "What is reason for selling? How long have you owned business?"
- "Length of lease, percentage of sales in each category: wine, beer and liquor."
- "Does the store cash checks? Does the store have lottery? Does the store sell fine wines? If so, it has higher margins. Is it a discount store? Does it sell lots of half- pints?"

Resources

Associations
- National Alcoholic Beverage Control Association: www.nabca.org

Little Caesar's Pizza	Franchise
Approx. Total Investment	$193,050 to $619,500
Estimated Annual Sales/Unit	$427,000
NAICS 722211	Number of Businesses/Units 2,700

Rules of Thumb

➤ 55 percent of annual sales plus inventory

Resources

Websites

- www.littlecaesars.com

Lock & Key Shops		
SIC 7699-62	NAICS 561622	Number of Businesses/Units 15,461

Rules of Thumb

➤ 40 to 45 percent of annual sales plus inventory

Benchmark Data

Statistics (Locksmiths)

Number of Establishments	15,461
Average Profit Margin	5.6%
Revenue per Employee	$60,100
Average Number of Employees	2
Average Wages per Employee	$20,477

Source: IBISWorld, March 2012

Products and Services Segmentation

Non-residential security system installation and repair	53.8%
Residential security system installation and repair	27%
Key duplication	7%
Security system rental and resale	6.6%
Other services	5.6%

Source: IBISWorld, March 2012

Industry Costs

Profit	5.6%
Wages	34.0%
Purchases	39.0%
Depreciation	3.0%
Marketing	2.0%
Rent & Utilities	5.5%
Other	10.9%

Source: IBISWorld, March 2012

Industry Trend

- "...he has consistent work from banks and realtors who need him for foreclosed properties all over the county. He estimates that nearly 75 percent of his business is related to foreclosures. 'A lot of the banks key their homes to a certain key, then if they trade it or sell it off to another bank, they have me re-key, so sometimes I get triple work off the same place.'"

  Source: "Foreclosures Provide Boon for Florida Locksmiths" by Laura Bowden Yang, *New-Journal* Daytona Beach, FL, May 3, 2010

Resources

Associations

- Associated Locksmiths of America: www.aloa.org
- Institutional Locksmiths Association: www.ilanational.org

		Franchise
Logan Farms Honey Glazed Hams		
Approx. Total Investment		$251,975 to $329,175
Estimated Annual Sales/Unit		Not Available
	NAICS 722211	Number of Businesses/Units 9

Rules of Thumb

➤ 30 percent of annual sales plus inventory

Resources

Websites
▪ www.loganfarms.com

Lumberyards (See also Building Materials/Home Centers)		
SIC 5211-42	NAICS 444190	Number of Businesses/Units 51,096

Rules of Thumb

➤ 40 percent of annual sales includes inventory

➤ 4 to 6 times SDE includes inventory

➤ 4 times EBIT

➤ 4 to 6 times EBITDA

Pricing Tips

▪ "The major buyers were offering to pay for the best yards 5.5 x EBITDA"

▪ There are several types of lumberyards: the publicly traded 'big box' Home Depot, Lowe's types, whose value is daily shown on the NYSE; and the more prevalent independently owned 'Pro' type lumberyard, usually in or close to a metro area with sales in excess of $5 million, that has as its customers primarily professional contractors (most new-home builders), remodel/repair contractors, and commercial/industrial customers. These Pro yards have a minimum of 80% of their business with professionals and a maximum of 20% with DIYers. The smaller town lumberyards generally serve DIYers (60%) and Pro accounts (40%). The demand for lumberyards since 2006 has diminished to now be almost nonexistent. With the housing 'meltdown' and poor economy, there is little interest in a capital-intensive business with a large, expensive, slow-turning inventory, expensive equipment and large accounts receivable. The value of a lumberyard has also changed drastically. It used to be, prior to 2006, that a good, profitable Pro type lumberyard would bring 1.5 times its book value, or from 5–6 times EBIT. Now a good lumberyard, if still profitable, would likely sell for its book value and, maybe even less, its liquidation value. Even a strategic acquisition may bring only these prices. I do not see anything on the horizon that would restore higher prices for these businesses. Home Depot and Lowe's are selling for about 50% to 60% of their highs of 2005–2006 so they too are showing signs of the tough economy ."

Expert Comments

"Most lumberyards sell most of their materials to new-home builders (contractors). This market, new homes, has been devastated and hardly exists. As a result lumber dealers' sales are off since 2006 from 20% to 80% and profits very slim, some not making it at all. There is basically no market for a lumberyard unless it is a stategic acquisition, or one of a few exceptional ones . . . this update dated April 2011."

"The new-housing market has crashed. Many dealers serving new- home builders have seen sales drop 50% or more and profitability disappear. It may be 2010 before the market returns to some normal level of activity, and profitability."

"Lumberyards are very difficult to duplicate. High dollar investment keeps most competition out of a market. It also requires a minimum of 2 acres to runs a $5 million lumberyard. Cost of land these days makes it impossible to start a new store. Most stores have been in existence for decades and have a very low cost basis on the facilities."

Benchmark Data

Statistics (Lumber & Building Material Stores)

Number of Establishments	51,096
Average Profit Margin	2.1%
Revenue per Employee	$211,400
Average Number of Employees	9.8
Average Wages per Employee	$28,678

Source: IBISWorld, June 2012

Products and Services Segmentation

Lumber and other structural building materials	65.4%
Hardware, tools, plumbing and electrical supplies	24%
Doors and windows	4.5%
Flooring and roofing materials	3.9%
Other	2.2%

Source: IBISWorld, June 2012

Major Market Segmentation

Professional contractors	54.4%
Household consumers (homeowners)	30.2%
Other	7.5%
Retailers for resale	4.5%
Wholesalers for resale	3.4%

Source: IBISWorld, June 2012

Industry Costs

Profit	2.1%
Wages	13.7%
Purchases	67.5%
Depreciation	1.6%
Marketing	1.0%
Rent & Utilities	2.9%
Other	11.2%

Source: IBISWorld, June 2012

- "Stores with 60% hardware and 40% lumber are considered home centers. If sales are 60% lumber or more and 40% hardware, it is a lumberyard.

Lumberyards earn 20–23% margin on lumber compared to 23–26% for home centers. Lumberyards have very high levels of accounts receivable (60–80% of monthly sales). When housing starts are in decline, contractors are slow to pay their bills. Lumberyards will see their receivables jump from 30–45 day turnover to 50–60 day. That can add $200,000 to receivables very quickly and kill any cash flow the lumberyard has. Bad debt write-offs can quickly run into the tens of thousands of dollars. LUMBERYARD OWNER SHOULD HAVE AN UNUSED LINE OF CREDIT EQUAL TO 50% OF MONTHLY SALES. This will allow him to weather receivable increases, winter sales declines and so on."

- "Sales per employee vary from $200,000 to $400,000."
- "Sales typically are over $500 per square foot and $300,000 per employee for lumberyards with retail space of more than 8,000 sq. ft."
- "Home centers typically have 2/3 sales in hardware and 1/3 sales in lumber and building materials. If lumber percentage is much higher, it is a lumber yard; much lower, it is a hardware store. 1.8 to 2.2 times SDE plus inventory. Home centers with SDE/Sales of 13 percent or more will be in the top range of multiplier. Those with less than 10 percent will be in low range.

Expenses as a Percentage of Annual Sales

Cost of goods	75%
Payroll/labor Costs	20%
Occupancy	03% to 05%
Profit (estimated pretax)	02% to 05%

Industry Trend
- "very tough . . . some of the worst times in the last 50 years"
- "Very tough, maybe in red for several years"

Seller Financing
- "Very few sell on owner financing; the sales are generally to existing lumber dealers."

Questions
- "Why selling? Have audited 5 years' financials?"
- "Look carefully at profit, and if future earnings are possible."

Resources
Associations
- National Lumber & Building Material Dealers Association: www.dealer.org

	Franchise
MAACO Auto Painting and Bodyworks	
Approx. Total Investment	$250,000 to $300,000
Estimated Annual Sales/Unit	Not Available
NAICS 811121	Number of Businesses/Units 457

Rules of Thumb

➢ 40 percent of annual sales plus inventory

Benchmark Data

- "Here's how the program works: If the Maaco location has not earned $750,000 after its first 15 months, the company will buy back the location, releasing the owner from his or her long-term commitment."
- "It's not a full guarantee, to be sure: Maaco will buy the location at a third of its gross revenue. It will also buy the equipment and assume the lease."

Source: "Guaranteed: Maaco program reduces risks for newbies" by Jonathan Maze, *Franchise Times*, September 2008

Resources

Websites

- www.maacofranchise.com

Machine Shops (See also Job Shops)		
SIC 3599-03	NAICS 332710	Number of Businesses/Units 20,700

Rules of Thumb

➤ 55 to 65 percent of annual revenues includes inventory

➤ 2 to 3 times SDE plus inventory

➤ 5 to 7 times EBIT

➤ 3 to 5 times EBITDA

Pricing Tips

- "Unique industry relative to valuation. Capital asset base, CAPEX, client concentration, value add services and industries served all contribute to fluctuations in value. Medical and aerospace concentration bringing highest multiples. EBITDA under $1M values 3-5X. Over $2M, 4-7X. Inventory typically included in Working Capital."
- "EBITDA under $1M will generate lower multiples while anything over $2M will generate 4-6X. CAPEX requirements and working capital may adjust price commensurately."
- "4–5 times SDE on a machine shop with sales trending in a positive direction"
- "Backlog, client concentration, client industries served"
- "Multiple of SDE seems to be a good starting point, backlog, AR, WIP; diversification boosts asking price"
- "WIP is extremely important as are raw materials. Certifications are becoming very important for strategic buyers."
- "Machine condition and level of technology are significant influences."
- "Wide range of customers a plus. Certifications extremely important most times.
- "Many are good solid businesses; important to remember work in progress when negotiating the transaction."
- "Multiples largely dependent on size of company, client concentration, backlog, industries served, etc."
- "Backlog, client concentration, WIP, CAPEX, line-item expense for repairs & maintenance, availability of qualified labor, client industry trends, etc. are all

issues a potential buyer should investigate in valuing a shop."

- "Short-run shops having design capabilities and doing prototyping may demand a premium. Different geographical areas will have varying availability of qualified machinists. Look for stable work force that is not near retirement. Be sensitive to difference between a machinist and a 'CNC machine operator.' Backlog, client concentration and industry(s) served can also have large effects on valuation."

- "Strategic buyers tend to look for excess capacity."

- "Short-run prototyping shops concentrating in the medical industry tend to sell for higher multiples."

- "Look for customer concentration. Determine sales mix between commercial and military/defense contractors. Age and type of equipment will affect valuation. Production capacity is important."

- "Condition of equipment; value equipment separately. Type of equipment very important. Any agreements or contracts?"

Expert Comments

"Backlogs are on the rise but net sales still relatively flat - off approx. 2% in 2012. Private equity investing more heavily in this space with roll-ups. Cost of new 4 and 5 axis machining centers increases barrier to entry. While the Northeastern US has its share, more machine shops in South and Midwest."

"Close attention should be paid to run rates per hour on machinery. Rent & labor will be split above and below COGS line. Percentages listed assume direct labor in COGS and admin labor below the line."

"Industry requires significant capital expenditures. Sales tied closely to demand from OEMs. "

"2011 is showing signs of strong improvement in sales and profits"

"Increasing global competition, OEM, customers driving down prices"

"It's not an easy business these days. On-time work that is high in quality is very important."

"Many small (<$1,000,000) machine shops grow dependent on 1–3 customers or industry single."

"A tough economy makes it a tough climate for many. Those with aerospace contracts do pretty well and seem to hold their own."

"CAPEX represents a large barrier to entry in today's robotic world. OEMs fuel the industry to a large extent. Proprietary processes can add value."

"Revenues and profitability are trending upwards in NE U.S. Barrier to entry high with well-equipped shops, low with antiquated equipment like retrofit CNC Bridgeports, etc. Abundance of bankers searching for businesses has grown demand as their background of lending to mfg. makes this industry 'seem' a fit. Risk of high client concentration always a concern with contract manufacturing."

"Need to be $10 million shop to get good buyers"

"Contract machining, while recovering slowly, continues to feel the ripple effect of the OEM's slowdown"

Benchmark Data

Statistics (Machine Shops)

Number of Establishments	20,700
Average Profit Margin	5.0%
Revenue per Employee	$168,500
Average Number of Employees	11.1
Average Wages per Employee	$53,829

Source: IBISWorld, June 2012

Products and Services Segmentation

Other machining	26%
Milling	13.4%
Turning	13.2%
Top and threading	12%
Drilling and boring	11.2%
Sawing	10.9%
Grinding	9.3%
EDM and ECM activities	4%

Source: IBISWorld, June 2012

Major Market Segmentation

Other clients	30%
Industrial machinery manufacturers	16.5%
Aerospace industry	13.4%
Defense industry	11%
Automotive part manufacturers	10.9%
Medical equipment manufacturers	10.5%
Construction sector	7.7%

Source: IBISWorld, June 2012

Industry Costs

Profit	5.0%
Wages	30.9%
Purchases	43.9%
Depreciation	6.0%
Marketing	0.8%
Rent & Utilities	7.0%
Other	6.4%

Source: IBISWorld, June 2012

- "$100,000 Sales/employee/year"
- "Geographic location is important to buyers since machinery is expensive to move."
- "Many shops like to get X dollars per hour per machine and then work towards 70%–80% capacity per machine or better."

Expenses as a Percentage of Annual Sales

Cost of goods	50% to 60%
Payroll/labor Costs	30% to 35%
Occupancy	03% to 07%
Profit (estimated pretax)	05% to 15%

Industry Trend

- "As small shops leave the market, there will be opportunities for the medium to large shops."
- "Trend appears to be upwards."

- "Looking good with lots of new business to good solid shops."
- "Declining"
- "Tough for the smaller shops"
- "Shrinking market based on overseas competition, declining manufacturing base, high operating costs"
- "As the economy gets stronger so will these businesses."
- "Increased competition from NAFTA partners and overseas production"
- "Highly cyclical industry, but most shops are staying fairly busy despite recent economy."

Seller Financing

- "Only small shops typically seller financed. Averages vary. Most deals SBA 7(a) 10 yrs. at P + 1- 2.5 pts."

Questions

- "Client concentration, capex needs, ISO certified, organized labor, WC modifier, OSHA issues,"
- "Backlog, client concentration, CAPEX, aging of receivables, organized labor, profit margins per category of equipment."
- "Any equipment need to be replaced, account concentration issues are very important to be informed of."
- "Personal salary & benefits, any unutilized or underutilized assets"
- "Will the owner stay on and will they finance, most important. Backlog and contracts also critical."
- "Customer concentration ratios, what % of capacity is being utilized?"
- "Any account concentration issues? Do you own ALL of the equipment?"
- "What capital equipment is on your wish list? What are your accounts receivable agings? What is your backlog? Do you ever have trouble meeting payroll?"
- "CAPEX requirements, backlog, client concentration, how much recurring revenues, value-added services."
- "Historical trends and future client relationships. Machinery obsolescence, etc."

Resources

Associations
- American Machine Tool Distributors' Association: www.amtda.org
- Fabricators and Manufacturers Association, International: www.fmanet.org

	Franchise
MaggieMoo's Ice Cream and Treatery	
Approx. Total Investment	$225,000 to $375,000
Estimated Annual Sales/Unit	$200,000

SIC 2024-98	NAICS 722213	Number of Businesses/Units 159

Rules of Thumb

> 25 percent of annual sales plus inventory

Industry Trend

- "The last MaggieMoo's ice cream shop in Orange County closed this week. Joe and Patrice Mudd of Coto de Caza owned four MaggieMoo's Ice Cream and Treatery franchises—on Balboa Island and in Lake Forest, Laguna Niguel, and Ladera Ranch—before the recession forced them to close or sell each parlor."

    Source: "Last MaggieMoo's ice cream shop in O.C. closes," by Rashi Kesarwani,
    The Orange County Register, January 29, 2010

Resources

Websites

- www.maggiemoos.com

		Franchise
Maid Brigade (See also Janitorial Services & Molly Maid)		
Approx. Total Investment		$25,995 to $27,995
	NAICS 561720	Number of Businesses/Units 420

Rules of Thumb

➢ 45 percent of annual sales

Resources

Websites

- www.maidbrigadefranchise.com

Maid Services (See also Janitorial Services, Maid Brigade, Molly Maid)		
	NAICS 561720	

Rules of Thumb

➢ 35 to 40 percent of annual sales plus inventory

➢ 1.5 times SDE plus inventory

Benchmark Data

- For Benchmark data see Janitorial Services
- "The Growing Residential and Commercial Cleaning Industry
    "The residential and commercial cleaning industry is a $94 billion market comprised of 500,000 companies, employing hundreds of thousands in labor force. The industry has enjoyed a 5.5% annual growth rate over the past five years and is projected to grow at a similar or greater rate over the next ten years.
    "Despite its extraordinary size and growth, the cleaning industry is largely dominated by family-owned, mom and pop operators. Over 80% of the cleaning services sector is comprised of small, family-owned business units that operate without a comprehensive set of standards and regulations.
    "According to Marketdata Enterprises, a research and analysis firm focused

on the services sector, an average cleaning company employs five or less employees and grosses under $150,000 in annual revenue. The cleaning business is a 'low tech' business characterized by ease of entry. An individual cleaning company can be started with as little as $1000 in capital and be in operation a few days later. As such, most of the operators lack the necessary knowledge, experience and training to deliver a professional standard of service.

"According to Marketdata Enterprises, the cleaning services sector has one of the highest customer loss rates, running as high as 45 percent per year. This translates into one of every two customers changing their cleaning provider at least once per year. Some studies indicate that more than 60 percent of building managers are not satisfied with their service provider. A recent survey conducted by the BSCAI Services Magazine identifies the low standard of quality' as the number one industry problem.

"One of the major reasons for the high customer dissatisfaction rate is the general lack of professionalism in the industry. The large majority of cleaning companies are small mom and pop¨ business units that lack the knowledge, training and experience demanded today. Frustrated with the low standard of quality, homeowners, renters, property management companies and commercial businesses are searching for a company that can offer them a service of uncompromising quality and professionalism.

Source: AW Cleaning Services, awcleaning.com. Although this site is a bit self-serving for AW, it is very informative.

Mail and Parcel Centers

(Also called Mail Receiving and Mailing & Shipping Services) (See also UPS Stores)

SIC 7299-18 7331-01	NAICS 561431	Number of Businesses/Units 26,909

Rules of Thumb

➤ 40 to 45 percent of annual sales includes inventory, less direct cost of goods sold (pass-throughs, e.g., stamps, money orders, UPS charges

➤ 2 to 3 times SDE for national franchises includes inventory

➤ 2.75 times EBIT

➤ 3 times EBITDA

Pricing Tips

- "Pre-paid mailbox rentals will need to be prorated and credited back to the Buyer unless negotiated out. Either way - it will affect value. Pass-throughs don't count toward annual sales."

- "Ratio of individual customers (only see them at Xmas) to business customers (regular- daily or weekly)."

- "The rental rate is very important to the valuation of mail and parcel centers. Some mail and parcel centers can be located off major streets because they are destination locations. Franchise businesses are usually worth more than independent stores because of name recognition, brand value. These businesses are appealing to people who want flexible hours and no night hours. Also, most stores are open only a few hours on Saturdays. Sales are usually fairly predictable for mature stores."

- "Since it is a generally low barrier to entry, an established store that has well passed the breakeven is the best situation. An owner operator in this industry can see near 30% SDE so long as fixed costs are not too damaging."
- "Desirable cities demand higher prices because box rental customers will pay more."
- "Franchises will sell for higher % of annual gross sales. High-volume UPS stores sell for over 1x STR (Subject to Royalty)."
- "Rent is a very important factor, as it is a fixed cost. Stores below a certain minimum of sales diminish in value exponentially as they find it more and more difficult to cover the fixed costs."
- "Length of time in business, sales are growing or declining, competition coming or going."

Expert Comments

"Easy to own and easy to operate."

"Risk can be high if owner does not audit the weekly Electronic Funds Transfers (EFT's)statements from the bank. The carriers make "mistakes" in their favor that you must then call & argue with them to change."

"Perception of mail centers is they are easy to learn and easy to run."

"This is a good service business that is somewhat recession resistant."

"The main suppliers to the industry are the biggest competitors. They give out accounts like candy. You can only make it if you provide a real service along with the shipping."

"These businesses are proven concepts today; and generally, mail and parcel centers are lower risk than many other businesses."

"Competition is high—even from the suppliers (UPS, FEDEX) providing individual accounts to your customers."

"Barriers to entry are not strong. A new store does not cost much to open. Establishing the business is the tough part. Competition is everywhere. Your suppliers (e.g., FedEx, UPS) are also your competition. All office supply houses are your competition."

"Buying a proven store with a steady track record may be a much better way to get into this business than opening a new one. It takes a long time to ramp up sales."

Benchmark Data

Statistics (Business Service Centers)

Number of Establishments	26,909
Average Profit Margin	5.0%
Revenue per Employee	$96,800
Average Number of Employees	4
Average Wages per Employee	$31,374

Source: IBISWorld, May 2012

Products and Services Segmentation

Photocopying, blueprinting, and other document duplicating services	65.9%
Postal, shipping and mailing services	27.1%

Source: IBISWorld, May 2012

Major Market Segmentation

Business	80%
Households	20%

Source: IBISWorld, May 2012

Industry Costs

Profit	5.0%
Wages	32.6%
Purchases	20.0%
Depreciation	4.0%
Marketing	10.0%
Rent & Utilities	4.0%
Other	24.4%

Source: IBISWorld, May 2012

- "Must have an AVERAGE 50% mark up on shipping (USPS, Fed Ex, UPS, etc.)"
- "There are a lot of startup stores or lower performing stores whose annual sales are under $200K. Be careful if it goes below $150K in annual sales, as fixed costs will eat up your profit."
- "Location is important, established nature, do not need a lot of SF. Keep the rent low."
- "Mailbox rentals should cover all operating expenses."
- "Must be earning at least 50% gross profit or better. The sales must exceed a certain level (usually 10 times rent) before a profit can really be seen. A good store has a decent budget for advertising."
- "Most stores must be doing at least $150,000 in annual sales before they start showing any real profit. Advertising is very important; stores should not skimp on advertising. The client base is primarily within a radius of a few miles."

Expenses as a Percentage of Annual Sales

Cost of goods	45% to 50%
Payroll/labor Costs	15% to 20%
Occupancy	10% or less
Profit (estimated pretax)	20%

Industry Trend

- "Trend toward more services—like opening, scanning and emailing mail to customers."
- "Trend is flat or down over the next few years."

Questions

- "What competition is nearby. Get a standard disclosure form completed."
- "Do you have an undercover DEA agent working at your store? Is the Notary income being reported? If not look at notary's journal to get idea of volume. Any accounts receivable (business accounts)? Any "trade" for mail box rental? Do you want to slap customers who bitch about you selling stamps for a penny or two more than the post office?"
- "Do they charge for packing labor? How much? If not, this is a pure profit area to explore! It does depend on their markup otherwise."
- "What services are offered? How many mailboxes do they have, how many are rented, how much are they rented for, and when was the last time they raised the rates?"
- "Do you know of any new competition coming soon?"

Resources

Associations
- Associated Mail and Parcel Centers: www.ampc.org

Mail Order		
SIC 5961-02	NAICS 454110	Number of Businesses/Units 64,021

Rules of Thumb

➢ 6 times EBIT

➢ 5 times EBITDA

➢ 80 percent of annual sales includes inventory

Pricing Tips

- "6 to 7 times EBITDA in 2005, $8 million transaction B-2-B mail-order house, $10 million in sales, national accounts, 100% interest transferred."
- "Valuation of firm typically based on house account quality (house database of customers) and EBITDA sustainability and growth"

Expert Comments

"Straightforward estimate of risk-reward. Margins declining, but from high past levels. Ease of replication reduces going concern values. Consolidation occurring."

Benchmark Data

Statistics (Mail Order)

Number of Establishments	64,021
Average Profit Margin	4.0%
Revenue per Employee	$719,600
Average Number of Employees	2.3
Average Wages per Employee	$42,276

Source: IBISWorld, September 2012

Products and Services

Drugs, health and beauty aids	23%
Clothing, jewelry and accessories	15%
Computer hardware, software and supplies	15%
Furniture and household goods	4.5%
Office and school supplies	4%
Toys, hobby goods and games	4%
Sport supplies and accessories	3%
Other	31.5%

Source: IBISWorld, September 2012

Industry Costs

Profit	4.0%
Wages	5.9%
Purchases	58.5%
Depreciation	1.2%
Marketing	2.8%
Rent & Utilities	1.5%
Other	26.1%

Source: IBISWorld, September 2012

- "$300,000 revenue per sales employee".
- "Sales personnel should generate revenue of about $1.3 million per employee."

Expenses as a Percentage of Annual Sales

Cost of goods	60% to 67%
Payroll/labor Costs	01%
Occupancy	01%
Profit (estimated pretax)	09% to 10%

Industry Trend

- "The emergence of e-mail marketing is also contributing to higher sales through mail orders. For instance, Internet/Mail Order sales for garden products in the U.S. are gaining increasing importance.
  "Excessive mail delivery cost, owing to higher postal costs for mail order businesses, is a major challenge for market participants. Players in the mail order market face challenge in the form of intense competition from other distribution channels such as departmental stores, discount stores, independent stores, mass markets, specialty stores, which also promise convenience and low prices to their customers."

  Source: "Convenience of Purchase, Payment & Delivery to Bolster Mail Order Market, According to a new report by Global Industry Analysts," www.acellphoner.com

- "'There are so many small operators today it's really impossible to be entirely accurate,' Schulte said. '(The Internet) has opened up new opportunity for entrepreneurs once again; it has lowered the cost to enter the mail-order business.'"

  Source: "Home Trends get post-recession makeover" by Mary Stone, March 29, 2011, www.rbi.net

- "Consolidation continuing. Profit margins diminishing. Overseas suppliers low priced but inconsistent."

Questions

- "What experience do you have in the catalog or direct marketing industry?"

Resources

Associations

- National Mail Order Association—an excellent site, loaded with information: www.nmoa.org

	Franchise
Mama Fu's Asian House	
Approx. Total Investment	$511,000 to $735,000
SIC 5812-08 NAICS 722211	Number of Businesses/Units 13

Rules of Thumb

➤ 30 percent of annual sales plus inventory

Resources

Websites

- wwwmamafus.com

Management Consulting

	NAICS 541611	Number of Businesses/Units 674,109

Rules of Thumb

➤ 2.5 times SDE

Benchmark Data

Statistics (Management Consulting)

Number of Establishments	674,109
Average Profit Margin	9.1%
Revenue per Employee	$127,800
Average Number of Employees	1.9
Average Wages per Employee	$52,766

Source: IBISWorld, July 2012

Products and Services Segmentation

Process and operations management	31%
Corporate strategy	17%
IT strategy	17%
Human resources and benefits	16%
Organizational design	11%
Financial advisory	6%
Marketing and sales	2%

Source: IBISWorld, September 2012

Major Market Segmentation

Financial services companies	22%
Other	18%
Consumer products companies	11%
Manufacturing companies	11%
Government and nonprofit agencies	10%
Telecommunications companies	10%
Energy and utilities companies	9%
Healthcare companies	9%

Source: IBISWorld, September 2012

Industry Costs

Profit	9.1%
Wages	58.3%
Purchases	4.1%
Depreciation	1.3%
Marketing	3.2%
Rent & Utilities	6.0%
Other	18.0%

Source: IBISWorld, September 2012

Market Share

Accenture Ltd.	3.5%
McKinsey	2.9%
Deloitte	2.5%
Marsh & McLennan	1.6%

Source: IBISWorld, September 2012

Manufacturing — Aluminum Extruded Products

	NAICS 331316	

Rules of Thumb

➤ 50 percent of annual sales plus inventory

➤ 6 times SDE plus inventory

➤ 5 times EBIT

➤ 4 times EBITDA

Pricing Tips

▪ "Nature of contract with metal supplier: this is a low added value business."

Benchmark Data

▪ "At least a ratio of added value/salaries cost (total) of 2.0."

Expenses as a Percentage of Annual Sales

Cost of goods	70%
Payroll/labor Costs	35%
Occupancy	05%
Profit (estimated pretax)	08%

Industry Trend

▪ "Growing"

Questions

▪ "Customer base, nature of metal contracts"

Manufacturing — Chemical

SIC 2899-05	NAICS 32599	Number of Businesses/Units 1,808

Rules of Thumb

➤ .5 to 2 times annual sales includes inventory

➤ 4 to 9 times EBITDA

Pricing Tips

▪ "Industry is very diverse (some businesses are state-of-the-art/cutting edge, some are very mature, and everything in between), therefore pricing depends on a variety of factors."

Expert Comments

"Chemical industry in the U.S. is by and large a mature industry."

Benchmark Data

Statistics (Chemical Product Manufacturing)

Number of Establishments	1,808
Average Profit Margin	6.0%
Revenue per Employee	$512,400
Average Number of Employees	43.6
Average Wages per Employee	$57,812

Source: IBISWorld, June 2012

Products and Services Segmentation

All other chemical products and preparations	45%
Sensitized photographic film, paper, plates and chemicals	33%
Custom compounding of purchased resins	22%

Source: IBISWorld, June 2012

Major Market Segmentation

Manufacturing industry	40%
Automobile industry	20%
Households	19%
Construction industry	18%
Other	3%

Source: IBISWorld, June 2012

Industry Costs

Profit	6.0%
Wages	11.1%
Purchases	49.0%
Depreciation	3.4%
Marketing	1.0%
Rent & Utilities	2.0%
Other	27.5%

Source: IBISWorld, June 2012

- "Benchmark Data are not common, given the diverse nature of the industry."

Expenses as a Percentage of Annual Sales

Cost of goods	25%
Payroll/labor Costs	n/a
Occupancy	n/a
Profit (estimated pretax)	10%

Industry Trend

- "In general, industry is on the uptick"
- "One of America's largest industries, the business of chemistry is a $720 billion enterprise that produces nearly one-fifth of the world's chemicals. The U.S. chemical industry also is one of the country's top exporters, with $171 billion in annual exports, accounting for more than 10 percent of total U.S. merchandise exports. The industry currently provides approximately 784,000 high-paying jobs in the United States, and each job in the chemistry industry also generates an additional 5.5 jobs in other sectors"

Source: ACC Publishes Comprehensive Economic Profile of $720 Billion Business of Chemistry, July 21, 2011, www.americanchemistry.com

Seller Financing

- 5 years

Questions

- "Normal due diligence type issues plus environmental/regulatory issues which are somewhat unique to the industry and impact of overseas competition."

Manufacturing — Contract		
(See Contract Manufacturing, Machine Shops, & Job Shops)		
	NAICS 332710	

Manufacturing — Custom Architectural Woodwork and Millwork		
	NAICS 337212	

Rules of Thumb

➤ 3 times SDE includes inventory

Pricing Tips

- "Pricing depends if company is growing or declining."
- "Growth and customer list affects multiple dramatically."

Expert Comments

"China is becoming a big factor."

Benchmark Data

Expenses as a Percentage of Annual Sales

Cost of goods	50%
Payroll/labor Costs	30%
Occupancy	10%
Profit (estimated pretax)	10%

Industry Trend

- "China will affect every aspect of this industry. Must have niche to prosper."
- "Most owners are getting older, and the industry will consolidate."

Manufacturing — Electrical		
	NAICS 33531	Number of Businesses/Units 2,169

Rules of Thumb

➤ 5 times EBITDA

Pricing Tips

- "Client relationships and strength of long-term contracts is a major factor. Patents and proprietary processes must be evaluated. Work force productivity factor, min. of $250K per man-year is essential."

Benchmark Data

Statistics (Electrical Equipment Manufacturing)

Number of Establishments.. 2,169
Average Profit Margin 5.8%
Revenue per Employee $399,400
Average Number of Employees... 47
Average Wages per Employee $52,444

Source: IBISWorld, August 2012

Products and Services Segmentation

Motors and generators.. 32%
Relays and industrial controls.. 26%
Switches 25.5%
Transformers.. 16.5%

Source: IBISWorld, August 2012

Major Market Segmentation

Utilities 35%
Wholesalers 31%
Downstream manufacturers.. 27%
Retailers.. 7%

Source: IBISWorld, August 2012

Industry Costs

Profit 5.8%
Wages 13.5%
Purchases.. 58.7%
Depreciation.. 1.2%
Marketing 0.8%
Rent & Utilities 1.7%
Other.. 18.3%

Source: IBISWorld, August 2012

Market Share

GE... 10.9%
Eaton 10.4%
ABB 5.8%

Source: IBISWorld, August 2012

- "Use of third-party contract manufacturers continues to grow as more and more traditional manufacturers outsource."

Expenses as a Percentage of Annual Sales

Cost of goods... 64%
Payroll/labor Costs..07% to 08%
Occupancy.. 04%
Profit (estimated pretax) 12%

Seller Financing

- "5 years"

Manufacturing — Electrical Connectors		
	NAICS 334510	

Rules of Thumb

➢ 3 times EBITDA

Pricing Tips

- "Transferring the customers and good accounting of inventory are very important."
- "Contract Mfg. companies sell for 3X SDE or under. Companies with proprietary products are 4–7 X SDE depending on growth."
- "The customer list and management talent are key."

Expert Comments

"The industry is very cyclical."

Benchmark Data

- "No customer bigger than 30%"

Expenses as a Percentage of Annual Sales

Cost of goods	40% to 45%
Payroll/labor Costs	30%
Occupancy	10% to 15%
Profit (estimated pretax)	10%

Industry Trend

- "Major consolidation"

Questions

- "How much engineering work do you do?"

Manufacturing — Food

	NAICS 311	

Rules of Thumb

➢ 4 to 7 times EBITDA

Pricing Tips

- "Earning multiples depend heavily on: Brand, Customer concentration, Size, Recurring revenue, Clientele, Vendor certifications, Working capital requirements, Earnings stability, Owner involvement, Product category and differentiation, Equipment age/condition (future CapEx), and barriers to entry."
- "Valuation driven by brand equity, by length of customer contracts for private label/copack businesses, and by the niche served, e.g., natural and organic."

Expert Comments

"Generally there is little or no proprietary content."

Benchmark Data

- "Wide range, depending on product category, sales channel, branded vs private label, etc."
- "Food manufacturing gross margins (after material costs and direct labor) should be at least 40%, and preferably at least 50%."

Expenses as a Percentage of Annual Sales

Cost of goods	30% to 40%
Payroll/labor Costs	10% to 15%
Occupancy	05%
Profit (estimated pretax)	05% to 10%

Industry Trend

- "Stable"
- "Food manufacturing businesses are somewhat recession-proof, making the industry appealing to buyers in the current economic environment."

Manufacturing — Furniture/Household

(See also Manufacturing—Wood Office Furniture)

SIC 2599-01	NAICS 33712	Number of Businesses/Units 5,741

Rules of Thumb

➤ 4 to 7 times EBITDA

Pricing Tips

- Size, growth, condition of plant, how profitable it is, place in the market, and management can play a part.

Benchmark Data

Statistics (Household Furniture Manufacturing)

Number of Establishments	5,741
Average Profit Margin	1.7%
Revenue per Employee	$163,400
Average Number of Employees	24.8
Average Wages per Employee	$33,853

Source: IBISWorld, July 2012

Products and Services Segmentation

Non-upholstered household furniture	38.0%
Upholstered household furniture	31.2%
Institutional furniture	18.4%
Metal household furniture	5.8%
Household furniture (except wood and metal)	4.6%
Wood TV, radio and sewing machine cabinets	2.0%

Source: IBISWorld, July 2012

Major Market Segmentation

Retailers	42.7%
Wholesalers	30.9%
Contract outfitters	13.1%
Exports	11%
End users	2.3%

Source: IBISWorld, July 2012

Industry Costs

Profit	1.7%
Wages	20.5%
Purchases	54.8%
Depreciation	2.5%
Marketing	2.6%
Rent & Utilities	5.1%
Other	12.8%

Source: IBISWorld, July 2012

Market Share

Ashley Furniture Industries Inc.	3.4%
Furniture Brands	4.7%

Source: IBISWorld, July 2012

Resources

Associations

- The Business and Institutional Furniture Manufacturers' Association—a worthwhile site: www.bifma.com

Manufacturing — General		
SIC 3999-03	NAICS 31	Number of Businesses/Units 11,500

Rules of Thumb

➢ 40 to 50 percent of annual sales includes inventory

➢ 3 times SDE (depending on size & quality) includes inventory

➢ 3 to 4 times SDE; must manufacture product; not be a job shop

➢ 3 to 4.5 times EBITDA

➢ 4 to 5 times EBIT

➢ Hard Assets + 1.5 to 2 times EBIT

Pricing Tips

- "Values higher for companies that have product lines versus job shops."
- "Several factors will affect the multiple including level of inventory, condition of equipment, years in business, management, back log and lease terms. Proprietary products and contracts will only increase the multiple."
- "What does the future look like in regards to the product manufactured?"
- "4–5 x SDE for product manufacturer. 3 x SDE & inventory & machinery & equipment."
- "Ask about obsolete inventory (raw materials, work in progress, and finished goods). The age and condition of the equipment could affect the ability to sell the business. The product lifespan must be evaluated as well."
- "Companies with larger EBITDA's command higher multiples."
- "Multiple would vary depending upon EBITDA range. For EBITDA's in excess of 4 million you might see a multiple of 4.5 or 5. EBITDA above $5 million would normally be a multiple of 6 or more."

- "Valuation is predicated on many variables and rules of thumbs should be used as a baseline or starting point. Companies with patented products, proprietary methods etc., would likely see higher multiples and those in highly competitive industries with significant price pressures and little or no product differentials would see lower multiples."

- "Most accurate method is to deduct cost of professional employees to replace current ownership, and then use a multiple of 4 to 6 times net earnings (EBIT) depending on industry, security of earnings, assets, growth potential, etc."

- "Multiple of EBITDA will range from 3 to 5 depending upon EBITDA. Multiple of 3 to 4 for EBITDA under $1 million, and 4 to 5 for EBITDA over $1 million."

- "The industry position and growth potential and exclusivity are other crucial factors. Age of equipment, trade name/branding, and intellectual properties also have a weight in determining value. Further considerations are leases or age of facilities, location, growth potential, backlog, contracts, relationships with suppliers, availability of credit lines. etc."

- "We look at the calculation for owner benefit/cash flow and apply a 2 to 3 times multiple plus the current market value of furniture, fixtures and equipment and inventory at cost. Since manufacturing is very equipment intensive, using a pure EBITDA or cash flow multiplier does not adequately give a fair evaluation, in our opinion."

- "Transferability of the customer base and maintenance capital expenditures are the two biggest issues to close a deal."

Expert Comments

"Companies that survived the economic downturn are now on an upswing due to less competition and increased demand."

"Most manufacturing companies saw declines in revenue in 2009."

"Profitability & sales trends important—FMV of equipment/machinery, inventory, real estate = financing."

"Unlike some industries, an unprofitable manufacturer may drive value due to its bolt-on capabilities. Overhead can be eliminated and capacity and customers can potentially be transferred to another company."

"Competition from Asia still beating down US manufacturing. Weakening dollar is helping."

"Niche products companies do very well."

"Manufacturing is typically a complex and expensive process, creating barriers to entry."

"The risk level is the most important factor in determining a multiple of earnings."

"I find that manufacturing facilities and more technological systems are much improved over the last 20 years. Cadcam systems and computerized equipment have greatly improved productivity in the industry. When I first started selling mfg, low-tech processes and poor working facilities were the rule."

"Every business is unique, but China is a big factor in California deals."

Benchmark Data

- "$100K in revenue per employee was a good number in the past, however many companies have found ways to downsize employees and are doing more with less."
- "40% or higher Gross Margins. 10% or higher EBITDA"
- "Sales per employee: $100,000"
- "Proprietary products are most important."
- "No customer bigger than 20%"
- "Gross margin >45%; Inventory turns >4"

Expenses as a Percentage of Annual Sales

Cost of goods	50% to 60%
Payroll/labor Costs	15% to 20%
Occupancy	03% to 05%
Profit (estimated pretax)	05% to 10%

Industry Trend

- "The strong have survived. Companies have made cuts so they are now more productive and efficient without some of the 'fat.'"
- "Growth consolidation of similar-size companies to acquire skilled employees and equipment."
- "Lower"
- "There will be companies going out of business due to banks not extending lines of credit that manufacturing companies have relied on in the past. However the strong will survive and be more profitable in the long run due to the consolidation."
- "Companies protected from off-shoring will command higher prices."
- "Niche businesses can grow rapidly. Some will be converted to distribution companies as the manufacturing process is moved overseas."
- "About the same; some sectors (labor-cost sensitive) will go down; other sectors (technology, medical equipment., etc.) will go up."
- "Volume will be the same, with profit margins declining, due to an increase in labor and other operational costs."
- "Many manufacturing companies have gone offshore, and we are left with the smaller and more closely held companies. On a resale basis, mfg. is much in demand and supply is low."
- "Outsourcing is putting a strain on manufacturing, as well as high labor and insurance costs."
- "China will continue to pose big, long-term pressures."

Seller Financing

- "3 to 6 Years"

Questions

- "What is the customer concentration? Are there any changes occurring in the industry that will change the demand? What are the annual capital expenditures and is the equipment in good condition?"

- "Revenue trends, competition, how much working capital is needed for the operations, are there any equipment upgrades needed soon?"
- "Customer concentration? Competition? International sales? Marketing strategy? Sales force? Patents/trade names?"
- "What is the customer concentration? What is the age of the machinery? When does the machinery need to be replaced or maintained and what are the costs associated with it? Are you subject to overseas competition? Is the work force union or non-union? What special skills are needed by the employees? What drives the customers' decision to purchase from you? How many competitors can manufacture what you produce? Do you have any exclusive products or patents on the products produced? Does your facility have any quality certifications? What processes and procedures are in place for quality control? How dependent are you on your supply base? Are there inventory control systems in place to manage raw material, WIP, and finished goods inventory?"
- "Inventory breakdown (WIP, raw FG), customer deposits, machinery & fixtures, number of customers, key employees, receivables (amount & days) and method of sales & distribution—all affect whether the multiple is high or low. Stock or asset sale is a function as to whether or not it is a C corporation. Most manufacturers selling are 20-plus years old and therefore are C corporations, which means a stock sale."
- "How is your business protected from off-shore competition?"
- "Insurance considerations—is the business properly insured?"
- "Value and margin of backlog; asset value and basis for value;. product line breakdown & mix; 3 to 5 years P&L and balance sheets."
- "What are the capital expenditures required to maintain and grow the business?"

Manufacturing — General Purpose Machinery		
	NAICS 333911	

Rules of Thumb

➢ 4.5 times EBITDA

Manufacturing — Guided Missile and Space Vehicle		
	NAICS 336414	Number of Businesses/Units 77

Rules of Thumb

➢ 100 + percent of annual sales

➢ 6 to 10 times EBIT

➢ 5 to 8 times EBITDA

Pricing Tips

- "Value increases with the company's ability to meet high quality controls and production deadlines as specified by military and military contractors. Extremely high barriers to entry in this industry keep values high."

Benchmark Data

Statistics (Space Vehicle & Missile Manufacturing)

Number of Establishments	77
Average Profit Margin	5.6%
Revenue per Employee	$503,200
Average Number of Employees	612.7
Average Wages per Employee	$120,228

Source: IBISWorld, July 2012

Products and Services Segmentation

Complete guided missiles	44.7%
Complete space vehicles	31.6%
Space vehicle propulsion units and parts	14.7%
Other guided missiles and space vehicle parts	9%

Source: IBISWorld, July 2012

Major Market Segmentation

Military	69.9%
Other U.S. government agencies	22%
Private corporations	6.5%
Foreign government	1.6%

Source: IBISWorld, July 2012

Industry Costs

Profit	5.6%
Wages	23.8%
Purchases	55.9%
Depreciation	2.1%
Marketing	1.5%
Rent & Utilities	2.3%
Other	8.8%

Source: IBISWorld, July 2012

Market Share

Lockheed Martin	25.2%
Northrop Grumman	14.9%
Boeing	13.4%
Raytheon	6.0%

Source: IBISWorld, July 2012

- "There are no common Benchmark Data or rules of thumb. Most businesses in this industry are unique, requiring special detailed analysis."

Industry Trend
- "Trend is up due to war on terrorism."

Manufacturing — Machinery		
	NAICS 333	

Rules of Thumb

➢ 100 percent of annual sales includes inventory

➢ 4 times EBIT

➢ 3 times EBITDA

Pricing Tips

- "Average of last 3 years' EBITDA plus stockholders comp, multiplied by 2 to 4 depending on profit history and Market Share."
- "Valuation method for work in process. Inventory turnover. Nature and situation of officer's account with business. Indebtedness. How easy for the firm to get bonded on basis of financial credibility."
- "A manufacturer of industry-specific machinery generally employs 50 to 500 people. A high price is 1 x sales figure (valid if market dominant worldwide). A good price is equal to total assets. A frequently observed price is twice net assets (Stockholder's Equity) or 5 times EBITDA for a firm in good standing. Multiple of net earning is meaningless since most owners minimize net earnings through various perks."

Expert Comments

"The machinery business is highly dependent on global Market Share (high), skills, reputation with customers based on customer service and availability of spare parts. Management predicament is: How to control a high global Market Share when you are a business with between 50 and 500 employees?"

"Any sales require customized engineering, manufacturing and assembly, plus installation and start-up which are always cursed with delays."

Benchmark Data

- "Take sales figure minus costs of raw materials and components, which is added value. Divide added value by total salaries cost including management. If result is consistently above 2.0, it is a well-managed business. Watch out: In figures in expenses below, we consider total salaries costs, not labor costs (meaningless)."
- "Added value/salaries cost >2. Added value/sales figure >50%. Sales per employee >$250,000. Identified competitors are few, and far away."
- "Sales per employee: $120,000 to 250,000; varies a lot as function of manufacturing integration. Our experience (300 clients during last 10 years) is that 80% of the world machinery industry is mismanaged because of lack of market focus and deficient customer service. The remaining can be highly profitable, and utilize market downturns to acquire competitors (most of our own business)."

Expenses as a Percentage of Annual Sales

Cost of goods	60%
Payroll/labor Costs	25%
Occupancy	5%
Profit (estimated pretax)	10%

Industry Trend

- "It is moving to fast-growing economies where the biggest market is: China, India, other NICs."
- "Favorable"

Questions

- "How many customers? Since when? How many customers amount to 50% of sales? How far away do they sell?"

- "Loans and advances to/from officers in balance sheet. Do they own their real estate (facility)? If so, is it undervalued in assets (historic value)?"

Manufacturing — Metal Fabrication

SIC 1791-04	NAICS 238390	

Rules of Thumb
➤ 6 times EBITDA

Pricing Tips
- "Typical 3–7 times EBITDA depending on the business, industry and the buyer. 1.5 times gross profit plus net book value combined with the normal three valuation approaches."
- "EBITDA must be adjusted to show owner's discretionary cash flow. The multiple that is used varies by industry, geographic location, and specific business, and must be determined in a subjective manner by one knowledgeable of current market conditions."

Expert Comments

"Proprietary products and processes can protect a company from competition, both domestic and overseas."

"Declining U.S. market"

Benchmark Data
- For additional Benchmark data see Metal Stamping
- "20% profit expected"

Expenses as a Percentage of Annual Sales
Cost of goods	30%
Payroll/labor Costs	30%
Occupancy	20%
Profit (estimated pretax)	20%

Industry Trend
- "Increased overseas competition"

Seller Financing
- "5 years"

Questions
- "Do you have any payment or performance bonds in place? Retainage? What is your backlog? Growing?"

Manufacturing — Metal Stamping

	NAICS 332116	Number of Businesses/Units 2,484

Rules of Thumb

➢ 5 times SDE plus inventory

➢ 3 times EBIT

➢ 4 times EBITDA

Pricing Tips

- "Length of time in business. Customer base and spread of customer base by percentage."

Expert Comments

"Depending upon products being developed"

Benchmark Data

Statistics (Metal Stamping & Forging)

Number of Establishments	2,484
Average Profit Margin	7.5%
Revenue per Employee	$313,500
Average Number of Employees	45.3
Average Wages per Employee	$48,079

Source: IBISWorld, July 2012

Products and Services Segmentation

Metal stamped products	35.6%
Custom roll formed products	23.6%
Iron and steel forged products	23.3%
Nonferrous forged products	9.7%
Powder metallurgy parts	4.3%
Crown and closure products	3.5%

Source: IBISWorld, July 2012

Major Market Segmentation

Automotive and truck markets	31.8%
Aircraft and aerospace markets	27%
Off-highway and agriculture markets	21.6%
Ordnance market	10.3%
Industrial, hardware and tools markets	4.9%
Valves and fittings markets	4.4%

Source: IBISWorld, July 2012

Industry Costs

Profit	7.5%
Wages	15.7%
Purchases	54.1%
Depreciation	6.3%
Marketing	0.1%
Rent & Utilities	4.5%
Other	11.8%

Source: IBISWorld, July 2012

Market Share

PCC	9.7%

Source: IBISWorld, July 2012

Expenses as a Percentage of Annual Sales

Cost of goods	50%
Payroll/labor Costs	15%
Occupancy	15%
Profit (estimated pretax)	20%

Industry Trend

- "Lots of this work is going to China."

Questions

- "How long in business? Cost of goods sold? Lease and rent? How long have employees been there? Diversification of customer base?"

Manufacturing — Metal Valve and Pipe Fitting

(See also Manufacturing—Valves)

	NAICS 332919	

Rules of Thumb

➢ 7 times EBIT

➢ 100 percent of annual sales

➢ Assets plus 1 to 2 times EBITDA

Expert Comments

"High capital investment"

Benchmark Data

- "Four inventory turns, 50 percent gross margin"

Expenses as a Percentage of Annual Sales

Cost of goods	50%
Payroll/labor Costs	20%
Occupancy	30%
Profit (estimated pretax)	15%

Manufacturing — Miscellaneous Electrical and Components

	NAICS 33599	Number of Businesses/Units 870

Rules of Thumb

➢ 8 times SDE

Pricing Tips

- "Customer concentration and special skills required by owner drive the price model."

Benchmark Data

Expenses as a Percentage of Annual Sales

Cost of goods	50%
Payroll/labor Costs	25%
Occupancy	15%
Profit (estimated pretax)	10%

Manufacturing — Office Products	
NAICS 33994	Number of Businesses/Units 2,487

Rules of Thumb

➤ 5 to 8 times EBIT

➤ 1 times sales plus inventory

Pricing Tips

- "Key to higher valuation is the company's customer base. Does it include either:

  (a) One or more office superstores? (Staples, OfficeMax or Office Depot)

  (b) One or more national wholesalers? (United Stationers, etc.)

  (c) One or more contract stationers?"

- "Customer concentration—many office-product manufacturers have one major customers—a Staples, for example. This may impact valuation if too dependent. Manufactured vs. imported product—companies whose manufacturing base is not vulnerable to imports (from China or Taiwan) are more valuable than those who are."

- "There is no rule of thumb for the office products industry, but in general, pricing is affected by the size of the company. The larger the EBIT, i.e., over $5 million, then the higher the multiple. If a manufacturer of office products sells half to Staples et al and half to Wal-Mart et al, it is not a pure play in the office products business, so the price would be discounted accordingly. A better, more valuable, company would sell 100 percent to office product dealers, not 50 percent to mass merchants, 50 percent to office products. Other factors: breadth of product line, channels of distribution—how broad and complete is that industry, customer and supplier mix (80/20)? Dependency on family members means lower value; union is negative. Is M&E up to date? Growth rate correlation. Is company financeable, or only soft assets?"

- "1. Customer profile—are the products well-entrenched in the office superstore channel? 2. Uniqueness of product—are items basic commodities or are they unique or distinctive? If the latter, valuation may go up."

Benchmark Data

Statistics (Art & Office Supply Manufacturing in the U.S.)

Number of Establishments	573
Average Profit Margin	11.5%
Revenue per Employee	$285,900
Average Number of Employees	20.3
Average Wages per Employee	$48,003

Source: IBISWorld, September 2012

Products and Services Segmentation

Pencils and art goods	36.1%
Pens and mechanical pencils	32.8%
Marking devices	16.4%
Carbon paper and linked ribbon	14.7%

Source: IBISWorld, September 2012

Major Market Segmentation

Wholesalers	58.5%
Exports	17.6%
Retailers	17.1%
Other industries	6.8%

Source: IBISWorld, September 2012

Industry Costs

Profit	11.5%
Wages	16.6%
Purchases	39.9%
Depreciation	2.2%
Marketing	4.3%
Rent & Utilities	2.0%
Other	23.5%

Source: IBISWorld, September 2012

Market Share

Newell Rubbermaid	34.9%
ACCO Brands Corporation	12.4%
Crayola	8.7%

Source: IBISWorld, September 2012

Seller Financing

- "Not very often. If it is a good company, it is a cash deal."
- "3 years"

Manufacturing — Ornamental & Architectural Metal

SIC 3446-04	NAICS 332321	

Rules of Thumb

➢ 3 to 7 times EBITDA depending on the company, industry and buyer.

Questions

- "Do you have to pay union or David-Bacon linked wages for government work?"

Manufacturing — Personal Health Products

Rules of Thumb

➢ 5 times SDE plus inventory

➢ 6 times EBIT

➢ 5.5 times EBITDA

Pricing Tips
- "30% of GPM [gross profit margin] X 5 should roughly equal a fair valuation."

Benchmark Data
- "$200,000 sales per employee"

Expenses as a Percentage of Annual Sales

Cost of goods	40%
Payroll/labor Costs	12%
Occupancy	5%
Profit (estimated pretax)	10% to 12%

Questions
- "Market Share and stability of GPM [gross profit margin]"

Manufacturing — Pharmaceutical Preparation & Medicine

NAICS 32541	Number of Businesses/Units 955

Rules of Thumb

- 75 percent of annual sales
- 5 times SDE
- 4 to 5 times EBIT
- 6 times EBITDA

Pricing Tips
- "Depends on the market size and developmental maturity of products in the pipeline"
- "Because of products manufactured, it is important that the products are not on the FDA hit list."
- "Much of what the company is valued at will depend on how many products they manufacture, the concentration of clients to the gross revenues, the cost margin for each product, the number of short runs versus the number of long runs, and the opportunity for expansion through existing clients."

Expert Comments

"High risk of product failure and high barriers to entry are hallmarks of the pharmaceutical and biotechnology industries. Profits for companies that manage to bring a drug to market are high."

Benchmark Data

Statistics (Brand Name Pharmaceutical Manufacturing)

Number of Establishments	955
Average Profit Margin	19.2%
Revenue per Employee	$960,100
Average Number of Employees	107
Average Wages per Employee	$108,507

Source: IBISWorld, August 2012

Products and Services Segmentation

Other pharmaceutical preparations	46.5%
Biological products (except diagnostic)	20%
Medicinal and botanical products	10%
In-vitro diagnostic substances	6%
Antipsychotic medications	4.9%
Lipid regulators	4.8%
Proton pump inhibitors	4.5%
Antidepressants	3.3%

Source: IBISWorld, August 2012

Major Market Segmentation

Wholesalers to chain stores	28%
Hospitals and clinics	16%
Third-party logistics providers	15%
Wholesales to mail-service retailers	13%
Wholesalers to independent stores	11%
Consumers	9%
Wholesalers to other markets	8%

Source: IBISWorld, August 2012

Industry Costs

Profit	19.2%
Wages	11.3%
Purchases	31.5%
Depreciation	4.5%
Marketing	7.0%
Rent & Utilities	2.0%
Other	24.5%

Source: IBISWorld, August 2012

Market Share

Pfizer Inc.	15.2%
Johnson & Johnson	14.3%
Merck and Co., Inc.	12.8%
Bristol-Myers Squibb	11.8%
GlaxoSmithKline PLC	9.4%
AstraZeneca PLC	8.3%
Eli Lilly & Company	7.4%

Source: IBISWorld, August 2012

Statistics (Generic Pharmaceutical Manufacturing)

Number of Establishments	1,345
Average Profit Margin	14.7%
Revenue per Employee	$717,300
Average Number of Employees	59
Average Wages per Employee	$82,543

Source: IBISWorld, July 2012

Products and Services Segmentation

Pharmaceutical preparations for other drugs	35%
Pharmaceutical preparations for metabolic drugs	14%
Pharmaceutical preparations for cardiovascular drugs	12%
Pharmaceutical preparations for central nervous system drugs	10.5%
Medicinal and botanical products	10%
Pharmaceutical preparations for psychotherapeutic drugs	6.5%
Biological products (except diagnostic)	6%
In-vitro diagnostic substance products	6%

Source: IBISWorld, July 2012

Major Market Segmentation

Wholesalers to chain stores	28%
Hospitals and clinics	16%
Third-party logistics providers	15%
Wholesalers to mail-order retailers	13%
Wholesalers to independent stores	11%
Consumers	9%
Other wholesalers	8%

Source: IBISWorld, July 2012

Industry Costs

Profit	14.7%
Wages	11.5%
Purchases	50.0%
Depreciation	4.5%
Marketing	5.5%
Rent & Utilities	3.0%
Other	10.8%

Source: IBISWorld, July 2012

Market Share

Teva Pharmaceutical Industries Ltd.	8.8%
Watson Pharmaceuticals, Inc.	6.3%
Sandoz Ltd.	6.2%
Mylan Inc.	6.1%

Source: IBISWorld, July 2012

- "Development stage: number of drugs in pipeline, and the stage of development"
- "Pharmaceutical businesses are premium now that many trademarked items are available and companies are getting top dollar. FDA requirements are hard, and it can take months to get a company approved for manufacturing."

Expenses as a Percentage of Annual Sales

Cost of goods	30% to 35%
Payroll/labor Costs	30% to 32%
Occupancy	15% to 20%
Profit (estimated pretax)	20% to 30%

Industry Trend
- "Consolidation of existing companies and emergence of many new entrants"

Seller Financing
- "5 years"

Manufacturing — Plastic and Rubber Machinery		
	NAICS 333220	

Rules of Thumb
➢ 9 times EBITDA

Pricing Tips
- "Look at customer concentration; determine age and condition of equipment; look at industry diversification."

Expenses as a Percentage of Annual Sales

Cost of goods	50%
Payroll/labor Costs	12%
Occupancy	08%
Profit (estimated pretax)	15%

Manufacturing — Plastic Products

SIC 3089-10	NAICS 32619	Number of Businesses/Units 6,914

Rules of Thumb

➤ 2.5 to 5.5 times EBITDA

Pricing Tips

- "Most sell for 4.0 to 5.5 times last 12 months' EBITDA. Low end for custom manufacturers; above the scale for companies with proprietary products."
- "Contract manufacturers are worth less than manufacturers of proprietary products. Value is also dependent upon the type of processes used by the manufacturer. In order of value, from lowest to highest, based on processes used, thermoformers are the lowest value range, then blow-molders, then extruders, then rotational molders, then injection molders. The size of the equipment also is a factor in value; manufacturers who only produce small parts are much less valuable than those who can produce large parts/products. Any company focused on the automotive industry will command less interest from acquirers."
- "Manufacturers who can produce their products from recycled materials also have an advantage."
- "4 to 5.5 times EBITDA less maintenance cap ex."

Expert Comments

"The plastics manufacturing industry in the U.S. has been heavily influenced by the automotive industry. With the decline of the U.S. 'Big 3' manufacturers, plastic products manufacturers have had a tough haul since 2005. There have been many failures, thus reducing the value of equipment since the market has been flooded by used equipment. We have seen a steady decline in values of the past few years. With many huge companies in bankruptcy (Collins & Aikman, et al), equipment values are depressed as are company values. Size matters as well. Furthermore, the resins used by plastics manufacturers are all petroleum based; the price of raw materials has doubled in the past 12 months. If a processor has fixed prices (as many suppliers to the Big 3 do), this is a death sentence."

Benchmark Data

Statistics (Plastic Products Miscellaneous Manufacturing)

Number of Establishments	6,914
Average Profit Margin	5.1%
Revenue per Employee	$265,000
Average Number of Employees	44.9%
Average Wages per Employee	$42,720

Source: IBISWorld, September 2012

Products and Services Segmentation

Other plastic products	25.4%
Fabricated plastic products for transportation applications	20.1%
Consumer, institutional and commercial fabricated plastic products	15.3%
Plastic packaging (except film, sheet, foam and bottles)	13.1%
Fabricated plastic products for building applications	8.9%
Fabricated plastic products for electrical/electronic applications	8.3%
Reinforced and fiberglass plastic products	5.4%
Plastic plumbing fixtures	3.5%

Source: IBISWorld, September 2012

Major Market Segmentation

Automotive manufacturers	30.1%
Hardware and home improvement wholesalers	23.7%
Electrical and electronic manufacturing	18.4%
Plumbing fixture wholesalers	13.4%
Furniture and furnishing wholesalers	10.1%
Other	4.3%

Source: IBISWorld, September 2012

Industry Costs

Profit	5.1%
Wages	16.4%
Purchases	57.5%
Depreciation	5.8%
Marketing	0.4%
Rent & Utilities	4.5%
Other	10.3%

Source: IBISWorld, September 2012

- "$125,000 sales per employee to be profitable."
- "Good companies should have at least $133,000 of sales per employee (all employees)."

Expenses as a Percentage of Annual Sales

Cost of goods	74%
Payroll/labor Costs	11% to 12%
Occupancy	06%
Profit (estimated pretax)	07%

Industry Trend

- "More and more interest in plastic-products manufacturers as OEMs look to replace steel & metal with plastic."

Questions

- "Customer concentration. Size, in tons, of equipment. How do they sell their products?"

Resources

Websites

- www.americanchemistry.com

Trade Publications

- Plastics News: www.plasticsnews.com

Associations

- Society of Plastics Engineers: www.4spe.org
- Society of the Plastics Industry: www.plasticsindustry.org

Manufacturing — Powder Metallurgy Processing	
NAICS 332117	

Rules of Thumb

➤ 50 to 60 percent of annual gross sales includes inventory

➤ 5 times EBIT

➤ 4.5 times EBITDA

Pricing Tips

- "Price could vary widely depending on growth prospects."
- "If EBIT is 12% of Sales...the multiple at 60%..is 5X...most of these business now are not bringing double digits down to the EBIT line... but they still have a lot of assets...most of which would be hard to sell."
- "Industry is under significant stress due to the concentration in the auto industry. Companies with less exposure are performing better and will be more marketable than businesses with auto exposure over 50%."
- "Prices vary widely by product type, primary customer markets, and gross margins achieved."
- "Industry and customer concentration is a major influence in transactions."
- "None have any merit due to profitability variations; sanity check at 80 percent of revenue."
- "Gross margins consistency and diversification of the customer base add value to PM business."
- "Value is and should be a function of projected future cash flow."
- "Investment value drives this and other manufacturing markets. 5 to 6 times EBITDA (adjusted for synergy) is typical, but never a firm rule."
- "Transactions are driven by technology fit, growth prospects, profitability and other attributes of the selling company. Other key factors are: management, technology & systems, markets, and equipment age & mix. Markets served may have an influence and older smelting furnaces may detract slightly."

Expert Comments

"Basic changes in the industry and individual company concentration will control the rate of recovery."

"The industry is 70% automotive based which has had a significant effect on companies with a high percent of sales in this market segment. Non-automotive PM manufacturers are experiencing much better results."

"Profit margins have been squeezed in recent years due to movement offshore and increased volatility in raw material costs. In addition, the cost of capital equipment has increased faster than industry sales growth"

"The current trend to move manufacturing to China and India is affecting the key customer groups of many PM companies."

Benchmark Data

- "Sales per employee = $125,000. (Varies with primary materials in products delivered.)"

Expenses as a Percentage of Annual Sales

Cost of goods	30%
Payroll/labor Costs	40%
Occupancy	20%
Profit (estimated pretax)	10%

Questions

- "Percent breakdown of customer types by market segment. How large are the top 10 customers? What percent of sales do the top 10 account for? How large is the engineering and tooling staff? What experience does the technical staff have? How long have they been with the company?"
- "Customer trends; industry concentration; changes in key technical, management personnel and direct production supervisors."

Manufacturing — Prefabricated Wood Buildings	
NAICS 321992	Number of Businesses/Units 1,090

Rules of Thumb

➢ 100 percent of annual sales includes inventory

Pricing Tips

- "Modular plants sell at a premium. Log home companies sell at a discount."
- "Dealer network is important, or if selling direct, quality of sales staff."

Expert Comments

"Difficult to develop designs and engineering and establish a reputation, so it is not easy to start business from scratch."

"The log and timberframe industry has suffered more than the building industry in general because it is such a custom building market that has a higher unit cost than more traditional construction and has been adversely affected (log structures in particular) by tightening energy and building code requirements."

Benchmark Data

Statistics (Prefabricated Home Buildings)

Number of Establishments	1,090
Average Profit Margin	2.9%
Revenue per Employee	$145,500
Average Number of Employees	43.8
Average Wages per Employee	32,658

Source: IBISWorld, August 2012

Products and Services Segmentation

Manufactured mobile homes	56.1%
Prefabricated wood buildings	35.2%
Nonresidential mobile buildings	8.7%

Source: IBISWorld, August 2012

Major Market Segmentation

Retail trade	58.5%
Wholesale trade	38.2%
Exports	3.3%

Source: IBISWorld, August 2012

Industry Costs

Profit	2.9%
Wages	22.4%
Purchases	52.7%
Depreciation	2.3%
Marketing	3.0%
Rent & Utilities	3.3%
Other	13.4%

Source: IBISWorld, August 2012

Market Share

Berkshire Hathaway Inc.	48.0%
Champion Enterprises Inc.	9.6%

Source: IBISWorld, August 2012

- "The last benchmarking study done by the Log Homes Council (2006?) suggested that successful operations generate sales in the range of $180K to $200K per employee."
- "Gross profit over 35%"
- "$1 million to $1.5 million sales per salesperson"

Expenses as a Percentage of Annual Sales

Cost of goods	50%
Payroll/labor Costs	15%
Occupancy	03% to 05%
Profit (estimated pretax)	05%

Industry Trend

- "Housing business is cyclical. Expect flat sales due to being in down cycle."

Questions

- "Warranty policy and expense. How much warranty exposure is there? Does company have a favorable reputation for taking care of warranties?"
- "What is your backlog? How many leads have you received over each of the last 5 years? How do you sell your product—through a dealer network or direct or both? What patented processed do you have? Do you have challenges meeting energy or structural/building codes? What info do you have for your sales performance by region for the last 5 years? How many competitors do you have and where are they located? Do you sell internationally? Brand name, length of time in business and type of building system are extremely important."

Resources

Trade Publications

- Building Systems magazine: www.buildingsystems.com

Associations

- Building Systems Council of National Association of Home Builders: www.nahb.org/page.aspx/category/sectionID=454

Manufacturing — Products from Purchased Steel

	NAICS 3312	

Rules of Thumb

> ➢ 3 to 5 times SDE includes inventory

Expert Comments

"Product line is the main importance along with the ability to deliver."

Benchmark Data

- "Payroll costs, equipment maintenance and age of equipment"

Expenses as a Percentage of Annual Sales

Cost of goods	15%
Payroll/labor Costs	35%
Occupancy	20%
Profit (estimated pretax)	20%

Industry Trend

- "If you have a niche business, you will do well. If you are a job shop, chances are you will struggle."

Questions

- "How many customers does he have and what is the percentage of his business?

Manufacturing — Scientific Instruments

	NAICS 339111	

Rules of Thumb

> ➢ "Company value is 3 to 6 times EBITDA."

Pricing Tips

- "Where are the products in the life cycle? What new products are about to be introduced? Do they have strong patents? What is the competitive situation?"

Expenses as a Percentage of Annual Sales

Cost of goods	50%
Payroll/labor Costs	25% to 30%
Occupancy	15%
Profit (estimated pretax)	10%

Manufacturing — Showcase, Partition, Shelving, and Lockers

	NAICS 337215	

Rules of Thumb

> ➢ 2 to 3 times SDE plus inventory

Pricing Tips

- "Customer concentration and any special skills required to operate can make for a big difference in pricing."

Expert Comments

"Economy changes the profitability very quickly here."

Benchmark Data

Expenses as a Percentage of Annual Sales

Cost of goods	35%
Payroll/labor Costs	40%
Occupancy	15%
Profit (estimated pretax)	10%

Manufacturing — Signs

SIC 7389-38	NAICS 339950	Number of Businesses/Units 5,600

Rules of Thumb

➢ 45 to 50 percent of annual sales plus inventory

➢ 2 to 2.5 times SDE plus inventory

Benchmark Data

Statistics (Billboard and Sign Manufacturing)

Number of Establishments	5,879
Average Profit Margin	5.5%
Revenue per Employee	$170,500
Average Number of Employees	13.1
Average Wages per Employee	$44,785

Source: IBISWorld, March 2012

Products and Services Segmentation

Alternative displays	55%
Billboards	30%
Transit displays	15%

Source: IBISWorld, March 2012

Major Market Segmentation

Automotive market	13.2%
Telecommunications market	12.7%
Financial services market	11.2%
Amusements and entertainment market	11.1%
Miscellaneous retailers	9.4%
Food and candy market	9%
Other	33.4%

Source: IBISWorld, March 2012

Industry Costs

Profit	5.5%
Wages	26.1%
Purchases	44.9%
Depreciation	4.0%
Marketing	1.0%
Rent & Utilities	2.1%
Other	16.4%

Source: IBISWorld, March 2012

Market Share

Daktronics Inc. 3.8%

Source: IBISWorld, March 2012

Industry Trend

- "ISA's 2012 State of the Industry survey shows that the signage industry continues to rebound, with most participants reporting they anticipate growth and plan to hire in the coming year. The survey polled more than 200 ISA International Sign Expo 2012 attendees and covered all segments: sign supply manufacturers, distributors, sign shops, and end users."
- "Nearly all—96%—anticipate growth in the coming year."

Source: "ISA Releases State of the Industry Report," International Sign Association (ISA), June 2012

Resources

Associations

- International Sign Association (ISA): www.signs.org

Manufacturing – Small (See Manufacturing—General)

Rules of Thumb

➢ 4 to 5 times SDE plus inventory

Pricing Tips

- "For manufacturing companies with sales of $1 million to $5 million, a crude rule of thumb is 3 to 4 times SDE, assuming the company is reasonably well established and viable. As company size goes up, the multiple will go up."
- Factors to look for: "Sales/profitability trends; SDE (and trends); industry trends; years in operation; fixed asset value, seller financing. Risk factors: technology, competition, industry trends."

Manufacturing — Specialty Vehicle

Rules of Thumb

➢ 4 times SDE includes inventory

Pricing Tips

- "Evaluate inventory closely as there is a tendency to accumulate difficult-to-use inventory."
- "Look for amount of booked business. Lead times from getting the order to shipping the finished vehicle can run 12 months or more."
- "Evaluate financials closely. Many in this industry do not know what their true costs are."

Expert Comments

"It is difficult to acquire the expertise to build these vehicles. Many can build them - few can build them well."

"Homeland Security issues make this a growth industry. It is fairly easy to replicate the 'physical facility,' but the real market advantage comes from experience in designing, building and using these vehicles."

Benchmark Data

- "Difficult to estimate sales per employee, but should probably be $175,000–$200,000 per hourly production employee."

Expenses as a Percentage of Annual Sales

Cost of goods	55%
Payroll/labor Costs	25%
Occupancy	05%
Profit (estimated pretax)	10%

Industry Trend

- "Much of the business is tied to Homeland Security. If there are attacks on our soil, demand will increase. Otherwise budget cutbacks will dampen demand."
- "The market for mobile command centers, bomb trucks, SWAT trucks, etc., will continue to be strong as long as the U.S. has to fight terrorists. Many corporations are developing mobile marketing vehicles which will also help drive demand."

Questions

- "What is the mix (govt, corp, private)? Who are key employees with industry experience? What is your sales/marketing plan?"
- "Who has design experience in the company? Who has the mfg. experience in the company? How do you accurately cost jobs?"
- "What portion of the business is municipal, corporate, & private? Who are the key employees with industry experience? What is your marketing/sales plan? What is your backlog of business?"

Resources

Websites
- www.vehiclesuccess.com/links

Manufacturing — Sporting Goods & Outdoor Products

Rules of Thumb

➢ 4 to 7 times EBITDA

Pricing Tips

- "Brand and customer concentration are extremely important factors in valuing a manufacturer of outdoor and/or sporting products. These consumer products include hunting equipment, ammunition, fishing equipment, camping gear, sporting goods, outdoor apparel, etc. Patents are also an important value driver by increasing barriers to entry and making these consumer products harder to imitate. Customer diversity and relationships with key distributors are important. Brand awareness and time in the market place also add value. Many manufacturers outsource to contract manufacturers overseas to control costs and create a variable cost model. It's important to understand the sustainability of these supplier relationships."

Expert Comments

"Trade association reports show that consumers continue to spend money on sporting goods, even in tough economic times."

Benchmark Data

- "Gross Margins tend to be very high for these manufacturers, well north of 50%, especially when they outsource manufacturing. Therefore, do not use revenue rules of thumb."
- "Cost of Goods — 30% to 50%"

Manufacturing — Stainless Steel Food Service Fabrication	
NAICS 333319	

Rules of Thumb

➢ 3 to 6 times EBITDA depending on the company, industry and buyer.

Questions

- "Are you a custom fabricator also? Do you install? Do you sell other food-service equipment? Do you sell to the cruise lines?"

Manufacturing — Turbine and Turbine Generator Set Units	
NAICS 333611	

Rules of Thumb

➢ 8 to 10 times EBITDA

Pricing Tips

- "Use cap rate, similar to pricing commercial real estate."

Expert Comments

"This industry is, for a number of reasons, going to grow dramatically over the next decade. The economic model is very similar to that of commercial real estate—high upfront capital costs followed by extremely consistent cash flows, with upside appreciation potential. Smart money will get in early and ride the wave."

Benchmark Data

- "Revenue per kilowatt hour, capacity factor, PPA rate"

Industry Trend

- "Significant growth as the industry consolidates and becomes institutionalized."

Manufacturing — Valves		
NAICS 332911	Number of Businesses/Units 1,235	

Rules of Thumb

➢ 5 times EBITDA

Pricing Tips

- "Special consideration given for special products, Market Share, industry recognition."

Expert Comments

"A lot of competition with 'commodity' type valves; the more specialized, the less competition"

Benchmark Data

Statistics (Valve Manufacturing)

Number of Establishments	1,235
Average Profit Margin	6.5
Revenue per Employee	$289,700
Average Number of Employees	81
Average Wages per Employee	$45,959

Source: IBISWorld, May 2012

Products and Services Segmentation

Industrial valves	42.1%
Fluid power valves and hose fittings	29.1%
Plumbing fixture fittings and trim	17.2%
Other metal valves and pipe fittings	11.6%

Source: IBISWorld, May 2012

Major Market Segmentation

Chemical and petrochemical industries	24%
Petroleum production and pipeline transmission	22%
Water and wastewater systems	19%
Power generation and electric utilities	15%
Construction	11%
Process industries	9%

Source: IBISWorld, May 2012

Industry Costs

Profit	6.5%
Wages	16.6%
Purchases	42.0%
Depreciation	5.0%
Marketing	1.2%
Rent & Utilities	11.5%
Other	17.2%

Source: IBISWorld, May 2012

Market Share

Emerson Electric Co.	11.9%
Tyco	7.0%

Source: IBISWorld, May 2012

- "Market Share, innovative products"

Expenses as a Percentage of Annual Sales

Cost of goods	60%
Payroll/labor Costs	20%
Occupancy	20%
Profit (estimated pretax)	15%

Industry Trend
- "Trends toward specialization"

Seller Financing
- "5 years"

Manufacturing — Wood Kitchen Cabinets and Countertops

	NAICS 337110	

Rules of Thumb
➤ 2 to 2.5 times SDE plus inventory

Pricing Tips
- "Some wood cabinet manufacturers have state-of-the-art equipment that increases the efficiency of the business. Analyzing and adding the value of the equipment is a component of the above."

Expert Comments
"The sales trends are determined on the general economy of the geographic area. When housing starts are booming demand is high."

Manufacturing — Wood Office Furniture

SIC 2499-02	NAICS 337211	

Rules of Thumb
➤ 2.5 to 3 times SDE includes inventory

➤ 2.5 to 3 times EBITDA

Pricing Tips
- "Very cyclical business"
- "Rules of thumb do not work well for an industry this diverse."
- "Customer list drives the value."

Expert Comments
"Really depends where you are on the food chain, these vary from high to low margin businesses."

"Very dependent on economic cycles and affected by China"

Benchmark Data

Expenses as a Percentage of Annual Sales

Cost of goods	40%
Payroll/labor Costs	30%
Occupancy	20%
Profit (estimated pretax)	10%

Industry Trend

- Forecast

  The IHS Global Insight industry forecast model is adjusted to focus on the value of the U.S. office furniture market defined as consumption rather than as the historical and traditional shipments, or production. This change was due to the increasing significance of international trade and its impact on the domestic market.

  Current U.S. Office Furniture Market Forecast

Year	Production	%Change
2012	$9.5 billion	+1.1%
2013	$9.8 billion	+2.9%

  Source:" The U.S. Office Furniture Market," The Business and Institutional Furniture Manufacturers Association, June 4, 2012, www.bifma.com

- "Getting better as we come out of recession"
- "More consolidation and offshore competition"
- "Historic Product Mix Ratios

  The chart below diagrams the gradual shift in total product mix. The overall Wood and Non-Wood product mix remains relatively constant at approximately 25% wood product and 75% non-wood product. However, the wood/non-wood mix will vary by specific product category. The chart is based on U.S. production rather than market consumption since comparable data is not available on the same basis for imports and exports.

  Annual U.S. Production by Product Category

  "Forecast

  The IHS Global Insight industry forecast model is adjusted to focus on the value of the U.S. office furniture market defined as consumption rather than as the historical and traditional shipments, or production. This change was due to the increasing significance of international trade and its impact on the domestic market.

  Current U.S. Office Furniture Market Forecast

Year	Production	%Change	Consumption	%Change
2011	$9.8 Billion	+ 17.5%	$11.4 Billion	+15.8%
2012	$10.7 Billion	+ 9.7%	$12.6 Billion	+10.5%

  Source: The Business and Institutional Furniture Manufacturer's Association (BIFMA International)

Questions

- "How much design work and fashion trends?"

	Franchise
Marble Slab Creamery	
Approx. Total Investment	$250,000 to $403,000
Estimated Annual Sales/Unit	$225,000
SIC 2024-98 NAICS 722213	Number of Businesses/Units 250

Rules of Thumb

➢ 45 percent of annual sales plus inventory

Resources

Websites
- www.marbleslab.com

Marinas (See also Boat Dealers)		
SIC 4493-06	NAICS 713930	Number of Businesses/Units 4,220

Rules of Thumb

> 10 to 12 times SDE plus inventory

> 10 times EBIT

> 12 times EBITDA

> 10 + times SDE plus inventory ("The real estate is included in the 10 + SDE figure. It is almost always owned. Very seldom is it leased, and then usually as part of a concession which has been bid out, say by the National Park Service or the TVA or something like that.")

Pricing Tips

- "Waterfront property makes the earnings multiple much higher than most businesses. That and the fact that marinas are very difficult to start from scratch anymore"

- "The value of a marina is greatly distorted in that a big component of the price can be attributed to waterfront property. Thus rules of thumb are just educated guesses. One method that works is to insure that the storage/slip rental component is sufficient to service the debt. If so, the other services offered would enable the buyer to make a living, knowing that their 'nut' is covered."

- "There are so many businesses within a marina that a % of gross is misleading at best. The pricing is driven by the real estate (waterfront property) and is usually at least 10 x EBITDA. The ROI is terrible. One is buying a lifestyle."

- "Sales are usually at least ten times or more EBITDA because we are talking waterfront property, and the buyer is looking for appreciation rather than immediate income. Also, in many cases, the buyer is purchasing a 'lifestyle.'"

- "A marina is a 'lifestyle' purchase, and the price is greatly influenced by the value of the waterfront land involved, hence most of the usual rules of thumb do not apply. It helps if you look at your various profit centers, i.e. slip rental & moorings, storage, repair facility, fueling, restaurant (if applicable), boat sales, ship's store, etc. as individual businesses and eliminate or enhance specific features. For example, it often makes sense to lease out the restaurant to an experienced restaurateur and just collect your rent payments. It is a huge burden off the marina owner who usually has no clue as to how to run a restaurant."

- "Rules of thumb are complicated because a marina is a combination of many businesses—berth rentals, service, perhaps a new or used boat sales, and sometimes even a restaurant."

- "As far as the marina part is concerned, I have a comfort level if the income from the slip rentals is enough to service the debt. The buyer's profit will then come from the ancillary businesses mentioned above. Fuel sales can also be a factor, as the markup is quite high."

Expert Comments

"Currently (2010) marinas have been encountering hard times as the first thing that goes when the economy is poor is the boat. Either it is sold, or ends up in the back yard or at a friend's dock. It is amazing how they disappear. Thus the risk is higher than the norm and the marketability is negatively impacted. However, replication remains very difficult mainly due to a punishing permitting process."

"It is a reasonably risky business, in that in bad times the boat is the first thing to go. They seem to end up at a friend's dock or in the back yard on blocks. It is 100% discretionary income for the boat owner."

"Profits are being squeezed as discretionary income is not quite as high. Marinas are hard to sell as one is looking for a buyer that is basically not dependent on the income stream from the marina. As you get more boats, there are fewer places to put them, and permitting issues make starting a marina from scratch ever more difficult."

"They are not making any more waterfront land, and permitting is increasingly difficult if one wishes to start a marina from scratch. Profit margins are generally dismal, hence marinas are very hard to market unless one can find a 'lifestyle' buyer with deep pockets."

Benchmark Data

Statistics (Marinas)

Number of Establishments	4,220
Average Profit Margin	12.1%
Revenue per Employee	$137,000
Average Number of Employees	6.9%
Average Wages per Employee	$33,486

Source: IBISWorld, August 2012

Products and Services Segmentation

Pleasure boat dockage, slip rental, launch fees and storage	40%
Fuel sales	18%
Boat repairs and maintenance	15%
Boat and marine equipment sales	10%
Food and beverage sales	8%
Membership fees and dues	4%
Other	3%
Boat and equipment rentals	2%

Source: IBISWorld, August 2012

Industry Costs

Profit	12.1%
Wages	24.1%
Purchases	30.0%
Depreciation	6.1%
Marketing	10.3%
Rent & Utilities	6.1%
Other	11.3%

Source: IBISWorld, August 2012

- "There are usually several businesses in a marina. Slip rental/boat storage, service, gas sales, ship's store, maybe new & used boat sales and sometimes a restaurant. Each activity has its own margins."

- "Slip rental income and storage fees should cover 100% of debt service. Owner compensation and other benefits would come from sales and service charges and appreciation of real estate value(s)."
- "My preferred benchmark is to make sure that the income from slip rentals, mooring & storage is sufficient to service the debt. If so, at least you have your 'nut' covered and any profit would come from ancillary activities."

Expenses as a Percentage of Annual Sales

Cost of goods	65%
Payroll/labor Costs	20%
Occupancy	05% to 10%
Profit (estimated pretax)	05% to 10%

Industry Trend

- "Every year, yard owners, the number of smaller boatyards in southern New Jersey seems to decrease, squeezed out by the combination of increased property values and competition from larger corporate maintenance yards.
- "Like Dolfin Dock, Barrett said, 'Most family-owned marinas now get by with bait shops and a few slips.'
- "As for the future, 'Who wants it' Barrett asked. 'Whoever buys any marina would have to rebuild the bulkhead and docks at half a million dollars. Who's going to buy a marina when you have to maintain those improvements? It's like a Catch – 22.'"

Source: New Jersey boatyards decline in number to rising development," June 21, 2011, www.marinadockage.com

- "Ocean Alexander Marine Center is the latest in a string of Seattle boatyards to fall victim to the economic downturn. The yard, located on the northwest shore of Lake Union, closed on Friday. It had been in business since 1991 and offered a full range of services for powerboats, from electrical work to hull extensions, heater installations to carpentry. 'There really wasn't very much we weren't capable of doing,' manager Ken Morris said.

"But after the recession started in late 2007, business dwindled and the company's workforce shrunk from 18 down to four. Eventually, Morris said, it was time to shut the doors. 'The economy is down right now and there's not a lot of work out there,' he said. Friday June 17, was the yard's last day of business. Machinery and other equipment will be auctioned off in late July, Morris said. Ocean Alexander's Seattle dealership, on South Lake Union, is separate from the boatyard and is not closing.

"Lake Union Yacht Center closed in December 2009, after business plummeted 60 percent over a two-year period. And Seaview East boatyard is closing at the end of June, its owner citing a combination of high rent and a slowdown in business. Seaview's other boatyards, including its west yard near Ballard Locks, remain open. There are plans to open another Seaview yard at a new location.

Source: "Another Seattle Boatyard Sunk By Recession," June 21, 2011 in *Business of Boating, Currents* by Deborah Bach, wwwthreesheetsnw.com

- "As the economy rebounds, so will the lot of the marina improve. We are looking at discretionary income here, and that disappears in a poor economy."

Seller Financing

- "15 years"

Questions

- "The number 1 question would be to cover all environmental issues. A Phase 1 would probably be called for."
- "Do you have any environmental issues, are your storm water plans up to date?"
- "Has the property been professionally appraised recently? Are there any environmental issues? Any lawsuits? Do you need to dredge?"
- "Why are you selling? Why would you not keep it in the family? What are your environmental issues? How about water depth and dredging?"

Resources

Associations

- Association of Marina Industries: www.marinaassociation.org
- Boat Owners Association of the U.S.: www.boatus.com
- National Marine Manufacturers Association: www.nmma.org
- American Boat Builders and Repairers Association: www.abbra.org

Marine/Yacht Services (Boat/Repair) (See also Marinas)

NAICS 811490	Number of Businesses/Units 40,458

Rules of Thumb

➤ 100 percent of annual sales includes inventory

➤ 2.3 times SDE includes inventory

Pricing Tips

- "Determine value of furniture, fixtures & equipment; any warranty work involved?"

Expert Comments

"The mega-yacht (80-foot to 180-foot boats) is a major growth industry, especially in south Florida."

Benchmark Data

Statistics (Boat Dealership and Repair)

Number of Establishments	40,458
Average Profit Margin	1.8%
Revenue per Employee	$182,200
Average Number of Employees	2.1
Average Wages per Employee	$23,450

Source: IBISWorld, April 2012

Products and Services Segmentation

New boats	56.3%
Used boats	10.7%
Other	14%
Boat repairs and maintenance	19%

Source: IBISWorld, April 2012

Why trust the value of your machinery and equipment to Nationwide?

Determining a value for machinery and equipment should be done by a *qualified* and *certified* professional.

An appraiser that has proven experience, professionalism, and most importantly, is certified.

The certified Machinery & Equipment Appraisers (CMEA) at Nationwide Valuations are widely known as a respected industry leader. Backed by experience and certification, our certified appraisals are prepared according to the ethics and reporting mandated by the Uniform Standards of Professional Appraisal Practice (USPAP), promulgated by Congress and the Appraisal Foundation. It is the leading authoritative source for appraisals.

You also should make sure that the appraisal company that you work with is USPAP compliant and prepares a certified Machinery & Equipment Appraisal as mandated by the IRS, CPAs, lenders, and the U.S. Small Business Administration. That way, you are assured that you are working with an industry leader who is a respected provider, widely accepted, and sought after by other professionals.

Who NEEDS an Appraisal?

Attorneys
need a certified Machinery & Equipment Appraisal for divorce, dissolutions and litigation to substantiate accurate and realistic values that will withstand IRS and court scrutiny.

CPAs
need a certified Machinery & Equipment Appraisal pursuant to AICPA's Standards of Valuation #1 in addition to the Pension Protection Act of 2006 and the Council of Foundations.

Lenders
need a certified Machinery & Equipment Appraisal in support of loan decisions.

Business Owners
need a certified Machinery & Equipment Appraisal for insurable value, selling, financing, buying, expansion, partnership dissolution, and property taxes and Converting from a C Corp to S Corp.

We 'VALUE' Our Clients

5445 DTC Parkway Penthouse 4
Greenwood Village, CO 80111

68 White Street, Suite 120
Red Bank, NJ 07701

26956 N. 90th Lane
Peoria, AZ 85383

2894 Pleasant Colony Dr, Suite A
Lewis Center, OH 43035

local: 303.750.5259
toll free: 888.750.5259   **fax:** 303.586.4554
web: www.nationwidevaluations.com
email: info@nationwidevaluations.com

Industry Costs

Profit	1.8%
Wages	13.1%
Purchases	69.5%
Depreciation	0.6%
Marketing	1.0%
Rent & Utilities	4.5%
Other	9.5%

Source: IBISWorld, April 2012

Market Share

Marine Max Inc.	3.9%

Source: IBISWorld, April 2012

Expenses as a Percentage of Annual Sales

Cost of goods	30%
Payroll/labor Costs	15%
Occupancy	07%
Profit (estimated pretax)	40%

Industry Trend

- "Growth"

Questions

- "Customer base, length of time in industry, employee turnover, specific services performed."

Markets (See Grocery Stores—Small to Medium Size)		
	NAICS 445110	

		Franchise
Martinizing Dry Cleaning (See also Dry Cleaning)		
Approx. Total Investment		$368,600 to $573,500
	NAICS 812320	Number of Businesses/Units 480

Rules of Thumb

➤ Note: Also known as One Hour Martinizing

➤ 55 to 60 percent of annual sales plus inventory

Benchmark Data

- "He said a franchisee could open a store for anywhere from $293,500 to $476,000, including the franchise fee and purchase of in-house dry cleaning equipment. A typical investment for a franchisee to open a store would be $390,000.

  "Four percent of the sales from a franchised store's gross sales go back to the company."

  Source: "Martinizing Cleans Up" by Jeff McKinney, www.greenearthcleaning.com

Resources

Websites

- www.martinizingfranchise.com

Masonry Contractors (See Contractors—Masonry)

	Franchise
McGruff's Safe Kids ID System	
Approx. Total Investment	$14,900 to $16,900
	Number of Businesses/Units 26

Rules of Thumb

➢ 52 percent of annual sales plus inventory

Resources

Websites

- www.mcgruff-tid.com/

Meat Markets

SIC 5421-07	NAICS 44521	Number of Businesses/Units 5,924

Rules of Thumb

➢ 40 percent of annual sales plus inventory

➢ 2.5 times SDE includes inventory

➢ 5 times monthly sales plus inventory

Benchmark Data

Statistics (Meat Markets)

Number of Establishments	5,924
Average Profit Margin	4.0%
Revenue per Employee	$124,400
Average Number of Employees	7
Average Wages per Employee	$20,069

Source: IBISWorld, October 2012

Products and Services Segmentation

Broilers	39.5%
Beef	30%
Pork	21%
Turkey	7.5%
Lamb and mutton	1%
Other chicken	0.5%
Veal	0.5%

Source: IBISWorld, October 2012

Industry Costs

Profit	4.0%
Wages	16.8%
Purchases	60.2%
Depreciation	1.0%
Marketing	1.0%
Rent & Utilities	4.8%
Other	12.2%

Source: IBISWorld, October 2012

Market Share

Omaha Steaks International Inc.	7.2%

Source: IBISWorld, October 2012

Expenses as a Percentage of Annual Sales

Cost of goods	50%
Payroll/labor Costs	15%
Occupancy	10%
Profit (estimated pretax)	15%

Resources

Websites
- www.meatami.org

Associations
- National Cattlemen's Beef Association: www.beef.org

Medical and Diagnostic Laboratories		
	NAICS 621511	Number of Businesses/Units 28,213

Rules of Thumb

➢ 1 times Annual Gross Sales

➢ 3.25 times SDE plus inventory

➢ 4 to 5 times EBIT

➢ 4 to 5 times EBITDA

Pricing Tips

- "Good diversity of accounts, Good 3rd party payer contracts a must"
- "Multiple of SDE increases with profit levels."
- "Client concentration, market penetration and ability to expand"

Expert Comments

"Difficult to acquire accounts since physician groups don't like to make changes. 3rd party payer contracts are difficult to obtain"

"This is a marketing business. Location, ease of service, and networking with doctors and attorneys is a must."

Benchmark Data

Statistics (Diagnostic & Medical Laboratories)

Number of Establishments	28,213
Average Profit Margin	11.9%
Revenue per Employee	$194,900
Average Number of Employees	8.9%
Average Wages per Employee	$63,597

Source: IBISWorld, September 2012

Products and Services Segmentation

Diagnostic imaging services	45%
Routine medical testing	31.5%
Anatomical pathology testing	12%
Other services	6.5%
Esoteric medical testing	5%

Source: IBISWorld, September 2012

Major Market Segmentation

Private insurance payments	43.5%
Medicare and Medicaid payments	19.5%
Hospital payments	10.5%
Health practitioners payments	8%
Out-of-pocket payments	5.5%
Other	7%
Workers' compensation payments	1.5%
Other healthcare providers payments	4.5%

Source: IBISWorld, September 2012

Industry Costs

Profit	11.9%
Wages	32.4%
Purchases	39.5%
Depreciation	7.0%
Marketing	1.5%
Rent & Utilities	6.5%
Other	1.2%

Source: IBISWorld, September 2012

Market Share

Quest Diagnostics Inc.	15.9%
LabCorp	11.8%

Source: IBISWorld, September 2012

- "Sales are measured on a per-technician basis. Each MRI tech should produce a certain level of revenue."
- "Broad, even client base a big plus. Ability to expand beyond immediate geographical region without significant working capital requirements."

Expenses as a Percentage of Annual Sales

Cost of goods	15%
Payroll/labor Costs	45%
Occupancy	03%
Profit (estimated pretax)	30%

Industry Trend

- "Flat to slightly growing"
- "More personal injury MRIs"
- "Somewhat declining revenue trends due to Medicare reimbursement cuts."

Resources

Associations

- American Society for Clinical Laboratory Science: www.ascls.org

Medical Billing		
	NAICS 541219	Number of Businesses/Units 9,467

Rules of Thumb

➢ 50 to 55 percent of annual sales plus inventory

Benchmark Data

Statistics (Medical Claims Processing Services)

Number of Establishments 9,467
Average Profit Margin 10.2%
Revenue per Employee $131,200
Average Number of Employees 2.8
Average Wages per Employee $32,698

Source: IBISWorld, October 2011

Products and Services Segmentation

Claims processing 60%
Claims investigations 15%
Policy and claims examinations 15%
Back-office, administrative support and consulting 10%

Source: IBISWorld, October 2011

Major Market Segmentation

Healthcare providers 60%
Government insurers 15%
Private insurers 25%

Source: IBISWorld, October 2011

Industry Costs

Profit 10.2%
Wages 25.2%
Purchases 2.5%
Depreciation 2.5%
Utilities 6.8%
Rent 4.5%
Other 48.3%

Source: IBISWorld, October 2011

Medical Practices		
SIC 8011-01	NAICS 621111	Number of Businesses/Units 143,295

Rules of Thumb

➢ 35 to 40 percent of annual gross sales includes inventory

➢ 1 to 3 times SDE includes inventory

➢ 1.5 to 2 times EBITDA

➢ 3.5 times EBIT

> "35 to 50 percent of annual fee revenue; applies to small practices; may require earnout"

> "20 to 60 percent of annual fee revenue; applies to practices with fee revenues of $125,000 plus; may require earnout"

> "45 to 55 percent of one year's gross collections, based on location, age and contracts"

Pricing Tips

- "Since there are a number of types of practices the tips vary. Primary care tends to sell for a higher multiple than a specialty practice. 1 to 1.5 times SDE plus inventory and accounts receivable would not be included in the pricing."

- "In medicine, there is such a physician shortage, that to have value a private practice needs income above FMV of labor. In other words there needs to be Dividends per the definition at IRS RR59-60. EBITDA rarely accurately applies due to the lack of capital invested in most service practices."

- "Often, after adjusting owner compensation at Fair Market Value, a lack of net economic benefit to be capitalized to value is determined, indicating a valuation premise of Value in Exchange rather than Value in Use as a Going Concern."

- "Adjusted expenses and adjusted SDE are critical to determining profit potential."

- "1.5 to 2 x Dividends as defined by IRS RR59-60"

- "Typically, after adjusting compensation to FMV, we find no positive cash flows and, therefore, perform an asset valuation."

- "Indeed, younger doctors—half of whom are now women—are refusing to take over these small practices. They want better lifestyles, shorter work days, and weekends free of the beepers, cell phones and patient emergencies that have long defined doctors' lives. Weighed down with debt, they want regular paychecks instead of shopkeeper risks. And even if they wanted such practices, banks—attuned to the growing uncertainties—are far less likely to lend the money needed.

  "Had he left a decade ago, Dr. Sroka might have been able to persuade a doctor to pay $500,000 or more for his roster of 4,000 patients. That he cannot give his practice away results not only from the unattractiveness of its inflexible schedule but also because large group practices can negotiate higher fees from insurers, which translates into more money for doctors."
  Source: "Family Physician Can't Give Away Solo Practice" by Gardiner Harris,
New York Times, April 23, 2011

- "If present doctor is retiring but staying on, then the value goes up."

- "1.5 times the annual revenue is the maximum in today's market. Specialists are worth more but not in elective-type medicine, i.e., cosmetic surgery."

- "Wide variety of sales price depending on type of practice. Primary care 30%–40%, specialty 20%–30%, non-physician owned (e.g., phys. therapy, NP/PA owned family practice) might sell for more 40%–50%. The more specialized the practice the harder to sell, x for goodwill, lower price ratios. Critical to compare after-debt service cash flow to doctor compensation range for that particular specialty. Different doctors have widely different compensation expectations. Focus on gross collections not gross billing."

- "VERY wide range of values depending on numerous characteristics. Primary care practices tend to sell for higher multiples (35%–50%) than specialty practices. Need to be especially cognizant of current compensation range for medical specialty in question. Some specialties may think a cash flow of $200K is good, other specialties won't consider practice with cash flow less than $400K. Payer mix/contracts is important. Revenue deriving from inpatient work (i.e., hospital work) may not count toward value as the hospital and not the selling doctor controls that revenue stream. Some specialties very susceptible to changes in technology. Stark Laws and Anti-Kickback Statutes can impact sales price/terms. The more specialized the doctor—or the more the practice relies on personal reputation of doctor—the harder to sell and lower value."

- "Correct pricing depends on specific specialty and appropriate treatment of intangibles, or lack, in the practice. Important intangibles include current health care, clinical and practice management systems in the practice; experienced, skilled workforce in place; effective management of referrals to the practice; etc."

- "The transferability of the value from the seller to the buyer is essential! Excellent clinical technology, management systems and managers, and effective relationships add value. A successful transition is critical to transferring value from the seller to the buyer."

- "Entirely dependent on facts and circumstances of SUBJECT PRACTICE, e.g., specialty, % ancillary services & technical component revenues, payer mix, etc."

- "1 to 1.35 times SDE plus inventory and accounts receivable are not included."

- "AGS, SDE, EBIT and EBITDA multiples really no longer apply. The best current formula is [2.5-4 times (SDE minus compensation for owner labor)]. The 2.5 multiplier is for insurance-based practices, and the 4 multiplier is for the best of cash practices. Insurance reimbursement trends are downwards, hurting values significantly. The reason AGS, SDE and EBITDA don't apply is the owner might be active or passive. It is illogical to think that a practice with $1,000,000 AGS has the same value to ownership if the owner works there 50 hours per week or is an absentee owner; which is why you have to subtract the market-rate comp for owner labor prior to applying the multiplier. Many specialties have merely liquidation value or close to it because of shortages, the ease of opening a competing practice, and hospital income & overhead guarantees via forgivable loans in lieu of practice purchase. Value issues are very, very localized. Rule of thumb: the sale should pay for itself to the buyer within 5 years with profits above comp for labor."

- "EBITDA is most important; % of Annual Gross Sales is generally irrelevant since profitability varies so widely. Rural practices are getting almost impossible to sell because of physician shortages. Watch out for big insurance reimbursement changes in 2008–12 due to Medicare changes and PPOs following their pricing. 501-C3 'not-for-profit' buyers will require formal appraisals. Maybe have to adjust value for lack of electronic health care record if it is needed locally within 1–2 years; $25,000–$40,000 per doc, reduces profits."

- "Current market information and terms are essential to understanding these transactions and values."

- "Payer mix, trade name, referral sources, physician compensation, noncompete, competition"

- "Medicare is always reducing the reimbursement amount, therefore a cash office is usually worth more than an office that depends a great deal on Medicare and other insurances."

- "Primary care practices (family practice, internal medicine, pediatrics) sell for higher multiples than specialty practices as there are more buyers, and goodwill transfers more easily. Any hospital based practice is almost entirely dependent on the hospital contract/privileges which the seller does not own/control. Brokers should be aware of Stark, AKS, and other regulations/constraints that can affect sale/value. Heavily regulated industry. Majority of sale price is goodwill value."

- "Jobs are paying more and gross income is often dropping, so the results of the Income Approach of valuation identifying dividends [(SDE minus market rate compensation of one working owner) x 3-4] is becoming more important for more specialties, and % of annual gross sales less important. Many practices can't even sell at the value of the liquidated assets, since jobs pay more without asset purchase. The impact of specialty and location is profound. Medicare is continually reducing reimbursement, which impacts other insurances, so dependence on insurance reimbursement is an important consideration in value. Cash and cosmetic practices are usually worth more since there is a higher profit for less work, and often a better lifestyle. Many specialties are having trouble attracting new doctors no matter the income, so wages are increasing, sales are becoming more difficult, and values dropping. Make sure to read the white papers on supply and demand available on many specialty professional association websites. Best overhead stats are usually available at http://www.healthcon.org. Best market rate compensation stats are usually available at http://www.mgma.com. The market rate comp data in the reports is often 1-2 years old and needs to be adjusted current. The Goodwill Registry is helpful in many cases, but the running average 10 year median needs close attention, as the average of many specialties reflects the midpoint of 10 years' steady decline (like in ophthalmology). Large multi-doctor practices can have higher values than solo and small practices. The effect of the temporary price spike by Physician Practice Management Company rollups in the 1990s can distort the Registry summary statistics and need to be removed; as may results from court valuations rather than sales transactions reported."

- "Prices vary widely depending on type of practice/physician. Most primary care practices (i.e., family practice, internal medicine, pediatric) sell in the 35%-50% of gross range. Primary care is easier to sell/transfer goodwill. Specialty practices sell in the 20%-30% of gross range. Referral patterns and transferability of goodwill is key in sale of specialty practices."

- "Minimum net profit of $100,000 before the doctor's salary."

- "Value varies widely by specialty and geographic location. The Goodwill Registry and Institute of Business Appraisers have databases on many sales, but beware of using historical data without considering current and upcoming issues, like Medicare's proposed reduction in reimbursement. Since other insurance company's base reimbursement on Medicare, this can significantly affect future profits in many specialties."

- "The healthcare industry has been experiencing margin compression over the past 5 to 7 years. Third-party payers/managed care companies (insurance companies, Medicare, Medicaid) have been reducing reimbursements, while office overhead has been growing. This has created stagnation in business valuations due to smaller buyer pool."

  "Depends on reason for selling— value is related to continuity of practice:

Retiring but stays on	value up
Death	value down
Loss of lease	value down
Divorce	value down:"

- "Pricing of health care professional practices is highly variable depending upon the specific type of health care service, geographical location (state), highly third party pay dependent versus fee for service or cash pay."
- "Multiple of SDE increases with profit levels."
- "Number of doctor referral relationships and strength of same"
- "Specialists have more value. Multi-physician practices have more value. Sales of past physician practices to large HMOs and hospitals are not viable comps, as none have done what they anticipated."
- "Located near a hospital or with other medical professionals. Positive reputation in the community. Established referral network. Type of medical specialty is a valuation factor."
- "Call around for waiting times to see a new patient. If local wait times are two weeks or more, opening from scratch may be an economically viable alternative to purchasing a practice, or setting a valuation comparable. Also, will the local hospital offer income guarantees via forgivable loans to a competitor to start from scratch (decreases demand and value, but alternatively may be a source of buyer-recruitment and support)?"
- "There are 23 specialties. Generally patient allegiances are salable, but doctor referrals are not. For example, a general surgery practice (based on referrals) would be worth quite a bit less than an ophthalmology practice (patients are transferable)."
- "Urban practices more popular than rural"
- "...Between 33 1/3 percent of gross to 55 percent depending on many things—or one times readjusted net—adding back discretionary items. Age of practice—how many provider contracts? Location—good or bad? Must show a net before doctor salary of over $100K."
- "45 percent to 68 percent of gross collected revenue. Type of patients? Collection history? Location? Age of equipment, staff?"

Expert Comments

"Gaining Market Share in this industry is time consuming."

"The industry is becoming less attractive without a great location. Medicare reimbursements are dropping and profits are more difficult to obtain than 2 to 4 years ago."

"Reimbursement is declining, business and malpractice risk are high, Health Reform will cause many docs to flee to hospital employment, reducing the # of buyers"

"There is always a demand for a good clinic with profit. The aging population will require more doctors and more care."

"The competition is greater now with the large regional chains that have emerged. Location is still very important to success."

"Medicare reimbursements dropping. Many practices picking up cosmetic and other ancillary profit centers."

"The insurance companies are reducing the profit levels."

"Reimbursement, regulatory, technological and competitive pressures in a dynamic healthcare delivery marketplace, undergoing significant reform initiatives."

"Each of these factors varies dramatically by specialty and by provider! Rules of thumb are not meaningful for medical practices in general because the cycles vary dramatically by specialty and by provider."

"The demand for these practices is growing but profits are more difficult to obtain than 3 to 5 years ago."

"Cost/barrier to entry is quite low for most practices."

"Risks are increasing and profits are decreasing, except in cosmetic practices."

"Competition is high and hospitals are offering better guarantees for startups."

"Medical practices differ dramatically in the above factors, and use of rules of thumb is risky! Value drivers differ substantially by specialty and payer mix."

"Location and facilities are usually OK except in rare circumstances. Rural locations are difficult. Profits are headed down."

"Competition for buyers from high-paying employment is high. Supply of buyers is dropping in certain specialties. Profits are dropping in many specialties. Hard to find buyers in many specialties for other than the most attractive locations. Whole industry is becoming less attractive to entrants. Easy to start competing business from scratch in many specialties and locations. Hospitals are often offering income guarantees to startups but not for purchases, making sales more difficult."

Benchmark Data

Statistics (Primary Care Doctors)

Number of Establishments	143,295
Average Profit Margin	3.1%
Revenue per Employee	$200,800
Average Number of Employees	6.2
Average Wages per Employee	$82,089

Source: IBISWorld, September 2012

Products and Services Segmentation

Diagnosis of general symptoms	20%
Diagnosis, screenings and preventative care	16.5%
Diagnosis of symptoms related to the respiratory system	16%
Diagnosis of symptoms related to the musculoskeletal	11%
Disease treatment	10%
Other	26.5%

Source: IBISWorld, September 2012

Industry Costs

Profit	3.1%
Wages	40.8%
Purchases	20.0%
Depreciation	1.5%
Marketing	5.0%
Rent & Utilities	5.0%
Other	24.6%

Source: IBISWorld, September 2012

Statistics (Specialist Doctors)

Number of Establishments	359,340
Average Profit Margin	23.4%
Revenue per Employee	$184,800
Average Number of Employees	6.8
Average Wages per Employee	$81,146

Source: IBISWorld, September 2012

Products and Services Segmentation

Other	45.5%
Internal medicine	20%
Pediatrics	9.5%
Anesthesiology	5.5%
Obstetrics and gynecology	5.5%
Dermatology and cosmetic surgery	5%
General surgery	5%
Emergency medicine	4%

Source: IBISWorld, September 2012

Industry Costs

Profit	23.4%
Wages	43.9%
Purchases	21.0%
Depreciation	1.5%
Marketing	1.5%
Rent & Utilities	5.0%
Other	3.7%

Source: IBISWorld, September 2012

- "Depreciation is at 1.2% to 1.6%, Average revenue should be from $1,000,000 to $1,300,000."
- "Staff efficiencies, patient flow trends"
- "Overhead under 65%, see benchmark studies at NSCHBC.org and MGMA.com"
- "The share of solo practices among members of the American Academy of Family Physicians fell to 18 percent by 2008 from 44 percent in 1986. And census figures show that in 2007, just 28 percent of doctors described themselves as self-employed, compared with 58 percent in 1970. Many of the provisions of the new health care law are likely to accelerate these trends."

  Source: "Family Physician Can't Give Away Solo Practice" by Gardiner Harris, *New York Times*, April 23, 2011

- "Net profit after doctor's salary of over $100,000."
- "Accounts receivable should be less than 30% in collections."
- "Typical SDE is 40%–65% of gross collections. Generally over 50% is decent. Expense ratios, procedures, amount of equipment, expense category costs change with practice type."
- "Revenue per FTE physician; physician compensation; procedures per physician; collections per physician; operating cost as a percent of revenue; charges, revenue, cost and productivity per work RVU; staffing per work RVU; staffing per FTE physician provider; etc."
- "Varies tremendously with specialty. Practice netting less than 50% likely underperforming. If netting over 60%, then probably above average practice."
- "Keep the A/R at less than 35% in collections."
- "A good office has less than 35% of collections in accounts receivable, and occupancy cost less than 7%."

- "Benchmark Data vary widely by specialty. You have to look up each specialty individually."
- "Procedure mix and payer mix are essential variables! Facilities ratios differ dramatically by specialty. Use of technology in the practice is an important indicator today."
- "75% reimbursement rate"
- "Family Practice: avg 44.8% of annual gross, with 22% std dev; Dermatology: avg 36%, with 16% std dev; Pediatrics: avg 50%, with 22% std dev; Specialty practices: avg 20%–30% of gross; Dentists: 60%–65% of gross, 11% std dev; Chiropractic: 65%–75% of gross, 23% std dev."
- "How many provider contracts? Age of practice and doctor if staying on with new owner. HMO or PPO contracts? Less than 40% of collections in accounts receivable."
- "Generally need at least 1000 SF space per doctor; primary care practice SDE normally in 50%–60% of gross collections; specialty care practices normally in 55%–70% gross collections."
- "All payroll and overhead together run between 40 to 60 percent, depending on specialty of doctor."
- "It depends upon the specialty, physicians, location, service mix, payer mix, regulations and reimbursement policy."
- "High profit margin"
- "Benchmark Data vary widely for 20+ specialties from pediatricians to neurosurgeons. Two good data sources by specialty are the National Association of Healthcare Consultants Statistics Reports (for practices with 10 or fewer doctors) at www.HealthCon.org, and the Medical Group Management Association at www.MGMA.com for larger groups."
- Note: www.healthcon.org is an excellent site and has a lot of data; however, one must purchase it, and non-members pay a lot more than members.

Expenses as a Percentage of Annual Sales

Cost of goods	n/a
Payroll/labor Costs	25% to 40%
Occupancy	05% to 10%
Profit (estimated pretax)	20% to 30%

Industry Trend

- "The industry is becoming less attractive without a great location. Medicare reimbursements are dropping and profits are more difficult to obtain than 2 to 4 years ago."
- "Serious shortage of new physicians, lots of reports about this online. Insurance reimbursement is generally down. Malpractice risks are increasing. Its hard to sell most practices, and pretty easy for new docs to startup cold without buying a practice."
- "If you thought it was hard getting a doctor's appointment now, just wait until 30 million more Americans join the line. Nearly 3 in 4 California counties already lack a sufficient number of family physicians, and by 2020 the U.S. faces an estimated shortage of 40,000 primary-care doctors with no way to remedy that in just a few years.

  "As a result, more consumers may soon find themselves getting their checkups and help in managing their high blood pressure, heart disease or diabetes at the local pharmacy or Wal-Mart as the Affordable Care Act extends health insurance to 30 million people and puts unprecedented strain on an already fragile network of primary care.

"Pharmacies giant CVS Caremark Corp., Target Corp. and other retailers are aiming to help alleviate the doctor shortage with hundreds of walk-in clinics run by nurses to treat ear infections and other routine ailments and increasingly help people suffering from chronic illnesses. These companies, after struggling to turn a profit from these clinics for the last decade, are now eager to capitalize on an influx of newly insured patients."

Source: "In-store clinics look to be a remedy for healthcare law influx" by Chad Terhune,
Los Angeles Times, July 30, 2012

- "Market and regulatory pressures and shrinking profits are leading many physicians to sell their practices and become salaried employees. Whether it's a good idea for you to remain independent or join forces with a hospital, insurer, or large multispecialty group depends on a range of factors, including the local market, the health of your practice, and, of course, your personal needs and interests.

"Whichever route you take, however, a rapidly changing healthcare landscape may require you to reevaluate your existing business model.

"With small groups of family, internal medicine, and general practice physicians under more pressure and living with less certainty than perhaps at any other time in history, it would be reasonable to think that doctors have widely changed their attitudes about practicing independently. In a recent survey of more than 5,000 physicians, however, the Doctors Company found that more than half — 56% — of respondents indicated that they are not likely to change practice models over the next 5 years.

"Only 20% say they plan to shift practice models or make other changes, such as practicing part-time, leaving medicine for a different career, or retiring. Nearly one-fourth of respondents (24%) did not select a future practice model at all. According to the Doctors Company, that 'suggests respondents feel substantial uncertainty about their prospects.'"

- "Lower supply of physicians/buyers, many practices going unsold, less people entering the field"

- "A Profession in Transition: American medicine is steadily shifting away from small, privately owned clinics and becoming an industry dominated by larger groups of doctors in salaried jobs.

"Fewer Self-Employed Doctors: Census data show that the number of doctors describing themselves as self-employed has fallen steadily since 1970.

"Fewer Small Practices: Doctor surveys suggest that small practices of one or two physicians are in decline and are now outnumbered by group practices.

"Harder to Balance Costs and Fees: Young doctors leaving medical school with large debts may be unwilling to risk solo practice because the costs involved with running a practice have risen faster than inflation over the past decade, while the rate at which Medicare reimburses doctors has lagged."

Source: "Family Physician Can't Give Away Solo Practice" by Gardiner Harris,
New York Times, April 23, 2011

- "While the economy begins to show signs of a slow recovery, many consumers continue to struggle with financial challenges, some of which could affect their health. A survey released today by the American Optometric Association (AOA) revealed that 36 percent of Americans say they are limiting their doctor visits because of the recession. When asked which doctors they are visiting less, the majority indicated dentist (63 percent), followed by primary care physician (59 percent) and eye doctor (52 percent). Only eight percent indicated that they are sticking to their regular health schedule."

Source: "Recession cutting into doctor visits, according to new consumer survey,"
American Optometric Association (AOA), www.aoa.org

Seller Financing

- "100% bank financing is usually available again so seller-financing is lessened."
- "5 to 10 years"
- "If Medicare patients are seen, limit payout terms to one year to comply with laws."

Questions

- "Hours worked, the payer mix, why are you selling, where do your patients come from, what type of management systems are in place."
- "It varies a lot by specialty and location, including: board certification, insurance panel memberships, sub-specialty interest, Medicare participation, local IPA and ACO action, hospital relationships, ancillary services offered, DME offered, office-based pharmacy, mid-level providers used, etc."
- "What are the ACO plans in this community? Is your ICD/CPT coding federally compliant? Are your provider employment and compensation plans and PECOS registrations state and federally compliant?"
- "History of staff, provider contracts, billing procedures type of patients"
- "Type of practice? Hours worked? Payer mix? Outpatient vs inpatient revenue? Patient encounters/week? Reimbursement trends?"
- "Hours worked. Use of mid-level providers/physician extenders payer mix reimbursement trends up/down ancillary profit centers."
- "Where are patients coming from? Payer mix—insurance and cash breakdown."
- "Sustainability of projected revenue stream, based on probability of patients remaining with practice, level of reimbursement yield, regulatory restrictions on ASTC, etc."
- "Many!! Really understand the specialty, procedures, technology, provider team, management systems and team, payment systems and concerns, regulatory requirements, etc."
- "Atypical services, local hospital trends, specialty trends, insurance plans of note, %Medicaid, % Medicare, hidden income, technology & surgical obsolescence, if hospital will help recruit or is a potential buyer."
- "Why are you selling? Are you willing to recommend me to your patients, colleagues, and the community? Are you willing to provide full disclosure and transparency and assist to the fullest extent in transferring the value in the practice?"
- "Where do you get patients?"
- "One should look at whether the business is primary care or surgery/specialty, and what portion of the business is professional (fees) vs. technical (diagnostic or pharmaceutical/medical goods). Specific reimbursement trends are based upon specialty, provider supply (i.e., the supply of physicians to the population) and other indicators of demand for services, such as utilization demand for services in the market service area of the practice. Things that make business sense are often illegal in medical practice, so services, leases, referral

sources, etc. need to be scrutinized for Stark II and Medicare compliance. CPT coding errors can greatly affect value."

- "# doctors? # support staff? any mid-level providers (e.g., PA, NP)? payer mix? How much Medicare/Medicaid? Collection ratio (i.e., how much does doctor get paid vs. amount of money billed) any special certifications, procedures, techniques performed in practice that might not be normal? How much income generated outside practice facility (i.e., hospital, ASC)? # patient encounters / day/week for each doctor? Get physician referral report to analyze referral patterns for those practices that rely upon referrals? Where do they have hospital privileges? How hard will it be for a new buyer to get privileges at same hospitals?"

- "Licensure, malpractice history, reimbursement forecasts for specialty,% of Medicare and Medicaid and HMO, waiting time for patient appointments in the specialty in the geographic area. Can insurance contracts be transferred? (difficult or impossible in some markets)"

- "Is this a primary care facility or specialty business? What portion is paid by cash, check, credit card or insurance companies? Do you have any workman's comp clients? Do you have all the current and updated billing with the major carriers?"

Resources

Trade Publications
- Medical Economics: www.memag.com
- Physicians Practice: www.physicianspractice.com
- The BVR/AHLA Guide to Healthcare Valuation: www.amazon.com

Associations
- Medical Group Management Association: www.mgma.com
- American Medical Association: www.ama-assn.org

Medical Spas		
	NAICS 713940	Number of Businesses/Units 21,500

Rules of Thumb

➤ 2.5 times SDE includes inventory

Pricing Tips

- "1) It is critical to understand if the business had prepaid services as a liability. Many med spas have balance sheet complications due to large prepaid services that are paid in advance and delivered over a year or more. Any assumed liability by the Buyer should be counted as consideration. 2) Because of equipment obsolescence, equipment leasing is common. 3.0 multiple assumes the Seller pays off the leases OR if the Buyer assumes the leases, the assumed amount counts as consideration/purchase price. 3) Med spas with niche services such as hair replacement MAY bring a higher multiple, especially if they have a relationship with a well-known Hair Restoration/Hair Replacement surgeon."

Expert Comments

"Med spas provide a niche between spa/beauty treatments and invasive plastic surgery. With the aging population of baby boomers, more women AND men are investing in non-invasive 'image enhancement.' Spending money on microdermabrasion, laser hair removal, botox and other services is considered more acceptable than ever. Medical doctors see the category as attractive, as the services are almost always elective and do not involve insurance money and its associated regulations."

Benchmark Data

- "Advertising expenses are generally 25% of revenue and drive the business. 2–3 sales consultants per million in sales. Owner is often helping sell for a single location. 1 clinician per $150,000–$200,000 in sales. Laser Hair Removal tends to be the largest revenue category (50%+)."

Expenses as a Percentage of Annual Sales

Cost of goods	05%
Payroll/labor Costs	30%
Occupancy	08%
Profit (estimated pretax)	25% to 30%

Industry Trend

- "Would you be tempted to head into a high-end salon for a chemical peel or botox shot for wrinkles? How about trying one of those new body-contouring devices advertised to shrink fat without pain or incisions?

   "The number of medical spas—hybrids of medical clinics and day spas—have grown by 80 percent in the past two years and is now up to an estimated 4,250 nationally, according to the International Medical Spa Association."

   Source: "Medical spas are booming" by Deborah Kotz, January 2012

Questions

- "1)Are there prepaids? 2) What UNIQUE services do you offer? 3) Equipment Leases 4) Revenue/Service Mix 5) Licensing/Regulatory requirements 6) Do you need doctor/nurse to oversee operations? 7) Insurance"

Resources

Associations
- Day Spa Association (DSA): www.dayspaassociation.com

Medical Transcription		
	NAICS 561410	Number of Businesses/Units 56,683

Rules of Thumb

➢ 75 percent of annual revenues

➢ 3 to 3.5 times SDE

Pricing Tips

- "The market for Medical Transcription companies will vary according to several factors: the higher the 'price per line' the more a buyer is willing to pay; technology can influence price if the work is highly automated; the size of the service with regard to annual revenue and diversity of its customer base. These factors in combination can create a range of value from 75% of gross sales to 120% of gross."
- "Size matters. MTSOs with revenue under $1M will generally get about 70% of revenue and as revenue exceeds $1M, sellers can expect 100% of revenue. Of course many factors will influence where on this continuum a given MTSO will sell—i.e., gross profit, technology, line rates and most importantly, how secure the buyer perceives the book of customers to be."

Expert Comments

"The overall market is growing but competition from overseas providers such as India, Pakistan, Philippines and South Africa are squeezing margins. Voice recognition software has also had some effect on portions of this business, especially in the radiology area."

"The MTSO industry faces many challenges, most notably: healthcare facilities moving away from transcription in favor of Electronic Medical Records (EMR/EHR), the ever increasing use of speech recognition technologies that significantly affect the amount of transcribing required by humans etc. Larger MTSOs have adapted to these changes by becoming experts at integrating their transcription work directly into the EMR and providing sophisticated speech recognition technologies paired with transcribing editors. Most of the active buyers looking to make acquisitions of US MTSOs are buyers with operations both onshore in the US and offshore generally in India or the Philippines, but sometimes also in Pakistan etc.."

Benchmark Data

Statistics (Medical Transcription)

Number of Establishments	56,683
Average Profit Margin	15%

Source: IBISWorld, June 2012

Products and Services Segmentation

Transcription and stenographic service	55%
Typing, word processing and desktop publishing	30%
Document editing and proofreading	15%

Source: IBISWorld, June 2012

Major Market Segmentation

Healthcare providers	40%
Other businesses	30%
Small service-related business	30%

Source: IBISWorld, June 2012

Industry Costs

Profit	15.0%
Wages	50.5%
Purchases	3.5%
Depreciation	3.9%
Marketing	6.0%
Rent & Utilities	4.0%
Other	17.1%

Source: IBISWorld, June 2012

Market Share

Nuance Communications Inc. 14.5%
MModal Inc. 9.9%
Source: IBISWorld, June 2012

- "Well run MTSOs with only onshore operations can see gross profit margins in the 30-40% range; those with offshore operations can increase these margins by 10 points to the 40-50% range."
- "Medical transcriptionists continue to be an aging population. Part of this is impacted by the aging nature of the US workforce overall. However, when compared to estimates of the 2006 age distribution of the US, the MT profession reflected in this survey trends older. This creates an immediate concern regarding the creation of not only a replacement workforce, but a workforce that can match the demands of the expanding healthcare industry."
- "Which of the following best describes your personal income before taxes last year"

Personal income	Percentage
Did not answer	4.8%
Under $10,000	9.5%
$10,000-19,999	13.0%
$20,000-29,999	22.6%
$30,000-39,999	23.0%
$40,000-49,999	13.2%
$50,000-59,999	6.5%
$60,000-69,999	3.3%
$70,000-79,999	1.8%
$80,000-89,999	0.9%
$90,000+	1.4%

Source: "2007 Survey of Medical Transcriptionists: Preliminary Findings" Released May 2008 and is the latest available.

Note: Both items above are from the source mentioned above.

- "The industry generally prices the transcription work on the basis of a 65 key strokes per line rate. Averages are running close to $.125 per line in the USA. The higher quality firms have been able to achieve as high as $.22 per line. This, of course, makes them more desirable and worth more to the buyer. Most of the firms use transcriptionists who are independent contractors and pick up the work from home based computers from the servers of the MT firm. Work is turned around on a 24-48 hour basis in most cases."

Expenses as a Percentage of Annual Sales

Cost of goods .... 50% to 70%
Profit (estimated pretax) .... 15% to 20%

Industry Trend

- "There are three trends in the industry that look to impact the future of the transcriptionist role. In no particular order, they are: (1) advances in voice recognition software; (2) more outsourcing of transcription functions overseas; and (3) new guidelines by the U.S. Department of Health and Human Services (HHS) regarding electronic health records (EHR).
- "In July of 2010, the HHS introduced rules that define 'meaningful use' of electronic health records. These rules basically lay the groundwork for a national initiative to adopt the widespread use of a standardized electronic format for health records. What does this mean to a transcriptionist? Simply

put, it means that the traditional process of dictating, transcribing, and generating a word-processed medical document is going to change sooner rather than later."

Source: "What Could Be The Future in Medical Transcription Industry?" a guest post by Brendan Cruickshank, March 1, 2011. www.mherald.com

Questions

- "Who are your customers—hospitals, clinics etc.? Do you have contracts with your clients? Have you lost any significant revenue in recent years to EMR? What line rates do you charge your customers? What line rates do you pay your MTs? Do you use offshore production? What technology platform, if any, are you using? What are the costs associated with the technology platform? Are you prepared to carry up to 50% of the purchase price in the form of an earn out?"

Resources

Associations

- Medical Transcription Industry Association: www.mtia.com
- The Association for Healthcare Documentation Integrity: www.ahdionline.org

		Franchise
Meineke Car Care Centers (See Also Auto Muffler & Midas)		
Approx. Total Investment		$125,000 to $398,000
	NAICS 811112	Number of Businesses/Units 966

Rules of Thumb

➤ 30 to 35 percent of annual sales plus inventory

		Franchise
Merry Maids		
Approx. Total Investment		$26,350 to $57,450
	NAICS 561720	Number of Businesses/Units 1,451

Rules of Thumb

➤ 45 percent of annual sales plus inventory

Resources

Websites

- www.merrymaids.com

Microbreweries (See Breweries & Brew Pubs)	
	NAICS 312120

	Franchise

Midas International (See Also Meineke & Auto Mufflers)

Approx. Total Investment		$88,500 to $390,970
	NAICS 811112	Number of Businesses/Units 2,194

Rules of Thumb

> ➤ 35 to 40 percent of annual sales plus inventory

Resources

Websites

- www.midasfranchise.com

Middle Market Businesses (In General)

Rules of Thumb

> ➤ 2 to 5 times SDE plus inventory
> ➤ 3 to 5 times EBIT
> ➤ 3 to 5 times EBITDA

Pricing Tips

- "Only accept audited financials. Always retain qualified legal and accounting professionals early on in the process to uncover any 'hidden' issues that you may not discover on your own. Determine whether the industry sector of the business you are considering is trending up or down and what the long-term direction of the specific businesses' product line(s), within that industry, is projected to be. Determine what your exit strategy would be if you were to obtain control of the business."

Expert Comments

"Middle market businesses have very sophisticated competitors and are quite risky. Therefore, they are historically more profitable than smaller, main street operations. Because of the high cost of entry, there is a limited market for many of these businesses. Additionally, these companies tend to often be quite specific in their product line and hold a large Market Share in their respective geographic location."

Benchmark Data

- "Look for 'visionary' leadership and highly structured accounting and marketing departments. Look closely at employee costs and how 'deep' the middle management is. i.e., is middle management highly motivational or just high cost? Are all processes and procedures of the company in place or is everyone 'flying by the seat of their pants'? And which of these will be better for your given situation?"

Expenses as a Percentage of Annual Sales

Cost of goods	20% to 30%
Payroll/labor Costs	25% to 30%
Occupancy	10%
Profit (estimated pretax)	30% to 40%

Questions

- "What are their companies' goals for the future and how have they prepared to make that a reality? Have they prepared a contingency plan in the event of unforeseen developments and what are their contingencies?"

	Franchise
Minuteman Press	
Approx. Total Investment	$100,000 to $150,000
Estimated Annual Sales/Unit	Not Available
	Number of Businesses/Units 975

Rules of Thumb

➢ 65 percent of annual sales plus inventory

Resources

Websites

- www.minutemanpress.com

Mobile Home Parks		
SIC 6515-01	NAICS 531190	Number of Businesses/Units 96,500

Rules of Thumb

➢ 3 to 8 times monthly income

Pricing Tips

- "Eight times gross or $8,000 per space (pad), depending upon the amenities, e.g., carports, recreation center, landscaping, paving, size of pad (space), closeness to city, etc."

- "City officials announced Thursday that Poway is selling Poway Royal Estates mobile-home park to a private, out-of-state company for $38.3 million. The move appears to end a six-year, often contentious effort by park residents to buy the 397-space mobile-home park at Metate Lane and Community Road. "A company that was trying to help the residents buy the 50-acre park submitted two bids. At just under $31.1 million and roughly $28.1 million, they were noticeably lower than the $38 million or more that Hometown America and two other private companies offered. Fuentes said city officials would not have been acting responsibly if they had accepted either of the residents' offers. 'They were significantly less than the market rate for Poway Royal,' she said. 'It would have been a gift of public funds.'"
  Source: "San Marcus: City to sell mobile-home park to private company for $38.3 million" by Andrea Moss, www.nctimes.com, April 30, 2010

- Note: Mobile-home parks are generally real-estate-intensive—a real estate license is probably necessary to handle the sale.

Benchmark Data

Statistics (Mobile Home Site & Other Leasing)

Number of Establishments	96,786
Average Profit Margin	12%
Revenue per Employee	$119,800
Average Number of Employees	1
Average Wages per Employee	$26,534

Source: IBISWorld, January 2011

Product and Services Segmentation (2010)

Lessors of home sites for manufactured and/or mobile homes (all ages)	44.3%
Lessors of home site for manufactured and/or mobile homes (Age 55+)	29.6%
Lessors of other real property	17.9%
Other real estate property income	8.2%

Source: IBISWorld, January 2011

Industry Costs

Profit	12.0%
Rent	3.4%
Utilities	8.5%
Depreciation	11.3%
Other	15.0%
Wages	22.4%
Purchases	27.4%

Source: IBISWorld, January 2011

Market Share

- There are no major players in this industry

Source: IBISWorld, January 2011

Industry Trend

- "With no dealers selling homes, and little lending for park purchases, many park sellers are becoming truly desperate. Day after day passes without any offers and, when they get one, the deal falls through, predictable during the financing contingency. Many sellers do not know how to get their parks sold. And the panic feeds on itself and on other similar parks. A lot of value is based on perception—and many sellers perceive their parks to be nearly valueless. Most notable are the parks that have less occupancy than is required for a bank loan (say 60%), yet show reasonable positive cash flow. Despite a lot of good, solid raw material, the seller may perceive that the park will never find a buyer despite the low asking price. And so the price just keeps dropping.
"The key buying opportunities in parks today are:
Parks that have just enough vacancy to be unable to get financing, yet can reach this occupancy level (normally about 80%) with the addition of only a few homes; parks that have sufficient occupancy, but have lousy financials due to mismanagement, and costs that can be reduced; parks that can attain an enormous rent boost upon closing without any changes in occupancy to attain attractive numbers; parks that come with additional real estate assets which can be subdivided and sold off, to reduce the basis in the park.
"These opportunities allow a buyer to increase the park income almost immediately, and with little risk. And they circumvent the weakness in the market (dealer sales/occupancy/financing issues) and allow the buyer to obtain a winning deal from the start."

Source: "The Best Time to Buy Mobile Home Parks In Decades" by Dave Reynolds, July 18, 2009, www.biggerpockets.com

Modeling Agencies

SIC 7363-01	NAICS 711410	Number of Businesses/Units 1,500

Rules of Thumb

➤ 20 percent of annual sales

Pricing Tips

- "Smaller agencies may be one-person businesses and the goodwill may be difficult to transfer. Earnouts may be necessary."

		Franchise

Molly Maid (See also Janitorial Services & Maid Brigade)

Approx. Total Investment		$164,800 to $175,000
	NAICS 561720	Number of Businesses/Units 618

Rules of Thumb

➤ 35 to 40 percent of annual sales plus inventory

Resources

Websites
- www.mollymaid.com

		Franchise

Money Mailer (See also Advertising Material Distribution Services)

Approx. Total Investment		$37,500
Estimated Annual Sales/Unit		Not Available
	NAICS 541870	Number of Businesses/Units 218

Rules of Thumb

➤ 45 to 50 percent of sales plus inventory

➤ "If a cooperative direct mail business, such as Money Mailer or Supercoups is making $100,000, it could be sold for $150,000 to $225,000, and $250,000 if it was a perfect situation. Now, on the other hand if it is a Valpak, I believe you could get up to 3 times what it is making because Valpak is the undisputed leader. They are owned by COX Publishing and they are within 50 franchises of being sold out."

Resources

Websites
- www.moneymailer.com

Montessori Schools (See also Schools & Day Care Centers/Children)

	NAICS 611110	

Rules of Thumb

➤ 1.5 to 2 times SDE

➤ 3 to 4 times EBITDA

Pricing Tips

- "The larger schools with enrollment of 100 tend to sell for 3 times EBITDA, perhaps 4 times if the facility is in a location not easily replicated; the owners typically run them semi-absentee. Smaller schools are typically run by an 'owner/director' and are sold as a typical service business 1.5 to 2 times SDE."
- "Montessori Schools with enrollment above 100 are in strong demand, and it is getting harder to get one listed as they are easily sold."

Expenses as a Percentage of Annual Sales

Cost of goods	N/A
Payroll/labor Costs	25% to 35%
Occupancy	30% to 45%
Profit (estimated pretax)	20% to 35%

Industry Trend

- "If Montessori was a stock, you would buy it. There are almost 4,200 private Montessori schools in the United States now, compared to 3,500 a quarter century ago. In the past 20 years, more than 140 charter schools have been founded on Montessori principles. A quarter century ago, 50 public schools used the Montessori method. That number is now 280."

  Source: "Succeeding at their own pace" by Alex Beam, *Boston Globe*, August 26, 2011

Seller Financing

- 5 years

Questions

- "Why are you selling?"
- "Tuition and comparison with competition, qualifications of teachers, teacher ratios. Do they accept toddlers or infants? Have there been any or is there now pending litigation? How is the revenue broken down?"

Resources

Websites

- www.montessori.org
- www.montessori.edu

Motels (See also Hotels)

SIC 7011-01	NAICS 721110	Number of Businesses/Units 40,000

Rules of Thumb

➤ 2.25 to 3.5 times annual revenues (sales); up to 5 times for resort properties

➤ 7 to 9 times SDE

➤ $20,000 per room

➤ 2.5 to 3 times room revenues

➤ 7.5 to 8 times SDE

➤ 8 to 10 times EBIT

➤ 8 to 10 times EBITDA

➤ 10 to 12 percent cap rate

Pricing Tips

▪ "Check contracted room business and QA score if franchised."

▪ "We use several approaches to establish value. One is the Performance Index Method—developing a valuation table showing (a) cap rate (b) economic value (c) value per room (d) multiple of room revenue and (e) multiple of total revenue. One can then determine economic value by using either desired cap rate (best method), per room rates, X gross or Y total revenue. We also use discounted future earnings, discretionary cash flow, book value, market value and rule of thumb. We usually provide a range of values based on profitability, income risk, desirability, business type, business trend in location, competition, industry, terms of sale, along with a few other factors."

▪ "Most ask 3 times, but sales result usually under 2.5 times—for larger and older properties, usually around 2 times gross. We usually use several approaches to establish value. We use the Performing Indexing Method showing: (1) cap rate percent (2) economic value (3) value per room (4) multiple of room revenue (5) multiple of total revenue. One can determine the economic value by selecting either the desired cap rate (best method) or the per-room rate, or the times room gross or times total revenue."

▪ "Our general analysis using a high and low range utilizes several approaches to value (1) the income approach (2) excess earnings (3) discounted future earnings (4) discretionary cash (5) book value (6) market value (7) rule of thumb—then we have value comparisons and then a correlation and final opinion of value range and finally an opinion of value. We base the above on: profitability, income risk, desirability, business type, leasehold, and product exclusivity. A factor is assigned to each of the above for both high and low range."

▪ "Limited-service operating expenses—50 to 65 percent; full-service operating expenses—75 to 80 percent (age influences pricing heavily). Current franchise status or possible entry? New competition coming into market?"

▪ "Room revenue multiplier (2x to 6x), net operating income multiplier (6x to 12x). The multiplier you choose determines the capitalization rate."

▪ "2.3 to 3 x annual gross sales. We try to avoid 'times gross' pricing. We prefer to price based on cap rate. The 'x' net room sales of 2.5 to 3 is better than using total sales. Location, age, structure, franchised or not, all make a difference in value. Some people (buyers and sellers) price based on $ per room."

▪ "Location—highway changes—age—obsolescence—market conditions—affiliation."

Benchmark Data

- For Benchmark data see Hotels

Expenses as a Percentage of Annual Sales

Cost of goods	01%
Payroll/labor Costs	20%
Occupancy	18%
Profit (estimated pretax)	22%

Industry Trend

- "With the slow economy the industry is hurting and prices in midmarket and below are going lower."
- "Slowly getting to be a buyer's market"

Seller Financing

- "10 to 20 years—depends on age and size of property. One assumption— seller financing seldom exceeds time of original note. Last five sales have all been different with different interest rates."

Questions

- "Punch list. Any new construction? Any new highway or closure coming down?"
- "Contract on the brand franchise? Age of equipment? Age of property? And all paperwork?

	Franchise
MotoPhoto	
Approx. Total Investment	$225,000 to $275,000
Estimated Annual Sales/Unit	Not Available
NAICS 81292	Number of Businesses/Units 30

Rules of Thumb

➢ 60 to 65 percent of annual sales plus inventory

Resources

Websites

- www.motophoto.com

Motorcycle Dealerships (See also Harley-Davidson Dealerships		
SIC 5571-06	NAICS 441221	Number of Businesses/Units 7,904

Rules of Thumb

➢ 12 to 14 percent of annual sales plus inventory

➢ 2 to 2.75 times SDE plus inventory

➢ 3 to 4 times EBITDA

Pricing Tips

- "2x to 5x SDE; includes parts, garments, & accessories inventory (PG&A); can include used vehicles, but not new vehicles. High multiples for Harley dealerships, and lower multiples for Japanese or other brands."
- "The EBIT multiple above assumes that all new vehicle inventory is subject to floor plan financing that will be assumed by the buyer. Normal working capital acquired."
- "The actual value of the franchise type of cycle business is fixtures and equipment plus the price of used cycles that have been taken in (prior to shop work being done) at the used motorcycle book price, plus the new cycles, plus 5 years' to ¾ year's net profit. One note of caution: contact franchisor to determine what is exactly required to satisfy their requirements for opening or buying a dealership; e.g., flooring requirements and financial strength."

Expert Comments

"Several years ago motorcycle dealerships were easy to sell. Some regions of the country have experienced a downward trend in sales. The southeastern U.S. is still very strong. Currently, smaller dealerships can be very difficult to sell."

"The original equipment manufacturers (Honda, Harley-Davidson, Yamaha, Suzuki, Kawasaki, etc.) control the number of dealers permitted in a marketplace. An existing dealership can block the establishment of a competing dealership of the same brand within a geographical proximity to the existing dealership."

Benchmark Data

Statistics (Motorcycle Dealership and Repair)

Number of Establishments	3,093
Average Profit Margin	1.3%
Revenue per Employee	$365,000
Average Number of Employees	7.8
Average Wages per Employee	$34,306

Source: IBISWorld, September 2012

Products and Services Segmentation

New motorcycles, motor scooters and motor bikes	48.5%
Motorized sports vehicles including all-terrain vehicles	23.5%
Other	14.5%
Used motorcycles, motor scooters and motor bikes	10.5%
Independent repairers (excluding dealerships)	03%

Source: IBISWorld, September 2012

Major Market Segmentation

Male consumers	72%
Government	1%
Business	13%
Female consumers	14%

Source: IBISWorld, September 2012

Industry Costs

Profit	1.3%
Wages	10.0%
Purchases	75.0%
Marketing	0.5%
Rent & Utilities	2.0%
Other	11.2%

Source: IBISWorld, September 2012

- "Vehicle sales 70% of gross; PG&A 15% of gross; service 12% of gross; finance & insurance sales 3% of gross."
- "GP% on new unit sales 18%
  GP% on used unit sales 20%
  F&I Income per major unit sold $500
  GP% on parts & accessories 36%–40%"

Expenses as a Percentage of Annual Sales

Cost of goods...85%%
Payroll/labor Costs 05%
Occupancy..01%
Profit (estimated pretax) ....02% to 03%

Industry Trend

- "2011 U.S. Motorcycle Sales Show Slight Increase

  July 30, 2011—U.S. motorcycle sales improved slightly in the first half of 2011 when compared to the same period in 2010.

  Motorcycle and scooter sales in the second quarter of 2011 rose 1.7%. Dual-sport sales improved by 13%; scooter sales improved by 28.9% and sportbike sales rose 3.3%. Off-road motorcycle sales continued a decline, down 17%. Overall sales were down 4.6% in Q2 and down by 1.6% in the month of June.

  Dual Sport motorcycles and scooter sales were up significantly.

  2011 U.S. Motorcycle Sales—January to June 2011
    ✓ Dual Sport 15,876 Units (2010: 14,045). Up 1,831 (13%)
    ✓ Off Road 37, 123 Units (2010: 44,673). Down 7,550 (-16.9%)
    ✓ Street Bikes 187,565 Units (2010: 181,542). Up 6,023 (3.3%)
    ✓ Scooter 18,198 Units (2010: 14,122). Up 4,076 (28.9%)
    ✓ Totals 258,762 Units (2010: 254,382) Up 4,380 (Approx. 1.0%)

  Source: Various Sources, Edited by webBikeWorld

Questions

- "PG&A inventory and new vehicle value requirements for a new buyer can be the most difficult and complex aspect to understand. A good deal of time should be spent understanding what inventory is there and how much is really needed. Inventory should turn on an average of 4x to 6X per year in a healthy dealership. Slower turns suggest the business is carrying too much inventory or is very seasonal."

	Franchise
Mountain Mike's Pizza (See also Pizza Shops)	
Approx. Total Investment	$197,000 to $598,000
Estimated Annual Sales/Unit	$525,000

SIC 5812-22	NAICS 722211	Number of Businesses/Units 132

Rules of Thumb

➢ 30% of annual sales plus inventory

Resources

Websites
- www.mountainmikes.com

Movie Theaters		
SIC 7832-01	NAICS 512131	Number of Businesses/Units 4,729

Rules of Thumb

➤ 4 times SDE

➤ 6 times annual adjusted earnings, 1000 plus seating

➤ 4 to 6 percent of annual sales; add fixtures & equipment

➤ 35 percent plus inventory for theaters with only one or several screens

Pricing Tips

- Concession sales usually make up 24 percent of movie-theater sales. It has been said that, without concession sales, the movie theater business would not be viable.

Benchmark Data

Statistics (Movie Theaters)

Number of Establishments	4,729
Average Profit Margin	5.2%
Revenue per Employee	$108,200
Average Number of Employees	28.4
Average Wages per Employee	$10,989

Source: IBISWorld, October 2012

Products and Services Segmentation

Admissions	67%
Food and beverage sales	28.7%
Other	4.3%

Source: IBISWorld, October 2012

Industry Costs

Profit	5.2%
Wages	10.2%
Purchases	39.2%
Depreciation	4.4%
Marketing	1.3%
Rent & Utilities	34.2%
Other	5.5%

Source: IBISWorld, October 2012

Market Share

Regal Entertainment	19.6%
AMC Entertainment	17.5%
Cinemark	11.6%

Source: IBISWorld, October 2012

Industry Trend

- "For Small Theaters, The Digital Future is Dark

"When Sanford Hess started running a century-old movie theater two years ago, he knew Hollywood was replacing celluloid with digital files.

"The 12-employee business, which had just over $300,000 in revenue in 2011, can't afford the pricey new projector and other equipment major studios want him to buy.

"Cinema owners are balking at the $65,000-plus price tag for new digital equipment.

"The biggest chains—Regal Entertainment, AMC Entertainment, and Cinemark Theatres, which account for just over half the $10.2 billion annual U.S. box office—expect to complete the conversion early next year. But 'for lower-grossing theaters, it's just not affordable,' says Fithian. 'I predict we'll lose several thousand screens in the U.S.'"

Source: "For Small Theaters, The Digital Future Is Dark," *Bloomberg Businessweek*, February 26, 2012

Resources

Trade Publications
- "Business of Show Business: The Valuation of Movie Theaters," published by the Appraisal Institute: www.appraisalinstitute.org

Associations
- National Association of Theater Owners: www.natoonline.org

Moving and Storage		
SIC 4214-01	NAICS 484210	Number of Businesses/Units 8,420

Rules of Thumb

➤ 50 percent of annual sales

Benchmark Data

Statistics (Moving Services)

Number of Establishments	8,420
Average Profit Margin	4.4%
Revenue per Employee	$142,400
Average Number of employees	12.4
Average Wages per Employee	$31,585

Source: IBISWorld, July 2012

Products and Services Segmentation

Long-distance moving	44%
Local moving	27%
Packing services related to motor-carrier moving or storage	7.5%
Other	7%
Contract warehousing and storage	5.0%
Other related motor-carrier and storage services	4.5%
General warehousing and storage	5.0%

Source: IBISWorld, July 2012

Major Market Segmentation

Private consumers	45%
Corporate customers	40%
Government	10%
Other	05%

Source: IBISWorld, July 2012

Industry Costs

Profit	4.4%
Wages	21.8%
Purchases	44.2%
Depreciation	4.6%
Marketing	2.5%
Rent & Utilities	11.8%
Other	10.7%

Source: IBISWorld, July 2012

Market Share

UniGroup Inc.	15.5%
SIRVA Inc.	7.9%
Atlas World Group Inc.	5.2%

Source: IBISWorld, September 2012

- "[Moving and Storage] is composed of mostly small businesses: 47.8% of industry companies employ fewer than 5 people. Only 8.5% of industry companies employ 100 or more people.

  "Industry revenue from these services totals more than $16.5 billion annually. The following three areas combined account for 97.3% of revenue:
    - ✓ 69.6% from local or long-distance transportation service
    - ✓ 20.2% from warehousing and storage services
    - ✓ 7.5% from packing and packaging services"

Source: www.promover.com

Resources

Associations

- American Moving and Storage Association—an informative site: www.promover.org

	Franchise
Mr. Jim's Pizza (See Pizza Shops)	
Approx. Total Investment	$75,000 to $150,000
Estimated Annual Sales/Unit	$440,000
SIC 5812-22 NAICS 722111	Number of Businesses/Units 75

Rules of Thumb

➢ 35% of annual sales plus inventory

Resources

Websites

- www.mrjimspizza.net

		Franchise
Mr. Payroll		
Approx. Total Investment		$75,300 to $151,000
Estimated Annual Sales/Unit		Not Available
	NAICS 522390	Number of Businesses/Units 112

Rules of Thumb

➢ 130 percent of annual sales

Resources

Websites
- www.mrpayroll.com

		Franchise
Mr. Rooter Plumbing		
Approx. Total Investment		$58,450 to $153,750
SIC 1711-05	NAICS 238220	Number of Businesses/Units 271

Rules of Thumb

➢ 1 to 4 times SDE plus hard assets; the number between 1 and 4 depends on several factors, such as the owner operating a truck, etc.

		Franchise
Mrs. Fields Original Cookies		
Approx. Total Investment		$179,100 to $251,100
SIC 5461-02	NAICS 311812	Number of Businesses/Units 300

Rules of Thumb

➢ 40 percent of annual sales plus inventory

Resources

Websites
- www.mrsfieldsfranchise.com

		Franchise
Murphy's Deli		
	NAICS 722211	Number of Businesses/Units 54

Rules of Thumb

➢ 50 percent of annual sales plus inventory

➢ Multiples have ranged from 40 percent to 60 percent

Resources

Websites
- www.murphysdeli.com

	Franchise
Music Go Around	
Approx. Total Investment	$253,550 to $325,300

SIC 5736-08	NAICS 451140	Number of Businesses/Units 34

Rules of Thumb

➢ 40 percent of annual sales plus inventory

Resources

Websites
- www.musicgoaround.com

Music Stores (Music and/or Instruments)		
SIC 5736	NAICS 451140	

Number of Businesses/Units Musical Instruments: 9,484 Record Stores: 2,606

Rules of Thumb

➢ 25 percent of annual sales. Retail is generally higher, but the trend of this business is decidedly down, especially for the small independent store.

➢ 1 to 2 times SDE plus inventory. If just a record/CD store it may be difficult to sell period. Music is now being downloaded over the Internet and records/CDs are becoming almost obsolete (see General Information below). If the music store sells sheet music, musical instruments, etc. SDE multiple might be higher.

Pricing Tips

- "Inventory of tapes, CD's, DVD's at FMV (used) is in addition to the above."
- "Usually in a store of this kind inventory turns about twice a year. The store should be located in an area where rent will not exceed 4 percent of the gross sales. National average shows a gross profit of approximately 54 percent before expenses of wages, repairs, maintenance, advertising, bad debts, utilities, insurance, taxes, etc. National average net profit is approximately 10 to 18 percent."
- "The leading music retailers are now box stores (Walmart and Best Buy), and music-only stores are no longer a player in the industry."

Source: www.en.wikipedia.org

Expert Comments

"Independent brick and mortar locations are a dying breed."

Benchmark Data

Statistics (Musical Instrument and Supplies Store)

Number of Establishments	9,484
Average Profit Margin	2.7%
Revenue per Employee	$164,400
Average Number of Employees	4.1
Average Wages per Employee	$25,461

Source: IBISWorld, July 2012

Products and Services Segmentation

Other musical instruments and accessories	53.4%
Audio equipment, components, parts and accessories	17.9%
Pianos	17%
Other goods (includes tapes, CDs and audiobooks)	4.3%
Instrument rentals	2.8%
Sheet music	2.8%
Organs	1.8%

Source: IBISWorld, July 2012

Major Market Segmentation

Hobbyists	35%
Professional	21%
Churches	1%
Students	43%

Source: IBISWorld, July 2012

Industry Costs

Profit	2.7%
Wages	15.4%
Purchases	70.0%
Marketing	1.0%
Rent & Utilities	3.9%
Other	7.0%

Source: IBISWorld, July 2012

Market Share

Guitar Center	34.5%

Source: IBISWorld, July 2012

Statistics (Record Stores)

Number of Establishments	2,606
Average Profit Margin	1.8%
Revenue per Employee	$149,900
Average Number of Employees	4
Average Wages per Employee	$22,560

Source: IBISWorld, January 2012

Products and Services Segmentation

Rock Music	28.2%
Other music	22.5%
Country music	12.9%
Pop Music	12.1%
Rap and hip-hop music	9.7%
R&B and urban music	9.2%
Religious music	5.4%

Source: IBISWorld, January 2012

Industry Costs

Profit	1.8%
Wages	14.2%
Purchases	68.0%
Depreciation	0.7%
Utilities	1.8%
Rent	5.3%
Other	8.2%

Source: IBISWorld, September 2012

Market Share

Trans World	11.85

Source: IBISWorld, September 2012

Expenses as a Percentage of Annual Sales

Cost of goods	35%
Payroll/labor Costs	25% to 30%
Occupancy	15%
Profit (estimated pretax)	20% to 25%

Resources

Associations

- International Music Products Association: www.namm.com

	Franchise
My Favorite Muffin	
Approx. Total Investment	$80,000 to $379,628
NAICS 722211	Number of Businesses/Units 70
Rules of Thumb	

> 30 to 35 percent plus inventory

Resources

Websites

- www.myfavoritemuffin.net

Mystery Shopping Companies	
NAICS 561990	Number of Businesses/Units 700
Rules of Thumb	

> 50 percent of annual sales—the larger the company, the higher the percentage of annual sales over 50 percent.

Pricing Tips

- Large mystery service companies can sell for considerably more than 50 percent of sales.
-

Benchmark Data

- "How much can someone realistically expect to earn as a mystery shopper? Compensation for mystery shopping significantly varies depending on a number of factors, including the type of industry, the level of difficulty required to complete the assignment and the detail required by the mystery shoppers. "Compensation for the typical shop ranges from $5 to $20. Some complex assignments, such as video mystery shop, can pay $75 or more.
  "It is hard to find out more specifics on which companies get mystery shopped and how much shoppers are paid because shoppers are not allowed to divulge specific information, such as the name of the company they've shopped or how much they make per assignment. The shoppers are required to sign confidentiality agreements at the request of the mystery shopping providers and their customers."

Source: www.mysteryshop.org

Resources

Associations

Mystery Shopping Providers Association (MSPA): www.mysteryshop.org

Nail Salons		
SIC 7231-02	NAICS 812113	Number of Businesses/Units 54,250

Rules of Thumb

➢ 25 percent of annual sales plus inventory

Benchmark Data

- For additional Benchmark data see Beauty Salons

Nail Tech Demographics

Ethnicity	Percentage
Vietnamese	45%
Caucasian	33%
Hispanic	10%
African-American	9%
Korean	2%
Other	1%

Gender	Percentage
Male	3%
Female	97%

Average number of clients per week	Percentage
10 or fewer	33.2%
11–20	22.3%
21–30	20.7%
31–40	14.7%
41–50	6.0%
More than 50	3.1%

Who are your clients?	Percentage
Girls under 20	7.4%
Women 21–25	12.4%
Women 26–35	19.5%
Women 36–45	28.0%
Women 46+	29.2%
Men	3.5%

What percentage of your business is appointments vs. walk-ins?	Percentage
Regular appointments	46.2%
Standing appointments	38.4%
Walk-in appointments	13.1%
Other (filling in for another tech, for example)	2.3%

What commission percentage do you receive on services?	57%

Average Weekly Income	Percentage
$150 or less	20.9%
$151–$250	12.4%
$251–$350	13.9%
$351–$450	21.1%
$451–$550	10.9%
$551–$650	9.1%
$651–$750	6.8%
More than $750	14.0%

Which best describes your compensation system?

I am the salon owner/manager and pay myself a salary	16.5%
I own the salon, but I also do nails and keep what I make from services I personally do	21.5%
I am a booth renter; I pay rent to the salon and I keep all my services fees	25.0%
I am a booth renter; I pay a percentage of service fees to the salon as rent	2.5%
I am an employee and I receive a salary	4.7%
I am an employee and I receive a salary plus a percentage of my service fees	3.0%
I am an employee and I receive just a percentage of my service fees	9.9%
I am an employee and my compensation is based on the number of clients I serve. I receive a higher commission if I bring in more clients	2.4%
Other	14.5%

Nail Salon Services	(figures represent % of weekly salon services)
all manicures	15.4%
all pedicures	21.3%
acrylics	17.9%
gels (all types)	25.9%
nail art	9.8%
wraps/other extensions	1.5%
Other	8.2%

Which title best describes your position

Nail technician/booth renter	23.0%
Nail technician/employee	14.9%
Salon owner (doing nails)	30.1%
Salon owner (not doing nails)	3.6%
Salon manager/nail dept. manager (doing nails)	6.1%
Salon manager/nail dept. manager (not doing nails)	1.4%
Student/apprentice	6.3%
Cosmetologist	7.3%
Other	7.3%

How many nail technicians work in your salon?

Just me 52.0%
2 nail techs 17.4%
3 techs 10.5%
4 techs 5.6%
5 techs 4.6%
6 techs 3.1%
7+ techs 6.8%

What is the square footage of your salon?

5,000 square feet or larger 4.2%
3,000–4,999 square feet 5.9%
2,000–2,999 square feet 9.1%
1,000–1,999 square feet 18.7%
501–999 square feet..15.0%
101–500 square feet..12.6%
less than 101 square feet 5.4%
I don't know...29.1%

Overall booth rental average $445/month

Source: "Nails Magazine," 2011–2012 The Big Book

Resources

Trade Publications

- Nails Magazine—interesting and useful site, has an interesting survey of the nail salon business: www.nailsmag.com

		Franchise
Nathan's Famous		
Approx. Total Investment		$50,000 to $1,000,000
	NAICS 722211	Number of Businesses/Units 305

Rules of Thumb

➢ 85 to 90 percent of annual sales plus inventory

Benchmark Data

- Units range from 120 sq. ft. to 3,000 sq. ft.

Resources

Websites

- www.nathansfamous.com

		Franchise
Natural Chicken Grill		
	NAICS 722211	Number of Businesses/Units 14

Rules of Thumb

➢ 25 to 30 percent of annual sales plus inventory

➢ Note: This a business opportunity rather than a franchise. There is also a $1,000-a- month charge after a unit has been open for three months. There is no royalty. The cost shown above is plus the build-out of the store. The cost includes training, set-up, consultation, etc. Units range from 1,500 sq. ft. to 3,500 sq. ft.

		Franchise

Nature's Way Cafe

Approx. Total Investment		$129,500 to $253,900
	NAICS 722211	Number of Businesses/Units 9

Rules of Thumb

➢ 45 percent of annual sales plus inventory

Resources

Websites
- www.natureswaycafe.com

Needlepoint Shops (See Fabric Stores)

SIC 5949-04	NAICS 451130	

Newspaper Routes

	NAICS 454390	

Rules of Thumb

➢ 90 to 100 percent of annual sales plus inventory

➢ $50 to $100 per daily/Sunday subscriber

Newsstands

SIC 5994-01	NAICS 451212	

Rules of Thumb

➢ 30 to 35 percent of annual sales plus inventory

Nurseries (See Garden Centers)

	NAICS 111421	

Nursing Homes (See also Assisted Living Facilities and Homes—Retirement)

SIC 8051-01	NAICS 623110	Number of Businesses/Units 16,406

Rules of Thumb

➢ 45 percent of annual sales plus inventory

➢ 2.5 times SDE plus inventory

➢ 3 times EBIT

➢ 4 times EBITDA

Pricing Tips

- "Return on investment—cash on hand is the guiding rule. Cost per bed varies from $20,000 to $60,000. Cost of upgrading facility a strong factor."
- "Pricing is based on a CAP Rate percentage based on NOI. NOI as defined in the HUD 232 analysis is much different than EBITDA. NOI calculates for management in place but also accounts for CAP EX or a "reserve" plus a proprietary income of 15% before you arrive at NOI. Then you need to look at national and regional comps to see what CAP Rate nursing homes are currently selling for and then you can do the math. This method is almost always spot on for value."
- "In Florida (and other states) the licensing requirements have changed drastically, making entry into this industry very difficult, which in turn may raise the pricing multiple somewhat."
- "Again, there is a substantial variance, depending upon the type of home and the type of patients, from $3,000 to $6,000 per bed. In addition to the amount of the rent, quality of the construction, condition and overall general appearance, and the number of beds are important as to whether or not the facility is licensed for Medicare."

Expert Comments

"Licensing issues"

"Many states have moratoriums on new licenses, so this means that if buyers want in they must buy an existing home or at least a license that is in limbo. We have found marketability to be very high having sold every one we've ever listed. Profits overall are probably slightly down but good homes will have some private pay and their profits are holding up just fine."

Benchmark Data

Statistics (Nursing Care Facilities)

Number of Establishments	16,406
Average Profit Margin	3.1%
Revenue per Employee	$67,300
Average Number of Employees	99.7%
Average Wages per Employee	$29,293

Source: IBISWorld, September 2012

Products and Services Segmentation

For-profit nursing homes	39%
For-profit skilled nursing facilities	25%
Nonprofit nursing homes	14%
Nonprofit skilled nursing facilities	10%
Hospice centers	7%
Government nursing homes and skilled nursing facilities	5%

Source: IBISWorld, September 2012

Industry Costs

Profit	3.1%
Wages	42.4%
Purchases	17.0%
Depreciation	2.5%
Marketing	7.5%
Other	27.5%

Source: IBISWorld, September 2012

- "With nursing homes the big thing is payor mix. Average to below average homes will run 90%+ Medicaid. An all Medicaid home will not be extremely profitable. A good home must have some private pay, at least 10%, and a good mix of Medicare, say around 20%. If this is the case you'll have a home doing 15%+ bottom line EBITDA. Another good benchmark is to look at average Medicaid rate. If the average Medicaid rate for a year is $140/day that home is struggling to make ends meet (unless there is a ton of private pay/Medicare). If the average Medicaid rate is $185/day then that's a home getting higher acuity residents and they will be very profitable."

- "National average rates for a private room increased by 4.4%, from $229 daily or $83,585 annually in 2010, to $239 daily or $87,235 annually in 2011. "Services provided at nursing homes typically include:
  - ✓ Room and board
  - ✓ Nursing care
  - ✓ Medication management
  - ✓ Personal care (assistance with ADLs)
  - ✓ Social and recreational activities"

Source: www.metlife.com/research/October 2011

Expenses as a Percentage of Annual Sales

Cost of goods	15%
Payroll/labor Costs	40% to 50%
Occupancy	10%
Profit (estimated pretax)	15% to 20%

Industry Trend

- "Washington, DC - At a time of economic struggle and continuous rounds of government funding reductions, skilled nursing facilities are in danger of falling into the red, finds a new study by the Moran Company. The analysis commissioned by the American Health Care Association (AHCA) reaffirms what previous studies have shown — that nursing homes are already operating under razor-thin margins. Additional cuts to the sector, which are plausible through end-of-the-year budget bills currently being debated in Congress, would result in a negative margin for facilities, threatening America's seniors and individuals' with disabilities access to skilled nursing care."

Source: "New Study Finds Nursing Homes on the Brink" by Claire Navaro, December 2011

- "While growth will continue in the industry in 2011, it could slow down a little. The main reason for that revolves around healthcare reform. Medicaid payments to facilities within the industry are predicted to be cut considerably over the next year or two as reform starts kicking in. For a while, there could be a lull in the growth and demand for nursing homes and rehab facilities. Chances are, though, that the slowdown will be minimal. Few facilities will be dramatically affected by the changes, at least during 2011; more dramatic impacts will be felt next year."

Source: "Nursing Home and Rehab Industry Outlook—2011 Report,"
www.nslpn.com/industry-outlook January, 2011

- "The health care legislation includes a list of changes to nursing services for seniors and the disabled, including an infusion of federal funding to help state programs provide more care through home- and community-based settings, which, presumably, will result in a reduction in nursing home care. The industry is expected to experience lower demand, which will be moderately offset by an increase in the number of insured. Overall, sales are expected to grow by 1.5 percent on average per year through 2015, reaching $109.5 billion. This is slightly lower than the previous five-year average growth rate of 1.7 percent annually.

"Snyder estimates that profits should remain healthy due to improved government reimbursement rates in the industry. Recognizing the disparity between Medicare and Medicaid reimbursement rates, the reform bill establishes supplemental payments to nursing facilities with high percentages of Medicare and Medicaid residents."

Source: IBISWorld: "Industry Insight: Nursing Facilities" June 2010

- "By 2010, the number of vacant positions in nursing homes is expected to reach 810,000.

"Not-for-profit organizations manage 31% of all nursing homes in the United States."

Source: www.aahsa.org (from Surveys conducted by Genworth Financial)

Seller Financing

- "10 years"
- "SBA will allow a seller to be ballooned at 7 years (amortization can be 7 years or longer). HUD will allow seller financing (up to 50% of the amount buyer puts down - example: 20% down buyer and seller can contribute 10% each) but it MUST be a non-recourse loan, which makes it very difficult for the seller to collect." if the buyer doesn't pay. If you're using SBA lending the seller note will have to be 7 years or longer.

Questions

- "SBA will allow a seller to be ballooned at 7 years (amortization can be 7 years or longer). HUD will allow seller financing (up to 50% of the amount buyer puts down— example: 20% down buyer and seller can contribute 10% each) but it MUST be a non-recourse loan, which makes it very difficult for the seller to collect if the buyer doesn't pay. If you're using SBA lending the seller note will have to be 7 years or longer."

Resources

Associations
- American Health Care Association: www.ahca.org

Office Staffing and Temporary Agencies		
SIC 7363-03	NAICS 56132	Number of Businesses/Units 32,590

Rules of Thumb
➢ 6 to12 times EBITA

Benchmark Data

Statistics (Office Staffing & Temp Agencies)

Number of Establishments	32,590
Average Profit Margin	2.5%
Revenue per Employee	$31,900
Average Number of Employees	92
Average Wages per Employee	$24,235

Source: IBISWorld, September 2012

Products and Services Segmentation

Industrial and factory staffing	26.7%
Office, clerical and administrative staffing	23.1%
Other staffing	14%
Healthcare staffing	13.9%
Information technology staffing	13%
Engineering and scientific staffing	5.4%
Accounting and financial staffing	3.9%

Source: IBISWorld, September 2012

Major Market Segmentation

Professional and business service companies	31.9%
Construction and manufacturing companies	31.8%
Education and health services companies	11.1%
Other	7.6%
Wholesale and retail companies	7.5%
Transportation, utilities and other service companies	6%
Financial companies	4.1%

Source: IBISWorld, September 2012

Industry Costs

Profit	2.5%
Wages	76.0%
Purchases	1.5%
Depreciation	1.0%
Marketing	2.0%
Rent & Utilities	8.0%
Other	9.0%

Source: IBISWorld, September 2012

Market Share

Adecco	SA 5.9%
Kelly Services Inc.	4.0%
Randstad Holding nv	4.0%
Manpower Inc.	3.3%

Source: IBISWorld, September 2012

Office Supplies and Stationery Stores

SIC 5943-01	NAICS 453210	Number of Businesses/Units 13,544

Rules of Thumb

➢ 25 percent of annual sales plus inventory

➢ 1.5 times SDE plus inventory

➢ 12 percent times EBIT

Pricing Tips

- "Check inventory levels and FF&E carefully. Owners of these types of businesses tend to hide cash flow in excessive inventory and FF&E."

Benchmark Data

Statistics (Office Supply Stores)

Number of Establishments	13,544
Average Profit Margin	1.4%
Revenue per Employee	$179.000
Average Number of Employees	8.8
Average Wages per Employee	$24,454

Source: IBISWorld, September 2012

Products and Services Segmentation

Office and school supplies	45%
Office equipment	24%
Stationery and computer paper	23%
Furniture	7.5%
Greeting cards	0.4%
Magazines and school supplies	45%

Source: IBISWorld, September 2012

Major Market Segmentation

Small businesses	28%
Households for education purposes	25%
Households for general purposes	17%
Large businesses	17%
Households for satellite work	8%
Federal, state and local government	5%

Source: IBISWorld, September 2012

Industry Costs

Profit	1.4%
Wages	13.6%
Purchases	65.3%
Depreciation	1.5%
Marketing	1.0%
Rent & Utilities	5.5%
Other	11.7%

Source: IBISWorld, September 2012

Market Share

Staples Inc.	39.2%
Office Depot Inc.	22.9%
Office Max	13.5%

Source: IBISWorld, September 2012

- "Historical sales against same store performance would be a good measurement. Adequate advertising budget (5% of gross is desirable.) Gross sales per square foot of $200/year would be good, $250/year would be very good, $300/year or more would be excellent."

	Franchise

Once Upon A Child	
Approx. Total Investment	$204,200 to $309,500

SIC 5932-05	NAICS 453310	Number of Businesses/Units 245

Rules of Thumb

➤ 20 percent of annual sales plus inventory

➤ 30 percent of annual sales includes inventory

Online Sales (See E-Commerce)

Optical Practices (See also Optical Stores)

SIC 5995-02	NAICS 446130	Number of Businesses/Units 11,500

Rules of Thumb

➤ 68 percent of annual sales plus inventory

Optical Stores (See also Optical Practices & Optometry Practices)

	NAICS 446130	Number of Businesses/Units 15,893

Rules of Thumb

➤ 50 to 60 percent of annual sales includes inventory (Sales do not include regular exam fees)

➤ 2 times SDE includes inventory (Sales do not include regular exam fees)

Pricing Tips

- "Another benchmark is 1 x SDE, plus tangible assets."
- "Adjust price up or down depending on how updated the equipment is."
- "How many days do they perform exams? For whom?"
- "Should have at least one lane (exam room). May be a finishing lab, but not a full lab. Exam fees are not included."

Expert Comments

"Very limited buyer pool; must have OD degree and state license."

"The aging population will increase the demand for eyecare."

"National chains seem to be weaker. Mom and pops seem to be hanging in there, so they may be keeping optometrists busy."

"Surgery has made the industry shrink. However many chains have contracted, giving independents some breathing room. Wal-Mart still looms."

"Industry has slowed. Big players have hurt mom-and-pop stores, however there seem to be fewer chains and the trend may be back in the small-store favor."

"Competition is stiff. Independents are getting squeezed."

Benchmark Data

Statistics (Eye Glasses & Contact Lens Stores)

Number of Establishments	15,893
Average Profit Margin	7.1%
Revenue per Employee	$122,600
Average Number of Employees	4.8%
Average Wages per Employee	28,348

Source: IBISWorld, June 2012

Products and Services Segmentation

Prescription lenses and lens treatments	28.7%
Eye examinations	17.2%
Contact lenses	13.8%
Sunglasses	7.9%
Frames	32.4%

Source: IBISWorld, June 2012

Industry Costs

Profit	7.1%
Wages	23.1%
Purchases	39.1%
Depreciation	1.6%
Marketing	7.0%
Rent & Utilities	10.0%
Other	12.1%

Source: IBISWorld, June 2012

Market Share

Luxottica Group S.p.A.	30%
Highmark Inc.	8.4%
National Vision Inc.	8.3%

Source: IBISWorld, June 2012

- "$300 average revenue per exam"
- "$250 revenue/patients is low. $500 is very good."
- "Should give exams at least one full day a week. The more days they offer exams, the better."
- "The retail optical industry in the U.S. includes about 14,000 retail stores with combined annual revenue of $7 billion, and 16,000 offices of optometrists with combined annual revenue of $6 billion. Large retailers include Cole National (Pearle Vision); Luxottica (LensCrafters); Eye Care Centers of America; U.S. Vision; and the optical divisions of mass merchants like Wal-Mart and Costco."

Source: www.findarticles.com

- "The retail industry is highly fragmented but concentrated at the top: 90 percent of companies operate a single store, but about a dozen chains operate more than 100 and account for half of industry revenue."

Source: www.findarticles.com

Expenses as a Percentage of Annual Sales

Cost of goods	35% to 45%
Payroll/labor Costs	10% to 15%
Occupancy	15% to 20%
Profit (estimated pretax)	25% to 30%

Industry Trend

- "Stable"
- "More group practices and fewer single-doctor practices"
- "Trend toward larger practices"
- "Perhaps stable. Surgery options will continue downslide."

Questions

- "Contact lens sales? Do they keep the profits from optician?"
- "Probability of staff retention. Number of active patient records."
- "Days they have exams. If only one or two, could be tough to generate sales."
- "What kind of equipment? Leased? Referral sources? Insurances accepted?"
- "How many days they have exams. Referral sources? Insurances accepted?"
  "Does he have a lab? How many lanes (exam room)? What type of finishing does he do? How many days is a doctor available for exams?"

Optometry Practices (See also Optical Stores)

SIC 5999-04	NAICS 621320	Number of Businesses/Units 37,729

Rules of Thumb

➤ 55% to 65% percent of annual revenues includes inventory

➤ 2 times SDE includes inventory

➤ 2.5 times EBIT

➤ 2 to 3 times EBITDA

Pricing Tips

- "Smaller practices under $400K in gross revenue will have more emphasis on asset values. Large practices over $1MM gross revenue and those with multiple doctors may have different value methods."
  "Another benchmark is 1 x SDE, plus tangible assets."
- "Adjust price up or down depending on how updated the equipment is."
- "How many days do they perform exams? For whom?"
- "Professional fee only offices have lower multiples"
- "Up-to-date equipment, increasing revenue, diverse patient base."
- "Smaller offices are more asset based."
- "1 times SDE plus inventory"
- "Offices without a dispensary typically have a lower multiple."
- "SDE + hard assets"
- "The intangible assets are difficult to value. Goodwill is 'the expectations of future profits under the ownership of someone other than the present owner.' According to the Internal Revenue Service, 'Goodwill is based upon earning capacity and its value, therefore it rests upon the excess of net earning over and above a fair return on net tangible assets...such factors as prestige and renown of successful operation over a prolonged period in a locality may be included in tangible value.' The American Medical Association simply defines goodwill as, 'the opportunity to take over the health care of a seller's patient base.'
  "There are 3 recognized formulas for determining the value of goodwill in an optometric practice. The first is simply calculating 25% of the last year's gross sales. The second method is calculating 25% of the average of the last 3 years' gross sales. The third method is a qualitative analysis. This is a series of value comparisons for the practice being appraised as it relates to the current market. [Such comparisons could include the factors listed below plus quality of records, office staff, etc.]"
  Source: "Optometric Practice Appraisals" by Michael Bacigalupi, OD, Assistant Professor, www.optometry.nova.edu/opep/articles
- "Sales prices range from 50% to 80% of gross or 1.5–2.25 times SDE. Variations are based on whether the office is professional fees only, specialty office or more retail oriented."
- "Optometry offices will typically sell for a multiple based on the SDE. This ranges from 1.5 to 2.25 times the SDE. This range is determined by the percentage of professional fees vs. dispensary (retail) revenue. If the practice grosses less than $300,000, then the cash flow method is not appropriate and may be valued based on assets."

Expert Comments

"Very limited buyer pool; must have OD degree and state license."

"The aging population will increase the demand for eyecare."

"National chains seem to be weaker. Mom and pops seem to be hanging in there, so they may be keeping optometrists busy."

"The chains are continuing to provide increased competition."

"Additional scope of licensing. General ophthalmic profession."

"Mom and pops may be coming back due to franchise failures."

"Depending on state, regulations may require OD or MD to own business."

"Years of experience in working with offices and in operating our own office."

"For optometry practice, must be licensed by state licensing board. Many states also require license for optical shop owners."

Benchmark Data

Statistics (Optometrists)

Number of Establishments	37,729
Average Profit Margin	27.5%
Revenue per Employee	$108,700
Average Number of Employees	3.5
Average Wages per Employee	$28,783

Source: IBISWorld, October 2012

Products and Services Segmentation

Patient care from visits and consultations	47%
Sale of optical goods	43%
Patient care from non-surgical interventions	5%
Patient care from other services	2%
Laboratory services and tests	1.5%
Patient care from surgical interventions	1.5%

Source: IBISWorld, October 2012

Industry Costs

Profit	27.5%
Wages	26.7%
Purchases	29.0%
Depreciation	2.0%
Marketing	2.0%
Rent & Utilities	7.0%
Other	5.8%

Source: IBISWorld, October 2012

- "Average optometry practice gross revenue nationwide is about $600K. Typically office show 30% adjusted net (owner benefit) before any debt service."
- "Net 30% of sales, $600,000 gross per OD."
- "Adjusted profit should be 30% with gross revenues in excess of $500,000."
- "Average revenue runs from $200 to $500 per patient. Offices focused on more retail high-end frames are higher."
- "$350 per patient"
- "Optometrists work mainly as solo practitioners or in small group practices. A typical group practice has less than $500,000 in annual revenue and four employees. About 1,000 practices have annual revenue over $1 million. Many optometrist practices include retail sales."

Source: www.findarticles.com

- "SDE is the biggest driver for buyers today."
- "Three to four staff per OD"
- "Typical benchmark for an average size office is 32% adjusted profit."
- "Incomes vary greatly, depending upon the geographic area, specialization, number of years in practice, professional reputation, and other factors. Earnings of new optometry graduates without experience range from $22,000 to $52,000 annually, while those with four to five years of experience range from $30,000 to $85,000 annually. Earnings of optometrists in private practice in major metropolitan areas can sometimes exceed $125,000 annually. Salary surveys show the average earnings for all optometrists range from $67,000

to $88,000, depending upon location and practice size. Optometrists who are employed by the state earn between $32,800 and $40,000 per year."

- "Average doctors may see a $250/per patient fee. Offices with premium eyewear selections will see a significantly higher per-patient revenue."

Expenses as a Percentage of Annual Sales

Cost of goods..30% to 35%
Payroll/labor Costs...10% to 20%
Occupancy...10% to 15%
Profit (estimated pretax) ....20% to 25%

Industry Trend

- "Trend to multi-doctor practices."
- "Flat growth"
- "Mom and Pops may be coming back."
- Excellent, increased licensure for doctors, added medical billings."
- "Continued stable growth"
- "Margins are diminishing, managed care."
- "The need for eye care services is expected to grow through 2012 in response to the vision care needs of a growing and aging population. Baby boomers will be more likely to visit optometrists because of the onset of vision trouble in middle age, including problems resulting from extensive computer use, according to the Bureau of Labor Statistics."

Source: www.aoa.org

- "Stable"
- "Over the long term, fewer single-doctor practices will be financially viable." "Additional revenue sources for optometrists as the scope of licensing is expanded (can perform more medical treatments of the eye)."

Seller Financing

- "10 years"
- "Partially seller financed with amortizations of 10 years and balloons in 3 to 5 years"

Questions

- "Contact lens sales? Do they keep the profits from optician?"
- "Probability of staff retention. Number of active patient records?"
- "Days they have exams? If only one or two, could be tough to generate sales."
- "What kind of equipment? Leased? Referral sources? Insurances accepted?"
- "How many days they have exams. Referral sources? Insurances accepted?"
- "Who are your insurance providers? Amount of frame inventory? Frame suppliers? What are your recall procedures? Number of active patient records? Type of practice management software?"
- "Get copies of fee schedule and insurance provider reports (revenue by provider)."
- "Typically this is straightforward, as both seller and buyer are doctors."

Resources

Associations

- American Optometric Association: www.aoa.org

	Franchise
Orange Julius	
Approx. Total Investment	$345,000 to $375,000

	NAICS 722211	Number of Businesses/Units 465

Rules of Thumb

➢ 32 percent of annual sales plus inventory

Resources

Websites
- www.orangejulius.com

	Franchise
Original Italian Pie	

	NAICS 722211	Number of Businesses/Units 14

Rules of Thumb

➢ 35 to 40 percent of annual sales plus inventory

Resources

Websites

www.italianpie.com

Outdoor Advertising (See Billboard Advertising Companies)

	Franchise
OXXO Care Cleaners (See also Dry Cleaning)	
Approx. Total Investment	$100,000 to $1 million

SIC 7212-01	NAICS 812320	Number of Businesses/Units 33

Rules of Thumb

➢ 65 percent of annual sales plus inventory

Resources

Websites
- www.oxxousa.com

Packaging (Industrial)	

	NAICS 561910	Number of Businesses/Units 1,926

Rules of Thumb

➢ 5 to 6 times EBIT

➢ 60 to 70 percent of annual sales plus inventory

Benchmark Data

Statistics (Packaging & Labeling Services)

Number of Establishments... 1,926
Average Profit Margin 5.3%
Revenue per Employee $195,700
Average Number of Employees 24.1
Average Wages per Employee $33,176

Source: IBISWorld, October 2012

Products and Services Segmentation

Other packaging and labeling service... 45.1%
Packaging and labeling services for retail 45.1%
Other... 7.6%
Resale of Merchandise 1.5%
Mailroom services and mailbox rentals... 0.7%

Source: IBISWorld, October 2012

Major Market Segmentation

Other retail product manufacturers 31%
Pharmaceutical companies... 23%
Retail food and cosmetics manufacturers... 22%
Other.. 15%
Government 9%

Source: IBISWorld, October 2012

Industry Costs

Profit 5.3%
Wages.. 17.1%
Purchases.. 45.0%
Depreciation... 3.4%
Marketing... 8.0%
Rent & Utilities 8.9%
Other.. 12.3%

Source: IBISWorld, October 2012

Expenses as a Percentage of Annual Sales

Cost of goods...60% to 65%
Payroll/labor Costs .... 08% to 10%
Occupancy.. 0
Profit (estimated pretax) .... 10% to 15%

Industry Trend

- "Consolidation will rule the packaging industry. Cheaper to buy than to grow Market Share in a mundane, non-innovative business, lacking pricing power and vulnerable to relocation of key accounts to offshore facilities."

Questions

- "How stable is your customer base—what is your customer retention record? What % of total sales do your top 10 accounts represent? Is there really any real 'free cash flow' in the business?"

Resources

Trade Publications

- Packaging Today: www.packagingtoday.com

Packaging and Shipping Services (See Mail and Parcel Centers)

Paint & Decorating (Wallpaper) Retailers

SIC 5231-07	NAICS 444120	Number of Businesses/Units 8,570

Rules of Thumb

➤ 20 percent of annual sales plus inventory

Pricing Tips

- "They should have nationally known brand name plus 2 competitive paint lines. A wide variety of wallpaper from lesser priced to higher priced lines should be offered. National averages tell us these stores make from 16 to 17 percent plus reasonable wages for the owner/operators. The average markup is 40 percent. These stores are sold for fixtures, equipment plus inventory at cost."

Benchmark Data

Statistics (Paint Stores)

Number of Establishments	8,570
Average Profit Margin	1.9%
Revenue per Employee	$253,300
Average Number of Employees	4
Average Wages per Employee	$42,858

Source: IBISWorld, April 2012

Products and Services Segmentation

Interior paint	39%
Exterior paint	22%
Stains, varnishes and other coatings	14%
Painting equipment and supplies	12%
Wallpaper and other flexible wall coverings	10%
Other merchandise	3%

Source: IBISWorld, April 2012

Major Market Segmentation

Professional contractors	57%
Do-it-yourself customers	22%
Do-it-for-me customers	18%
Other	3%

Source: IBISWorld, April 2012

Industry Costs

Profit	1.9%
Wages	16.6%
Purchases	64.3%
Depreciation	1.0%
Marketing	1.2%
Rent & Utilities	3.1%
Other	11.9%

Source: IBISWorld, April 2012

Market Share

The Sherwin-Williams Company	60.2%

Source: IBISWorld, April 2012

Industry Trend

- "Oscar Gonzalez dreamed of starting a paint company in the United States but decided that the established way of operating was too drab, so, he's opened his first Internet-based paint company, ThePaintDrop.com, in San Antonio with a decided twist. The customer does not have to go to the store or even know the exact color.

  "The store, in the form of a delivery truck filled with Benjamin Moore paints and pigments and with mixing equipment in the back, will go to the customer and help him or her choose the best option at the home. The company also handles commercial projects. 'It's the evolution of purchasing things,' said Gonzalez, president and founder. 'It's like taking your room to the paint store.'"

  Source: "Paint store at your door" by William Pack, www.mysanantonio.com May 3, 2011

Resources

Associations

- Paint and Decorating Retailers Association (PDRA): www.pdra.org

		Franchise
Pak Mail (See Mail & Parcel Centers)		
Approx. Total Investment		$135,000 to $166,000
	NAICS 561431	Number of Businesses/Units 430

Rules of Thumb

➢ 50 percent of annual sales plus inventory

Resources

Websites

- www.pakmail.com

		Franchise
Panera Bread		
Approx. Total Investment		Net Worth of $7.5 million
Estimated Annual Sales/Unit		$2,200,000
	NAICS 722211	Number of Businesses/Units 1,250

Rules of Thumb

➢ 35 to 40 percent of sales plus inventory

Industry Trend

- "Drive-thru expansion: Panera plans to add drive-thrus to about 80 new or retrofitted stores this year. The company ended 2011 with 119 drive-thrus.

  "Catering: Catering sales grew 25 percent in the first quarter on top of 26-percent growth in the first quarter of 2011, Moreton said. The company is working on targeted marketing efforts in catering, he added.

  Source: "Panera co-CEOs Ron Shaich and Bill Moreton outline company plans" by Ron Ruggless, nrn.com/article/panera, April 25, 2012

Resources

Websites
- www.panerabread.com

Franchise

Papa John's Pizza (See also Pizza Shops)	
Approx. Total Investment	$115,823 to $549,523
Estimated Annual Sales/Unit	$745,000

	NAICS 5812-22	Number of Businesses/Units 4,490

Rules of Thumb
➢ 38% to 40% of annual sales

Benchmark Data
- See Pizza Shops

Resources

Websites
- wwwpapajohns.com

Franchise

Papa Murphy's Take 'N' Bake Pizza (See also Pizza Shops, etc.)	
Approx. Total Investment	Minimum net worth $250,000
Estimated Annual Sales/Unit	$550,000

	NAICS 722211	Number of Businesses/Units 1,100

Rules of Thumb
➢ 35 to 40 percent of annual sales plus inventory

Benchmark Data
- See Pizza Shops

Resources

Websites
- www.papamurphys.com

Franchise

Parcel Plus	
Approx. Total Investment	$206,720 to $245,795

	NAICS 488991	Number of Businesses/Units 59

Rules of Thumb
➢ 25 percent of annual sales plus inventory

Resources

Websites
- www.parcelplus.com

Parking Lot Sweeping		
SIC 1611-04	NAICS 561790	Number of Businesses/Units 12,000

Rules of Thumb

➤ 60 to 70 percent of annual sales includes inventory

➤ 3 to 4 times SDE includes inventory

➤ 5 to 5.5 times EBIT

➤ 5 to 6 times EBITDA

Pricing Tips

- "Some value factors are..... Types of accounts? Large box stores, nat'l shopping centers, small strips, construction, colleges, corp....? The stronger the account base with good contracts ....the higher the value. Condition of equipment, quality of labor force and quality of service to the accounts separate the top companies from the rest."

- "Most of the time, prospective buyers for a sweeping company will primarily look at two factors, your sweeping equipment and your accounts. For the former, that's when you'll want to have preventative and scheduled maintenance documents on each piece of equipment available. If you know you're putting your business onto the market, you may even want to go through your sweepers and improve their cosmetics, installing items like seat covers and floor mats. These are low-cost items that provide a better overall impression to prospective buyers. It's best if you have all safety and normal operational items working, as well.

  "When it comes to your contracts, savvy buyers will want to look at several areas of your accounts. Although quantity and margin are important, their perception of the quality of your accounts is perhaps even more so. This includes such factors as longevity on the books, ease of cancellation, whether or not escalation clauses are in the contract and more. For example, if all of your contracts allow for a 30-day, 'no reason required' cancellation by the customer, your business won't be worth as much when you want to sell it.

  "In most buy/sell transactions, at least for sweeping businesses that have been operational for a number of years, 'goodwill' is also a factor. The seller typically wants money to compensate for having developed the business to its current state. As a buyer, your goal is to keep this amount to a minimum.

  "'Everyone wants lots of money for the business they've put however many years of blood, sweat and tears into,' said Presutti. The reality, however, is often different.

  "That will often become apparent when, as a buyer, you sit down with the owner and go through the actual current valuations of both contracts and depreciated equipment. This is central to the negotiation process.

  "Since most business owners plan ahead to sell, the machinery has typically not been replaced recently. Contracts usually have a 30-day cancellation clause where the customer can cancel for no reason. You have to ask yourself what that type of contract is really worth to you. 'In my view, giving more than 60 days of revenue to such an account is really a crapshoot.'"

Source: "Operate Your Business With a Resale in Mind" by Jay Presutti and Ranger Kidwell-Ross, October 2005, http://www.worldsweeper.com/ This is a very informative site and should be visited by anyone who has an interest in this business. Don't let the date fool you, still excellent information.

Expert Comments

"Some regional consolidation occurring, but mostly smaller local companies still exist."

"This industry has been unable to support national or regional consolidation. Mostly local, statewide, or small regional players."

Benchmark Data

- "$125K/employee or $150–$200K/driver"
- "Very generally speaking, using 2005 prices, it is not uncommon for a contractor with a smaller parking area sweeper, such as a three-yard-capacity sweeper on a 1-ton chassis, to be able to charge between $55 and $65 per hour, for a gross earnings of between $9,000 and $11,000 per month.

  "For a larger sweeper, one which is suitable for performing a variety of duties other than parking lot cleanup, the same rule of thumb is a charge of between $65 and $75 per hour; this should net you a gross of between $11,000 and $14,000 per month. Street sweeping pricing should be about $90, since it is harder on your equipment, and the sweepers cost substantially more.

  "Again, these are simply generalizations, and actual earnings are quite dependent upon work performed, charges in your area, etc. They are definitely, however, numbers which have been attained by many in the industry who have worked hard at developing their businesses."

Source: Schwarze Industries, Inc. Although this information is dated, it is still interesting.

Expenses as a Percentage of Annual Sales

Cost of goods	20%
Payroll/labor Costs	15%
Occupancy	05%
Profit (estimated pretax)	10% to 12%

Questions

- "Must establish the quality of the accounts, condition of equipment, review contracts, examine labor force, etc. Is the owner tied to any special interests, people or other connections responsible for a significant portion of his company's business? If so how will this affect these accounts/sites? Future growth in a local area or region? Competition?"

Resources

Websites

- www.worldsweeper.com

Associations

- North American Power Sweeping Association (NAPSA) :
  www.powersweepping.org

Parking Lots and Garages	
NAICS 812930	Number of Businesses/Units 19,246

Rules of Thumb

➤ "[In some cities] they have been selling for 1.5 times their annual net before taxes, plus the value of fixtures, equipment and inventory at cost—plus real estate."

Benchmark Data

Statistics (Parking Lots and Garages)

Number of Establishments	19,246
Average Profit Margin	17%
Revenue per Employee	$66,400
Average Number of Employees	7.2
Average Wages per Employee	$17,268

Source: IBISWorld, April 2012

Products and Services Segmentation

Parking facility management	54%
Valet service	20%
Parking meter enforcement	16%
Billing and collection	5%
Parking consulting services	5%

Source: IBISWorld, April 2012

Major Market Segmentation

Daily commuters	50%
Corporate drivers	25%
Leisure drivers	20%
Government drivers	5%

Source: IBISWorld, April 2012

Industry Costs

Profit	17.0%
Wages	26.2%
Purchases	3.5%
Depreciation	1.9%
Rent & Utilities	48.4%
Other	3.0%

Source: IBISWorld, April 2012

Market Share

Central Parking Corporation	32.3%
Standard Parking	8.0%
ABM Industries Inc.	6.7%

Source: IBISWorld, April 2012

- "Total parking revenues grew in 2010 for several sectors including college/ university and municipal operators, while hotels remained stable and CBD, hotel, and on-and off-airport facilities declined. Not all operators are reporting the same results: for example CBD operators generally report the same revenues (27%), a slight (22%), or substantial decrease (18%), or a slight increase (25%).

"Average CBD 12-hour daily parking rates in 2010 were $15.92 and $8.48 for the most and least expensive rates in the respondent's metro area, while early bird averages were $10.99 and$6.47. The maximum 12-hour rate decreased from the last study, but the other rates represent slight increase. Average CBD monthly rates were $169 and $91 for unreserved and $240 and $148 for reserved most and least expensive rates.

"Average CBD municipal hourly rates were $0.88.

"Average overnight hotel rates in 2010 were $23.71 and $16.13 for self-park and $30.44 and $24.60 for valet (most and least expensive), all increases over 2009 averages.

"Average daily hospital patient/visitor rates were $8.61 and $5.72 for self-park and $7.68 and $5.85 for valet.

"Average educational facility rates per student per semester were $203 and $120, and per year were $481 and $235, while average faulty rates per year were $581 and $250 (most and least expensive).

"Average first hour on-airport rates were $2.92 (long term), $2.80 (short term), and $2.67 (economy) for self-park and $12.07, $13.03, and $4.50 for valet. All hourly self-park rates declined from 2009.

"Average off-airport 24 hour rates were $11.46 and $9.84 for self-park and $15.62 and $13.70 for valet while weekly rates were $75 and $65 for self-park and $92 and $77 for valet. These are sharp declines from average 2009 rates."

Source: "2010 Parking in America," National Parking Association. An excellent site!

- "2009/Latest FY Revenue (millions)

"The average revenue by city/metro area by type of parking facility was $8.35 million for CBD operators, municipal ($2.86 million), hotel ($7.94 million), hospital ($3.1 million), college/university ($4.99 million), off airport ($12.86 million), and on airport ($23.33 million)."

On airport	$23,334
Off airport	$12,865
CBD	$8,351
Hotel	$7,941
Coll/University	$4,998
Hospital	$3,137
Municipal	$2,863

"Revenue per space

"CBDs report average revenue per space of $1,510. These figures are lower among municipal respondents ($1,249), hospitals ($1,331), and colleges/universities ($635). Hotels report the highest revenue per space of $3,098, while off-airport ($2,254) and on-airport facilities ($2,483) report higher revenue per space.

"Average Total Spaces per Facility/Operation

"CBDs report managing an average of 6,836 in the metropolitan area. This is considerably higher than the number reported by off airports (4,977), hospitals (2,704), municipal operators (2,159), and hotels (1,597). Only colleges/universities (8,938) and on-airport facilities (8,184) are larger.

"City/Metro Area Overall Change in Parking Revenues in the Past Year

"Operators are split in terms of the recent direction of their total revenues. For example, 32% of CBD operators report an increase, while 40% report a decrease.

"Municipal operators fared much better, with 46% reporting an increase and 23% a decrease.

"Airport facilities show similar patterns: 30% of on-airport operators report increases and 56% decreases; 40% of off-airport operators report increases and 44% decreases.

Most college/university operators (66%) report an increase, and only 16% a decrease.

"Hospitals remained largely unchanged, with 30% reporting an increase, 19% a decrease, and 51% staying the same. Hotels were also relatively stagnant: 28% reported an increase and 35% a decrease."

Source: "2010 Parking in America," National Parking Association. An excellent site!

Industry Trend

- "Improved traffic management: Traffic flow is enhanced through wireless sensing devices indicating space availability in parking facilities as well as with mapping devices in cars that show parking locations.

  "Parking access control: License plate recognition (LPR) uses specialized cameras and software to recognize license plates, capture tag images, and transform the characters into a data stream. Municipalities, universities, airports, medical centers, military bases and other sectors use LPR to confirm authorized vehicle access to parking facilities.

  "E-payment: The parking industry is moving away from cash payment to e-payment. Increasingly, parking operations accommodate credit cards and even cell phones that access e-payment accounts or possess credit card capability with an electronic chip on the subscriber identity module (SIM) card.

  "Recharging stations for electric vehicles: As the number of electric vehicles is expected to grow, parking areas are installing recharging stations.

  "Integration of parking with planning: Parking operators are increasingly recognized as able to bring specialized expertise to urban improvement projects and economic redevelopment. They need to have a seat at the table with architects, engineers, developers, and planning officials."

  Source: "Emerging Trends in Parking," The International Parking Institute, www.parking.org June 2012

- "It's a reflection of the economic times that parking professionals cited increased demand for finding ways to increase parking revenues as the top trend impacting the parking industry. Cash -strapped cities and states are demanding that parking revenues—which traditionally were re-invested in parking and transportation related maintenance and services—are now being diverted to fund other non-parking related services.

  "Demand for green and sustainable parking solutions is the second leading trend, cited by more than one-third (36%) of respondents. In a related concern, 19% specifically identify the need to accommodate electric cars and provide charging stations in the near future.

  "The survey identifies a very strong trend toward technological solutions. Large numbers of professionals see increased demand for cashless or electronic payment (32%). More than one-quarter anticipate increased use of cell phones to find, reserve, or pay for parking (27%). A similar number see a move toward innovative technologies to improve access control (24%).

  "Typical operational issues such as customer service and security appear prominently on the list. Different models such as public-private partnerships and alternative uses of the facility during off-peak hours also emerge as trends."

- "Technology is the next big thing in parking. Professionals offer many specific visions of the coming technology, whether it is smart phone apps, cashless parking, automatic vehicle identification, or simply a continued push to integrate and expand technology to make both operations and traffic flow more efficient. When you add it all up, nearly half of all respondents mention one of these technological solutions as the next big thing in parking.

  "Sustainability and green initiatives are the next big thing and will bring more energy-efficient plug-ins for electric vehicles and accommodations for alternative fuel vehicles.

  "Nearly one-fifth mention revenue-producing measures, new pricing models, or alternatives like public-private partnerships. Parking professionals are also paying significant attention to changes in parking demand, whether brought about through transportation demand management to relieve stress on facility capacity, or through consumers' shifting to alternatives such as mass transit."

  Source: International Parking Institute, 2011

Resources

Associations

- National Parking Association: www.npapark.org
- International Parking Institute : www.parking.org

Pawn Shops (See also Used Goods)		
SIC 5932-29	NAICS 522298	Number of Businesses/Units 11,403

Rules of Thumb

➤ 3 times SDE includes inventory

➤ 3 to 5 times EBIT

➤ 3.5 times EBITDA

➤ 40 to 70 percent of annual sales plus inventory. Since money is loaned using items of value belonging to the customer and said items serve as collateral for the loan, inventory against money loaned has to be taken into account.

Pricing Tips

- "Quality of inventory is very important. Stores with lots of unwanted "junk" will not be of interest to educated pawn buyers. Need to understand pawn renewal rate, average loan, do they buy gold and at what rate."
- "Years in business, quality of pawn balance, and quality of inventory are very important."
- "A very large factor for selling pawn shops is what we call 'money on the street.' Some owners feel as though they should be able to collect 1–3 months' interest on this. It can be considered A/R, but keep in mind the national average is that 75% of this will be collected at anywhere from 200% to 300% APR. Yes, you read that right."

Expert Comments

"Economic factors have created an environment where many individuals do not have access to credit other than pawn shops or other sub-prime lenders. This trend will continue for the next 1 to 3 years at a minimum."

"Risk is actually very low IF you make educated loans on a daily basis. There are many factors that weigh in on this and typically 'EDUCATION' in this field comes from 'learning the hard way,' but several large chains have been very successful in training personnel quickly to run shops successfully."

"Some people use a necklace like others would a Visa card. You just use it continuously to get loans as you need them."

Source: "Off the Skids" by Rob Walker," *Boston Globe Sunday Magazine*

Benchmark Data

Statistics (Pawn Shops)

Number of Establishments	11,403
Average Profit Margin	17.5%
Revenue per Employee	$228,600
Average Number of Employees	2
Average Wages per Employee	$30,232

Source: IBISWorld, September 2011

Products and Services Segmentation

Merchandise sales 58%
Secured loans for personal collateral 42%

Source: IBISWorld, September 2011

Industry Costs

Profit 17.5%
Rent 1.5%
Utilities 1.0%
Depreciation... 3.0%
Other... 19.8%
Wages... 13.2%
Purchases 44.0%

Source: IBISWorld, September 2011

Market Share

Cash America International, Inc. 11.2%
EZCORP, Inc.. 6.5%

Source: IBISWorld, September 2011

- For additional Benchmark data see Used Goods
- "The National Pawnbrokers Association reports that there are over 30 million pawn store customers per year and they appreciate this unique form of credit and tend to borrow only what they need, as evidenced by the relatively low national average loan amount of $80. NPA President and pawn shop owner Dave Crume says, 'Pawn customers repay their loans and redeem their collateral at a correspondingly high average national redemption rate of 80 percent. These parameters appear to be holding constant, despite the current economy."
- "Most of the 13,000+ pawn stores in the US are small, privately owned businesses and do not report their earnings publicly."

Source: "Pawn Shops: Economic Barometer?," National Pawnbrokers Association, www.pawnshoptoday.com

- "Typically when a shop has $100,000 'on the street,' the shop becomes very very profitable and easier to sell."
- "As a rule of thumb, over 80% of a pawn shop loan base will come from within an 8 mile radius of the location. Therefore, in your business plan it is important to spell out your estimated default rate on your loan base (usually around 25%) and your estimated effective yield on your income producing loans. This makes it much easier to sell the idea to your investor on borrowing cash from him at 10% per year and loaning it out to your customers at a return of 10% per month."

Source: Cloud Ten, Inc., a leading pawn shop consulting firm, www.startapawnshop.com, this appeared on the Web site of the National Pawnbrokers Association, a very informative site

- "The rise of the Internet allows employees to quickly determine what an item being pawned is worth—a skill that once took years to develop."

Source: "Left Behind: Pawn Shop Franchise Has Right Economy" by Matt Bolch, *Franchise Times*,

- "Our business is simple: We are in the loan and storage business. The cost of making a $100 loan can best be explained by using current Georgia pawn laws in effect. We currently charge 2% interest and 23% storage fee or $25.00 total. The following is an analysis of what it costs to make the $100.00 loan: To meet the State of Georgia and city and county requirements, we must execute a full disclosure loan contract. Then we must describe the content in full detail, including serial numbers, etc. Then the customer must submit a fingerprint and affix it to the contract. Then the information must be transferred in full detail to a list that is furnished each day to the local and state law enforcement. A small percentage of the loans are lost to claims by law enforcement or others who have legal ownership of the item used as collateral for the loan. In most cases this is a total loss to the pawn shop owner. Pawn shops are required by law and 3000 years of history to keep the item in storage that we make loans on. A good example is a $300 loan recently made on a riding lawn mower for a customer who has a small yard-service business to repair his truck. We were his only hope to keep his business going. Now a 400+ pound lawn mower has to be stored. To understand the cost, if you as an individual stored this large lawn mower at a mini warehouse complex, it would cost $42.00 per month for a 5' x 10.' One of our largest expenses is the safe and secure storage of all items that are used for collateral. We also have insurance to cover the value of the items against fire, theft or loss. We have 26 employees who average over 12 years each as employees at a cost average of $21.00 per hour each for whom we furnish health insurance (included is a copy of June 2009 bill in the amount of $3740.99.) Add rent, utilities, all related expenses, federal payroll taxes, state taxes and occupation tax, and out of the $25.00 charged on the $100.00 loan we showed a taxable profit of +/- $6.79. Our statistics show that 79% of our 30-day loans are repaid on or before the 30 days. The remaining 21% include outright purchases that customers wanted to sell, however, under state law they must be shown as pawn loans so reports, fingerprints, police reports are properly executed, etc. Less than 10% of our loans are extended over the original 30-day period. The idea of someone making a 30-day $100 loan for $3.00 (36% APR) is a noble idea but an impossible reality."

Source: An open letter to U.S. Senator Durbin, Reference Senate Bill 500 and H.R. 1608 from a pawn shop owner, from a blog in www.pawnshopstoday.com—a very informative site with some fascinating material.

- "Pawn shops are a combination of a friendly loan office and a retail store selling goods at rock-bottom prices. Where else can you get a loan of less than $225 at 13.3% interest for four months—and with a 10-day grace period? Interest rates for larger loans are comparable to high-interest credit cards. A typical loan is in the $40 to $60 range, made on jewelry and intended to tide the borrower over for a short period. The typical patron is a white woman, under 30 years old, and a repeat shopper. Customers are most likely to come back for their jewelry and TVs or VCRs, and are least likely to get their clarinets, keyboards or skis out of hock."

  Source: "The New Pawn Shop" by John Erhlich, www.Psychologytoday.com from Sussex Publishers

- "A typical loan is small, averaging $75 to $100. The interest rate charged by a pawnbroker is controlled by the state and varies widely across the nation. The pawnbroker is also required to hold the merchandise for a specific period of time, giving the borrower time to repay the loan. This hold period also varies widely but is typically in the 60 to 90 day time frame.
  "On average, about 80 percent of all loans are repaid. Repeat customers make up most of the business, similar to any other lending or retail establishment.

- "Less than half of one percent of all loans are identified as stolen goods. Thieves and robbers are a pawnbroker's worst enemy.
  "What is the difference between buying at a pawnshop and buying at a retail store? Mainly price. If you go to a pawnbroker, gold can be found for about 40 percent less than at retail outlets, and other products are usually 30 to 50 percent less.
  "Since 15 to 20 percent of a pawnbroker's customers elect not to repay their loans, they are forced to turn 'bad debt' into a retail center to recover their costs."

  Source: National Pawnbrokers Association, www.nationalpawnbrokers.org

Expenses as a Percentage of Annual Sales

Cost of goods	62%
Payroll/labor Costs	09%
Occupancy	04%
Profit (estimated pretax)	18%

Industry Trend

- "Maybe it's the original artwork displayed around the office or the soft lighting, paneled walls, Persian rugs and leather furniture. The receptionist adds to the aura, too. So does the TV screen turned to a financial-news channel. Whatever the reason, Biltmore Loan and Jewelry feels more like a stock brokerage or private-banking office than a pawn shop.

  "'We're seeing an increase in these kind of stores in Beverly Hills and other affluent neighborhoods,' said Emmett Murphy, a spokesman for the National Pawnbrokers Association. 'People in all walks of life are in need of short-term credit.'"

  Source: "Pawn Shops Go Upscale for Affluent Clients," *USA Today*, July 17, 2012

- "Most of the 13,000+ pawn stores in the U.S. are small, privately owned businesses and do not report their earnings publicly."

- "Trend is more competition and a steady customer base."

- "The pawn business model is diverse, including retail, jewelry sales and pawn loans. While one element of the pawn business may thrive in a slow economy, such as pawn loans, other elements such as retail sales, will decrease. Dave Crume notes, 'While many of our association members are making it through the dip in the economy, there are many pawn shops in the U.S. that are struggling and closing. Just like all sectors of the American economy, the pawn industry is challenged by the recent economy, the pawn industry is challenged by the recent economic trends.'"

  Source: www.pawnshopstoday.com

Questions

- "What type of software do you use to track pawn receivables and inventory? How do you value pawned items? What is the quality of your pawn receivable? How do you measure and track bad inventory? What are the state laws regarding pawn shops, gun sales, and interest rates on loans?"

- "Do you have a good POS program and do you use it correctly? How is your accounting done? What type of software and is all income recorded?"

Resources

Associations

- National Pawnbrokers Association: www.nationalpawnbrokers.org

---

Payday Loans (See also Check Cashing Services)	
NAICS 522291	Number of Businesses/Units 17,525

Rules of Thumb

➤ 70 percent of annual sales

Benchmark Data

Statistics (Check Cashing & Payday Loan Services)

Number of Establishments	17,525
Average Profit Margin	16.6%
Revenue per Employee	$105,000
Average Number of Employees	6
Average Wages per Employee	$20,853

Source: IBISWorld, May 2012

Products and Services Segmentation

Consumer loans	64%
Check cashing	36%

Source: IBISWorld, May 2012

Industry Costs

Profit	16.6%
Wages	20.1%
Depreciation	2.0%
Marketing	6.6%
Rent & Utilities	4.1%
Other	50.6%

Source: IBISWorld, May 2012

Market Share

DFC Global Corp	5.9%

Source: IBISWorld, May 2012

- "Pew Charitable Trusts has released a new report, 'Payday Lending in America: Who Borrows, Where they Borrow, and Why.' In it, the organization calculates that U.S. consumers spend $7.4 billion annually on payday loans, forking out interest at an average of $520 per borrower for eight $375 loans or extensions. Payday loans often are considered a 'last resort,' but a majority of short-term borrowers cited several alternatives they would use if payday loans become unavailable. Nick Bourke, project director for Pew's Safe Small-Dollar Loan Research Project, notes that while payday loan regulations have effectively curtailed storefront operations, they have not prompted consumers to seek such loans online. 'In states that restrict storefront lending, 95 percent of would-be borrowers have elected not to use payday loans at all. Just five percent went online or elsewhere,' he reports. Pew's survey about payday borrowing found that most users are employed, white, female, and 25 to 44 years old. A disproportionate amount of consumers who use payday loan products, however, lack a four-year college degree, are home renters, are African American, earn less than $50,000 annually, and are separated or divorced. Pew also discovered that most consumers use payday loans for everyday living expenses— including shelter and utilities—rather than for emergencies."

  Source: "Nationwide Pew Survey Challenges Conventional Wisdom on Payday Loans," MarketWatch, July 18, 2012

- "Among the findings of the Ernst & Young study:
  - ✓ The average revenue for multi-line payday advance lenders for every $100 loaned is $15.26. At the same time, the store-weighted average cost to lenders equaled $13.89 for every $100 loaned.
  - ✓ On a pre-tax and pre-interest basis, multi-line payday advance lenders earn an average profit of $1.37 per $100 of loan principal issued—that represents a modest margin of 9.1% before taxes.
  - ✓ There are no collateral requirements for a payday loan, so lenders in this

industry face a much greater risk than lenders offering loans requiring some form of collateral. According to the Ernst & Young report, the store-weighted average bad debt costs equaled $3.74 per $100 loaned, or 26.9% of the total cost of each loan issued.

"The following chart breaks down these costs and illustrates them in relation to the revenue and pretax profit generated from the typical payday loan.

"Revenue, cost, and pretax profit for the average payday advance of the E&Y survey

Payday advance revenue, cost and profit (pre-tax basis)
Store-Weighted Average Per $100 Loan

Revenue	$15.26
Operating cost	$9.41
Cost of Loan Capital	$0.07
Cost of Supplementary Capital	$0.67
Bad Debt Cost	$3.74
Loan Cost	$13.89
Profit (pretax)	$1.37

Source: Ernst & Young." National Study Confirms Pricing of Payday Loans is Fair and Reasonable," October 13, 2009

- "For the payday lending industry, and as previously discussed, smaller loans cost more to originate than larger ones on a cost-per-dollar basis. This is because lenders, regardless of their structure, incur fixed costs in originating a loan, whatever its size. In the case of payday lending, these costs include:
  - ✓ Defaults on extensions of unsecured credit to borrowers of moderate means;
  - ✓ Operating costs, such as salaries, facilities, processing applications, and collection of payments;
  - ✓ Taxes; and
  - ✓ Return on investment capital.

"Available data on defaults suggest that unpaid obligations to payday lenders amount to about 10 to 20 percent of the finance charges they levy over the course of a year.

"The operating costs, which represent the largest part by far, are fixed and are not affected by the loan amount. While the fixed costs of facilitating a $200 loan are not substantially different from those likely to be incurred to facilitate and place a $20,000 home equity loan or $5,000 cash advance on a credit card, actual labor costs associated with servicing payday loans are higher.

"Within the parameters of the marketing proposition—i.e., a quick, convenient loan, as an alternative to credit card borrowing—payday lenders can be expected to do as much as they can to ensure that the risk of default is low.

"For example, payday lenders require borrowers to produce proof of a checking account, identification and a pay-stub; some lenders screen for histories of bounced checks.

"For payday loans—as for other unsecured, subprime loans—the costs relating to collection of payments is significant. Our reading of Prof. Caskey's analysis suggests that payday lenders are exceptionally close to their borrowers.

"Payday loans are generally originated and serviced by local loan offices."

Source: www.CIFA.net, Community Financial Services Association of America. This is a very informative site.

Industry Trend

- "Online payday lenders throughout the country are increasing political contributions, retaining lobbyists, and rallying Congress to transfer oversight of the industry from states to the U.S. Office of the Comptroller of the Currency

(OCC). Peter Barden, a spokesman for the Online Lenders Alliance, said the $11 billion online loan industry is also working on shedding the 'payday lenders' label. A memo to lenders advised them to refer to the loans as 'short term' and 'small-dollar' loans when lobbyists visit the Hill."

Source: "Payday Lenders Seek U.S. Oversight to Avoid State Rules," *Bloomberg* July 24, 2012

Resources

Associations
- Community Financial Services of America: www.cfsa.net

Personnel Staffing Agencies

(See also Office Staffing & Temporary Agencies, & Staffing Services)

	NAICS 561310	

Rules of Thumb

➤ .75 times annual sales; includes equipment

Resources

Associations
- American Staffing Association: www.staffingtoday.net

Pest Control

SIC 7342:01	NAICS 561710	Number of Businesses/Units 24,878

Rules of Thumb

➤ 90 percent of annual sales includes inventory

➤ 4 times SDE plus inventory

➤ 4 times EBIT

➤ 5 times EBITDA

Pricing Tips
- "Length of time in business, methods used in treating, % of profit on total sales (higher =more value), annual contracts add value, increased sales each year adds value, no tax liens or other liens, good reputation with competitors and customers add value."
- "It is all about transferring profit from one company to the other. Profit being 10 to 45% how much is transferable to the new owner? The more transferable, the higher the price."
- "It's not as easy as putting a percentage to a business or simply using a multiple of EBIT. Each business is different. It is more than likely a sum of the various positives and negatives of the business. A first class, growing, well established business with good books, good cash flow, newer vehicles, and long- time employees will bring a better price than one without these attributes."
  "Profitability must be transferred to new owner."

- "The following was asked by Frank Andorka, Editorial Director of PMP Buzz Online eNewsletter: 'What criteria do you use to determine whether a company is a good acquisition target?'
    - ✓ "Stephen Good, Terminix International: 'We look at a high percentage of recurring revenues versus one-time revenues. We also look at a company's pricing relative to Terminix's pricing. Finally, we look at how a company may augment our geographic penetration and enhance our competitive position in a market or given region.'
    - ✓ "Kevin Burns, Arrow Exterminators: 'At Arrow, we typically consider the transaction more of a merger than an acquisition, as the integration phase is really a merger of employees and customers into the Arrow family. We pay particular attention to the owners and the culture of the company they have created over the years with their employees and the customer service they perform. We look at top-line revenue and revenue growth over the past three years, the mix of business, the service schedule, the mix of commercial vs. residential, detailed expenses and of course, net income. We consider the return on investment in the first year and each year thereafter based on typical revenue growth and net profit we've experienced at Arrow.'
    - ✓ "Victor Hamel, Rentokil North America: 'The most critical criteria for us is the cultural fit. This is most important for sellers as well. It is critically important that we share the same values.'
    - ✓ "Bob Hines, Orkin: 'The initial answers are reputation and length of time in the industry, size of the company and type of services rendered. There are times where we have left a company as a stand-alone, but had it assigned to one of our regions. We would do this with a large, well-run, multimillion dollar company that has a good reputation in an area. It wouldn't make sense to drop those key assets—the name and reputation.'"

    Source: "Online Exclusive: Meet You on the Other Side," PMP Buzz Online eNewsletter

- "Range .60 to 1.15 times sales, as high as 1.5 annual sales for commercial pest control."
- "Pricing is based on recurring contractual revenue. Pest control companies generally sell for about 100% of recurring sales and between 20% and 50% of nonrecurring sales. SDE is generally not applicable to pest control companies, rather, use EBITDA. A company with a high degree of contractual recurring revenue will sell for the closer to 5 or 6 times EBITDA, whereas a company with a low proportion of contractual recurring revenue will sell for the low end of the range of 2 to 3 times EBITDA."
- "Profit on most pest control companies with 3 or more employees = 30%. $1 million to $5 million profit = 18 to 25%. One-man pest control ($100K volume) profit = 85%."
- "One-person pest control companies normally sell for approximately 1.25 times cash flow (SDE). One-man operations usually sell for 75% of annual sales. A good one-man route sells for close to one year's annual sales. Larger businesses normally sell for 2 to 3 times SDE as in most service businesses."
- "Normally no more than 1 year's gross sales for a good business. However, Terminix is paying in excess of 1.5 times gross on a pest control business (w/no termites). 1.5 times cash flow is another figure often used, based on monthly accounts with charges of $25 to $32 for average residential. Annual contracts might go for as high as 2 times cash flow."
- "$1 to $5 million in annual sales should make 18% to 22%."
- "Profit is the main determining factor. Size of business is a determining factor. Potential for expansion is a determining factor. Time in business is a

determining factor; the transfer of the seller's profit to the buyer's profit is a determining factor."

- "Pest control with contracts—most valuable; Termite renewals—2nd; Lawn & ornamentals with contracts—3rd; Fumigation value = equipment value only."
- "In Arizona it's what the market will allow. With Terminix, Orkin and other large companies aggressively pursuing the industry, prices presently are high."
- "Price depends on profit, efficiency, category, location—volume is a big factor. Most buyers prefer to buy pest control as opposed to termite. Some companies in the South do exclusively lawn & ornamental."

Expert Comments

"There are more buyers than sellers. Have to train for three years in most productive states. Demand is extremely high and the supply is extremely low."

"Location and facilities are not important in this industry as long as they meet the needs of the business. Customers rarely visit the business."

"Have to be licensed; SBA will not loan to a non-licensed pest control business buyer. .All states require a license and apprenticeship 1 to 3 years".

"License takes from 1 to 3 years to obtain. You must study and pass a test after putting the time in. You must know the state guidelines and how to identify and treat insects."

"There is a high degree of competition in the industry and the barriers to entry are low, except for the fact that it requires a license to perform pest control work."

Benchmark Data

Statistics (Pest Control)

Number of Establishments	24,878
Average Profit Margin	7.9%
Revenue per Employee	$106,500
Average Number of Employees	4.6
Average Wages per Employee	$36,200

Source: IBISWorld, April 2012

Products and Services Segmentation

Termite control	41.5%
Bed bug control	15.7%
Roach control	15.3%
Rodent control	8.1%
Other services	6.6%
Ant control	6.1%
Mosquito and flying insect control	4.0%
Bird and other wildlife removed	2.7%

Source: IBISWorld, April 2012

Major Market Segmentation

Residential home	65.6%
Commercial establishments	31.8%
Government institutions	2.6%

Source: IBISWorld, April 2012

Industry Costs

Profit	7.9%
Wages	34.6%
Purchases	21.3%
Depreciation	2.7%
Marketing	2.4%
Rent & Utilities	2.8%
Other	28.3%

Source: IBISWorld, April 2012

Market Share

Service Master	10.9%
Rollins Inc.	10.1%

Source: IBISWorld, September 2012

- "Companies over $1 million profit should be 18 to 24 percent of annual volume."
- "Production per employee minimum $100K up to $150K."

Expenses as a Percentage of Annual Sales

Cost of goods	10% to 15%
Payroll/labor Costs	25% to 30%
Occupancy	n/a
Profit (estimated pretax)	20% to 30%

Industry Trend

"Increasing, and major companies buying smaller companies."

Seller Financing

- "Financing is directly related to the profits of the business. The buyer needs to feed his family and pay the debt service. When the seller is willing to finance a portion of the sale, it is normally between 3 to 7 years."
- "40% down financed 2 to 5 years depending on size."
- 3-5 years

Questions

- "Why are you getting out of the business? What is your employee turn over rate? Have you paid all of you federal and state taxes and can you prove it."
- "Like most businesses, a quality company sells for more. New equipment, good books and records, and a high profit margin make a business worth more. Repeat commercial accounts also affect the bottom line positively when pricing a business."
- "Breakdown of services: commercial versus residential; general pest versus wood destroying."

Resources

Websites

- This is the Website of Al Woodward, a specialist in the pest control brokerage business; the site is informative and interesting: www.servicebusinessconsulting.com/al-woodward-broker/

Trade Publications

- Pest Management Professional—an excellent site with lots of informative articles: www.mypmp.net

Associations
- National Pest Management Association: www.pestworld.org
- National Pest Control Association:
  www.urbanwildlifesociety.org/UWS/BrdCtrl/NatlPestAssnHabtatMod.html

Pet Boarding (See Dog Kennels & Pet Grooming)

Pet Grooming (See also Dog Kennels)

SIC 0752-04	NAICS 812910	Number of Businesses/Units 82,056

Rules of Thumb

➤ 40 to 45 percent of annual sales plus inventory

➤ 1.5 times SDE plus inventory

Benchmark Data

Statistics (Pet Grooming and Boarding)

Number of Establishments	82,056
Average Profit Margin	7.4%
Revenue per Employee	$38,300
Average Number of Employees	2
Average Wages per Employee	$12,298

Source: IBISWorld, July 2012

Products and Services Segmentation

Pet boarding	42.2%
Pet grooming	31.6%
Other services	14.4%
Pet training	7.5%
Merchandise sales	4.3%

Source: IBISWorld, July 2012

Industry Costs

Profit	7.4%
Wages	33.9%
Purchases	25.0%
Depreciation	1.7%
Marketing	2.1%
Rent & Utilities	4.4%
Other	25.5%

Source: IBISWorld, July 2012

Establishments by Employment

# of Employees	# of Establishments	Share of total %
1 to 4	7,039	70.80
5 to 9	1,847	18.60
10 to 19	774	7.80

Source: IBISWorld, July 2012

Market Share

PetSmart Inc.	15.5%

Source: IBISWorld, July 2012

- "Annual sales revenue remained steady and slightly increased over 2010 in a survey of 1,252 independent U.S. grooming businesses.

  Less than $25,000 .... 08%
  $25,001 to $50,000 .... 17%
  $50,001 to $100,000 .... 58%
  $100,001 to $200,000 ....11%
  More than $200,000 .... 06%

  Source: "eGroomer Journal Pet Grooming, March 2012, www.stallionPublishers.com

Industry Trend

- "The pet grooming seems to be faring better than many business sectors. Three out of ten grooming business said their business was up (10% average) in 2011, and four out of ten said their business was unchanged in 2011."

  Source: "eGroomer Journal Pet Grooming, March 2012, www.stallionPublishers.com

- "The pet grooming industry seems to be faring better than many business sectors. Three out of ten grooming business said their business was up (10% average) in 2011, and four out of ten said their business was unchanged in 2011."

- "Which best describes how the economy affected your business in 2011?

  Business was better in 2011 than 2010 .... 29.7%
  Very little difference 54.2%
  I had to hire more employees to keep up with demand 12.3%
  I had to let one or more employees go 7.7%
  Clients are cutting back about one appointment a year .... 44.1%"

- "Less than 8% of employers reduced staff in 2011, and 37% reported an ongoing chronic shortage of skilled groomers to fill open positions.

  "Only 2% of grooming business owners surveyed are considering closing their doors if business doesn't improve."

- "No specific grooming business type bucked these trends. Mobile reported the highest level of confidence (84%)."

- "In the current economic climate how confident are you in the future of your grooming business?

  Strong 76%
  Good .... 15%"

- "A majority of business owners (60%) continue to describe their businesses as grooming shops (includes groomers that groom in their homes) or a full-service salon. Although by a small margin, pet spas with grooming increased from 5% to 7%, and mobile groomers increased from 11% to 12%."

Resources

Websites

- www.petgroomer.com

Associations

- American Pet Products Association: www.americanpetproducts.org
- National Dog Groomers Association of America: www.nationaldoggroomers.com

Pet Stores		
SIC 5999-30	NAICS 453910	Number of Businesses/Units 17,247

Rules of Thumb

> ➤ 25 to 30 percent of annual sales plus inventory

> ➤ 2 times SDE plus inventory

Pricing Tips

- "Be sure to check inventory turnover rate to make sure inventory is saleable."
- "Dealing with reputable breeders increases value."
- "If they have an 'acceptable' system for acquiring pets for sale, increase the price by 5%."
- "Retail—treat like any other retail business."

Expert Comments

"This takes into consideration that the store would be privately owned and not a 'big box' store. Many of these privately owned businesses have been able to successfully compete on price against the big box stores. Stores in small towns tend to do well."

"Location is a key factor in pricing, as many people travel to pick out the 'right' dog. Location to major intersections is a definite plus. Although it is fairly easy to duplicate a pet or pet supply store, knowing the mechanics of the industry can be tricky. Risk is primarily associated with dealing with reputable breeders that stand by their product; diseases such as parvo and kennel cough can cost quite a bit."

"Unless there is a big box pet supply close by, a single ownership shop will do well in any dense residential area."

Benchmark Data

Statistics (Pet Stores)

Number of Establishments	17,247
Average Profit Margin	4.3%
Revenue per Employee	$135,900
Average Number of Employees	6.6%
Average Wages per Employee	$18,050

Source: IBISWorld, July 2012

Products and Services Segmentation

Pet food	58%
Pet supplies	27.3%
Pet services	10.2%
Live animals	4.5%

Source: IBISWorld, July 2012

Industry Costs

Profit	4.3%
Wages	13.1%
Purchases	70.3%
Marketing	1.6%
Rent & Utilities	4.0%
Other	6.7%

Source: IBISWorld, July 2012

Market Share

PetSmart Inc.	43.1%
PETCO Animal Supplies Inc.	20.7%

Source: IBISWorld, July 2012

- "According to the 2011–2012 APPA National Pet Owners Survey, 62% of U.S. households own a pet, which equates to 72.9 million homes.

  "In 1988, the first year the survey was conducted, 56% of U.S. households owned a pet as compared to 62% in 2008.

  "Total Number of Pets Owned in the U.S. (millions):

  Bird: 16.2
  Cat: 86.4
  Dog: 78.2
  Equine:.. 7.9
  Freshwater Fish: 151.1
  Saltwater Fish:.. 8.61
  Reptile:.. 13.0
  Small animal: 16.0

- "Estimated 2012 Sales within the U.S. Market:

  For 2012, it estimated the $52.87 billion will be spent on our pets in the U.S. Estimated breakdown:

  Food:... $20.46 billion
  Supplies/OTC Medicine: .... $12.56 billion
  Vet Care:.. $13.59 billion
  Live animal purchases: .... $2.15 billion
  Pet services: grooming and boarding: .... $4.11 billion"

  Source: 2011–2012 APPA National Pet Survey, www.americanpetproducts.org/press

- "Los Angeles—Americans spent $50.96 billion on their pets in 2011.

  "Food and vet costs accounted for about 65 percent of the spending. But it was a service category—one that includes grooming, boarding, pet hotels, pet-sitting, and day care—that grew more than any other, surging 7.9 percent from $3.5 billion in 2010 to $3.79 billion in 2011.

  "Spending in 2011 was up 5.3 percent from 2010, when it totaled $48.35 billion, Vetere said. He estimated 2012 sales would total $53 billion.

  "In 2011, people spent $19.85 billion on food, $13.41 billion on vet care, $11.77 billion on supplies and over-the-counter medicines, $3.79 billion on other services and $2.14 billion on live-animal purchases."

  Source: "Pet spending in US hits peak, but sales of animals level off" by Sue Manning, Associated Press, *Boston Globe*, March 3, 2012

- "The keys to success in this industry are low rent, knowledgeable and caring employees, spotlessly clean store, publicly accepted pet sales system, and competition in price against 'big box' stores.

  "According to the 2011–2012 National Pet Owners Survey, 62% of U.S. households own a pet which equates to 72.9 million homes."

  Source: Industry Statistics and Trends, American Pet Products Association 2009–2010 Survey

- "1,000 sq. ft.; 5–7 rotating part-time employees; biggest profits are in the accessories, but the food products must be high volume."

- "Costs of goods should not exceed 75%."

Expenses as a Percentage of Annual Sales

Cost of goods..50% to 60%
Payroll/labor Costs ....08% to 10%
Occupancy...04% to 05%
Profit (estimated pretax) ....20% to 25%

Questions

- "Where do you get your puppies from and what is their guarantee?"
- "Do they have a publicly accepted way of selling pets?"

- "Do your customers have a desire to know about the food products? (This will give you an idea of the service the seller is providing.) How do you go about recruiting employees?"

Resources

Websites
- Pet Industry Joint Advisory Council: www.pijac.org

Associations
- American Pet Products Association: www.americanpetproducts.org
- World Pet Association: www.worldpetassociation.org

Pet Supply (Wholesale)		
SIC 5199-32	NAICS 422990	Number of Businesses/Units 1,300

Pricing Tips
- "Treat like any other distribution company."

		Franchise
Petland		
Approx. Total Investment		$299,000 to $900,000
	NAICS 453910	Number of Businesses/Units 135

Rules of Thumb
➢ 50 percent of annual sales plus inventory

Resources

Websites
- www.petland.com

Pharmacies and Drug Stores		
SIC 5912-05	NAICS 446110	Number of Businesses/Units 52,193

Rules of Thumb
➢ 18 to 42 percent of annual sales—depending on profits and includes inventory
➢ 70 times average daily sales (range 60 to 80 times) plus inventory
➢ 25 percent of annual sales (range 20% to 30%) plus inventory
➢ 6.5 times EBIT (range 5 to 8 times) plus inventory

Pricing Tips
- "Average total Rx filled daily, % new, % ref, & total Rx average price for year, % Rx third-party insurance & Medicaid & % cash sales, % charge sales. Inventory

value in date & salable. Inventory turns per year; total cost of goods sold + inventory on hand (8 times); age analysis of all accounts receivable including welfare, Worker's Comp; hours open per day, per week, per month, # days per year open; lease."

- "Good front business, e.g., gifts and greeting cards that improve profits. Look for niche business & profits."
- "Number of prescriptions filled daily, monthly, annually; divide by number of days open to arrive at number of prescriptions filled per day. Retail & cost of ingredients. In medical professional building—number of physicians in building. Does pharmacy do its own prescription compounding, & what percentage of business is third party; i.e., Medicare (welfare) & insurance company paid?"
- "Try 22% of [annual] sales. Net income, i.e., return on investment. Future income of business at least 5 years down the line. Demographics and customer review."

Benchmark Data

Statistics (Pharmacies and Drug Stores)

Number of Establishments	52,193
Average Profit Margin	2.2%
Revenue per Employee	$313,700
Average Number of Employees	14.9%
Average Wages per Employee	$36,900

Source: IBISWorld, October 2012

Products and Services Segmentation

Branded prescription drugs	31%
Over-the-counter non-prescription medication	24%
Specialty prescription drugs	12%
Other merchandise and photo processing services	8%
Personal health goods	7.5%
Generic prescription drugs	7%
Cosmetics and toiletries	6.5%
Food and beverages	4%

Source: IBISWorld, October 2012

Industry Costs

Profit	2.2%
Wages	11.7%
Purchases	76.0%
Depreciation	3.5%
Marketing	1.5%
Rent & Utilities	3.0%
Other	2.1%

Source: IBISWorld, October 2012

Market Share

Walgreen Co.	30.9%
CVS Caremark	27.0%
Rite Aid Corporation	11.0%

Source: IBISWorld, October 2012

- "You might think of doctors, who have to go to medical school, as making six figures or more, but not pharmacists. In fact, the median salary for pharmacists in the U.S. is $113,000, according to Salary.com. It's not just filling out prescriptions, it's offering advice on dosage and side effects and interacting with doctors. Becoming a pharmacist requires a bachelor's degree and an advanced degree in pharmacy. The job prospects are expected to be good over the next decade—the number of pharmacist jobs is expected to jump 17 percent, according to the Labor Department."

Source: HTTP://www.salary.com

"Average number of prescriptions per pharmacy:...........54,427 annually, 174 per day.
Average independent pharmacy sales:... $2.855 million.
Average prescription sales:... $2.55 million.
Average independent pharmacy employs................2.6 pharmacists (including owner) and 3.3 technicians."

Source: National Community Pharmacists Association (NCPA)

- "Independent pharmacies comprise the largest segment of the retail pharmacy market. Chains follow, comprising 31 percent of the market with 18,279 drugstores. Supermarket pharmacies make up 15 percent with 8,790 pharmacies, and mass merchandisers comprise 11 percent with 6,695 pharmacies.

  "Among multi-store owners, the average number of pharmacies owned is 2.8. For the independent sector as a whole, the average is 1.2 pharmacies."

Expenses as a Percentage of Annual Sales

Cost of goods	75%
Payroll/labor Costs	09%
Occupancy	02% to 03%
Profit (estimated pretax)	03% to 04%

Industry Trend

- "As companies push to save money on health care expenses, more Americans are getting their medications from the mailman instead of the pharmacist. But the movement toward mail-order drugs is inciting a debate over patient care and patient choice.

  "The results of this shift may be far-reaching. Not only does it change the way millions of Americans get their prescriptions, but if it continues, it will jeopardize the health of some independent pharmacies. And, it makes the already competitive pharmacy business even more so.

  "Mail-order pharmacies can afford this because, by relying on computers and automation, they can fill as many as 80,000 prescriptions in a day. It could take a year before the average retail pharmacy filled that many. They also save money by working with drug companies to set prices."

  Source: "Patients, pharmacies adapt to drugs by mail," wwwnewsobserver.com, April 11, 2010

- "Rural residents across the country are seeing pharmacies shuttered as customer volume fails to keep pace with financial challenges. The losses pegged at more than 500 pharmacists nationwide in a recent two-year period mean more than empty storefronts. Rural pharmacists 'do a lot of triage, telling people when they need to go to the doctor and when they don't,' said pharmacist Jeff Seabloom, who works at Walgreens in Rhinelander after having sold the struggling pharmacy in Elcho. Of the 500 rural pharmacies that vanished recently across the country, more than 200 were their community's only pharmacy, according to the Missouri-based Rural Policy Research Institute. At least six small towns in Wisconsin lost their only drugstore during that time."

  Source: "Disappearing drugstores: Small-town health suffers…" www.pharmacychoice.com, April 25, 2010

Seller Financing

- Mostly all cash sales. Owner finance 3 to 7 years with interest at prime +/- 1% or 2 %
- 10 years

Questions

- "Number of years on lease? Do you own the building?"

Photographers & Photographic Studios (See also Camera Shops)	
NAICS 541921	Number of Businesses/Units 146,535

Rules of Thumb

➤ 45 to 50 percent of SDE; add fixtures, equipment & inventory

➤ 2.5 to 3 times monthly sales; add inventory

Pricing Tips

- "They are usually sold for the new cost of fixtures and equipment, plus inventory, plus 30 percent of one year's net profit. National average states the gross profit usually runs about 62 percent, leaving a net profit of about 24 percent after expenses."

Benchmark Data

Statistics (Photography)

Number of Establishments	146,535
Average Profit Margin	8.8%
Revenue per Employee	45,800
Average Number of Employees	1.4
Average Wages per Employee	$23,102

Source: IBISWorld, September 2012

Products and Services Segmentation

Wedding photography	52.9%
Commercial photography	25.6%
School portrait photography	11.2%
Other photography services	9.8%
Passport portrait photography	0.5%

Source: IBISWorld, September 2012

Industry Costs

Profit	8.8%
Wages	49.4%
Purchases	25.6%
Depreciation	1.8%
Marketing	1.4%
Rent & Utilities	5.0%
Other	8.0%

Source: IBISWorld, September 2012

Market Share

Lifetouch Inc.	14.1%

Source: IBISWorld, September 2012

Resources

Associations

- PhotoMarketing Association International—this contains valuable information on the photography business including the school market, the portrait business, etc. : www.pmai.org

Physical Therapy

	NAICS 621340	Number of Businesses/Units 112,084

Rules of Thumb

➢ 75 percent of annual sales

➢ 2 to 2.5 times SDE

➢ 1.5 to 2 times EBIT

➢ 1.5 to 2 times EBITDA

Pricing Tips

- "Physical therapists depend on physician referrals, mostly primary care and orthopaedic. Those two specialties are top targets for inclusion in ACOs under the Accountable Care Act. PTs are typically insurance-reimbursement-dependent, so are at the mercy of insurance companies, similar to physicians. I find that sales have been at a cap rate of 65% on pre-tax dividends (per IRS RR59-60 definition) for most, at best (except for larger chains).

  "Private Practice Physical Therapy Clinics: We have valued over 300 in the last 20 years. My valuation rules of thumb are based on this experience. Value is typically 60% to 100% of annual collected fees, 3–4 times amount available to owner (SDCF) and 2–3 times (SDCF less reasonable replacement salary for owner)."

- "U.S. Physical Therapy, Inc. (NASDAQ: USPH), a leading national operator of outpatient physical and occupational therapy clinics, has acquired a 70% interest in a five-clinic outpatient physical therapy group. The practice presently has more than 58,000 patient visits per year and produces approximately $6.9 million in annual revenue. The purchase price of the acquisition was $9.0 million, which was financed with borrowings under the Company's credit line and a seller note."

  Source: "U.S. Physical Therapy Makes Acquisition," www.businesswire.com, March 1, 2010

Expert Comments

"Competition is the biggie, particularly if a large health care provider decides to enter the market. Relationships with physicians are key."

"Competition is highly dependent on location, with higher competition in urban areas. Rural practices frequently can't sell at any price, but buyers in urban areas can be hard to find too. Risk is higher due to medical malpractice, but certainly not as high as for physicians."

Benchmark Data

Statistics (Physical Therapists)

Number of Establishments	112,084
Average Profit Margin	8.8%
Revenue per Employee	$99,300
Average Number of Employees	2.7
Average Wages per Employee	$52,527

Source: IBISWorld, July 2012

Products and Services Segmentation

Orthopedic physical therapy	48.1%
Speech therapy and audiology	10%
General physical therapy	9%
Geriatric physical therapy	8.7%
Pediatric physical therapy	8.1%
Sports physical therapy	6.7%
Neurological physical therapy	6.5%

Source: IBISWorld, July 2012

Industry Costs

Profit	8.8%
Other specialty physical therapy	2.9%
Wages	52.0%
Purchases	8.0%
Depreciation	3.0%
Marketing	1.5%
Rent & Utilities	8.5%
Other	18.2%

Source: IBISWorld, July 2012

- "Collected fees per full-time employed physical therapist should be $200,000 to $300,000 per year. Net profit after reasonable salary to owner should be 25%–35%. Collected fee per visit should be close to $100 and patient visits per PT should be 3000–3500."

- "Total clinic operating costs were $149,678,000 or 74.3% of net revenue as compared to $143,588,000 or 76.5% of net revenue in 2008. Clinic salaries and related costs as a percentage of net revenue were 52.5% for 2009 versus 53.4% for 2008. Rent, clinic, supplies, contract labor and other costs as a percentage of net revenue were 20.1% for 2009 versus 21.2% for 2008. The provision for doubtful accounts was 1.7% of net revenue versus 1.6% for the prior year."

  Source: "U.S. Physical Therapy Reports Record Results for 2009," http://markets.on.nytimes/research, March 4, 2010

- "According to 2008 data from the BLS, the mean annual salary for physical therapists is $74,000 and $46,300 for physical therapist assistants. Salaries appear to have nowhere to go but up. According to APTA research, 13% to 18% of physical therapy positions are open."

  Source: "Looking for a New Career? Try Physical Therapy, www,businessweek.com"

Expenses as a Percentage of Annual Sales

Cost of goods	27%
Payroll/labor Costs	21%
Occupancy	07%
Profit (estimated pretax)	12%

Industry Trend

- "Employment of physical therapists is expected to grow 27 percent from 2006 to 2016, much faster than the average for all occupations. The impact of proposed Federal legislation imposing limits on reimbursement for therapy services may adversely affect the short-term job outlook for physical therapists. However, the long-run demand for physical therapists should continue to rise as new treatments and techniques expand the scope of physical therapy practices."

  Source: http://www.bls.gov/oco/ocos080.htm#empty

Seller Financing

- 2 to 5 years

Questions

- "Source of patients, local ACO trends, insurance impacts, dependence on PTs and PTAs and their availability."

Resources

Websites
- medicalpracticeappraisal.com

Associations
- American Physical Therapy Association: www.apta.org

Physicians (See Medical Practices)

Picture Framing		
SIC 5999-27	NAICS 442299	Number of Businesses/Units 1,003

Rules of Thumb

➤ 45 percent of annual sales plus inventory

Pricing Tips

- "Not a lot of activity to report in the framing industry. While there have been some transactions, most involve private sales where numbers aren't reported. I have valued a few businesses in the past year and found the same formulae apply as in the past. Values were less, but that is as a result of lower sales, inventories and other assets."
- "Perhaps most critical is the impact of a change in ownership. If the shop is small, that is the owner is the face of the business, rarely is the business worth any more than 10% of sales."

Expert Comments

"Location and co-tenancy is extremely important to value as long as lease is secure."

Benchmark Data

Statistics (Picture Framing Stores)

Number of Establishments	1,003
Average Profit Margin	8.6%
Revenue per Employee	$1,102
Average Number of Employees	2
Average Wages per Employee	$44,643

Source: IBISWorld, May 2012

Products and Services Segmentation

Custom framing	74.5%
Other sales	25.5%

Source: IBISWorld, May 2012

Industry Costs

Profit	8.6%
Wages	4.0%
Purchases	74.2%
Depreciation	1.2%
Marketing	1.0%
Rent & Utilities	6.0%
Other	5.0%

Source: IBISWorld, May 2012

Market Share

Michaels Stores Inc.	32.7%

Source: IBISWorld, May 2012

- "COGS (direct materials only) should be at or below 25% of sales."

Expenses as a Percentage of Annual Sales

Cost of goods	25%
Payroll/labor Costs	12%
Occupancy	10%
Profit (estimated pretax)	14%

Industry Trend

- "With much competition eliminated from recession, we expect to see steady growth over the next 3 to 5 years"

Questions

- "In addition to the usual financial questions, you should conduct a market evaluation to determine the viability of the present pricing structure."

Resources

Associations

- Professional Picture Framers Association (PPFA): www.ppfa.com

	Franchise
Pillar to Post — Home Inspection (See also Home Inspection)	
Approx. Total Investment	$19,900 to $24,900
		Number of Businesses/Units 400

Rules of Thumb

➢ 25 to 30 percent of annual sales plus inventory

Resources

Websites

- www.pillartopost.com

	Franchise
Pizza Factory (See also Pizza Shops)	
Approx. Total Investment	$137,000 to $426,000
Estimated Annual Sales/Unit	$375,000

	NAICS 722211	Number of Businesses/Units 140

Rules of Thumb

➢ 30% to 35% of annual sales plus inventory

	Franchise
Pizza Inn (See also Pizza Shops)	
Approx. Total Investment	$80,000 to $764,000
Estimated Annual Sales/Unit	$460,000

	NAICS 722211	Number of Businesses/Units 318

Rules of Thumb

➢ 45 percent of annual sales plus inventory

Resources

Websites
▪ www.pizzainn.com

Pizza Shops		
SIC 5812-22	NAICS 722211	Number of Businesses/Units 76,932

Rules of Thumb

➢ 35 percent of annual sales plus inventory for independent shops

➢ 38 percent of annual sales plus inventory for franchised or chain pizza shops

➢ 1.5 to 2 times SDE; plus fixtures, equipment and inventory

➢ 4 times monthly sales plus inventory

Pricing Tips

▪ "Typical pricing is 20 to 24 times weekly gross sales. Industry insiders and purchasers use this barometer consistently."
▪ "A 2x multiple is sometimes the best case scenario, often a 1.5x is the reality, of chief importance is the length of the lease, rent as well as location and parking for customers and delivery persons. Lots of creative ways to understand cash flow, including pizza box purchases, cheese and tomato purchases as examples. An important part of due diligence should include on-site observation of the operation for several days."
▪ "Domino's Formula—45 percent of the first $400K in annual sales, 50 percent of the next $100K ($400 to $500K) in annual sales, then 55 percent of the next $250K of annual sales (from $500–$750k)"

P - Rules of Thumb

- "Sole ownership in this type of business results in numbers that are hard to decipher their basis in reality. Be cautious and spend a great deal of time with the owner to truly understand the earnings of the business."

- Pizza Franchise Rules of Thumb—Quick Check

Blackjack's Pizza	40% of annual sales
Domino's Pizza	50% of annual sales
Gatti's Pizza	30%–35% of annual sales
Godfather's Pizza	25%–30% of annual sales
Hungry Howie's Pizza	35% of annual sales
Little Caesar's Pizza	50% of annual sales
Mountain Mike's Pizza	30% of annual sales
Mr. Jim's Pizza	35% of annual sales
Papa Murphy's Take 'N' Bake	35% to 40% of annual sales
Pizza Factory	30% to 35% of annual sales
Pizza Inn	45% of annual sales
Sarpino's Pizza	50% of annual sales

Note: Several of the businesses had a percentage multiple of, for example, 35% to 40%. The lower figure was the one used in tabulating an average. This produced an average rule of thumb of 38% of annual sales = the "ballpark" price. The above represent an average rule of thumb for franchised pizza restaurants. As you can see from the information in this section, independent pizza shops have an average rule of thumb of 35%. This slight difference may be due to more information being available for franchised units than independents.

Benchmark Data

Statistics (Pizza Shops)

Number of Establishments	76,932
Average Profit Margin	6.4%
Revenue per Employee	48,700
Average Number of Employees	11.8
Average Wages per Employee	$16,306

Source: IBISWorld, March 2012

Products and Services Segmentation

Quick service pizza restaurants	66.2%
Full service pizza restaurants	29.4%
Other	4.4%

Source: IBISWorld, March 2012

Industry Costs

Profit	6.4%
Wages	33.4%
Purchases	42.6%
Depreciation	2.5%
Marketing	4.7%
Rent & Utilities	8.6%
Other	1.8%

Source: IBISWorld, March 2012

Market Share

Yum! Brands Inc.	11.6%
Domino's Inc.	9.8%
Papa John's International Inc.	6.3%

Source: IBISWorld, March 2012

- How many units do you own?
  - 1 .... 79.1%
  - 2 to 3 .... 13.3%
  - 4 to 10 .... 5.1%
  - 10 to 20 .... 1.3%
  - More than 20 Units 0.6%
  - More than 50 Units 0.6%

- What type of location do you own?
  - Stand-alone 47.5%
  - Shopping center 13.9%
  - Strip mall 33.5%
  - C-store 0.6%
  - Other 4.4%

- What percentage of your business is delivery?
  - 5 to 10% 10.9%
  - 11 to 20% 10.3%
  - 21 to 30% 14.1%
  - 31 to 40% 15.4%
  - More than 40% 17.3%
  - Don't offer delivery 32.1%

- What are the average yearly sales at each of your stores?
  - Less than $250,000 .... 24.3%
  - $300,000 to $500,000 .... 36.8%
  - $550,000 to $750,000 .... 14.5%
  - $750,000 to $1 million 8.6%
  - $1 million to $2 million 6.6%
  - More than $2 million 0.7%
  - More than $5 million 0.0%
  - Decline to answer 8.6%

- Which segment of your sales, as reported above, has seen the most growth during the last year?
  - Dine-in 22.4%
  - Takeout 35.9%
  - Take and bake 0.6%
  - Delivery 18.6%
  - Catering 3.2%
  - Buffet 1.9%

- How many direct competitors do you have within a 10-mile radius?
  - Less than 5 .... 30.4%
  - 5 to 9 .... 36.1%
  - 10 to 15 .... 13.3%
  - More than 15 .... 20.3%

- In general, are your sales increasing, decreasing or about the same compared to last year?
  - Increasing 51.9%
  - Decreasing 20.3%
  - Same 27.8%

- Do you offer pizza by the slice?
  - Yes 53.8%
  - No 46.2%

- What percentage of your budget is spent on advertising?
  - Less than 2% 32.9%
  - 2% to 5% 37.5%
  - 6% to 7% 10.5%
  - 8% to 10% 9.2%
  - More than 10% 5.9%
  - We don't advertise 3.9%

The above is from a 2011 Survey conducted by Pizza Monthly Quarterly (PMQ.com). This is a wonderful site and should be used by anyone involved in the pizza shop business or wanting to get into the business.

- "Nearly half (48%) of respondents this year own a standalone store, and the next-biggest group (33.6%) own a strip-mall location. Almost half of the pizzeria operators in our survey also live in small towns. Meanwhile, nearly a third (31.6%) are newbies in the business, reporting that they've owned their store for less than five years."
- "58.6% of pizzeria operators don't serve any alcohol in their restaurants."
- "Store averages. During the period between January 2010 and December 2010, the average per-unit sales for all U.S. pizzerias equaled $538,738, which is a slight decrease of $19,933 from 2009's reported $558,671. The Top 50 per-unit sales numbers increased from $636,507 in 2009 to $661,053 in 2010."
- "Independent pizzerias, on the other hand, are most often patronized by those who earn more than $75,000 per year, according to several studies, so a down economy might not hit them as hard."
- "The top 50 pizza chains own 43% of pizzerias and control 52% of the sales.

Pizza Hut	12%
Domino's	8%
Little Caesar's	4%
Papa John's	4%
Other Top Chains	15%
Independents	57%

Source: The above is from a 2011 Survey conducted by Pizza Monthly Quarterly (PMQ,com).
- "The top 50 franchises/chains per-unit sales averaged $636,507 for the period June 2009 to June 2010. The average for the prior period was $642,290.

"The per-unit sales for independent stores averaged $501,314 for the same period. For the prior period the average was $470,426, 'showing that many consumers still favor the customized service they receive at a mom-and-pop shop.'

"The per-unit sales for all stores averaged $558,671 for the same period.

"Independents own 58 percent of pizzerias—and control 51.66 percent of the sales.

"The top 50 chains/franchises own 42 percent of pizzerias and control 48.34 percent of the sales."

Source: Pizza Power Report 2010 published by PMQ. The above information is for comparison purposes.
- "Keep food costs below 30 percent, and labor, not counting manager's salary, below 20 percent."
- "Luke Bailey, owner of the two-unit Pizza Company in Davison, MI, keeps 10 to 14 days' worth of inventory on hand and schedules a running inventory only sporadically. 'If I can keep 61 percent on food and payroll, I'm OK,' he said."

Food Cost	28% to 30%
Payroll/Labor	25% to 30%
Occupancy	06% to 08%

- Here are some franchised pizza operations and their approximate annual sales per unit for 2012:

Chuck E. Cheese's Pizza	$769,000
CiCi's Pizza	$884,000
Domino's	$700,000
Gatti's Pizza	$900,000
Godfather's Pizza	$384,000
Hungry Howie's Pizza	$484,000
Little Caesar's	$427,000
Marco's Pizza	$540,000

Mazzio's Pizza	$756,000
Mountain Mike's Pizza	$525,000
Papa Gino's	$830,000
Papa John's Pizza	$748,000
Papa Murphy's Take 'N' Bake	$550,000
Pizza Factory	$375,000
Pizza Hut	$675,000
Pizza Inn	$425,000
Round Table Pizza	$770,000
Sbarro Pizza	$660,000
Shakey's Pizza	$1,000,000

Source: Franchise Times, *Nation's Restaurant, Pizza Marketing Quarterly,*
Top 400 Restaurant Chains for 2012 and various other publications.

Note: Figures are rounded.
The figures above are 2012 estimated annual figures. Our calculations have indicated that annual sales of franchised pizza stores have increased from 2011 to 2012. Keep in mind that they are educated estimates. The highest grossing franchise and the lowest grossing one were eliminated when figuring an average. This produced average annual sales of approximately $645,000.

Expenses as a Percentage of Annual Sales

Cost of goods	28%
Payroll/labor Costs	25%
Occupancy	08%
Profit (estimated pretax)	12%

Resources

Trade Publications
- *Franchise Times*: www.franchisetimes.com
- Guide to a Successful Pizza Business & Pizza Business Manual by Paul Shakarian: www.pizzabusiness.com
- Nation's Restaurant News—this is one publication you must have if you're marketing any type of food operation, including pizza stores: www.nrn.com
- Pizza Marketing Quarterly—this is a wonderful site. If you are serious about selling pizza businesses, you have to visit it.: www.pmq.com

		Franchise
Planet Beach (See also Tanning Salons & Medical Spas)		
Approx. Total Investment		$140,800 to $281,000
	NAICS 812199	Number of Businesses/Units 324

Rules of Thumb

➢ 35 to 40 percent of annual sales

➢ Planet Beach franchises day spas in the U.S, Canada, and Australia.

Resources

Websites
- www.planetbeach.com

	Franchise

Play It Again Sports

Approx. Total Investment	$240,500 to $390,700

	NAICS 453310	Number of Businesses/Units 324

Rules of Thumb

➢ 40 to 45% of annual sales plus paid-for inventory

Benchmark Data

- "Specializing in the resale of used sports equipment and gear, Play It Again Sports has grown to about 350 stores since their founding 25 years ago. The retailer has primarily grown through franchising, as it is part of the Winmark Corporation's family of franchise companies. According to CoStar Tenant, at least 13 new Play It Again Sports stores have opened since the start of the recession. The size of these new store leases range from 2,600 to 19,200 square feet, with an average size of about 6,300 square feet."

    Source: www.costar.com. "Second Time Around" by Sasha M. Pardy, August 19, 2009

Industry Trend

- "'With the rise in the number of sporting goods stores that emphasize used equipment sales and the growing use of the Internet, it is important for NSGA to look at the impact of these changes in channels of distribution,' NSGA Vice President of Information & Research Thomas B. Doyle said. 'The purchase of used equipment is a two-edged sword. It may take away from new equipment purchases initially, but it also may provide the entry point for future purchasers of upgraded equipment.'"

    Source: National Sporting Goods Association, 2007, www.nsga.org

Resources

Websites

- www.playitagainsports.com

Plumbing and Heating Contractors (See HVAC)

Podiatrists

SIC 8043-01	NAICS 621391	Number of Businesses/Units 11,905

Rules of Thumb

➢ 35 to 40 percent of annual sales plus inventory

➢ 3 to 4 times SDE plus inventory

➢ 1.5 times EBITDA

Pricing Tips

- "Inventory varies widely. Some podiatrists sell products and some don't. Product sales can be profitable, but surgical podiatry is usually the most profitable."

- "You can view podiatry as similar to orthopaedics, but limited to the foot and ankle. Many of the same guidelines apply, as they also are dominated by insurance reimbursement, but their incomes are frequently lower as they are outside the direct allopathic referral loop."

Expert Comments

"Medicare and insurance dominated revenues and profits"

"An aging population will result in increased foot related issues. There will be increased growth in outpatient surgery."

"Competition in the primary markets is high, but low in rural markets. Risk is high due to medical malpractice issues, just like other specialties of surgery."

Benchmark Data

Statistics (Podiatrists)

Number of Establishments	11,905
Average Profit Margin	11.5%
Revenue per Employee	$121,800
Average Number of Employees	3.4
Average Wages per Employee	$43,697

Source: IBISWorld, May 2012

Products and Services Segmentation

Other service	35%
Care of musculoskeletal connective tissue	34%
Care of skin and subcutaneous tissue	23%
Care of injuries and adverse effects	8%

Source: IBISWorld, May 2012

Industry Costs

Profit	11.5%
Wages	35.5%
Purchases	20.0%
Depreciation	2.0%
Marketing	5.0%
Rent & Utilities	10.0%
Other	16.0%

Source: IBISWorld May 2012

- "A sole practitioner should generate around $250,000 in gross income. A doctor will treat over 94 patients per week."
- "3 to 4 staff per doctor"
- "Variables include whether 'midlevels' like nurse practitioners or P.A.'s are employed; orthotic sales or referral; surgical components."

Expenses as a Percentage of Annual Sales

Cost of goods	05% to 06%
Payroll/labor Costs	21% to 23%
Occupancy	06% to 07%
Profit (estimated pretax)	40% to 43%

Industry Trend

- "Increasing demand by baby boomers"

- "There will be a trend to fewer solo practices and more group practices. There will be a trend toward group practices involving other health care disciplines."

Seller Financing
- "Financing term of 5 to 7 years"
- "2 to 5 years"

Questions
- "State and Federal compliance"
- "Do you have nursing home contracts? Do you have Medicaid patients?"

Resources

Trade Publications
- Podiatry Today: www.podiatrytoday.com

Associations
- American Podiatric Medical Association: www.apma.org
- American Academy of Podiatric Practice Management: www.aappm.org

Pool Service (Swimming)		
SIC 7389-09	NAICS 561790	Number of Businesses/Units 52,351

Rules of Thumb

> 10 to 12 times the "Monthly Service Only Gross Income"— swimming pool routes throughout the country sell for this multiple.

> "Note: The monthly service gross income is just that. It does not include income from maintenance or repair.

> "This is already considered in the multiple, because most pool service technicians agree that whatever your monthly service billing is, half of that again will translate into maintenance/repair income."

> 50 to 55 percent of annual sales plus inventory

Pricing Tips

- "As stated, there are two main sources of income, monthly service billing and maintenance/repair income. Throughout the United States the purchase price of a pool service route is based on a multiple times the Monthly Service Billing Only income. The multiple will vary from state to state and even within some states. However, it is an industry standard to use a multiple times the Monthly Service Billing Only income. In other words, the maintenance/repair income should not be included to arrive at a fair purchase price. Any other method of appraising the value of a pool route would be contrary to the industry standards. The maintenance and repair income is already considered in the multiple, because most pool service technicians agree that whatever your monthly service billing is, half of that again will translate into maintenance/repair income.

  "We have been selling businesses for over 28 years. Pool routes are our specialty. We can tell that the most important step in purchasing a pool route is in verifying the monthly service billing. Financial statements, profit and loss statements, and balance sheets are usually not available, mainly because it is not necessary to keep an expensive bookkeeping system for one person operating out of their home. Therefore, there are not usually records available to satisfy a bank or financial institution to borrow the money to buy the route. Individual tax returns usually will not help either, because if you were buying 50 accounts of a route of 100, the tax returns would not be broken down that way. Also, if he is a pool builder or does a lot of business in major pool repairs or pool remodeling, again the tax returns would reflect all this income. What if he had 100 accounts and sold 50 accounts? His tax return would show an income for 100 accounts and you would have no way of knowing this. The next couple of paragraphs will discuss what we find to be the best way to verify the income of the accounts you are purchasing.

"Pool routes are sold for cash and no terms are generally available. Therefore, you should have the funds available at the time of purchase, unless you are arranging for an equity loan, line of credit or other means to enable you to purchase a pool route.

"While most pool routes have the same expenses, they do not have the same income. Income is what you will be purchasing. One of the best ways to get a handle on the monthly service income, as well as what the owner is charging for repairs, is to look at his ledger cards. A ledger card is a monthly history for each account. A ledger card should show when an account was billed and when the account was paid. The payment history of the customer is one of the most important items to review during purchase. Who wants an account that does not pay his or her bill? The ledger card also shows what the account was billed for repairs. This part of the ledger card will show if the owner is charging for the proper extras. In addition, the ledger card will show how long the account has been on service. While this is very important to some, the length of time on service is not as important as the payment history. If the average age of the accounts is over a year and they have a good payment history that would be a good account.

"Another big question on the minds of most potential purchasers is the radius of the route and the quality of the neighborhoods. The overall radius of a pool route is not as important as the daily radius. Almost everyone has to drive to work or the office. Some people drive 30 minutes, some an hour, some much more. If you purchase a pool route that is within an overall radius of twenty miles but is under a five-mile daily radius, this would be considered a good route in the industry. Try to keep your pools clustered tight by service day. The neighborhood of your accounts is not as important as the way they pay their bills. There are several high-priced neighborhoods where collection is a problem. Most people in just average neighborhoods have a far better collection record than some so-called upper class neighborhoods."

Source: Contributed by Frank Passantino, Pool Route Brokers, Inc. Frank is a veteran business broker and the information provided has been taken from his Web site—www.poolroutebrokers. He is one of the country's leading pool route brokers. His firm is in California and the phone number is 800-772-6002

Benchmark Data

Statistics (Swimming Pool Cleaning Services)

Number of Establishments	52,351
Average Profit Margin	6.0%
Revenue per Employee	$47,100
Average Number of Employees	1
Average Wages per Employee	$33,378

Source: IBISWorld, January 2012

Products and Services Segmentation

General cleaning services	41.2%
Equipment cleaning and maintenance	28.1%
Chemical adjustments	18.6%
Other	12.1%

Source: IBISWorld, January 2012

Industry Costs

Profit	6.0%
Wages	69.8%
Purchases	17.8%
Depreciation	1.5%
Utilities	1.0%
Rent	2.0%
Other	1.9%

Source: IBISWorld, January 2012

- "How many pools can I service in a day? A good question, but difficult to answer. The average pool service technician will service approximately 16 full-service pools a day, while some can service 25 to 30 in a day. It depends on the individual and what type of pools he or she is servicing. The average pool service technician will service two pools an hour including driving time. If the accounts are chemical only, he can do many more. If the accounts are commercial, he or she will do less.

  "The average pool service technician, if running his route correctly, should be netting between $75,000.00 and $80,000.00 per year. If you have a monthly gross service billing income of $4,000.00 per month, that equates to $48,000.00 per year generated from weekly 'service only.' Your expenses should be approximately 2 months of your service income or in this example $8,000.00. This will cover your three major expenses, gas, insurance and chemical replacement. Therefore, your service income totaling $48,000.00 for the year, less estimated expense of $8,000.00, should produce a net profit of $40,000.00, assuming you are operating in a diligent manor. In addition to this profit, you will have a second income on the same accounts for maintenance (filter cleaning, algae, conditioner treatments and other preventive maintenance) charges that you will bill your account extra, plus repairs (motors, pumps, heaters, etc.) This second income should be fifty percent of your service net. If your net income from service is $40,000.00 then your net from maintenance and repairs should be $20,000.00. This is assuming that you are providing full service to your accounts."

  Source: Contributed by Frank Passantino, Pool Route Brokers, Inc. Frank is a veteran business broker and the information provided has been taken from his Web site—www.poolroutebrokers. He is one of the country's leading pool route brokers. His firm is in California and the phone number is 800-772-6002

Industry Trend
- "This business has been on a steady up since I have been selling them over 30 years."

Questions
- "How long have the pool service accounts been established? What is the average monthly service fee? How many times a week do they service the account? Do they charge extra for filter cleaning, conditioner and other treatments?"

Portable Toilet Companies

SIC 7359-22	NAICS 56299	Number of Businesses/Units 4,050

Rules of Thumb

➢ $1,000 per unit

➢ 85 to 90 percent of annual revenues

Pricing Tips

- "An interesting statistic is that experienced purchasers anticipate the loss of customers when buying a company. The percentage, although not a scientific number, has been expressed as high as 25%. In terms of fast numbers, a business with gross sales of $500,000 along with a price conscious customer base could fall to $375,000 as fast as the ink dried on the check.

- "In reality, it has been more common during the last three to five years for portable restroom businesses to sell for approximately 90.62% of annual sales.

- "In revealing the percentage rate, it is important to note that the average percentage rate includes transactions where businesses sold for as little as 50% and as high as 150% of annual sales. Consideration for profitability is included with a highly profitable portable sanitation business demanding a higher price. Again, as an example, a business that does $500,000 in annual sales and is not a good fit or is not running profitably might fall into the lower percentage rate, while a company running the same numbers and showing an annual profit of $125,000 with good equipment and verifiable records might attract a buyer for 100% of annual sales."

Source: "What Is My Portable Restroom Business Worth?" *Sanitation Journal*, www.sanitationjournal.com

Benchmark Data

Statistics (Portable Toilet Rental & Septic Tank Cleaning)

Number of Establishments	4,050
Average Profit Margin	5.2%
Revenue per Employee	$109,200
Average Number of Employees	9.7
Average Wages per Employee	$37,510

Source: IBISWorld, October 2012

Products and Services Segmentation

Portable toilet rentals	46.3%
Septic tank maintenance services	34.5%
Other	14.7%
Cleaning and maintenance services	4.5%

Source: IBISWorld, October 2012

Major Market Segmentation

Businesses, farms and nonprofit organizations	44.2%
Individuals	42.5%
State and local governments	11.1%
Federal government	2.2%

Source: IBISWorld, October 2012

Industry Costs

Profit	5.2%
Wages	34.5%
Purchases	41.6%
Depreciation	4.4%
Marketing	2.1%
Rent & Utilities	5.2%
Other	7.0%

Source: IBISWorld, October 2012

- "... said the company has about 4,000 toilets, and he estimated as many as 200 of them a month are rendered unusable after being set on fire, spray-painted or tipped. It can take $500 to $750 to replace a standard portable toilet and as much as $2,000 for a handicapped stall, he said."

  Source: Carey Mack, operations manager for Readilite & Barricade in an article, "Got the Urge to blow up a portable toilet? Sit on it" by Sarah Ovaska, June 24,2009, www.newsobserver.com

- Route Units: On a construction site, each weekly serviced toilet unit can accommodate 10 workers (working a single 40-hour shift).

- Special Event Units: Each unit can accommodate approximately 200 uses with 4 hours between uses before service is required. The American with Disability Act requires that 5% of all units ordered be wheelchair accessible, or a minimum of one per each order.

- The minimum established standard for route units is weekly service and for special event units when at 1/3 tank capacity.

- 1. Pumping or evacuating the effluent from the portable toilet receptacle into the truck holding tank.
  2. Recharging the portable toilet receptacle.
  3. Cleaning the interior of the portable toilet by scrubbing with brushes and towel drying.
  4. Providing toilet tissue.
  5. Performing minor repairs to the portable toilet as needed.

- Effluent is disposed of at licensed and approved disposal sites as needed. Officially approved disposal sites can be found by consulting with local health officials.

  Source: PSAI.org, September 2008

Industry Trend

- "For decades, renting a portable toilet has meant asking elegantly dressed guests to brave one of those unsightly plastic boxes typically associated with construction sites, recreation areas and rock concerts. But as the $1.5 billion U.S. portable-sanitation industry chases the luxury market, the port-a-potty is getting a makeover. Rental companies are rolling out upscale 'restroom trailers,' equipped with amenities such as marble counters, wall-to-wall carpeting, satellite radio and flat-panel TVs."

  Source: www.nwfdailynews.com

Resources

Associations

- Portable Sanitation Association International: www.psai.org

Power/Pressure Washing

	NAICS 561790	

Rules of Thumb

➢ 50 percent of annual revenues

		Franchise

Precision Tune Auto Care

Approx. Total Investment		$123,000 to $208,075
	NAICS 811118	Number of Businesses/Units 411

Rules of Thumb

➢ 35 to 40 percent of annual sales plus inventory

Resources

Websites
- www.precisiontune.com

Print Shops (General)

SIC 2752-02	NAICS 323114	Number of Businesses/Units 26,567

Rules of Thumb

➢ 30 to 45 percent of annual sales plus inventory

➢ 2 to 3.5 times SDE plus inventory

➢ 3.5 to 4 times EBITDA

Pricing Tips

- "EBIT, EBITDA 3-5 years of financial statements, outsourced industry specific appraisal, best to have audited statements every 5 yrs."
- "In Southern California there is tremendous over-capacity in commercial sheet-fed printing firms. I separate them into two categories: 1) Profitable 2) Underperforming (unprofitable). The profitable firms transact as always although financing and underwriting is much tougher. The underperforming firms need to be liquidated. selling equip for cash and selling accounts with an earn out note tied to gross sales retained. Normally paid monthly for 2-3 years at 6-9% of gross."
- "Market Share in region, quality of accounts, no more than 20% of annual revenues per key account. Profit margin vs. industry Benchmark Data"
- "Owner benefit add-backs, IP protection, key account loyalty, key employees and non-compete agreements."
- "There are two primary methods of valuing printing companies. A multiple of EBITDA and fair market value of assets plus half times a multiple of EBITDA. If everything is equal, these two methods should come relatively close."
- "What is trend of business for the subject company?"

Expert Comments

"Talent pool, key sales relationships, special capabilities, owner financing"

"Key accounts, brand awareness, strong sales force, experience of leadership, documented business plans and vision, funding and vendor relationships, diversity of markets, product mix."

"Some areas of printing are declining, which will cause support services to decline."

"Focus on specialty, lean operations, financial metrics, marketing/sales investment, growth strategies, cash flow and cash."

"Contrary to what you might read, print is still growing slightly. It remains top 10 in GDP in the United States. It has changed and some segments are way off. Manuals and Business Forms are examples of segments hit hard. Direct Mail and Digital Printing are still growing. Technology continues to drive the industry with digital encroaching on conventional litho printing."

Benchmark Data

Statistics (Printing)

Number of Establishments	26,567
Average Profit Margin	4.1%
Revenue per Employee	$164,900
Average Number of Employees	17.3%
Average Wages per Employee	$41,850

Source: IBISWorld, August 2012

Products and Services Segmentation

Commercial lithographic printing	54.7%
Other printing	9.3%
Commercial screen printing	9.1%
Commercial flexographic printing	7.6%
Digital printing	6.6%
Book printing	5.3%
Commercial gravure printing	4.1%
Quick printing	3.3%

Source: IBISWorld, August 2012

Major Market Segmentation

Advertisers	31%
Consumer goods manufacturers	17.5%
Magazine and periodical publishers	14.5%
Stationery and textile manufacturers	12%
Retailers	11%
Book publishers	9%
Financial and legal firms	5%

Source: IBISWorld, August 2012

Industry Costs

Profit	4.1%
Wages	25.2%
Purchases	41.0%
Depreciation	3.9%
Marketing	0.4%
Rent & Utilities	2.5%
Other	22.9%

Source: IBISWorld, August 2012

Market Share

R. R. Donnelley & Sons Company.. 10.0%
Quad/Graphics Inc. 4.1%

Source: IBISWorld, August 2012

- "Using Breakeven to understand profits, Gross margins, Net Margin, ROI expectation"
- "$180,000 per employee for a profitable business"
- "Sales per employee varies by size of company but should exceed $150k/ employee in any case."
- "According to the Printing Industries of America (PIA), the print industry consists of nearly a million small business people. The average commercial printer has about 25 employees and revenue in the $4.5 million range. This is no longer true, as many of these printers have been hit hard by the recession and are seeking work wherever they can find it. Government work keeps many in business, especially when developed as a secondary market to complement commercial printing, Snider said.
"Approximately 10,000 print companies are registered to do work for GPO. The value of GPO work awarded to the private sector is approximately $425 million a year."

Source: "Government Printing Office Work to Private Sector Declines from 1Q09 to 1Q10,"
www.quickprinting.com

- "$200, 000.00 per employee; great target"
- "Sales per employee $200,000"
- "Having contracts and exclusive relationships"
- "Due to decreased margins, revenue per employee should be $150K+."

Expenses as a Percentage of Annual Sales

Cost of goods..35% to 45%
Payroll/labor Costs 25%
Occupancy.. 05%
Profit (estimated pretax) 20%

Industry Trend

- "2009–2014—2.2.5% per yr. mixed services"
- "Growth 9% to 11%"
- "Higher capability and lower cost for in-house equipment to handle short-run requirements."
- "Printing establishments will continue to decline and over-capacity will continue."

Seller Financing

- "Two years maximum or don't do it."
- "3 to 5 years"

Questions

- "Competitive advantages? Retained talent pool for transitions? Last year of 3rd party valuation of business? Reasons for selling? Best identified and suited buyers of your business?"
- "What is the business plan? Vision of business? Key employees secured by non-compete? IP status? What do the next 3 years look like in contacts, sales revenues?"

- "Systems, controls, leadership team, competitive advantages, ideal clients."
- "Who are your largest customers and what percentage of the total do they account for? Are these relationships personal and can they be transitioned to a new owner? What has been done to grow the business? "
- "What is customer mix? What is age and type of equipment?"
- "Client concentration? Who services the client relationships? How current is the equipment?"

Resources

Trade Publications
- Print Shop by John Stewart: www.quickconsultant.com

Associations
- National Association for Printing Leadership: www.napl.org

Print Shops/Commercial Printers (See also Print Shops/General)		
SIC 2752-02	NAICS 323114	Number of Businesses/Units 47,500

Rules of Thumb

➤ 50 to 55 percent of annual sales plus inventory

➤ 2 to 3 times SDE includes inventory

➤ 2.5 to 3 times recast EBITDA if sales under $2 million

➤ 2.5 to 3.5 times recast EBITDA if sales $2 to $5 million

➤ 3.5 times recast EBITDA if sales $5 to $25 million

➤ 4 times EBIT

➤ 1 to 1.5 SDE plus fair market value of assets (for smaller companies)

➤ 5 times EBITDA for Commercial Flexographic Printing (See also Printing/ Flexographic)

Pricing Tips
- "Print for Pay is declining as volume users have purchased equipment and produce in-house. Walk-in trade is inconsistent, commercial accounts provide stability. Newer equipment is important to allow a greater range of products delivered in an efficient manner."
- "Be careful of long term contracts that might go away if the business ownership changes."
- "Having current technology in computer to plate is a big plus."
- "There are two primary ways of valuing printing companies. Fair value of assets plus a half multiple of EBITDA for goodwill and customer lists. The other is 2–4 times EBITDA depending on size, profitability, equipment, sector, etc."
- "Current viability of equipment is an important consideration."
- "Equipment value, and how up-to-date, will have a large influence on price and salability."
- "There are two common ways to value printing companies: a multiple of EBITDA and fair market value of assets plus 1 times EBITDA. In a perfect world they would come pretty close"

- "The bigger the printer, the higher the multiple"
- "What investment has been made in digital equipment for short-run jobs? Has the company moved forward technologically to at least match the competition?"
- "Generally printing companies are sold as a multiple of EBITDA (less capex) ranging from 2 times to 6 times. The multiple will depend on size, profitability, segment of the industry, growth factors, number and percentage of clients to total sales. For companies with few earnings you can use fair market value of assets plus 1 times seller's discretionary income."
- "There are two common ways to value printing companies: a multiple of EBITDA and fair market of assets plus 1 times EBITDA. In a perfect world they will come pretty close."
- "Age of equipment is big issue and customer base"

Expert Comments

"Industry is consolidating. Low barriers to entry created supply imbalance/excess. Demand for outside services is declining due to less printing and more in-house production."

"Person to person relationships are still very important."

"The current regional market shows excess capacity and possibly short-term declines in sales. There is brisk competition, but capitalization costs are high to replicate these businesses. Consolidations are needed."

"Declining industry, overcapacity, printing switching from offset to digital"

"The printing industry is changing to shorter runs and from traditional printing to digital. That doesn't mean it will go away—it won't. The segment the company is in is also a factor; Web printers are having a difficult time. Also other forms of advertising are also taking printing away from the traditional printer."

"Trend is toward large online providers. Level of technical knowledge is critical."

"Customer base important. Hard to steal customers from competition."

"There is a lot of over-capacity in this industry that is only growing slightly and that depends on the segment. For some segments the barrier to entry is low. A person can buy a small press and equipment for a few thousand dollars and he is in business in the lower end of the business. Web printers continue to face huge challenges."

"Printing is a mature industry that is growing at barely the growth in population."

"Price competition from on-line providers. Short-run color work is being done on in-house printers and copiers. 'Pleasing quality' has become acceptable for the small-business owner."

Benchmark Data

- For additional Benchmark data see Print Shops (in general)
- "Margins used to be very good. For example, a color copy was $0.99 years ago with a cost of $0.15. With Kinko's, Staples, etc. entering the market, price per copy has been driving down over the years—now as low as $0.19 at some low-cost providers, with a cost of $0.07. So, a good print shop should still show

a 75% Gross Margin on core printing/copy products."
- "Sales per employee is $100K to $150K to $3 million gross."
- "Sales per employee should exceed $200k."
- "Revenue per employee should be at least $175,000."
- "Sales per employee approx. $125,000"
- "Payroll less than 30% of sales"
- "Sales for employee averages about $200,000. It is on the higher side for Web printers and a little lower for sheet-fed printers."
- "Sales per employee should be in the $150,000 range."
- "No customer bigger than 10%, and direct-to-plate image making"
- "Profit (estimated) 0 to 17 percent depending on segment. Digital printing will be on high side, commercial printing will be much less."
- 2007 PIA/GATF Ratios Show Printing Industry Profits Increasing
- "The average printer's before-tax profit on sales was 3.4% for the typical Ratios participant over this past year. This was an increase compared to 2.7% for 2006; it also is within the 3.0–3.4% range experienced from 1995 to 2001. "Profit leaders, printers in the top 25% of profitability, saw profits decrease slightly to 10.1% as compared to 10.3% in 2006. Despite the small decrease, profit as a percentage of sales for profit leaders remained at the same level it was at in the mid to late 1990s.

  "In 2007 materials accounted for the largest single cost category for the typical U.S. printer, approximately 35.4% of sales. Paper alone consumed more than one-in-five sales dollars last year. Other major costs incurred by printers last year included factory payroll (24.95% of sales), factory expenses (16.77% of sales), administrative expenses (9.57% of sales), and selling expenses (8.77% of sales).

  "Total materials expenses increased from 35.12% of sales in 2006 to 35.44% of sales in the 2007 survey. Printers also spent slightly less on factory expenses in 2007) constituting most of the decline. Selling expenses in 2007 decreased from 9.09% in 2006 compared to 8.77% in 2007, while administrative expenses crept up slightly from 9.46% of sales in 2006 to 9.57% of sales in 2007."

  Source: "2007 PIA/GATF Ratios Show Printing Industry Profits Increasing," www.gain.net

Expenses as a Percentage of Annual Sales

Cost of goods	40% to 50%
Payroll/labor Costs	35% to 45%
Occupancy	05% to 10%
Profit (estimated pretax)	05% to 10%

Industry Trend
- "Flat with consolidations happening"
- "The industry is splitting into two distinct segments: specialty wholesale printers 'gang running' for the trade (other printers) and full-service B2B printers incorporating design, Web services, etc. as part of their offerings."
- "Traditional printing declining and digital printing increasing."
- "Greater competition from large online providers"

Seller Financing
- " 5 years"

Questions

- "Commercial account base? Outside salespeople? What role(s) does owner fill? Product mix? Specialty vs. commodity."
- "Look for any niche they serve; client concentration is a risk; client contracts are rare and would be a premium multiple."
- "Is production equipment leased or owned?"
- "Client concentration is an important risk to evaluate. The facility should have some digital equipment in this day and age."
- "How up-to-date is their equipment? Do they have a niche? Do they do digital printing? What is their salesperson(s) situation? Do they have non-compete agreements with salespeople?"
- "How tied to the customers is the owner, why do customers use this printer over others, does any customer account for more than 10% of revenue."
- "How has the business been trending over the past five years?"
- "Who does the selling?"
- "Why would a customer do business with you, other than quality, price and turnaround time?"

Resources

Websites

- Parker-Nelson publishes a valuation software program especially for the printing industry called Valuware: www.bizbooksoftware.com
- Printing Industries of America: www.printing.org
- www.irs.gov/businesses/small/article/0,,id=108149,00.html

Trade Publications

- "Valuing Printing Businesses, Handbook of Business Valuation," West & Jones, 2nd Edition: www.wiley.com
- American Printer: www.americanprinter.com
- Printing Impressions, an online publication: www.piworld.com

Associations

- National Association for Printing Leadership: www.napl.org
- National Association of Quick Printers: www.naqp.com

Print Shops/Quick Print (See also Print Shops/Commercial Printers)			
SIC 2752-02	NAICS 323114	Number of Businesses/Units	5,126

Rules of Thumb

- ➤ 45 to 55 percent of annual sales plus inventory
- ➤ 2.5 to 3.5 times SDE plus inventory
- ➤ 2 to 5 times SDE plus inventory—SDE (Owner's compensation) treats depreciation as an expense and thus it is not included in SDE.
- ➤ 4 times EBIT
- ➤ 3 to 4 times EBITDA

Pricing Tips

- "Fair market salary adjustment required prior to calculating SDE or excess earnings."
- "Excess earnings should exclude a fair-market salary for a new owner/ manager."
- "Quick printer valuations have been on the decline."
- "The terms of the leases on the digital equipment will affect the operating income and price."
- "2 to 4 times EBITDA but trends are on the low end."
- "The business should be a solutions provider to their clients."
- "Competitive equipment is very important, including lease terms and click charges."
- "The condition of the equipment and whether or not it is up-to-date makes a big difference in the selling price. The buyers normally have industry experience and are knowledgeable about the equipment."
- "Review replacement cost of assets. Percentage of business with top ten clients. Receivable turn."
- "The price can vary significantly with how up-to-date the equipment and software are. A desirable quick printer should have offset and digital equipment and an up-to-date pre-press department."

Expert Comments

"Printing customers today do not necessarily buy on price, but they are buying small quantities and cutting back . . . this favors smaller printers."

"Industry is equipment intensive and requires a high degree of marketing skills to succeed."

"Strong trend in the printing industry from offset to digital printing."

"Quick printers that don't adapt have been declining. The ease of publishing and printing with computers and various printing devices have taken business from the quick printers."

"These are marketable companies suitable for corporate dropouts or general business people."

"I'm not sure that 'Quick Printer' is a relevant category or that the answers to the questions relate to this as a classification. I recently sold a $3,000,000-per-year-sales digital printer that operates out of a retail location. Much of their printing is same day, about $800,000 is retail. I think of this business as 'digital.' I have a newspaper printer under agreement—over $4 million in sales. Within 6 hours of receiving files from the newspaper, the newspaper is printed, addressed, and at the post office. Is this a quick printer? I don't tend to think of it as a quick printer."

"There is a trend from offset printing to digital printing."

"The quick printer has been declining partly because of computers and a failure to adapt to a changing market."

"A business that gives good service can compete effectively with Kinko's and other chains."

"It is easy to obtain the equipment, but much harder to get people, since many need special skills. Customers are not easy to obtain; they have to be taken from the competition."

Benchmark Data

Statistics (Quick Printing)

Number of Establishments	5,126
Average Profit Margin	4.5%
Revenue per Employee	$103,200
Average Number of Employees	5.5
Average Wages per Employee	$31,633

Source: IBISWorld, June 2012

Products and Services Segmentation

Document photocopying	37%
Custom promotional materials	23%
Document printing	16%
Custom stationery material	10.5%
Prepress services	7.5%
Other services	6%

Source: IBISWorld, June 2012

Major Market Segmentation

In-store customers	47%
Small businesses	23.5%
Non-employing businesses	18.5%
Online customers	11%

Source: IBISWorld, June 2012

Industry Costs

Profit	4.5%
Wages	31.7%
Purchases	41.0%
Depreciation	3.9%
Marketing	0.4%
Rent & Utilities	3.8%
Other	14.7%

Source: IBISWorld, June 2012

Market Share

FedEx Corporation	20.2%

Source: IBISWorld, June 2012

- "Sales Per Employee highly indicative of potential success . . . $120,000 minimum and is calculated by dividing gross annual sales by total # of employees including working owners."

- "Sales per employee is a large factor in determining profitability. Over $125,000 is desirable."

- "A successful quick printing firm ought to have a Sales Per Employee, including owner, of at least $125,000 to be considered productive and profitable. However, there are numerous good opportunities for buying companies that are underperforming."

- "Sales per employees $200,000"

- "One that goes out and gets business instead of waiting for it to walk in the door; one that is more creative"

- "Sales per employee (SPE) is a good indicator of overall productivity. SPE is annual sales divided by total # of employees, including all working owners. A good SPE would be in the $125,000–$140,000 range."

- "Owner's compensation 13%"
- "Sales per employee, medium in industry, $107,000. Seven percent increase over last year. Top percentile $110,000."
- "Sales per employee are more a measure of automation and type of work than a meaningful value. Net profit after allowance for equipment is the main factor."

Expenses as a Percentage of Annual Sales

Cost of goods	30% to 40%
Payroll/labor Costs	25% to 30%
Occupancy	05% to 10%
Profit (estimated pretax)	10% to 20%

Industry Trend

- "Moderation of profits and growth"
- "Slight decline for companies unprepared to take necessary steps to modernize."
- "Very good for someone who is technically literate regarding computers and networks and has specific skills found in the printing industry."
- "Growing"
- "Continued decline as it becomes even easier to do much of the work on computers."
- "Digital equipment is taking over this segment of the printing industry. Quick turns and high quality are important."
- "Sales and marketing skills important"
- "Continued decline as people do more with computers and advanced printers."
- "Trend is up"
- "Large asset investment in equipment. Continued growth at 4%–6% annually."
- "More consolidation, declining number of printers"

Questions

- "Percent of sales represented by top 3–5 customers?"
- "How did the seller arrive at his initial asking price? What was the basis for this price, and what references did he refer to?"
- "Describe competition, percentage of sales by category (products & customers)."
- "Information on leases, click charge, customer concentration,"
- "What percentage of customers makes up 80% of the business?"
- "Type of equipment, lease terms, click charges. What related services do they offer? How do they get and maintain sales?"
- "Concentration of customer base. Amount of sales in digital printing vs. offset printing. Age and condition of equipment. Are digital copiers leases or owned? Click charge? How good is the staff."
- "Top 10 client list to see what percentage of sales. Receivables turn. Type and age of equipment."
- "Sales per employee, how old is the equipment—and number of impressions. How long have the employees been with the business? How up-to date is the pre-press department?"

Resources

Trade Publications
- Quick Printing Magazine: www.myprintresource.com/

Associations
- NAPL: www.napl.org
- National Association of Quick Printers: www.naqp.com

Printing/Flexographic		
	NAICS 323112	

Rules of Thumb

➢ 2 to 5 times EBITDA

➢ 3 times EBIT

➢ Note: "It is a different area—they print labels on Web presses using plates that are made of curved rubber. Web presses use rolls of material rather than sheets. Think newspaper printing. However, it is my understanding that the pricing multiples are similar."

Pricing Tips
- "Depending on size EBITDA ranges from 2 to 4 unless special circumstances are present like exceptional profit or none"
- "Multiples range from 2 to 5 depending on size and sector."

Expert Comments

"It is probably the most stable section of the printing industry but it is not growing"

"There is generally lots of competition but less than those of commercial printers. Profits have stabilized in recent years. Marketability is generally high. Replication is relatively easy but can you get the business and can you keep going until you make a profit? This is a good sector of the printing industry."

Benchmark Data
- "Look for stable customer base with no heavy concentration with one or two clients."
- "Sales $200,000 per employee"

Expenses as a Percentage of Annual Sales

Cost of goods	43%
Payroll/labor Costs	43%
Occupancy	05%
Profit (estimated pretax)	05% to 09%

Industry Trend
- "Business should continue stable with not a big increase or decline."

Questions

- "Does the owner handle major customers personally and can they be transitioned to a new owner? Do they have contracts? What sets this company apart from others? Do you have non-compete agreements with your salesmen?"

Resources

Websites

- www.greenevilleplateservices.com

Printing/Silk Screen		
SIC 7336-09	NAICS 541430	

Rules of Thumb

➤ 40 to 45 percent of annual sales plus inventory

➤ 2.5 to 3 times SDE includes inventory

➤ 3.5 to 4 times EBITDA

➤ 3.5 to 4 times EBIT

Pricing Tips

- "SDE 2.5–3.0 range. Sales growth, market potential, age/quality of equipment, staffing, lease will determine which end of range to use."
- "Note age of production equipment, as recent technology has improved production efficiencies."
- "Value affected by equipment, customer base, skilled labor, location and sales growth"
- "Value of any long-term contracts that are in place. Are contracts assignable?"
- "Age of digital printing equipment should be taken into consideration, as new technology is more desirable."
- "National/Corporate accounts as customers increases value vs. small local accounts"

Expert Comments

"Can be high capital investment to start up."

"Anyone can open a small screen printing shop or store. Most companies do screen printed and embroidered products. They also sell small signs, graphics, etc. This industry can be capital intensive. High speed equipment is necessary to produce larger volume and some companies add a second and third shift."

Benchmark Data

- "$60,000 to $90,000 sales per employee, depending upon area of country located, type of printing and products manufactured."
- "$100,000/employee. $175–$200 sq. ft."
- "Sales $75–$100K/employee"

Expenses as a Percentage of Annual Sales

Cost of goods	60%
Payroll/labor Costs	20% to 25%
Occupancy	05%
Profit (estimated pretax)	05% to 10%

Industry Trend

- "Economic downturn has lowered profitability."
- "Consolidation as weaker competitors are either sold or shut the doors."
- "Continued slow growth"
- "Increased competition & pressure on margins"
- "Growth due to U.S. society continuing to be more visually oriented"
- "Transition from traditional screen printing to digital printing output"
- "Flat small companies will go out of business. Med/large companies will grow via an acquisition or investing capital for new equipment."

Questions

- "Sales & profit trend over past 3 years, and especially over most recent 12 month period."
- "Monthly revenue over past 3 years to gauge seasonality of business and to analyze competitive environment"
- "Provide concentration of customers. Any range, one-time orders in sales figures? Maintenance schedule for all equipment?"
- "How are sales generated? Competition? Breakdown of revenues? Condition of equipment? Maintenance records? Seasonality? Sales Structure? Website?"

Resources

Trade Publications

- Screen Printing Magazine: www.stmediagroup.com

Produce Markets (See Fruit & Vegetable Markets)

		Number of Businesses/Units: 8,800

Propane Companies (See Liquefied Petroleum Gas)

	NAICS 211112	

Property Management Companies

SIC 6531-08	NAICS 53131	Number of Businesses/Units 159,518

Rules of Thumb

➤ 100 percent of annual revenues

➤ 6 to 7 months' revenues for firms selling under $500K

➤ 10 to 12 months' revenues for firms above $500K

➤ 2.5 to 5 times SDE based on a cash sale

➤ 3.5 to 6 times SDE with sales involving notes and/or contingencies

P - Rules of Thumb

Pricing Tips

- "Key item is the longevity of accounts (i.e., any property managed for more than 3 years is good). Also, the transition period should have the owner (seller) remain visible for 2 to 3 months."

Expert Comments

"Not much competition. Expenses are low."

Benchmark Data

Statistics (Property Management)

Number of Establishments	159,518
Average Profit Margin	13.5%
Revenue per Employee	$83,500
Average Number of Employees	3.8
Average Wages per Employee	$42,433

Source: IBISWorld, October 2012

Products and Services Segmentation

Residential property management	51.7%
Non-residential property management	25.6%
Other	16.1%
Real estate brokerage	3%
Land management	2.2%
Construction	1.4%

Source: IBISWorld, October 2012

Major Market Segmentation

Residential properties	63.8%
Office buildings	20%
Retail buildings	9.5%
Industrial buildings	3.7%
Other non-residential properties	3.0%

Source: IBISWorld, October 2012

Industry Costs

Profit	13.5%
Wages	51.7%
Purchases	2.8%
Marketing	1.0%
Rent & Utilities	3.8%
Other	27.2%

Source: IBISWorld, October 2012

Market Share

CB Richard Ellis Group Inc.	7.5%
Jones Lang LaSalle Inc.	3.3%

Source: IBISWorld, October 2012

- "Most property management firms earned 10 to 30 percent of their revenue from non-management activities, e.g., lease fees, maintenance contracts."

Expenses as a Percentage of Annual Sales

Cost of goods	n/a
Payroll/labor Costs	40% to 50%
Occupancy	07% to 10%
Profit (estimated pretax)	15% to 20%

Seller Financing

- "Seller financing is less common for property management companies larger than $500,000 gross income, but for smaller companies would be 3 to 5 years."
- 4 years. Note typically has fixed amortized payment, but may be contingent upon payments based on retention of accounts."

Questions

- "Why are you selling? Have there been any lawsuits or complaints?"

Resources

Websites
- www.irem.org

Associations
- National Property Management Association: www.npma.org
- Property Management Association: www.pma-dc.org

Publishers –Books (See also Publishers in General)		
SIC 2731-01	NAICS 511130	Number of Businesses/Units 3,077

Rules of Thumb

> 70 percent of annual sales plus inventory

> 4 to 6 times EBIT

> 4 to 6 times EBITDA

Pricing Tips

- "Professional publishing is valued higher than educational publishing, and both are valued higher than consumer publishing. Proprietary and niche-specific publishing is most attractive."

Benchmark Data

Statistics (Book Publishing)

Number of Establishments	3,077
Average Profit Margin	10.8%
Revenue per Employee	$334,200
Average Number of Employees	25.3%
Average Wages per Employee	$69,807

Source: IBISWorld, June 2012

Products and Services Segmentation

Textbooks	26.4%
Scholarly, professional and technical books	23%
Other services	22.3%
Other books	17.6%
Children's books	10.7%

Source: IBISWorld, June 2012

Industry Costs

Profit	10.8%
Wages	20.6%
Purchases	53.0%
Depreciation	0.6%
Marketing	12.4%
Rent & Utilities	0.5%
Other	2.1%

Source: IBISWorld, June 2012

Market Share

Pearson PLC	10.4%
The McGraw-Hill Companies Inc.	5.7%

Source: IBISWorld, September 2012

- "On a typical hardcover, the publisher sees a suggested retail price. Let's say it is $26. The bookseller will generally pay the publisher $13. Out of that gross revenue, the publisher pays about $3.25 to print, store and ship the book including unsold copies returned to the publisher by booksellers. For cover design, typesetting and copy-editing, the publisher pays about 80 cents. Marketing costs average around $1 but may go higher or lower depending on the title. Most of these costs will decline on a per-unit basis as a book sells more copies. Let's not forget the author, who is generally paid a 15 percent royalty on the hardcover price, which on a $26 book works out to $3.90. For big best-selling authors – and even occasionally first-time writers whose publishers have taken a risk – the author's advance may be so large that the author effectively gets a higher slice of the gross revenue. Publishers generally assume they will write off a portion of many authors' advances because they are not earned back in sales.

  "Without accounting for such write-offs, the publisher is left with $4.05, out of which it must pay overhead for editors, cover art designers, office space and electricity before taking a profit."

Source: *New York Times*, "Publishers Making Their Case for E-Book Prices" by Motoko Rich, March 1, 2010

- "Sales per employee should be $200,000 or over. Returns should be below 15 percent. Mostly valued on cash flow, the balance sheet is rarely considered unless the company is losing money. Company needs to have clear rights to their intellectual property."

Source: IBISWorld, April 2009

Industry Trend

- "A 40-year-old Secaucus company that says it prints 1.5 million books a day will soon close and lay off 105 employees, the latest victim of the shift towards digital media that is transforming the publishing industry.

- "Command Web Offset Co., a division of McNaughton Lithograph Co. Inc., that prints soft cover books, directories, catalogs and other publications, said it will close on Nov. 15, and will sell its assets.

- "The company will lay off pressmen, material handlers, managers and other employees, according to a letter filed with the New Jersey Department of Labor and workforce Development in line with the federal WARN Act.

- "Andrew Merson, the company president and owner, called it a 'difficult decision' forced by 'the impact of e-books, and various other digital media, on offset printing coupled with changing technology' as well as other factors."

Source: "Squeezed by digital media, Secaucus printer to close, lay off 105" by Hugh R. Morley, www.northjersey.com/news, September 2011

Resources

Associations
- American Booksellers Association: www.bookweb.org
- Association of American Publishers: www.publishers.org
- Independent Book Publishers Association: www.pma-online.org

Publishers — In General	
NAICS 511130	

Rules of Thumb

> 100 percent of annual sales includes inventory

> 3.5 to 4 times SDE includes inventory

> 5 times EBITDA

Pricing Tips

- "Publishing valuations vary significantly by niche segment. The lowest valuations would be trade book publishing, as low as 3 times EBITDA, up to scientific/technical journals which might be valued on a multiple of sales, as much as 3 to 4 times revenue. Consumer magazines would range up to 7 times EBITDA and B to B magazines 5 times. The latter is impacted by the significant difficulties which B to B magazines are having in the current economic environment. Internet publications, if well established, would have a higher valuation given the movement of print to the Internet."

- "Publishing is quite diverse, making it difficult to generalize about a multiple. For example, business-to-business magazines are generally worth more than consumer magazines, due to low level of competition. On the other hand, the Market Share of a business-to-business magazine is critical in valuation. Scientific journals of reasonable size command very high multiples. Books, being very low margin, command low multiples."

- "The larger the publishing entity, the higher the multiple. There is a major variation in multiples between different 'niches' in publishing. For example, educational publishing versus business-to-business magazines versus consumer magazines. Local consumer magazines, such as city magazines, generally have a lower valuation than a national enthusiast consumer magazine. Strategic buyers are very active for larger national publications. There are quite a few PEG financed strategic buyers who, if they have an existing property, or the property works with an existing property, will pay a premium. Multiples of EBITDA as high as 10 times are common in these situations. And publishing is a fixed-cost business—once you have exceeded a breakeven point, significant profit falls to the bottom line, fostering the willingness of strategic buyers to pay a premium for the 'right' property. You need to know the industry to sell a publishing business—who are the players."

- "Niched publishers demand higher multiples. Publishers that are in demand from strategic buyers can demand much higher multiples, particularly if the revenue exceeds $10 million."

- "Business are essentially goodwill, with little consideration of fixed assets. Strategic and financial buyers (PEGs) figure predominantly in valuation with considerably higher valuations, some as high as 8 to 10 times EBITDA, possible for a publisher of strategic interest. Size is also a critical factor in valuation, as most strategic buyers will not be attracted to publishing business with gross revenue less than $3 to $4 million annually."

Expert Comments

"Publishing is a risky, competitive but profitable business for those who are successful. There are some declining segments which you should be aware of, such as general book publishing."

"Publishing is high risk, with high profit margin and returns. Very important that publisher have a reasonably high Market Share in its niche. This may mean a highly defined niche, such as log-home enthusiasts, but to be #2 in the market would demand a far lower price than #1."

Benchmark Data

- "Revenue per page for magazines, cost per page."
- "A general benchmark has been one times sales but this is more difficult to measure now because of declining sales."
- "In magazine publishing there are numerous indicators for efficiency such as revenue per page, cost per page. Beyond these, publishing Associationscollect data from publishers so that statistics such as G & A as a % of revenue are available. These are, for the most part, not available to those outside the association members."
- "Publishing cost of goods solely will be based on the type of publication, as will labor and occupancy costs. Profits will range from 10% to 30% based on type of publication. Publishing is undergoing a change. Successful publishing companies will be in a growth industry and will have an interactive presence."

Expenses as a Percentage of Annual Sales

Cost of goods	25%
Payroll/labor Costs	20% to 25%%
Occupancy	05% to 08%
Profit (estimated pretax)	20%

Industry Trend

- "Internet will continue to negatively impact many segments of the publishing business."

Questions

- "For magazines, what is the definition of your market segment and what is your rank in the segment? Number 1 can be worth considerably more than number 2 for a business-to-business magazine. Where do you print, who are your suppliers? Questions about subscribership are critical for consumer magazines. Newsstand distribution is difficult for consumer magazines—how do you do it? Is the magazine paid or free, and so on."

Resources

Trade Publications

- Publishers Weekly: www.publishersweekly.com
- Booklist: www.booklistonline.com
- Circulation Management: www.audiencedevelopment.com

Publishers — Internet (and Broadcasting)

	NAICS 514191	

Rules of Thumb

➢ 100 percent of annual revenue includes inventory

➢ 6 times SDE includes inventory

➢ 6 times EBIT

➢ 5 times EBITDA

Pricing Tips

- "Size matters. Multiples for larger companies >$5 million will be in the 10X range. Same goes for companies with a subscription base that represents recurring revenues."
- "Faster growing companies will provide higher multiples. Higher multiples will also be paid for companies that can document recurring revenue streams, such as subscriptions or annual advertiser contracts. Publishers that provide original content or who own assets such as proprietary databases also can expect greater buyer interest."
- "Subscription based businesses create recurring revenues. Revenue per subscriber and renewal rates are key metrics for publishing businesses; number of listeners and longevity of advertisers are important criteria for broadcasting sites."
- "Larger companies and those with high renewal rates for subscription-based services command a premium. Also companies with long-term agreements and/or verifiable recurring revenue streams should be valued on the high end of the multiple."

Expert Comments

"Ease of replication; it really depends on the content provided. The best businesses have proprietary content and/or a market niche in which they operate."

"Online publishing is a popular business. The barriers to entry are low and the financial reward can be great. The key is developing something original that keeps users coming back to a site. Competition is growing, a factor that will make good sites more valuable while leading to the demise of weaker ones."

"The Web is the world's largest printing press. Everyone wants to be a publisher and competition for eyeballs, ad dollars, subscribers and Market Share is intense. Barriers to entry are low. On the flip side, publisher and broadcaster audiences tend to be loyal. If they like your site they will stay with you. This leads to lots of repeat business and higher profit margins."

"The ease of replication depends on the content being published. The more unique, the more valuable, the more timely—the better."

Benchmark Data

- "A successful Internet business will generate revenues at the rate of 2x employee costs."

- "Revenue per employee should be at least 2 times employee costs."
- "For every dollar in employee expense, a successful Internet publishing company should generate at least two dollars in sales."

Expenses as a Percentage of Annual Sales

Cost of goods	10%
Payroll/labor Costs	65%
Occupancy	05% to 10%
Profit (estimated pretax)	20%

Industry Trend

- "Businesses will continue to grow as 'old' media ad dollars continue to migrate to Web-based 'new' media."
- "There will be significant consolidation as smaller operations are rolled into larger ones."

Questions

- "I would ask about stability of earnings, renewal rates, staff turnover, number of advertising contracts, and if there is any revenue/customer concentration."
- "1. How much of your revenue base is recurring? 2. What is your renewal rate? 3. How much do you spend on customer acquisition?"

"I'd want to know about revenue growth, subscriber/advertiser diversification and renewal rates. Professional publications/broadcasts should be in the 80% range; consumer oriented services should be at 50%. These are rough metrics, but demonstrate 'stickiness.'"

Publishers — Magazines/Periodicals (See also Publishers—In General)	
SIC 2721-02 NAICS 511120	Number of Businesses/Units 6,248

Rules of Thumb

➢ 7 times SDE includes inventory

➢ 2 to 5 times EBIT

➢ 2 to 5 times EBITDA

Pricing Tips

- "Publishers are generally selling for 2 to 5 times EBITDA down from where they once were."
- "Publishing companies are generally based on a multiple of EBITDA, and the range can go from 3 to as high as 12 depending on size, growth, industry served, etc."
- "Publications generally sell for a multiple of EBITDA and have very little inventory. Depending on size, industry, if it is a consumer publication or business to business, profitability, etc. smaller ones will sell in the 2 to 5 times range, while the large companies will sell for as much as 12 times EBITDA."
- "Magazines generally fall into two categories, trade and consumer. Both are valued by a multiple of EBITDA generally ranging from 3 to 10 depending on size, industry trend and profitability. Trade magazines are suffering because people no longer want to wait a month to get their news. In some cases, consumer magazines are suffering as well, but not nearly as much."

- "Circulation questions are key, including various details of subscriptions and newsstand. Advertisers—number, new advertisers. Share of market in the specific specialty area such as log-home magazines, fishing — # of pages and revenue dollars."
- "Prices have been hurt due to low advertising and magazines not embracing an Internet strategy."
- "In magazine publishing, operating profits or EBITDA (earnings before interest, taxes, depreciation and amortization) of 15 to 20 percent are desired and frequently exceeded, while paid subscription renewals above 50 percent and newsstand 'sell-through' above 35 percent will support a higher selling price."

Expert Comments

"Publishing, especially trade publishing, is declining rapidly. People are looking to the Internet for trade information because it can be delivered daily and weekly and be received long before a magazine can even be produced."

"Competition will depend on the industry and market served. Risk for startups are high for established publications, in the consumer space relatively little. Profits on b-to-b publications are declining as advertisers and readers look more to magazines and Web-based information. At the present time there is a good market for publications. Easy to replicate but stiff competition."

Benchmark Data

Statistics (Magazine & Periodical Publishing)

Number of Establishments	6,248
Average Profit Margin	3.1%
Revenue per Employee	$304,400
Average Number of Employees	19.1
Average Wages per Employee	$81,890

Source: IBISWorld, September 2012

Products and Services Segmentation

Academic and professional periodicals	28.9%
Entertainment	27.9%
General-interest magazines	14%
Home and living magazines	13.1%
Business journals	7.5%
Political journals	7.5%
Other periodicals	1.1%

Source: IBISWorld, September 2012

Industry Costs

Profit	3.1%
Wages	26.2%
Purchases	45.2%
Depreciation	0.8%
Marketing	3.4%
Rent & Utilities	5.6%
Other	15.7%

Source: IBISWorld, September 2012

Market Share

Time Warner Inc.	7.0%
Advance Publications, Inc.	6.7%

Source: IBISWorld, September 2012

- "Publishing costs of goods sold will vary based on the type of publication as well as labor and occupancy costs. Profits have ranged from 10% to 30% based on type of publication but are declining. Publishing is undergoing a change. Successful publishing companies will be in a growth industry and will have an interactive presence."

Expenses as a Percentage of Annual Sales

Cost of goods	50%
Payroll/labor Costs	35%
Occupancy	05%
Profit (estimated pretax)	10%

Industry Trend

- "Publishing will continue to decline with the exception of the publishers that can embrace the Internet. Consumer magazines will fare better."

Questions

- "What are advertisers telling you? Look at circulation trends and costs."
- "What have you done to grow the company and how would you grow it in the future?"

Resources

Websites
- www.editorandpublisher.com

Associations
- The Association of Magazine Media: www.magazine.org

Publishers — Newsletters		
	NAICS 511120	

Rules of Thumb

➢ 1 times revenues

Pricing Tips

- "High renewal rate (70 percent plus) increases value"

Publishers — Newspapers—Dailies		
(See also Publishers—Weeklies & Newspapers)		
SIC 2711-98	NAICS 511110	Number of Businesses/Units 5,081

Rules of Thumb

➢ 50% of annual sales includes inventory (only very large will get higher)

➢ 4 times EBITDA

➢ 4 times EBIT

➢ 5 times SDE includes inventory

Pricing Tips

- "EBITDA valuation multiples for mid and small market papers range from 3x to 6x — Publishing company values are currently in the 3x to 6x trailing EBITDA range with most transactions at 4x to 5x. Prices over 5x tend to be strategic acquisitions. Buyers typically look at the most recent performance, and the multiples indicated here are based on stable or improving performance. Companies with declining revenues and EBITDA tend to be valued at the lower end of the multiple scale."

  Source: www.cribb.com—an excellent site, full of valuable information on the publishing business, especially newspapers.

- "In today's market, most valuation methods for newspapers are out the window."

- "Multiples are average. Price can vary + or -50 percent depending on profit margins, market potential and competition. Daily newspapers generally sell for more than weeklies. Amount of paid circulation versus free circulation can affect value."

- "Multiples for newspapers can range from four to ten times EBITDA depending on size and type. Dailies can easily sell at 10 times while smaller weekly publications will be at the lower range."

- "5x EBITDA is a current average for newspaper properties with a history of stable earnings. Number may be considerably higher if publication is positioned for sale to a strategic buyer."

- "Key factors include: size of market, years in business. Is the newspaper geographically desirable by contiguous publishers or buyers looking to roll-up smaller publications into larger groups and take advantage of economies of scale? How active and dominant is the publication in its market and how dominant are its online activities?"

- "Six to 12 times depending on size, profitability, circulation and advertising trend. Some smaller weekly papers will have lower multiples in the 3 to 5 EBITDA area. Current trends in revenue and profitability will have an impact on multiple. Recent large daily newspaper transactions have gone at 11 plus times EBITDA."

Expert Comments

"While the industry is certainly on a decline, there are still many strategic consolidation opportunities."

"Competition generally comes from other media such as TV and cable rather than other newspapers. As newspapers face new challenges, the risk will increase. Profits have historically been very high, reaching 30% EBITDA. Marketability is still strong but will probably decrease. Industry trend is down as circulation and advertising decline. You can replicate but you must sustain the losses for some time."

"Established newspapers with 10+ year track record tend to be extremely stable and low risk. Competition from Internet has not had a material impact on revenues or valuations . . . at least not yet."

"Subscriber acquisition and gaining solid market position takes many, many years for paid circulation newspapers, therefore time is the greatest barrier to entry."

"There is very little competition in newspapers. The days of cities having two newspapers is long gone, with only a handful of exceptions. Newspapers are still getting high multiples. In recent years, the trend has been for newspaper circulation to decline. For most of the last 30 years, average daily circulation was 62 million; two years ago that slipped to 60 million."

Benchmark Data

Statistics (Newspaper Publishing)

Number of Establishments	5,081
Average Profit Margin	7.5%
Revenue per Employee	$147,200
Average Number of Employees	42.1
Average Wages per Employee	$42,215

Source: IBISWorld, October 2012

Products and Services Segmentation

Daily newspapers	44.6%
Other newspapers and services	30.7%
Printing services	11.7%
Other publishing	3.7%
Specialized newspapers	3.2%
Archives	2.3%
Merchandise for resale	1.9%
Daily newspapers	44.6%

Source: IBISWorld, October 2012

Industry Costs

Profit	7.5%
Wages	28.8%
Purchases	19.7%
Depreciation	1.2%
Marketing	2.8%
Rent & Utilities	4.3%
Other	35.7%

Source: IBISWorld, October 2012

Market Share

Gannett Co. Inc.	10.6%
Tribune Company	6.7%
The *New York Times* Company	6.0%

Source: IBISWorld, October 2012

- "There are none in today's economy."
- "Benchmark Data vary greatly by type of publication. For instance, sellers of daily paid circulation newspapers may find that valuations based on subscriber base may be most advantageous. Publishers of free distribution publications are often tied to multiple of discretionary cash flow."
- "Generally multiple of EBITDA. Another is $50 to $400 per paid subscriber."
- "Sales per subscriber, number of subscribers, revenue per household reached (if free distribution publication)"

- "Ratios, Benchmark Data, etc. vary according to the type of publication and geographic area. Daily newspapers, weekly newspapers, free circulation newspapers, coupon book, local magazines, niche magazines, etc."

Expenses as a Percentage of Annual Sales

Cost of goods	50% to 55%
Payroll/labor Costs	30%
Occupancy	05%
Profit (estimated pretax)	15%

Industry Trend

- "Other question responses tended to be positive with 'Would you consider buying a newspaper currently?' up slightly from 46% 'yes' to 49% 'yes.' However a little over half of the respondents would not currently purchase a newspaper."

"Also up are executives who think next year's bottom line will be higher than this year — from 39% in 2011 to 52% in 2012; and those who feel advertising revenue will be higher in 2013 — up from 38% in 2011 to 51% in 2012.

"But publishers are more pessimistic on whether their bottom line will be better than in the past [prior to the recession] as the economy improves — 46% thought it would be better in 2011, down to 42% in 2012. In 2012 33% think their bottom line will be worse than in the past."

Source: www.cribb.com—an excellent site, full of valuable information on the publishing business, especially newspapers.

- "It's the year of the paywall: American newspapers have committed, for better or worse, to making readers pay for the news online, after years of giving away on the web what they charge a fortune for in print. Previously, Ebyline looked at statistics of paywall adoption and discovered that larger newspapers are building paywalls at significantly higher rates. But examining paywalls by newspaper size only tells part of the story.

"The metered paywall approach (allowing readers to read, say, 5 or 10 articles before they have to pay for content) is the most popular, with 84% of the newspapers listed in NAA's database. It's also the paywall strategy used by The *New York Times*, which recently changed the number of free articles readers can access to 10, down from 20, earlier this year. On average, newspapers allow 11.2 free articles before readers encounter the paywall."

Source: "Newspaper Paywalls Accelerating" by Susan Johnston, July 2012

- "*The Daily*, News Corp.'s attempt to create a digital newspaper for the iPad age, is laying off nearly a third of its staff.

"News Corp. officials have publicly defended *The Daily*, which News Corp. CEO Rupert Murdoch thought would serve as a template for newspapers' transition to the tablet era. Murdoch's team worked closely with Apple and its late CEO Steve Jobs to produce a publication initially tailored for the iPad.

"The cuts come at the same time as News Corp. examines costs at other properties in its newspaper portfolio, in advance of its corporate divorce. News Corp.'s flagship Dow Jones unit, which publishes the *Wall Street Journal*, has quietly been letting go of some of its business executives; last month, Dow Jones shuttered the print edition of its SmartMoney personal finance magazine."

Source: "The Daily Lays Off a Third of Its Staff," www.allthingsd.com, July 2012

- "Cribb, Greene & Associates has released the Publisher Confidence Survey Spring 2010 with results that may surprise newspaper industry observers.

Newspaper executives clearly feel that the industry is improving quickly. Seventy one percent (71%) of executives polled believe their advertising revenues will be up in 2011 and 25% more think they will be about the same as this year. Only 4% think next year's ad revenues will be down.

"Most newspapers believe their local market economies are improving or stable (94%); their profits will be up in 2011 (68%); and with an improving economy feel their profit margin will be the same or better than in the past (69%). However a substantial number of respondents—31%—think their profit margin will be lower than it was prior to the economic downturn."

Source: "Publisher Confidence Survey Results," Cribb, Greene (April 21, 2010) www.cribb.com

- "Just trying to stay alive"
- "They say big metros also are discussing a wide range of other radical notions. Among them: making home deliveries only on certain days of the week, shrinking additional weekday print editions, and even cutting out paid papers entirely on certain days of the week in favor of a smaller and free product. (The executives promise their Web sites will pick up the slack on days when the print edition is skimpier.) . . . Dean Singleton, said that, in his estimation, 19 of the top 50 U.S. newspapers are losing money. And, he warned 'that number will continue to grow.'"

Source: "The Daily Shrinking Planet" by Jon Fine, *Businessweek*, June 23, 2008

Seller Financing

- "5 years"

Questions

- "How effectively are you competing with online media? How are your renewal rates compared to your competitors'?"
- "How he would increase the circulation and advertising revenue and why he has not been successful if that is the case? Is the circulation audited?"

Resources

Websites
- www.cribb.com

Trade Publications
- Editor & Publisher: www.editorandpublisher.com

Associations
- Association of Free Community Papers: www.afcp.org
- Newspaper Association of America: www.naa.org
- National Newspaper Association: www.nnaweb.org

Publishers — Newspapers—Weeklies/Community Papers		
(See also Publishers—Newspapers—Dailies)		
	NAICS 511110	

Rules of Thumb

- ➤ "100 percent of annual sales"
- ➤ "Some smaller weekly papers will have lower multiples in the 3 to 5 EBITDA area."
- ➤ "Community monthlies will sell for 3 x SDE if they produce at least $150,000 in SDE. Otherwise, multiple comes down to the 2 x SDE area."
- ➤ 3 times SDE
- ➤ 3 times EBIT
- ➤ 3 times EBITDA
- ➤ 1 times annual income for mid-sized weekly newspaper

Pricing Tips

- See Newspapers (In General)

Expert Comments

"Barriers to entry are low. This is a selling business. Getting good salespeople is very difficult. The buyer of this type of business should expect to spend half of their time selling."

Benchmark Data

- For additional Benchmark data, see Publishers—Newspapers—Dailies
- "Advertising to editorial should run 2/3rd to 1/3rd for maximum profitability."
- "Look for businesses where the owner does very little selling. You have to make a negative adjustment to SDE to account for sales commissions to replace an overactive seller."

Expenses as a Percentage of Annual Sales

Cost of goods	25%
Payroll/labor Costs	25%
Occupancy	05%
Profit (estimated pretax)	20%

Industry Trend

- "Most say revenues are down 10%-15%, and are making expense cuts to compensate. EBITDA margins can still be in the 15%-25% range, although 5%-15% is closer to the norm. The industry may not have hit the bottom in revenue decline, but it appears it may be getting close. Certainly, these are ugly numbers compared to what newspapers are used to, but they are not disastrous."

  Source: "Mid and small market newspapers are not failing" by John Cribb, June 16, 2009, www.cribb.com

- "Up. Local merchants are looking for a cost-effective way to reach their local customers. Major dailies are too expensive and provide too much reach for the local markets."
- "Community papers are following the rise in the housing market. New communities are receptive to local papers that educate them as to local restaurants, salons, etc. This trend will continue."

Questions

- "How many salespeople do you have?"

Resources

Websites

- www.cribb.com

Associations

- National Newspaper Publishers Association (NNPA): www.nnpa.org

Publishers — Software	
NAICS 511210	Number of Businesses/Units 25,868

Rules of Thumb

➢ "Varies widely, particularly on multiple (revenue, earnings) of historical performance. Many acquisitions are strategic in nature."

Expert Comments

"Market momentum of software products can change quickly, both up and down. With specialized niche firms, buyers can be international companies. This is a trans-national market."

Benchmark Data

Statistics (Software Publishing)

Number of Establishments	25,868
Average Profit Margin	29.4%
Revenue per Employee	$435,800
Average Number of Employees	16.8
Average Wages per Employee	$139,407

Source: IBISWorld, September 2012

Products and Services Segmentation

Operating systems and productivity software	37.5%
Business analytics and enterprise software	20.3%
Database, storage and backup software	19.3%
Video games	8.7%
Security software	7.1%
Design, editing and rendering software	6.1%
Smartphone apps	1%

Source: IBISWorld, September 2012

Major Market Segmentation

Finance and insurance	22.4%
Other business	16.4%
Manufacturing	14.1%
Information	12.4%
Households	10%
Retail and wholesale trade	8.5%
Professional, scientific and tech services	8.2%
Governments	8.0%

Source: IBISWorld, September 2012

Industry Costs

Profit	29.4%
Wages	30.6%
Depreciation	2.0%
Marketing	12.0%
Rent & Utilities	3.0%
Other	23.0%

Source: IBISWorld, September 2012

Market Share

Microsoft Corporation	20.9%
Oracle Corporation	7.0%
International Business Machines Corporation	5.6%

Source: IBISWorld, September 2012

Industry Trend
- "Increasingly competitive"

Publishing — Monthly Community Magazines

Rules of Thumb

➢ 65-85 percent of annual sales includes inventory

➢ 3 times SDE includes inventory

➢ 3.5 EBIT

➢ 3.5 times EBITDA

Pricing Tips
- "The page count of the magazine and the size of the distribution is a key to attaining the higher number and the greater multiple suggested above. Most Publications in this segment will be focused on an area or group within a geographical area, i.e., 'Lake Norman Woman,' 'Carolina Living,' or 'Iredell County Life' and will require that targeted readers identify themselves with the title implication and market. The attraction to a segment of the market creates a loyalty that should translate into long-time advertisers. Make sure the renewal rate is over 75% to confirm this loyalty is real & present."

"If gross revenues exceed $500,000 then 1X sales is common. That usually equates to 3X SDE. A monthly that has the owner doing all of the sales is worth less than one with a good sales staff. Publications under $500,000 will sell closer to 2X SDE or 50% to 75% of sales."

Expert Comments

"The advertising industry as a whole is very competitive, which will show in the last 3 years' sales, but there is a strong opportunity for a great salesperson to make good money. Hiring great salespeople is very hard and a new owner should not count on a salesperson making a material difference in sales. This is the owner's primary responsibility."

"Monthlies are easy to start up and competition is great. Look for the thickest book (largest number of pages). Advertising should be around 70% of total pages. The thinner books will have the hardest time staying alive.

Advertisers tend to stick with the publication they are in, so it's hard to be the new kid on the block."

Benchmark Data

- "The average cost is about $700 a page to print and distribute. The average sales commission should not exceed 25% of the sale. Most vanity magazines will operate out of a home or key-man office space with the occasional use of conference rooms for sales meetings. In any case, occupancy cost should not exceed 5% of sales."
- "Look for sales per salesperson of around $20,000 a month. That should pay a commission of $4,000 which is the minimum you need to keep good salespeople."

Expenses as a Percentage of Annual Sales

Cost of goods	25%
Payroll/labor Costs	25% to 30%
Occupancy	05%
Profit (estimated pretax)	20% to 30%

Industry Trend

- "The boutique magazine industry trend is positive as a larger number of people see this industry as attractive because it affords them the opportunity for a specific lifestyle in a targeted community setting without a significant liability and risk"
- "Soft. Real estate advertising usually makes up a big percentage of monthly publications. That is very soft right now. Financial advertising is also down. Trends will be soft until the economy picks up and real estate starts selling again."

Questions

- "What are the top five advertisers? How long have they been with you? Could you grow the circulation? How long have you been with your current printer? Describe your 'layout' process."

  "How long have you been publishing and what are your historical trends? How many salespeople and how long have they worked for you? Who do you consider your competition?"

Publishing — Newspapers (In General)

SIC 2711-98	NAICS 511110	Number of Businesses/Units 5,400

Rules of Thumb

➢ 25 percent of annual sales includes inventory

➢ 3 times SDE plus inventory

➢ 3 to 5 times EBIT

➢ 3 to 5 times EBITDA

Pricing Tips

- "Newspaper multiples have been weak the last few years, but 2011 has started off with a significant increase in activity."
- "I no longer see multiples of revenue as a realistic way of pricing a media business."
- "Depends on size and segment, for example it would be very hard to sell a daily newspaper in today's environment."
- "Price can vary greatly depending on the size and frequency of publication, i.e., weekly, daily publication, if the company has its own printing plant and the value of printing equipment and approximately 50% of gross revenue for recurring outside print work."
- "Market at a Glance
  - ✓ Daily newspapers: All dailies actively sought at 6 to 10 times EBITDA. Dailies over 10,000 circulation at 7 to 10 times EBITDA or 1.5 to 3 times publishing revenues. Smaller dailies at 5 to 8 times EBITDA or 1 to 2 times publishing revenues.
  - ✓ Weekly Groups, free or paid circulation: Sought at 5 to 8 times EBITDA or 1 to 2 times publishing revenues.
  - ✓ Large Weekly & Twice Weekly Newspapers and Shoppers: (over $1 million revenues) Sought at 4 to 7 times EBITDA or 1 to 1.5 times publishing revenues.
  - ✓ Small Weekly Newspapers and Shoppers: (under $1 million revenues): Moderate activity at 4 to 6 times EBITDA or 0.5 to 1 times publishing revenues.
  - ✓ Specialty & Niche Publications: Specific niches sought at 3 to 5 times EBITDA or 0.5 to 1.25 times publishing revenues. Wide pricing variation depending on niche."

  Source: "Newspaper market in upheaval," Cribb Greene Report, published by Cribb, Green & Associates, Summer, 2008. Note: This firm has an excellent site and is very informative. www.cribb.com

- "A stable weekly will sell for 5 to 7 times EBITDA. A strong weekly in a growth area can sell for as much as 9 to 11 times EBITDA. Variation in price is based upon age of property, market potential, competition, stability, growth history, community acceptance, reputation and market penetration. If printing equipment is owned, add value of equipment. If income is generated from outside printing, the profits for the printing portion of the business need to be separated and valued at 3 to 5 times EBITDA. "
- "Each newspaper is unique and its strengths and weaknesses must be analyzed in order to arrive at a Fair Market Value. There are industry rules-of-thumb that apply to Gross Revenues and EBITDA, which change according to the dictates of the market."

Expert Comments

"The growth of online advertising has significantly reduced profitability and gross revenues of newspapers"

"Online media and the recession have significantly impacted performance."

"Newspapers need to find a way to reinvent themselves. Traditional print is declining, most young people today don't get a newspaper. Newspapers need to embrace the Internet and the whole interactive scene. Newspapers are competing for the same advertising dollars that other media is trying to get. Profits are down significantly and many newspapers that have been used to great profits are facing something they have never faced: declining sales, profits or no profits."

"Amount of competition from all media in the market is important because there is a limited amount of advertising dollars to go around. Historic performance and competition will be large factors in determining the amount of risk. Location is of minor importance because the customer rarely goes to the business. Most publications with reasonable profits are marketable as there are sufficient buyers in the market for local community operations. While the trend in large metro dailies is declining revenue and profits, smaller community publications continue to do well. It is easy to start a new publication, but a lot more difficult to build a reader and advertising base."

"Competition generally comes from other media such as TV and cable rather than other newspapers. Profits have historically been very high, reaching 30% EBITDA, but have been falling recently. Marketability is decreasing."

"Competition is a key element because there is a limited amount of advertising dollars in any market. If a publication has a history of increasing profits they are taking advantage of the market growth, likely have a good reputation and less risk of a new competitor breaking into the market. Starting a publication is easy, getting established is difficult. Location has almost no effect on profitability or value."

"The industry is in a state of turmoil and transition. Large metro dailies are being hardest hit, while smaller community newspapers have been able to weather the perfect storm of Internet competition and a changing economic environment."

"Newspapers live in a competitive world, but in the majority of cases there is only one dominant newspaper in each community."

Benchmark Data

- For additional Benchmark data see Publishers — Newspapers — Dailies
- "At one time $200 per daily newspaper subscriber, but not anymore. It is a matter of profitability. Some smaller newspapers in rural areas have a better chance because there are not as many advertising options."
- "The ratio of advertising space to editorial space has a lot to do with profitability. Ideally one should have two-thirds advertising, one-third profit."

Expenses as a Percentage of Annual Sales

Cost of goods	35% to 45%
Payroll/labor Costs	25% to 35%
Occupancy	05% to 10%
Profit (estimated pretax)	15% to 25%

Industry Trend

- "Tough times will continue for this sector."

Seller Financing

- "About 50% of sales are financed. Larger papers generally sell for cash. Smaller papers will sell for as little as 30% down with terms averaging seven years."
- "Seller financing is typical with terms of five years or longer."

Questions

- "What is your online market position and share of market in each market that you serve?"
- "What are the reasons why you feel your media will continue to be relevant in the years to come?"
- "How would you increase the circulation and advertising? Why haven't you been successful in doing so?"
- "Revenue by category, cash flow, paid circulation and free circulation, average advertising percentage, competition, owner's duties, who sells the ads, number of ad contracts in place and dollar value.?"
- "What contracts do you have; how are you handling the changes in the newspaper environment? Is it an all-cash sale or is the owner willing to carry some of the sale price?"
- "Subscription base, number of subscribers, subscriber retention, revenue trends, strength of online initiatives, years established"
- "Why they are selling; what their daily involvement is; what investment has been made to adapt to new technologies; how do they reach the individual reader and advertiser. Many more."
- "How are you positioned in your market relative to competition in the online market? How are you protecting your employment and classified advertising base from online competition?"

Resources

Trade Publications
- Editor and Publisher Magazine: www.editorandpublisher.com

Associations
- Newspaper Association of America: www.naa.org

	Franchise
Pump It Up	
Approx. Total Investment	$297,550 to $646,900
NAICS 713990	Number of Businesses/Units 175

Rules of Thumb

➤ 30 percent of annual sales plus inventory
➤ (Provides children's parties with inflated/bouncy toys)

Resources

Websites
- www.pumpitupparty.com

Purrfect Auto

	NAICS 811118	Number of Businesses/Units 100

Rules of Thumb

> ➢ 45 percent of annual sales plus inventory
> ➢ Note: This franchise is on the West Coast

Quick Print (See Print Shops/Quick Print)

	NAICS 323114	

Quizno's Classic Subs

Approx. Total Investment		$157,547 to $217,527
Estimated Annual Sales/Unit		$330,000
SIC 5812-19	NAICS 722211	Number of Businesses/Units 2,500

Rules of Thumb

> ➢ 25 to 30 percent of annual sales plus inventory

Benchmark Data
- For Benchmark data see Sandwich Shops

Resources

Websites
- www.quiznos.com

Racquet Sports Clubs (See Fitness Centers)

Radio Stations

SIC 4832-01	NAICS 513112	Number of Businesses/Units 8,672

Rules of Thumb

> ➢ 8 to 10 times EBITDA
> ➢ 10 to 12 times cash flow in medium markets
> ➢ 15 times cash flow—large markets
> ➢ 1.5 to 6 times annual sales

Pricing Tips
- "BROADCAST STATION 'STICK' VALUATION OR THE CONUNDRUM OF HOW TO VALUE A STATION THAT HAS NEVER MADE ANY MONEY...EVER

"Broadcast station valuation is usually done by using a multiple of the station's broadcast cash flow (BCF). Of course this assumes the station is producing a cash flow. Where there is no cash flow, it is the perceived value of what the license is worth plus any hard assets the station may have ... commonly referred to as the 'stick' or base value. There are several scholarly tomes on broadcast or radio station valuation (Search: broadcast station valuation). The problem here is that many stations have gone through a succession of owners and have never shown any positive cash flow or just enough to keep the power on until the next sale/transfer. What is a station like this worth? Many new construction permits (CP) are coming on the market as a result of the recent FM allocation auctions. What are these worth?

"In the case of a station that has never shown a positive cash flow you need to determine the reason. Is it an unfortunate combination of circumstances that has led to a succession of owners who had no clue as to what to do with the station? Poor market conditions? Improper format? Poor signal? Also, some stations can be artistic successes and commercial failures. Such a station might have a format that appeals to a significant audience but the station is unable to sell enough advertising to capitalize on the station's own success. This is frequently because the station has not developed a proper sales force. As any broadcast owner knows, the hardest positions to fill at a station are good sales representatives. I talk to would-be broadcasters all the time that have no clue as to what it takes to put together a sales staff ... but that will have to wait for another commentary.

"Back to how to evaluate a non-cash flowing station or a dark station ready to go back on the air. A common industry approach has been to factor the amount of revenue a particular facility may generate by looking at the amount of advertising revenue the station may be able to secure out of the total revenue available for radio in the market if it reaches a particular audience level ... whew ... got that? The problem here is there are many pieces of the puzzle that have to be put together to get an idea of what the numbers should be. What is the financial condition of the market? Power of the station? Is it AM or FM? Is the ownership/management talented? In today's market we have to contend with how much advertising revenue is going to other competitors on the Internet. This is where the question is asked... 'Is the Internet going to be a foe of the station or a tool to be used by it?' To stream or not to stream? Interactive Web site or not? Maybe even podcasts?

"Another major factor to look at in evaluating a start-up property is the technical condition of the station. Failure to conduct an engineering inspection can be a costly mistake. What looks like a cheap price for an AM property could be a pig in a poke with some nasty surprises. Questions that need to be answered: What is the condition of the AM ground system and tower? Do either need to be painted (tower), repaired or even replaced? Are the copper radials in the ground damaged or corroded away? If the AM station is a directional system, is the pattern still in compliance? Has there been lightning damage to the phasor system and other transmitter/audio processing components? What is the age of the transmitter? Will it need to be replaced? To get the answers, hire a competent broadcast engineering firm to do an evaluation. You will need to pay for this but it can save you big money and headaches later."

Source: David Garland, Media Brokerage, www.radiobroker.com.
Garland is one of the most successful radio brokers in the country.

- "Normally depends on historical (and projected) Broadcast Cash Flow, or EBITDA plus certain non-recurring charges and management-unique expenses. Value of the intangible rights to the license can vary widely with supply and demand.

"Some advice to sellers—you are not going to get 22 times cash flow on a small market station. Yes, I know that some stations recently, and one in particular in Texas, were reported as having sold for 22 times cash flow. This is only going to happen in probably the top 50 markets. Most banks will only (if you can get them to look at the deal) do 4 to 5 times cash flow. That means the buyer will have to put in the balance in cash unless you carry the paper yourself (and be in 2nd position behind the bank). The only way you are going to get a big premium is if your FM station has the potential to upgrade into a much larger market. My associate Burt Perrault has been in discussions with the owner of a small market combo, billing in the $150,000 range, about listing the stations for sale. The market has about 6,000 population, with 40,000 or so in the county. There are 3 other radio stations in the county also. He wants close to $1,000,000 for the combo. In a market this size, to bring $1million he needs to cash flow $125K to bring 8 times cash flow (which is a realistic multiple) in a market this size. He also does not want to do the work to bring his station's cash flow, and, as a result, the value, up to where he wants it. That is to be left to the hoped-for buyer to do. Yes his combo may be worth $1million one day but not on a present 'as is...where is' basis. There are lots of people wanting to get into the radio station ownership business, but pricing has got to be realistic in relation to market size. That's the way it is...deal with it."

Source: David Garland, Media Brokerage, www.radiobroker.com

- "A multiple of broadcast cash flow (revenues minus operating expenses before interest, depreciation, taxes). Multiple varies by service (AM/FM/TV) & market size. All broadcasters need to own tower site. Consolidation opportunities within a market add value."
- "Try 8 to 12 times cash flow depending on market size."
- "With rapid consolidation taking place in the radio industry sellers and buyers are happy with the multipliers they are achieving—buyers of multiple properties can reduce expenses. Ask about buyer's investment horizon. What expenses are in the business of the owner/operator that an investor may not have?"

Expert Comments

"More competitive"

Benchmark Data

Statistics (Radio Broadcasting)

Number of Establishments	8,672
Average Profit Margin	4.8%
Revenue per Employee	$163,900
Average Number of Employees	12.2
Average Wages per Employee	$55,058

Source: IBISWorld, July 2012

Products and Services Segmentation

Contemporary music	35.2%
Other programming	25.7%
News and talk radio	12.6%
Country music	12.5%
Classic rock music	4.7%
Classic hits music	3.9%
Sports programming	2.5%
Mexican regional programming	2.9%

Source: IBISWorld, July 2012

Industry Costs

Profit	4.8%
Wages	33.5%
Purchases	27.7%
Depreciation	2.9%
Marketing	6.8%
Rent & Utilities	8.8%
Other	15.5%

Source: IBISWorld, July 2012

Market Share

Sirius XM Radio Inc.	19.8%
CC Media Holdings Inc.	18.8%
CBS Corporation	7.7%

Source: IBISWorld, July 2012

Industry Trend

- "There is a credit crunch in the land if anyone has noticed. It started when home loan lenders started making stupid loans. I have been in this business long enough to have seen this happen two or three times. Home loan sharks in some cases have constructed loan vehicles where the monthly payment on a house was not enough to cover both principal and interest…the deficit each month is tacked on the back end of the loan principal to generate even more interest….How stupid is this? Now the lenders are whining because the poor schmucks they conned into taking out such a loan are unable to make the nut every month. This is now spilling over into my business. Banks and other lenders are turning off the loan spigot to potential borrowers for media transactions. Merger and Acquisition deals of all types are being scrutinized closely…many are being delayed or canceled altogether….Unless, and this is where it gets good…you have the cash.

"Cash deals are king. Just think… no monthly payment to that nasty, ill-tempered banker who really does not understand your business anyway. He/she gave you the loan in the first place only because you promised him/her the marriage of your first born Dartmouth/Stanford/Harvard etc. business school educated son/daughter to their loser offspring. But I digress….What I am getting at is if you want to get into the Radio/TV business and can raise the equity… step right this way.

"In reference to email…I am now including a 'read' receipt to be sent back to me on all email I now send out. Due to problems with anti-spam software both on my end and folks I respond to I find this necessary. I have tried to avoid it for a long time but have finally seen the need."

Source: David Garland, Media Brokerage, www.radiobroker.com.

Seller Financing

- "Rarely is there seller financing except for smallest of deals."

Questions

- "Can your signal be upgraded or moved to cover a larger market? How are you spending your revenue? How much do you do in trade? Can any barter be converted to cash? Do you really need to buy that new gadget, just because you have a few extra bucks this month? Spend the money to find out what can be done to expand or move that signal to more ears. Are you being a partner in your advertisers' business? The more you expand your advertisers' businesses, the more you expand yours and are therefore able to ask for more dollars on the selling market."

Source: www.buysellradio.com

Resources

Websites

- www.buysellradio.com—this is a brokerage site loaded with good information
- www.radiobroker.com

Real Estate Offices

SIC Real Estate 6531-18; SIC Business Brokerage 7382-22

	NAICS 531210	Number of Businesses/Units 702,174

Rules of Thumb

> ➤ 2 times SDE; may require earnout
> ➤ 33 percent of annual sales (real estate offices) includes inventory

Pricing Tips

- "Price will depend on agent splits."
- "Time in the market and number of listings"
- "This industry has taken a huge hit. The multiples must be on SDE that is sustainable."
- "Must factor out owner's personal production. Smaller brokerages (under $1M in gross commissions) are about 1x SDE."

Expert Comments

"Easy to replicate. Marketability will be down until economy and house sales rebound."

"RE brokerages are going to be soft for the next year or so. Business brokerages may sell easier."

"Easy to replicate small offices"

Benchmark Data

Statistics (Real Estate Agency Franchises)

Number of Establishments	31,331
Average Profit Margin	7.5%
Revenue per Employee	$22,900
Average Number of Employees	9.3
Average Wages per Employee	$3,705

Source: IBISWorld, August 2012

Products and Services Segmentation

Residential real estate agency franchises	68.5%
Commercial real estate agency franchises	31.5%

Source: IBISWorld, August 2012

Industry Costs

Profit	7.5%
Wages	16.1%
Purchases	30.0%
Depreciation	1.1%
Marketing	5.0%
Rent and Utilities	2.3%
Other	38.0%

Source: IBISWorld, August 2012

Major Market Segmentation

Sellers	45%
Lessors	30%
Buyers	25%

Source: IBISWorld, August 2012

Market Share

Realogy Corporation	9.0%
RE/MAX LLC	3.2%
Keller Williams Realty	2.7%

Source: IBISWorld, August 2012

Statistics (Real Estate Sales and Brokerage)

Number of Establishments	702,174
Average Profit Margin	8.8%
Revenue per Employee	$109,300
Average Number of Employees	1.3
Average Wages per Employee	$23,581

Source: IBISWorld, September 2012

Products and Services Segmentation

Residential sales	48%
Commercial sales	21.1
Residential rentals	14.6%
Commercial leases	13.3%
Other (including sale or lease of land)	3%

Source: IBISWorld, September 2012

Major Market Segmentation

Sellers	45%
Lessors	30%
Buyers	25%

Source: IBISWorld, September 2012

Industry Costs

Profit	8.8%
Wages	60.2%
Purchases	1.0%
Depreciation	1.0%
Marketing	5.0%
Rent & Utilities	2.3%
Other	21.7%

Source: IBISWorld, September 2012

Market Share

Realogy Corporation	4.4%
CB Richard Ellis Group Inc.	4.3%

Source: IBISWorld, September 2012

- "Should have 5 closings per agent annually"

- "Need to get to about $1million in gross commissions."

Expenses as a Percentage of Annual Sales

Cost of goods	65% (commission payout)
Payroll/labor Costs	10%
Occupancy	05% to 10%
Profit (estimated pretax)	15%

Industry Trend

- "Should increase"
- "Indications RE will be soft. However that may mean more brokers get listings. Business brokers should be strong."
- "Growing, but may still see a decline in the short run."

Questions

- "Are you in production? What contract do you have for advertising and services? Where do you get your leads? Have you recently lost top-producing agents?"
- "Do you produce? What are your splits? Do you have non-competes?" "Will the owner be available?"

Records Management		
	NAICS 541611	

Rules of Thumb

➤ 8 times SDE

➤ 200 percent of annual sales

Pricing Tips

- "Pricing [above] specifically for Records Management businesses"

Benchmark Data

- "Internal account growth of 5 to 7%. Sixty percent storage revenues with 40% service revenues."

Expenses as a Percentage of Annual Sales

Cost of goods	0%
Payroll/labor Costs	35%
Occupancy	25%
Profit (estimated pretax)	30%

Industry Trend

- "Continued industry growth with emphasis on document-destruction services"

Recruiting Agencies		
SIC 7361-03	NAICS 56131	Number of Businesses/Units 74,846

Rules of Thumb

➤ 50 percent of annual revenues; may require earnout

1 to 1.5 times SDE; add fixtures equipment & inventory; may require earnout

Benchmark Data

Statistics (Employment and Recruiting Agencies)

Number of Establishments	74,846
Average Profit Margin	3.7%
Revenue per Employee	$55,100
Average Number of Employees	3.6
Average Wages per Employee	$37,871

Source: IBISWorld, August 2012

Products and Services Segmentation

Permanent placement services	58.2%
Contract staffing services	26.5%
Temporary staffing services	5.9%
Other	4%
Online job listing services	1.6%
Online resume listing services	3.8%

Source: IBISWorld, August 2012

Major Market Segmentation

Professional and service industries	30%
Healthcare industries	15%
Other	15%
Technical industries	15%
Construction and manufacturing industries	10%
Finance and accounting industries	10%
Government industries	5%

Source: IBISWorld, August 2012

Industry Costs

Profit	3.7%
Wages	70.7%
Purchases	1.5%
Depreciation	1.0%
Marketing	3.0%
Rent & Utilities	3.7%
Other	16.4%

Source: IBISWorld, August 2012

Recycling

NAICS 56292	Number of Businesses/Units 1,451

Rules of Thumb

> 3 to 5 times SDE includes inventory
> 3 to 6 times EBIT
> 3 to 6 times EBITDA

Pricing Tips

- "Once the EBITDA exceeds $1,000,000 most buyers will assume that normal levels of inventory, A/R, and FFE will be included in the transaction as working capital. The key is to understand how the buyer is structuring their offer and how they are accounting for these values."
- "Must consider if this is a commodity product that is sold. If so, consider the consistency of the source of the product as an important risk factor."

Benchmark Data

Statistics (Recycling Facilities)

Number of Establishments	1,451
Average Profit Margin	8.6%
Revenue per Employee	$288,800
Average Number of Employees	13.6
Average Wages per Employee	$37,742

Source: IBISWorld, August 2012

Products and Services Segmentation

Recyclable material recovery and preparation	67.6%
Other	25.6%
Waste Transfer facility services	4.5%
Resale of merchandise	2.3%

Source: IBISWorld, August 2012

Major Market Segmentation

Consumer product manufacturers	52.6%
Paper and paper packaging companies	37.4%
State and local government	10%

Source: IBISWorld, August 2012

Industry Costs

Profit	8.6%
Wages	13.3%
Purchases	51.4%
Depreciation	12.3%
Marketing	1.1%
Rent & Utilities	3.9%
Other	9.4%

Source: IBISWorld, August 2012

Market Share

Waste Management Inc.	29.0%%
Republic Services Inc.	8.2%%

Source: IBISWorld, August 2012

Industry Trend

- "Companies associated to the waste management industry will continue to be attractive as they provide a 'green' business opportunity to both individual and strategic buyers."
- "Trend is overall growth in the recycling industry with a consolidation with middle to large sized companies seeking to purchase smaller competitors."

Questions

- "What kind of contracts do you have with your paper suppliers? Are you contracted to sell your paper to certain mills or brokers? Who is your competition within 100 miles?"

Red Robin Gourmet Burgers		Franchise
Approx. Total Investment		$1,800,000 to $3,000,000
Estimated Annual Sales/Unit		$2,650,000
	NAICS 722211	Number of Businesses/Units 454

Rules of Thumb
➤ 30 to 35 percent of annual sales

Resources
Websites
▪ www.redrobin.com

Registered Investment Advisors		
	NAICS 523930	Number of Businesses/Units 137,742

Rules of Thumb
➤ 150 percent of annual sales
➤ 3 to 5 SDE

Pricing Tips
▪ "The structure of your deal will depend on the willingness of the seller to hold an earnout vs. a note and cash down payment at closing."

Expert Comments
"There will be continued major consolidation in the industry."

Benchmark Data

Statistics (Financial Planning and Advice)
Number of Establishments	137,742
Average Profit Margin	17.9%
Revenue per Employee	$199,400
Average Number of Employees	1.8
Average Wages per Employee	$93,315

Source: IBISWorld, October 2012

Products and Services Segmentation
Business and government planning and management	45.1%
Personal financial planning and advice	23.7%
Other services	21.2%
Personal investment management	10%

Source: IBISWorld, October 2012

Major Market Segmentation
Individuals and households	33.7%
Number of Businesses/Units	31.6%
Other clients	21.1%
Governments	13.6%

Source: IBISWorld, October 2012

Industry Costs
Profit	17.9%
Wages	51.0%
Depreciation	2.0%
Marketing	1.0%
Rent & Utilities	4.0%
Other	24.1%

Source: IBISWorld, October 2012

Market Share

Morgan Stanley Smith Barney LLC	14.3%
Wells Fargo & Company	12.7%
Bank of America Corporation	10.1%
Ameriprise Financial Inc.	8.%

Source: IBISWorld, October 2012

- "Average account per client"

Expenses as a Percentage of Annual Sales

Cost of goods	05% to 10%
Payroll/labor Costs	10% to 20%
Occupancy	05% to 15%
Profit (estimated pretax)	20% to 45%

Industry Trend

- "Continued major consolidation. Large players absorbing smaller operators for their higher margins. However, smaller players will have a disadvantage due to size."

Questions

- "Gross commissions? Net? Broker-dealer? Overhead? Fee-based or commission-based? Average fees? Average client investment, net worth?"

Remediation Services		
	NAICS 562910	Number of Businesses/Units 5,571

Rules of Thumb

➢ 4 to 5 times EBITDA

➢ 40 percent of annual sales includes inventory

➢ 2 to 3 times SDE includes inventory

Pricing Tips

- "Union vs non-union work force. Private vs. public projects."
- "Contract and client direct relationships will be worth more than those performed as a subcontractor for a general contractor. Size makes a big difference in price—larger Number of Businesses/Units with $1 million + EBITDA sell for higher multiples."
- "Value of future jobs under contract is a major factor in value and salability."

Expert Comments

"Industry has become increasingly competitive as more players are chasing fewer projects."

"Demand for remediation services is tied to the construction remodeling and improvement market. As demand for building modifications has decreased with the economic crisis, so too have remediation services."

"Competition varies based on union vs. non-union, and public vs. private market. Revenue varies with commercial real estate renovation and development."

Benchmark Data

Statistics (Remediation & Environmental Cleanup Services)

Number of Establishments	5,571
Average Profit Margin	8.7%
Revenue per Employee	$229,900
Average Number of Employees	16.2
Average Wages per Employee	$65,609

Source: IBISWorld, July 2012

Products and Services Segmentation

Site remediation services	39.7%
Building remediation services	32.6%
Other	17.2%
Environmental emergency response services	10.5%

Source: IBISWorld, July 2012

Major Market Segmentation

Number of Businesses/Units	41%
Federal government	34.4%
State and local government	14.7%
Individuals	9.9%

Source: IBISWorld, July 2012

Industry Costs

Profit	8.7%
Wages	34.0%
Purchases	42.0%
Depreciation	1.0%
Marketing	1.0%
Rent & Utilities	1.5%
Other	11.8%

Source: IBISWorld, July 2012

Market Share

The Shaw Group Inc.	9.0%
CH2M Hill Companies Ltd.	9.2%

Source: IBISWorld, July 2012

- "Owner compensation 3% of sales"
- "Flat management structure with an engaged owner will be much more profitable. Sales, estimating and production responsibility for each project should be with the same manager."
- "Gross margin should be 25%–30% and SDE 20% of revenue."

Expenses as a Percentage of Annual Sales

Cost of goods	70%
Payroll/labor Costs	07%
Occupancy	04%
Profit (estimated pretax)	03% to 05%

Industry Trend

- "Project opportunities are a function of the overall commercial construction industry. Business will pick up when commercial renovation work picks up."
- "Demand will decline with the commercial construction market."

Questions

- "Have there been any DEP violations? Workers comp claims?"
- "Check for hidden liabilities. Union vs. non-union is important difference. Reputation is also important—how many jobs have they abandoned? or not completed on time?"
- "BOD rate for workers comp, and if there have been any DEP fines"

	Franchise
Renaissance Executive Forums	
Approx. Total Investment	$75,500 to $110,000
NAICS 611430	Number of Businesses/Units 50

Rules of Thumb

➢ 75 percent of annual sales includes inventory

Resources

Websites

- www.excutiveforums.info

Rent-to-Own Stores (See also Rental Centers)	
SIC 7359-30	NAICS 532310	Number of Businesses/Units 6,136

Rules of Thumb

➢ 55 percent of annual sales includes inventory

Pricing Tips

- "Eight (8) times monthly gross receipts (tops), includes lock, stock (inventory) and barrel. All underlying debts would be paid off by seller at this price. I think the multiple is now less because the industry has sustained a shakeout."

Benchmark Data

Statistics (Consumer Electronics & Appliances Rental)

Number of Establishments	6,136
Average Profit Margin	5.2%
Revenue per Employee	$199,900
Average Number of Employees	4.9
Average Wages per Employee	29,490

Source: IBISWorld, July 2012

Products and Services Segmentation

Electronics rentals	36.3%
Full-term rentals	2%
Appliance rentals	34.5%
Computer rentals	15.5%
Merchandise sales	9.6%
Financial services	2.1%

Source: IBISWorld, July 2012

Industry Costs

Profit	5.2%
Wages	18.7%
Purchases	36.2%
Depreciation	12.0%
Marketing	3.4%
Rent & Utilities	5.9%
Other	18.6%

Source: IBISWorld, July 2012

Market Share

Rent-A-Center Inc.	31.7%
Aaron's Inc.	23.9%

Source: IBISWorld, July 2012

- "The average store has annual revenue of $736,000 and serves 360 customers each year."

- "Operating costs for rent-to-own businesses are higher than traditional retail because of the ultimate return of merchandise, merchandise repair and replacement expenses and the need to continually market the industry's services to a rotating customer base."

Product Breakdown

Furniture	36.7%
Appliances	18.6%
Electronics	24.9%
Computers	10.7%
Jewelry	.06%
Other	7.6%

Source: Association of Progressive Rental Organizations (APRO), www.rtohq.org, 2010

- The following data is a bit dated, but still may help.

"Rental Revenue per Employee—Rent-A-Center 2007 Rental Revenue per employee rose to its highest level ever—$153,930.54, up from $121,209.57 in 2006.

"Rental Revenue per Home Office Employee—after declining for four consecutive years, Rent-A-Center's Rental Revenue per Home Office Employee increased to $5,402,090.57 up from $4,843,475.71 in 2006.

"Monthly Revenue per Location—Rent-A-Center's 2007 average monthly rental revenue per location reached its highest level ever at $77,439.90, up from $58,540.74 in 2006. Note: Based on store count at the end of 2007. If based on weighted average store count, average revenue per location for 2007 would have been $70,673.08. Rent-A-Center's lowest average monthly rental revenue per location ($29,797.00) was reported in 1998, the year Renters Choice acquired Rent-A-Center. For the entire 12-year period—1996 through 2007—Rent-A-Center's average monthly revenue per location is $58,701.53.

"Rental Revenue per Square Ft.—Rent-A-Center's 2007 Rental Revenue per Square Ft., increased sharply to $202.02 up from $152.71 in 2006.

"Average Store Size—Rent-A-Center's average store size remained at 4,600 square ft. in 2007. The company's average store size has grown from a low of 3,800 square ft. in 1998."

Source: Rent-to-Own Industry Statistics, www.rtoonline.com.

- "The average total revenue of Aaron's top performing stores is $2,019,535, and the average pretax cash flow of Aaron's top performing stores is $371,527."

Source: An Aaron's ad in *Franchise Times*, October 2008

Resources

Websites
- www.rtoonline.com

Associations
- Association of Progressive Rental Organizations (APRO)—a very good site with lots of data and information: www.rtohq.org

Rental Centers (See also Rent-to-Own Stores)		
SIC 7359-59	NAICS 532310	Number of Businesses/Units 8,597

Rules of Thumb

➤ 95 to 100 percent of annual sales includes inventory

➤ 3 times SDE includes inventory

➤ 4 times EBITDA

➤ Depending on type of business (general, tool, construction, industrial, party) values will range from 3.0 to 5.5 EBITDA, $1.00 to $2.00 per annual revenues.

➤ 5 times SDE (party and tent rental)

Pricing Tips

- "Age of equipment, depreciation expense. If age of equipment is old and depreciation expense getting lower each year, then examine equipment carefully. Equipment may be old and worn out requiring replacement with new."
- "Age of equipment fleet will determine future depreciation and maintenance cost."
- "A. Type of rental business: tool versus construction equipment versus party/event rental—earnings have a different set of criteria. B. Key ratios: rental equipment inventory; rental revenues; EBITDA percent of net revenues."
- "Percentage of rent to sales; capitalization versus expense policy for equipment purchases; age of rental fleet (inventory for rent); rental inventory is a fixed asset, not a current asset such as inventory for sale."
- "ROI—Return on Investment (annual rental revenues divided by original cost of equipment). Varies from $0.70:$1.00 to $2.00:$1.00, 1:1 depending on whether equipment is construction, general tool, or party. Values primarily based on multiple of EBITDA, net revenues, value of assets plus goodwill factor, customer base, organizational structure/employees & staff, physical plant facilities, including location and expansion area availability."
- "Areas to look at: Rental equipment inventory mix, type, unit investment, ROI, revenues, net earnings, EBITDA, customer (type) base, location, physical plant facilities, organization structure, market position, and overall thrust of the business."
- "To be successful, a general equipment rental store should be doing a minimum of $800,000 gross sales per year."

Expert Comments

"Business location is very important relative to competition and accessibility for customers."

"EBITDA 20%–35%."

Benchmark Data

Statistics (Tool and Equipment Rental)

Number of Establishments	8,597
Average Profit Margin	8.0%
Revenue per Employee	$151,400
Average Number of Employees	4.0
Average Wages per Employee	$35,755

Source: IBISWorld, July 2012

Products and Services Segmentation

Contractor equipment	38.1%
Building tools and equipment	22.5%
Other miscellaneous rental items	13.3%
Aerial lifts	12.4%
Garden tools and equipment	7.6%
Merchandise sales and repairs	6.1%

Source: IBISWorld, July 2012

Major Market Segmentation

Construction firms	24.8%
Industrial firms	21.2%
Independent builders and contractors	19.6%
Private households	18.1%
Other	8.9%
Government	7.4%

Source: IBISWorld, July 2012

Industry Costs

Profit	8.0%
Wages	23.5%
Purchases	40.1%
Depreciation	15.5%
Marketing	1.0%
Rent & Utilities	5.0%
Other	6.9%

Source: IBISWorld, July 2012

Market Share

United Rentals Inc.	25.2%
Hertz Global Holdings Inc.	16.1%

Source: IBISWorld, July 2012

Statistics (Party Supply Rental)

Number of Establishments	4,003
Average Profit Margin	5.4%
Revenue per Employee	$70,300
Average Number of Employees	8.5
Average Wages per Employee	$22,721

Source: IBISWorld, September 2011

Products and Services Segmentation

Wedding rentals	34.8%
Corporate event rentals	31.3%
Other event rentals	18.7%
Birthday rentals	15.2%

Source: IBISWorld, September 2011

Industry Costs

Profit	5.4%
Rent	3.5%
Utilities	2.0%
Depreciation	4.3%
Other	12.2%
Wages	32.4%
Purchases	40.2%

Source: IBISWorld, September 2011

- "For tool and equipment, labor costs should be less than 25%. Party and tent rental less than 35%. $100.000 annual sales per employee."
- "The U.S. construction and industrial equipment segment is expected to account for the largest share of the total U.S. rental revenue at 66.2 percent of the total. General tool follows with rental revenue of U.S. $8.0 billion in 2009, accounting for 26.4 percent of total U.S. rental revenue, while at U.S. $2.2 billion the party and event segment has the smallest share of the total U.S. market with 7.4 percent. Although the relative size of the construction and industrial equipment rental industry is impressive, its share has declined substantially from the mid-1990s when it was close to 80 percent."

  Source: "State of the Equipment Rental Industry Outlook 2009-2014," *Rental Management Magazine*
- "Revenues of $100,000 per employee"
- "A well-run store will have approximately $100,000 in net revenues per full-time equivalent employee."
- "Rental revenues should be $0.70 to $2.00 the value of inventory at cost and be in reasonable rental condition."

Expenses as a Percentage of Annual Sales

Cost of goods	<10%
Payroll/labor Costs	<30%
Occupancy	<10%
Profit (estimated pretax)	05% to 15%

Industry Trend

- "Industry has been under profit squeeze with recession of last two years. Large % of rental businesses have shown profit declines."
- "Growing industry with growth areas. Dependent on construction cycle."

Seller Financing

- "Limited to 20 percent of the sales price"
- "7-year amortization"

Questions

- "Get a depreciation schedule and verify equipment age and condition. Do a thorough due diligence. If a stock sale find out about lawsuits and environmental issues."
- "How does business account for equipment maintenance—expense or capitalize?"

Resources

Trade Publications

- Rental Management: www.rentalmanagementmag.com
- AssociationsAmerican Rental Association: www.ararental.org

Repair Services

Pricing Tips

"General type—When establishing a price for a repair business which caters to the general public, the selling price should be fixtures and equipment; inventory, which is usually rather small; plus two-thirds of one year's profit."

Repossession Services

	NAICS 561491	

Rules of Thumb

➤ 85 to 95 percent of annual sales includes inventory

➤ 4 times SDE

➤ 2.5 to 3.5 times EBITDA

Pricing Tips

- "Some industry consolidation is happening by various large conglomerates."
- "Be careful of the depreciation associated with trucks. Towing is also a supplement of this industry."

Expert Comments

"There are barriers to entry in certain states which require licensing. The insurance costs are very high."

Benchmark Data

- "A successful company tracks on average how much fuel is consumed per recovery and also makes an allocation for insurance cost."
- "The average repo fee is $275.00."

Expenses as a Percentage of Annual Sales

Cost of goods	10% to 15%
Payroll/labor Costs	35% to 45%
Occupancy	10% to 15%
Profit (estimated pretax)	35% to 45%

Industry Trend

"The business will grow as the economy continues to improve."

Resale Shops

(See also Used Goods, Clothing Stores—Used, & Consignment Shops)

	NAICS 453310	Number of Businesses/Units 30,000

Rules of Thumb

➤ 40 to 45 percent of annual sales plus paid-for inventory

Benchmark Data

- For additional Benchmark data see Used Goods
- "According to America's Research Group, a consumer research firm, about 16%–18% of Americans will shop at a thrift store during a given year. For consignment/resale shops, it's about 12%–15%. To keep these figures in perspective, consider that during the same time frame, 11.4% of Americans shop in factory outlet malls, 19.6% in apparel stores and 21.3% in major department stores.

  "Resale is a multi-billion-dollar-a-year industry. First Research estimates the resale industry in the U.S.to have annual revenues of approximately $13 billion. Goodwill Industries alone generated $2.69 billion in retail sales from more than 2,500 Not For Profit resale stores across America in 2010. Another NATS member, Buffalo Exchange, who began with a 450 sq. ft. shop in 1974, has grown to 43 stores plus 2 franchises in fifteen states. They employ more than 700 people and generated annual revenues of $64.4 million in 2010. Longtime NARTS member, Crossroads Trading Co., based in Berkeley, CA, rang up over $20 million in sales last year at its 27 stores with plans to add additional locations. Add to this the many thousands of single location shops, hundreds of multi-location chains, franchises and Not For Profit stores and you begin to realize the vast scope of this growing industry."

  Source: "Industry Statistics & Trends," The Association of Resale Professionals, 2012

Industry Trend

- "While many businesses close their doors every day, resale remains healthy and continues to be one of the fastest growing segments of retail. With new stores entering the industry and current establishments opening additional locations, the industry has experienced a growth—in number of stores—of approximately 7% a year for the past two years. This percentage reflects the estimated number of new stores opening each year, minus the businesses that close."

  Source: Industry Statistics & Trends, http://www.narts.org/

- "Name Brand Exchange, another resale company based in Phoenix, also is doing well. 'Every hanger in the store is being used,' said Tamra Thomas, sales manager for the Mesa store. 'But we never turn it away, even though we have no room in the stores.' Thomas said the resale turnover and customer traffic at Name Brand are very high. 'It is crazy busy right at this time,' she said. 'People are selling clothes to get money for vacation, save up for college or for gas.' As a result, sales have increased at the two Name Brand locations. 'We make at least $10,000 to $15,000 more a month in sales than we did five years ago.' Traci Nelson, another manager at the Mesa location, said business depends on the economy. 'Everyone is trying to get something any way they can to get extra gas money,' she said."

  Source: "Business is booming at used clothing, consignment shops during economic downturn" by Ashley Macha, www.bizjournals.com/phoenix/stories

- "The resale industry is one of the few recession-proof segments of retailing. Not only does it survive during economic slowdowns, but it grows and thrives. The appeal is twofold... consumers are attracted to buying quality merchandise at a fraction of the original cost, and the financial incentive to sell, consign, or donate their unused or unwanted items."

  Source: www.narts.org

- "Increased consumer commitment to resale has resulted in new shops being opened throughout the country at a rate of about 5% a year. NARTS members have also been expanding and opening additional locations. Some members are increasing their space to include specialty categories such as bridal, sporting goods, or furniture. A number of clothing stores have opened additional locations catering to teens or specializing in furniture—two of the fasting growing segments of the resale industry. We believe our members will come out of this recession in a stronger position with a larger customer base as a broader section of consumers explore the options the resale industry has to offer."

Source: www.narts.org

Restaurants (Asian)

NAICS Full Service 722110; NAICS Limited Service 722111

Number of Businesses/Units 62,000

Rules of Thumb

➤ 30 to 32 percent of annual sales plus inventory

Benchmark Data

Statistics (Sushi Restaurants)

Number of Establishments	3,943
Revenue per Employee	$88,200
Average Number of Employees	5
Average Wages per Employee	$3,412

Source: IBISWorld, April 2012

Products and Services Segmentation

Full-service dining sushi sales	62%
Beverage sales	26%
Take-out sushi sales	12%

Source: IBISWorld, April 2012

Industry Costs

Profit	5.0%
Wages	5.2%
Purchases	76.8%
Depreciation	4.8%
Marketing	2.2%
Rent/Utilities	2.0%
Other	4.0%

Source: IBISWorld, April 2012

Name	Annual Sales
Benihana of Tokyo	$3.5 million
Pei Wei	$1.8 million
PF Chang's Chinese Bistro	$4.5 million
Panda Express	$1.0 million
Sarku Japan/Sushi Bar & Teriyaki	$900,000

Source: Nation's Restaurant News, 2012—As we have said many times, if you are involved in anything related to the food business, you have to subscribe to Nation's Restaurant News: www.nrn.com

Industry Trend

- "And Asian in general is one of the fastest growing categories in the U.S., though it's very fragmented.

  "Other Asian fast-casual concepts include the 168-unit Pei Wei Asian Diner brand, owned by P.F. Chang's China Bistro Inc.; the 90-unit Pick Up Stix chain owned by Carlson Restaurants Worldwide; and the Flat Top Grill and Stir Crazy brands owned by Chicago-based Flat Out Crazy Restaurant Group, which operates about 28 locations of the two brands combined."

  Source: "Chipotle to open Asian fast-casual concept" [in mid-2011], by Lisa Jennings, www.nrn.com/article

Resources

Trade Publications

- Asian Restaurant News: www.a-r-n.net/

Restaurants — An Introduction

State of the Restaurant Industry — 2012

Contributed by Charles Perkins, Boston Restaurant Group

CASUAL DINING

- Casual dining restaurants were the rage from the 1980s into the mid 2000's— Applebee's, Chili's. T.G.I Friday's, etc.—however, the advent of fast casual concepts like Chipotle, Panera, Five Guys, etc. and the upgrades at McDonald's have changed the landscape; especially since the recession:
  - ✓ The service is faster
  - ✓ The meal is less expensive
  - ✓ The quality of the ingredients is equally good
  - ✓ The customer does not have to leave a tip

MCDONALD'S

- McDonald's, the gold standard by which other restaurants are measured, owns 45% of all of their sites and they own 70% of all of their buildings.

  Source: Restaurant Finance Monitor, April 2012

FINANCIAL BENCHMARKS

- Dennis Monroe, a leading franchise attorney, noted the following Benchmark Data in an article for Restaurant Finance Monitor in January 2012:
  - ✓ Valuation
    Formerly a multiple of 4 to 6 times cash flow was the accepted approach. Today the trend is a multiple of sales.
  - ✓ Unit Economics
    Many franchise businesses are looking for a minimum of from 15 to 20 percent EBITDA
  - ✓ Occupancy Costs
    The numbers haven't changed: Full Service 6% and Fast Food 9%.

VALUATION

- "Shannon Pratt agrees with Perkins that the market approach, using a multiple of sales and a multiple of earnings based on transaction data from other restaurants, is best for smaller independent restaurants."

  Source: Shannon Pratt's Business Valuation Update, Feb 1999 (It hasn't changed)

FAILURE RATE

- "... a Cornell University study of restaurants in three major markets showed a first year failure or closure rate of 27 percent, with only a 4 percent difference between the closure ratios of franchised and independent restaurants.
  Source: Nation's Restaurant News, March 6, 2006, p.23

MARKET SHARE

- According to an article in the March 17, 2012 issue of Nation's Restaurant News, chains have a 46 percent Market Share while the Independent operator still controls 54 percent of the market.

WHAT ARE THE HOT CONCEPTS

- Burger Bars
- Food Trucks
- Anything Asian
- Mexican
- Burritos

ACTION IN THE SUBURBS

- Pretty much dinner is over by 9:00 PM
- Fast Food has taken much of the lunch business from full service
- The biggest issues are maintaining consistency and inexperienced employees

INTEREST RATES

- Declining interest rates have been a boom for many home owners and commercial property owners; however, it has had a limited impact on restaurant valuation and higher selling prices. The reason being the difficulty in getting financing from risk adverse commercial lending institutions.

PERSONAL GUARANTEES

- This can be a major sticking point in lease negotiations today. Landlords want a five year guarantee, given the amount of closings during the recession. Some landlords will accept a three year guarantee that decreases, "burns off", 33% every year. The least exposure for the tenant is a one year guarantee (the best is one month)

EBITDA

- In the sale of company owned stores to franchisees, Applebee's CEO Julia Stewart confirmed that the average multiple, since 2008, has been between 4.5 times and 6.0 times EBITDA.
  Source: Restaurant Finance Monitor, March 16, 2012, p. 7

LIFESTYLE CENTERS

- Twenty years ago the big guns in retail were the regional malls. Today the action is in the Lifestyle Centers. These are open air shopping plazas, somewhat similar to the strip center that was popular in the 1960s and 1970s, only with much more diversity and a retail mix tailored toward an upscale consumer.

EMPLOYMENT

- Today, besides competition with the national chains for customers, the independents are also competing for employees. Your better staff—kitchen workers, servers, managers, bartenders, etc.—are following the money. They find more opportunity and stability working for high-volume chain restaurants.

MARKET RENT

- Ten years ago, base rent in excess of $30 psf was pushing the envelope. Today, $40 to $50 psf NNN seems to be the norm, with term sheets getting $40 to $50 psf plus CAM and real estate taxes.

ANNUAL RENT INCREASES

- In years past, leases were written in five year increments with options of five additional years each. Base rent was flat for each five year term, with increases of from 10 percent to 15 percent with the exercise of each option period. Today many landlords are looking for bumps of from 3 percent to 5 percent every year.

LOCATIONS

- It is no longer location, location, location. Today the mantra is location, the right concept at that location and the right sales to investment ratio. A good benchmark is that first year sales, for an independently owned restaurant, should be at a minimum 2.5 times the cost of the investment for the build-out and equipment.

OBSERVATIONS

- It has been my experience that the success or failure of many restaurants is determined before the business even opens. Issues relating to the concept, the amount of the investment, the terms of the lease, the implementation of a sound business plan and the use of the right professional are key issues. Consider the following:
  - ✓ Many owners have no idea as to what their costs should be
  - ✓ Many owners do not really work the business, rather they "put in time."
  - ✓ Many restaurants operate at less than 75 percent efficiency
  - ✓ Many operators leave as much as 5 percent on the bottom line. For a business doing a million dollars, that represents $50,000.

PIZZA

- The pizza industry has been hard hit in the last ten years. The industry is highly competitive and has relied very heavily on aggressive discounting during the recession.

CUSTOMER SERVICE

- From Jim Sulivan, a restaurant consultant:
  "Good service can save a bad meal; however, a good meal cannot save bad service."

Source: Nation's Restaurant News, June 13, 2012

FLAT SALES

- One of the major contributors to flat sales has been rising gas prices over the past 4 years. At President Obama's inauguration gas prices were $1.84 per gallon. Today the prices are $3.80+/-per gallon.

CAM CHARGES

- CAM charges are in many projects, no longer based upon an exact measurement of the leased space. They are more of a profit center for the landlord with 5% increases each year.

SHOPPING MALLS

- Of more than 1,000 enclosed shopping malls in the United States, an estimated 30 percent, generate less than $300 per square foot: the minimum standard for a profitable center. The national average estimated at $370 per square foot.

Source: *Wall Street Journal*, August 29, 2012

FOOD COSTS

- Restaurant chains are caught in a bind between escalating ingredient costs and a reluctance to increase prices for fear of alienating today's budget conscious customer. Full service operators are better able to protect their bottom line with either selective price increases or reduced portion sizes, while limited service restaurants, with value driven menus, have less margin to work with.

Source: *Wall Street Journal*, August 29, 2012

Restaurants-QUICK CHECK-2012

Bagels	30% of annual sales (Not as much interest today)
Bars	50% of annual sales (Very much in demand)
Bar & Grill	(50% liquor) 40% of annual sales (Very popular)
Barbecue	30% of annual sales (Limited pool of buyers)
Bistros	30% of annual sales (Typically chef owned)
Brew Pubs	40% of annual sales
Billiard Parlors	40% of annual sales (Limited pool of buyers)
Cajun	30% of annual sales (Not big in New England)
Catering	30% to 40% of annual sales (Seller may have to stay)
Caribbean	30% of annual sales
Chicken	30% of annual sales
Chinese	30% of annual sales (Of reported sales)
Coffee Houses	30% of annual sales (Higher ingredient cost)
Continental	30% of annual sales (Heavy/rich menues not in vogue today)
Delis	30% to 40% of annual sales (Higher value if only5/6 days)
Diners	30% of annual sales
Fine Dining	30% of annual sales
Gourmet Shops	20% of annual sales (+ cost of inventory which can be expensive)
Hamburgers	30% of annual sales
Ice Cream	35% to 40% of annual sales (Higher volume in warmer climate)
Irish	40% of annual sales (If higher liquor sales)
Italian	30% of annual sales (Value down today)
Mexican	30% of annual sales
Night Clubs	20% of annual sales (High risk rate lowers value)
Pancake Houses	30% of annual sales
Pizza (if delivery)	30% of annual sales
Pizza (if no delivery)	40% of annual sales
Sandwiches	40% of annual sales
Seafood	30% of annual sales (Very high food costs)
Sports Bars	40% of annual sales (Beverage sales over 40%)
Steakhouses	30% of annual sales (Very high food costs)

Source: Business Brokerage Press and the Boston Restaurant Group, September 2012

Points to consider when drafting a Business Plan for a new restaurant opening.

Sources of Information

- The following publications provide excellent information about the industry:
  - *Nation's Restaurant News* .... Lebhar-Friedman Publication
  - *The Restaurant Planning Guide* .... Upstart Publishing Company
  - *Restaurant Management* .... Prentiss Hall
  - *Restaurant Dealmaker* .... through Amazon

Lease Negotiations

- A partial checklist of salient points:
  - ✓ Have lease reviewed by an attorney
  - ✓ Length of the lease – 10 years +
  - ✓ Base rent at Industry Average
  - ✓ Scope of Landlord/Tenant Improvements
  - ✓ Right of Assignment
  - ✓ Condition of space at delivery
  - ✓ Options to extend
  - ✓ Extent of Personal Guarantee

Site Selection Criteria

- Representative points to be considered:
  - ✓ Demographics
  - ✓ Competition
  - ✓ Activity generators
  - ✓ Demand for concept
  - ✓ Zoning Ordinances & Variances
  - ✓ Signage, Visibility and Accessibility

The Restaurant Facility

- Representative points to be considered:
  - ✓ Availability of licenses and permits
  - ✓ Condition of the space & past history
  - ✓ Cost of renovations
  - ✓ Utilities – gas, water, electric, etc.
  - ✓ Workable Layout and Design
  - ✓ Rent, lease terms & R.E. Taxes

Buying a Restaurant

- Documents to be requested:
  - ✓ Copy of the Lease
  - ✓ Tax Returns for 3 years
  - ✓ Financial Statements for 3 years
  - ✓ Complete Equipment List
  - ✓ Latest Health Inspector's Report

Valuing an Existing Restaurant

- These factors determine the value:
  - ✓ The potential for sales growth
  - ✓ The potential for cash flow growth
  - ✓ The condition of LHImp & FFEq.
  - ✓ The length of the lease – 10 year minimum
  - ✓ Base rent as a percent of sales

The Professional Team

- Select professionals with experience:
  - ✓ Attorney
  - ✓ Accountant
  - ✓ Contractor

Unit Level Economics

- Representative operating expenses:

Sales	100%
Cost of Goods	32%
Payroll Cost	32%
Other Expenses	20%
Rent	6%
Cash Flow	10%

Restaurant Concepts

- The concept needs to be well defined:

Fine Dining	Ruth's Chris, Capital Grill
Casual Dining	Applebees, Chili's
Family Dining	Friendly's, Denny's
Fast Food	McDonalds, Wendy's
Quick Casual	Panera, Baja Fresh
Bars, Pubs	Bennigan's, Houlihan's
Coffee	Dunkin Donuts, Starbucks
Other	Ice cream, Deli, Pizza, etc

Target Food and Beverage Costs

- Percentage will vary based on concept:

Food	29% - 32%
Beer	22% - 25%
Wine	29% - 32%
Liquor	22% - 25%

Business Plan Outline

- Samples available on the Internet:
    - ✓ Executive Summary
    - ✓ Company/Concept Description
    - ✓ Industry Analysis
    - ✓ Products and Services
    - ✓ Target Market
    - ✓ The Competition
    - ✓ Market/Sales Strategies
    - ✓ Operations
    - ✓ Management & Organization
    - ✓ Long Term Development/Exit Strategy
    - ✓ Financial Data & Projections

Source: Charles Perkins, The Boston Restaurant Group

VALUING A RESTAURANT

FAIR MARKET VALUE

"The asking price is what the seller wants. The selling price is what the seller receives. Fair Market Value is the highest price the buyer is willing to pay and the lowest price the seller is willing to accept."

There is no formula for valuing a restaurant. Each business needs to be considered on an individual basis. There are, however, certain Benchmark Data and valuation approaches and methods that enable an experienced appraiser to determine the most probable price for which the business could be sold on the open market.

INCOME STATEMENT ANALYSIS

The restaurant's operating expenses will be consolidated into four categories to more accurately reflect industry format and to allow for more meaningful comparisons with the industry averages:

SALES	$	%	COMMENTS
Cost of Goods			
Payroll/Benefits			
Other Expenses			
Occupancy Costs			
Income			

CASH FLOW ANALYSIS

When valuing a company it is customary to analyze the financial statements and make adjustments, where necessary, to better indicate the true earnings capacity of the business:

ADJUSTMENTS

1.

2.

3. etc.

Total Adjustments

VALUATION ANALYSIS

The following approaches and methods should be considered in the valuation of any restaurant:

APPROACHES / METHODS	Sales/Cash Flow		Multiple	Indicated Value
Multiple of Sales		X		
Multiple of Cash Flow		X		
Sales to Investment Ratio		÷		
Appraisal Databases		X		
Industry Rules of Thumb		X		

Source: Charles Perkins, The Boston Restaurant Group

WHY RESTAURANTS FAIL

A Cornell University study noted that the first year failure rate for restaurants is between 20 percent and 25 percent. Major contributors to a restaurant's failure in today's market: 1. The concept is not well defined – you know what you are going to get at Five Guys Burgers. 2. Poor management and lack of leadership skills. 3. Inconsistent customer service and product preparation 4. The business being undercapitalized. 5. Ownership being unable or unwilling to react.

Source: Charles Perkins, The Boston Restaurant Group

Benchmark Data

- "2011 Restaurant Industry Overview
    - ✓ Sales: $604 billion
    - ✓ Locations: 960,000
    - ✓ Employees: 12.8 million—one of the largest private-sector employers
    - ✓ Restaurant-industry share of the food dollar: 49%"
    - ✓ 46 percent of restaurant employees say they would like to own their own restaurant some day
    - ✓ 47 percent of adults say they would patronize food trucks"

Source: "2011 Restaurant Industry Pocket Factbook," www.restaurant.org

- "Small Number of Businesses/Units with a Large Impact
  - ✓ Restaurant-industry sales are projected to total $604 billion in 2011 and equal 4 percent of the U.S. gross domestic product.
  - ✓ The overall economic impact of the restaurant industry is expected to exceed $1.7 trillion in 2011.
  - ✓ Every dollar spent by consumers in restaurants generates an additional $2.05 spent in our nation's economy.
  - ✓ The restaurant industry is projected to employ 12.8 million people in 2011, or nearly 10 percent of the U.S. workforce.
  - ✓ The restaurant industry is expected to add 1.3 million jobs over the next decade, with employment reaching 14.1 million by 2021.
  - ✓ Every additional million dollars in restaurant sales generates an additional 34 jobs for the economy.
  - ✓ 93% of eating-and-drinking place Number of Businesses/Units have fewer than 50 employees.
  - ✓ 7 out of 10 eating-and-drinking place establishments are single-unit operations
  - ✓ Average unit sales in 2008 were $862,000 at full-service restaurants and $737,000 at quick-service restaurants."
    Source: "2011 Restaurant Industry Pocket Factbook," www.restaurant.org

Industry Trend

- "In addition, the restaurant industry will continue to fuel U.S. employment in the year ahead as the nation's second largest private sector employer. Overall restaurant industry employment will reach 12.9 million in 2012, representing 10 percent of the total U.S. workforce. "While the industry is expected to grow in 2012, the top challenges cited by restaurateurs are food costs, building and maintaining sales volume, and the economy."
  Source: "Restaurant Industry Set to Outpace National Job Growth, Reach Record Sales in 2012,"
  National Restaurant Association, www.restaurant.org
- "The top 10 menu trends for next year will be:
  - ✓ Locally sourced meats and seafood
  - ✓ Locally grown produce
  - ✓ Healthful kids' meals
  - ✓ Hyper-local items
  - ✓ Sustainability as a culinary theme
  - ✓ Children's nutrition as a culinary theme
  - ✓ Gluten-free/food allergy-conscious items
  - ✓ Locally produced wine and beer
  - ✓ Sustainable seafood
  - ✓ Whole grain items in kids' meals"
- "About one-quarter of the chefs (26 percent) ranked smartphone apps as the hottest technology trend in restaurants in 2012, and another quarter (25 percent) said tablet computers (i.e., iPads for menus and wine lists) will be the top technology trend. Sixteen percent said social media would be the top trend, and the same percentage said mobile/wireless/pay-at-the-table payment options, while 4 percent said QR codes."
  Source: "Hottest Restaurant Menus Trends in 2012," National Restaurant Association,
  www.restaurant.org, December 8, 2011

Restaurants — Full Service

(See also Restaurants—an Introduction & Limited Service)

SIC 5812-08	NAICS 722110	

Rules of Thumb

➤ 25 to 35 percent of annual sales includes inventory

➤ 1.8 to 2.5 times SDE includes inventory

➤ 2 to 3 times EBIT

➤ 2.5 to 3 times EBITDA

➤ Note: California restaurants seem to be receiving higher multiples than the rest of the country with the possible exception of New York City. For example: 35 to 40 percent of annual sales and 2 to 5 times SDE.

Pricing Tips

- "Lease is a big one, if the lease exceeds 10% of sales it will be a tough sale, also, location, the condition and what equipment, type of cuisine, if the establishment sells liquor, what type of liquor license, etc. all factor in to the value."
- "Asset sales - non-profitable restaurants or those without cash flow may be factored at 20 to 30 cents on the dollar. Additional items affecting pricing are: saturation of concepts, franchise or independent, geography and/or desired locations."
- "The multiple drops as the SDE drops below $100k."
- "Occupancy cost and lease terms are the overriding factor in today's economy, where buyers have a choice to walk in to a closed fully equipped restaurant versus buying an existing and operating restaurant. The lease is key because even a 'great deal' going into the project is not a deal at all if the restaurant cannot make money."
- "The most important aspect to pricing is location and facility condition."
- "You can value higher price on franchise restaurants if their royalty, marketing and advertising fees and other costs are reasonable."
- "Quality of financial data will impact pricing."
- "Add liquor license value + FFE + inventory to SDE"
- "It's important to look at how many hours the owner and owner's family are putting in. The SDE will need to be adjusted to reflect accurate staffing costs."
- "Restaurants under $500K sales volume seem to go for around 1.5 times SDE. If they have below $75K SDE depending on the build-out, rent, and location I am seeing just over 1X SDE. Restaurants over $500K in sales with decent margins, location and build out may fetch as much as 2 times SDE. Often Owner records are not pristine and the above quoted multiples are based off of that consideration. Theoretically with higher sales figures, good books and records, favorable lease and location we should be able to get larger multiples than stated, but it appears that few restaurants right now are meeting this criteria. Please note that my multiples are assuming 50% financing."
- "In the current market environment a 2 times provable cash flow is the best yardstick for a sales price"

- "Compare COG to industry standards. Rent factor vs. sales. Extraneous cost to generate sales, e.g., music, price deals, advertising, hours of operation"
- "Including real estate the sale price should be close to 1 x gross"
- "Number of meals served, average meal ticket, location, age of equipment"
- "You need to understand the value of the liquor license."
- "Common sense applies. If the business is named after a chef or the menu requires special skills, then it will be a riskier transition and will sell at the low end of a multiple. In contrast, a simple operation such as a coffeehouse or deli may sell at a higher multiple given the same SDCF. The operating hours will also be a factor in how the multiple is applied.
- "Gross sales multiples are most relevant. Everyone thinks they can run it better themselves."
- "With the recent economic conditions and excess market supply, most non-profitable restaurants are rarely valued over $100,000."
- "While gross revenue and SDE is important, one factor that may be easily overlooked is the number of days and hours the establishment is operated to achieve those numbers."
- "Including the real estate, the sale price should be about 1 x gross sales."
- "Food cost, wages, management costs"
- "Pay close attention to the location and competition. Also, occupancy cost has never been more important than now. Note that if occupancy cost is over 10%, adjust accordingly."
- "Some closed restaurants represent excellent opportunities to buyers with 'better ideas.'"
- "The terms of the lease—assignability, relationship to market rent, remaining term and solid renewal options are key to the value of the restaurant."
- "Business averaging less than $750K in sales normally can be sold for 2.5 times EBITDA, but anything above normally gets sold to a pro operator, and most of them are not willing to go higher than 2 times EBITDA."
- "Make sure that it is making a profit."
- "Only add back what you can prove."
- "Location is very important in this current economy. Annual revenue should exceed $300,000; otherwise it should be listed as an asset sale."
- "There are 5 critical criteria for restaurants to meet. #1 is location: busy location, high traffic, booming business in the area and finally mid to high income population. #2 is rent: it should not exceed 10% of gross revenue. #3 is conversion potential: can the restaurant be converted into another concept that will not compete with other restaurants within same particular center? #4 is condition of equipment: are they NSF approved and in good condition? Since they are expensive, we shouldn't overlook that. #5 is asking price: the most important is percentage of gross revenue, which shouldn't exceed 30%–40%, that's what experienced restaurant owners/buyers look for; and the gross annual revenue shouldn't be less than $500,000 for a full-service restaurant, otherwise it should sell as an asset sale. If you have all these 5 criteria, the business will sell for market value."
- "Lease terms and liquor license are important factors that can affect the value. If the facility is relatively new and up to current codes, it can be sold as an asset sale even with negative cash flow."
- "1. Occupancy cost should not exceed 10% of annual gross sales. 2. Watch accounts- payable aging. Restaurant operators tend to drag vendors out to 60–90 days. 3. If cost of sales exceeds 35%, there is probably some skimming going on."

- "Currently a buyers' market: must be profitable or will sell for depreciated asset value only. Lease obligations are a large part of negotiations."
- "2 times EBITDA plus value of FFE + Liquor License + Inventory"
- "Be wary of comparing industry statistics against smaller mom & pops which do not have equal purchasing power. Fuel charges are pushing costs much higher."
- "Most restaurants will sell for 30%–35% of gross sales, but the bigger the business the better. Over $2 million in annual sales normally needed to make real money."
- "Adjust for exceptionally low operating hours vs. extremely long hours."
- "Restaurants with small profits are worth more as an asset sale than based on sales or net cash flow. The cost of opening a new restaurant makes over 50% of the restaurants for sale only worth what the buyer feels he would have to spend to open a new one. The cost of permits and fees has driven the cost of new restaurants through the roof, and buyers should always consider taking over an existing one even if not profitable."
- "Non-franchise restaurants are worth 30%–40% of annual sales. Franchise sit down have been selling for 50% of annual sales, if they make a profit big enough to justify the price. Johnny Rockets are now selling for around 1 year's gross income. Franchise food not making money; before debt service, they are worth the value of the assets in place."
- "The last 100 full-service restaurants sold were sold for an average of 2.2x Seller's Discretionary Cash Flow (SDCF), or cash flow available to a full-time working owner. The range was 0.0x (simply taking over a lease for a non-profitable venture) to 5.0x SDCF (well-established community icon with unique and non-duplicatable concept). Lease rate and term, and competitive environment are the most critical. In certain geographies, availability of liquor licenses may be even more critical."
- "If real estate is included the sale, the price should be about 1x gross sales depending on condition and quality of the building. Any of these rules of thumb should be confirmed by deducting the debt service on 80% of the sale price (20% down) from the seller's discretionary cash and determining then what is left over for owner's income. This also needs to make sense to a buyer."
- "Due to the high cost of creating a restaurant, we are seeing more conversion sales or asset sales. For unprofitable newer restaurants (with recent build-outs and newer equipment) having long-term leases in place, we can often recoup 1/3 to 1/2 of the total cost of creation."
- "5-day breakfast, lunch, or alcohol-only bar: 40% of sales. Large full-service over 6000-sf and $1 million in sales: 25% of sales. All others: between 30–35% of sales depending on profitability and condition of facility."
- "May require reverse gross margin proofing. EBITDA formulas typically larger restaurants."
- "Minimum length of lease: 10 years; consistent sales history over three years. Assumes no major renovations required. Pricing for going concern only with market rent."
- "75% food sales and 25% beverage sales—40% of sales for a sports bar"
- "60% food sales and 40% beverage sales—50% of sales for a bar"
- "Since a buyer will probably introduce their own concept, the most important factors tend to be lease term and rate, equipment and condition, and type of liquor license."
- "Full-service restaurants rarely sell above 40% of sales with 30% (or less) being common. Remember the lease must be at market or below. Restaurants

with over-market leases rarely sell. Always remember to normalize wages as many operators over or under pay themselves. EBITDA is true EBITDA with management in place, not owner's cash flow. SDE is owner's cash flow. Big problem with overstated value due to misstating earnings. Also, for restaurants that are losing money, conversion method is best. Don't try to 'create' cash flow. Our company has used the conversion method for years and now I am teaching it. Simply, the conversion value of a restaurant is based on the value of the infrastructure and FF&E in place. It is common for a full- service restaurant operator to spend $100–$200 per square foot to build out (a leased space) and equip a restaurant. So based on our experience, we estimate the value another operator will recognize for the space. Another operator will utilize the plumbing, electrical, hood, grease trap and some of the FF&E. It is subjective but has been very accurate. We assign a dollar-per-square-foot value to a fully equipped restaurant that has a long-term market (or below) lease. Rarely is this number higher than $40 per square foot. The conversion method will not work in depressed markets where many empty restaurant properties exist.

Expert Comments

"Lease is key, at least 5years with at least one 5 year option."

"1—Competition: Very easy to get in 2—Risk: Very risky to start a new restaurant concept, especially in the first year. Requires a lot of dedication, hard work, long hours, lots of energy, & in many cases not much in return 3—Historical Profit trend: 10%–20% most of the time with owner(s) participating long hours in the operation of the business 4—Location & facilities: Location could make or break many restaurants in the industry, & it is added value for many others with great food, right price, good ambiance & service. Facilities: Majority of the chain stores have to update & renew the appearance of the facility whereas many of the mom & pop do not see this as necessary, or they do not want to commit such an investment, or they do not have the reserve for such a venture or they rather to spend that money on personal stuff, & they do not believe that some customers take their business somewhere else who keep the atmosphere very pleasant & the facility very presentable. Also when it comes to selling, the buyers know the difference between a presentable place & ignored & rundown place. 5—Marketability: To market a restaurant to sell is very easy & extremely hard at the same time. It is easy since a majority of prospective buyers are familiar with the restaurant business to a certain extent. However they cannot understand how come two similar restaurants may be as close as two sides of an intersection and have different prices even though they serve similar food, & are the same sizes. It is very hard to market some intangible features such as ambiance, different side of street, easy access, ample parking, & so on. Majority of the buyer prospects in this industry are financial buyers, especially in medium to low range prices, & rarely a strategic buyer will show up for these businesses who appreciate intangible values. 6—Industry Trend: Probably is growing all the time, more it is because of change & constant new concepts phenomena. People never get tired to try a new concept in this industry. 7—Ease of Replication: Very easy to replicate a concept, & of course many more in the outside think that way with no success at all."

"The amount of risk in the restaurant industry is high so viewing one opportunity against another, does not overly impact most valuations. The industry trend is more volatile relative to pricing since concepts come and go. Those exceeding industry norms have been unfairly punished from a pricing perspective in the past three years. At the same time, those that follow the 'me too' model of business and park themselves in the latest trend, i.e. frozen yogurt, can find themselves in a market saturation situation that depresses pricing."

"Historical profit trend is less important than in some other industries, because many will buy the restaurant as a conversion opportunity, although the profit trend does impact the price. It is true that many restaurants and bars do not show a profit on the books or tax returns, but this is less of a factor today due to the dominance of debit and credit card revenues and POS systems."

"It is a high-risk business; more chains open up giving the independents more competition."

"Marketability is still high even with low growth and profit due to ease of entry/replication and exception deals. The industry trend has been steadily declining over the last few years . . . minor comeback in the last year but no terrific outlook."

"In Colorado sales are trending up but COGS are increasing."

"Restaurants continue to be risky investments. Purchases and conversions of existing restaurants continue to require less capital than new restaurant build outs."

"The rental rate per the lease agreement is very important. Watch out for percentage rent clauses as well. A below market lease with years to go is a big benefit. A short lease or above market rent is a problem."

"Barrier to entry can be restricted by number of pouring licenses in town or municipality."

"Competition in the surrounding area is not much of a factor because more restaurants together become a reason to visit a location (provided they are different concepts)."

"Highly competitive area, trends change; big national chains dominate"

"Food costs vary somewhat depending on the type of food served. Mexican and Italian tend to have lower food costs. Steaks and seafood will be higher."

"More and more emphasis must be placed on quality of food and service to survive these days."

"1. The restaurant industry is extremely competitive and difficult. 2. Because of its competitive nature the industry is also extremely risky, especially for the uninitiated. 3. Profits have been trending downward in the current economy as many restaurateurs have found it necessary to reduce prices while suppliers are raising prices. 4. Location and physical facility are imperative. Customers want convenience and ambiance along with quality and price. 5. Marketability is difficult at best if you are to deliver a truly qualified buyer in a financial situation where the seller is almost invariably going to be asked to carry some or all of the paper. 6. Mom-and-pops are falling by the wayside and being crushed by the chains. The chains can afford to lose money in a market while destroying the local competition. 7. The physical plant, equipment and decor are fairly easy to replicate. What is difficult to replicate is employee attitude and customer service as well as some KEY menu items and recipes."

"1. Competition is daunting. Big chains can & do kill independents. 2. Very risky business due in large part to competition but also changing customer attitudes and the media. 3. Profit trends are down due to increasing labor costs and competition. 4. Location, location, location! 5. Tough to sell due to all other factors. 6. The field is growing but is being diluted by grocery and big discount stores selling pre-packaged meals. 7. Most any concept can be fairly easily replicated in menu and design. The key is in quality, quantity and service."

"You never know why one concept works or doesn't, but location is key and you're only as good as your servers!"

"Competition is very heavy between different food concepts. As gas prices go up, restaurant sales continue to go down."

"Competition and risk are both high because it's rather easy to enter the industry (getting harder) and too many novices attempt owning a restaurant. The economy is definitely affecting the bottom line. Due to the high cost of recent construction, the rent factors have increased and are cutting into the restaurant's profitability and also hindering the opening of new restaurants in prime locations. In the high-rent areas of Metro Orlando the costs have risen from $25.00/S.F. to as much as $60.00/ S.F. My office sales still constitute approx. 45% food-related businesses. The industry is still growing although more difficult to replicate than in past years."

"The location and quality of the assets and facility add value, even if the current concept is not profitable. Historical profitability is a key factor for determining the actual price. The more simple concepts translate to lower risk and this also results in a higher price. A restaurant requiring a skilled chef, or one closely associated with an owner's name and reputation, can be difficult to sell and the price will reflect the higher risk of transfer."

"The hard truth is that most restaurants fail. It is often the 2nd or 3rd restaurateur that makes a location work. Part of the reason is that that party has a lower initial cost than the original party that did the build-out, purchased new equipment, etc. Buyers benefit tremendously from seller's losses."

"Competition is high; there is an attraction to the restaurant business by a lot of people. They think it's like entertaining friends and a lot of fun. Of course, they find out differently, usually too late. Risk is also high because of competition, inexperience, high employee turnover and national chains taking a bigger chunk of the pie. Historical profit trends are in most cases increasing, more & more people eat out. Location & facilities are also improving and are now more important. Marketability is very good; my office sales are about 35% to 40% food-related sales. Personally, over 50% of my sales are restaurants. Industry trend is on the upswing, as cooking at home habits are changing to eating out. Ease of replication is thought to be easy, therefore there are a lot of new 'wannabe' restaurateurs and their inexperience adds to the high mortality rate in this industry."

"Large amount of competition and risk, especially in metropolitan and populated suburban areas"

"Franchises have continued to increase product lines, and in some case combine products. Many now sell their food products directly to consumers in the supermarkets. Franchises generally maintain the better locations."

"Location is critical in most restaurants and it helps to have other ones around you to give the customers a choice."

"It generally takes at least 2 years for a new restaurant to reach its initial potential."

"There is nothing proprietary about any restaurant concept in the country today. The chains have the financial wherewithal and technical expertise to replicate anything that exists."

"Restaurants are not as attractive as bars due to the food component. Food automatically can drive gross margins up 15-20%. Most restaurants purchased will require a full 'face-lift' for an opportunity to do well."

"Highly competitive industry, management experience is very important."

Benchmark Data

Statistics (Chain Restaurants)

Number of Establishments	34,587
Average Profit Margin	6.3%
Revenue per Employee	$42,500
Average Number of Employees	39.2
Average Wages per Employee	$12,965

Source: IBISWorld, September 2012

Products and Services Segmentation

Varied cuisine restaurants	40%
Asian food	20%
American food	12%
European food	10%
Pizza shops	10%
Mexican food	08%

Source: IBISWorld, September 2012

Industry Costs

Profit	6.3%
Wages	31.7%
Purchases	.8%
Depreciation	4.4%
Marketing	3.0%
Rent & Utilities	6.2%
Other	19.6%

Source: IBISWorld, September 2012

Market Share

Darden Restaurants Inc.	15.8%
Bloomin' Brands Inc.	6.0%

Source: IBISWorld, September 2012

Statistics (Single Location Full-Service Restaurants)

Number of Establishments	206,462
Average Profit Margin	6.2%
Revenue per Employee	$37,800
Average Number of Employees	12.4
Average Wages per Employee	$12,910

Source: IBISWorld, September 2012

Products and Services Segmentation

Casual dining	40%
Asian food	20%
American food	12%
European food	10%
Pizza shops	10%
Mexican food	08%

Source: IBISWorld, September 2012

Industry Costs

Profit	6.2%
Wages	34.7%
Purchases	22.4%
Depreciation	2.5%
Marketing	3.0%
Rent & Utilities	5.5%
Other	25.7%

Source: IBISWorld, September 2012

Statistics (Premium Steak Restaurants)

Number of Establishments	1,276
Average Profit Margin	4.9%
Revenue per Employee	$99,000
Average Number of Employees	44.7
Average Wages per Employee	$20,539

Source: IBISWorld, October 2011

Products and Services Segmentation

Classic steak restaurants	35%
Steak and seafood restaurants	32.6%
Other premium steak restaurants	22%
Premium Brazilian steak restaurants	10.4%

Source: IBISWorld, October 2011

Industry Costs

Profit	4.9%
Rent	4.3%
Utilities	3.9%
Depreciation	3.8%
Other	20.4%
Wages	20.9%
Purchases	41.8%

Source: IBISWorld, October 2011

- "Sales per square foot- $500 + Food costs 30 to 32 percent, Labor costs 30 to 32 percent, Profit 8 to 12 percent."
- "Food Costs should be between 25-30% of sales depending on the concept (i.e., low meat concepts like a burrito store will have lower food costs than white tablecloth restaurants focused on farm to table). Labor costs should be around 25% of sales Total occupancy (including CAMS) should be between 8-10% of sales."
- "Important factors: 1-Location 2-Food Quality 3-Pricing 4-Ambiance 5-Presentation 6-Service 7-Accebility 8-Cleaness of the place 9-Sales Level 10-Rent 11-Food Cost 12-Labor Cost."
- "Cost of food + payroll cannot exceed 60% of sales = Prime Cost"
- "Owner operated places should keep payroll and food cost below 60% Rent should be no more than 9%."

- "The kitchen tour and lounge visit, deployed late in the meal, also solved a problem that bedevils every restaurateur: how to get people up from the table so that the next customers can be seated, a feat known as 'the turn.' Fast-food places, which must turn every few minutes, use bright primary colors and loud, fast music to encourage people to eat faster.

  "Before a fork is lowered after a course, cooks watching from the kitchen can insure that the next dish is ready, shaving vital minutes off the meal."
  Source: The New Yorker magazine, 2012

- "Finding Food costs for Breakfast/Lunch and basic pizza/Italian 26%-28%, American restaurants depending on menu around 30-32%, fine dining 35%."

- "According to the rule that every new restaurateur learns, the combined costs of food and labor must not exceed seventy per cent of expenses; ideally, food should be thirty."

- "I like to earn half of the food costs."

- "Food costs below 35%. Calculate the sales per seat on an annual basis. This number should be at least $7,000 or there might be a problem."

- "Seeing an average of about $8k–$10k sales per seat in a full-service; if liquor is heavy, can be a little higher. Limited service about $5k–$8k. Sales per seat—low end $250 to high end $400 per foot."

- "Food costs usually between 28 and 35% depending on concept. I have found in this area, profit to be around 15% or in some cases higher If it is not a franchise. Franchises run closer to 10%"

- "It is difficult in California to achieve occupancy cost of 6% which seems to be the national industry target, but 8% for full-service and 10% for quick service is a target here. Food costs range greatly based on concept, from 20% to 35%."

- "Average ticket price targets for most full-service restaurants with beer and wine licenses are $25–$30 per person. Restaurants with liquor licenses tend to target average ticket prices of $40–$50 per person, as they may also provide additional entertainment such as sports bar concept, club, or live music."

- "Median sales per full-time employee should be between $55,000 and $60,000 and sales per square foot should be over $300 per square foot."

- "Sales range $48k–$55k per employee, $250–$300 per sq. ft. Per seat like to see $8k–$10k; again above will be variable based upon concept and style."

- "Keep Prime Cost (COGS + Payroll divided by sales) below 60%"

- "Depending on style of restaurant, each seating should have at least 2 turns breakfast & dinner."

- "Occupancy costs need to be under 10% or you'll need to re-negotiate the lease prior to selling."

- "Food cost should be about 33% and liquor should be 25%. Higher percentages of COGS usually indicates theft."

- "Ideally prime costs (cogs & labor) should be 60% of sales. Seldom can a restaurant be profitable if prime costs are over 65% and never over 70%."

- "Food cost should be at 33% & liquor at 25%."

- "Although 6% occupancy cost is a benchmark, 8% is most common. This should include all net charges."

- "Food costs can range from 20% to 40% for most concepts, so it is hard to generalize. The occupancy cost is the most important factor since it may be fixed, although there are opportunities to renegotiate leases at this time. In California it is still difficult to have occupancy cost in line with national averages."

- "Some may argue that the most important factor to succeed in the restaurant business is the lease. If you can pay the rent with the gross sales of one strong day, you will definitely make it. Updated numbers for costs in a full-service restaurant: Food: 27% to 35%; Liquor: 22% to 28%; Beer: 28% to 35%; Wine: 30% to 36%. Most restaurants are heavily discounting pricing through daily food and drink specials, coupons and special promotions to keep the sales volume at a higher cost of goods sold"
- "Sales $350 to $400 per sq. ft. Food cost should be 28% to 35% of sales depending on the concept, except for seafood restaurants."
- "Look for maximum utilization of space. $300-400 per square foot for multi-meal operations."
- "A good full-service operator should drive 10% to the bottom line if the total occupancy costs are 8% (of sales) or less in major markets. 6% has always been the benchmark but this cannot be achieved in larger markets due to cost of real estate. The theory is simple; controllables (cogs & labor) must be within industry standards. If the occupancy cost is high (as a percentage of sales) the controllables must be lower to achieve the same earnings."
- "Combined food and labor costs should not exceed 55%–60%."
- "You've got to find a way to compete with the buying power of the chains and the big stores or you cannot compete on a COGS basis."
- "If food costs exceed 30% you are in trouble. If rent is more than 10% it is hard to make a profit."
- "Food cost should be about 33% and liquor cost should be about 25%. Often (like the IRS) you can figure out how much cash is missing from the recorded sales. This won't help at the bank but might influence a buyer at to how much sales are not being recorded."
- "'No prudent restaurant operator allows his lease to get down to two to four years, because if he has been there a number of years before that and he is doing good business, he will be walking on egg shells,' says Richard Lackey, president of the Lackey Cos. and a founder of the CIRB. 'On the other side of the coin, if the market is declining, but you want to stay in that neighborhood and still upgrade your facility, I think you should approach your landlord like you are in it together. "We've been in this marriage for 15 or 20 years, and I need a lower rent if I'm going to survive." If the landlord is smart, he'll work with you.'"

Expenses as a Percentage of Annual Sales

Cost of goods	30% to 35%
Payroll/labor Costs	25% to 30%
Occupancy	06% to 10%
Profit (estimated pretax)	08% to 12%

Industry Trend

- "Lots of menu changes with more sophisticated dishes."
- "1-More of the current restaurants will be closing down, since the sales are down, occupancy cost is increasing 2-Food cost is on the rise 3-Downward pressure on the menu prices will force many more to exist the industry faster 4-Lack of investment & attention to facility will drive away some customers to other places like chain restaurants. 5-If the economy gets better so the restaurant industry, & if not many more will be out of business & closing down. 6-Many companies & individuals are scared to implement their new concept under the current economic environment, & are waiting for the better time."

- "As long as there are a plethora of food and restaurant reality TV shows, I see more and more buyers entering the market. Also, more and more customers are becoming 'foodies,' which encourages the market."

Seller Financing

- It ranges from 3 to 7 years, with most industry experts reporting 5 years.
- "Sellers will generally know how much debt service the business can handle. The sellers don't typically want the business back after someone has run it and or changed the business. The length of financing is a moving bar today. It depends on how long the seller to wait for their funds and how confident the seller feels about the buyer's ability. Buyers like to go out 3-5 years but sometime the buyer wants the seller out of the business sooner. I have seen promissory notes written for as short as 6-12 months. In all cases, the buyer will insist on a no penalty provision for early pay off in the note."
- Restaurants are often seller financed, as unless they have gross sales of $1 million, bank financing is not available. The average term is 1–5 years.

Questions

- "Would you do it again? What would you do differently?"
- "1-P&L 2-Name 3 most important things that you like about this business 3-Name 3 most important things that you do not like about this business 4-What is the sales & profitability trend in the last 3 years & why 5-How do you see the sales & profitability trend in the next 3 years & why 6-WHY ARE YOU SELLING?"
- "Explain bad online reviews if any. Have there been any health code violations? Is the restaurant in compliance with local laws or a CUP (Conditional Use Permit)?" "What needs to be fixed."
- "Lease and terms. Review concept, food cost, staff. Do they sell liquor, beer/ wine, none? Hours of operation. Length of time in business. Role of owner in the business. Is it a franchise? What are franchise terms and support?"
- "Why are you selling? Who are the key employees? Any liquor license violations? Get a copy of the most recent health department report."
- "Is the price/sq ft of the lease within market?"
- "Ask the sellers what they could have done differently. Do not waste an opportunity to capitalize on sellers' missed opportunities."
- "Which equipments are leased and which are paid, and the condition of the equipment. Is there a grease trap? What kind and what size? Any key employee, specially the cook, and whether he or she wants to stay."
- "We ask over 60 questions, including normal items: how long in business, liens, loans . . . all the way to size of hot water heater, HVAC service, telephone, etc."
- "Cost and expense breakdown. Customer breakdown. Facilities description (w/ asset list). Competition—describe in detail."
- "The tenure of all employees, but especially key employees. What kind of marketing/advertising works for the seller?"
- "Make sure to review the Conditional Use Permit (CUP) if applicable. Also, check the lease for use restrictions for menu changes."
- "Pay attention to what kind of food they serve. What is the cost of goods? That way, as brokers, you can usually get a sense of how good the books and records are when comparing their answer to the tax returns. How much is rent?"

- "How long have your employees been with you? How old is the equipment and are you having any issues with it?"
- "Is there any competition coming to the area?"
- "Will the owner offer financing, training, non-compete (for how many miles); is the lease assignable; is all equipment approved by the NSF (many states do not allow domestic appliances in a commercial location); are trade name, Web site, recipes and training manuals included in the deal?"
- "Reason for sale. Be aware of promotional advertising discounts that may increase sales but not profit. Make sure to understand the labor and staffing as there are often family members working with no pay, or there may be employees that are key to the business (chef or bartenders even, as examples). Know if Health Dept. is going to expect modifications to bring the facility or equipment up to code."
- "How many hours do they work?"
- "What is the real reason (not given reason) you want to sell?"
- "How long since menu/price change?"
- "Can you provide me with your most recent health inspection reports? Both operation inspections and structural!"
- "What are the real costs of doing business and are the reported costs real?"
- "If the equipment is owned or leased/rented, make sure it is in good and working condition. If the chef/cook will stay. The reason for sale. "
- "Ask about the lease."
- "Where is the labor pool? Who are key suppliers? What is the demographic base? Who are major employers in the market? Who are the competition?"
- "What is the gross annual revenue? Are all equipments paid or leased and NSF approved? Are there any governmental issues, including city and health departments?"
- "It is useful to know if the owner has experimented with different hours (breakfast, lunch, dinner, weekend brunch, late night entertainment). Of course the reason for sale is good to know. Any expected modifications from health dept. or franchisor? Any liquor license violations or restrictions?"
- "Is there any competition coming to the area?"
- "Review the lease in advance. Sellers often perceive, knowingly or not, that they have a more favorable lease than they do."
- "Real financial information"
- "Why are you selling? Tell me about your lease. What type of books do you keep?"
- "Bring a tire iron and a pry bar and dig as deeply as possible."
- "Blend of sales food/liquor"
- "Ask about cash payroll. May sellers pay all or part of their payroll in cash. Check if the POS computer is connected to the corporate headquarters or franchise. How long the seller has owned the business might be a good indication that after they bought it they decided that they made a mistake and want out."
- "I really think you have to ask as many as it takes to understand the operation, the employees, the financials, the seller discretionary earnings and verify it. More importantly the buyer needs to determine if he/she can do a better job than the present owner or at least match it."
- "Ask about the competition in the area, both current and future/pending. Know

if the marketing includes coupons which deeply discount the pricing. Take a close look at the labor expenses to determine if this is properly reflected. Realize that cost of goods can be distorted if the business is on a cash basis and does not count inventory regularly. Make sure to understand the lease terms including options to renew."

- "How long have the employees been working there?"
- "Why are you selling? Ask questions about the hours and days of operation to determine if there may be room for increasing sales based on changing the hours. Find out about coupons, discounts and promotions, to be aware of whether these may be increasing the sales without increasing the profits."
- "Work histories of staff? Staffing resources? What vendors should I NOT deal with and why? Suggestions for growth or expansion?"
- "Who is chef and how long has he/she been in place? Does chef have total control of menu?"
- "Do they have good and current tax returns; are the federal, state and payroll taxes current; and does the family have non-essential employees on the payroll? Are sales taxes and gratuities being included in the sales? Some accountants will permit the operator to do that, then remove them as an expense."
- "Which equipment do you own that is leased? Do you have any gift-card programs?"
- "Why did you get in the business and why are you getting out?"
- "How much of your income is in cash? How much of your payroll is paid in cash?"
- "Does a refurbishment need to occur? Why are you selling now?"
- "How to explain the high food and liquor costs and what type of marketing has and has not worked for him."
- "How many hours a week do you work? If they say anything less than 50, don't believe them."
- "What is your strongest area in your business? What part of your business needs the most improvement?"
- "Vendor relationships, tenure of key help, rumored new competition, how long current menu/prices, outstanding gift certificates, lease restrictions,"
- "Are you participating in any credit card advance programs? What equipment leases do you have in place?"
- "What is the condition of the equipment, and how old? What type of liquor license will transfer with this establishment? Check the history with the health department."
- "How long in business? How many employees? PT/FT? Gross Sales? Cost of Goods? Personal expenses paid by the business? Complete Lease Information. A list of all other business expenses. Reason for sale. Non-compete miles and years. etc."

Resources

Trade Publications
- "Appetite for Acquisition": www.wesellrestaurants.com
- Nation's Restaurant News: www.nrn.com
- Restaurant Finance Monitor: www.restfinance.com
- Restaurant Dealmaker: through Amazon

- Restaurant Start-up and Growth: www.rsgmag.com
- Practitioners Publishing Company: www.ppc.thompson.com
- Associations
- National Restaurant Association: www.restaurant.org

Restaurants — Limited Service

(See also Restaurants—Full Service & An Introduction)

SIC 5812-08	NAICS 722211	

Rules of Thumb

➤ 30 to 40 percent of annual sales for independents; 45 to 60 percent for many franchises—plus inventory

➤ 1.5 to 2.5 times SDE plus inventory

➤ 2 to 3 times EBIT

➤ 2.5 to 3.5 times EBITDA

➤ For a rule of thumb for many Limited Serve Franchises see Franchises and the specific franchise listing, if available.

Pricing Tips

- "Add liquor license cost & value of FF&E"
- "Today ('10) it is 1 1/2 times owner's benefit"
- "Lease is the key."
- "Food and labor costs are value drivers."
- "Not all restaurants are valued the same—each segment has their own value"
- "2 to 2.5 times SDE is around what we are seeing, lower for sandwich and pizza right now."
- "Analyze food costs - ideally, they should be less than 30%. Industry average ranges from 30-40%. Look for non-operating assets and unreported cash."
- "5-day breakfast/lunch: 40% annual sales; alcohol only (no food) bar: 40% annual sales; national franchises: 50% sales (if profitable also); full service over $1 million sales or facility >6,000 sq. ft.: 25% sales"
- "Location and history are important. Independents are less attractive but often more profitable than franchises. The key is low overhead, and most franchises have high overhead. Considering owner financing is a must."
- "Food cost and payroll must be meticulously controlled."
- "Limited-service may be lower volume than a full-service restaurant allowing for some higher rent as a % of sales. Make sure that true profitability is over 20% (near 25%)."
- "Independent restaurants priced to sell should be around 1.5 to 2.0 times EBITDA (real estate not included) and owner must be willing to consider some sort of owner financing. Franchised limited-service restaurants may go for as high as 3 times EBITDA but be prepared to go through the franchise-transfer process. You will need patience."
- "Price: twice the yearly net income"
- "We will look for approx. 3.5 times annual cash flow (EBITDA add back owner's salary), then look at 45% to 55% of annual revenue and the sales prices should be between those two. Higher prices are recommended for length of lease & franchise agreement, well-trained crew, good scores on Franchisor's

evaluations (cleanliness, service and product quality), and appearance of the location (paint, remodel, equipment condition etc.) Once this is established, we look at outside influence on that unit in terms of economic and social and other influences, town coming towards the location, or moving away, etc."

- "3.0 x SDE and 75% of sales assumes that the owner operator can make a 25% cash to owner."
- "You arrive at two sets of figures, based on profit and sales. Price tends to move towards higher figure when a new store, has length of lease, volume increasing, and favorable market placement. Price tends to go lower if short lease, declining volume, no franchise term, equipment old, store tired, dropping profitability."
- "Gross revenue is the key, but if the SDE doesn't support the debt service requirements and a reasonable salary, then the % of gross will have to come down."
- "Pricing should be tempered by the type of restaurant (drive thru, sit down, franchise or nonfranchise) and the location. Pricing is adjusted up or down in relationship to the rent factor and length of lease."
- "2.5 times SDE and 50 percent of annual sales are aggressive for independent quick- service restaurants. Most franchises such as Subway, Quizno's etc. sell at these numbers. Nonfranchised sell closer to 2 times SDE. Biggest problem with comps: some brokers state EBITDA without a manager's salary, which is really SDE."
- "35 percent of annual sales for independents and 50 percent for franchises"
- "Sales are a much better indicator of value than bottom-line numbers. Different operators can have huge a impact on food and labor costs running the same business."
- "Popular business, sandwich shops can create high gross profits."
- "Limited menu a bonus; delivery and length of lease major considerations."
- "Look for dramatically out-of-line cost of sales. Often indicates owner skimming."
- "Location, lease, concept, operating manuals, recipes"
- "If business is a franchise, usually priced between 45% and 50% of annual sales."
- "Normal situation—I would take last year's net plus any adjustments such as cars, insurance for owner, depreciation and interest, and make it a multiple of .72 to 2 times that number depending upon location, growth or decline of sales, age of fixtures and condition of building, then add value of FF&E, liquor license and other assets for a good value number."
- "Increase in upcoming rental amount; ease of menu; delivery and competition in the market"

Expert Comments

"Operations closing, which will help the ones left as long as consumers keep spending. Expensive to equip and furnish without knowing if the concept will go. Takes a lot of money to find out. Controlling overhead is key."

"Established independents often are better deals than the franchises as far as net cash flow."

"Tough to compete against national chains and big franchises"

"Highly competitive industry, relatively strong demand from new entrants.

Lenders often require industry experience."

"Most chains realize over 60% of their business through this one window [drive-thru]. That's like saying we get 60% of our business on one product."

"Neal Moro, the napkin business leader at Kimberly-Clark, said the standard rule of thumb at a fast-food restaurant is that a couple will have dinner for two and napkins for 12."

Source: Boston Globe

- "Most models project labor as a percentage of total sales, but I find this method highly inaccurate. I view the majority of labor as a fixed expense. A restaurant needs the majority of its staff whether or not any customers are served. As a result, unpredictable sales generate high labor cost as a percentage of sales. Sending an hourly employee home can reduce labor only slightly. Therefore I recommend treating labor as a fixed expense."

Source: "The New Restaurant Entrepreneur" by Kep Sweeney

- "Highly competitive; tied to economic outlook"
- "Large capital investment in equipment required. Makes resales a bargain!"
- "Increasing food costs squeezing profits"
- "Low-price menus helps during difficult economic times."
- "Restaurants are tough work. They are usually profitable but owners tend to burn out very quickly. Too many owners have a good thing, try to expand, and then spread themselves too thin and end up failing at both locations. One good location does not assure you the 2nd one will be as profitable. KEEP YOUR OVERHEAD UNDER CONTROL".
- "Any food service is risky, however, there are always people looking to buy these types of businesses."
- "By limited service, one would think of something like a smoothie shop. With limited offerings, however, keep in mind sales may hit a peak. Must keep an eye on food cost and labor cost as well as fixed costs."
- "Ease of replication is normally not a consideration, unless buyer is interested in popping out more units. In a franchised world, this does not even enter the equation, since it's controlled by Franchisor. As for location, it's been found that if you got an A location, but substandard product and service, you will do poorer than a B location with excellent fresh product and great service. Others are standard."
- "Easy to open, hard to master. Very difficult to run absentee, owner must be present."
- "Competition is very heavy from chains, franchises as well as independents."
- "Very much location driven"
- "Heavy foot traffic, locations like malls, airports, office buildings"
- "Fast food is here to stay. People like the fast route, and fast food is it. There is a ready work force always coming up with the next generation of young people and first-time workers."
- "Lots of competition. Risk factor: must give consistent product, with good quality. Catering a plus for today's business environment. Many sandwich shops add catering. Some catering-only locations with delivery, in low-rent areas with little highway exposure."
- "Great service followed by good food are keys to success."

Benchmark Data

Statistics (Fast Food Restaurants)

Number of Establishments	268,431
Average Profit Margin	3.3%
Revenue per Employee	$48,700
Average Number of Employees	13.3
Average Wages per Employee	12,690

Source: IBISWorld, July 2012

Products and Services Segmentation

On-premises limited-service restaurants	42.9%
Drive-thru limited-service restaurants	34.4%
Off-premises (take-out) limited-service restaurants	18.1%
Cafeterias and buffets	4.6%

Source: IBISWorld, July 2012

Industry costs

Profit	3.3%
Wages	26.3%
Purchases	31.0%
Depreciation	3.6%
Marketing	3.0%
Rent & Utilities	9.0%
Other	23.8%

Source: IBISWorld, July 2012

Market Share

McDonald's Corporation	12.9%
Yum! Brands Inc.	9.6%
Doctor's Associates Inc.	8.2%
Wendy's International Inc.	4.4%
Burger King Corporation	2.1%

Source: July 2012

Statistics (Coffee & Snack Shops)

Number of Establishments	51,436
Average Profit Margin	5.9%
Revenue per Employee	$57,400
Average Number of Employees	9.8
Average Wages per Employee	$13,014

Source: IBISWorld, October 2012

Products and Services Segmentation

Coffee shops	42%
Other snack shops	21%
Donut shops	15%
Ice cream shops	13%
Bagel shops	05%
Cookie shops	02%
Frozen yogurt shops	02%

Source: IBISWorld, October 2012

Industry Costs

Profit	5.9%
Wages	22.7%
Purchases	31.0%
Depreciation	3.6%
Marketing	4.5%
Rent & Utilities	9.0%
Other	23.3%

Source: IBISWorld, October 2012

Market Share

Starbucks Corporation 35.6%
Dunkin' Brands Inc. 24.5%

Source: IBISWorld, October 2012

Establishments by Employment Size

Number of Employees	Share
1 to 4	32.6%
5 to 9	15.3%
10 to 19	21.6%

Source: IBISWorld, June 2012

- "Drive-thru is the operational heart of the fast-food industry, as central to a brand like Taco Bell as the kitchen itself, maybe more so. According to the National Restaurant Assn., the fast-food industry will do $168 billion in sales for 2011, and about 70 percent of that will come in through drive-thru windows. The technology deployed at order stations and pick-up windows has evolved to meet that demand. Every step is measured, every movement calculated, every word scripted. Taco Bell, with more than 5,600 locations in the U.S., currently operates some of the fastest and most accurate drive-thru windows in the industry, at least according to QSR magazine's last survey, in 2009, though for years they lagged. The system is the result of a 15-year-plus focus on the window as the core of the business."

  Source: "Fast and Furious," by Karl Taro Greenfeld, *Bloomberg Businessweek*, May 9–May 15, 2011

- "Prime cost (cost of goods plus payroll costs divided by sales) must remain below 60%"
- "Food costs—sub shops < 30%, fine dining 35% +, breakfast/lunch < 30%, pizza & pasta 29%–32%."
- "Food costs under 33% are critical, and labor costs under 30% are important."
- "Restaurants (non-franchise) should net 15% with professional operator."
- "2 times EBITDA plus real estate is most often used."
- "An owner-operated place should keep labor costs below 15%. Food cost should never go over 32%, the lower the better. Rent can be 10%–12% of sales."
- "With food and labor rising, you need to look to cut costs elsewhere. Owner-operators are a must with an independent restaurant. If you don't think the employees are stealing ... they are."
- "Food costs should be in 28% to 30% range."
- "Food costs range to a very high of 35%, average of 29 to 31%, low of 21 to 26%. Coffee and pizza sites tend to have favorable food costs, while some of the deli's tend to have mid to high mid-range food costs."
- "Again sales must be at a point that there is enough margin to cover fixed costs and then some."
- "Food costs should run 33%, not higher. Rent or lease cost runs 7% to 9% maximum, and the raw labor without mgmt. should run about 17% to 18%, with mgr. accounting for 3% to 6%, depends on site's volume. The payroll taxes at 2.7 to 2.9, final bottom line cash flow at least 11%."
- "Combined food cost, labor and occupancy (the big 3) must not exceed 70% in total."
- "Food costs need to be kept under 38%. Rents need to be kept under 10%."
- "Lower quartile per seat is $5,115, median is $7,510, and $14,293 is upper. $10,000 per seat is a benchmark for a successful quick-service restaurant."
- "Better operators keep food costs down closer to 30%, adds to bottom line."

- "Food usually maximum of 35%. Sandwich shops very popular today. Catering a plus, hard to prove without good reliable records."
- "I look for a 20% plus EBIT and 'Prime Costs' (Cost of Sales & Labor) combined below 50%."
- "Good menu can add to success. Location, visibility, and parking key ingredients for profitable business."
- "Mall fast food should be $1,000 + per square foot."
- "Ownership of real estate very desirable. Franchise stores more marketable than independents. Franchise presence in marketplace very important."
- "Median sales per full-time employee = $55,240; sales per square foot = $291"

Expenses as a Percentage of Annual Sales

Cost of goods	28% to 32%
Payroll/labor Costs	25% to 35%
Occupancy	08% to 12%
Profit (estimated pretax)	15% to 20%

Industry Trend

- "Slow sales, higher expenses"
- "Good food, good service at fair price will always survive."
- "Highly competitive; national chains continue to expand"
- "Lots of turnover"
- "Sales should be increasing starting late 2010; overall sales and profit should be around the same levels as last year."
- "Many units with expensive leases are likely to close."
- "Lots of restaurants out of business with recession. Chains can absorb more, so you will see a decline in independent upscale restaurants."
- "Less upscale dining, more family-oriented businesses"

Seller Financing

- "Five years—8 percent"
- "3 to 4 years"
- "7 to 10 years with a 3 to 5 year stop"
- "Average of 5 years and prime plus 2 percent"
- "Depends on size and cash flow; 8 years is an average of our last 20 restaurant transactions."

Questions

- "What can be done to improve the business that you are not doing?"
- "Sales, purchase invoices, detail of expenses"
- "Food costs & payroll costs"
- "Who are your key people? How many hours per week do you work? How long have you been in business?"
- "Tax issues. Relationship with franchisor if applicable. Any mandatory remodeling in near future. Lease terms and length. CAM charges."
- "Gross sales, food cost, total itemized expenses, payroll breakdown, all income including cash."
- "When was the last time you had a menu change or price change?"

- "Cost %, profit %, length of lease, length of franchise agreement, length of time employees are with him, or turnover %, training methods for employees, franchisor/ franchisee relationship, age of business, age of his ownership, what does honesty mean to him, why he got in this site in first place, what does he plan to do after sale, and other such things."
- "Definitely dig into ALL the expenses, including monthly recurring but especially less frequent items like CAM adjustments from landlord or repairs and maintenance."

Retail Businesses (In General)

Rules of Thumb

➢ 30 to 35 percent of annual sales plus inventory

➢ 1.5 to 2 times SDE plus inventory

Pricing Tips

- "Occupancy—lease terms"
- "It's very common. Wall Street pressures you to show growth. There's a certain seduction to opening up more stores, because that's an easy way to show growth. But in a downturn, you wish you hadn't. It's like overeating at Thanksgiving. Sharper Image was guilty of that sin.

"Private-equity people have thought for 10 years that retailing was an easy way to make money, and it's proving not to be so easy the moment you get a slight tick-down in the economy."

Source: "Priority: Losing an Edge," Interview with Richard Thalheimer, founder of the Sharper Image, *INC Magazine*, July 2008

Benchmark Data

- No business lends itself more to benchmarking than retailing. Two important Benchmark Data for retail operations that may measure profitability, or just how a particular business may stack up against its peers, are Sales per square Foot and Sales per Employee.
- *Pat O'Rourke, the creator of BizStats, has written a very interesting—and informative —article titled "Why Sales per Foot Is the Critical Benchmark for Retailers." Here are a few excerpts.*

"Think of Sales per Foot in terms of sun protection factor—SPF—a healthy SPF will help prevent you from getting burned in a retail business. SPF is one of many retail Benchmark Data, but I believe it's the best gauge of a retailer's efficiency, and, ultimately, its profitability. It's also easy to compute—just divide sales by the store's gross square feet. Some retailers calculate SPF based on selling feet (excluding in-store administrative, storage and other space), but this can be subjective and impair meaningful comparisons.

"SPF differs among industries. For example, a big box discounter with high inventory turnover (such as Costco) is going to have a much higher SPF than a clothing chain or sports equipment outlet. Another key element is location, SPF is typically much higher for merchants in a destination mall, than for similar stores in a local shopping center—of course you pay much higher rent in the big mall.

"An upward trend in SPF is almost always a positive sign of a retailer's health, whereas a downward trend in SPF is often a warning sign that business performance is suffering—even if the company's total sales are increasing.
"There can be many reasons for a low SPF. The first reason is obvious—the retailer simply has too much space. By having excessive space, a retailer will be adversely impacted by high fixed costs:

✓ Rent costs are excessive
✓ Labor costs are excessive, since additional floor space requires additional personnel
✓ Flooring costs are excessive, since additional space requires additional merchandise

- Insurance utilities and theft costs all increase with additional floor space
- "Assuming the store size is reasonable, there are many reasons for a poor SPF relative to competitors. Here are 10 primary reasons for a low SPF—these are considerations for retailers of all sizes:
  1. Poor product/merchandising mix
  2. Insufficient floor inventory (e.g., empty shelves, missing sizes)
  3. Un-competitive pricing
  4. Poor location
  5. Poor sales and customer service personnel
  6. Non-optimal store hours
  7. Poor store layout and design
  8. Cannibalization of nearby owned stores
  9. Insufficient/poor marketing
  10. Fixed consumer perception"

Expenses as a Percentage of Annual Sales

Cost of goods	25%
Payroll/labor Costs	20%
Occupancy	18%
Profit (estimated pretax)	28%

Industry Trend

- "Even though the number of retail store openings by major U.S. retail industry chains is expected to far outnumber the number of store closings in the 2011 calendar year, both large and small retail chains will still be struggling to hold onto their domestic retail presence, keep stores open, and grow sales and turn a profit. The number of U.S. retail industry store closings planned for 2011 will not be insignificant, particularly in an economy that is still plagued by high unemployment.
"Many experts believe that the number of retail establishments per capita in the United States was excessive even before the economy recessed. According to the 2007 Economic Census, there were 1,122,703 retail establishments in the United States and a total of 14.2 billion square feet of retail space. That means that there is approximately 46.6 square feet of retail space per capita in the U.S., compared to two square feet per capita in India, 1.5 square feet per capita in Mexico, 23 square feet per capita in the United Kingdom, 13 square feet per capita in Canada, and 6.5 square feet per capita in Australia."

Source: "Retail Store Closings Roundup: U.S. Retailers Closing or Liquidating Stores, www.retailindustry.about.com

Retail: "If your product isn't different, then how you sell it must be different if you are going to survive."

Retail Stores (Small Specialty)

		Number of Businesses/Units 117,832

Rules of Thumb

➢ 15 to 20 percent of annual sales plus inventory

➢ 1.8 to 2.2 times SDE plus inventory

Pricing Tips

- IBISWorld includes such businesses in this category as tobacco stores, artists' materials, souvenirs & collectibles, coin & stamp shops, religious goods (not books), occupational supplies and other similar type businesses. Approximately 85 percent of them are single-owner/small family businesses. Eighty-eight percent of these businesses have 9 or fewer employees.

Benchmark Data

Statistics (Small Specialty Retail Stores)

Number of Establishments	117,832
Average Profit Margin	3.0%
Revenue per Employee	$120,300
Average Number of Employees	2
Average Wages per Employee	$17,490

Source: IBISWorld, July 2012

Products and Services Segmentation

Tobacco products and smokers' accessories	36.3%
Other	24.2%
Art materials and supplies	16.7%
Collectible items	10.4%
Occupational supplies	6.6%
Religious goods (except books)	5.8%

Source: IBISWorld, July 2012

Industry Costs

Profit	3.0%
Wages	14.5%
Purchases	61.9%
Depreciation	1.5%
Utilities	1.0%
Rent	4.3%
Other	13.8%

Source: IBISWorld, July 2012

Distribution of Enterprises by Staff Size

Number of Employees	Enterprise Share
1 to 4	68.5%
5 to 9	18.4%
10 to 19	8.0%

Source: IBISWorld, February 2012

Retirement Homes

(See Homes—Retirement, Nursing Homes, & Assisted Living)

	Franchise
Rita's Italian Ice	
Approx. Total Investment	$199,400 to $378,400
Estimated Annual Sales/Unit	$230,000

	NAICS 722213	Number of Businesses/Units 550

Rules of Thumb

➢ 80 percent to 1.3 times annual sales plus inventory

Resources

Websites
- www.ritasice.com

	Franchise
Rocky Mountain Chocolate Factory (See also Candy Stores)	
Approx. Total Investment	$158,451 to $592,265

	NAICS 311330	Number of Businesses/Units 235

Rules of Thumb

➢ 60 to 65 percent of annual sales plus inventory

Resources

Websites
- www.sweetfranchise.com

	Franchise
Roly Poly Sandwiches (See also Sandwich Shops)	
Approx. Total Investment	$101,050 to $220,200

	NAICS 722211	Number of Businesses/Units 120

Rules of Thumb

➢ 35 percent of annual sales plus inventory

Benchmark Data
- For Benchmark data see Sandwich Shops

Resources

Websites
- www.rolypoly.com

Route Distribution Businesses

	NAICS 4224	

Rules of Thumb

➤ 50 percent of annual sales plus inventory

➤ 1 to 4 times SDE plus inventory

➤ 3 times SDE plus inventory—3 to 4 times for name brands; 1 to 2 times for no name brands

➤ 1 to 4 times EBIT

➤ 10 to 20 times weekly gross plus inventory

Pricing Tips

- "The going rate on most franchised routes is about 2.5–3 times a year's net income, while non-franchised routes sell for 1–2 times a year's net income."
- "Major factors involved in pricing a route include: (1) Where the route is located; (2) What is the year & condition of the vehicle included? (3) Is the truck owned or leased? (4) How many years the route is established; (5) Is the route protected stops territory or is it an unprotected route? (6) What is the brand of the product that the route is distributing? (7) How close to the depot is the route?"
- "Each category (bread, coffee, chips, candy/nut, cookie, dairy, juice, paper, pie/pastry, provisions, soda/beverage, vending, package delivery {FedEx, etc.}) of route businesses is priced differently. Even within categories such as 'Soda/Beverage' a Snapple route will go for a higher multiple than an independent beverage route. Other major factors involved in pricing a route include: (1) where the route is located; (2) the year & condition of the vehicle included; (3) how many years the route has been established; (4) if the route is protected stops territory or an unprotected route; (5) the brand of the product that the route is distributing. Bread routes typically use a multiple of weekly sales. Beverage & juice routes usually use a price/case. Majority of routes are multiple of annual net profit."
- "Franchised Routes: Approximately 2 times SDE. Note that franchised routes, which usually exist on the more consumer-recognized products, have 'Distribution Agreements' in force between wholesales and distributor."
- "Non-Franchised Routes: Approximately 1 times SDE. Non-franchised routes have no such contracts [Distribution Agreements] and they usually distribute staple items and/or non-consumer recognized products."

Expert Comments

"Easy to check out business, learn business, operate business and grow business."

Benchmark Data

- "Cost of goods should never be more than 35 percent."

Expenses as a Percentage of Annual Sales

Cost of goods	70% to 80%
Payroll/labor Costs	n/a
Occupancy	n/a
Profit (estimated pretax)	15% to 20%

Industry Trend

- "Since this business is not linked to 'high rent' real estate market, it can still flourish even though 'per store' sales are down."
- "Has been growing for the past 75 years and the trend is definitely up"

Seller Financing

- "3-10 years"

Questions

- "Ask the Seller to point out problem customers & CAREFULLY check the route's receivables & parables policies."
- "Documentation of purchases, sales and expenses."

Resources

Websites

- www.routebrokers.com

Routes – Newspaper (See Newspaper Routes)

RV Dealerships

SIC 5561-03	NAICS 441210	Number of Businesses/Units 6,954

Rules of Thumb

➢ 15 percent of annual sales plus RV inventory & parts, etc.

Benchmark Data

Statistics (Recreational Vehicle Dealers)

Number of Establishments	6,954
Average Profit Margin	1.1%
Revenue per Employee	$436,800
Average Number of Employees	6.1
Average Wages per Employee	$44,560

Source: IBISWorld, October 2012

Products and Services Segmentation

Fifth-wheel trailers	31.5%
Travel trailers	28%
Class A	26.6%
Class C	7.9%
Parts and services	3.2%
Folding trailers	2.3%
Class B	0.5%

Source: IBISWorld, October 2012

Industry Costs

Profit	1.1%
Wages	10.1%
Purchases	82.5%
Depreciation	0.2%
Marketing	1.9%
Rent & Utilities	1.7%
Other	2.5%

Source: IBISWorld, October 2012

Resources

Associations
- Recreational Vehicle Industry Association (RVIA)—a very informative site: www.rvia.org

RV Parks (See also Campgrounds)		
SIC 7033-02	NAICS 721211	Number of Businesses/Units 6,954

Rules of Thumb

➢ 3.3 percent of annual sales plus inventory

➢ 8.5 times SDE plus inventory

Pricing Tips
- "4.2 times gross profit. I would use the same guidelines as "Campgrounds". The more important differences would be if the park is a "resort", "overnight park" or a "monthly park". Do not use cap rates that are intended for a real estate investment property. Most RV Parks and Campgrounds are run as a mom and pop business until they reach maybe $600,000 in revenue and have full time managers. Also, the number of sites is not a good indicator of value or income."
- "The industry is getting more sophisticated at marketing and pricing. Many hotel/motel pricing strategies are starting to work for campgrounds."
- "Too variable for rules of thumb. Cap rates of 9 to 15 percent. Urban parks at low end of cap rate spectrums. Destination parks are at higher end. Number of ancillary revenue sources will affect cap rates on destination parks—more revenue sources, lower cap rates. Parks with fewer than 100 sites are very inefficient, and value tends to be exclusively in the real estate, with little or no intrinsic value."

Expert Comments
"See campgrounds for more info"

"It is difficult to build new facilities due to permitting."

Benchmark Data
- "Below 5,000 camper nights per year is difficult to operate the business and make a profit."

Expenses as a percentage of sales
Marketing	10%
Utilities	14%
Payroll	25%
G&A	05%

- "Expenses should run between 40 and 60% of gross profit"
- Note: See Campgrounds for additional Benchmark data

Expenses as a Percentage of Annual Sales
Cost of goods	10%
Payroll/labor Costs	10%
Occupancy	40%
Profit (estimated pretax)	40%

Industry Trend

- "The Baby Boomers have arrived at the nation's RV parks and resorts, which now offer a growing variety of activities and entertainment as well as healthy activities, from water aerobics and bocce ball to classes in Tai Chi. Some RV resorts even have onsite health and wellness centers.

  "The Baby Boomers have arrived," said Paul Bambei, president and CEO of the National Association of RV Parks and Campgrounds, the Denver-based trade association that represents the outdoor hospitality industry.

  "And RV parks and resorts are responding by providing a greater variety of activities and entertainment. Some have even established health and wellness centers."

  Source: "America's Snowbirds are Getting Younger and More Active," www.arvc.org February 2012

- "Gradually better "
- "The National Association of RV Parks and Campgrounds, for its part, plans to create a listing of parks that offer electric vehicle refueling services on its Go Camping America website."

  Source: "Electric Car Owners Are Increasingly Using Campgrounds as Refueling Stops on Longer Journeys," National Association of RV Parks and Campgrounds, April 6, 2011

- "Affordable travel that should grow. Retired baby boomers should keep the business strong for several years."

Seller Financing

- 50% of all sales

Resources

Trade Publications

- Guide to Appraising Recreational Vehicle Parks published by the Appraisal Institute: www.appraisalinstitute.org
- RV Life—an industry publication: www.rvlife.com

Associations

- National Association of RV Parks and Campgrounds: www.arvc.org

			Franchise
Safe Ship			
Approx. Total Investment			$29,000 to $88,000
	NAICS 561431		

Rules of Thumb

➢ 40 percent of annual sales

Sales Businesses (In General)			
			Number of Businesses/Units 750,000

Rules of Thumb

➢ 1 times SDE plus inventory

Sales Consulting

SIC 8748-08	NAICS 541613	

Rules of Thumb

➤ 33 percent of annual sales includes inventory

Pricing Tips

- "Price paid should be affected by current accounts surviving the exit of the owner."

	Franchise

Samurai Sam's Teriyaki Grill

Approx. Total Investment	$125,350 to $506,300
NAICS 722110	Number of Businesses/Units 51

Rules of Thumb

➤ 45 percent of annual sales

➤ 1.5 times SDE

Resources

Websites

- www.samuraisams.net

Sand and Gravel Mining

SIC 5032-11	NAICS 212321	Number of Businesses/Units 2,384

Rules of Thumb

➤ 100 percent of annual sales plus inventory

➤ 5 times EBITDA

Benchmark Data

Statistics (Sand and Gravel Mining)

Number of Establishments	2,384
Average Profit Margin	34.2%
Revenue per Employee	$295,200
Average Number of Employees	12.7
Average Wages per Employee	$48,152

Source: IBISWorld, October 2012

Products and Services Segmentation

Construction sand and gravel	68.5%
Industrial (silica) sand	15.0%
Common day	9.1%
Kaolin	3.8%
Other clays and ceramic minerals	3.6%

Source: IBISWorld, October 2012

Industry Costs

Profit	34.2%
Wages	16.9%
Purchases	24.4%
Depreciation	9.0%
Marketing	0.1%
Rent & Utilities	6.5%
Other	8.9%

Source: IBISWorld, October 2012

Market Share

CRH PLC	11.4%
Heidelberg Cement AG	8.9%
Martin Marietta Materials, Inc.	6.8%
Vulcan Materials Company	4.9%

Source: IBISWorld, October 2012

- "At least 150,000 tons/year is the minimum usually necessary for a profitable site."

Sandwich Shops (See also Individual Franchised Sandwich Shops)

SIC 5812-19	NAICS 722211	

Rules of Thumb

➢ 40 to 50 percent of annual sales plus inventory

➢ 2 times SDE plus inventory

➢ 3 times EBIT

➢ Bllimpie's	45% to 50% of annual sales
Lil' Dino's	50% of annual sales
Quizno's	25% to 30% of annual sales
Roly Poly	35% of annual sales
Jimmy John's	60% to 65% of annual sales
Jersey Mike's	50% of annual sales
Subway	60% to 65% of annual sales

All above rules of thumb are plus inventory

Average Rule of Thumb for above franchises is 47% of annual sales plus inventory

Note: In averaging the rules of thumb for some of the larger franchised sandwich shops, it turns out that it is just about the same as sandwich shops in general— independent or franchised. However, they seem to be more saleable than independents.

Benchmark Data

Statistics (Sandwich & Sub Store Franchises)

Number of Establishments	34,527
Average Profit Margin	5.5%
Revenue per Employee	$40,600
Average Number of Employees	14
Average Wages per Employee	$14,029

Source: IBISWorld, March 2012

Products and Services Segmentation

Limited-service restaurants	46.8%
Cafeteria restaurants	33.5%
Takeout restaurants	19.7%

Source: IBISWorld, March 2012

Industry Costs

Profit	5.5%
Wages	34.4%
Purchases	35.0%
Depreciation	3.6%
Marketing	4.5%
Rent & Utilities	8.5%
Other	8.5%

Source: IBISWorld, March 2012

Market Share

Doctor's Associates Inc.	73.6%
Quizno's	10.0%

Source: IBISWorld, March 2012

- For additional information on the following franchises, see the entry for it.

For informational Purposes

Jimmy John's—Average Annual Sales	$820,000
Quizno's—Average Annual Sales	$330,000
Firehouse Subs—Average Annual Sales	$650,000
Jersey Mike's—Average Annual Sales	$530,000
Penn Station East Subs—Average Annual Sales	$580,000
Subway—Average Annual Sales	$470,000
Cousin's Subs—Average Annual Sales	$430,000
Port of Subs—Average Annual sales	$370,000
Average Annual Sales	$522,000
Average Rule of Thumb	47% plus inventory
Average Price	$245,000

Sandwich Franchise Compared (Failure % to pay back SBA loans)

Jimmy John's	4%
Subway	10%
Firehouse Subs	15%
Quizno's	35%
Blimpie's	45%

Source: SBA, May 2011, www.bluemaumau.org. Note the information above is from 2001 to 2010

Expenses as a Percentage of Annual Sales

Cost of goods	28%
Payroll/labor Costs	22%
Occupancy	10%
Profit (estimated pretax)	20%

Industry Trend

- "Sandwich chains' 37,903 units, for example, grew just 1 percent last year versus bakery-café's 3,643 units and 3.2 percent growth rate, according to Technomic's Top 500 Chain Restaurant report.'"
- "A few chains have continued to struggle, leading to what some are calling a 'shakeout' in the sandwich segment. Quizno's lost more than 1,000 units. Blimpie, once the second-largest sandwich chain in the country and a Subway rival, has fallen to under 1,000 restaurants nationwide."

- "Jimmy John's is the second-fastest-growing restaurant chain in the country, thanks in large part to its delivery system, combined with humorous radio ads promoting its 'freaky fast' speed."

  Source: "Spicing up a Pickle," Franchise Times, June/July 2011

	Franchise
Sarpino's Pizzeria (See also Pizza Shops, etc.)	
Approx. Total Investment	$188,095 to $274,895
SIC 5812-22 NAICS 722211	Number of Businesses/Units 25

Rules of Thumb
> 50 percent of annual sales plus inventory

Resources
Websites
- www.sarpinosfranchise.com

Schools — Educational/Non-Vocational	
NAICS 61	Number of Businesses/Units 14,270

Rules of Thumb
> 40% to 50% of Annual Gross Sales

> 2.5 to 3 times SDE includes inventory

> 1.5 times EBIT

Pricing Tips
- "Use cash flow to determine price and what the lenders will do with that figure."
- "One of the safest ways to price is based on the cash flow of the business and the ability to service a loan size based on the cash flow. If you know the size of the loan your cash flow supports, you know the price."

Expert Comments
"Overall there are more childcare centers in the country than private schools, adult- ed schools, and other types of schools.There is a market for schools."

"There are no physical barriers to entry, but creating a quality school or day care takes more than a facility. It takes quality teachers and leaders. Finding these is the real barrier to entry."

Benchmark Data
Statistics (Business Certification & IT Schools)
Number of Establishments	14,270
Average Profit Margin	3.9%
Revenue per Employee	$85,900
Average Number of Employees	2.3
Average Wages per Employee	$28,935

Source: IBISWorld, May 2012

Products and Services Segmentation

General computer and IT courses	45%
Product-specific computer and IT certification courses	30%
Other	10%
General administrative training	7.5%
Specialized administrative training	7.5%

Source: IBISWorld, May 2012

- "Phoenix now boasts 458,600 students, with more than 200,000 in its two-year online program. Enrollment in for-profit colleges went from 673,000 in 2000 to 1.8 million in 2008. Revenue rose from $9 billion in 2000 to an estimated $29.2 billion this year, says Jeffrey Silber, an analyst for BMO Capital Markets in New York. Operating margins averaged 21% in 2009; schools typically charge $10,000 to $20,000 a year, well above comparable programs at community colleges."

    Source: "Hardselling the Homeless" by Daniel Golden, *Bloomberg Businessweek*, May 3, 2010

- "Cash flow of the school will determine price. It's hard to use per employee, per student or per foot."
- "Some people use a crude measure to value of between $1,500 and $2,500 per student enrolled for childcare facilities in leased space."

Expenses as a Percentage of Annual Sales

Cost of goods	20%
Payroll/labor Costs	40%
Occupancy	20%
Profit (estimated pretax)	15% to 20%

Industry Trend

- "Slow the last few years, starting to pick up. SBA lending helped."
- "High- and middle-school online education is going to grow at a very fast rate. Cost to offer is low and do not need facility to provide services. Currently 2 million take some type of online schooling; in the next 5 years, it will be 10 million."
- "New Student Loan Source

    To ensure a stream of new students in the current credit crunch, some profit-making career colleges and technical schools will offer students loans or guarantee them."

    Source: *New York Times*, February 19, 2008

- "Demand for good schools for sale."
- "There is plenty of growth as the population increases. Franchises and corporate-owned schools are increasingly popular."
- "The demand for educated and trained staff is high. Education leads to a better job."
- "Always students who need help fall behind, need passing grades to pass"

Seller Financing

- "5 years"

Questions

- "What type of programs do you have with government agencies?"
- "What is your market area?"

Schools — Tutoring & Driving Schools

(See also Schools—Educational & Vocational)

		Number of Businesses/Units 114,769

Rules of Thumb

➢ 40 to 45 percent of annual sales

➢ Driving Schools/Instruction

➢ 1 times SDE + fair market value of fixed assets

➢ 40 to 45 percent of annual sales + fair market value of fixed assets

Pricing Tips

▪ Driving Schools/Instruction

"High barrier to entry due to increasingly higher and stricter state regulations and standards"

The rule of thumb above applies to "learn-to-drive schools" that primarily teach teenagers to drive and pass a state driving test. It is mandatory in many states. However, there are many other types of driving schools such as: winter driving, commercial driving (trucks, etc.), race driving, etc.

Benchmark Data

Statistics (Tutoring & Driving Schools)

Number of Establishments	114,769
Average Profit Margin	N/A
Revenue per Employee	$38,700
Average Number of Employees	2
Average Wages per Employee	$21,010

Source: IBISWorld, June 2011

Products and Services Segmentation (2011)

Exam preparation and tutoring	49.5%
Driving schools	10.2%
Other schools	40.3%

Source: IBISWorld, June 2011

Enterprises by Employment Size (2011)

No. of Employees	No. of Enterprises	Share (%)
1 to 4	6,836	58.6
5 to 9	1,997	17.2

Source: IBISWorld, June 2011

Industry Costs

Profit	10.0%
Rent	2.0%
Utilities	1.0%
Depreciation	3.0%
Other	14.8%
Wages	54.4%
Purchases	14.8%

Source: IBISWorld, June 2011

Market Share

The Washington Post Company	4.6%

Source: IBISWorld, June 2011

Schools — Vocational/Training

(See also Schools—Educational/Non-Vocational)

	NAICS 611410	Number of Businesses/Units 40,153

Rules of Thumb

➤ 75 to 100 percent of annual sales plus inventory

➤ 2 to 4 times SDE plus inventory

➤ 1.5 times EBIT

➤ 3 to 5 times EBITDA

Pricing Tips

- "Accreditation and Title IV funding provides for higher pricing."
- "Pricing is all over the board because of the size of a facility. The larger the school the more the owners profit."
- "I am in the process of closing a second sale on truck-driver-training schools in Missouri and Alabama. Unfortunately the same buyers of Franklin College are my buyers for the Missouri and Alabama schools. Their criteria are straight up and simple, and I quote:

  'Invested capital has to come back to buyer 100 percent + Cost of Money (Interest) in 24 months or less.'

  "My sale, being a truck-driver-training school, is a somewhat different business than a typical trade school where the 'class' time or number of months to complete school would be say 1 year or 2 years. The CDL licensing school is a 'short' 3-week, high-turn business. Asset/Liability structure is much different for other 'long-term' schools, as they invest higher percentages in fixed assets and typically do not get the margin as the CDL licensing schools.

  "The 'deal' on Franklin College was an equity purchase of $2,600,000+, plus cash payments to owner principals of $120,000. In the following, I will use the $2.6 million as a sale price.

  Amount and % Seller financed: $1,000,000 or 38.46%

  Term Financed: 5 years

  x Historical Cash Flow 3.43 x (based on last two years' average)

  x Forecasted Two Yr. Cash Flow 2.5x (buyer's forecast)

  x Book Equity 98.48% (net depreciation and amortization)

  x Blue Sky 0%

  x Annual Gross Revenue 1x

  x Cost of Goods % to Gross Revenue* 16.6%

  x Recruitment Expense** 18.00%

  x Administrative Expense 17.8%

  x All Other & Misc. 6.9%

  x Net Operating Income 40.7% (before income tax)

  *(Cost of teaching supplies for training, including instructor/teacher wages and wage burden)

  **(Cost of commissioned salesmen, advertising)

  "The buyer of this particular school has never owned or operated a truck-driver-training school or been involved in the trucking industry. I had earlier sold them a structural-steel-fabrication company, and they wanted to look at ALL my sell deals and became interested because of the high margins of this particular school and the well-known truck driver shortage, nationally. Since that date, they have acquired 7 other operating schools in 5 states and are now in the process of purchasing 2 more in 2 states, as I earlier mentioned.

"Until this buyer came along, my best offer came from PGT Trucking, a Northeast, PA firm that was not considered acceptable to the sellers. It is also interesting to note that I marketed to 14 different truck-driver-training schools and only had one principal to inquire, without an offer of any kind."

- "Value is driven by type of program (longer, more expensive programs are more valuable), enrollment, and enrollment growth."

Expert Comments

"Great industry with room to grow. The childcare, private school and adult education industry is on the move."

Benchmark Data

Statistics (Trade and Technical Schools)

Number of Establishments	40,153
Average Profit Margin	8.9%
Revenue per Employee	$104,700
Average Number of Employees	3.7
Average Wages per Employee	$40,220

Source: IBISWorld, July 2012

Products and Services Segmentation

Other professional development programs	30.8%
Flight training programs	20%
Healthcare training programs	15%
Apprenticeship training programs	14.1%
Cosmetology and barber schools	11.1%
Management	9%

Source: IBISWorld, July 2012

Industry Costs

Profit	8.9%
Wages	39.0%
Purchases	13.1%
Depreciation	3.5%
Marketing	9.6%
Rent & Utilities	9.9%
Other	16.0%

Source: IBISWorld, July 2012

- "Sales per license cap can range from $6,000 to $ 14,000. An example: a 100-student licensed school could sell for as much as $1.4 million. Most schools sell based on Cash Flow."

Expenses as a Percentage of Annual Sales

Cost of goods	20%
Payroll/labor Costs	40%
Occupancy	05%
Profit (estimated pretax)	20%

Industry Trend

- "Generally increasing revenues"

Seller Financing

- "10 years"

Questions

- "Is the school accredited and what is the status?"

Resources

Websites

- www.schoolsforsale.com

Franchise

Sears Carpet and Upholstery Care & Home Services	
(See also Carpet Cleaning)	

Approx. Total Investment		$25,960 to $191,550
	NAICS 561740	Number of Businesses/Units 140

Rules of Thumb

➢ 35 percent of annual sales plus inventory

Resources

Websites

- www.searsclean.com

Secretarial Services	
	NAICS 561410	

Rules of Thumb

➢ 50 percent of annual revenues includes inventory

Security Services/Systems	
(See also Guard Services & Alarm Companies)	

SIC 7382-02	NAICS 561621	Number of Businesses/Units 55,829

Rules of Thumb

➢ 50 percent of annual sales includes inventory

➢ 2 times SDE includes inventory

➢ 3 times EBIT

➢ 4 times EBITDA

➢ 24 to 28 times monthly revenue based on an average $25 mo. per account plus inventory

Pricing Tips

- "Weighted monthly billing times 4"

Benchmark Data

Statistics (Security Services)

Number of Establishments	55,829
Average Profit Margin	8.1%
Revenue per Employee	41,800
Average Number of Employees	12.7
Average Wages per Employee	$23,961

Source: IBISWorld, August 2012

Products and Services Segmentation

On-site security guard services	69.2%
Investigation services	16.3%
Armored vehicle services	9.9%
Security personnel at special events	3%
Other services	1.6%

Source: IBISWorld, August 2012

Major Market Segmentation

Major corporations	26%
Retail clients	23%
Financial institutions	21%
Government clients	16%
Other clients	9%
Residential clients	5%

Source: IBISWorld, August 2012

Industry Costs

Profit	8.1%
Wages	57.9%
Purchases	3.6%
Depreciation	4.0%
Marketing	0.6%
Rent & Utilities	3.0%
Other	22.8%

Source: IBISWorld, August 2012

Market Share

SecuritasAB	12.6%
G4S PLC	9.7%
Allied Security LLC	5.8%

Source: IBISWorld, August 2012

Expenses as a Percentage of Annual Sales

Cost of goods	40%
Payroll/labor Costs	40%
Occupancy	10%
Profit (estimated pretax)	10%

Seller Financing

- "3 to 5 years and an average of 20 to 50 percent of transaction value financed by seller"

Questions

- "What are the contract terms? How long have you had this account? Buyers do not like government contracts."
- "Type of guard services and customer list. Most guard companies have one major client."

Resources

Websites
- The American Society for Industrial Security (ASIS): www.asisonline.org

Trade Publications
- Security Distribution and Marketing magazine—an excellent site with lots of good information and data. It's everything one needs to know about the security industry: www.sdmmag.com

Associations
- Security Industry Association (SIA): www.siaonline.org
- National Burglar & Fire Alarm Association: www.alarm.org

Self Storage (Mini Storage)		
	NAICS 531130	Number of Businesses/Units 48,170

Rules of Thumb
➢ 1 times EBITDA

Pricing Tips

- "These are difficult because they are often a means of holding land until it reaches the point where it is more profitable to redevelop it for another use. Most buyers look for a cash on cash return of about 20% on the amount they must invest to purchase the property compared to the purchase price/financing that can be obtained."

- "Transaction velocity (in south central states) has slowed approximately 10 percent over the last year, though activity remained steady during the first half of 2009. Despite more consistent market velocity, prices have fallen 36 percent year over year to $37 per square foot. The median price has declined 29 percent to $45 per square foot during the past 12 months.(southern states) "Transaction velocity (in the Northeast) has declined 29 percent over the past year, with the median price falling 5.9 percent to $64 per square foot, as of the third quarter."
  Source: "Self-Storage Performance Trends Nationwide: Occupancy, Concessions and Development" by Greg Wendelken. www.insideselfstorage.com. January 7, 2010

- "We are presently seeing rigorous value underwriting (12 months trailing income, 60% to 70% as max loan to value ratios, full recourse, real net worth), short amortizations and shorter terms. In this market having your financing relationships tied down is probably the single most important thing you can do, both for yourself and to convince the seller that you have the financial capacity to do the deal; it will make the negotiations easier and close faster. Once you have this date, you can then run your numbers and develop values that you think are appropriate for the deal. We are seeing deals in cap rate ranges anywhere from 9% to 11% and maybe more in some instances. Give yourself a little room because the current market is so unique and volatile that there are very few sales where an exact cap rate is easily determined."
  Source: "Inside Self Storage" by Michael L. McCune — July 2009. The Argus Self-Storage Sales network, www.selfstorage.com

- "Key factors are vacancy and turnover of units. Buyers want to get at least a 20% cash-on-cash return."

- Western States—$74 per square foot
  South Central States—$57 per square foot
  Southeastern States—$74 per square foot
  Northeast—$103 per square foot
  North Central States—$60 per square foot"
  Source: Self-Storage Research, Marcus & Millichap, First Half 2007. This firm is very active in the sale of self-storage firms and is a wonderful resource: www.marcusmillichap.com
- "Most involve the real estate"
- "Pricing is driven by capitalization rates and expense ratios."
- "The typical buyer is looking for about a 20% cash-on-cash return plus an opportunity to eventually sell the ground for a profit when development reaches the area."
- Cap Rate Adjustments
  The little chart that follows is about the best thing we have seen in pricing a business. It outlines specific business issues and assigns them an adjustment to the cap rate. What is so good about this chart is the specific areas it covers and that it essentially assigns a rating to each one that impacts the valuation or pricing of each business.

Item	9.50 - 10.00	10.00 - 11.00
Occupancy (last 2 years)	95%-100%	90%-95%
Rates (last 2 years)	Continuous Rise	Steady
Size	>45,000	30,000-45,000
Competition (3 mile radius)	None	One
Competition's Vacancy	95%-100%	90%-95%
Surrounding Area	Growing Metro	Large City
Density (5 mile radius)	>200,000	100,000-200,000
Median Household Income	Above Average	Average
Manager	Full-time	Full-time
Records (last 3 years)	Computerized & Professionally Audited	Computerized
Computer System	Computers & SS Accounting Software	Computers
Construction	Concrete or Brick	Combination Brick & Metal
Maintenance	Pristine	Little Deferred Maintenance
Security	Full Gate & Card Access	Full Gate
Access	Very Direct	Clear, but Not Direct
Visibility	Can see Sign & Facility	Can see Sign & Entrance
Drives	Concrete	Paved

Note: This is from an excellent article by Michael L. McCune, Cap Rates and Sales Prices. For more information visit www.selfstorage.com—an excellent site. The above is a bit dated but still of interest.

"You can look at it a couple of different ways. It depends on your location; but here in southern Indiana, mini-storage facilities are being appraised based upon the number of units. Age, condition and income are also looked at. Our appraiser just today told us that they are ranging from $3,000 to $3,500 per unit. So your 131-unit facility would appraise for around $393,000 if it were located here.

"Another way to figure out what your potential income will be: if you are totally full, then multiply that number by 60 to 75 percent, because of the reality of occupancy. Use those numbers to figure out what your income/expense ratio will be. Your income should be at least 1.25 over your debt service (if it's not, then you're paying too much for the property). That extra 25 percent will help cover vacancies, utilities, labor, etc."

Source: www.autocareforum.com

- "We sold a 195-unit mini-storage in Idaho last year. It had annual gross receipts of $105,000 and an annual net cash flow of $80,000. It sold for $640,000 with $235,000 cash down payment and the balance at 8.3 percent over 15 years.

  "We have another mini-storage in the process of being sold. It looks like it will go for $500,000 with $150,000 cash down payment, the balance over 20 years at 8.5 percent. It has annual gross income of $70,000 and cash flow debt service of $61,000.

  "I believe that a cash-on-cash return of 15 percent to 20 percent is required to sell one of these mini-storage projects. A minimum of 15 percent seems to be required."

Expert Comments

"Storage units are a great way to warehouse land until the highest and best use changes."

"This is a real estate purchase with a business element attached to it. The value of the underlying real estate controls a large part of the value of the property. Management is more important than most people realize."

Benchmark Data

Statistics (Storage and Warehouse Leasing)

Number of Establishments	48,170
Average Profit Margin	17.0%
Revenue per Employee	$148,700
Average Number of Employees	3.5
Average Wages per Employee	$22,797

Source: IBISWorld, July 2012

Products and services Segmentation

10-by-10-foot storage spaces	16%
10-by-15-foot storage spaces	15.3%
Other	15.3%
10-by-20-foot storage spaces	13.7%
10-by-30-foot storage spaces	11.3%
20-by-40-foot storage spaces	10.5%
5-by-10-foot storage spaces	9.1%
5-by-15-foot storage spaces	8.8%

Source: IBISWorld, August 2012

Major Market Segmentation

Long-term residential customers	41.1%
Short-term residential customers	32%
Commercial firms	19%
Other	4.9%
Military	3%

Source: IBISWorld, August 2012

Industry Costs

Profit	17.0%
Wages	15.5%
Purchases	25.7%
Depreciation	15.8%
Marketing	3.1%
Rent & Utilities	10.2%
Other	12.7%

Source: IBISWorld, August 2012

Market Share

Public Storage Inc. 7.1%

Source: IBISWorld, July 2012

- "The distribution of U.S. self storage facilities (Q4-2011) is as follows: 32% urban, 52% suburban and 16% rural.
  "The average revenue per square foot varies from facility to facility: however, here are the year-end data for 2011: Traditional facility: $8.65 psf; Hybrid facility: $9.85 psf; Big Box facility: $11.52 psf; Conversion facility: $10.89 psf.
- "Primary U.S. self storage facility gross revenues for 2011 were approximately $22.45 billion [or a national average (mean) of $449,540 per facility or national average (mean) of $9.76 of gross annual revenue per rentable sq. ft. (all types of facilities combined)]"
- "The average (mean) size of a 'primary' self storage facility in the U.S. is approximately 46,600 square feet."

Source: www.selfstorage.org/ssa/Content/AboutSSA

- "The 2010 Self Storage Expense Guidebook"
  2009 National Operating Expenses
  Range

	Low $/SF	High $/SF	Average $/SF	% of Expenses
Taxes	$0.03	$3.54	$0.52	14.17%
Insurance	$0.01	$2.33	$0.18	4.75%
Repairs & Maintenance	$0.01	$3.14	$0.24	6.49%
Administration	$0.01	$4.76	$0.44	11.91%
On-Site Management	$0.01	$5.58	$0.86	23.30%
Off-Site Management	$0.01	$2.12	$0.49	13.19%
Utilities	$0.01	$5.59	$0.30	8.16%
Advertising	$0.01	$4.80	$0.25	6.85%
Miscellaneous	$0.01	$5.62	$0.41	11.19%
Total Expenses	$0.09	$37.48	$3.69	100.00%

Expense/Income Ratio* 41.80%
$/SF Change from 2008: .... -9.73%
Total Facilities Responding 571
Total Rentable Area (SF) 29,509,563
Average Rentable Area (SF) 51,590
Average Concessions Cost (%) 4.49%
Average Vacancy Cost (%) 11.27%

* The data as expressed as a percentage of income is indicated in a range and average.

- "East: As a result, occupancy will finish 2012 at 87 percent, marking a 210-basis point improvement from year-end 2011. Landlords will lift asking rents 4.8 percent this year to $1.10 per square foot.
  "Midwest: Occupancy levels will rise 80 basis points this year to 80.8 percent, while asking rents will jump 2.8 percent to $0.77 per square foot.
  "South: As a result, occupancy will climb 130 basis points in 2012 to 81.3 percent, bolstering asking rents by 1.3 percent to $0.76 per square foot.
  "West: Occupancy will increase 160 basis points in 2012 to 83 percent, while owners will gain sufficient leverage to hike asking rents 1.8 percent to $1.12 per square foot.

Source: Self-Storage Research Semi-Annual Report, Marcus & Millichap, Midyear 2012

- "Primary U.S. self storage facility gross revenues for 2010 were approximately $22.0 billion [or a national average (mean) of $444,000 per facility or national average (mean) of $9.52 of gross annual revenue per rentable sq. ft. (all types of facilities combined)]."

Source: "As 0f 6/30/11 Fact Sheet" www.selfstorage.org

- "The average rent for self-storage space (south central states) is $0.72 per square foot, unchanged over the last year. Occupancy levels, meanwhile, have declined steadily since the second quarter of 2008, despite limited new inventory."

  Source: "Self-Storage Performance Trends Nationwide: Occupancy, Concessions and Development" by Greg Wendelken. www.insideselfstorage.com. January 7, 2010

- "20% cash on cash return"

- "The most common 'state-of-the-art' facility will be about 60,000 to 80,000 net rentable square feet, cost $25-50 per square foot, outside of existing land costs, to construct and have break even operating expenses in the 25 to 40 percent range (not including debt service) of total stabilized income.
  "A well-designed and located facility will successfully operate in the 83-93 percent occupancy range, with many projects having been successful at occupancies as low as 70 percent, depending upon cost, rental rates and the method of financing applied and age of project. As a general rule, the investor should open his facility in the spring of the year and allow at least 18 to 24 months for it to realize its potential in a competitive market, 36+ months for 'jumbo' 1000,000 square foot size facilities to reach stabilization."

  Source: Self Storage Association, www.selfstorage.org

Sample facility

"Size	40,000 SF
Average Rent	$71/month
Rent/SF	$8.52/yr.
Current Occupancy	88%
Market Occupancy	70%
Potential Rent	$341,000
Rents Collected @ 88%	$300,000/yr.
Expenses	$100,000
Net Operating Income	$200,000/yr.
Value @ 9.5	$2,100,000
Loan Amount @ 75%	$1,575,000
Debt Service @ 6.5%	$128,000/yr."

Source: "The State of Self Storage Real Estate" by Michael L. McCune, Argus Self-Storage Sales Network

Expenses as a Percentage of Annual Sales

Cost of goods	0
Payroll/labor Costs	0
Occupancy	0
Profit (estimated pretax)	05%

Industry Trend

- "This is more apparent today than ever before as we are seeing large operators winning business away from smaller operators whether by pricing, advertising or property amenities. I would also note that in general, the large operators are able to get a rent premium over the small operators that have similar properties in the same market. This leads me to believe that the self-storage industry has reached a crossroads and operators need to make the necessary adjustments in order to compete as the industry continues to mature.
  "The effects of the continuing low interest rate environment have had a very dramatic impact on self-storage investments over the last six to nine months. The most obvious and positive result is that owners are able to sell their properties at close to historically high prices once again (reflecting back on 2006-2007) or refinance and keep a larger share of their hard-earned income by paying less to the lenders."

  Source: "Extraordinary Times — How Long Will They Last?" by Ben Vestal, www.argusselfstorage.com

- "Large units developed by professionals in the industry are the trend."
- "Demand continues to grow."
- "More units will be built in many areas."

Seller Financing

- "10 to 15 years"

Questions

- "Who manages the site and are they willing to stay on. Can existing financing be assumed."
- "How long has the manager been in place?"
- "Occupancy and waiting list"
- "Management turnover"

Resources

Websites
- Argus Self-Storage Sales Network: a large real estate firm that specializes in the self-storage industry. Their Web site contains a lot of articles and research on the industry: www.argusselfstorage.com/

Trade Publications
- Mini Storage Messenger—they provide excellent resources for the self-storage business. Their publications are published by Mini Co., Inc.: www.selfstoragenow.com

Associations
- Self Storage Association—an excellent site with lots of information: www.selfstorage.org

			Franchise
Senior Helpers (See also Home Health Care—Care Giving)			
Approx. Total Investment			$75,000 to $99,000
	NAICS 621610	Number of Businesses/Units 300	

Rules of Thumb

➢ 40 to 45 percent plus inventory

Service Businesses (In General)

Rules of Thumb

➢ 50 percent of annual revenues [sales] plus inventory; however it is not unusual for service businesses to sell for a much higher figure

➢ 72 percent of annual sales plus inventory

➢ 2 times SDE

Pricing Tips

- "Consider the last 3 to 5 years—is it an up or down trend? Is the business expandable or is it at its peak?"

- Valuation Issues for Service Companies

  "On the plus side, almost all service companies have recurring revenue. Some, like funeral homes, have very little, while others, like Paychex (payroll service), Cintas (uniform rental) and Dun & Bradstreet (credit reports) have a lot of recurring revenue with each customer. Another plus is that service companies usually have modest capital equipment requirements resulting in a high return on assets. Expansion and geographic roll-outs like retail and restaurant chains can be readily expedited.

  Additionally, service companies are less impacted by foreign competition. From a macro-economic view, the U.S. had a $65 billion service trade surplus in 2002 while the U.S. had a large manufactured goods deficit in 2002. And, from a competitive point of view, large service companies can source services off-shore just as manufacturing companies have done in order to reduce costs. For example, the annual cost for a computer-related employee in the U.S. is $61,600 compared to India at $5,800.

  "On the minus side, service companies are largely dependent on their management team and employees. They are, by and large, the assets of the company... so imagine what would happen to the value of an architectural firm or a law firm if the people walked off their job. Since labor is the major expense of service companies, they are more difficult to substantially increase sales (or scale-up) compared to manufacturing companies where labor might only represent 20% of sales.

  "From a service owner's perspective, rarely can they fully cash-out at closing or rarely can they walk away from the business at closing, as service companies are highly relationship driven... not only with the customers but with the employees. Further, unlike some small niche manufacturers, many service companies need to reach a higher revenue threshold of $10+ million to prove the company's viability of not being dependent on just a few key people or a few key customers.

  "The valuation multiples vary widely across the various sectors and equally divergent are the various structures of the transactions. Of course, the critical issues in the valuation of service companies include the extent of their profitability, relative size, proprietary nature of the service firm's capabilities and the potential growth. Conventional wisdom dictates that service firms are valued between .5 x to 1.0 x revenues, but a closer look at the following sectors shows a wide differential of valuation metrics based on Last Twelve Months (LTM) of revenues and EBITDA."

Expert Comments

"Competition and the industry trends (growing or constant) are important for calculating the ROI on the intangible part."

Service Stations (See Gas Stations)

Franchise

ServiceMaster Clean

Approx. Total Investment	$47,860 to $156,025
NAICS 561720	Number of Businesses/Units 4,450

Rules of Thumb

➢ 55 to 60 percent of annual sales plus inventory

Resources
Websites
- www.ownafranchise.com

Franchise

Servpro

	Number of Businesses/Units 1,400

Rules of Thumb

➢ 90 to 95 percent of annual sales plus inventory

Shoe Stores

SIC 5661-01	NAICS 451110	Number of Businesses/Units 30,460

Rules of Thumb

➢ 15 to 20 percent of annual sales plus inventory

Benchmark Data

Statistics (Shoe Stores)

Number of Establishments	30,460
Average Profit Margin	4.0%
Revenue per Employee	$209,010
Average Number of Employees	6.9
Average Wages per Employee	$17,587

Source: IBISWorld, May 2012

Products and Services Segmentation

Women's casual shoes	30%
Women's dress shoes	21%
Children's shoes	18%
Men's shoes	14%
Women's boots and sandals	9%
Slippers and other shoes	8%

Source: IBISWorld, May 2012

Major Market Segmentation

Women aged 35 and older	48.7%
Men aged 35 and older	15%
Women aged 25 to 34	13%
Children aged 14 and younger	10%
Men aged 25 to 34	8.7%
Women aged 15 to 24	3.3%
Men aged 15 to 24	1.3%

Source: IBISWorld, May 2012

Industry Costs

Profit	4.0%
Wages	14.5%
Purchases	65.8%
Depreciation	1.1%
Marketing	5.6%
Rent & Utilities	5.9%
Other	3.1%

Source: IBISWorld, May 2012

Market Share

Foot Locker Inc.	15.9%
Designer Shoe Warehouse Inc.	8.1%
Collective Brands Inc.	13.9%
Brown Shoe Company Inc.	6.9%

Source: IBISWorld, May 2012

Shoe Category Market Share

Women's casual shoes	17%
Women's dress shoes	13%
Women's athletic shoes	10%
Men's athletic shoes	20%
Men's casual shoes	9%
Men's dress shoes	6%
Other styles	25%

Source: National Shoe Retailers Association, U.S. Census, January 2012

Industry Trend

- "Though the number of independent shoe retailers has fallen to about 6,000 from 30,000 in the 1930s—reflecting such trends as the growth of big-box stores and discount chains—there will always be a place for independent niche retailers, said Madelyn Rygg, vice president of the National Shoe Retailers Association in Columbia, MD.

  "Rygg did not have figures on how many independent stores open each year, but said her organization sells about 220 start-up kits to potential store owners annually.

  "'The independent retailers will always be there,' she said, 'They are much more customer-service oriented and tend to deal with high-end shoes.'"

  Source: "The Shoe Business Fits Her Just Fine" by Maureen Costello, *Boston Globe*, April 5, 2007.
  Dated but interesting.

Resources

Associations

- National Shoe Retailers Association: www.nsra.org

Short Line Railroads		
	NAICS 482112	

Pricing Tips

- "These are highly regulated businesses that, as businesses, tend to be basically real estate businesses. Many buyers tend to be hobby buyers. Historically, buyers have grossly overpaid to purchase these businesses, then not exploited the potential of the real estate business. Buyers are almost always industry related in some way. Sellers are mainly large operating corporations who cannot operate these units economically."

- "Buyers are quoting 1.6 to 1.85 times gross revenues and in most cases it is a seller's market."
- "If it's for sale, that pretty much guarantees that someone with expertise has determined that they cannot operate it profitably and/or make the capital investments required. Sellers have usually deferred capital investment and maintenance to an extreme degree prior to sale."

Industry Trend

- "America's short line railroads provide fuel savings and environmentally friendly shipping for small businesses and communities around the country. One freight rail car can carry a ton of cargo 436 miles on just one gallon of fuel. Short line railroads take the equivalent of nearly 33 million truck loads off the highways, saving the country over $1.4 billion annually in highway repair costs and improving highway safety and congestion."

Source: American Short Line and Regional Railroad System (ASLRRA)

Shuttle Services & Special Needs Transportation	
NAICS 485999	Number of Businesses/Units 480

Rules of Thumb

➤ 3 times EBITDA plus the value of the vehicles

Benchmark Data

Statistics (Airport Shuttle Operators)

Number of Establishments	480
Average Profit Margin	9.7%
Revenue per Employee	$84,000
Average Number of Employees	15.1%
Average Wages per Employee	$20,810

Source: IBISWorld, December 2011

Major Market Segmentation

Short-haul consumers	55%
Long-haul consumers	40%
Business travelers	5%

Source: IBISWorld, December 2011

Products and Services Segmentation

Short-distance shuttle services	65.9%
Long-distance shuttle services	34.1%

Source: IBISWorld, December 2011

Industry Costs

Profit	9.7%
Rent	2.0%
Utilities	2.6%
Depreciation	8.2%
Other	16.5%
Wages	25.4%
Purchases	35.6%

Source: IBISWorld, December 2011

Sign Companies (See also Manufacturing—Signs)

	NAICS 339950	Number of Businesses/Units 30,000

Rules of Thumb

> 50 percent of annual sales includes inventory

> 2.5 times SDE includes inventory

Pricing Tips

- "Most sign companies are small independents—SDE is a better calculation than EBIT or EBITDA. Inventory is not usually an excessive number, and usually included as part of a 2.5–3 x multiple of SDE."

Expert Comments

"The recession of 2009 did take a toll on the sign industry, but growth has occurred in 2010 and forward. Other than the dip in 2009 and recovery through part of 2010, profitability in the industry has been fairly consistent. Technology has advanced considerably over the past 10 years or so, allowing for more efficiency and therefore keeping overall margins of profitability consistent."

Benchmark Data

- "Typical sales/employee statistic is $100K–$125K per employee. Anything below $100K/employee would suggest additional capacity available for growth or inefficiency in the sales or production process. The size of facilities varies considerably and is not necessarily relative to sales productivity."

Expenses as a Percentage of Annual Sales

Cost of goods	25% to 28%
Payroll/labor Costs	20% to 25%
Occupancy	15% to 20%
Profit (estimated pretax)	20% to 25%

Seller Financing

- "3 to 5 years"

Questions

- How do they secure customers? What kind of repeat customer base do they have? How much of the business/sales depends on their personal relationship with customers.

Resources

Trade Publications
- Sign & Digital Graphics Magazine: www.sdgmag.com

Associations
- Specialty Graphic Imaging Association: www.sgia.org

		Franchise
Signarama (See also Manufacturing—Signs)		
Approx. Total Investment		$160,000–$164,000
	NAICS 339950	Number of Businesses/Units 875

Rules of Thumb

➤ 55 to 60 percent of annual sales plus inventory

Resources

Websites
- www.signarama.com

Silk Screen Printing (See Printing—Silk Screen)	

		Franchise
Sir Speedy Printing		
Approx. Total Investment		$275,000 to $350,000
	NAICS 323114	Number of Businesses/Units 502

Rules of Thumb

➤ 55 to 60 percent of annual sales plus inventory

Resources

Websites
- www.sirspeedy.com

Ski Shops		
SIC 7011-10	NAICS 532292	Number of Businesses/Units 500

Rules of Thumb

➤ 1.8 to 2.5 times EBIT; very rare 3.0 times (plus inventory), unless store is very exclusive with no competition in area.

➤ 40 percent of gross annual sales plus inventory

➤ 2.5 to 3.5 times SDE plus inventory

Pricing Tips

- "Key is long-term lease, since location is so important in resort retail sales. If lease is less than 3 years, a heavy discount in percentage of gross sales is appropriate. The price goes down the higher the inventory—which is always in addition to price [calculated on rules of thumb]. Every store is different. Be careful, the trend is for ski companies to get into the retail business and compete with independent shops."

- "In resort businesses, location is key. Businesses must be in the tourist foot traffic areas. A strong lease securing such a location is the key in determining the multiple of cash flow. Since most areas have limited real estate, competition plays a large factor in determining price; e.g., how many ski shops are in your immediate area?"

Benchmark Data

Statistics (Ski & Snow Board Resorts)

Number of Establishments	469
Average Profit Margin	7.1%
Revenue per Employee	$45,800
Average Number of Employees	125.5
Average Wages per Employee	$11,915

Source: IBISWorld, December 2011

Products and Services Segmentation

Lift tickets	50.5%
Food and beverage sales	12.3%
Other revenue	9.5%
Snowsports instruction	8.9%
Season pass sales	7.3%
Merchandise sales	5.9%
Equipment rental	5.6%

Source: IBISWorld, December 2011

Major Market Segmentation

18 to 24 years old	20%
45 to 54 years old	19%
35 to 44 years old	18%
25 to 34 years old	16%
Under 17 years old	14%
55 years and older	13%

Source: IBISWorld, December 2011

Industry Costs

Profit	7.1%
Wages	26.4%
Purchases	25.0%
Depreciation	6.4%
Utilities	5.0%
Rent	6.0%
Other	24.1%

Source: IBISWorld, December 2011

Market Share

Vail Resorts Inc.	29.2%
Fortress Investment Group LLC	14.7%
Boyne Resorts	8.7%

Source: IBISWorld, December 2011

Expenses as a Percentage of Annual Sales

Cost of goods	45% to 50%
Payroll/labor Costs	22% to 28% (Rising due to labor shortages)
Occupancy	08% to 12% (Seeing some 18% to 20% in very hot locations
Profit (estimated pretax)	0

Seller Financing
- "3 years maximum"

Smartbox Portable Self-Storage (See also Self Storage)		Franchise
Approx. Total Investment		$750,000 to $2 million
		Number of Businesses/Units 19

Rules of Thumb

➢ 45 to 50 percent of annual sales includes inventory

Resources

Websites
- www.smartboxusa.com

Smoothie King		Franchise
Approx. Total Investment		$139,900 to $322,000
	NAICS 722213	Number of Businesses/Units 611

Rules of Thumb

➢ 40 to 45 percent of annual sales

Resources

Websites
- www.smoothieking.com

Snack Bars (See Sandwich Shops & Restaurants—Limited Service)

Snap Fitness (See also Fitness Centers)		Franchise
Approx. Total Investment		$77,000–$242,000
	NAICS 713940	Number of Businesses/Units 1,912

Rules of Thumb

➢ 40 percent of annual sales plus inventory

Resources

Websites
- www.snapfitness.com

Soft Drink Bottlers

	NAICS 312111	Number of Businesses/Units 800

Rules of Thumb

➤ $10/case sold annually

Benchmark Data

Statistics (Soda Production)

Number of Establishments	946
Average Profit Margin	7.4%
Revenue per Employee	$356,900
Average Number of Employees	47.0
Average Wages per Employee	$42,315

Source: IBISWorld, November 2012

Products and Services Segmentation

Coke	16.7%
Pepsi-Cola	9.2%
Diet Coke	9.1%
Mountain Dew	6.5%
Dr. Pepper	6%
Other	52.5%

Source: IBISWorld, November 2012

Major Market Segmentation

Supermarkets and general merchandisers	48%
Food service and drinking places	20%
Vending machine operators	12%
Convenience stores and gas stations	11%
Other	7.6%
Exports	1.4%

Source: IBISWorld, November 2012

Industry Costs

Profit	7.4%
Rent	4.5%
Utilities	3.2%
Depreciation	3.6%
Other	16.7%
Wages	12.3%
Purchases	52.3%

Source: IBISWorld, November 2012

Market Share

The Coca-Cola Company	42.4%
PepsiCo Inc.	35.2%
Dr. Pepper Snapple Group Inc.	16.4%

Source: IBISWorld, November 2012

Software Companies

	NAICS 511210	

Rules of Thumb

➤ 1 to 3 times revenue (trailing 12 months) plus inventory

➤ 5 times EBITDA

➤ 6 times EBIT

Pricing Tips

- "Selling prices can vary significantly because the businesses and buyers can vary significantly. An industry buyer may have significant costs to convert a seller's customers to their software. SaaS software and recurring revenues are desirable."
- "Pricing is determined by the type of software and customers a tech company seeks. Two major areas are web-based/consumer centric vs. mission-critical/commercial based. Web based has pre-determined value based upon subscriber base, whereas mission-critical based gain value from growing maintenance (recurring) revenue that organically grows over time."
- "There is no 'typical' rule of thumb because individual software companies can have widely different cycles and growth phases. Classic measures focus on revenue amounts, consistency, and growth, although revenue recognition policies vary and market conditions can change quickly."
- "Usually no bank financing involved, companies can be unprofitable or have negative net worth and still sell. Average deal is 50 percent liquid, 2 year employment agreement—3 to 4 year non-compete. Most buyers are public and hi tech in order to leverage the purchase—35 percent international buyers."

Expert Comments

"Tech companies rely on skilled professional, primarily at the technical ranks. These are high paid individuals whose creation of intellectual property is difficult to reproduce in a short period of time. This can limit competition, but also encourages others to try and make a better 'mouse trap' because of the typically high gross margins. In order to encourage a limited qualified personnel pool, many companies have a higher benefit cost to employee ratio and offer better than average benefits including bonuses, time-off, health, dental, 401K, and for certain companies, options. Location is important in the overall scope of attracting qualified employees."

Benchmark Data

- "Gross profit is very high on software. Typically companies will sell software and related services. Software typically 70% of revenues, services 30%."
- "Quality companies who are already earning a return on investment for an established time should have a greater than 75%-80%+ gross margin. Typical R&D allocation can/should be up to 25% allowing for future growth of product line, as well as maintenance substantiation. Number of salespeople should be relative to the marketplace being addressed."

Expenses as a Percentage of Annual Sales

Cost of goods	05%
Payroll/labor Costs	60%
Occupancy	10%
Profit (estimated pretax)	25%

Industry Trend

- "Technology is growing. More businesses are bringing their products to market using domestic employees due to need for speed to completion, allowance for cultural requirements, and rising compensation for overseas programmers. Technology plays an important role in expense recovery, securing competitive advantages, and addressing lifestyle needs. Care should be taken in due diligence of web-based organizations who lack a validated model. Established companies, with a base of customers/maintenance revenue are increasing, but harder to find for acquisition."

- "Growth Drivers (percent answering 'important' or 'most important')
  Developing New Upgraded Products & Services 87.4%
  New Distribution Channels/Key Partnerships 76.4%
  Acquisition of Companies ....35.4%"
  Source: Spencer Stuart/Software & Information Association

Seller Financing

- "Given the competitive landscape for this type of business, sales typically have significant cash or stock components. Sellers are requested to hold notes that vary in scale based upon the maturity of the product and customer base."

Questions

- "Ask for a pro-forma income statement to maintain business. Industry trends. Competition and how the business/software compares. Similar questions as you would ask any business owner."
- "1. Explain the product(s) you have, and the benefits to the end users. 2. Who ARE the end users? 3. What R&D do you allow for? What percentage of the company's revenue or investment dollars are allocated to R&D? 4. How long has your product been available? 5. How many releases have you had? How often do you provide updates to your products? Explain your development cycle. 6. What percentage do you charge for maintenance? 7. What monthly/ yearly fee do you charge for online access? 8. Do you offer your products on a SaaS (Software as a Service) basis? If not, what will it take to re-engineer to do this? 9. Describe your staff. How many? What positions? Areas of technical expertise? Domain experience? Average age of technicians? 10. What software platforms do you use? 11. What does your business plan call for in terms of monetizing the product, revenue growth, and personnel needs to achieve this, over time? 12. What impediments do you currently need to overcome in developing/selling the product? 13. What competition do you have, do you see coming down the pike which could jeopardize any investment in the company or allocation of income to future R&D?"
- "Calculations of net cash flow, consistently applied, are good for historical analysis. Discounted cash flow models vary widely, but commonly use higher rates because of risk and uncertainty. Premiums for control, discounts for illiquidity are usually magnified from more 'stable' industries. The broker/ intermediary should inquire about capitalization policies of the software 'asset.' Many companies will not capitalize their product; others will be based on cost accumulation. 'Niche' software with an established client base will attract buyers because of the ongoing service revenues."

Resources

Websites
- Industry/Company Analysis (fee-based): www.factset.com

Trade Publications
- How to Evaluate a Software Company:
  www.essensys.ro/LinkClick.aspx?fileticket=JUOMzPERupg%3D&tabid=178

Associations
- Software & Information Industry Association: www.siia.net

Sound Contractors

SIC 5065-07	NAICS 235420	

Rules of Thumb

➤ 75 percent of annual sales includes inventory

➤ 2 to 3 times SDE and/or 30 to 60 times monthly contract billing for music services includes inventory

➤ 5 times EBIT

➤ 3 times EBITDA

Pricing Tips

▪ "Most contractors in this industry supply some type of music service; if it is a recurring base and the contractors are on their paperwork, then this company will have more value to a buyer."

▪ "Any inventory over 24 months is dead inventory and should not be part of sale."

Expert Comments

"If company is a commercial contractor, the economy does not have much effect on industry. If they give good service and have experience in technical support, business will be stable."

"There are few good sound contractors with a great customer list."

Benchmark Data

▪ "Recurring services are a key in value to this industry."

▪ "One tech per $400K in revenue"

Expenses as a Percentage of Annual Sales

Cost of goods	35%
Payroll/labor Costs	35%
Occupancy	10%
Profit (estimated pretax)	20%

Industry Trend

▪ "5% to 10% growth each year"

▪ "Business is stable."

Seller Financing

▪ "5 to 8 years"

Questions

▪ "Inventory, how much is dead and on the books?"

▪ "Relationship to customers"

Franchise

Soup Man (The Original) (See also Restaurants—Limited Service)

	NAICS 722211	

Rules of Thumb

➤ 30 percent of annual sales includes inventory

Resources

Websites

- www.originalsoupman.com

Souvenir and Novelty Stores (See Retail Stores—Small Specialty)

Specialty Food Stores (See also Food Stores—Specialty)

Benchmark Data

Statistics (Ethnic Supermarkets)

Number of Establishments	22,894
Average Profit Margin	2.8%
Revenue per Employee	$203,700
Average Number of Employees	6
Average Wages per Employee	$19,427

Source: IBISWorld, December 2011

Products and Services Segmentation

Other food items	38.9%
Meats	16.5%
Produce	14.0%
Non-food items	9.7%
Beverages (including alcohol)	9.3%
Dairy items	7.4%
Frozen foods	4.2%

Source: IBISWorld, December 2011

Major Market Segmentation

Asian	50.1%
Hispanic	48.2%
Other ethnicities	1.7%

Source: IBISWorld, December 2011

Industry Costs

Profit	2.8%
Rent	4.5%
Utilities	3.2%
Depreciation	1.3%
Other	8.6%
Wages	9.1%
Purchases	70.5%

Source: IBISWorld, December 2011

Industry Trend

- "Some Highlights
    - ✓ Natural food stores are the fastest growing retail channel, boasting a sales increase of 19.8 percent between 2009 and 2011.
    - ✓ Cheese and Cheese Alternatives is the largest specialty food category, at $3.44 billion.
    - ✓ Manufacturers say that specialty food stores and natural supermarkets are the fastest growing retail channels for specialty foods.
    - ✓ The average transaction size for specialty food stores was $41.49 in 2011, up 11.4 percent over 2010.

✓ Three-quarters of retailers say that Local is the most influential product claim today and two-thirds report the claim will grow the most in the next three years.

✓ Retailers say the fastest emerging cuisine is Latin; importers report that Eastern European and Indian are growing."

Sporting Goods Stores

SIC 5941-13	NAICS 451110	Number of Businesses/Units 41,997

Rules of Thumb

➢ 25 percent of annual sales plus inventory

➢ 4 times EBIT

Pricing Tips

- "Add or subtract based on nearby competition"
- "Inventory should be excluded due to rapid obsolescence."

Expert Comments

"Increasing competition from on-line retailers"

"Declining profitability due to ability of customers to comparison shop online"

Benchmark Data

Statistics (Sporting Goods Stores)

Number of Establishments	41,997
Average Profit Margin	4.0%
Revenue per Employee	$171,800
Average Number of Employees	5.5
Average Wages per Employee	$18,220

Source: IBISWorld, October 2012

Products and Services Segmentation

Sporting equipment	46%
Athletic footwear	34%
Athletic apparel	20%

Source: IBISWorld, October 2012

Industry Costs

Profit	4.0%
Wages	10.6%
Purchases	70.0%
Depreciation	1.0%
Marketing	1.8%
Rent & Utilities	7.4%
Other	5.2%

Source: IBISWorld, October 2012

Market Share

Dick's Sporting Goods Inc.	13.6%
Foot Locker Inc.	10.3%
The Sports Authority Inc.	8.8%

Source: IBISWorld, October 2012

- "Cost of goods sold should be no more than 55%"

Expenses as a Percentage of Annual Sales

Cost of goods..45% to 55%
Payroll/labor Costs 17%
Occupancy..15% to 20%
Profit (estimated pretax) 08%

Industry Trend

- "Increasing competition from on-line retailers"
- "Short term declining due to economic climate, longer term return to moderate growth due to increased interest in sports/leisure activities."

Questions

- "Are the sales personnel knowledgeable in their specific areas?"

Resources

Associations
- National Sporting Goods Association: www.nsga.org

Staffing Services (See also Employment Agencies)		
SIC 7361-03	NAICS 561320	

Rules of Thumb

➤ 2 to 5 times SDE

➤ 2 to 5 times EBITDA

➤ 3 to 4 times EBIT

Pricing Tips

- "Two to two and half SDE for Light Industrial staffing net of receivables. Must have a minimum Gross Profit of 16%."
- "Clerical\admin have lower multiple that MEDICAL staffing or IT agencies. Medical and IT at 3-4X. Home healthcare at 2-3X (Home workers)"
- "The multiple will vary significantly based upon temporary, contract or permanent staffing, and it will vary based upon specialty area (light industrial, clerical, professional, IT, etc.). Thus, multiple may range from 1 to 4.5 to 5.0. Revenues size, concentration etc. are major factors as well."

Expert Comments

"The staffing industry is directly impacted by the economic environment. The last 2 years have been difficult but there are increasing signs of a positive turnaround."

"Entry into the industry is relatively easy. Competition can be tough but the market is big. The industry has been on a strong upswing over the last couple of years but is very susceptible to economic conditions."

Benchmark Data

- For additional Benchmark data see Employment Agencies
- "Hours billed per branch. Recruiting cost per employee. Workers Comp mod factor."
- "A key is the gross margin %. Buyers will look at that very closely. Here again, margin and markups will vary based upon the specialty area."
- "Multiple of SDE: 2 to 5; Gross Profit: 22% to 30%"

Expenses as a Percentage of Annual Sales

Cost of goods	0%
Payroll/labor Costs	75%
Occupancy	05%
Profit (estimated pretax)	15%

Industry Trend

- "Growing industry in MEDICAL staffing and some IT areas. Heavy competition in the home care workers segment."
- "In a word(s): The 'big squeeze' in the staffing industry will continue in 2012 as clients maintain downward pressure on rates, reduce the number of staffing vendors and recruiters they work with and demand perfection from an American workforce of uneven quality."
  Source: "How Staffing Companies Will Stand Out in 2012" by John Rossheim, www.hiring.monster.com
- "In the two years after the Great Recession ended in June 2009, U.S. staffing firms created more new jobs than any other industry. According to the U.S. Bureau of Labor Statistics, the temporary help services industry added nearly half a million workers and accounted for 91% of total nonfarm job growth from June 2009 through June 2011."
  Source: "Staffing Statistics," www.www.americanstaffing.net
- "Trend should be good once we get past the current downturn in the economy."

Questions

- "Customer composition. Bad debt experience. Do they factor receivables."
- "Closeness of relationships to clients; length of transition; recent changes to business or competition; staff retention."
  "1) Concentration 2) Competition 3) Infrastructure"

Staffing Services (Health Care)

(See also Employment Agencies, Staffing Services

Rules of Thumb

- ➢ "Barry Asin, chief analyst at Staffing Industry Analysts, in Los Altos, California, says that most health care staffing firms sell for four to five times EBITDA."
  Source: "Businesses For Sale" by Elaine Appleton Grant, *Inc Magazine*, January 2008

	Franchise
Subway (See also Sandwich Shops)	
Approx. Total Investment	$116,000 to $300,000
Estimated Annual Sales/Unit	$470,000

SIC 5812-06	NAICS 722211	Number of Businesses/Units 36,000

Rules of Thumb

> ➢ 60 percent of annual sales includes inventory
> ➢ 3.5 times SDE includes inventory
> ➢ 3.5 times EBIT
> ➢ 3.5 times EBITDA
> ➢ 35 to 40 times weekly sales

Pricing Tips

- "Factor in costs of high rent (>12%), remodel costs, short lease, new store coming nearby"
- "70% of asking price minus remodel cost if any."
- "Deduct for remodel expense; deduct for high rent; deduct for less than 7 yrs on lease. C-Store and Walmart locations need an adjustment too."
- "If sales less than $400,000, price is less than 50% of sales. If sales over $400,000 and closer to $500,000 and above, can get 60%. Subject to lease term over 7 yrs. and remodel done, rent 10%–12% of sales."
- "Influx of many Subway restaurants and similar competitors has caused a decline in the attractiveness of this franchise. Franchises grossing over $8,000 per week are attractive and profitable. The business is very dependent on location, many of which have been compromised in an effort to add additional units."
- "60%–70% of sales. I have seen higher and lower, depends on lease, compliance issues, remodel issues and proximity to other stores or impending new store construction."
- "Lease of less than 8 years diminishes the value. This is typical valuation for Subway type store."
- "I would suggest for Subway, in New England and maybe all of New England, due to the high number of pizza restaurants, Subways tend to sell for a much lower of percentage of sales than 47%—sometimes as low as 20% to 25%."

Expert Comments

"Outstanding brand name, huge buyer demand, seller's market, great resale value, profitable and profits very predictable"

"Very high demand, low number of opportunities."

"Good franchise, happy owners"

"Simple business to establish and duplicate. Many similar competitors in the marketplace."

Benchmark Data

- For additional Benchmark data see Sandwich Shops
- "Food cost 30%, labor costs 20% if owner operated"
- "Food costs 30%, labor 20% as an owner operator, net 15%–20%, rent should be below 10% ideally."
- "Most stores are 1,000 s/f, have approximately 20 seats and are owner operated. Food cost is controllable."

- "Food costs-30% or below, rent 10% or below, average sales per store per week over $10,000 makes a good store. Subway average nationwide is about $7300 per week in store sales."
- Sales per square foot—"Average sq. ft. per location—1,200/at $300/sf (malls significantly higher)"

Expenses as a Percentage of Annual Sales

Cost of goods	30%
Payroll/labor Costs	20%
Occupancy	10%
Profit (estimated pretax)	15% to 25%

Industry Trend

- "Steady sales increase"
- "Far too many Subways on every block."
- "Overbuilt and oversold....resale of existing franchises will be challenging. New franchises, unless in major shopping mall or high-traffic 'city' location, have less appeal."
- "Flooding of market…reduction in old-fashioned delis"

Seller Financing

- "Rarely seller financed"
- "5 years"

Questions

- "Lease length and terms, trend of gross sales, years established"
- "Store coming nearby?"
- "Remodel due? Rent and CAM? Combo report?

Resources

Websites
- www.subway.com

Sun Room and Awning Installation		
SIC 1521-22	NAICS 326199	Number of Businesses/Units 5,000

Rules of Thumb

➢ 35 percent of annual sales plus inventory

Pricing Tips

- "Strong, knowledgeable managers who have been with this specialty business for a long time can add a lot of value to the company. This would also increase the buyer pool greatly. A buyer with no knowledge or experience in this business could purchase it and be successful."

Expert Comments

"Competition—this is a specialty business; risk—there is an abundance of work in this field; profit trend—sales have shown steady increases;

location—a shop and a central location is all you need; marketability—there is a high demand for this type of work; industry trend—new housing boom and damages from hurricane have this business booked for years; replication—this being a specialty business, most construction workers don't have the necessary knowledge to do these jobs."

Benchmark Data

- "30%+ net income based on gross sales"

Expenses as a Percentage of Annual Sales

Cost of goods	15%
Payroll/labor Costs	25% to 30%
Occupancy	15%
Profit (estimated pretax)	30%

Industry Trend

- "Growing due to housing boom in area"

Questions

- "What contracts do you have with whom?"

Resources

Websites

- www.nationalsunroom.org

			Franchise
SuperCoups (See also Coupon Books, Valpak)			
Approx. Total Investment			$26,000–$50,000
	NAICS 541870	Number of Businesses/Units 160	

Rules of Thumb

➤ 40 to 45 percent of annual sales plus inventory

➤ "If a cooperative direct mail business, such as Money Mailer or SuperCoups is making $100,000, it could be sold for $150,000 to $225,000, and $250,000 if it was a perfect situation. Now, on the other hand, if it is a Valpak, I believe you could get up to 3 times what it is making because Valpak is the undisputed leader. They are owned by COX Publishing and they are within 50 franchises of being sold out."

Resources

Websites

- www.supercoups.com

Supermarkets (See also Grocery Stores)	
NAICS 445110	

Rules of Thumb

➤ 3 times SDE plus inventory

➤ 15 percent of annual sales plus inventory

Pricing Tips

- "There are different departments within a supermarket, with some departments having a gross profit of 30% or more and others having lower than 10% and even negative gross profit on sale items; so depending on the store customers' buying habits and how these departments are managed, the selling price will be adjusted."
- "3 times yearly net income"

Benchmark Data

- For additional Benchmark data see Grocery Stores—General
- "Larger and better. Full-service grocery store in a larger strip center. Plenty of parking."

Expenses as a Percentage of Annual Sales

Cost of goods	70%
Payroll/labor Costs	05%
Occupancy	05%
Profit (estimated pretax)	15%

Industry Trend

- "Small neighborhood supermarkets are fading away, with big box retailers and big chains moving into a lot of neighborhoods that never had them."

Seller Financing

- "5 years"

Questions

- "Why are you selling? Check the store order history to determine what kind of clients are shopping the store. A store with high ad ordering and low everyday items ordering is not a good store, and you have to examine the P&L very carefully."

Sustainable Businesses (See Green Businesses)		
	NAICS 541620	

		Franchise
Swisher (Restroom Hygiene Service)		
Approx. Total Investment		$100,000 to $150,000
	NAICS 561720	Number of Businesses/Units 110

Rules of Thumb

➤ 75% of annual sales plus inventory

Industry Trend

- "With today's announcement that it has acquired South Florida-based Q Linen Service, Swisher Hygiene Inc., a provider of hygiene and sanitation products and services, has acquired three laundry service companies in three separate deals in the past two weeks."

  Source: "Swisher Hygiene Acquires Three Laundry Services Firms in Southeast," American Laundry News, April 11, 2011

Taco John's		Franchise
Approx. Total Investment		$627,000 to $1,071,000
Estimated Annual Sales/Unit		$700,000
	NAICS 722211	Number of Businesses/Units 430

Rules of Thumb

➢ 30 percent of annual sales plus inventory

Resources

Websites

- www.tacojohns.com

Tan USA (Business Opportunity)		
SIC 729944	NAICS 812199	

Rules of Thumb

➢ 45 to 50 percent of annual sales plus inventory

Pricing Tips

- Liquid Capital Required $99,000 to $150,000. This a license agreement not a franchise.

Tanning Salons		
SIC 7299-44	NAICS 812199	Number of Businesses/Units 19,152

Rules of Thumb

➢ 2 to 2.5 times SDE includes inventory

➢ 50 to 55 percent of annual sales plus inventory

➢ 2 times EBIT

➢ 2 times EBITDA

Pricing Tips

- "Salons with standup beds and spray tanning have higher gross margins and levels of profitability. These type salons can command a multiple of 3.0"

- "To arrive at a value for the company, we then apply a multiple to the SDE. According to Scott Gabehart, a certified business appraiser with Gabehart Valuation Services, tanning salons typically sell for 2 to 2.5 times SDE—or in Linda's case, between $116,000 and $145,000. If sales were $400,000 or higher, the multiple would likely be 3 to 4 times SDE, mainly because the larger the company, the less likely it will fail."

  Source: "How to Value a Tanning Salon" by Tom Tauli, *Forbes*, April 7, 2010

- "The recently imposed federal 10% surtax on tanning will most likely reduce the demand for services and thus impact cash flow."

- "How To Value A Tanning Salon

  As a general rule, tanning beds that are 3 years old and are properly maintained will have a value of about $.15 to $.20 on the dollar. For example: if the purchase price of the bed was $10,000 new, then the value of that bed is around $1500, $2000 after 3 years provided it is in an average condition.

  "The value of a tanning salon business is sometimes determined by multiplying its net profit by 2.5, plus the depreciated value of its assets. So if a tanning salon earned $40,000 net profit last year, and has $50,000 in depreciated assets, the estimated value of that business is $150,000.

  "The Main Valuation Drivers:

  "Equipment: Tanning beds can run to $30,000 apiece and require significant maintenance.

  "Utilities: While newer models are more energy efficient, utility costs can still be a large part of operating costs.

  "Taxes: As part of President Obama's massive health care bill, there is now a 10% tax on tanning services.

  "Health Concerns: There are concerns that tanning can lead to skin cancer. Some states even have laws that place age limits on who can go to a tanning salon.

  "Seasonality: Business tends to ramp up from January through June, given the weather.

  "Competition: Barriers to entry are small and there are a variety of alternatives, such as gyms, spas, and apartment complexes.

  "How many outstanding tans have yet to be delivered to both active and inactive clients? This is probably the most overlooked element when negotiating the purchase of a tanning salon. If a decision is made to buy the salon and a large number of outstanding tans exist, the previous owner will have had the benefit of depositing the money of those sales into their account while the new owner will have the burden of delivering the service and paying for the overhead associated with it. The buyer should always negotiate the value of outstanding tans out of the purchase price of the salon."

  Source: www.insun.us/negotiate-salon-purchase.php

- "Most tanning salons sell between 1.5 and 2.5 X SDE. There are various factors that will shift value along this spectrum. These factors include the following: age/type/brand of equipment, strength of lease, and local competition. However the most important factors are profitability and owner involvement. Buyers are willing to pay more if the owner is absentee or semi-absentee."

- "Make and age of tanning beds is paramount. Quality salons tend to use the best tanning beds. Some tanning beds can cost as much as $35,000 or more."

- "If equipment is very new, calculate FMV less debt outstanding."

- "Pricing may vary based on the time of year the salon is sold, due to seasonality. Higher multiples will be achieved in the December to February time frames, as peak season is March until June. Buyers will seek to get in and implement changes prior to the busy season. Salon values are then depressed from June until November, as the salons are far less lucrative (or even operating in the red) during these months."

- "Price varies based on time of year purchase is made. If salon is purchased in February, multiple should be 3 times SDE, since the 'season' starts mid-February and runs through June. If a salon is bought in July the multiple should be 2, since the prime season has passed."

- "Most tanning salons sell between 1.5 and 3 x SDE (Seller's Discretionary Earnings). There are various factors that will shift value along this spectrum. These factors include the following: age/type/brand of tanning equipment, whether equipment is fully owned or leased, location and strength of lease (term and increases) and threats of competition. Other factors which may have a more subtle influence on value are the current and potential electrical capacity and A/C tonnage. If a buyer is looking to run large, high-pressure tanning equipment these factors will come into play. They may not directly influence value since it is going to be dominated by cash flow, however, it can make a salon more attractive to a high-end buyer."

Expert Comments

"Concern with skin cancer has dampened public interest. Also parents are controlling their teenage daughters from going to salons."

"The tanning industry is shifting to more modern high-end salons versus the traditional 'mom and pop' style locations. This is helping to eliminate weak competitors, however the downside is that the competition is getting better."

"Gyms, nail salons and beauty shops continue to add single tanning beds, so perceived competition or threat of new entrants is high due to the low cost in doing so. Such novice entrants are rarely successful in tanning, however, the perception may differ."

"While the industry is growing overall, competition has created saturation in many markets, especially high-growth areas that experienced a recent housing boom. New commercial development has enticed many new operators to enter the market. The older 'mom and pop' site locations are being overtaken by more upscale, higher end facilities."

"Locations are often difficult to replicate, but they are one of the most important factors in valuation. Adjacent anchor tenants, nearby gyms, or complementary neighbors such as hair and nail salons or day spas also influence value and provide a business a sustainable competitive advantage."

"Tanning salons can vary greatly. People prefer the most modern beds and/or stand-up booths. Also spray-on is very popular. An ideal location would be next to or near a health club like LA Fitness and/or a massage facility like Massage Envy."

"Local competition is key in determining a location's competitive environment. A competitor cannot replicate an ideal location next to a gym or next to a grocery store."

"In a highly competitive industry like tanning, the ability to market to your target market is your business's life blood. The client base can be very fickle, so customer service is of the utmost importance."

"Tanning salons are a cash business but are heavily capital intensive. Customers want the newest state-of-the-art stand-up equipment, while most equipment is lay-down beds. It is very expensive to replace old equipment, and it takes a long time to recover your investment."

"Tanning salons may be easily duplicated but require strategic marketing and service techniques to succeed."

"Competition varies greatly by location. California, Nevada, Arizona, Texas, and Florida are highly competitive in most areas. Some college towns (i.e., Ann Arbor, Michigan) also see a great deal of competition."

Benchmark Data

Statistics (Tanning Salons)

Number of Establishments	19,152
Average Profit Margin	10.2%

Source: IBISWorld, July 2012

Products and Services Segmentation

UV tanning	58.7%
Sunless tanning	21.8%
Merchandise sales	16.6%
Other	2.9%

Source: IBISWorld, July 2012

Industry Costs

Profit	10.2%
Wages	28.3%
Purchases	35.1%
Depreciation	6.3%
Marketing	2.4%
Rent & Utilities	8.6%
Other	9.1%

Source: IBISWorld, July 2012

Statistics (Tanning Salon Franchises)

Number of Establishments	10,058
Average Profit Margin	10.5%
Revenue per Employee	$32,300
Average Number of Employees	5
Average Wages per Employee	$13,581

Source: IBISWorld, June 2012

Products and Services Segmentation

UV tanning	58.7%
Sunless tanning	21.8%
Merchandise sales	16.6%
Other	2.9%

Source: IBISWorld, June 2012

Industry Costs

Profit	10.5%
Wages	42.1%
Purchases	22.1%
Depreciation	3.0%
Marketing	5.5%
Rent & Utilities	7.1%
Other	9.7%

Source: IBISWorld, June 2012

Market Share

Palm Beach Tan..6.4%

Source: IBISWorld, June 2012

- "Rent, payroll, COGS, and utilities should account for approximately 90% of total expenses."

- "Statistics indicate there are roughly 20,000 professional indoor tanning salons and another 15,000 to 20,000 locations—such as health clubs, spas, video stores and beauty salons—that house one or two tanning units. In keeping with tradition, the Midwest and Southeast have the highest number of tanning salons per capita, with Ohio, North Carolina, Michigan, South Carolina, Illinois, Indiana and Florida leading the charge.
  "The majority of U.S. indoor tanning facilities are small businesses, and more than 50 percent of them have female ownership, compared to 25 percent of businesses in other industries, according to the U.S. Census. Indoor tanning also provides jobs for approximately 160,000 employees annually.
  "Today's salon owner is a professional with long-term commitment to the future of the tanning industry. Statistics support that the average salon has been in business for about 10 years, however, some salons have experienced a turnover in ownership. The majority of growth is from individuals staying in the business longer, which equates to more maturity of ownership, experience and stability."

- "One general manager and two (rotated) employees per store. If multi-unit, also include a regional manager."

- "It will be worthwhile to determine bed utilization, electrical power capacity utilization, sales per square foot, and percentage of sale percentages from monthly electronic fund transfers, recurring memberships or single sessions."

- "There are few industry Benchmark Data, as the industry has a broad spectrum of competitors."

- "Roughly 20% of sales should be derived from retail sales. Retail sales levels are a good indicator of how aggressively a seller is incentivizing employees to maximize profits. Rent, payroll, utilities and COGS should account for 90% of an operation's expenses."

- "The following four categories will usually comprise about 90% of the salon's expenses: Rent, Payroll, COGS, Utilities."

- "Annual sales of $250,000 should lead to a successful salon. Payroll should be heavily weighted on bonus and incentive programs, versus salaries and fixed wages."

Expenses as a Percentage of Annual Sales

Cost of goods	10%
Payroll/labor Costs	25%
Occupancy	25%
Profit (estimated pretax)	30%

Industry Trend

- "The California Indoor Tanning Trade Organization (CITTO) is bracing for change, helping salon owners in The Golden State to prepare for proper implementation of the new UV minimum age.
  "Effective January 1, 2012, the minimum age for UV-light tanning in California will increase to 18. (There is no age limit on UV-free spray tanning.) CITTO recommends that if they haven't already, salons should immediately begin to

prepare their staff and clientele—especially those ages 14 to 17 years old—for this change.
"Customers looking to tan in 2012 need to have a birth year of 1994 or earlier (of the corresponding month/day of service) to be of legal age for UV tanning. CITTO suggests creating a salon policy of carding those 21 and younger to ensure proper age verification is taking place."
Source: "California Braces for a New Tanning Age'" www.lookingfit.com December 2011

- "There will always be a demand to 'look beautiful' regardless of the risk"
- "There's just no doubt that last year's random imposition of a double-digit tax as an unjustified and un-researched part of the Health Care bill has cost the economy thousands of jobs in the tanning market alone."
Source: "Tanning Businesses Cut Staff in 2011," www.smarttan.com September 2011

- "The industry continues to grow, however, so does competition. Unsophisticated buyers and franchise chains that are not looking out for their franchisee's best interest saturate some markets."
- "The overall industry continues to grow; larger chains are gaining the majority of new Market Share."
- "Consolidation is the trend"
- "As the industry matures, buyers and sellers are 'graduating' to higher end prime locations. We've recently seen salons with rent of $20,000 per month, adjacent to high-end bars and restaurants"
- "The high-end salons that cater to high demographic clientele and offer state-of-the-art stand-up equipment will do well. The average tanning salon will barely survive or will go out of business."
- "While the overall industry grows, owners in more saturated markets are experiencing diminishing returns. Saturated markets will see consolidation in the next 10 years."
- "Overall growth in industry"
- "While the majority of freestanding tanning salons have 10 beds or less, the industry saw a shift in business tactics as a number of savvy salon chains acquired smaller facilities, improved them, made them bigger and added them into their tanning fold. Industry experts predict this consolidation trend will continue in larger markets but not in smaller, rural markets that don't have the populace to support bigger salons."

Questions

- "Have any of your competitors gone out of business within the last 12 months? Who has opened up within the last 12 months? How old are each of the beds? How old are the bulbs in each bed?"
- "Are there any new competitors that have recently entered the market?"
- "How many hours are truly worked by owner? Are there any new competitors?"
- "How old are the beds? How often are bulbs changed? Do you have spray-on beds? Who is the competition?"
- "Revenue trends"
- "How many members have you lost in the last 12 months? What is your retention percentage? How old is each piece of equipment? Do you have every bed metered? How do you check on your employees to make sure they are not giving away free time?"
- "How old is the equipment? How often is maintenance performed? Is there an EFT system in place?"

Resources

Trade Publications
- Looking Fit: www.lookingfit.com
- Smart Tan: www.smarttan.com

Associations
- The National Tanning Training Institute (NTTI): www.tanningtraining.com

Tattoo Parlors		
SIC 7299-43	NAICS 812199	Number of Businesses/Units 21,000

Rules of Thumb

➤ 50 percent of annual sales includes inventory

Benchmark Data

Statistics (Tattoo Removal)

Number of Establishments	504
Average Profit Margin	6.1
Revenue per Employee	65.6
Average Number of Employees	2
Average Wages per Employee	21,287

Source: IBISWorld, January 2012

Products and Services Segmentation

Removing colors	30.0%
Removing black ink	70.0%

Source: IBISWorld, January 2012

Industry Costs

Profit	6.1
Wages	32.8
Purchases	39.5
Depreciation	5.5
Utilities	2.5
Rent	2.5
Other	11.1

Source: IBISWorld, January 2012

Tattoo Statistics

Annual amount of U.S. spending on tattoos	$1.65 billion
Total percent of Americans (all ages) who have at least one tattoo	14%
Percentage of U.S. adults 18–25 who have at least one tattoo	36%
Percentage of U.S. adults 26–40 who have at least one tattoo	40%
Total number of Americans that have at least one tattoo	45 million
Number of tattoo parlors in the U.S.	21,000
Average cost of a small tattoo	$45
Average cost of a large tattoo	$150/hour
Percentage of people with a tattoo who are getting or have had one removed	11%

Source: Pew Research Center, Tattoo Finder, Vanishing Tattoo, www.statisticbrain.com/tattoo-statistics
July 2012

Industry Trend

- "The *Wall Street Journal* has a story about how tattoo parlors are showing up in more malls around the country. They cite a study from Pew Research that says 36% of 18-to-25-year-olds have a tattoo while only 10% of their parents' generation have a tattoo. The article says a company named Tattoo Nation has set a goal to have 400 stores in malls and be as common as Victoria's Secret. "Tattoo Nation says it has enough funds set aside to open at least three more stores immediately and hopes to raise more capital as additional leases are signed. 'Our goal is to have 400 stores—to be as common as Victoria's Secret,' says Chief Executive Heath Wolfson, 31, who has a Chai—the Hebrew symbol that signifies life in Judaism—tattooed inside his lip."

Source: "Tattoo Parlors Coming to a Mall Near You," from an article in the *Wall Street Journal.*
www.shoppingblog.com

Taverns (See Bars, Cocktail Lounges, & Restaurants)		
		Number of Businesses/Units 53,250

Tax Practices (See Accounting/Tax Practices)	
SIC 7291-01	NAICS 541213

Taxicab Businesses		
SIC 4121-01	NAICS 485310	Number of Businesses/Units 137,306

Rules of Thumb

➤ 4 times EBITDA plus value of vehicles

Pricing Tips

- "Selling price should be between 1 year's and 2 years' net profit, depending upon the number of cabs and their respective ages."

Benchmark Data

Statistics (Taxi & Limousine Services)

Number of Establishments	137,306
Average Profit Margin	12.4%
Revenue per Employee	$55,600
Average Number of Employees	1.3
Average Wages per Employee	$30,725

Source: IBISWorld, August 2012

Products and Services Segmentation

Taxi services	55.1%
Leasing to taxi operators	23.7%
Luxury and corporate services	7.2%
Stretch limousine services	5.8%
Other	5.7%
Special needs transportation services	2.5%

Source: IBISWorld, August 2012

Major Market Segmentation

Private consumers	54.5%
Corporations	29.5%
Tourists	13.2%
Other	2.8%

Source: IBISWorld, August 2012

Industry Costs

Profit	12.4%
Wages	57.1%
Purchases	19.5%
Depreciation	2.7%
Marketing	3.9%
Rent & Utilities	0.3%
Other	4.1%

Source: IBISWorld, August 2012

- "Here's one for the Guinness World Records people: Two New York City taxi medallions were sold last month for $1 million apiece. That's the highest price ever paid for the right to operate a car as a taxicab in 'The City That Never Sleeps.' It's also an expensive lesson in the harm caused to consumers and would-be entrepreneurs by over-regulation and the strangling of competition. "By law, every cab in New York has to have an official medallion—the numbered metal plate nailed to the hood—but the number of medallions is fixed at 13,237. When the city first issued taxi medallions in the 1930s, they cost $10 each. But before long the demand for taxi ownership had outstripped the limited supply of medallions. Since City Hall wasn't issuing new ones, the only way to get a medallion was to buy one from an existing owner. Over time the value of those metal tags went through the stratosphere.

  "New York isn't alone in blighting its taxi market like this. In Boston, which also adopted a medallion system in the 1930's, the little metal plates now sell for $400,000 and cab fares for most rides are the highest of any big city in North America. The number of cabs is limited to 1,825, which is why trying to get a taxi in Boston's outlying neighborhoods can be so tough. Cabbies—most of whom can't afford a medallion of their own and instead must pay stiff fees to lease somebody else's—naturally gravitate to the most lucrative routes.

  "Even more obnoxious is the government-protected monopoly in Milwaukee, which in 1991 imposed a citywide cap of just 321 taxis, yielding a ration of 1 taxi for every 1,850 residents. (By comparison, the ration in Boston is about 1 to 340; in Washington, D.C., where the number of cabs is not artificially limited, it's 1 to 90.) The cost of a taxi permit has soared from $85 to $150,000, which is well above the price of an average Milwaukee house."

  Source: "Medallion madness" by Jeff Jacoby, *Boston Sunday Globe*, November 6, 2011

- "Drivers absorb a 5 or 6 percent processing fee on credit-card fares, while many also must pay $1.50 each time they withdraw cash from an account in which card payments are deposited.

  "But New York's density makes it a more lucrative place to be a cabdriver, Derebala said. While his friends who drive taxis in New York might clear $400 before expenses during a busy shift, Boston cabdrivers say they are lucky to collect $250.

  "But even as the fare increase was meant to put more money in drivers' pockets, the city allowed fleet owners to raise the rent they charge on cabs, from $77 to $95 per 12-hour shift, intended to subsidize newer and more fuel-efficient taxis."

  Source: "Credit card use frustrates cabdrivers," by Eric Moskowitz, *Boston Globe*, May 16, 2011

	Franchise
TCBY	
Approx. Total Investment	$142,000 to $347,200
NAICS 722213	Number of Businesses/Units 900

Rules of Thumb

➤ 40 to 45 percent of annual sales plus inventory

Technology Companies — Information

Rules of Thumb

➤ 100 percent of annual sales plus inventory

➤ 3 times SDE plus inventory

➤ 3 times EBIT

➤ 3 times EBITDA

Pricing Tips

- "Renewal rates are paramount, whether the business is advertiser supported or subscription supported."

Benchmark Data

- "The sales ratio to employee expense should exceed 1.5 to 1."

Expenses as a Percentage of Annual Sales

Cost of goods	40%
Payroll/labor Costs	25%
Occupancy	05%
Profit (estimated pretax)	20%

Industry Trend

- "I see continued consolidation as smaller providers are rolled into larger companies. It is easier for larger companies to buy than to build."

Seller Financing

- "5 years"

Technology Companies — Manufacturing

	NAICS 334111	

Rules of Thumb

➤ Niche market—4.25 to 4.75 adjusted net plus inventory

➤ PCB—4.65 to 5.0 plus inventory

➤ Software—4.50 to 6.0 plus inventory

➤ Non-niche—4.35 to 5.5 plus inventory

Pricing Tips

- "Adjusted net times [EBIT] 4 to 5.5 (depending on prior growth curves)"
  "Additions: location, 1st impression on walk-through, how competitive is marketplace, how clear P&L is. High tech or low tech? How much is straightforward in P&L & how much has to be recast?"

Technology Companies — Service

	NAICS 541	

Rules of Thumb

➤ Temporary Agencies—1.25 to 3.5 EBITDA

➤ Test Services—2.75 to 3.35 EBITDA

➤ Design Services—2.5 to 3.5 EBITDA

➤ 3 to 7 times EBITDA
   (Adjusted net for large companies is EBITDA, for smaller ones SDE is used as adjusted net)

Pricing Tips

- "There is usually no rule of thumb. Right combination of technology and customers can push deal prices up significantly. Typically financed by cash, stock and earnouts."
- "Usually goes for multiple of revenues—especially when the company is not highly profitable but has valuable technology."

Expert Comments

"Software services are typically very sticky and high value add. At the same time technology changes rapidly and risk of obsolescence is high. Customer concentration tends to be high."

Seller Financing

- "Typically sellers get a good party of value on earnouts, non-competes, etc."

Questions

- "Focus should be on strategic value of the business because most of the times the value has very little to do with current financials"

Tee Shirt Shops

SIC 5699-17	NAICS 448190	Number of Businesses/Units 11,500

Rules of Thumb

➤ 30 percent of annual sales plus inventory

Telecommunication Carriers (Wired)

	NAICS 517110	

Rules of Thumb

➤ 2.5 times SDE includes inventory

Pricing Tips

- "Need to understand how the carrier commission structure will impact the current client base and future sales. Trained, knowledgeable and professional sales staff are critical—this is not an order-taking environment."

Expert Comments

"Very robust competitive landscape but a savvy operator can carve out a healthy Market Share."

Benchmark Data

- "Sales per employee"

Expenses as a Percentage of Annual Sales

Cost of goods	40%
Payroll/labor Costs	24%
Occupancy	12%
Profit (estimated pretax)	17%

Industry Trend

- "Continued growth, especially in smart phones and data services"

Questions

- "Trends for client counts. Cancellation rates and velocity."

Telecommunications		
	NAICS 5133	

Rules of Thumb

➢ $700 to $1,400 per line

➢ 3 times SDE includes inventory

➢ 5 times EBITDA

Pricing Tips

- "Depends on the amount of equipment involved as well as the quality. Differentiate from Fiber Optic splicers and diggers."
- "Three variables—$1,000 to $2,000 per installed port; 20 to 40 percent of annual revenues, depending upon sales mix & earnings; earnings impact selling price, but on a case by case basis relating to the first two variables plus cash flow analysis. This industry is far from exact, as Market Share , client base revenues, product line exclusivity, market potential (saturation) & earnings all impact market value. The old adage 'beauty is in the eye of the beholder' definitely applies to the telecom industry. Client (installed) base revenue mix & profit margin? New system sales product mix? Competition? Service reputation? Customer retention rate? Inventory obsolescence factor? Overall pretax profit?"

Industry Trend

- "These businesses are growing exponentially as the demand is starting to catch up with the amount of fiber in the ground"

Seller Financing

- "3-5 Years"

Questions

- "Point of differentiation. Where do your customers come from?"
- "Are there any Competitive Local Exchange Carriers (CLECs) operational in market area? Do they have their own facilities or are they reselling?"

Resources

Trade Publications

- Telephony Magazine: www.tmcnet.com

Telemarketing (See Call Centers)

Telephone Companies/Independent

	NAICS 513310	

Rules of Thumb

➢ "Sales price throughout the nation has been established at between $800 and $1,200 per subscriber."

Television Sales & Service

(See also Appliance Stores & Appliance Repair)

	NAICS 443112	

Rules of Thumb

➢ 2 times monthly sales plus inventory

Television Stations (See also Radio Stations)

SIC 4833-01	NAICS 513120	Number of Businesses/Units 4,000

Rules of Thumb

➢ 9 to 12 times EBITDA

Temporary Agencies (See also Office Staffing)

SIC 7363-04	NAICS 56132	Number of Businesses/Units 11,000

Rules of Thumb

➢ 1 to 2 times annual sales plus inventory

➢ 3 times SDE plus inventory

➢ 2 to 5 times EBIT (smaller deals under $25 million)

➢ 5 to 7.5 times EBIT (larger deals over $25 million)

➢ 6 to 9 times EBIT (Information Technology)

➢ 3 to 6 times EBITDA—Depending on revenues

Pricing Tips

- "The price depends on the industry served."
- "Multiple depends on size of company."

Expert Comments

"Very nice business for financial buyer"

"Easy to start, and smart owners can really grow these quickly."

Benchmark Data

- For Benchmark data see Office Staffing

Expenses as a Percentage of Annual Sales

Cost of goods	10%
Payroll/labor Costs	70%
Occupancy	10%
Profit (estimated pretax	10%

Seller Financing

- "3-year earnouts are most typical"
- "2 to 5 years"

Questions

- "What industry do you serve?"
- "Who does the sales?"

Resources

Associations

- American Staffing Association: www.americanstaffing.net

	Franchise
The Maids (See also Janitorial Services, Maid Brigade, & Molly Maid)	
Approx. Total Investment	$92,000 to $125,000
NAICS 561720	Number of Businesses/Units 1,118

Rules of Thumb

➢ 40 to 45 percent of annual sales plus inventory

Resources

Websites

- www.maids.com

Thrift Shops (See Consignment Shops & Used Goods)		
SIC 5932-22	NAICS 453310	

Ticket Services

SIC 7999-73	NAICS 561599	Number of Businesses/Units 1,600

Rules of Thumb

➢ 4 times EBITDA for small to midsize operations; 5 times EBITDA for larger companies

Pricing Tips

- "Due to StubHub, RazorGator and private equity shops, multiple has increased."
- "Number of corporate clients?"
- "Length of time in business? Stability of earnings? How do they get tickets? Average markup? Repeat business?"

Resources

Associations
- National Association of Ticket Brokers: www.natb.org

Tire Stores (See Auto Tire Stores)

	NAICS 441320	Number of Businesses/Units 20,000

Title Abstract and Settlement Offices

SIC 6541-02	NAICS 541191	Number of Businesses/Units 25,000

Rules of Thumb

➢ 60 percent of annual sales

➢ 3 times SDE

➢ 5 times EBIT

➢ 4.5 times EBITDA

Pricing Tips

- "'Affiliated Business Arrangements' (ABAs) are in vogue. Make sure the ABA is transferable upon sale. Title agencies will command higher prices in states with higher filed premiums."
- "Criteria include the sales history and trends. Title companies' revenues are affected by interest rates, but the stronger ones will maintain profits through the ups and downs by adjustments of variable expenses."

Expert Comments

"Although there is significant competition, this is a highly profitable industry with relatively low barriers to entry."

"Buyers for title agencies have increased due to legislative changes."

Benchmark Data

Statistics (Conveying Services)

Number of Establishments.. 23,103
Average Profit Margin 4.8%
Revenue per Employee $145,700
Average Number of Employees 4
Average Wages per Employee $48,818

Source: IBISWorld, December 2010

(These reports are the latest reports that IBISWorld did on this business. We left them as it may be of interest.)

Products and Services Segmentation

Conveyancing and title abstract consulting 38.0%
Property, document and other intellectual document filing 5.9%
Other legal services 15.1%
Title search consulting 20.0%
Settlement and closings consulting 21.0%

Source: IBISWorld, December 2010

Industry Costs

Profit 4.8%
Rent 3.5%
Utilities 2.0%
Depreciation.. 1.1%
Other... 55.6%
Wages.. 33.0%

Source: IBISWorld, December 2010

Distribution of Establishments by Employee Size

No. of Employees	No. of Establishments	Percentage
1 to 4	8,975	65.4
5 to 9	2,750	20

Source: IBISWorld, December 2010

Market Share

Fidelity National Financial, Inc. 9.3%
The First American Corporation.. 6.2%
Stewart Information Services Corporation 4.9%

Source: IBISWorld, December 2010

- "Title companies typically retain 70% of the premium on title insurance policies issued, with remaining 30% going to the underwriter."
- "Labor/Gross Revenues = <35% for metropolitan markets
Labor/Gross Revenues = <30% for rural markets"

Expenses as a Percentage of Annual Sales

Cost of goods.. 30%
Payroll/labor Costs 20%
Occupancy.. 07%
Profit (estimated pretax) 35%

Questions

- "How many referral sources does the company have solid relationships with?"

Tobacco Stores (See also Retail Stores—Small Specialty)

SIC 5993-01	NAICS 453991	Number of Businesses/Units 10,000

Rules of Thumb

> ➤ 15 percent of annual sales plus inventory

Benchmark Data

Statistics (Cigar Lounges)

Number of Establishments	5,892
Average Profit Margin	4.5%
Revenue per Employee	$306,600
Average Number of Employees	2.2
Average Wages per Employee	$17,243

Source: IBISWorld, May 2012

Products and Services Segmentation

Cigars	56.9%
Accessories	22.7%
Food and drink	14.3%
Other tobacco products	6.1%

Source: IBISWorld, May 2012

Industry Costs

Profit	4.5%
Wages	5.5%
Purchases	75.0%
Depreciation	1.5%
Marketing	1.0%
Rent & Utilities	3.4%
Other	9.1%

Source: IBISWorld, May 2012

- For additional Benchmark data see Retail Stores—Small Specialty
- "The survival of a tobacco store is based on having a little bit of everything, so we have not cut back on tobacco products at all. If you start limiting your tobacco products, if you don't carry this style or that brand, you'll have brand-loyal smokers go look elsewhere. We try to have high inventory in our stores and we try and carry all the cigarettes, although no fourth tier.

  "We can't rely on tobacco and tobacco products anymore. There are plenty of other things you can merchandise in this business. Candles are really popular; fragrance oil lamps are really popular with the ladies. It all depends on your clientele. We sell shoes, purses in some stores, flip flops; we sell the devil out of them in some stores. In two of my bigger stores I'm putting deli's in; all the equipment's been ordered."

  Source: www.tobonline.com. Tobacco Outlet Business Online, George Frichter, President, TBM Management

Industry Trend

"Charleston, WV—Loose tobacco has come a long way since Prince Albert was trapped in a can. Roll-your-own cigarette stores are opening nationwide, turning out smokes that look and taste like big-name brands for a fraction of the price. But the cheap cigarettes may cost business owners a fortune as state officials investigate the shops' creative take on tobacco taxes.

"The stores don't sell cartons of cigarettes, but machine-rolled 'carton runs' manufactured by consumers. Steincamp said he guarantees 190 cigarettes, though most patrons leave with between 195 and 205. It takes about eight minutes to complete a run.

"'People love it. They're getting a prime cigarette that is a full tobacco cigarette, that doesn't have the fire paper and doesn't have the additives,' Steincamp said. Customers also appreciate the price. First-time Ciggy Shack patrons pay about $26 for their first carton run. Returning customers pay $30, except on their birthdays. Then, it's half-off.

"A quick comparison for non-smokers: a carton of Marlboro cigarettes costs $42.45 at Smoker Friendly in Southridge. Cartons of Camel or Winston cost $45.45. Marlboro Special Blend costs $34.95, and Pall Mall costs $32.99. A carton of Pyramid cigarettes, the cheapest sold by Smoker Friendly, retails for $27.10.

"Steincamp said roll-your-own shops are popping up around the country. There are currently 15 stores in West Virginia alone, he said. But how can Ciggy Shack and similar stores set their prices so low?"

Source: "State sniffs out tobacco shop smokes" by Zack Harold, www.dailymail.com July 2011

Resources

Associations
- Tobacco Merchants Association (TMA): www.tma.org

		Franchise
Togo's Eatery		
Approx. Total Investment		$257,813 to $419,796
	NAICS 722211	Number of Businesses/Units 249
Rules of Thumb		
➢ 60 percent plus inventory		

Resources

Websites
- www.togos.com

		Franchise
Topz Healthier Burger Grill		
Approx. Total Investment		$350,000 to $500,000
		Number of Businesses/Units 75
Rules of Thumb		
➢ 40 percent of annual sales plus inventory		

Resources

Websites
- www.topz.com

Tour Operators

SIC 4725-01	NAICS 561520	Number of Businesses/Units 2,643

Rules of Thumb

➢ 2 to 4 times SDE plus inventory

➢ 3 to 5 times EBITDA — multiple expands as profits go up.

Pricing Tips

- "Upscale or mid-grade?"
- "Average mark up? Wholesale or direct?"

  "Length of time in business? Single destination operators warrant a bit higher; type of travel (golf, ski, scuba, etc.)—specialist vs. generalist. Wholesale via agents or direct business? Inbound or outbound?"

Expert Comments

"Travel & tourism is universal. World is shrinking. Huge inheritance in USA to fuel 20- year boom."

Benchmark Data

Statistics (Tour Operators)

Number of Establishments	2,643
Average Profit Margin	6.0%

Source: IBISWorld, February 2012

Products and Services Segmentation

Arranging, assembling and marketing package tours (international)	47%
Arranging, assembling and marketing package tours (domestic)	34%
Commissions and fees from the sale of transport or accommodations	11%
Reselling tours acquired from other tour operators	6.8%
Other	1.2%

Source: IBISWorld, February 2012

Major Market Segmentation

Travel agents	70%
Tour wholesalers	30%

Source: IBISWorld, February 2012

Industry Costs

Profit	6.0%
Wages	31.8%
Purchases	31.8%
Depreciation	2.2%
Utilities	3.0%
Rent	5.0%
Other	20.2%

Source: IBISWorld, February 2012

Market Share

Flight Centre Ltd.	21.1%
The Mark Travel Corporation	9.8%

Source: IBISWorld, February 2012

Expenses as a Percentage of Annual Sales

Cost of goods	80%
Payroll/labor Costs	55% (after COG)
Occupancy	15% (after COG)
Profit (estimated pretax)	20%

Industry Trend

- "Moderate — economy is not robust."

Questions

- "Which key employees stay post-sale? Are wholesale contracts transferable?"

Resources

Associations

- National Tour Association: www.ntaonline.com

Towing Companies		
SIC 7549-01	NAICS 488410	Number of Businesses/Units 8,468

Rules of Thumb

- 70 percent of annual revenues plus inventory
- 2.75 times EBITDA

Pricing Tips

- "Extreme care with adding back depreciation, and/or allowance to replace trucks. Define which segment of industry, and check to see if the insurance premium is fair market value. Small companies and those in non-consent business are hard to sell."
- "The last of the consolidators has liquidated its acquisitions at a loss. The implication is that there are negative economies of scale at both ends of the scale, large and small, i.e., above some size these businesses based on revenue etc. have a declining value, and that optimal values are found within the span of control of one person. Ease of entry has been increasing, so going-concern values have been declining."

Expert Comments

"These businesses vary widely. Hands-on management is almost always a critical element. Control of operating real estate is usually a major element in profitability."

Benchmark Data

Statistics (Automobile Towing)

Number of Establishments	8,468
Average Profit Margin	3.5%

Source: IBISWorld, August 2012

Products and Services Segmentation

Passenger car towing services	41.6%
Light duty truck towing services	41.4%
Roadside assistance services	17%

Source: IBISWorld, August 2012

Major Market Segmentation

Individuals	43%
Local and state governments	35%
Commercial customers	22%

Source: IBISWorld, August 2012

Industry Costs

Profit	3.5%
Wages	41.5%
Purchases	22.4%
Depreciation	4.4%
Marketing	1.2%
Rent & Utilities	6.0%
Other	21.0%

Source: IBISWorld, August 2012

Expenses as a Percentage of Annual Sales

Cost of goods	30%
Payroll/labor Costs	30%
Occupancy	08%
Profit (estimated pretax)	20%

Industry Trend

- "Trend is positive, but competition is fierce. Many companies come and go."
- "More than 85 percent of all tows in the U.S. involve passenger cars and light trucks. The majority of these tows are provided by small, family-owned towing businesses."

Source: Towing and Recovery Association of America (TRAA)

Seller Financing

- "5 years"

Resources

Trade Publications

- Tow Times Magazine: www.towtimes.com

Toy Stores (See also Hobby Shops)

SIC 5945-17	NAICS 451120	Number of Businesses/Units 6,500

Rules of Thumb

➤ 20 to 25 percent of annual sales plus inventory

Benchmark Data

- For Benchmark data see Hobby Shops

Industry Trend

- "A slate of hot new toy trends for 2012 that keep pace with advancements in the tech world, mirror societal trends and aim to produce well-rounded, lifelong learners were unveiled today by the Toy Industry association (TIA) at its 109th American International Toy Fair."

Source: www.toyassociation.org February 2012

Resources

Associations
- Toy Industry Association—good site: www.toyassociation.org

Translation and Interpretation Services		
SIC 7389-20	NAICS 54193	Number of Businesses/Units 49,429

Rules of Thumb

➤ 40 to 45 percent of annual sales plus inventory

Benchmark Data

Statistics (Translation Services)

Number of Establishments	49,429
Average Profit Margin	6.8%
Revenue per Employee	$49,600
Average Number of Employees	1.3
Average Wages per Employee	$27,338

Source: IBISWorld, May 2012

Products and Services Segmentation

Written translation services	50%
Interpretation services	42.5%
Other	7.5%

Source: IBISWorld, May 2012

Major Market Segmentation

Marketing and advertising firms	15%
Technology and IT	12%
Medicine	11%
Finance	9%
Engineering and natural sciences	7%
Other	6%
Business and retail	22%
Legal and government	18%

Source: IBISWorld, May 2012

Industry Costs

Profit	6.8%
Wages	55.1%
Purchases	2.0%
Depreciation	2.3%
Marketing	7.2%
Rent & Utilities	3.6%
Other	23.0%

Source: IBISWorld, May 2012

Market Share

Language Line Services 11.9%
Lionbridge 6.6%

Source: IBISWorld, May 2012

- "It's all about supply and demand and since the U.S. became involved in Afghanistan after the Sept. 11 attacks, there has been demand for linguists or interpreters of the two main Afghan languages, Dari and Pashto. The average salary for a linguist or interpreter who speaks Dari is $187,000 and it's $193,000 for those who speak Pashto, according to Indeed.com. The jobs range from an interpreter for military personnel to a media desk officer who would translate Afghan news stories and communicate with Afghan media."

Source: HTTP://www.salary.com

Travel Agencies

SIC 4724-02	NAICS 561510	Number of Businesses/Units 14,510

Rules of Thumb

➢ 25 to 30 percent of annual gross profit

➢ 2 to 2.5 times SDE plus inventory

➢ 2 to 3 times EBIT for small to mid-size agencies

➢ 3 to 5 times EBITDA for larger agencies

➢ "Small operations, $1 to $3 million—35 percent of annual commissions and fees; $4 to $8 million—40 percent; $9 to $20 million—45 percent; 3.5 times EBITDA above $20 million in volume; 5 times EBITDA for shops earning over $1 million net profit."

➢ "For agencies with $1 to $4 million in sales, 1.5 to 2.0 SDE is customary. If $5 to $10 million, then 2.0 to 2.5 SDE"

Pricing Tips

- "Top importance is : 1. The Gross income not gross sales 2. In-house Income not Independent agent income. Income verification is easy in this business as there is a paper trail for all transactions."

- "Gross Sales with more in-house agents is better than independent/outside sales agents"

- "Profitability? Agency more than 3 years old? Agency does not depend on more than one account for more than 10 percent of gross? Agency does not rebate? Manager stays on?"

- "Would need last 18 months' financials to spot any trends"

- "Today a common formula for the pricing of travel agencies is paid via earnout with a minimal down payment applied to the overall earnout. 25% of revenue over two years is a common multiplier. For example if gross sales were $5,000,000 and gross commission income were $500,000, it would be calculated as follows, assuming the sales remain stable over the two year earnout: 25% of $500,000=$125,000 multiplied by 2 for two years, give a total purchase price of $250,000. With the current economic situation, we are seeing multipliers of 20% the first year and 15% the second year applied to this formula in some cases."

- "The market is soft, however business volume is growing. Travel industry is the biggest industry in the world, and people love to be in it for the lifestyle it provides. Profits are slimmer; however the bigger volume brings overrides & incentives."
- "Buyers simply need to receive what they pay for. With zero tangible assets, all transactions now include performance-laden contracts."
- "20 year value:
  1990—100% of gross profit
  2009—33% of gross profit"
- "Always include service charges, fees and markups to the gross sales. These are becoming a more and more important part of agencies' income."
- "Several factors. Most important staff, goodwill. Airline contracts for net rates, specialty clients, etc."
- "Look at commission and fee income; both are important."
- "Most important are long-term good employees, long-term goodwill, owner's covenant not to compete, high volume and special contracts net or override with the vendors. It's important to count all service fees as well as commissions from suppliers when calculating SDE. Also overrides and CRS money."
- "One-quarter down, balance earned out over 24 months"
- "Earnouts are very common, with a percentage of the income generated from the selling agency's customer list paid over a 2-year period—maximum."
- "99 percent of deals are earnouts versus fixed price."
- "Gross Income is more important than Gross Sales. Management team to stay. Higher commission structure and specialty is the key."

Expert Comments

"The small Travel agency's income has declined due commission cuts & internet, however the Industry is growing due to more people travelling and many people willing to pay service fees for good travel agents. It is good to have Corporate & Leisure mix to weather all possibilities. The bigger the volume, the bigger the ratio of income."

"Service is most important, ARC & IATAN appointments transfer require 2 years' experienced manager. Better to purchase an agency with goodwill."

"Due to economy the travel industry is in a crunch, profit margins are lower."

"Very risky to be brick and mortar generalists."

"Competition is high as it is an easy business to learn. Fully licensed agencies are more difficult due their financial requirements. Location is not important; services & cost are more important."

"Agents are vanishing—no new blood is entering the industry."

"Earnouts are becoming more and more the norm."

"The travel industry's volume is higher as more people are traveling; however, with commission cuts and direct Internet sales from the airlines, revenue has shifted. Major sources of revenue are service fees, commissions paid by cruise, hotels, car and other vendors. Belonging to a good consortium is important for higher revenue."

Benchmark Data

Statistics (Travel Agencies)

Number of Establishments	14,510
Average Profit Margin	7.6%
Revenue per Employee	$187,600
Average Number of Employees	7.1%
Average Wages per Employee	$56,353

Source: IBISWorld, October 2012

Products and Services Segmentation

Domestic airline travel reservations	22%
Packaged tour reservations	18.4%
Other	16.7%
International airline travel reservations	15%
Cruise reservations	12.8%
Lodging reservations	9.1%
Vehicle rental reservations	3.9%
Rail reservations	2.1%

Source: IBISWorld, October 2012

Major Market Segmentation

Domestic travel	61%
International travel	39%

Source: IBISWorld, October 2012

Industry Costs

Profit	7.6%
Wages	29.3%
Purchases	18.0%
Depreciation	6.0%
Marketing	6.5%
Rent & Utilities	10.8%
Other	21.8%

Source: IBISWorld, October 2012

Market Share

Carlson Companies Inc.	22.8%
Expedia Inc.	11.1%
Priceline.com Incorporated	10.1%
American Express Company	9.1%
Sabre Holdings Corporation	9.8%
Travelport	6.1%

Source: IBISWorld, October 2012

- "The best is $800,00 to one million gross sales per employee."
- "One million or more gross sales is very good for 1 employee."
- "Corporate agents should book $1M in volume per year; leisure agents should book $700K volume per year."
- "Sales per employee should be high. Most important factor the ratio between inside(salary) or outside(independent contractor) employees. On sale of the business independent employees can leave & goodwill will be lost."
- "SDE should equal 20% of Gross Commissions in a well-run agency."
- "$1 million sales per employee; specialty groups, corporate accounts and low rent."
- "Sales per agent"
- "A top inside full-time employee should be managing $1 million in sales volume or at least $70,000 in gross revenue. Too many independent/outside sales employees could be negative for the sale price of the business."

T - Rules of Thumb

- "Typically an 'average' travel agent, if there is such a thing, should generate a gross of $1 million and a gross profit of $100K."
- "Higher net commissions due to special contracts. Service fee income. Overall control on expenses."
- "Look for preferred supplier and override agreements, written contractual agreements with corporate customers, relationships with wholesalers on airline tickets. GDS (airline computer system) contract situation is a key factor."

Expenses as a Percentage of Annual Sales

Cost of goods	20%
Payroll/labor Costs	50% to 60%
Occupancy	15% to 20%
Profit (estimated pretax)	05% to 10%

Industry Trend

- "'The travel industry continues to be one of the prime drivers of the nation's economy,' David Huether, senior vice president of economics and research at U.S. Travel, said in a statement.

  "The 9,200 jobs added to the travel industry in July marked the largest increase the sector has seen in four months. A total of 63,700 jobs were added to the U.S. travel industry, or an average of 9,100 jobs per month, since January of this year.

  "Job growth in travel was mainly driven by increases in the restaurant and lodging sectors, according to U.S. Travel.

  "The domestic travel industry now directly employs 7.6 million people, U.S. Travel reported."

  Source: "Travel outpacing other sectors of the economy in job growth" by Michelle Baran,
www.travelweekly.com August 2012

- "According to those in the travel agent industry, clients like Ms. Griffin are not alone, and are in fact helping to stanch the bloodletting the industry has experienced since the onset of D.I.Y. booking more than a decade ago. Nearly one in three leisure agencies is hiring, according to PhoCusWright, a travel research firm. And in 2011 travel agencies experienced a second consecutive year of growth; their bookings account for a third of the $284 billion United States travel market.

  "This comes after years during which all signs seemed to be suggesting that travel agents would soon go the way of telex operators. And it's true that the numbers are stark: During the industry's peak years of the mid-1990s, there were about 34,000 retail locations booking trips. Today, there are 14,000 to 15,000, according to PhoCusWright. In 2009 alone, in the throes of the recession, bookings through traditional agencies plummeted by 23 percent."

  Source: "Are Travel Agents Back?" by Michelle Higgins, *New York Times*, April 22, 2012

- "Online giants (Expedia, Travelocity, Orbitz, Priceline) continue to soar, taking Market Share."
- "Consolidations. Potential for tremendous growth with world travel increasing."
- "More and more people seem to be turning back to traditional brick-and-mortar travel agencies, especially as the baby boomers age. Baby boomers seem to be especially interested in learning while traveling, so customization is important to them."

Seller Financing

- "2 to 5 years"

Questions

- "Reason for sale, covenant not to compete a must as most are addicted to stay. Ratio of inside & outside sales income."
- "The breakdown of revenue for salary & independent employees. Covenant not to compete clause."
- "Who stays on post-sale? Any client over 10% of biz? How long have your key accounts and employees been on board? Are you 100% credit card? Willing to do earnout on performance basis?"
- "Will the staff stay?"
- "What are your GDS and override contracts?"
- "Do you have contractual agreements with your corporate accounts? What is your override program with preferred suppliers? Do you belong to a co-op or a consortium? When does your GDS contract expire?"
- "Ask about who controls the business, is it under contract? Length of GDS contract, location, lease expiration date? Any net pricing? Do customers have written contracts to use the agency? Is there a database of past leisure customers? How often is this database contacted? The net commissions earned, service price charged, special override commission contracts from the vendors. Employees' goodwill, inside or independent contractors, all licenses, covenant not to compete."

Resources

Trade Publications
- Travel Weekly: www.travelweekly.com
- Travel Agent Magazine: www.travelagentcentral.com

Associations
- American Society of Travel Agents (ASTA): www.astanet.com
- U.S. Travel Association: www.ustravel.org

Travel Wholesalers/Consolidators		
	NAICS 561520	

Rules of Thumb

➤ 3 times EBITDA for small to midsize companies; 4 times EBITDA when profits exceed $350,000

Pricing Tips

- "Airlines not giving out as many contracts as they have in the past due to 90 percent of all airline seats being filled as number of aircraft has decreased. Airlines pushing more direct channels to own Web sites. Value of wholesaler is under some pressure."

Questions

- "Are the contracts owned or are they subcontracted?"
- "Length of time in business? Salary vs. commission? Who controls the business? How long are contracts valid?"

Trophy Studios		
	NAICS 453998	Number of Businesses/Units 7,000

Rules of Thumb

➢ 40 to 45 percent of annual sales plus inventory

Industry Trend

- "Should be about the same as it has been, but technology is changing the business."

		Franchise
Tropical Smoothie Café		
Approx. Total Investment		$164,500 to $398,000
Estimated Annual Sales/Unit		Approximately $525,000
	NAICS 722211	Number of Businesses/Units 308

Rules of Thumb

➢ 50 to 55 percent of annual sales plus inventory

Truck Stops (See also Gas Stations)		
SIC 5541-03	NAICS 447190	Number of Businesses/Units 3,000

Rules of Thumb

➢ 75 percent of annual sales

➢ 5 times SDE plus inventory, may deduct cost of cosmetic update.

➢ 5 times EBITDA

Pricing Tips

- "The rule of thumb for truck stops is going to be between 5-6 times EBITDA with the factors coming into play like the quality of the assets, and are any environmental issues that will need to be deducted from the value of the truck stop. However, to arrive to an EBITDA one must add up all of the different profit centers that comprise of the truck stop. Such as: income from the scales, truck wash, video games, gift shop, restaurant income or restaurant lease income if the unit is leased out and sometimes there are other ancillary forms of income that will all need to be added together to get to the EBITDA of the truck stop."
- "A lot of people will try to pump up the value of a truck stop by stating how much property is comprised by the truck stop, because it takes several acres to make a truck stop, but anything beyond the basic amount of property needed that is being used to support the business should not be included as additional value.

  "For example there may be a truck stop that sits on a 10-acre tract of ground and the seller has another 5 acres that he thinks add additional value to the truck stop, but it doesn't. Only the property that is being used at the present time."

"Be sure to check to see if they have any additional profit centers such as scales and if the scales are leased or owned. Other profit centers such as gambling machines (video poker etc.) that sometimes are not included in the P & L's due to skimming."

- "Due to the multiple streams at one location the goodwill can go for a premium."
- "The current formula for the pricing of a truck stop/travel plaza is EBITDA which currently is between 5 to 5.5 times."
- "Limited buyers who buy this kind of business, due to the large number of employees and size of operation."
- "The only thing that comes to your house that wasn't delivered by a truck is your children."

Source: Tony Love, a trucker, in the *Chicago Tribune*, July 9, 2006

- "Business Only 2.5 to 3.5 times the Net/EBITDA; Real Estate + Business 7 to 10 times Net/EBITDA."
- "I only do cash deals. Environmental risk can turn into nightmare on contract sales."
- "Net profit median is 2 to 2.5 percent of sales; high net profit truck stops make 5 to 7 percent of sales. Note: Truck stops have an overall higher gross profit because there are various departments—restaurants, trucker's store, motel, scale, C-store, laundromat, showers, movies, phones, gas, diesel, repairs, truck wash, barber shop, shoeshine shop, check cashing and much more sometimes."

Expert Comments

"The truck stop industry has taken a severe beating lately due to the increased diesel fuel prices. Plus added to that the fact that the major truck stop operators such as Love's, Petro, Flying J, and Pilot are ruthless on their competition and have decreased the fuel margins considerably. Plus the majors that I just mentioned have made it a point to have fueling agreements with most of the major truck carriers across the country leaving only the independent truckers who will stop at the independent truck stops."

"Very expensive to replicate and build, few buyers, due to the heavy labor involvement and the 24X365 days business, yet very profitable."

"The truck stop/travel plaza industry is in turmoil as is the convenience store industry. High fuel prices, credit card fees, low margins and increased competition are taking their toll. Many convenience store operators have thought they would try their hand at a truck stop thinking that they are the same thing only larger with more volume. Not so. A truck stop is a different animal with a completely different customer base, nothing like that of a convenience store. In a truck stop the main seller is diesel fuel and the wants and needs of the customers are totally different. A convenience store deals mostly with local people and is really a little grocery store with gas, whereby a truck stop is a small city having to furnish more complete services to individuals that are going to be staying for an extended period of time, unless the truck stop/travel plaza, as they are known now, is something like a Love's that has formed an alliance with McDonalds and is selling their fuel at rock bottom prices because of their volume discounts and agreements made with national carriers."

"Even though the travel plazas are profitable, the size of operation and management acumen required can be daunting. Also the upfront monies required are pretty hefty as compared to most small businesses."

"The average return on investment for a truck stop is 6 to 8 percent. The high profit return on investment for a truck stop is 16 to 17 percent. In order for a buyer to determine a good deal—12 to 15 percent ROI for a truck stop should provide a good rule of thumb."

"Replication is difficult because 5 to 25 acres of prime real estate is required, and the cost can be between $5 million and $10 million to build one. Truck stops/travel plazas have been steady, but also the older or small mom/pops are being eliminated due to competition."

Benchmark Data

- "To be a profitable truck stop it seems inevitable that there is a restaurant connected to the facility. Many of the truck stops are now partnering with Hardee's, Wendy's, McDonald's, Arby's etc. while the others have a sit-down restaurant."
- "$500 sales per sq. ft."
- "Convenience/Retail combined is approx. $500 per sq. ft."
- "Per employee sales annually: $135,000

  Gross Profit Margins: 24%

  Net Profit Margins: 1.8%"
- "Average annual sales are nearly $7 million with the larger, high-profit centers doing in excess of $20 million annually with a net of 6% of sales."
- "Typical Full-Service Travel Plaza Statistics

  At a typical full-service travel plaza you will find:
  - ✓ Convenience or retail stores (97%)
  - ✓ Check cashing (98%)
  - ✓ Private showers (89%)
  - ✓ Free parking (93%)
  - ✓ Buses welcome (82%)
  - ✓ Public fax machines (81%)
  - ✓ Restaurants or delis (77%)
  - ✓ Platform scales (59%)
  - ✓ Laundry facilities (58%)
  - ✓ Truck repair (50%)
  - ✓ Emergency road service (63%)
  - ✓ ATM machines (91%)
  - ✓ Security/local police patrol (54%)
  - ✓ Load boards (75%)
  - ✓ Postal service (53%)
  - ✓ Truck washes (28%)
  - ✓ Hotels or motels (28%)
  - ✓ Driver lounges (48%)
  - ✓ Recreational vehicle facilities (23%)
  - ✓ On-site fast food (51%)
  - ✓ Church services (38%)
  - ✓ Food court (15%)
  - ✓ Internet services (39%)"

- "Employment: The typical travel plaza or truck stop employs 75 to 95 individuals. The largest percentage work in restaurants, followed by retail/ convenience stores, administrative offices and maintenance shops.
"Sales: The average travel plaza or truck stop has annual sales of about $7.8 million (median $6.6 million).
"Fuel: NATSO member travel plazas and truck stops average 6.5 diesel islands and 3.0 gasoline islands. A typical fuel stop sells an average of 250,000 gallons of diesel fuel per month, while a typical full-service truck stop sells an average of 1 million gallons per month. Sales of gasoline at fuel stops average 150,000 gallons per month, while sales at full-service truck stops average 100,000 gallons.
"Restaurants: Almost all NATSO travel plazas and truck stops operate a restaurant as part of their facility—90 percent operated by the facility itself, with 10 percent either leased or franchised. The average travel plaza or truck stop restaurant has a seating capacity of 132, with 60 percent of the restaurants designating separate sections for professional drivers. Truckers account for the greatest share of truck stop restaurant business (57 percent), followed by local patrons (26 percent) and tourists (17 percent). The average meal ticket is $4.97.
"Retail Operations: The typical travel plaza or truck stop convenience store or retail store measures 2,100 square feet. The most common retail offering is a combined convenience and retail store (70 percent), followed by in-store fast food, separate retail stores, and separate convenience stores."

> Source: National Association of Truck Stop Operators(NATSO). (The figures in the data above are from an industry survey of 1999, but the information is still of interest).

Expenses as a Percentage of Annual Sales

Cost of goods	63%
Payroll/labor Costs	08%
Occupancy	02% to 03%
Profit (estimated pretax)	04%

Industry Trend

- "There are not many independent truck stops left in the country with Pilot acquiring Flying J and making deals with other operators like Road Ranger to sell their Pilot fuel. It has been said that Pilot alone controls almost 60% of the diesel fuel sales in the United States."
"The trend has been going down due to increased competition and reduced margins. The independents are dropping out because they cannot compete with the major players who are expanding. Many of the independents have overbuilt and cannot compete."
- "Large chains will survive and mom and pops will have to specialize or get out."
- "Very slow growth due to the nature of the business. Large lots of 10+ acres required, and investments upwards of $10+ million per site make the field of players very limited."

Seller Financing

- "Property and land included: 10 to 15 years (8% to 11%)"
- "Business only: 3 to 8 years (8% to 10%)"

Questions

- "Do they own the restaurant or lease it out? What is the environmental situation?
- "Does he have any fuel agreements with any trucking lines? Does he have Fuel Man or similar fuel agreements that would be in place to draw regional or national trucking companies to him? Any hidden income, i.e., video machines, laundry, showers etc.?"
- "As much paperwork as possible including tax returns."
- "When valuing the business be sure to question the Seller about ALL of the sources of income. Most units have income from video games which is very lucrative, but that doesn't make it to the P & L; scale income and do they own the scales or lease them, any contracts with carriers, do they have Mr. Fuel or other recognized fuel discount programs, shower income etc.? The money is still made on the inside so the higher the fuel volume, the more people that visit the facility, the more money they will spend inside. Is the unit branded with Shell, BO, TA etc.? If so how much time is left on the contract with them and what are their costs to them? Who do they buy their fuel from? To purchase fuel you must have a fuel purchase agreement with your supplier and what is the length of the term and the charge for the fuel? Most agreements are for 7–10 years and if it is a branded unit you will be required to pay them back if you do not fulfill the length of the agreement, and this can be very costly. Are there any rebates coming back from the fuel supplier? How much over rack are they charging you? Very important that you know what the cost to buy fuel is. If you are doing 400,000 gallons of fuel per month and you are paying 1 cent over the posted rack price, that is $4,000 per month plus freight to bring it to your facility. The seller will know this and the buyer should know it too."

Resources

Websites

- www.truckernews.com
- www.npnweb.com
- www.aitaonline.com

Associations

- National Association of Truck Stop Operators—an excellent site, full of interesting information and data: www.natso.com

Trucking Companies		
	NAICS 484230	Number of Businesses/Units 507,466

Rules of Thumb

➢ 50 percent of annual sales

➢ 5 times EBIT

➢ 2 to 3 times EBITDA

➢ 1 to 2 times SDE + market value of assets

➢ $4,000 to $6,000 per driver

Pricing Tips

Operating Ratio (EBIT divided by gross sales)

Excellent	85% or less
Good	86% to 92%
Fair	93% to 96%
Poor	97% or greater

Revenues per Mile

Excellent	1.40 or more
Good	1.35 to 1.39
Fair	1.30 to 1.34
Poor	1.29 or less

- "Focus should be on strategic value of the business because most of the times the value has very little to do with current financials"

- "Gross Sales important of course, understand ALL costs involved from licensing, broker (trucking brokers) fees, fuel surcharges, trailer and truck parking and driver salaries are all important to understand. Very Understanding the length of contracts, some contracts are not for actual work, but allow for bids to do the work/deliveries."

- "Special Equipment +15 percent; special services +5 to 25 percent; routes & relationships +10 to 25 percent."

Expert Comments

"This is difficult because of the variations in different types of motor carriers."

Benchmark Data

Statistics (Long-Distance Freight Trucking)

Number of Establishments	311,808
Average Profit Margin	4.9%
Revenue per Employee	$144,100
Average Number of Employees	3.6
Average Wages per Employee	$45,103

Source: IBISWorld, October 2012

Products and Services Segmentation

Truckload carriers	58.8%
Less-than-truckload carriers	31.7%
Other services	9.5%

Source: IBISWorld, October 2012

Major Market Segmentation

Wholesale sector	19.9%
Other	16.4%
Retail sector	11.9%
Oil refiners	6.8%
Chemical companies	4.2%
Agricultural sector	2.6%
Manufacturing sector	38.2%

Source: IBISWorld, October 2012

Industry Costs

Profit	4.9%
Wages	31.2%
Purchases	15.3%
Depreciation	4.7%
Marketing	3.7%
Rent & Utilities	5.8%
Other	34.4%

Source: IBISWorld, October 2012

Market Share

YRC Worldwide Inc.	3.5%
J. B. Hunt Transport Services Inc.	3.1%
Con-way Inc.	2.5%
Swift Transportation	1.6%

Source: IBISWorld, October 2012

Statistics (Local Freight Trucking)

Number of Establishments	195,658
Average Profit Margin	6.4%
Revenue per Employee	$44,300
Average Number of Employees	1.7
Average Wages per Employee	$45,065

Source: IBISWorld, October 2012

Products and Services Segmentation

Truckload services	72.4%
Less-than-truckload services	27.6%

Source: IBISWorld, October 2012

Major Market Segmentation

Manufacturing sector	36.7%
Retail and wholesale sectors	31%
Agricultural sector	12.1%
Other	9.7%
Mining sector	6.7%
Energy sector	3.8%

Source: IBISWorld, October 2012

Industry Costs

Profit	6.4%
Wages	42.9%
Purchases	25.1%
Depreciation	3.8%
Marketing	4.0%
Rent & Utilities	2.9%
Other	14.9%

Source: IBISWorld, October 2012

Market Share

YRC Worldwide Inc.	5.0%
J. B. Hunt Transport Services Inc.	3.5%
Con-way Inc.	3.3%
Swift Transportation	3.0%

Source: IBISWorld, October 2012

Expenses as a Percentage of Annual Sales

Cost of goods	0
Payroll/labor Costs	40% to 60%
Occupancy	0
Profit (estimated pretax)	08% to 15%

Industry Trend

- "Trucking is becoming even more important as internet sales and the need for packages to be moved from place to place increase."
- "In the 1980's there were approximately 300,000 trucking companies. That number has ballooned to over 675,000 carriers currently operating in the US. Additionally the miles driven and the trucks on the road at these carriers have increased. Freight volume shipped by trucks in the US is expected to grow 50% over the next 20 years, and the country's infrastructure will not even come close to keeping up."

Source: www.truckinjurylawyerblog.com

- "The United States has about 1.3 million drivers of long-haul, heavy trucks, roughly 20,000 fewer than needed, according to American Trucking Associations, an industry group based in Alexandria, VA. A 2005 study the Associationscommissioned projects a shortage of 111,000 drivers by 2014, a gap attributed partly to retirements and inadequate recruitment, plus increased demand for trucking."

Source: The Wilmington (NC) *Star-News*, May 13, 2007

Seller Financing

- "2 years, up to 50%. Earn-Outs can work in this industry."

Questions

- "How old are the trucks, who owns the trailers. Where do you park and do you offer warehousing."

Resources

Associations

- America's Independent Truckers Association: www.aitaonline.com

	Franchise
Two Men and a Truck (See also Trucking Companies)	
Approx. Total Investment	$158,000 to $460,910
NAICS 484210	Number of Businesses/Units 210

Rules of Thumb

➤ 40 to 45 percent of annual sales plus inventory

Resources

Websites

- www.twomenandatruck.com

	Franchise
U Save Car & Truck Rental (See also Auto Rental)	
Approx. Total Investment	$60,000 to $681,300
NAICS 532111	Number of Businesses/Units 195

Rules of Thumb

> "10 percent of annual sales (price does not include cost of vehicles, and revenues do not include auto & truck sales)"

Resources

Websites
- www.usave.net

Uniform Rental (See also Hospital Laundry—Supply)

NAICS 812331	Number of Businesses/Units 2,912

Rules of Thumb

> 40 to 45 times weekly sales plus inventory

Pricing Tips
- An industry expert says that if there are contracts with the accounts serviced, the rule of thumb will be 70 percent of gross annual sales.

Benchmark Data

Statistics (Industrial Laundry & Linen Supply)

Number of Establishments	2,912
Average Profit Margin	5.1%

Source: IBISWorld, May 2012

Products and Services Segmentation

Uniform rental and cleaning	33.6%
Linen rental and cleaning	22.6%
Other	16.9%
Linen supply garments rental and cleaning	11.5%
Industrial mats rental and cleaning	11%
Industrial wiping cloths rental and cleaning	4.4%

Source: IBISWorld, May 2012

Major Market Segmentation

Manufacturing	34.2%
Healthcare	25.2%
Hospitality and lodging	17.3%
Government	9.9%
Food services	9.1%
Other industries	4.3%

Source: IBISWorld, May 2012

Industry Costs

Profit	5.1%
Wages	35.3%
Purchases	34.0%
Depreciation	2.3%
Marketing	1.7%
Rent & Utilities	7.0%
Other	14.6%

Source: IBISWorld, May 2012

Market Share

Cintas Corporation	27.2%
Aramark Corporation	11.6%
UniFirst Corporation	8.1%
G&K Services Inc.	5.6%

Source: IBISWorld, May 2012

		Franchise
UPS Store (Mail Boxes, Etc.) (See also Mail & Parcel Centers)		
Approx. Total Investment		$150,196 to $371,022
	NAICS 561431	Number of Businesses/Units 4,705

Rules of Thumb

➤ 35 to 40 percent of annual sales plus inventory

➤ 2 to 3 times SDE plus inventory

➤ "Franchises will sell for higher % of Annual Gross Sales. High volume UPS stores sell for over 1 times annual sales. (STR Subject to Royalty)"

Resources

Websites

▪ www.theupsstore.com

Used Goods		
(See also Clothing Stores—Used, Consignment Shops, & Resale Shops)		
	NAICS 45331	Number of Businesses/Units 84,174

Rules of Thumb

➤ 20 to 25 percent of annual sales plus inventory unless it is on consignment

Benchmark Data

Statistics (Used Goods Stores)

Number of Establishments	84,174
Average Profit Margin	5.3%
Revenue per Employee	$69,400
Average Number of Employees	2.5%
Average Wages per Employee	$14,81

Source: IBISWorld, July 2012

Products and Services Segmentation

Women's wear	19%
Children's products	16%
Furniture	14%
Kitchenware and home furnishings	10%
Books	8%
Men's wear	8%
Jewelry	4%
Other	21%

Source: IBISWorld, July 2012

Industry Costs

Profit	5.3%
Wages	20.3%
Purchases	54.9%
Depreciation	1.1%
Marketing	1.2%
Rent & Utilities	6.8%
Other	10.4%

Source: IBISWorld, July 2012

Market Share

Goodwill Industries International Inc.	21.5%
Winmark Corporation	5.9%
The Salvation Army National Corporation	3.9%

Source: IBISWorld, July 2012

Franchise

Valpak Direct Marketing Systems

(See also Coupon Books & SuperCoups)

Approx. Total Investment	$32,500 to $1,500,000
NAICS 541870	Number of Businesses/Units 170

Rules of Thumb

➤ 40 to 45 percent of annual sales plus inventory

➤ 2 times SDE plus inventory

➤ "If a cooperative direct mail business, such as Money Mailer or Supercoups is making $100,000, it could be sold for $150,000 to $225,000, and $250,000 if it was a perfect situation. Now, on the other hand if it is a Valpak, I believe you could get up to 3 times what it is making because Valpak is the undisputed leader. They are owned by COX Publishing ..."

Resources

Websites

▪ www.valpak.com

Franchise

Valvoline Instant Oil Change (See also Auto Lube/Tune-up)

Approx. Total Investment	$178,000 to $1,739,000
NAICS 811191	Number of Businesses/Units 760

Rules of Thumb

➤ 50 percent of annual sales

Resources

Websites

▪ www.viocfranchise.com

776

Vending Machine Industry (See also Routes)

SIC 2599-02	NAICS 454210	Number of Businesses/Units 30,111

Rules of Thumb

➢ 65 to 75 percent of annual sales plus inventory

➢ 2 to 3 times SDE plus inventory

➢ 3 to 4 times EBIT

➢ 2 to 3 times EBITDA

➢ "Smaller, one-man operations sell for less than one year's gross sales. Larger vending businesses are based on cash flow and asset value. A common rule of thumb would be 1 to 2 times SDE plus assets. Again, companies with new assets would be closer to 2 times SDE plus hard assets."

➢ "Listing price should be less than 1 year's gross. Some vending businesses are heavy in assets, so assets plus 1 to 1½ times cash flow. Highly profitable may sell for 2 to 3 times cash flow."

Pricing Tips

- "Routes grossing less than $200k typically go for 2X SDE; Routes grossing more than $200k typically go for between 2X-3X SDE; Routes grossing over $500k for 3X SDE"
- "Type of vending (bulk vs. full line vs. crane, etc. >0; are machines owned; age of equipment; commissions paid to customers"
- "Age of equipment and accounts under contract are value factors"
- "Price could be 70 to 80 percent of last year's sales if business is well established."
- "New equipment"
- "Take a pricing survey of what is sold...soda selling for less than $1 or candy selling for less than .75 is not good."
- "Are machines owned or leased? How new are they? Are any customer contracts in place? Commissions paid to customers and how much."
- "Major factors involved in pricing a route include: (1) Where the route is located; (2) What is the year & condition of the vehicle included? (3) Is the truck owned or leased? (4) How many years the route is established; (5) Is the route protected stops, territory or is it an unprotected route? (6) What is the brand of the product that the route is distributing? (7) How close to the depot is the route? (8) Value of equipment included (vending machines, validators, step-climbing hand trucks, coin & bill counters?)"
- "How much does a route cost? The net profit of the route is the main factor in determining its value. Other significant factors include the type of route, the gross, the area, days and hours, and the vehicle. A general rule to keep in mind for the purchase of a route is 'double net.' The amount that you net in one year will be the approximate down payment amount, and double that figure will be the total purchase price. (Example: route netting $1,000/wk. would cost approximately $100,000 with $50,000 down.) As a rule of thumb, the bigger the name a brand route is, the more the route will cost. Independent routes and service routes, on the other hand, cost usually 1 to 1 ½ year's net as opposed to 2 years' net (double net)."

Source: Mr. Route, www.mrrouteinc.com—a very informative Web site

- "These factors will also influence price determination: ownership status of the machines coming with the sale; are they leased, owned, financed; the type of machines that the route consists of and the service schedule that they would need to have the machines produce income (sandwiches need daily servicing … soda/snacks many need weekly servicing); the locale of the machines … inside, outside, 24-hour access, limited access; is the commission paid to accounts above the normal 10% to 15%?"

- "As in all businesses, the size of the business, the value of the equipment and the provable cash flow by the business must be considered. It is difficult to value this type of business on cash flow basis alone."
- "Ratios of investment dollars (borrowed or asset) and estimated length of return"
- "Caution should always be prime in price of equipment, location risk, and percentage of payouts."

Expert Comments

"Risk is low as machines can be relocated to more profitable locations. Replication difficult due to high cost of equipment and marketing to secure good locations. Industry trend will parallel the economy-as the economy improves, companies hire more people increasing the number of breakroom customers for the machines. Opposite is true as well."

"De-industrialization, c-store competition are factors"

"It is a relatively easy business to enter, but its potential for growth is limited (mostly due to increasing product costs versus consumer resistance to higher vending prices)."

"The vending industry (at least in the metro New York area) is dominated by several large companies. However, the market usually views this business as being a 'good part-time,' making it generally a highly desirable business opportunity."

Benchmark Data

Statistics (Vending Machine Operators)

Number of Establishments	30,111
Average Profit Margin	5.0%
Revenue per Employee	$108,000
Average Number of Employees	2.3
Average Wages per Employee	$19,072

Source: IBISWorld, August 2012

Products and Services Segmentation

Soft drinks	40.4%
Food	39.8%
Other	17.2%
Toys	1.0%
Games	0.9%
Tobacco products	0.7%

Source: IBISWorld, August 2012

Major Market Segmentation

Manufacturing sites	27.3%
Schools and colleges	16.0%
Other	15.0%
Offices	14.7%
Hospitals and nursing homes	12.2%
Retail sites	8.0%
Military bases	6.8%

Source: IBISWorld, August 2012

Industry Costs

Profit	5.0%
Wages	28.8%
Purchases	45.6%
Depreciation	3.1%
Marketing	1.0%
Rent & Utilities	1.1%
Other	15.4%

Source: IBISWorld, August 2012

Market Share

Compass Group PLC	11.9%
Aramark Corporation	11.7%

Source: IBISWorld, August 2012

Operator Sales

Size	Revenue Range	% of 2010 Operators	Projected 2010 sales	% of 2010 sales
Small	under $1M	77%	$1.65 B	9%
Medium	$1M to $4.9M	15%	1.1 B	6%
Large	$5M to $9.9M	5%	2.38B	13%
Extra Large	$10M+	3%	13.17 B	72.0%
Total			$18.3Billion	

Does not include 5 percent of total industry revenue for machines owned and operated by locations.

Source: Automatic Merchandiser, AMonline.com, August 2011

Machines by Location

Manufacturing	26.8%
Offices	28.5%
Hotels/motels	4.7%
Restaurants, bars, clubs	1.3%
Retail sites	9.1%
Hospitals, nursing homes	8.8%
Schools, colleges	12.7%
Military bases	0.4%
Correctional facilities	0.9%
Other	7.0%

Source: Automatic Merchandiser/AMonline.com, August 2011

- "Route average $8,000 to $10,000 per week"
- "Bulk machines should sell at least $100 per month/per location to be considered viable; soda machines should vend at least four cases per week to be considered viable, and snack machines should produce a minimum of $50 per week/per location to be viable."
- "Gross sales in vending businesses are directly related to the number of employees per location. A few locations with 100 or more employees normally make for a good business."
- "Profit depends on volume and percentage paid to customer providing space & power."

Industry Profitability

Item	<$1M	$1–$3M	$3–$5M	$5–$10M	>$10M
Sales	100%	100%	100%	100%	100%
Product Cost	50%	49.9%	47.4%	47.5%	44.5%
Gross Margin	50%	50.1%	52.6%	52.5%	55.5%
Labor Costs	22.6%	22.6%	21.8%	23.8%	21.7%
Commissions	5.2%	6.4%	8.0%	7.6%	10.1%
Other Costs	24.7%	19.9%	19.2%	18.1%	18.4%
Op. Profit	(2.5%)	1.2%	3.6%	3.0%	5.3%

Expenses as a Percentage of Annual Sales

Cost of goods	35% to 45%
Payroll/labor Costs	25% to 30%
Occupancy	10%
Profit (estimated pretax)	15% to 20%

Industry Trend

- "NAMA said this year's State of the Industry Report (SOIR), recently released in Automatic Merchandiser, indicates that a turnaround in the industry may be coming sooner than expected.

  "Industry research from NAMA (the national trade association for the vending and refreshment services industry) revealed that Gen Y is an ideal target for the industry because these consumers prefer vending over convenience, grocery and drug stores for snacks and cold beverages, and because they enjoy machines that offer a tech-based experience. These findings are from a NAMA quantitative research study among users and non-users of vending conducted by Synovate Inc."

  Source: "NAMA: Vending Industry Report Indicates Turnaround May Be in Store," www.tmcnet.com, August 2012

- "Fiscal 2009 marked the biggest 1-year decline in vending sales and the first double-digit drop in the industry's recorded history. According to the Automatic Merchandiser State of the Vending Industry Report, vending sales fell 10 percentage points in 2009, sending aggregate sales to just below the $20 billion mark.

  Medium-size vendors hurt the most.

  "The medium-size operators, those with $1 million to $5 million in annual sales, continued to lose sales to small (under $1 million) and large ($5 million to $10 million) competitors in 2009, as indicated in chart 2. Where medium-size operators once did more aggregate sales than large operators, the overhead for a medium-size operation has increased to the point that more sales are necessary to cover the overhead."

  Source: "The Great Recession has led to the Great Restructuring," www.VendingMarketWatch.com July, 2010

- "Growing in popularity as more individuals look for secondary sources of income"
- "Current trend is down"

Seller Financing

- "50% financed for 3-5 years.
- "3 to 5 years. A seller will need to carry for a longer period if the cash flow is low and assets high. Could carry for 5 to 7 years—10 percent interest."

Questions

- "Are machines owned or leased? How new are they? Ask for maintenance records? Commissions paid out & how they are paid out (by check, cash, monthly, etc.)"
- "What are your vend prices? Are you third party with Coke and/or Pepsi? Are your machines DEX capable? How many machines and locations do you have? Do you pay commission on any accounts?"
- "Accounts by size?"
- "Head count at the particular location & permissible servicing time for each account."

- "Do you have contracts?"
- "How many people work at a location? How close are accounts? Are commissions paid to all or some customers? Do you pay commissions to accounts; do machines carry perishable food stuffs?"
- "Will seller finance the deal? Lenders do not want to own a lot of vending machines in case the loan would go bad."

Resources

Websites
- www.vendingmarketwatch.com—excellent site

Trade Publications
- Automatic Merchandiser—www.vendingmarketwatch.com/magazine/
- Vending Times: www.vendingtimes.com

Associations
- National Automatic Merchandising Association (NAMA)—good site with lots of educational informational: www.vending.org
- Amusement & Music Operators Association (AMOA): www.amoa.com

Veterinary Hospitals

Rules of Thumb

➤ 65 to 70 percent of annual revenues plus inventory

Veterinary Practices

SIC 0742-01	NAICS 541940	Number of Businesses/Units 40,921

Rules of Thumb

➤ 70 to 75 percent of annual sales includes inventory

➤ 2 to 3 times SDE for small-animal practices includes inventory

➤ 2 to 3 times EBIT

➤ 3 times EBITDA

➤ "Usually 70 to 80 percent of past 12 months' gross revenues [sales] (includes tangible and intangible assets)"

Pricing Tips
- "The price will be skewed downward for mixed animal and large animal practices. The absence of a nearby emergency clinic would have a depressing effect on the sale price of a practice. A practice generating a profit lower than a competitive full-time veterinarian salary will be valued downward."
- "Ranges from 40% - 80% depending on cash flow, condition of equipment and location. Often smaller practice grossing under $300,000 have much lower value. Offices grossing over $700,000 could attain a premium in price."
- "Type of vet practice is important. Small-animal (dog/cat) sell well as do ER practices. Large- or mixed-animal practice can be tougher to sell. Mobile

practices, and racetrack equine practices have little to no transferable goodwill value. Examine profit centers other than professional services; many practices have boarding/kennels, grooming, drug wholesaling, retail, pet food, or acupuncture/chiropractic components.These have lower profit margins than profession vet med services. Must adjust for this."

- "Examine the client/patient profile: small-animal vs. large-animal. Look for ancillary services such as boarding and/or grooming. Retail (food/supplies) and insurance can be significant."
- "Sale price ratios very wide above/below average. Common range is 40%–100% of gross."
- "Rural and small offices have lower values"
- "Multiples are based on offices doing $500K or more. Smaller offices and ones over $1 million will have values based on assets alone or on excess earnings."
- "Larger practices usually apply a higher multiple."
- "Wide range of sales prices compared to gross income. Typically 60%–80%, but might be as wide as 50%–100%. Practices grossing over $750K tend to sell for more...75%–80% average. This is for asset sale and includes inventory."
- "Average is 72% of gross. Wide variance of plus/minus 35%. Higher grossing practices & multidoctor practices tend to sell for more than solo practice. Practices grossing under $350K difficult to sell (not enough cash flow). Large-animal, mixed, and equine-only practices may have little transferable goodwill."
- "Small-animal practices sell for 1.5 to 3.0 SDE. Other types of veterinary practices sell for varying amounts, and market demand varies."
- "Inventory included in the sale is usually a working level or 30-day supply. Most sales are asset sales and include equipment, furniture, removable fixtures, working levels of consumable inventory, and intangibles (goodwill)."
- "Small-animal (i.e. dog/cat) practices grossing under $500K sell for about 72% of gross. Practices grossing over $500K tend to sell for about 76% of gross. There is about +-35% variability in sales price due to various factors: profit margin, equipment, inventory, practice type, location, etc. SDE for average practice is 30%–35% of gross. Better practices have SDE 36%–40%. Well-managed practices can have SDE of 41%–48%, but these are a small percentage of practices. Large-animal, mixed-animal, equine, ER practices are harder to sell because there are fewer buyers. Mobile practices and ambulatory equine practices tend to have very little transferable goodwill value. Statistical income/expense data can be purchased from American Veterinary Medical Association, and American Animal Hospital Association."
- "Small-animal practices typically sell for 50%–70% of revenues. Other types of practice vary significantly due to demand and resale/retail activity. Sales prices can appear independent of revenues and profitability. Demand for urban practices greater than rural practices."
- "Range 50% to 90% of gross revenues; 1.5 to 3.0 SDE. Multi-doctor, small-animal practices in urban areas bring higher prices than most others. Mixed practice (large and small animal) are very difficult to sell as there are few buyers and they are generally less profitable. The above rules of thumb are probably inappropriate for mixed or large-animal practices."
- "Small-animal practices are much easier to sell than larger animal practices. Most small animal practices grossing less than $500K will be sold for 50 to 70 percent of gross revenue. Small animal practices grossing more than $500K will sell for 70 to 90 percent of gross revenue. Large, or predominately large, animal practices with significant retail/resale/dispensing activity will be discounted significantly from what small-animal practices sell for, due to limited market and low profitability."

- "Small-animal clinics in good locations can command premium prices. Generally, these practices can sell for 75 to 125 percent of the last year's revenues for the goodwill, equipment, and supplies."

Expert Comments

"Doctors are able to obtain 100% financing to buy or start-up an office. A DVM license is required, but the hospital can be owned by a non-licensed professional in most states. However, offices are not suited for investment / absentee ownership unless the gross is well above $1 million dollars."

"Long-term growth industry. For small-animal practices fairly low risk. Practices in metro areas sell well. Hard to sell in many rural locations. Good financing up to 100% if px cash flows."

"Vet school is very difficult to get in to. Boomers are selling their practices."

"Many practices owned by baby boomers are being transferred to recent graduates; usually with a buyout."

"Competition is keen in most urban areas with significant investment required for facilities, equipment, drugs and supplies needed. Profitability is trending lower due to increased costs of care and decreasing revenues in a challenging economic environment. Facilities vary by location. There are fewer buyers today wanting to purchase veterinary practices and this is due to changes in attitudes regarding business ownership and greater emphasis on quality-of-life issues. Great opportunities exist in many rural areas for those desiring large-animal and mixed-animal practice opportunities."

"Female veterinarians numbered close to 45,000, while male veterinarians numbered just over 43,000. In another trend, more veterinarians are becoming specialists."

"Goodwill for dog/cat day practices tends to transfer pretty well. Specialty practices may not transfer as well. Gross trend has been up (10.7% avg.), except for 2009 with economic downturn. Many practices are flat or down in gross income."

"Fairly good market for profitable small-animal practices"

"Fewer young veterinarians desire their own business. The costs of veterinary practice are increasing."

"Stable pet care market but more competition for the discretionary dollars used to underwrite the cost of care. Costs to provide services are increasing."

"Risk is low. Loan default rates very low. Can get up to 100% financing. Cost of entry for vet practice is higher than for human medical practice."

"Competition varies by location. Most urban areas are well represented. Huge opportunity exists in rural areas. Demand for services is good. Business risk is relatively low for those purchasing established profitable practices. Profit trend is up as demand for services increases and veterinarians are charging better for their services. Facilities vary significantly depending upon practice. Many older practices are outdated and need upgrades. Demand for practices for purchase is decreasing. This is especially true for practices with limited revenues and rural nature."

"Easier to sell because of 100% financing. General industry growth."

"Some states now allow non-vets to own vet practices, providing that the licensed vet runs the medical practice."

Benchmark Data

Statistics (Veterinary Services)

Number of Establishments	40,921
Average Profit Margin	10.0%
Revenue per Employee	$101,700
Average Number of Employees	7.6
Average Wages per Employee	$34,478

Source: IBISWorld, August 2012

Products and Services Segmentation

Routine veterinary services	20%
Diagnostics	19.5%
Surgical procedures	18%
Vaccinations	15.5%
Product sales	13.5%
Non-invasive procedures	12%
Other	1.5%

Source: IBISWorld, August 2012

Major Market Segmentation

Households with children	35%
Households without children	30%
Owners of food animals	9.5%
Colleges or universities	8.5%
Other public and private clients	8%
Owners of equine animals	5%
Federal, state or local government	4%

Source: IBISWorld, August 2012

Industry Costs

Profit	10.0%
Wages	37.6%
Purchases	35.0%
Depreciation	2.0%
Marketing	4.5%
Rent & Utilities	6.5%
Other	4.4%

Source: IBISWorld, August 2012

Market Share

VCA Antech Inc.	5.7%%

Source: IBISWorld, August 2012

Private Clinical Practice	Percent of Total 2009 Earnings	Median Professional Income Before Taxes
Food animal exclusive	1.8%	$103,000
Food animal predominant	6.3%	$91,000
Mixed animal	7.0%	$85,000
Companion animal predominant	9.7%	$91,000
Companion animal exclusive	67.3%	$97,000
Equine	6.1%	$85,000
Other	1.8%	$79.000
Total Private Practice	100%	$97,000

Source: "U.S. Veterinarians—2010" www.avma.org/reference/marketstats.asp February 2011

- "A full-time doctor should generate in excess of $550,000 annual revenue. 1,200 active clients per full-time doctor. 28 new clients per month per full-time doctor."
- "Major expenses: Rent 6-12% depending on city and area Labor (excluding

doctors): 15- 22% Medical supplies/ costs of goods: 20% Profit (before doctor salaries): 20%-30% Profit after doctor salaries: 10% (provided office has sufficient gross revenue)."

- "Good benchmark data from AVMA and AAHA. Can be purchased for $100–$200. Staff, drugs, and rent expense are 3 biggest expenses."
- "Key Facts
  - ✓ Competition in this industry is medium.
  - ✓ Volatility is low (revenue fluctuations less than 3 points.)
  - ✓ The life-cycle stage is growth.
  - ✓ The top 1 player accounts for 5% of industry revenue: VCA Antech, Inc. 4.6%
  - ✓ The U.S. Veterinary Services industry is expected to generate revenue of $29.3 billion and employ 315,963 people in 2010.
  - ✓ Overall, 80% of total industry revenue is estimated to be derived from providing care to dogs and cats and other small animals. According to the American Pet Products Manufacturers Association's 2009-10 National Pet Owners Survey, 62% of U.S. households had at least one pet (compared with 56% of U.S. households in 1988)."
- "Sales per FT Vet = $300 to $500k"
- "Small-animal practice SDE is typically 25%–35% today. Other types of veterinary practices tend to be lower."
- "30% profit with revenue over $600,000."
- "SDE of 30%–35% typical. 35%–40% above average. Over 40% very good. Biggest expenses are usually, salary 32%, drugs 15%–17%, rent 5%–9%."
- "Profit after accounting for a reasonable return on professional labor or reasonable salary for the doctor's efforts should be 10%–20%."
- "Practice should gross about $400K–$5450K per FTE DVM."
- "Today, the practice is devoted 100 percent to small animals, mostly dogs and cats, Tucker [Robert Tucker, veterinarian, co-owner of Concord Animal Hospital, Concord, MA] said. 'Many of the families we see have several pets.' Some 2,500 dogs and 2,500 cats are treated every year, he said. "Because many clients don't have animal health insurance, 'we try to charge what's reasonable,' he said, pointing out that fees range from less than $50 for a routine office visit to more than $1,000 for a major procedure."
- "Income/DVM: $402K; Avg. Transaction Charge: $83; Avg. staff/DVM: 3.5; Rent: 5%–9% Drug expense: 15%–18%; Non-DVM staff expense: 21%; 1600–2000 SF typical facility size for sole practice."
- "Sales per full-time employed doctor in small-animal practice is $350,000 to $500,000."
- "Seller's discretionary cash flow typically is 30%–35% for small-animal practices. Other types of practice vary with degree of retail/resale activity."
- "3.4 employees per FTE veterinarian"
- "Vet wages should be approximately 23% of gross vet professional fees generated."
- "Revenues of $250,000 to $500,000/doctor typical. Compensation of doctors should be 20% to 25% of revenue production. High end of this range if managing practice; lower end if just being a doctor."

Expenses as a Percentage of Annual Sales

Cost of goods	15% to 20%
Payroll/labor Costs	20% to 30%
Occupancy	05% to 10%
Profit (estimated pretax)	20% to 30%

Industry Trend

- "The trend will continue toward larger practices with more upscale facilities."
- "Stable trends with near term flat growth. Last 2 years many offices experience down trends due to the economy."
- "Positive. Some slowdown with economy but now holding their own"
- "Boomers selling, younger vets seem to prefer working for another owner rather than taking on the burden of debt to start or buy a practice."
- "Continued decreases in numbers of potential buyers and greater number of practices coming on the market as 'baby boomer' doctors retire."
- "Good stable revenue. Smaller offices exhibit downward pressure on values."
- "An increase in consumer demand for better access, convenience, technology, diagnosis, and feedback will continue to shape veterinary practices."
- "More women DVMs. General industry growth."
- Fewer young veterinarians want to own practices and many older veterinarians are approaching retirement age. Many smaller or unprofitable practices will close or liquidate."
- "Good demand for services. Demand for veterinary practices decreasing as young doctors prefer to be employed rather than own their own practice. Demographics of young doctors changing as graduating classes are commonly 60%–80% female."

Seller Financing

- "Specialty lenders off 100% financing. Sellers may carry up to 20% usually for 10 yrs. Real estate portion may be 25 years"
- "Financing can be 100% (no down payment) with 7- to 10-year notes if credit is good."
- "10 years"

Questions

- "Gross hours worked, type of patients seen, and percentage mix; ancillary profit centers support staff info; number active clients in last 2 years"
- "What is the turnover rate, large vs. small animal, surgery vs. treatment, retail sales, inventory size, payroll costs."
- "Ask what medical services they do not provide that could be added"
- "Review cash flow. Check conditional use permits. Fees schedule and list of procedures."
- "What percentages of revenues are from: vaccines, surgery, boarding, retail sales and grooming?"
- "Are they willing to sign a covenant not to compete? Can they work in the practice after the sale? How was price arrived at and justified? What is the value of the real estate and how was the price arrived at? What is being sold for the asked price? How many hours per week are worked by the owner/ doctor? How are emergencies calls covered?"
- "At least 5 years of financial statements and tax returns, current detailed depreciation schedule, practice management and production reports, and payroll and staffing information to begin analysis. Then follow up information and details. Site visit is extremely informative!"
- "# hours worked/week; ancillary profit centers (grooming, boarding); non-Western therapy procedures (i.e., acupuncture, chiropractic, holistic); type of practice (small, mixed, large, equine, ER, referral, mobile)?"
- "Be sure to understand how the price was determined and be sure cash flows allow for a reasonable salary after debt. Be sure the seller agrees to a

covenant not to compete where legal."
- "Type of practice (small, mixed, large, equine)? Gross? Hours worked each week? Any significant grooming/boarding? Do associates have noncompetes?"
- "Gross income? # Full time equivalent DVMs? Hrs/week worked by DVMs? Production $ of each DVM? % of revenue from non-tradition western therapy professional services (i.e., chiropractic, acupuncture, grooming, kennel)? # exam rooms? Any large clients? (i.e., humane society, corporate cattle ranches, breeders)"
- "Will they agree to covenant not to compete? If financing, how much down money is desired? Will they stay on after sale for transition? What assets are they selling? How much inventory is included in the sale?"
- "Standard recasting info for sellers. Types of surgery performed? 1 or 3 vaccination schedule? Relationship with local shelters/humane societies? How are emergencies handled?"

Resources

Websites
- Vet Quest Classifieds: www.vetquest.com
- www.vin.com

Trade Publications
- DVM Magazine: www.veterinarynews.dvm360.com/
- Veterinary Economics: www.veterinarynews.dvm360.com/
- Veterinary Practice News: www.veterinarypracticenews.com/

Associations
- American Animal Hospital Association: www.aahanet.org

Video Stores

SIC 7841-02	NAICS 451220	Number of Businesses/Units 9,053

Rules of Thumb

➤ Most buyers want to recover their investment within 24 months, so 2 times SDE is a safe bet, including inventory.

➤ "It used to be one year's SDE plus the fair market value of the tapes and games, but inventory drops in value too dramatically after the 'new release' prime period (90 days) has passed."

➤ "1 to 2 times SDE to a working owner plus fair market value for videos, games & DVDs"

➤ .65 to 1.0 annual revenues plus inventory

Pricing Tips

- "I have sold more mom-and-pop video stores in the state of Georgia than anyone else. But these stores are not coming on the market very frequently, and when they do, they typically are making very little money if any. This, of course makes them unsaleable. The video industry is primarily composed of the chains like Blockbuster, Hollywood Video, etc."

- "The inventory price of the videos and games drops drastically from its original retail. Unit prices can be as low as $5.00 or less."
- "If the current owner can computer-generate a video rental report that shows you how many times each video in inventory has been rented and the income associated with it, you will see how much 'dead inventory' could be replaced to increase revenues. Special- interest videos and games like Nintendo and PlayStation 2, etc. would be good profit generators."

Expert Comments

"The industry has changed with the switch to games."

Benchmark Data

Statistics (DVD, Game & Video Rental)

Number of Establishments	9,053
Average Profit Margin	2.7%
Revenue per Employee	$84,300
Average Number of Employees	6.8
Average Wages per Employee	$14,476

Source: IBISWorld, May 2012

Products and Services Segmentation

Kiosk rentals	41.4%
Subscription-based rentals	33.2%
Brick and mortar rentals	20.4%
Other products and services	5%

Source: IBISWorld, May 2012

Industry Costs

Profit	2.7%
Wages	17.4%
Purchases	54.2%
Depreciation	1.8%
Marketing	12.3%
Rent & Utilities	2.0%
Other	9.6%

Source: IBISWorld, May 2012

Market Share

Coinstar Inc.	36.8%
Dish Network Corporation Inc.	12.6%
Netflix Inc.	16.8%

Source: IBISWorld, May 2012

- "Retail: The report provides an update on the industry's leading retailers including Amazon, Best Buy, DISH, GameStop, Hastings, Redbox, Netflix, Target and more.

"The rental business models for consumer spending in 2011 are projected to be 22% in traditional stores, 50% through subscription and 28% at kiosks."
Source: "Annual Industry Report," vsda.org

- "Stores should have well-stocked concession areas including popcorn, candy, soft drinks. They should be close to cash registers."

Expenses as a Percentage of Annual Sales

Cost of goods	33%
Payroll/labor Costs	27%
Occupancy	15%
Profit (estimated pretax)	25%

Industry Trend

- "The future of the traditional home-video store looks bleaker than ever. Rentals of movies from DVD-by-mail services like Netflix and kiosks run by Redbox and newer startups have surpassed the number of films borrowed from stores operated by the likes of Blockbuster for the first time, according to NPD Group. "Netflix and other subscription services comprised 41% of video rental turns in the third quarter of 2010, followed by kiosk rentals at 31%, and in-store rentals at 27%, the research firm said."
  Source: "NPD report says customers prefer mail, kiosks" by Marc Graser, January 18, 2011
- "Redbox, meanwhile, which will operate more than 30,000 kiosks by the end of the year, according to Arrington, now represents 18.9 percent of the market."
  Source: "Video rental stores play final reels" by Taryn Plumb, *Boston Sunday Globe*, December 12, 2010

Seller Financing

- "12 to 24 months"
- "3 years"

Resources

Associations
- Entertainment Merchants Association: www.entmerch.org

Visa/Passport Companies

	NAICS 561510	

Rules of Thumb

➢ 3 times EBITDA for small to midsized operations, 4.5 times EBITDA for larger ones.

Pricing Tips

- "Total number of applications processed year over year (up or down?)"
- "Due to new U.S. Government requirements, this industry multiple has increased."

Expert Comments

"This industry deals as expeditors of government travel documents."

Questions

- "How do they execute quick turnaround? How long does it take them to fulfill applications?"

Waste Collection

NAICS 56211	Number of Businesses/Units 8,878

Rules of Thumb
- ➢ 95 percent of annual sales
- ➢ 3 times SDE
- ➢ 5 times EBIT
- ➢ 4 times EBITDA

Pricing Tips
- "For a company with predictable repeat earnings with service contracts, eleven (11) times the last twelve months' revenue. For a company involved in the construction industry, there may be a holdback of an amount multiple to adjust for homebuilder risk. The most valued are ongoing commercial accounts, which might have an adjustment or an earnout up or down. The best buyers are the 'big boys' in waste management."
- "Eleven times gross earnings for the last twelve months"

Expert Comments
"This has been a very difficult business dominated by a few large companies."

Benchmark Data

Statistics (Waste Collection Services)
Number of Establishments	8,878
Average Profit Margin	9.4%
Revenue per Employee	$262,700
Average Number of Employees	20.7
Average Wages per Employee	$45,010

Source: IBISWorld, September 2012

Products and Services Segmentation
Non-residential waste collection services	28.2%
Residential waste collection services	21.7%
Transfer facility services	12.2%
Recyclable material collection services	7.8%
Other	30.1%

Source: IBISWorld, September 2012

Major Market Segmentation
Commercial and business firms	37%
Municipal government and individuals	32%
Industrial firms	19%
Construction and demolition firms	12%

Source: IBISWorld, September 2012

Industry Costs
Profit	9.4%
Wages	17.5%
Purchases	8.5%
Depreciation	10.5%
Marketing	1.0%
Rent & Utilities	3.0%
Other	50.1%

Source: IBISWorld, September 2012

Market Share

Waste Management Inc.	29.9%
Republic Services Inc.	18.1%

Source: IBISWorld, September 2012

Expenses as a Percentage of Annual Sales

Cost of goods	20%
Payroll/labor Costs	50%
Occupancy	05%
Profit (estimated pretax)	25%

Industry Trend

- "Growing by leaps with no bounds"

Water Companies		
	NAICS 22131	Number of Businesses/Units 53,000

Rules of Thumb

➤ "The market price varies greatly, between $75 and $150 per metered customer. The normal meter hookup charge is approximately $100. These are not saleable unless they have a minimum of 250 customers with growth potential."

		Franchise
We The People (Legal Document Preparation)		
Approx. Total Investment		$123,200 to $169,500
	NAICS 561410	Number of Businesses/Units 100

Rules of Thumb

➤ 85 percent of annual sales plus inventory

Resources

Websites

- www.wethepeopleusa.com

Web-Based Companies

Rules of Thumb

➤ "Right now it's 2 times SDE maximum or asset liquidation value. ISP's are being sold for 3 – 6 times monthly gross sales."

Pricing Tips

- "It depends on if there is any profit. If there is, about 2 times SDE."

Seller Financing

- "Very short—2 to 4 years"

Wedding Stores (See Bridal Shops)

Weight Loss Services/Centers

SIC 7299-34	NAICS 81219	Number of Businesses/Units 27,237

Rules of Thumb

➢ 50 to 55 percent of annual sales

Benchmark Data

Statistics (Weight Loss Services)

Number of Establishments	27,237
Average Profit Margin	11.4%
Revenue per Employee	$54,600
Average Number of Employees	1.9
Average Wages per Employee	$14,422

Source: IBISWorld, October 2012

Products and Services Segmentation

Weight loss services	60.6%
Merchandise sales	38.7%
Other	0.7%

Source: IBISWorld, October 2012

Industry Costs

Profit	11.4%
Wages	26.6%
Purchases	20.0%
Depreciation	1.0%
Marketing	16.0%
Rent & Utilities	5.2%
Other	19.8%

Source: IBISWorld, October 2012

Market Share

Weight Watchers International Inc.	39.4%
NutriSystem Inc.	15.1%
Nestle SA	11.6%

Source: IBISWorld, October 2012

Industry Trend

- "The latest figures from Marketdata, Inc., which analyses ten major segments of the US diet industry, put the current annual total at $58 billion spent on weight-loss products and services. In a 393-page study entitled: 'The US Weight Loss & Diet Control Market (9th edition),' Marketdata projects 6 percent annual growth for total US weight loss market, to $68.7 billion by 2010, followed thereafter by lower overall growth.

  "The analysis includes ten major segments of the US diet industry: diet drugs, diet books and exercise videos, diet soft drinks, artificial sweeteners, diet dinner entrees and meal replacements, health clubs, diet websites, commercial chains, hospital, RD and MD-based programs, kid's weight loss camps and bariatric surgeries. Of these, diet soft drinks gets the largest share at 29.5 percent and was worth $19 billion in 2006. Bariatric surgeries reached record levels with a total of 177,000 in 2006, representing a $4.4 billion market.

Prescription diet drugs claimed $459 million of the 2006 market. Among diet companies, market leaders are Weight Watchers ($1.2 billion), NutriSystem ($568 million), LA Weight Loss ($500 million), Jenny Craig ($462 million), Slim-Fast ($310 million), and Herbalife ($271 million)."

Source: "Weight loss market to reach $58 Billion." www.healthyweightnetwork.com

Wholesale/Distribution — Durable Goods

NAICS 423	

Rules of Thumb

➢ 4 times EBITDA

➢ 2 to 2.5 times SDE plus inventory

Pricing Tips

- "Worth approximately one-half of sales volume; watch out for large, stale inventory."
- "% of annual gross sales is a poor guide to follow. EBITDA drives ROI and ability to service debt."
- "Add cost of replacing current ownership with professional management to SDE, and then multiply this number by 4 to 6 to get price. Variance is for security of earnings, competition, assets, etc."

Expert Comments

"There are significant competitive cost barriers to entry into this industry, where size does matter along with quantity and quality of product lines, adequate logistical distribution channels, good supplier pricing and terms, adequate facilities sizing and location. Solid, well-diversified customer base mitigates risk and wards off competitive challenges."

Benchmark Data

- "Cost of goods should be less than 74%, with 70% as ideal; operating expenses of less than 20%; sales/assets ratio of 3.0; W/C ratio of 13% to 15% of revenues; current ratio of 3.0 or greater; A/R turnover ratio of 12.0; inventory turns of 6.0 or greater; sales per employee greater than $250,000; sales per sq. ft. in excess of $300,000."

Expenses as a Percentage of Annual Sales

Cost of goods	70% to 72%
Payroll/labor Costs	15% to 20%
Occupancy	03% to 08%
Profit (estimated pretax)	08% to 15%

Industry Trend

- "Self-service options will change the way you do business with customers and transform your sales force. Customers will roam online, searching for information and taking over more of the pre-sales and transactional activities typically handled by their wholesaler-distributors. Distributors will not have a lock on information needed by customers to make purchasing and sourcing decisions, since manufacturers and online sources will make such information readily available.

"In response, wholesaler-distributors of all sizes will complement their traditional selling methods with online technologies. Wholesaler-distributors will catch up to larger companies by 2008, as the costs and complexity of today's technologies drop.

"Customer self-service will also significantly erode the perceived value of the wholesale distribution sales force in educating customers about new products. The majority of wholesale distribution executives believe the Internet could actually replace their sales force as a source of product information. Manufacturers will seriously question the effectiveness of the distributor's sales force going forward. As a result, sales positions in wholesale distribution are forecast to grow at half the rate of overall U.S. job growth over the next five years.

Source: The Road to Opportunity in Wholesale Distribution by Adam J. Fein, Ph.D.,
Pembroke Consulting, Inc., www.pembrokeconsulting.com

Wholesale/Distribution — Fuel Dealers (See Fuel Dealers)

	NAICS 424720	

Wholesale/Distribution — Green Groceries

(See Fruits & Vegetables—Wholesale)

Wholesale/Distribution — In General

(See also Distribution/Wholesale—In General)

Rules of Thumb

➤ 65 percent of annual sales plus inventory

➤ 2.75 times SDE plus inventory

➤ 3.2 times EBIT

➤ 3 times EBITDA

Pricing Tips

▪ "Assumes SDE in excess of $500K. Where less than $500K, lower multiples; where over $1M, multiples exceed 3 and escalate as SDE increases"

▪ "Suppliers, how many, and will that continue for a new owner, under the same or better terms. Current contracts with customers and account concentration issues all of high importance in determining value."

▪ "Debt service will have great impact on ultimate rule of thumb multiple considering 'living wage' necessary by locality after debt is serviced."

Expert Comments

"Easy to market with use of the Web. For a savvy new owner with more technical abilities, an existing wholesale/distribution business can market to the world."

"Can be easy to replicate, the sales force is often key to success."

"Distributor with large, developed customer base is difficult to duplicate, thus enhancing the value. Seller-based financing is essential with the limitation on SBA financing where the major business asset is inventory."

Benchmark Data

- "Cost of goods sold usually 60% or higher depending on source of goods and the competitive nature of the marketplace."
- "Low rent can be easy to achieve for these type of 'warehouse' businesses."
- "Cost of goods sold varies from 60%–70% depending on product."

Expenses as a Percentage of Annual Sales

Cost of goods	68%
Payroll/labor Costs	12%
Occupancy	03%
Profit (estimated pretax)	12% to 15%

Industry Trend

- "Highly competitive . . . unless a unique product, specifically manufactured. Margins are declining as competition increases."
- "Always a demand for wholesale and distribution businesses."
- "Sales are declining in 2009 due to economic conditions, although those product lines which are more essential will recover."

Questions

- "Get financials for past 3 years and year to date. What has changed in your industry? Do you sell to distributors? If so, what are the margins? What is the source of your product and is there an agreement to assure continued supply?"
- "What is the current method of finding and keeping customers? How do they expect the current sales to grow? Does China or overseas production cause any future issues for the current products sold?"
- "How many clients do you have and how many are 'regularly' serviced?"

Resources

Associations

- National Association of Wholesaler-Distributors: www.naw.org

Wholesale/Distribution — Paper	
NAICS 422130	Number of Businesses/Units 672

Rules of Thumb

➢ 3 to 4 times SDE plus inventory

➢ 4 to 5 times EBIT

➢ 5 times EBITDA

Pricing Tips

- "Use 25–30% of GPM [Gross Profit Margin] times 4 to arrive at goodwill price including all FF&E. To this number, add the dollar amount of net working capital to be included in the sale."

Benchmark Data

Statistics (Paper Wholesaling)

Number of Establishments.. 672
Average Profit Margin 1.9%

Source: IBISWorld, September 2012

Products and Services Segmentation

Printing and writing paper... 43.9%
Fine roll paper.. 28.8%
Other.. 15.1%
Newsprint... 12.2%

Source: IBISWorld, September 2012

Major Market Segmentation

Commercial printing.. 27.6%
Book and magazine publishers... 22.2%
Exports... 16.9%
Paper Converters... 11.7%
Newspaper publishers 11.5%
Other industries 10.1%

Source: IBISWorld, September 2012

Industry Costs

Profit 1.9%
Wages... 3.9%
Purchases.. 82.1%
Depreciation.. 0.6%
Marketing 0.4%
Rent & Utilities 1.4%
Other... 9.7%

Source: IBISWorld, September 2012

Market Share

International Paper Company 19.5%

Source: IBISWorld, September 2012

- "$285,000–$300,000 sales per employee would be a good benchmark for a successful wholesale distributor."

Expenses as a Percentage of Annual Sales

Cost of goods.. 70% to 75%
Payroll/labor Costs.. 10%
Occupancy... 04%
Profit (estimated pretax) .... 08% to 10%

Industry Trend

- "Stable"

Questions

- "Stability of gross profit margins, number of inventory turns per year. Percentage of slow moving inventory and the need for adjustments thereof."

	Franchise
Wienerschnitzel	
Approx. Total Investment	$350,000 to $1,100,000
Estimated Annual Sales/Unit	$625,000
NAICS 722211	Number of Businesses/Units 325
Rules of Thumb	
➢ 30 to 35 percent of annual sales plus inventory	

Wild Bird Shops	
NAICS 453910	
Rules of Thumb	
➢ 30 percent of annual sales plus inventory	

	Franchise
Wild Birds Unlimited	
Approx. Total Investment	$99,832 to $157,344
	Number of Businesses/Units 280
Rules of Thumb	
➢ 30 to 35 percent of annual sales plus inventory	

Resources

Websites
- www.wbu.com

Wind Farms (Energy)	
NAICS 333611	Number of Businesses/Units 300
Rules of Thumb	
➢ 10 times EBITDA	

Pricing Tips
- "Use a cap rate, similar to pricing commercial real estate."

Expert Comments

"This industry is, for a number of reasons, going to grow dramatically over the next decade. The economic model is very similar to that of commercial real estate—high upfront capital costs followed by extremely consistent cash flows, with upside appreciation potential. The smart money will get in early and ride the wave."

Benchmark Data

- "More good news: Eight of the ten wind turbine manufacturers with the largest share of the U.S. market had at least one factory in the United States at the end of 2011, helping drive up the percentage of domestically sourced equipment used in U.S. projects from 35 percent in 2005 to 67 in 2011.

  "The equipment is also becoming less expensive—20 percent to 30 percent less expensive than in 2008, the report said—a trend that's beginning to nudge down project costs, with cheaper wind power the result.

  "'Among a sample of wind power projects with contracts signed in 2011, the capacity-weighted average levelized price is \$35 per megawatt-hour, down from \$59 per megawatt-hour for projects with contracts signed in 2010, and \$72 per megawatt-hour for projects with contracts signed back in 2009,' Berkeley Lab said in a statement that accompanied the report's release."

  Source: "On Wind, Obama Sees a Clean Energy Winner" by Pete Danko, www.greentechmedia.com
  August 2012

- "Revenue per kilowatt hour, capacity factor, PPA rate."
- "A megawatt of wind-generated electricity can power about 300 homes."

  Source: "On land, wind farms growing" by Erin Ailworth, Globe Staff, *Boston Globe*, July 9, 2012

Industry Trend

"Significant growth as the industry consolidates and becomes institutionalized."

Window Cleaning		
	NAICS 561720	

Rules of Thumb

➤ 60 percent of annual sales

Resources

Websites
- www.windowcleaningdirectory.net

Associations
- International Window Cleaning Association: www.iwca.org

Window Treatment/Draperies		
	NAICS 442291	

Rules of Thumb

➤ 35 to 40 percent of annual sales plus inventory

Resources

Trade Publications
- Draperies and Window Coverings: www.dwconline.com

	Franchise

Wine Kitz (Canada)

Approx. Total Investment	$70,000 to $88,000 (Retail Only)
	$116,000 to $145,000 (In-Store Winery)

		Number of Businesses/Units 85

Rules of Thumb
➤ 55 percent of annual sales plus inventory

Resources
Websites
- www.winekitz.com

Wineries

SIC 2084-01	NAICS 312130	Number of Businesses/Units 7,069

Rules of Thumb
➤ 25 percent of annual sales (This does include real estate)
➤ 10 times SDE
➤ 60 times EBIT (Does include real estate)
➤ 89 times EBITDA (Does include real estate)

Pricing Tips
- "Napa land values, which average $150,000 to $200,000 an acre for a vineyard planted with red varietals, have fallen 15% from the 2007 peak. Falling land prices, of course, make it harder to refinance mortgages. Adding to their woes is the sudden frugality of the American wine drinker." (See comment below)
  Source: *Bloomberg Businessweek*, "Napa Valley's Grapes of Wrath" by Dan Levy, March 22 & 29, 2010

Expert Comments
"Wineries take 1–2 years to sell if they are priced well."

Benchmark Data

Statistics (Wineries)

Number of Establishments	7,069
Average Profit Margin	7.5%

Source: IBISWorld, August 2012

Products and Services Segmentation

Chardonnay	19%
Other red wine	19%
Blush wine	10%
Cabernet Sauvignon	9%
Dessert wine and brandy	8.5%
Merlot	8%
Sparkling wine	4.5%
Other white wine	22%

Source: IBISWorld, August 2012

Major Market Segmentation

Wholesale and retail traders	59.2%
Licensed drinking places	28.2%
Exports	8.2%
Direct to public	4.4%

Source: IBISWorld, August 2012

Industry Costs

Profit	7.5%
Wages	9.9%
Purchases	45.5%
Depreciation	4.5%
Marketing	9.5%
Rent & Utilities	2.5%
Other	20.6%

Source: IBISWorld, August 2012

Market Share

E. & J. Gallo Winery	21.8%
Constellation Brands Inc.	15.2%
The Wine Group, Inc.	8.1%

Source: IBISWorld, August 2012

Expenses as a Percentage of Annual Sales

Cost of goods	59%
Payroll/labor Costs	20%
Occupancy	20%
Profit (estimated pretax)	10%

Industry Trend

- "The U.S. surpassed France as the world's largest wine-consuming nation in 2010, with wine shipments to the U.S. from California, other states and foreign producers growing 2% from the previous year to nearly 330 million cases, a record high for the industry, according to wine industry consultants Gomberg, Fredrikson & Associates in Woodside. The estimated retail value of these sales was $30 billion, up 4% from 2009. Total French consumption was 320.6 million cases in 2010.

  Source:www.wineinstitute.org

- "After a two-year slump, domestic wine retail sales in 2010 increased 7% from the prior year; U.S. wine exports jumped 26%. And for the first time, the U.S. consumed more wine than France.

  "Shoppers, who shifted to wines that cost less than $7 during the height of the recession, are reaching for pricier bottles, analysts said. According to the wine Institute, sales of wine in the $7 to $14 category grew 5% in 2010."

  Source: "U.S. wine sales rebound," by P.J. Huffstutter, *Los Angeles Times*, June 1, 2011

- "Greater divide between small family business and global corporations is increasing."

Questions

- "Will you [the seller] stay on as a consultant?"

Resources

Websites

- California Wineland: www.winesandvines.com

Trade Publications

- Wine Business Monthly: www.winebusiness.com

Associations

- Family Winemakers of California: www.familywinemakers.org
- American Society for Enology and Viticulture: www.asev.org

	Franchise
Wingstop Restaurants	
Approx. Total Investment	$332,500 to $550,000
Estimated Annual Sales/Unit	$1,480,000

	NAICS 722211	Number of Businesses/Units 420

Rules of Thumb

> 30 to 35 percent of annual sales plus inventory

Resources

- Websites www.wingstop.com

Wireless Communications		
(Carriers, dealers & resellers of cellular, PCs, & paging)		
SIC 5999-02	NAICS 517210	Number of Businesses/Units 14,000

Rules of Thumb

> 30 percent of annual gross sales

> 2 to 3 times SDE plus inventory

> 3 to 5 times EBITDA includes inventory

> $50 to $130 per pop for operational market—less if naked license

Pricing Tips

- "It is important to consider revenue per customer"
- "Strong employee technical base/tenure desirable along with non-competes for key personnel"
- "Trend upward in volume and downward in service income is not abnormal"
- "Subscribers, physical plant capacity, client retention and gross margins"
- "Calculating furniture, fixtures and equipment value along with any real estate involved"

Expert Comments

"Difficult to replicate due to technical nature of business as well as myriad supplier relationships required"

"Expanding into synergistic product lines is becoming the norm."

"This is a fairly mature market, however, the advent of the Internet and Voice over Internet Protocol are changing the landscape of the wired telecommunications market. While core services (long distance and data) have become a commodity, there is plenty of opportunity to differentiate with platform applications and custom architecture."

Benchmark Data

- "35%–40% percent gross profit"
- "COG 25%, payroll 20%, profit 28%, occupancy cost 18%"
- "Sales per employee"
- "Number of years owner has operated the business, along with how long they will stay and train. Are the employees staying or leaving? Location of the business and any customer lists they may have are all similar factors."
- "Gross profit of 34 percent"

Expenses as a Percentage of Annual Sales

Cost of goods	60%
Payroll/labor Costs	20%
Occupancy	05% to 10%
Profit (estimated pretax)	10%

Industry Trend

- "Trend toward commodity-based marketing and addition of synergistic product lines in an effort to offset eroding equipment profits"
- "There will be large consolidations of operators, and wireless penetration in U.S. will continue to increase. More use of data."
- "Increasing competition, need for international services, data and cell services will see dramatic increases."
- "Continued growth in wireless communications and launch of new products increases."

Questions

- "Ask if market is built out (to what percentage of population and geography) and if it is operational (how long)."
- "Number of activations per month currently doing? How many deactivations per month? What is advertising budget? How long at this location? Are employees on commission or salary or both? Number of locations?"
- "Pricing strategy and debt owed"

Resources

Trade Publications
- Wireless Week: www.wirelessweek.com
- RCR Wireless News: www.rcrwireless.com
- Wireless Dealer Magazine: www.wirelessdealermag.com

	Franchise
Wireless Toyz	
Approx. Total Investment	$215,370 to $693,050
Estimated Annual Sales/Unit	$650,000
NAICS 443112	Number of Businesses/Units 160

Rules of Thumb

➤ 45 to 50 percent of annual sales plus inventory

Women's Clothing (See also Clothing Stores—Retail)	
SIC 5621-01	NAICS 448190	Number of Businesses/Units 53,940

Rules of Thumb

➤ 20 percent of annual sales plus inventory

➤ 2 times monthly sales plus inventory

Benchmark Data

Statistics (Women's Clothing Stores)

Number of Establishments	53,940
Average Profit Margin	6.8%
Revenue per Employee	$109,600
Average Number of Employees	6.8
Average Wages per Employee	$15,140

Source: IBISWorld, July 2012

Products and Services Segmentation

T-shirts, knit and woven shirts, blouses and sweaters	32%
Pants, jeans, shorts and skirts	24%
Dresses	18%
Coats, jackets and suits	17%
Sports apparel (including swimwear and sweatshirts)	6%
Other apparel (including fur and custom garments)	3%

Source: IBISWorld, July 2012

Industry Costs

Profit	6.8%
Wages	13.7%
Purchases	61.4%
Depreciation	4.5%
Marketing	7.1%
Rent & Utilities	4.8%
Other	1.7%

Source: IBISWorld, July 2012

Market Share

Ann Taylor Stores Corporation	6.0%
Charming Shoppes Inc.	4.8%

Source: IBISWorld, July 2012

W to Y - Rules of Thumb

Franchise
World Wide Express

Approx. Total Investment		$25,000 to $150,000
	NAICS 488510	Number of Businesses/Units 143

Rules of Thumb

➤ 50 to 55 percent of annual sales plus inventory

Resources

Websites
- www.wwex.com

Yardage Shops (See Fabric Shops)	
	NAICS 451130

Franchise
You've Got Maids (See also Janitorial Services, Molly Maid, etc.)

Approx. Total Investment		$16,500 to $23,000
SIC 7349-23	NAICS 561720	

Rules of Thumb

➤ 60 percent of annual sales plus inventory

Resources

Websites
- www.youvegotmaids.com

Franchise
Your Office USA

Approx. Total Investment		$200,000 to $500,000+
	NAICS 531120	Number of Businesses/Units 100

Rules of Thumb

➤ 60 percent of annual sales plus inventory

Resources

Websites
- www.youroffice.com

Franchise

Ziebart International (auto services)

Approx. Total Investment		$75,000 to $250,000
	NAICS 8111	Number of Businesses/Units 358

Rules of Thumb

➢ 42 percent of annual sales plus inventory

Resources

Websites
- www.ziebart.com

Franchise

Zoo Health Club

Approx. Total Investment		$73,899 to $278,499 (equipment purchased)
		$48,399 to $189,249 (equipment leased)
	NAICS 713940	Number of Businesses/Units 15

Rules of Thumb

➢ 20 percent of annual sales

Resources

Websites
- www.zoogym.com

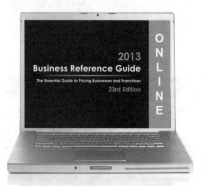